CALIFORNIA
POLITICAL
ALMANAC

CALIFORNIA
POLITICAL
ALMANAC
1989 -90 EDITION

Dan Walters, Editor

Amy Chance • Thorne Gray
Stephen Green • Rick Kushman • James Richardson
Rick Rodriguez • Ray Sotero
Contributors

John Hughes and Lori K. Richardson, Copy Editors
Shirley Bittante, Cover Design

Published by
Pacific Data Resources

ISBN 0-944158-02-1

Contents

Preface

In the autumn of 1988, as political campaigns raged throughout California, a few Sacramento Bee political journalists were discussing the paucity of reliable political information about the state.

Every time someone wanted to write about a particular congressional or legislative campaign, or a state agency, or a lobbyist, he or she had to conduct elaborate research from several sources.

California needed, someone suggested, a book that did for state politics what *The Almanac of American Politics* did for the national political situation: provide one source of basic information. From that discussion very quickly grew an idea: produce our own almanac that would fill the need. Eventually, 10 Bee staffers would volunteer to compile, write and edit such an almanac, drawing on our own experience and data, acquiring new information and including what we considered to be most interesting and useful about politics and government in California.

As the seasons changed, we chugged away at the the project. It was made immeasurably easier by cooperation from the editors and managers of The Sacramento Bee, who understood the value of the project and generously allowed us to use the newspaper's computer systems.

We don't expect the first edition to be perfect. It represents our best judgment about what is important now. In future editions, we will not only update the material, chronicling the flow of politics in the state, but add sections to expand the usefulness of the book. Ideally, it will be a living organism that grows and develops as circumstances dictate and allow, and needs input from its readers/users to fulfill that long-term goal.

Dan Walters
Sacramento
September, 1989

1

California–a state of change

California is the planet's most diverse society.

At no time in mankind's history have so many people of so many ethnic and national groups, practicing so many different religions, speaking so many different languages and engaged in so many different kinds of economic activities gathered in one place. It would follow, therefore, that California's politics would be equally complex. And they are, but not exactly in the ways that one might think. Rather than reflecting the incredible socioeconomic and demographic diversity, the state's politics have become the almost exclusive province of California's relatively affluent and aged Anglo – non-Hispanic white – population.

Proposition 13, the successful campaign to oust liberals from the state Supreme Court and a seeming lock on the state's electoral votes by Republican presidential candidates are just three indications that California's politics have been edging rightward in recent years, thus creating a growing tension between the aspirations of the emerging majority and the limits laid down by the politically dominant soon-to-be minority. That tension manifests itself in an untold number of specific struggles and issues, ranging from reapportionment to fiscal policy, that form the murky political climate of California as the state approaches the 21st century.

As it functions as a living social laboratory, so does California test the ability of the traditional American system of government to cope with social and economic change beyond the wildest imagination of the system's creators. A major question for the 1990s and beyond is whether features of government developed in the 18th and 19th centuries – the two-party system, separately elected legislative and executive branches of government, counties and cities formed along traditional lines – can function amid such a range of social and cultural values.

To understand the political currents flowing through California in the late 20th century, one must first understand its social and economic currents. And if one accepts the wave theory of social development – each wave consisting of economic change, followed by social change, followed by political change – California is in the third, or political phase, of its third wave.

The first wave lasted for roughly a century, from the early days of white settlement in the 1840s to the onset of World War II. The gold rush aside, that century was one in which California was a relatively unimportant place in the larger scheme of things. Its economy was resource-based – mining, agriculture, timber – and it had a decidedly rural ambiance. Los Angeles, with its orange groves, vegetable fields and low buildings, resembled an overgrown Midwestern farm city – the presence of a few movie studios after World War I and the Pacific Ocean notwithstanding. San Francisco had a more cosmopolitan reputation, along with its cable cars and Chinatown, but it was the socioeconomic exception. California was white, Republican and quiet. It was largely ignored by the rest of America, whose population was centered in the East and had, if anything, a European outlook.

All of that changed, suddenly and dramatically, on Dec. 7, 1941, when the Japanese bombed Pearl Harbor and plunged the United States into world war. Suddenly, America was forced to consider Asia as a factor in its future, and the window through which the nation viewed the war in the Pacific was California. Overnight, seemingly, the state was transformed into an industrial giant to serve the war effort, sprouting countless dozens of aircraft assembly lines, shipyards, steel mills and all of the other paraphernalia needed to fight a modern war. And it became a staging point for the war, a training ground for soldiers, sailors and airmen.

A WAR BRINGS ECONOMIC AND SOCIAL CHANGE

It was war, but it was also a sudden economic change for the state; California was jerked into the industrial 20th century. And that economic transformation had an equally rapid social impact: hundreds of thousands and then millions of Americans were drawn or sent to the state to participate in the war effort.

While there had always been a steady flow of domestic emigrants to the state (some of whom, like the ill-fated Donner Party, regretted the decision to move), it was nothing compared to what happened during World War II and continued almost unabated after the war. "Gone to California" became a terse explanation for the sudden absence of families in hundreds of Midwestern, Southern and Eastern communities. It was one of history's great migrations, and one that actually began a few years before the war when refugees from the Dust Bowl, as chronicled in John Steinbeck's *Grapes of Wrath*, came to California in a desperate search for work and formed the nucleus of life and politics in agricultural areas of the state, such as the Central Valley.

As the expanding industrialism of California created jobs, it drew emigrants and they, in turn, formed the nucleus of a new industrial middle class. These young emigrants had vast ambitions for themselves and their families. They wanted schools, highways, parks and homes. And they provided, during the postwar years, the core backing for politicians who promised to fulfill those desires. A political change was under way.

California's prewar Republicanism was of a particular variety. Rooted in the abolitionism of the Civil War era and the prairie populism of such men as William Jennings Bryan and Robert LaFollette, California's Republicans were reformist and progressive.

The state's great Republican reformer, Hiram Johnson, set the tone for the 20th century when he led efforts to break the stranglehold that Southern Pacific Railroad and other entrenched economic interests had on the state Legislature.Small farmers had battled for decades with the railroad over freight rates, the clashes being both political and, in one instance, violent. With Johnson – governor and later a U.S. senator – marshaling public opinion, California enacted a series of pioneering political reforms that included the initiative, referendum and recall, all designed to increase popular control of politicians. Decades later, the initiative was to become a tool of special interests, rather than a barrier, but that was after social and political developments beyond Johnson's ability to foresee.

Johnson set a tone of high-minded Republicanism that survived for decades. Democrats were weak, able to elect only one one-term governor, Culbert Olsen, in 1938, despite the dramatic rise of the Democratic Party nationally after Franklin Roosevelt became president.

Olsen's Republican successor, Earl Warren, was out of the Johnson mold, and he became the only governor ever elected three times, going on to even greater fame as chief justice of the U.S. Supreme Court from 1953 to 1969.

Warren was governor during and immediately after World War II, when the state underwent its big economic and social evolution. He responded to the demand that California's growth brought with far-reaching investments in public infrastructure, schools, highways, parks and other facilities that not only served the state's fast-growing population but laid the foundation for even greater public works in the future.

THE POLARIZATION OF POLITICS

It was during this period that California began developing a national reputation for political unpredictability as it became a battleground for the ideological wars sweeping through America. Postwar California politics revolved mainly around Cold War issues, typified by the 1950 U.S. Senate contest between a young Republican congressman named Richard Nixon and a liberal political activist named Helen Douglas, the wife of actor Melvyn Douglas. Nixon won after a brutal campaign in which he implied, at least, that Douglas was sympathetic to communism. It was a polarizing political battle that launched Nixon on his way toward political immortality – and some would say, immorality. And it marked a turn away from centrist politics by both parties.

The Democrats began veering to the left through such organizations as the California Democratic Council, which was established by liberals to strengthen party identification in a state where "cross-filing" allowed candidates to obtain the nominations of both parties and to do battle with the more conservative elements then in control of the party. And the Republicans took a turn to the starboard, with conservatives such as U.S. Sen. William Knowland, an Oakland newspaper publisher, assuming a larger role in the party as moderates of the Earl Warren-Goodwin Knight faction fell from grace in the absolutist atmosphere of the day.

At the time, in the mid- and late-1950s, social change favored the Democrats. The emigrants who had come to California to take jobs in the expanding industrial economy, their ranks swollen by returning veterans, put down roots and became politically active. As they did, they expanded the Democratic Party's base – especially since the Republicans were in the process of turning right, alienating voters who had supported Warren and his centrist philosophy.

THE NEW BREED

Jesse Unruh was archetypical of the new breed. Unruh came to California from Texas during the war, remaining to attend the University of Southern California, where he became active in campus politics as leader of a band of liberal veterans. Within a few years of graduating from USC, Unruh was heavily involved in politics on a larger scale and won a seat in the state Assembly. It was the perfect territory for the consummate political animal, coinciding with the general rise of Democratic fortunes in the 1950s.

The 1958 election was the pivotal event in the postwar rise of the state's Democratic Party, a direct result of the social and economic changes brought about by World War II. Sen. Knowland, who had led the right-wing Republican contingent in the Senate during the early- and mid-1950s, was openly hostile to President Dwight Eisenhower's "modern Republicanism," which included Warren's appointment to the Supreme Court. Knowland saw Eisenhower, Warren, Thomas Dewey and other Republican leaders from the East as leading the party, and the nation, astray, refusing to confront expansionist communism around the globe and temporizing on such domestic issues as labor union rights and welfare spending.

Knowland wanted to take the party back to the right and hoped to do it by running for president in 1960, when Eisenhower's second term would end. But he thought the governorship of California would be a more powerful platform for a presidential campaign than the Senate. Knowland's major impediment was the moderate Republican governor of the time, Goodwin Knight, who didn't want to give up the governorship. Knight had been Warren's lieutenant governor, had inherited the top spot when Warren was appointed to the Supreme Court and had then won a term on his own in 1954. He wanted to run for re-election in 1958.

Knowland solved his problem by simply ordering Knight to step aside. With the rightists firmly in control of the party machinery, Knight was forced to obey, agreeing, with obvious reluctance, to run for Knowland's Senate seat.

But Knowland, in his preoccupation with Eisenhower, Communist expansionism and other weighty matters, didn't bother to consider whether his forced switch with Knight would sit well with California voters. With an arrogance that bordered on stupidity, he assumed that the voters would do whatever he wanted them to do. He was wrong. Democrat Edmund G. Brown Sr., the liberal attorney general, was elected governor and Democratic Rep. Clair Engle was elected to the Senate. Knight might have been re-elected governor and Knowland given another term in the Senate, but both were instead retired by the voters.

THE DEMOCRATS TAKE OVER

It was a banner year for the Democrats. In addition to winning the top two spots on the ballot, they also took firm control of the Legislature. Over the next eight years, during this peak of Democratic hegemony, the most ambitious policy agenda in California history became reality. With Unruh at the helm of the Assembly as speaker, the early Brown years saw a torrent of liberal, activist legislation ranging from an ambitious water development scheme to pioneering civil rights and consumer protection measures.

While Unruh sharpened the ideological focus of the Assembly, taking it to the left, the state Senate remained a bastion of rural conservatism. For a century, the Senate's 40 seats had been distributed on the basis of geography, rather than population, in a rough approximation of the U.S. Senate's two-to-a-state system. No senator represented more than two counties and giant Los Angeles County, with a third of the state's population, had just one senator.

With most of California's 58 counties being small and rural, it gave the Senate a decidedly rural flavor. Conservative Democrats and Republicans formed a solid majority. Even so, Pat Brown guided much of his progressive legislative agenda through the upper house, using his unmatched skills of personal persuasion on Democratic senators.

In 1966, as Brown was winding up his second term, the U.S. Supreme Court, still under the leadership of Earl Warren, handed down its far-reaching "one-man, one-vote" decision requiring legislative seats to be apportioned on the basis of population, even though the U.S. Senate retained its two-to-a-state makeup. And as the Senate's districts were redrawn in response to the ruling, there was a huge shift of power from rural counties to urban areas, strengthening not only Democrats generally but liberals within the party. But that didn't take effect until after another man had assumed the governorship, the result of another clash between two big-name politicians.

Brown wanted to run for a third term in 1966 but Jesse Unruh thought – or so he said later – that Brown had promised to step aside in his favor. Whatever the precise truth of the matter, there was a big rupture between the two most powerful California politicians of the day, and in the long run, both would suffer from it. Brown ran for his third term, but his break with Unruh, some public fumbles, a rising level of social unrest and the appearance of an ex-movie actor named Ronald Reagan spelled disaster for those ambitions.

Reagan, who had had a moderately successful career as a B-movie leading man and television actor, was enticed to run against Brown by a consortium of wealthy

Southern California businessmen. At the time, television had become a new and powerful factor in political campaigning. Televised debates had doomed Richard Nixon's bid for the presidency in 1960, which was followed by a hopelessly desperate run against Brown for the governorship in 1962. In 1964, Reagan had made a powerful television speech for Barry Goldwater, the Republican presidential candidate. Reagan was, the businessmen decided, just the man to take on non-telegenic Pat Brown in 1966.

THE RISE OF RONALD REAGAN

They were right. Even though the Democratic phase of the postwar political era was not yet concluded, and even though a large majority of California voters were Democrats, Reagan buried Pat Brown and his bid for a third term by emphasizing Brown's shortcomings and stressing a conservative, get-tough attitude toward civic and campus unrest. The strength of Reagan's win swept several other Republicans into statewide offices.

Two years earlier, Reagan's old chum from Hollywood, song-and-dance-man George Murphy, had defeated Pierre Salinger for a California Senate seat. Salinger, who had been John Kennedy's press secretary, was appointed to the Senate by Pat Brown after Clair Engle died during his first term.

With Murphy in the U.S. Senate (he was defeated in his second-term bid by John Tunney in 1970), Reagan in the governor's office and Republicans holding other statewide offices, the GOP appeared once again to be on the ascendency. But it all proved to be a short-term spurt. It would take another socioeconomic cycle for the Republicans to begin a real, long-term rise in influence among the voters.

The GOP won control of the Assembly (for two years) in 1968, but for most of Reagan's eight years as governor, he had to deal with a Democratic-controlled Legislature. Unruh was gone after losing his own bid for the governorship in 1970, but another Southern California liberal, Bob Moretti, took his place. There were occasional compromises between the conservative governor and the liberal legislators, most notably on welfare reform, but it was a period remarkable for its dearth of serious policy direction from Sacramento. The Pat Brown-Jesse Unruh legacy was not undone, Reagan's rhetoric notwithstanding. But neither could liberals advance their agenda. It was a time of stalemate.

Even as Reagan and Moretti did battle in Sacramento, another cycle, largely unnoticed at the time, was beginning to manifest itself.

The period of intense industrialization in California began to wind down in the 1960s. Asia, principally Japan, had risen from the devastation of the war to become a new industrial power. Californians began buying funny-looking cars stamped "Made in Japan" and domestic automakers began shutting down their plants in California. The steel for those cars was made not in Fontana but in Japan or Korea. Even tire production began to shift overseas. One factory at a time, California began to de-industrialize.

California was not the only state to experience damaging foreign competition in basic industrial production in the 1960s and 1970s, but what happened there was unusual. The state underwent a massive economic transformation, from a dependence on basic industry to an economy rooted in trade (much of it with the nations of Asia), services and certain kinds of highly specialized manufacturing, especially of the high-tech variety centered in the Silicon Valley south of San Francisco. Computers and associated devices and services – including a huge aerospace industry tied to Pentagon contracts – became the new backbone of the California economy. By the late 1980s, in fact, California's economy, on a per capita basis, was probably the most productive in the world, even more so than that of much-vaunted Japan.

But there was a lull, a period of adjustment between the apex of the industrial era and the onset of the postindustrial period. That occurred in the 1970s, and it resulted in a social lull as well.

The rapid population growth that California had experienced during the postwar years, driven by domestic immigration, slowed markedly in the 1970s as industrial job opportunities stagnated. California was still growing, even growing a bit faster than the nation as a whole, but it was much less dramatic than what had occurred earlier. And California began to experience another phenomenon: an outflow of residents to other states.

A DIFFERENT KIND OF POLITICIAN

In retrospect, that lull in population growth may have been politically misleading. It persuaded the state's political leaders, first Reagan and then his successor, Democrat Jerry Brown, that the infrastructure of services and facilities that had been built after World War II was adequate, that it was time to retrench, to tighten budgets and cut back on public works, whether they be state buildings in Sacramento or freeways in Los Angeles. It was a collective and indirect policy decision that was to have serious and adverse consequences in later years.

Jerry Brown, son of the man Reagan had defeated for governor in 1966, burst into state politics in 1970 by getting himself elected secretary of state, a mostly ministerial office with few powers or opportunities for publicity. But Brown, a young former seminarian who was the personal antithesis of his back-slapping father, seized the moment.

The Watergate scandal that erupted in 1972 and destroyed Richard Nixon's presidency two years later focused public attention on political corruption. Brown grabbed the issue by proposing a political reform initiative and shamelessly pandering to the media, especially television. He bested a field of relatively dull Democratic rivals, including Bob Moretti, to win the party's nomination for governor and then took on Houston Flournoy, the Republican state controller, who was a throwback to the earlier era of Republican moderation but who came across in media terms as dull.

Even so, it was a whisker-close race. Ultimately, Brown was elected not so much on his political acumen, but because of his name and because the post-Watergate political climate had raised Democratic voter strength to near-record levels. At the height of Democratic potency in California, which occurred during the early years of Jerry Brown's governorship, 59 percent of California voters identified themselves as Democrats in an annual party preference poll while just over 30 percent said they were Republicans. Democrats ran up huge majorities in the Legislature; at one point, after the 1976 elections, Republicans fell to just 23 seats in the 80-member Assembly. Even Orange County, the seemingly impregnable bastion of Republicanism, had a Democratic registration plurality.

With the younger Brown sitting in the governor's office and big Democratic majorities in the Legislature, there was a spurt of legislative activity, much of it involving issues, such as farm labor legislation and bread-and-butter benefit bills, that had been stalled during the Reagan years.

Brown preached a homegrown political philosophy that defied easy categorization. It was liberal on civil rights, labor rights and environmental protection but conservative on taxes and spending. Brown defined the philosophy in a series of slogan-loaded speeches, in which he talked of teachers being content with "psychic income" rather than salary increases and California facing an "era of limits," that seemed to directly contrast with the expansionist policies of his father and most other postwar governors.

THE PROPERTY TAX REVOLT

At first, Brown was a hit. The words and a rather odd personal lifestyle that included late-night visits to Mexican restaurants drew attention from national political reporters starved for glamour in the post-John F. Kennedy world of Jerry Ford and Jimmy Carter. Soon, there was a steady stream of pundits to Sacramento and a flurry of effusively praiseful articles in national media. Brown was a star, it seemed; a Democratic Reagan. Brown believed it. And scarcely more than a year after becoming governor, he was running for president. As Brown turned his political attention eastward – or skyward, according to some critics – Brown neglected California politics. And they were changing again.

While the state's economy roared out of a mid-1970s recession, property values soared. And as they rose, so did property tax bills. It was an issue too prosaic for Jerry Brown, whose sights by then were firmly fixed on the White House. But it was just the ticket for two aging political gadflies, Howard Jarvis and Paul Gann.

Raising the specter of Californians being driven out of their homes by skyrocketing property tax bills, Jarvis and Gann placed on the ballot a radical measure to slash property taxes and hold them down forever. Republican candidates, seeking an issue to restore their political power, seized upon Proposition 13, as the measure was numbered on the June 1978 ballot. Belatedly, Brown and legislative leaders devised a milder alternative for the same ballot.

Proposition 13 was enacted overwhelmingly and Brown, then running for re-election against the state's terminally dull attorney general, Evelle Younger, did a 180-degree turn. Sensing that the tax revolt could be his political downfall, Brown proclaimed himself to be a "born-again tax cutter" and pushed a state tax cut as a companion to Proposition 13.

Younger failed to exploit the opening and Brown breezed to an easy re-election victory. Almost immediately, Brown began plotting another run for the White House in 1980, this time as an advocate of balanced budgets, spending limits and tax cuts. Brown was nothing if not ambitious and opportunistic, qualities that were to be his political undoing in the long run.

Brown's re-election aside, the 1978 elections marked the beginning of a long slide for the Democratic Party after it had enjoyed two decades of dominance. Democrats suffered major losses in legislative races that year and a flock of conservative Republicans, dubbing themselves "Proposition 13 babies," came to Sacramento – out of caves, liberals said – prepared to conduct ideological war.

A REBIRTH FOR THE REPUBLICANS

In the years since, Republicans have continued to gain legislative seats, even in the face of a Democratic reapportionment plan in 1982 that was designed specifically to keep the party in power. And the Democrats have suffered a massive hemorrhage of voter strength. Since the Democrats' high point in the California Poll's annual survey of party identification, 59 percent to 32 percent in 1976, the margin has eroded year by year. In the most recent polls, the parties are tied at about 45 percent each. There's been a corresponding shrinkage in the voter registration gap as well, although it's not as dramatic.

In the mid-1970s, voter registration favored Democrats by, at most, a 57 percent to 34 percent margin. But in more recent years it has dipped to about 50 percent to 40 percent on the official rolls. Democrats even lost a fraction of a point in 1988 when they committed $4 million to a huge voter registration drive in support of Michael Dukakis' presidential campaign.

But the unofficial voter registration numbers are even worse for the Democrats. It's estimated that at least 1 million, and perhaps as many as 2 million, of California's 14 million registered voters don't exist. The official euphemism for those phantom names is "deadwood," and it exists because California's voter registration laws make it relatively difficult to drop people from the rolls when they die or move. Some mobile Californians may be counted two or three times as registered voters in different jurisdictions. And because Democrats are more likely to change addresses than Republicans, an adjustment for the deadwood tends to reduce their ranks more.

It's generally acknowledged among political demographers and statisticians that stripping the voter rolls of duplicate or missing names would reduce official Democratic registration to below 50 percent, an important psychological level, and raise Republican registration to well above 40 percent. That's why Democratic legislators have resisted efforts to purge the rolls of non-persons. But no one agrees on just how far to adjust the figures in trying to estimate the real split among voters. Some believe that Democrats should be dropped two or three percentage points and

Republicans raised by that much, which would bring registration closer to the 45 percent to 45 percent identification margin garnered in recent polls. The state's leading public pollster, Mervin Field, adjusts the voter registration split to 49 percent to 41 percent in his polling, saying the number is based on surveys of actual registration.

THE DEMOCRATS' CRISIS

Whatever the real number may be, the Democratic side has been declining and the Republican side gaining. And some Democratic officials, most notably Secretary of State March Fong Eu, are warning that the party is in danger of slipping into minority status. The big question asked among political insiders in California is why the Democrats are failing. Democratic leaders ask the question themselves, even though most deny the existence of the trend.

The roots of the trend may be found in the socioeconomic currents evident in California during the late 1970s and 1980s. As the state's postindustrial economy shifted into high gear in the late 1970s, it created millions of jobs and, like the postwar period of industrialization, began attracting new waves of immigrants to fill them. But these immigrants didn't come from Indiana, Tennessee and Texas with their political consciousness already formed. They came from Mexico, Taiwan, Korea and the Philippines.

By the late 1980s, California's population was growing by some 2,000 people a day and half of them were immigrants, mostly from other nations of the Pacific Rim with whom California was establishing ever-stronger economic relations. California was developing, in short, into the new American melting pot in which dozens of languages and cultures were represented.

As the newcomers to California poured into the central cities, especially Los Angeles, San Francisco and San Jose, there was a commensurate outpouring of Anglo families into the suburbs. And as those suburbs filled and as their home prices soared, there was an even more dramatic movement into the new suburbs, located in former farm towns such as Modesto and Stockton in the north and Riverside and Redlands in the south. These newly minted suburbanites – white and middle-class – shifted their political allegiance to the Republicans and their promises of limited government and taxes. Areas that had once been dependably Democratic in their voting patterns, such as Riverside and San Bernardino counties, evolved into Republican registration majorities as they suburbanized and exploded with population. Prosperity encouraged the conversion, as did the popularity of Ronald Reagan in the White House.

A 1988 California Poll revealed that Anglo voters favored Republicans by a 50 percent to 41 percent margin. And that was critical because non-Anglos, while identifying with the Democratic Party by substantial margins, were not voting in numbers anywhere close to their proportions of the population. Exit polls in 1980s elections revealed that more than 80 percent of California's voters were Anglos, even though they had dipped to only about 60 percent of the population as a whole.

At the other extreme, Asians doubled their numbers in California between the late 1970s and the late 1980s, surpassing blacks to become almost 10 percent of the population. Yet Asians accounted for just 2 percent of the voters. The fast-growing Hispanic population was approaching one-fourth of the total by the late 1980s, but were only 6 percent or 7 percent of the voters. Among non-Anglo minorities, only blacks voted in proportion to their numbers – roughly 8 percent of both population and electorate. But they are also the slowest-growing of the minority populations.

Thus, the 1980s saw a widening gap between the ethnic characteristics of California as a whole and those of voters, who not only were white but better educated, more affluent and – perhaps most important – markedly older than the non-Anglo non-voters. By 1986, half of California's voters were over 50 years old, a reflection of the rapid aging of the Anglo population.

THE CHARACTERISTIC GAP

In brief, while California's population was moving in one direction – toward a multiracial, relatively young profile – the electorate was moving in another. And this characteristic gap was driving California politics to the right, toward a dominant mood of self-protection and reaction. Republicans scored well among these older voters with appeals on crime and taxes. Democrats, hammered on these and other hot button issues, scrambled to find some response and were mostly unsuccessful.

The characteristic gap makes itself evident in a wide variety of specific issues and contests, but is most noticeable when it comes to issues of taxes and spending. The Proposition 13 property tax revolt in 1978 and the subsequent passage of a public spending limit measure promoted by Paul Gann in 1979 were the first signs that the climate had changed. Republican George Deukmejian's 1982 election to the governorship on a no-new-taxes, tough-on-spending platform (along with tough-on-crime) was another indication. Deukmejian, a dull-as-dishwater former legislator and attorney general, represented a 180-degree change of style from the unpredictable Brown.

The demands for more spending were coming from and for a growing, relatively young non-Anglo population, while the political power was being held by a relatively old, Anglo bloc of voters. By the late 1980s, a majority of California's school children were non-Anglo, but only about a quarter of California's voters had children in school – one example of how the characteristic gap affected political decision-making.

A 1987 poll conducted for the California Teachers Association revealed that older voters would kill any effort to raise state taxes for education. A CTA consultant told the group that even "arguments about grandchildren and overall societal need don't work." And if education was losing its basic political constituency – voters with children in public school s– other major spending programs, such as health and welfare services for the poor, had even smaller levels of public support.

Deukmejian slashed spending for these and other programs repeatedly and saw his popularity among voters soar. He was re-elected by a landslide in 1986, defeating for the second time Los Angeles Mayor Tom Bradley. Even Deukmejian, who gloried in the "Iron Duke " image, relented in 1989 as the Gann spending limit enacted by voters 10 years earlier gripped the state budget. He was under pressure from business interests to spend more to relieve traffic congestion, but he refused to raise gasoline taxes. And even if he had agree to a tax boost, the spending limit would have prevented the money from being spent.

Finally, the governor and legislative leaders reached agreement on a complex package that would place a measure that would loosen the Gann limit and increase the gasoline tax directly before voters in 1990. But chances of passage were rated at less than 50-50, and if the measure fails, it will reinforce the view that California voters don't want higher taxes, even for something as seemingly popular as highways.

JERRY BROWN'S RE-ENTRY

The essential public policy question facing California in the 1990s, therefore, is whether an aging Anglo population will continue to dominate the political agenda, even in the face of pressure from business executives for more spending on infrastructure to maintain the state's business climate.

One might think that the solution to the Democrats' political woes would be to register and organize millions of non-Anglo voters, rather than continue to face an erosion of support among white middle-class Californians. Ex-Gov. Jerry Brown, who went into political exile after losing a U.S. Senate bid in 1982, returned to the stage in 1989 by running for and winning the state Democratic Party chairmanship on a promise to bring minorities and economically displaced whites into the party in record numbers and thereby reverse its decline. The unfaithful, Republican-voting Democrats would, in effect, be banished from the party as it took a couple of steps to the left.

But as simple as that sounds, it's a very complex task. There are barriers of citizenship, of language and of a tendency among refugees from authoritarian regimes not to stick their necks out politically. That's a tendency most evident among Asians, who have very high levels of education and economic attainment but very low levels of political involvement.

And there are problems in creating a party image that is attractive to minorities who may be social and political conservatives. Republicans regularly garner about 40 percent of the Hispanic vote, for instance, and some Democratic Party positions, such as being pro-choice on abortion, are hard-sells among Hispanics.

There are also internal barriers, such as the traditionally powerful role that blacks have played within the Democratic Party. Rhetoric about a "Rainbow Coalition " notwithstanding, minority groups do not automatically cooperate on matters political and there is, in fact, some friction.

If these weren't serious enough problems, Brown also faces continued skepticism among more traditional elements of the party, who see him as a loser with an image that repels many would-be Democratic voters. Brown's attempt to centralize fund-raising activities as one step toward his goal of creating a powerful party apparatus has been rebuffed by other influential figures, who have refused to cooperate and have insisted on running their own fund-raising and "soft money " operations.

Political number-crunchers in California generally believe that in the short run – to the mid-1990s at least – Republicans will continue to gain market share and Democratic strength will continue to erode. A major question is whether that trend will be reflected in real power.

REAPPORTIONMENT REDUX

Democrats maintained their hold on the Legislature and expanded their control of the state's congressional delegation with a highly partisan reapportionment plan after the 1980 census. In effect, they preserved their power in the face of real-world trends. The plans were approved by then-Gov. Brown and a state Supreme Court dominated by liberal Brown appointees. Conditions are not likely to be as favorable after the 1990 census and the stakes will be much, much higher.

The relative lull in California population growth during the 1970s meant that the state was awarded only two new congressional seats after the 1980 census, its delegation increasing from 43 to 45. Prior to reapportionment, the 43-member delegation had been divided 22-21 in favor of Democrats. It was a fair division of the seats in terms of both overall party identification and total congressional vote in the state, both of which were evenly divided between the parties.

But after the late Rep. Phil Burton completed what he called "my contribution to modern art, " a plan rejected by voters via referendum but ordered into use by the state Supreme Court for the 1982 elections, the delegation was 28-17 in favor of Democrats. That result was stark evidence that gerrymandered reapportionment of district boundaries works. And it was so well done that Republicans were able to gain only one seat in subsequent elections, leaving the delegation at 27-18. The margin held even though the total vote for Democrat and Republican congressional candidates in California continued to run almost dead even (and in some elections the GOP ran ahead).

California's population growth has been much, much higher in the 1980s, especially so in relationship to the rest of the nation. Roughly a quarter of all U.S. population growth has occurred in California during the decade. That means the state will be awarded six, and perhaps even seven, new congressional seats after the 1990 census.

Republicans want redress. They believe, with statistical evidence on their side, that they should have roughly half of the California seats, which would mean that they would receive all of the new ones. And it will be very, very difficult for the Democrats to pull a repeat of 1982, not only in congressional reapportionment, but in the redrawing of legislative districts.

Initially, Republicans pinned their hopes vis-a-vis reapportionment on

Deukmejian's running for a third term in 1990. Thus, he would have been available to veto any gerrymander drawn by majority Democrats in the Legislature. But after dropping hints that he was interested in a third term, Deukmejian eventually announced in early 1989 that he would retire after his second term was completed.

GOP leaders, stretching as high as the White House, then engineered a strategic coup. They persuaded Pete Wilson, the one-time mayor of San Diego who had defeated Jerry Brown for a U.S. Senate seat in 1982 and won a second term handily in 1988, to run for governor in 1990. The early pre-1990 polling favors Wilson over either of the Democratic candidates, Attorney General John Van de Kamp and Dianne Feinstein, the ex-mayor of San Francisco.

So it's a better-than-even bet that the governorship will continue to be occupied by a Republican, who could protect the party's position on reapportionment. The congressional stakes are so heavy that the Republican National Committee has made Wilson's election its No. 1 priority for 1990. And Republicans are also promoting a series of ballot measures for the 1990 ballot that would either impose new standards for redistricting or take the job away from the Legislature and give it to a supposedly independent commission. Finally, the state Supreme Court is now dominated by Deukmejian appointees and is less likely to automatically validate a Democratic reapportionment plan.

A final factor in reapportionment is that minority groups, especially those representing Hispanics, believe they too were damaged by the 1982 reapportionment. So they will be pressuring Democrats for new representation in both congressional and legislative seats.

For all of those reasons, reapportionment is likely to be a nastier squabble than it was a decade earlier. And given the underlying trends, Republicans could become the dominant party by the mid-1990s if they get a fair shake on reapportionment.

ARE REPUBLICANS READY?

Expansion of the Republican Party's market share among voters in California has meant a subtle broadening of the party's base, and that has brought internal discord. The right-wingers who were dominant in the party for years have seen their influence slip during the 1980s. The 1982 elections were a watershed of internal party power. George Deukmejian, denounced by some rightists at the time as a "closet liberal," defeated then-Lt. Gov. Mike Curb for the gubernatorial nomination and went on to win the election. Pete Wilson, who is a little to the left of Deukmejian in ideological terms, defeated several conservatives to win the nomination, and then won the seat.

With patronage from the governor's office and the Senate, Republican moderates have enjoyed a rebirth of influence within the party, and right-wingers have been complaining privately and publicly about being ignored. Their only bastion is the Assembly Republican caucus, which continues to be dominated by the "Proposition 13 babies" or "cavemen," as some dub them.

The conservatives have stopped short of open revolt and the party has remained relatively unified at the top of the ticket. Conservatives haven't complained, for instance, about having Wilson as their candidate for governor in 1990 because they want a winner who will protect the party on reapportionment. But there are certain issues that could divide the party bitterly and thus lessen its chances of taking full advantage of the opportunity to become dominant in state politics.

Chief among those issues is abortion. The right-wingers are adamantly opposed to it and want laws to make it illegal. But the newer recruits to the party, as well as the moderate leaders, favor the so-called pro-choice position, Wilson among them. The issue, however, was moot as long as national law favored abortion rights. That changed in 1989 when the U.S. Supreme Court ruled that states could make their own laws on abortion. It had an immediate impact. There was vicious in-fighting among Republicans in the summer of 1989 over abortion as they vied to fill a vacant state Assembly seat from San Diego County in a special election. What happened in San Diego, a contest between pro-life and pro-choice Republicans (the pro-choicer won in a district of white suburbanites) could be repeated dozens of times if abortion becomes an issue for the Legislature to decide.

Success, then, may become a Catch-22 for the Republicans. They can only become the majority party by expanding their base to include a wider variety of cultural and ideological viewpoints, but that expansion could mean that Republicans will squabble more among themselves – just like the Democrats have been doing. Conversely, if the Democrats slip into minority status in the 1990s, they may find it easier to project a unified and integrated philosophical image, having rid themselves of elements – conservative whites – who are unhappy with the party's liberal ideology.

LEGISLATURE FALLS DOWN ON THE JOB

In the last decade, reapportionment, as partisanly slanted as it may have been, was one of the Legislature's few decisive actions. Increasingly, the Legislature drew within itself, preoccupied with such games of inside baseball as campaign strategy, fund-raising and partisan and factional power struggles. It seemed unable, or unwilling, to cope with the huge policy issues raised by the dynamics of the real world outside the Capitol: population growth, ethnic diversification, transportation congestion, educational stagnation, environmental pollution.

The Legislature, which Jesse Unruh had recast as a full-time professional body in the 1960s, had once been rated by most authorities as the finest in the nation. The 1980s saw not only policy gridlock but a rising level of popular disgust with antics in the Legislature, fueled by several official investigations into corruption and a much more critical attitude of the Capitol press corps.

California's political demography is at least partially responsible for the Legislature's lethargy. Legislators are torn between the demands and aspirations of California's new immigrant-dominated population and the limits set by white, middle-class voters. But the very professionalism that was Unruh's proudest achievement also has contributed to the malaise. Full-time legislators, many of them graduates of the Legislature's own staff, are naturally preoccupied with their personal political careers. Thus legislative duties that conflict with those careers are shunted aside.

Throughout the decade, reformers have proposed institutional changes to restore the Legislature's luster, such as imposing limits on campaign spending and fund raising (which have increased geometrically) and providing public funds to campaigns. Voters endorsed a comprehensive reform initiative in 1988, but they also approved a more limited version placed on the ballot by some legislators and special-interest groups. The first provided public funds for campaigns while the second specifically barred such spending, and the second gained more votes. The final result was that most of the first initiative was negated.

As a years-long federal investigation of Capitol corruption erupted in indictments in 1989, the Legislature itself began drafting reforms designed to raise its standing with an increasingly cynical public.

Mostly, however, the impotence of the Legislature manifested itself in an explosion of initiative campaigns that took issues directly to voters, bypassing the Capitol altogether. Initiatives became so popular that lawmakers and even candidates for governor began sponsoring them as vehicles to make policy or gain favorable publicity. Gubernatorial hopeful John Van de Kamp proposed, for instance, a political reform initiative that would take advantage of the popular disdain for the Legislature, and another to deal with environmental matters. The Republican candidate for governor in 1990, Pete Wilson, has trumpeted his own initiative to deal with crime. In addition to their publicity-generating value, initiatives sponsored by candidates allow them to slide around voter-imposed limits on direct campaign fund raising.

THE INITIATIVE EXPLOSION

The "initiative entrepreneurs," as some dubbed them, emerged during the decade as powerful new political figures, and the Legislature was reduced to reacting to the policy directives they issued. The syndrome began when Howard Jarvis and Paul Gann sponsored Proposition 13, demonstrating how initiative campaigns could be self-financing through direct-mail appeals, and continued unabated through the 1980s, with causes emerging from both sides of the political spectrum.

The most notable example of the syndrome was auto insurance, the subject of no fewer than five measures in 1988. Four were defeated but one, championed by a consumer group coalition in sometime alliance with trial lawyers, won approval. Proposition 103 was only slightly less revolutionary than Proposition 13, the prototype for bomb-thrower initiatives. It promised big cuts in auto insurance rates and created an entirely new state regulatory system for insurers, including an elective insurance commissioner's position.

Proposition 103 was also something else: an indication that the political left might score points with a generally conservative electorate if it picked its issues carefully. Proposition 103, like Proposition 13, appealed to personal economic motives. Other initiatives from the left side of the political spectrum, such as a series of special tax and bond measures to benefit health and environmental causes, were also successful. Harvey Rosenfield, the young consumer activist who promoted Proposition 103, is trying to keep his string going with a 1990 measure that would change Proposition 13, removing limits on property taxes for non-residential property but keeping them for homes.

But the right isn't silent. Republicans are working on reapportionment initiatives for 1990, some of them tied to legislative reform that also would take advantage of the Legislature's declining public image.

As many as three dozen measures could confront California voters as the orgy of initiatives continues in a perverse exploitation of the reforms that Hiram Johnson instituted more than 75 years ago. The initiative petition has become the political weapon of choice as the Legislature's ability to respond to conflicting demands has diminished.

AN UNCERTAIN FUTURE

California politics, having undergone so many evolutions in the past two generations, remains in a state of flux. In the short run, the state is likely to continue its slow movement toward the right as the dominant Anglo electorate ages. While half of California's current voters are over 50, it could reach 60 percent by the turn of the century.

Republicans could become the dominant party by the mid- to late-1990s, especially if they get a fair shake on the post-1990 reapportionment of legislative and congressional seats. And the current trends could carry that into the first or even second decade of the new century. California will become increasingly important in presidential politics as it continues to gain congressional seats and electoral votes and if it moves up its presidential primary election to March or April, a virtual certainty since leaders of both parties, including Gov. Deukmejian, have endorsed the shift. In general, given previous California voting trends, these changes would favor Republicans, making it that much more difficult for Democratic candidates to win enough electoral votes to capture the White House.

California Democratic leaders are pushing the earlier primary in hopes of using the state's huge delegate clout to create a candidate more acceptable in California and other Sun Belt states and thus arrest the party's national decline in presidential politics. The 1988 presidential election demonstrated anew that when it comes to electing presidents, even without a Californian on the ticket, the state leans Republican.

In the longer run, the Democrats' best hope in California is to organize the unorganized – principally the fast-growing and low-voting Hispanic and Asian population blocs. But it will be a slower process than many party leaders publicly contend, perhaps taking a generation or even two of Americanization. And it will demand some internal changes within the party that its leaders are not now willing to concede. Republicans, in fact, might also take advantage of the social conservatism of the new Californians.

A major factor may be the development of some charismatic leaders among Hispanics and Asians who could move their latent political power in one direction or another, much as Martin Luther King and Jesse Jackson mobilized the latent power of blacks. But so far, none has emerged.

Thus, the real story of California's 21st century political development will be the extent to which today's newcomers become tomorrow's voters and how their cultural values change the political landscape.

2

Congress: Biggest and the weakest

Rep. Chet Holifield was built like a rhino and had the disposition to match. In 29 years in Congress, the Montebello Democrat became legendary for blistering rebukes of both staff and fellow officeholders.

On this particular day, however, he was in a relaxed and expansive mood as three Whittier College coeds quizzed him about his life in Congress and his role as dean of the California delegation.

One asked how often all the Californians vote the same way on a bill.

Holifield wrinkled his brushy eyebrows in thought. "Well, yes," he finally replied. "There was a wine bill two or three sessions ago."

That was 1972. But the current dean, San Jose Democrat Don Edwards, agrees that little had changed until recently. California has long had the most impotent of the large state delegations.

Although House Republican and Democratic caucuses try to meet weekly during sessions, the entire delegation doesn't even get together socially. It's not enough to say that the 45 members are badly divided by differences involving geography and ideology. They're scattered. Some have likened the delegation to the cartoon image of a huge dust cloud rolling along the ground with feet and hands sticking out here and there.

Membership ranges from the Republican bombasts of Orange County, Robert Dornan and William Dannemeyer, to brittle liberals such as Berkeley Democrat Ron Dellums. They not only can't, but won't, work together even when obvious interests of the state are at stake.

Add to that the intense bitterness over reapportionment battles earlier in this decade when the Democrats successfully gerrymandered the state and made it stick.

The late Rep. Phil Burton of San Francisco drew lines to guarantee 28 Democratic seats and with Democrats in the governor's chair and running both houses of the Legislature – including longtime Burton ally Willie Brown in the Assembly – there was never any question that Burton's plan would be approved.

The current breakdown is 27 Democrats and 18 Republicans. Had district lines been drawn with even a pretense of fairness, Republicans could easily hold three to five more seats today. As it stands, only one Democratic seat has been taken away by a Republican, the 38th District where Dornan ousted Jerry Patterson. This hardly reflects Republican registration, which has been creeping upward all through the decade. Total GOP vote for Congress matches, and sometimes surpasses, the Democratic total.

Burton's gerrymandering was in the worst tradition of the 19th century political bosses. District lines stop in the middle of city blocks, cut through backyards and snake down alleys. In San Pedro Harbor, the boundary loops across the bay, snatches a Republican stronghold in a Democratic district, and jogs back across the water. Burton, who drew the lines personally and kept them secret from just about everyone, laconically referred to the plan as "my contribution to modern art."

As a result, "There's a lack of trust," said ex-Rep. Tony Coelho, D-Merced. "We're the nation's largest delegation and we could never pull together."

That's led to great frustration for Edwards and his senior Republican counterpart, Carlos Moorhead of Glendale, who get along well and attempt to provide some cohesion.

LOWER-LEVEL ALLIANCES

On a less senior level, another working alliance has been formed in recent years between two men who are the de facto leaders of their caucuses – Republican Jerry Lewis of Redlands and Democrat Vic Fazio of West Sacramento. In a short period of time for Congress, Lewis has become the third-ranking member of his caucus as chairman of the House Republican Conference. Fazio is vice chairman of the Democratic Caucus, the No. 5 position in his ranks.

Both are affable men who've ingratiated themselves to House leaders by tending to thankless chores such as congressional pay raises and producing policy papers. They talk regularly and have put together loose coalitions on parochial areas involving trade, immigration and defense. They are also ranking members of a key Appropriations subcommittee which gives them standing to deal for the state.

Edwards and Moorhead, however, believe they've finally found the vehicle for bringing unity to the delegation. And the California Business Roundtable, an association of top business leaders, has put up $200,000 to see if it will fly.

Last fall, they launched the California Institute, a bipartisan research group to pursue issues important to the state. Office space was rented on Capitol Hill and a full-time staff was recruited. Half of the 18 policy board members were named by Republicans in the state delegation and the others by Democrats. Officeholders were ineligible.

In the short term, the institute is to mobilize support for pork-barrel projects that come along from time to time. The latest is the proposed $27.4 million Army computer research center. The University of California, San Diego, is vying to become the host school along with universities in Pennsylvania, West Virginia and New Mexico.

But in the long term, the institute is to concentrate on economic issues that would tend to unite the delegation. It's expected to develop strategies for dealing with California needs 10 to 20 years from now in areas such as trade, transportation and waste disposal. There have been similar attempts to put such an organization together, but they've always collapsed amid partisan suspicion.

Nonetheless, other areas of the country have had considerable success with such associations. Texans have been delivering for their home state in such a manner for years. There's also the Northeast-Midwest Institute which takes in 18 states and operates with a $1.4 million-per-year budget. The Sunbelt Institute represents 16 states and operates on $160,000 per year.

Such cooperation is credited with winning Texas two of the major federal plums of the 1980s – the $4.1 billion Superconducting Super Collider to be built near Dallas and the $125 million Sematech semiconductor research facility which went to Austin. A third project was a $25 million earthquake research center which ended up in Buffalo, N.Y.

California was in the running for each of those, but it's not fair to say incoherence in the congressional delegation was the chief reason they went elsewhere. For the collider, in particular, there was plenty of blame to be shared with the state Legislature and the governor's office.

Nonetheless, three stunning losses in a row plus a weak attempt to snare one of three new federal centers on updating manufacturing technology was not lost on the state's business leaders. They've demanded something better.

California's delegation, after all, is the nation's largest, comprising 11 percent of the membership in Congress. Only New York has ever had 45 delegates and that was in the 1930s and '40s. After reapportionment, California could get another six or even seven seats because of rapid population growth during the 1980s. And the Census Bureau estimates that California is likely to continue that growth until well into the 21st century, which would expand its congressional delegation to nearly 70 members by 2010.

But that, too, can be a liability, Fazio points out. Small delegations fear California's potential dominance. "They want to gang up on the big guy," he explained. "Our numbers make them paranoid."

STRENGTH ON PAPER

On paper, at least, the delegation looks strong. Alan Cranston's long service and No. 2 position in the Senate puts him in a unique position to aid the state's industries and special-interest groups. He also chairs the Veterans' Affairs Committee.

Aside from Lewis, House Republicans hold few important positions. Only one, William Thomas of Bakersfield, is the ranking minority member of a committee, but his House Administration panel is not a power base. Rep. Duncan Hunter of Coronado chairs the Republican Research Committee, which develops House GOP strategies on emerging issues.

Democrats, however, hold a number of important committee posts: Augustus Hawkins of Los Angeles chairs Education and Labor, Glenn Anderson of Long Beach heads Public Works and Transportation, Leon Panetta of Carmel has Budget, Edward Roybal of Los Angeles chairs the Select Committee on Aging, Julian Dixon of Los Angeles has the ethics committee and Anthony Beilenson of Los Angeles heads Intelligence. George Miller of Martinez chairs the Select Committee and Children, Youth and Families. He's also in line to head Interior when ailing Rep. Morris Udall of Arizona retires. Miller has made good use of his subcommittee posts as has Henry Waxman of Los Angeles who's a major force on health issues. Tom Lantos of San Mateo used his housing subcommittee to pry open the HUD scandals.

The question, said Coelho, is whether the institute will help them pull together instead of in so many separate ways.

Much of the answer won't come until the 1990 elections. Californians may decide on one of several proposed ballot measures that would remove most of the overt politics from the reapportionment process. A fair reapportionment unquestionably means that the 1992 election would then pit Democratic incumbents against each other in some parts of the state as Republicans claim a half-dozen or more new seats.

Even if the ballot measures fail, the election of a Republican governor in 1990 would assure that Democrats won't be able to dominate the process as they did in the early 1980s. Any deal would have to be acceptable to both parties or there could be a standoff that would eventually force a court to reapportion the state. Either way, Democrats could be losers.

A third possibility would be the election of a Democratic governor and the presumed continuance of Democratic dominance of the Legislature. That could assure a gerrymander and yet another decade of bitterness. But things aren't all rosy for Democrats even in that version. Most of the state's growth in the last decade has been in suburbs represented by Republicans. Those districts will shrink in 1992. But some Democratic districts will have to expand.

Burton drew the lines so tightly in 1982 that a number of the Democratic districts have no place to grow except into Republican strongholds. That's particularly true in the Bay and Los Angeles areas.

So, regardless of who draws the lines after the 1990 census, the election of 1992 promises to be exactly the kind of barnburner Burton worked so hard to avoid. And the first casualty of any such contest would undoubtedly be any new-found, bipartisan unity.

BIOGRAPHICAL PROFILES

Following the political and biographical sketches of the state's two senators and members of the House of Representatives are election results from their most recent campaign. To the right of the results is the amount of money raised for the campaign.

Ratings from a selection of lobbying organizations are also given. A score of 100 indicates the officeholder voted in agreement 100 percent of the time on bills of interest to that organization. Lower scores indicate fewer votes in agreement. The organizations are:

ADA - Americans for Democratic Action Inc., 1511 K St., N.W., Suite 941, Washington D.C. 20005, (202) 638-6447. Liberal. Issues include civil rights, handgun control, hate-crimes statistics, gay/lesbian discrimination, and opposition to the death penalty, Contra aid and defense spending.

ACLU - American Civil Liberties Union, 122 Maryland Ave., N.E., Washington, D.C. 20002. Seeks a strict interpretation of the Bill of Rights. Most members are liberal, although the union takes some positions favored by conservatives.

ACU - American Conservative Union, 38 Ivy St., S.E., Washington, D.C. 20003, (202) 546-6555. Conservative on foreign policy, social and budget issues.

AFL-CIO - Department of Legislation, 815 16th St., N.W., Room 309, Washington, D.C. 20006. The nation's biggest union confederation promotes labor, health and civil-rights issues.

CFA - Consumer Federation of America, 1424 16th St., N.W., Washington, D.C. 20036, (202) 387-6121. Consumer, health and ₄ousing issues.

LCV - League of Conservation Voters, 2000 L St., N.W., Suite 804, Washington, D.C. 20036. Political arm of the environmental movement.

NTU - National Taxpayers Union, 325 Pennsylvania Ave., S.E., Washington D.C. 20003, (202) 543-1300. Conservatives devoted to reduced federal spending.

USCC - United States Chamber of Commerce, 1615 H St., N.W., Washington, D.C. 20062, (202) 659-6000. Pro-business and trade. Issues also include South Africa sanctions, welfare reform and civil-rights restrictions.

All ratings are based on 1988 votes.

U.S. Senate – Alan Cranston (D)

There are slow days, even in the writing game. Yet political writers always have spare arrows in their quivers for those times when no inspiration strikes. And for a good many years, many of them have had an arrow with Alan Cranston's name on it.

Cranston's political obituary has been updated countless times in newspaper columns throughout California. The senior senator has been counted down and out more often than anyone else on the state political scene except, perhaps, for Richard Nixon.

Yet Cranston's also one of the most enduring political figures in California's history. Except for a two-year hiatus, he's held state-wide elective office since 1959. Cranston and Hiram Johnson are the only Californians who've ever been

Alan Cranston

popularly elected to four terms in the U.S. Senate. When non-elected public service is counted, Cranston has been active since 1939, which is longer than either Nixon or Ronald Reagan.

Cranston was again stumping backwater areas of the state in the past year, making preparations for another Senate campaign in 1992. He'll be 78 then and probably looking more cadaverous than ever before. But if his health is good – Cranston runs almost daily and still competes in track meets for his age group – most observers believe he'll be on the ticket.

Some Democratic party leaders make no secret of the fact that they'd like him to retire. After a very close race in 1986 and ethical questions involving his ties to a junk bond king and a shady savings and loan operation, there's fear that Cranston could lose to a Republican challenger in 1982 and at least one, ex-Congressman Ed Zschau, already is making noises. It was Zschau who gave Cranston a scare in 1986. But Cranston has heard a lot of advice like that over the years and never paid it much heed. The ethics charges, he insists, are just so much "hullabaloo."

Instead, he's out carefully tending his political fences and reinvigorating his campaign organization. It's no accident that one of his chief causes in recent years has been voter registration drives in areas where Democrats are most likely to be found. In the meantime, the man so many have branded as a lightweight has built a solid power base in the Senate. Since 1977, Cranston has been majority whip, the No. 2 position in the Senate hierarchy. That also puts him on the Democratic Policy Committee and the Democratic Steering Committee. He chairs the Veterans' Affairs Committee and has key positions on both the Foreign Relations and the Banking, Housing and Urban Affairs Committees. Recently, he added the Intelligence Committee to his list, which helps bolster his influence in foreign affairs.

A LIBERAL PRAGMATIST

From his first days in Congress, Cranston has shown the ability to work in a bipartisan way to achieve his legislative goals. Cranston, the New Deal and Great Society liberal, has co-authored legislation with unlikely allies such as Sen. Strom Thurmond, R-S.C., and former Sen. Barry Goldwater, R-Ariz.

"I look for an issue where I can work with them," Cranston has said, such as veterans or defense. "From that, you form relationships that can lead to other positive things."

Cranston's ability to work with senators of all political stripes, and with not only the power brokers but the wallflowers, has earned him great respect. At the same time, he's developed a legendary ability to count votes, which is an indispensable talent for the majority whip.

It's notable that none of his colleagues promoted him for the majority leader's job early in 1989 when Sen. Robert Byrd of West Virginia stepped down. Yet he had only a brief challenge for the whip's post from Sen. Wendell Ford of Kentucky. It suggests that Cranston's colleagues don't see him as their leader, but as a complement to the Democratic leadership. And he hasn't any strong enemies, either.

Cranston and the new majority leader, George Mitchell of Maine, have a good working relationship. But South Dakota's Tom Daschle seems to have emerged as Mitchell's closest deputy.

That's also somewhat of a reflection of Cranston's standing in California. As Washington Post columnist Lou Cannon has said, "Californians like Alan Cranston, but there's no deep affection for him."

Even at Democratic functions, there's no clatter of high heels around Cranston or office seekers pawing to have their picture taken with him. He's essentially a shy man who finds small talk tedious and comes across to many as cold-blooded. Cranston make his presence felt by skillful use of his position to assist California interests and to blunt sources of discontent.

When Cranston moved to Washington in 1968, for example, his dovish stand on the Vietnam War had made him the sworn enemy of both veterans and aerospace groups. But he soon established himself as a champion of veterans' health concerns and formed a shrewd alliance with then-Gov. Reagan's administration to bring

Space Shuttle development home to California. Even his worst antagonists in those areas soon learned that Cranston was the man to see if they wanted something in Washington. When Lockheed's solvency depended upon a federal loan guarantee, Cranston delivered.

He's worked to broker problems for the state's financial, computer electronics, and agricultural industries while proving in vote after vote that he's a solid friend of labor. He's championed park and environmental causes even when it has cost him with loggers and other conservative Democrats.

FINANCIAL SCANDAL TOUCHES

Through all that, he has steered clear of any personal scandal until recently. In 1989, it was revealed that Cranston helped win delays in federal regulatory action against Lincoln Savings & Loan Co. of Irvine, a subsidiary of American Continental Corp. of Phoenix, owned by Charles H. Keating Jr.

Lincoln Savings was eventually declared insolvent, sticking the taxpayers with a $2.5 billion liability, but not before Keating raised $40,000 for Cranston's 1986 re-election campaign, $85,000 for the California Democratic Party, and $850,000 for three voter registration groups allied with Cranston, including one for which the senator's son, Kim, was the unpaid chairman.

Cranston also wrote the Securities and Exchange Commission asking relief for junk-bond king Michael Milken, who has since been indicted for alleged securities fraud. Milken ran his operation out of Drexel Burnham Lambert's Beverly Hills office and Drexel kicked in $10,000 to one of Cranston's voter registration operations.

Cranston maintains that his actions were similar to those performed for some 300,000 constituents over the years. And in Lincoln's case, Cranston says he had no knowledge that the S&L was in such serious trouble.

The S&L problems took on a bipartisan hue when it was revealed that state regulators failed to investigate Lincoln's dealings in junk bonds. Los Angeles attorney Karl Samuelian, Gov. George Deukmejian's chief fund-raiser, represented Lincoln's parent company in dealing with the regulators. Also, Keating had donated $75,000 to Deukmejian's re-election campaign. Deukmejian denied any impropriety as well.

While the story continued to unfold in late 1989, there were no revelations that Cranston got Cadillacs or personal investment opportunities as kickbacks – the stuff that has lead to the downfall of other politicians. Nonetheless, the links have angered many taxpayers and elderly people who lost savings. It remains to be seen how much liability he will carry into the 1992 campaign.

The irony is that Cranston got into trouble helping business. For years, critics have been painting Cranston as a foe of business although his record in Congress shows anything but an anti-industry bias. Many of those are the same critics who consider Cranston too liberal for California. That's generally the camp that equates liberalism with being soft on defense and naive in foreign affairs.

Cranston, though, has been in office long enough to see some of those arguments come full circle. In 1973, for example, he proposed START – Strategic Arms Reduction Talks with the Soviet Union as the logical extension of the ongoing Strategic Arms Limitation Talks, or SALT. The criticism was withering. But in the late 1980s, START has become one of the pillars of Reagan-Bush foreign policy.

Cranston, however, has done some policy shifting of his own. In 1980, for instance, as he prepared to run for re-election against the late tax cut leader Paul Gann, Cranston delivered a series of hawkish foreign policy addresses that condemned the Soviets and called for a massive military buildup. After he was re-elected, and as he ran for the Democratic nomination for president in 1984, Cranston shifted back to the left, calling for arms reduction and a lowering of East-West tensions.

Cranston still faces the liability shared by every other statewide politician in California: the difficulty of projecting a positive image to a diverse population of 28 million. But grass-roots organizing has been a Cranston specialty for 40 years.

A PIONEER IN LIBERAL CAUSES

It began in the late 1940s during his tenure as president of the United World Federalists, a national organization devoted to enhancing world law. From coffee klatches in Cranston's Palo Alto home, a statewide organization evolved for boosting liberal causes. The California Democratic Council, which he founded in 1952, became the dominate liberal force in the state during the 1950s and put Cranston into the state controller's office in 1958.

Cranston ran for the U.S. Senate in 1964 but was elbowed out in the primary by Pierre Salinger, who had been President Kennedy's press secretary. Salinger subsequently lost to Republican actor George Murphy in the runoff and left the state.

Two years later, Cranston was turned out of the controller's office by Republican Assemblyman Houston Flournoy. Cranston moved to Los Angeles and went into the housing development business, but kept his campaign organization together.

In 1968, he filed for the U.S. Senate seat held by Republican Whip Thomas Kuchel. Cranston personally admired Kuchel, but doubted the incumbent could survive the primary fight with right-wing state School Superintendent Max Rafferty. Cranston was right and went on to defeat Rafferty that November.

Cranston had an easy race against former state Sen. H.L. Richardson, R-Glendora, in 1974. Six years later, he beat Gann while garnering more votes than anyone who has ever been elected to the Congress.

In 1984, Cranston took a fling at the presidency. Some of his staff people still don't understand why he did it.

It was a disastrous campaign in which his only victory was the straw vote in Wisconsin. In 1989, he was still battling with the Federal Elections Commission over another questionable contribution during that campaign. He eventually paid a

$50,000 fine, the second largest up to that time, for accepting an illegal contribution of $54,000 from another Beverly Hills commodity broker.

In the midst of the presidential campaign, Cranston tried to dye the scant fringe of hair around his shiny dome. The hair turned orange. Cranston ended the campaign with a $2 million debt and Republicans salivating for what was left of his scalp when he ran for re-election two years later. Rep. Ed Zschau of Palo Alto emerged from a crowded Republican primary and ran a tough race. Cranston's margin was 3 percent or 104,868 votes out of nearly 7.2 million cast. The senator credited his voter registration efforts with providing the margin. But he also was helped by conservative apathy toward Zschau, a moderate with a libertarian approach to lifestyle issues.

Zschau lost to Cranston in his home turf on the San Francisco Peninsula. But he immediately announced he'd be a candidate for Cranston's seat again in six years. He went back to the Silicon Valley where he once made an electronics fortune and has busied himself in trade-association work.

If Zschau runs again in 1992, it seems likely that he'll face a crowded primary of GOP hopefuls as he did in 1986. Cranston, at least, hopes he will. But if Cranston's political problems discourage him from running, there'll be no shortage of Democratic candidates, including Congressman Mel Levine and, perhaps, ex-Gov. Jerry Brown.

PERSONAL: elected 1968; born June 19, 1914, in Palo Alto, Calif. ; home, Los Angeles; education, attended Pomona College and University of Mexico, B.A. Stanford University 1936; Protestant; twice divorced; one living child.

CAREER: journalist, International News Service in Europe and Africa, 1936-39; Washington lobbyist, Common Council for American Unity, 1939; language specialist, Department. of War, 1942-44; U.S. Army, 1944-45; Realtor, home developer, 1947-68; state controller, 1959-67.

COMMITTEES: chairman, Veterans' Affairs; Foreign Relations; Banking, Housing and Urban Affairs; Select Committee on Intelligence; Democratic Policy Committee, Democratic Steering Committee.

OFFICES: Suite 112, Hart Building, Washington, D.C. 20510, (202) 224-3553. Suite 980, 1390 Market St., San Francisco 94102, (415) 556-8440. Suite 515, 5757 West Century Blvd., Los Angeles 90045, (213) 215-2186. Suite 5-S-31, 880 Front St., San Diego 92188, (619) 293-5014.

1986 CAMPAIGN:

Cranston - D	50%	$11,037,707
Zschau - R	47%	$11,781,316

RATINGS:

ADA	ACLU	ACU	AFL-CIO	CFA	LCV	NTU	USCC
95%	46%	75%	15%	42%	70%	52%	77%

U.S. Senate – Pete Wilson (R)

In November of 1988, Sen. Pete Wilson did something that none of his predecessors had been able to do for 36 years: He held onto his seat for a second term.

It appeared that the "jinxed seat" from California finally had an occupant who would make a career of the Senate. Sen. William Knowland last won a second term in 1952. He was followed by Clair Engle, who died in office and was replaced briefly by Pierre Salinger. Following them were a trio of one-termers who seemed to forsake politics for ethereal causes once they were in office – George Murphy, John Tunney and S.I. Hayakawa.

Pete Wilson

Arguably, all Wilson had to do was show up for Senate hearings and stay awake and he'd have been assured a more prominent place in history than "Snoozing Sam" Hayakawa.

Wilson spent his first term working mostly anonymously on legislative issues and making himself useful to business interests at home. He also worked well with Alan Cranston, California's senior senator, something which Murphy, Tunney and Hayakawa seldom bothered to do.

After a comfortable win over Lt. Gov. Leo McCarthy in the 1988 race, (53 percent to 44 percent) Wilson seemed to be settling in for another productive six years.

But then came Republican Gov. George Deukmejian's announcement that he wouldn't seek a third term. GOP leaders, desperate to have a Republican in the governor's chair when the state is reapportioned after the 1990 census, cast about for someone electable. With no other Republicans holding statewide office, most agreed that only Wilson fit the bill.

And Wilson was delighted.

He ran unsuccessfully in the GOP gubernatorial primary in 1978 and has "wanted to be governor for a long time," Wilson said. "I see it very likely as a career capper – and a damn good one. Administrative challenges are more interesting than legislative ones. You see the end result right away."

Wilson had five years in the Assembly where he quickly showed leadership ability. As San Diego mayor for nearly 12 years, he ran a clean administration and was innovative in some areas.

A SLOW TRACK IN THE SENATE

In the Senate, he faces the likelihood of working his way slowly up the seniority ladder in the minority party for the balance of his career. During the two years the Republicans held the Senate ('85-'87), Wilson was too junior to play much of a role. His major committee assignments – agriculture, commerce and Armed Services – are important to California, but are not the glamour committees of the Senate.

As long as Republicans control the White House, Wilson can depend on having friends in the administration to assist in achieving his goals. The fact remains, however, that junior status in the minority caucus can be pleasant work if one doesn't mind seeing few tangible fruits of one's labor.

Wilson didn't exactly win the seat Hayakawa vacated in 1982 – Jerry Brown lost it. Brown, who was finishing eight years as governor, made two quixotic runs at the presidency and showed little interest in running the state during his second term. Despite a spirited Senate campaign that showed signs of producing an upset, Brown was carrying too much baggage into the November runoff. Voters choose Wilson by a half-million votes.

Wilson wasn't the favorite of many Republicans, either. In the 1976 presidential campaign, he endorsed Gerald Ford over Ronald Reagan. At the 1985 Republican state convention, conservatives almost booed him off the stage.

A CONSERVATIVE PARIAH

Through most of Wilson's career, he's been more centrist than conservative, causing the right wing to regard his Republican credentials as suspect. Being one of the few Republican senators to ridicule supply-side economics also didn't help enhance his reputation among conservatives.

At the same time, he's courted the environmental vote with consistent stands on coastal protection, limits on offshore oil drilling, expansion of transit systems and planned growth. Calling himself a "Teddy Roosevelt Republican," Wilson helped work out a compromise on Alan Cranston's wilderness bill, which added 1.8 million acres to California's roadless areas. But in the process, he angered Gov. Deukmejian, who wanted half as much acreage set aside.

Yet in the governor's race, Wilson's environmental constituency probably will be soft since he worked in Congress to block Sen. Cranston's Desert Protection Act which would create a huge federal park and wilderness area in the Mojave Desert.

On other matters, Wilson generally supported Reagan administration policies and was an early backer of George Bush's candidacy. On Armed Services, he's been a reliable vote for the Pentagon and CIA aid to the Contras.

He's worked for California industry, particularly agriculture, aerospace and computer electronics. One important setback came in 1984 when he lost efforts to get favorable trade restrictions for the U.S. tuna fleet, which is based San Diego.

THE HOLLYWOOD CONNECTION

One early success has also turned into a fund-raising plus. He backed Hollywood studios in a fight with the Federal Communications Commission over plans to allow television networks to own programs they broadcast. The plan was effectively killed when Wilson announced President Reagan's opposition at a 1983 hearing.

Producer Lew Wasserman, a long-time fund-raiser for Democrats, thanked Wilson by throwing a Beverly Hills party that brought Wilson more than $100,000. More importantly, it gave him entree to a number of show business personalities who seldom, if ever, had supported Republicans. Wilson's entertainment industry connections have muted the support that Democratic foes could expect from the liberal Hollywood community, a factor that helped Wilson win a second term in 1988 and will help him in 1990.

Probably the most memorable moment in Wilson's first term came when he was recovering from an emergency appendectomy. The Senate was considering a complex budget measure and it appeared that Vice-President Bush would be needed to break a tie. At the critical moment, pajama-clad Wilson was wheeled onto the Senate floor to cast the deciding vote in favor.

Much more significant, however, was Wilson's maneuvering on an immigration measure when he beat Wyoming Sen. Alan Simpson, the Senate's No. 2 Republican. That came in 1985 when Simpson, the assistant majority leader, was carrying a pet bill to restrict the number of foreigners allowed in the United States.

The chief opposition came from California growers who rely on an annual migration of "guest workers" from Mexico to harvest crops. Wilson took up their cause, insisting that Simpson's reforms have provision for 350,000 guest workers.

Simpson, who'd been kicked once too often by California growers, condemned them for their "greed" and insisted that a guest worker provision "would gut the intent" of his bill. When it came to a floor vote, Simpson won 50-48.

Wilson, however, invoked a rarely used procedural rule and got a second vote five days later. In the interim, he teamed with agricultural lobbyists to work every soft vote. On the second roll call, Wilson prevailed 51-44.

A ROCKY BEGINNING

Early in his Senate career, staff gaffes and lack of preparation caused Wilson public embarrassment several times. Those problems seemed to be behind him until mid-1989 when some over-zealous staff work put Wilson in the middle of the Department of Housing and Urban Development influence-peddling scandals.

A letter came to light bearing Wilson's signature which had been sent to HUD in support of a Minnesota apartment complex for senior citizens. HUD's regional office had turned down a $5 million grant for the project. But the day after Wilson's letter arrived, the decision was reversed.

The letter was written at the request of Robert Weinberger, a consultant to the Minnesota developer and politically well-connected nephew of former Defense Secretary Caspar Weinberger.

Wilson insisted he'd never seen the letter and blamed its existence on an aide who made too liberal use of an autopen. Though the truth of the statement wasn't disputed, Wilson's answer didn't sit well with California developers who were competing for the same scarce HUD money.

Wilson also was embarrassed by revelations that he accepted round-trip air fare from defense contractors and others who regularly lobby committees on which he serves. His wife flew gratis on a number of the flights as well. Most of the trips were coast-to-coast and involved legitimate speaking engagements requested by the firms involved, Wilson contended.

"What votes are those (trips) tied to, what actions?" Wilson demanded. "Senators do it routinely, and they do it because it is entirely within the law."

Those may be embarrassments, but they're hardly big-time scandals. Although they're sure to be issues in his gubernatorial race, voters are more likely to remember the pictures of Wilson being wheeled into the Senate chamber in his bathrobe. Or more recently, they'll recall he was the one who attempted to wrest away part of the fund senators use to send their constituents newsletters and give it to programs that help pregnant dope addicts.

Like most successful pols, Wilson postures well.

PERSONAL: elected 1982; born Aug. 23, 1933, in Lake Forest, Ill.; home, San Diego; education, B.A. Yale University 1955, J.D. UC Berkeley 1962; Protestant; wife Gayle.

CAREER: U.S. Marine Corps, 1955-58; attorney, 1963-66; Assembly, 1966-71; San Diego mayor, 1971-83.

COMMITTEES: Agriculture, Nutrition and Forestry; Armed Services; Commerce, Science and Transportation; Special Committee on Aging; Joint Economic.

OFFICES: Suite 720, Hart Building, Washington, D.C. 20510, (202) 224-3841.
1130 O St., Fresno 93721, (209) 487-5727.
Suite 915, 11111 Santa Monica Blvd., Los Angeles 90025, (213).209-6765.
4590 MacArthur Blvd., Newport Beach 92660, (714) 756-8820.
401 B St., San Diego 92101, (619) 557-5257.
450 Golden Gate Ave., San Francisco 94102, (415) 556-4307.

1988 CAMPAIGN: Wilson - R   53% $12,969,294
McCarthy - D 44% $ 6,986,294

RATINGS:

ADA	ACLU	ACU	AFL-CIO	CFA	LCV	NTU	USCC
15%	46%	75%	15%	42%	70%	52%	77%

1st Congressional District

Douglas H. Bosco (D)

California's 1st Congressional District sweeps down the north coast from the Oregon border and into the heart of the wine country north of San Francisco Bay. To the north, it's an area dependent on tourism, lumber, fishing and small farms. That gives way to the lush vineyards, mammoth poultry farms and inflated real estate values of Mendocino, Sonoma and Napa counties at the southern end.

Most of the small towns of the north coast are chronically depressed. Lumbermen are constantly at war with fishermen, although almost no one likes offshore oil development. There's a thriving counterculture which is usually held in check politically by conservative small town merchants and a growing number of traditionally

Douglas H. Bosco

oriented families who've escaped from the Bay area into southern reaches of the district, although the region evolved during the 1970s from Republican-voting to Democratic. State officials considered marijuana to be the area's largest cash crop – a situation that couldn't exist without some tolerance by the establishment.

Rep. Douglas Bosco, a conservative Democrat who served in the Assembly until winning the congressional seat in 1982, manages to keep the area's ardent liberals angry most of the time. Yet at election time, it's a choice of voting for Bosco or a Republican with even more conservative views.

Bosco's political base is in Sonoma County, which is more in step with his centrist views. But in three terms as an assemblyman, he's also proved to be a good friend of North Coast fishing, lumbering and farming interests, which gives him a solid support there as well. Often that puts him at odds with environmentalists whose causes such as pesticides, herbicides and old-growth timber are so intertwined with the economy of the region. But he's worked on solutions to sewage problems in the Russian River and for protection of coastal marshes.

Bosco, who was a page in Congress during his high school days, beat a 10-term Republican incumbent for the seat. It's probably safely his as long as he wants it.

PERSONAL: elected 1982; born July 28, 1946, in New York City; home, Occidental; education, B.S. Willamette University 1968, J.D. 1971; Roman Catholic; unmarried.

CAREER: attorney, 1971-78; Assembly, 1978-82.

COMMITTEES: Merchant Marine and Fisheries; and Public Works and Transportation.

OFFICES: Suite 225, Cannon Building, Washington, D.C. 20515, (202) 225-3311.

Suite 329, 777 Sonoma Ave., Santa Rosa 95405, (707) 525-4235.
Eureka Inn, 7th and F Streets, Eureka 95501, (707) 445-2055.
DISTRICT REGISTRATION: 56% D, 33% R
1988 CAMPAIGN: Bosco - D   63% $247,779
                 Vanderbilt - R   28% $ 6,633
RATINGS: ADA ACLU ACU AFL/CIO CFA LCV NTU USCC
         80%   74%   8%   79%   73% 56% 30% 36%

2nd Congressional District

Wally Herger (R)

The southern Cascade Range and Trinity Alps, the Sacramento Valley north of Sacramento and a small piece of the wine country in Napa County make up this increasingly conservative district. Some of the most remote parts of California are found within its boundaries where there are clear vistas to the giant volcanoes, Mounts Lassen and Shasta.

Tourism, timber and farming are the mainstays of an economy that is healthy on the valley floor and is often on the slide in wooded sections. Water is plentiful and residents expect their representatives to keep any more of their liquid gold from being siphoned off to other parts of the state.

Wally Herger

The mountains and remote villages make it an expensive area in which to campaign, a fact that favors incumbents. Rep. Wally Herger comes from the agricultural heartland of the district, which gives him an added edge in both fund raising and name identity.

Despite the safety of the seat, Herger shows no inclination toward activism. During three terms in the Assembly, he was a conservative backbencher who consistently voted "no" on most measures. In Congress, he's shown the same posture. He initiates a few farm bills but little else. He has vocal critics among owners of small logging companies who claim he favors the timber giants at their expense. Fishermen are angry that he's done nothing to change the operations of federal facilities that have been killing salmon runs on the upper Sacramento River. But his inaction sits well with many of his constituents who prize self-reliance and less government. In recessionary times, however, that could spell trouble if voters decide he's done too little to help them from his seat on the Agriculture Committee.

PERSONAL: elected 1986; born May 20, 1945, in Yuba City; home, Rio Oso; education, A.A. American River College 1968, attended CSU Sacramento; Mormon; wife Pamela; eight children.

CAREER: rancher and operator of family petroleum gas company, 1969-80; Assembly, 1980-86.
COMMITTEES: Agriculture; Merchant Marine and Fisheries.
OFFICES: Suite 1108, Longworth Building, Washington, D.C. 20515, (202) 225-3076.
Suite B, 20 Declaration Dr., Chico 95991, (916) 893-8363.
Suite 410, 2400 Washington Ave., Redding 96001, (916) 246-5172.
Suite 20, 951 Live Oak Blvd., Yuba City 95991, (916) 673-7182.
DISTRICT REGISTRATION: 46% D, 43% R

| **1988 CAMPAIGN:** | Herger - R | 59% | $696,748 |
| | Meyer - D | 39% | $193,915 |

| **RATINGS:** | ADA | ACLU | ACU | AFL/CIO | CFA | LCV | NTU | USCC |
| | 0% | 17% | 92% | 20% | 27% | 0% | 63% | 93% |

3rd Congressional District

Robert T. Matsui (D)

Robert T. Matsui

The 3rd District includes most of Sacramento and its suburbs, stretching east to the Sierra Nevada foothills. With the state Capitol and some 41,000 state wage earners, the Sacramento area is more strongly identified with government than any other part of California. But the government influence doesn't stop with the state. There are nearly 20,000 more federal paychecks from two Air Force Bases in or adjacent to the district plus 5,000 at an Army depot and 2,400 more at regional federal offices.

Such a strong civil service presence normally means friendly turf for a Democrat and Rep. Robert Matsui represents them ably. Yet the economy is diversifying and the district is turning more conservative along with it. Electronic industries and distribution centers are sprouting up in areas where rice and tomatoes once grew. Cheap land, by California standards, is feeding a boom that hardly noticed there was a recession in the early 1980s. In the 19 months ending in August 1989, the median cost of a home shot up 34 percent to $116,967.

It's a tribute to Matsui's strength that he could advocate shutting down Mather Air Force Base (5,600 jobs) as a cost-cutting move and no one even mentioned the word "recall." He's considered one of the brighter lights in the congressional delegation and has shown interest in statewide office, although he's never mustered the fortitude to take the plunge. And like most California House members, he's virtually unknown outside his district.

As an infant, Matsui was sent to a Japanese-American internment camp during

World War II. In Congress, reparations for victims of the relocation became one of his causes. His legislative interests are quite diversified, however, ranging from foster care and job training to medical care for elderly people. On the Ways and Means Committee, he's had an important role in shaping tax reform.

Matsui keeps a wary eye on the eastern suburbs of his district which are increasingly Republican, but no strong challengers have emerged. With each election, he wins in a walk.

PERSONAL: elected in 1978; born Sept. 17, 1941, in Sacramento; home, Sacramento; education, A.B. UC Berkeley 1963, J.D. Hastings College of Law 1966; United Methodist; wife Doris, one child.

CAREER: attorney, 1967-78; Sacramento city councilman, 1971-78.

COMMITTEES: Ways and Means.

OFFICES: Suite 2419, Rayburn Building, Washington, D.C. 20515, (202) 225-7163.

Suite 8058, 650 Capitol Mall, Sacramento 95814, (916) 440-3543.

DISTRICT REGISTRATION: 53% D, 35% R

1988 CAMPAIGN: Matsui - D   71% $638,688
Landowski - R   29% $ 7,695

RATINGS:	ADA	ACLU	ACU	AFL/CIO	CFA	LCV	NTU	USCC
	90%	86%	4%	88%	91%	81%	22%	36%

4th Congressional District

Vic Fazio (D)

One of the districts clearly targeted for shrinkage in the next reapportionment is the 4th, which stretches from Sacramento and some of its near suburbs west across the valley floor to Vallejo. Growth is booming on the eastern edge around Sacramento and Davis. From the west, Bay area workers are spilling into the Cordelia, Fairfield and Vacaville areas in search of affordable home sites.

The area's vast agricultural tracts are rapidly being paved over along the I-80 corridor. Yet the district also includes the sleepy villages of the Delta where life still revolves around cattle, pears, row crops and fishing. More retirees live in the area now, but that's the chief demographic change in recent years.

Vic Fazio

The district is safe Democratic country, but increasingly conservative. Nonetheless, Vic Fazio didn't even draw a Republican opponent last time out. Fazio has flowered into one of the House's most promising members. Several publications have called him the most skillful legislator in the 45-member California House delegation. With Rep. Tony Coelho's departure in 1989, Fazio became California's most influential House member. He was easily elected vice chairman of the Democratic Caucus, the No. 5 position in the House's Democratic hierarchy and a frequent stepping stone to greater things.

Fazio, a former assemblyman, came to Washington well schooled in the workings of legislative bodies. He caught the notice of party leaders by doing many of the thankless chores that others eschew such as facilitating congressional pay raises and serving on the ethics committee. In 1989, he was instrumental in keeping Congress' free mailing privileges intact despite efforts by Sen. Pete Wilson to divert a chunk of newsletter funds elsewhere.

He also quickly became known as a consensus builder. As Fazio's power has increased, he's used it to solidify relationships with other congressmen. One of the keys to his strength is the chairmanship of the Legislative subcommittee of Appropriations. That gives him enormous say on which programs get funded and which do not. He has a reputation for being the man to see in the delegation when there's a difficult political or legislative problem to resolve.

At the same time, he has diligently worked his district and has been a friend of the two huge Air Force bases located there, even though he publicly supports cutbacks in Pentagon spending. Neither is on the list of those to be shut down. He serves on another Appropriations subcommittee with jurisdiction over energy and water projects. That's an extremely important post for his district, but it also has made Fazio the chief mediator in one of the longest-running, no-win disputes in California – whether to build the Auburn Dam on the American River. But then again, no-win issues are one of his specialties. After the 1990 election, Fazio will have charge of representing House Democrats in the state's reapportionment battle.

Fazio's voting in Washington tends to be more liberal than his posturing in the district, but none of his opponents has been able to use that issue effectively.

PERSONAL: elected 1978; born Oct. 11, 1942, in Winchester, Mass; home, West Sacramento; education, B.A. Union College in Schenectady, N.Y., 1965, attended CSU Sacramento; Episcopalian; wife Judy.

CAREER: congressional and legislative staff, 1966-75; co-founder, California Journal magazine; Assembly, 1975-78.

COMMITTEES: Appropriations; Select Committee on Hunger.

OFFICES: Suite 2433, Rayburn Building, Washington, D.C. 20515, (202) 225-0354.

Suite 330, 2525 Natomas Park Dr., Sacramento 95833, (916) 978-4381.

844-B Union Ave., Fairfield 94533, (707) 426-4333.

DISTRICT REGISTRATION: 58% D, 35% R

1988 CAMPAIGN: Fazio - D   99% $529,334
                   No opponent

RATINGS:	ADA	ACLU	ACU	AFL/CIO	CFA	LCV	NTU	USCC
	85%	100%	0%	88%	64%	69%	17%	29%

5th Congressional District
Nancy Pelosi (D)

All but the northwest corner of San Francisco lies within the district the late Congressman Phil Burton drew for himself. Burton was a labor Democrat who missed becoming House speaker by one vote in 1976. His roots were in San Francisco's tough labor community, but he also was a messiah for the Sierra Club and mingled well with the city's financial and developer barons. His death in 1983 could have set off a raucous fight among the new constituencies that had been gaining political power for some time in the city – gays, Asians and Hispanics. But his wife, Sala, stepped in and the scepter was passed. She succumbed to cancer in 1987. The fight to replace her pitted straight liberals against gays in the Democratic primary. Long-time party activist Nancy Pelosi was the victor over gay county Supervisor Harry Britt.

Nancy Peolosi

But there was no lingering bitterness. Pelosi had many gay supporters and also was an acceptable choice for the city's Roman Catholic, society, environmental and labor factions. If anything, the election showed how seriously San Francisco's gay political leadership had been ravaged by the AIDS epidemic. The gay community simply couldn't mobilize itself as it had in recent years.

Pelosi came to Congress a wealthy housewife who long ago paid her dues licking envelopes and walking precincts in Democratic campaigns. Her father, a congressman from 1939-47, and a brother were mayors of Baltimore. Pelosi had been state Democratic chairwoman, a member of the Democratic National Committee and chaired the Democratic National Convention in 1984. Although new to Congress, she has been quickly learning the ropes and has been willing to take on the thankless chores that make friends and increase visibility. She's Northern California Democratic whip and a member of the executive board of the Democratic Study Group.

PERSONAL: elected 1987; born March 26, 1940 in Baltimore; home, San Francisco; education, B.A. Trinity College, Washington, D.C., 1962; Roman Catholic; husband Paul, five children.

CAREER: public relations executive, 1984-86.

COMMITTEES: Banking, Housing and Urban Affairs; Government Operations.

OFFICES: Suite 1005, Longworth Building, Washington, D.C. 20515, (202) 225-8259.

Suite 13407, 450 Golden Gate Ave., San Francisco 94102, (415) 556-4862.

DISTRICT REGISTRATION: 65% D, 19% R

1988 CAMPAIGN: Pelosi - D   76% $616,936
                       O'Neill - R   19% $ 19,245
RATINGS: ADA ACLU ACU AFL/CIO CFA   LCV NTU USCC
             100% 95%   0%   96%   100% 79% 15% 21%

6th Congressional District

Barbara Boxer (D)

Some of the great mortgages of the Western World
are nestled among the fir and redwood trees of Marin
County, which makes up half of the 6th District electorate. The remainder of the district is scattered. To the
south, it includes the northwest corner of San Francisco,
once a predominantly middle-class area which is becoming increasingly affluent and Asian. There are extremely expensive homes with sweeping sea views near
the Presidio. Poor blacks inhabit the Fillmore District.
To the north, the district swings around the top of San
Francisco Bay to the one-time socialist, blue-collar city
of Vallejo. It also takes in the farms, small towns and
counter-culture havens that dot slices of Solano and
Sonoma Counties.

Barbara Boxer

The district lines were originally gerrymandered for John Burton, Phil Burton's
brother, whose tenuous hold on his seat was complicated by drug and alcohol
problems. The younger Burton decided not to run for re-election in 1982. The lines
were altered somewhat and the seat came close to going Republican in that election.
Marin County Supervisor Barbara Boxer, once John Burton's aide, won the seat
with only 52 percent of the vote, but has never had trouble since.

It's a district of informed people who turn out to vote. Marin is still the trend-
setter, a bastion of yuppie attitudes long before the term was coined. Voters tend to
be environmentally aware and economically conservative. It's a good fit for Boxer,
who as a freshman exposed the Air Force purchase of the $7,622 coffee pot.

Almost overnight, Boxer became one of Congress' experts on defense procurement issues. By her third term, she was on the Armed Services Committee which
was once one of the most exclusive old-boy clubs of the House. But she's also
worked her staff to exhaustion on a variety of other issues which are popular in her
district such as AIDS research, transportation, dial-a-porn, consumer protection,
abortion rights, off-shore oil bans and high-school dropouts. She was elected
president of her freshman class and has been moving up the leadership ladder in a
variety of areas ever since. She currently is whip-at-large for the Democratic caucus.

Boxer is one of the few California congressional members who is developing a
national following. In a Democratic administration, she could be considered for a

cabinet post. And if she ever found herself in a tough race, she could expect dollars to flow in from women's groups throughout the country.

PERSONAL: elected 1982; born Nov. 11, 1940, in Brooklyn, N.Y.; home, Greenbrae; education, B.A. Brooklyn College 1962; Jewish; husband Stewart, two children.

CAREER: stockbroker and financial researcher, 1962-65; reporter for the weekly Pacific Sun, 1972-74; aide to Rep. John Burton, 1974-76; Marin County Supervisor, 1976-82.

COMMITTEES: Armed Services; Budget; Select Committee on Children, Youth and Families.

OFFICES: Suite 307, Cannon Building, Washington, D.C. 20515, (202) 225-5161.

Suite 300, 3301 Kerner Blvd., Greenbrae 94904, (415) 457-7272.

450 Golden Gate Ave., San Francisco 94102, (415) 626-6943.

DISTRICT REGISTRATION: 59% D, 27% R

1988 CAMPAIGN: Boxer - D   73% $351,687

                 Steinmetz - R   27% $ 50,532

RATINGS:	ADA	ACLU	ACU	AFL/CIO	CFA	LCV	NTU	USCC
	80%	91%	5%	97%	82%	88%	25%	27%

7th Congressional District

George Miller (D)

The 7th District begins in the backwaters of San Francisco Bay and stretches inland along the south shore of the Carquinez Straight. The grubbiest of the industrial towns in the district is Richmond, which is more than 50 percent black. To the east lie a series of roughneck refinery and factory towns – Pinole, Hercules, Rodeo, Martinez, and Pittsburg.

To the south are the affluent suburbs of Concord and Pleasant Hill. Those areas of Contra Costa County traditionally have been populated by youngish couples in search of affordable starter homes. But prices there have become so outlandish in recent years that young families are fleeing to further suburbs. Some of the more adventurous are rehabilitating homes in the industrial areas.

George Miller

The trend in the district is toward more conservative voters, but that seems to be of little threat to George Miller, the district's long-time liberal congressman. Miller is a strong environmentalist, but not a dogmatic one. He knows practically every civic and labor leader in the district by first name and works tirelessly on behalf of middle-class social and economic concerns. It's a grass-roots approach that he learned from his father, a long-time state senator.

As chairman on Interior's Water and Power Resources Subcommittee, Miller is one of the more powerful members of the delegation. Interior Chairman Morris Udall, who has Parkinson's disease, is expected to retire soon. That would give Miller the Interior chairmanship and even more clout to wage his battles – against water giveaways in the San Joaquin Valley, among many others. In a Democratic administration, he'd probably be a contender for Interior Secretary as well.

PERSONAL: elected 1974; born May 17, 1945, in Richmond; home, Martinez; education, A.A. Diablo Valley College 1966, B.A. San Francisco State College 1968, J.D. UC Davis 1972; Roman Catholic; wife Cynthia, two children.

CAREER: legislative aide, 1969-74; attorney, 1972-74.

COMMITTEES: Education and Labor; Interior; chairman of Select Committee on Children, Youth and Families.

OFFICES: Suite 2228 Rayburn Building, Washington, D.C. 20515, (202) 225-2095.

Suite 14, 367 Civic Dr., Pleasant Hill 94523, (415) 687-3260.

Suite 280, 3220 Blume Dr., Richmond 94806, (415) 222-4212.

DISTRICT REGISTRATION: 55% D, 34% R

1988 CAMPAIGN: Miller - D   68% $269,887

               Last - R   32% $ 14,710

RATINGS:	ADA	ACLU	ACU	AFL/CIO	CFA	LCV	NTU	USCC
	95%	96%	4%	90%	100%	88%	29%	31%

8th Congressional District

Ron Dellums (D)

Few voters in the 8th District have ambivalent feelings about Rep. Ron Dellums. In election after election, a third of the voters are solidly against him and the other two-thirds are solidly for him. Occasionally, splinter-party candidates also make a respectable showing on Election Day. Dellums, perhaps the most liberal member of the California delegation, has a polarizing effect on people. It is a posture that was effective in the quirky arena of the Berkeley City Council, where Dellums spent four years. But it has served him less well in Congress.

The favorable vote comes from the flatlands and low hills near San Francisco Bay – Oakland, Berkeley, Albany, Kensington and El Cerrito. They tend to be

Ron Dellums

black, blue-collar workers or underpaid professionals employed at the University of California and related enterprises. The rest of the voters tend to live in mostly-white Republican outposts high on the ramparts of the Berkeley hills or just over the crest in the wooded ravines of Lafayette, Orinda and Moraga.

Dellums' gift for oratory gave him unusual visibility when he first went to Congress, but it led to few constructive advances for him and his district. He wouldn't help boost the flow of federal money to the university, which is its life-blood. Other parochial concerns seemed to bore him. Like-minded colleagues tended to regard him as an unreliable ally.

In time, Dellums succeeded in pushing Congress to impose sanctions on South Africa – perhaps his greatest legislative victory.

He also learned to work with senior leaders, but had the misfortune of backing some of the wrong horses when Wisconsin Rep. Les Aspin was shaking the mossbacks off the Armed Services Committee in 1984.

In the 1980s, he developed a protective attitude over the huge military bases in Oakland and Alameda. But that feeling doesn't extend to Hunter's Point in San Francisco with its predominantly black community. He helped kill the proposal to home-port the battleship Missouri there.

Today, he chairs the District of Columbia Committee. That gives him great stature in the black community, but little elsewhere.

PERSONAL: elected 1970; born Nov. 24, 1935, in Oakland; home, Berkeley; education, A.A. Oakland City College 1958, B.A. San Francisco State College 1960, M.S.W. UC Berkeley 1962; Protestant; wife Leola, three children.

CAREER: U.S. Marine Corps, 1954-56; social worker, poverty program administrator and consultant, 1962-70.

COMMITTEES: Armed Services; chairman of District of Columbia Committee.

OFFICES: Suite 2455 Rayburn Building, Washington, D.C. 20515, (202) 225-2661.
Suite 105, 201 13th St., Oakland 94617, (415) 763-0370.
Suite 6, 1720 Oregon St., Berkeley 94703, (415) 548-7767.
Suite 160, 3732 Mount Diablo Blvd., Lafayette 94549, (415) 283-8125.

DISTRICT REGISTRATION: 64% D, 24% R

1988 CAMPAIGN: Dellums - D 67% $1,174,676
Cuddihy - R 31% $ 7,071

RATINGS:

ADA	ACLU	ACU	AFL/CIO	CFA	LCV	NTU	USCC
100%	100%	0%	92%	91%	94%	26%	23%

9th Congressional District

Fortney H. "Pete" Stark (D)

At its western edge, the 9th District takes in some neighborhoods of Oakland, plus Alameda and the scruffier suburbs to the south such as San Leandro, San Lorenzo and Hayward. Then it sweeps across the hills through more affluent neighborhoods to Pleasanton and Livermore. It's in the latter areas that rapid growth has occurred in recent years, bringing a conservative bent to one of the more liberal districts in the state.

The working-class areas also are seeing the beginning of a renaissance as the demand for housing has boosted the price of stucco bungalows beyond the reach of middle-income people. This could be an unpleasant change for a liberal such as Rep. Pete Stark. Yet his growing seniority and clout in tax and health matters

Forney "Pete" Stark

provide a solid platform from which to assist the district. Stark has become a chief lieutenant of Illinois Rep. Dan Rostenkowski on the powerful Ways and Means Committee. One day he may chair it. That's made him a key player in tax reform and a factor in almost any California issue that comes before Ways and Means.

Stark is also used to swimming against the tide and winning. He started his own bank in Walnut Creek and pulled in deposits throughout the Bay Area by using peace symbols on his checks during the Vietnam era. But he sold his bank stock once he became a member of the House Banking Committee. In 1986, the political arm of the American Medical Association spent some $200,000 to bankroll an opponent. But Stark crushed him with 70 percent of the vote and continues to be a consistent "no" vote on issues that pit the AMA against consumers.

PERSONAL: elected 1972; born Nov. 11, 1931 in Milwaukee, Wis.; home, Oakland; education, B.S. Massachusetts Institute of Technology 1953, M.B.A. UC Berkeley 1960; Unitarian; wife Carolyn, four children.

CAREER: U.S. Air Force, 1955-57; 1961-72, founder and president of a bank and a savings and loan institution.

COMMITTEES: District of Columbia; Ways and Means; Select Committee on Narcotics Abuse and Control; Joint Economic Committee.

OFFICES: Suite 1125 Longworth Building, Washington, D.C. 20515, (202) 225-5065.

Suite 1029, 22300 Foothill Blvd., Hayward, 94541, (415) 635-1092.

DISTRICT REGISTRATION: 59% D, 30% R

1988 CAMPAIGN: Stark - D   73% $410,540

                 Hertz - R   27% $ 0

RATINGS: ADA ACLU ACU AFL/CIO CFA LCV NTU USCC
90% 100% 0% 90% 82% 88% 27% 42%

10th Congressional District
Don Edwards (D)

In the early days of the Vietnam War, one of the few voices of opposition anywhere in the Congress came from an eloquent member from San Jose. Rep. Don Edwards' brand of militant liberalism has shown no sign of waning during nearly three decades in Congress.

Edwards, a one-time Republican and FBI agent, is the same forceful spokesman for civil liberties and social justice that he always was. The Fair Housing Act of 1980 is a triumph that he wears like a peace symbol in his lapel. But that's just one of many. He was a prime mover behind the Equal Rights Amendment, the Voter Rights Act, the fight to abolish the House Un-American Activities Committee and others. He's been a stalwart against attacks on forced busing and abortion, as well.

Don Edwards

Yet Edwards also is a fair man who insists on procedural integrity in all he does. That reputation has helped him exert some leadership over the fractious California delegation, of which he is the dean but not a whip-cracking leader of the Phil Burton sort. It's a job that tries even Edwards' patience. The California delegation isn't a house divided. It's a rabbit warren.

As the district's prune orchards and dairy farms have given way to electronics plants and housing tracts, Edwards' philosophy as been less in vogue. But he rarely even draws a Republican opponent any more and is immensely popular among the Hispanic people who makes up nearly a third of the district. His turf takes in central and east San Jose, and then stretches up the east side of San Francisco Bay to Milpitas, Union City, Newark and Fremont. It's essentially a working-class district, but is being rediscovered by yuppies who've been priced out of the area's more affluent residential areas.

Edwards makes effective use of his seniority on the Judiciary and Veterans Affairs committees to assist the district. And despite the fact that he's in his mid-70s, he enjoys good health and shows no sign of slowing down.

PERSONAL: elected 1962; born Jan. 6, 1915, in San Jose, Calif.; home, San Jose; education, B.A. Stanford University 1936, L.L.B. 1938; Unitarian; wife Edith.

CAREER: FBI agent, 1940-41; U.S. Navy 1941-45; title company executive, 1945-62.

COMMITTEES: Judiciary; Veterans Affairs.

OFFICES: Suite 2307 Rayburn Building, Washington, D.C. 20515, (202) 225-3072.
Suite 100, 4210 West Hedding St., San Jose 95126, (408) 247-1711.
38750 Paseo Padre Pkwy., Fremont 94536, (415) 792-5320.
DISTRICT REGISTRATION: 58% D, 29% R
1988 CAMPAIGN: Edwards - D   86% $173,537
　　　　　　　　　No opponent
RATINGS: ADA   ACLU   ACU   AFL/CIO   CFA   LCV   NTU   USCC
　　　　　　 100%   100%   0%   94%   100% 94%   25%   23%

11th Congressional District

Tom Lantos (D)

From the San Francisco city limits to Redwood City, the 11th District includes all of the Peninsula except for the extremely wealthy (and Republican) communities of Hillsborough, Woodside, Portola Valley and Atherton.

At the northern end are the boxy, working-class homes of Daly City and San Bruno plus Colma, the graveyard for more than a million San Franciscans. South of the airport, the suburbs become ritzier and more wooded. But congestion is everywhere – on the freeways, the streets and even the bicycle paths.Residents tend to be pro-environment, well educated and not particularly burdened by a social conscience.

But the lack in social conscience didn't rub off on Rep. Tom Lantos who, as a youth, fought the Nazis in the

Tom Lantos

Hungarian underground. Lantos is a strident spokesman for human and workers' rights. Unlike most congressmen, he'll wade into a state issue such as the fight to restore the Cal-OSHA worker safety program. He stridently opposes any totalitarian regime and fights tirelessly for increased security for Israel.

In 1989, he was Congress' point man on the Housing and Urban Development agency scandals. His intense questioning of HUD officials kept the pot stirring for months and gave him enviable visibility on nightly news programs. Yet he's shown considerable independence in Congress, often tending to vote his conscience rather than the party line.

The former economics professor came from behind in 1980 to unseat a Republican who'd served less than a year. Once in office, he immediately began to amassed a large campaign war chest and has had no serious opposition since.

PERSONAL: elected 1980; born Feb. 1, 1928, in Budapest, Hungary; home, Burlingame; education, B.A. University of Washington 1949, M.A. 1950, Ph.D UC

Berkeley 1953; Jewish; wife Annette, two children.

CAREER: economics professor and administrator for San Francisco State University and the California State University system, 1950-80; part-time bank economist and television commentator.

COMMITTEES: Foreign Affairs; Government Operations; Select Committee on Aging.

OFFICES: Suite 1526 Longworth Building, Washington, D.C. 20515, (202) 225-3531.

Suite 820, 400 El Camino Real, San Mateo 94402, (415) 342-0300.

DISTRICT REGISTRATION: 55% D, 32% R.

1988 CAMPAIGN: Lantos - D   71% $269,510

                Quraishi - R   24% $ 95,575

RATINGS:	ADA	ACLU	ACU	AFL/CIO	CFA	LCV	NTU	USCC
	85%	73%	8%	94%	82%	94%	21%	31%

12th Congressional District

Tom Campbell (R)

Lines for the 12th District were drawn to cram as many south Bay Area Republicans as possible into one district. It takes in some of the richest communities in the state (Hillsborough, Atherton, Woodside and Portola Valley), the heart of the Silicon Valley in San Mateo and Santa Clara Counties, and then skirts San Jose and runs down Highway 101 to the garlic capital of Gilroy. Despite that, the voters show increasing independence. For years, it was the stronghold of liberal Republican Pete McCloskey. He was replaced by another liberal-to-moderate, Ed Zschau. But Alan Cranston, whose father made a fortune as a real estate agent there, carried the district against Zschau in the 1986 Senate race.

Tom Campbell

Rep. Ernest Konnyu, a fringe conservative, became a one-term wonder when sexual harassment of his staff became public. He was replaced in 1988 by a brilliant Stanford economist and law professor, Tom Campbell, another liberal Republican who had the backing of both Zschau and electronics mogul David Packard.

Campbell appeals to the wealthy, egghead and electronics factions in this district. He brings to Congress trade and tax knowledge that could be used to forge favorable trade opportunities for the district's computer electronics industries. As a freshmen and member of the minority party, it may be a long time before Campbell can put his knowledge to practical use. But if he settles in for a career in Congress, it could be a productive one.

PERSONAL: elected 1988; born Aug. 14, 1952, in Chicago, Ill.; home, Palo Alto; education, B.A. and M.A. University of Chicago 1973, J.D. Harvard University 1976, Ph.D University of Chicago 1980; no religious affiliation; wife Susanne.

CAREER: attorney, 1978-80; White House and U.S. Justice Department positions, 1980-81; Federal Trade Commission, 1981-83; Stanford law professor, 1983-88.

COMMITTEES: Science, Space and Technology; Small Business.

OFFICES: Suite 1730 Longworth Building, Washington, D.C. 20515, (202) 225-5411.

Suite 105, 599 North Mathilda, Sunnyvale 94086, (415) 321-9154.

DISTRICT REGISTRATION: 45% D, 42% R

1988 CAMPAIGN: Campbell - R   52% $1,440,639
                               Eshoo - D   46% $1,089,570

RATINGS: None as of yet.

13th Congressional District

Norman Y. Mineta (D)

The 13th District is compact and probably will shrink more after the next reapportionment. It includes most of San Jose, which surpassed San Francisco to become the state's third largest city in 1989, and the suburbs of Campbell, Santa Clara and Los Gatos.

Most of the growth as been in the more affluent suburbs, but sky-rocketing housing values in San Jose are changing the economic mix of this region. The area's computer electronics industries produce an increasing number of dinks (double-income, no kids) and fewer of the lower-paid workers in those industries can afford to live near their jobs. Despite the conservative trend, Norm Mineta consistently runs ahead of the Democratic registration in the district. The popular former San Jose

Norman Y. Mineta

mayor seems fully recovered from a heart attack in 1986 and has a solid place in the House leadership as one of 10 deputy majority whips.

As a senior member of the Public Works Committee, he's the Californian to see for airport development money and other aviation issues. He also has a reputation for finding soft spots in the budget.

Like Rep. Matsui, Mineta spent part of his youth in a Japanese detention camp during World War II. He's led the fight to redress those wrongs. In another arena, however, he's been in the forefront of efforts to open up Japanese markets to Silicon Valley products. He's also pressured the Japanese to end whaling and protect arctic wildlife.

PERSONAL: elected 1974; born Nov. 12, 1931, in San Jose, Calif.; home, San Jose; education, B.S. UC Berkeley 1953; United Methodist; wife May, two children.

CAREER: U.S. Army 1953-56; insurance agency owner, 1956-74; San Jose City Council, 1967-71; San Jose Mayor, 1971-74.

COMMITTEES: Public Works and Transportation; Space, Science and Technology.

OFFICES: Suite 2350, Rayburn Building, Washington, D.C. 20515, (202) 225-2631.

Suite 310, 1245 South Winchester Blvd., San Jose 95128, (408) 984-6045.

DISTRICT REGISTRATION: 49% D, 38% R

1988 CAMPAIGN: Mineta - D   67% $521,674
                Sommer - R   30% $ 25,511

RATINGS:

ADA	ACLU	ACU	AFL/CIO	CFA	LCV	NTU	USCC
95%	90%	4%	89%	91%	81%	21%	31%

14th Congressional District
Norman Shumway (R)

One of the state's largest congressional districts, the 14th takes in pieces of San Joaquin County and swings north through the Sierra Nevada and its foothills to the Oregon border. It contains most of the state's least-populated counties (Alpine, Plumas, Sierra, Lassen and Modoc), but also the booming foothill communities of the northern Mother Lode and the agricultural towns around Stockton.

Since the late 1960s, refugees from smog-belt counties have been streaming into the foothills in search of cleaner air, less congestion, and more traditional lifestyles free of crime and drugs. The irony, however, is that the foothills have become the state's second most pro-

Norman Shumway

ductive marijuana-growing region and are distinguished by some of the most bizarre criminal activity in the state. The foothills seems to attract a unique population of mass murderers, renegade bikers, grave robbers and cult worshipers.

Rep. Norman Shumway, however, typifies the more traditional values that many residents revere. He's a former Morman bishop and strong family man who espouses conservative economics and less government. In the last reapportionment, a good chunk of his home base in Stockton was taken away, but Shumway was re-elected handily anyway. He had a credible and well financed opponent in the 1988 election, but still came away with 63 percent of the vote.

Shumway concentrates on public works issues that benefit the Port of Stockton and Delta reclamation efforts. He's a tireless supporter of building the Auburn Dam and reducing product liability. He'd like to export California's English-is-the-official-language law to the national scene. But he personally speaks both Japanese and Spanish, the language of two important minorities in his district.

PERSONAL: elected 1978; born July 28, 1934, in Phoenix, Ariz.; home, Stockton; education, A.A. Stockton College 1954, B.S. University of Utah 1960, J.D. UC Hastings College of Law 1963; Mormon; wife Luana, six children.

CAREER: attorney, 1964-78; San Joaquin county supervisor, 1974-78.

COMMITTEES: Banking, Finance and Urban Affairs; Merchant Marine and Fisheries; Select Committee on Aging.

OFFICES: Suite 1203 Longworth Building, Washington, D.C. 20515, (202) 225-2511.

Suite 1-A, 1150 West Robinhood Dr., Stockton 95207, (209) 957-7773.

Suite B, 11899 Edgewood, Auburn 95603, (916) 885-3737.

DISTRICT REGISTRATION: 47% D, 43% R

1988 CAMPAIGN: Shumway - R   63% $492,349

                Malberg - D   37% $103,678

RATINGS:

ADA	ACLU	ACU	AFL/CIO	CFA	LCV	NTU	USCC
0%	4%	100%	6%	27%	6%	67%	92%

15th Congressional District
Gary Condit (D)

If written a year earlier, this passage would be devoted to the golden boy of the delegation. In just eight years, Rep. Tony Coelho went from freshman to majority whip, the No. 3 Democratic position in the House.

He got there through hard work, extreme partisanship and fund-raising ability that was staggering even by Washington standards. But now he's gone from Congress, and perhaps from the political scene as well. As part of the long-running scandal that drove House Speaker Jim Wright, D-Texas, from office, Coelho's financial dealings came under intense scrutiny as well. The probers didn't have to look very far to find a questionable junk bond purchase and personal loan among other embarrassments. Coelho, rather than face a gauntlet like the one Wright ran, simply resigned.

Gary Condit

With help from Coelho, Assemblyman Gary Condit, D-Ceres, easily won the post in a special primary election with 57 percent of the vote. His chief opponent was former state Sen. Clare Berryhill, R-Los Banos, who also headed the state agriculture agency during part of the Deukmejian administration.

Condit established conservative credentials during his seven years in the Assembly. Crime and drug bills occupied most of his time and he was one of the dissident "Gang of Five" who made life unpleasant for Assembly Speaker Willie Brown, D-San Francisco. His legislative record, however, was far from distinguished. The question now is whether he'll settle into a long career as a backbencher in the House of Representatives.

The district twists up the San Joaquin Valley from western Fresno County to the San Joaquin County line, taking in all of Merced, Stanislaus and Mariposa counties along the way. Fast-growing Modesto is the population center. It includes the most fertile agricultural region in the valley and is growing both more Hispanic and more politically diverse as Bay Area workers filter into the valley in search of cheaper housing. Nearly a quarter of the residents now have Spanish surnames. The district has been safe turf for conservative Democrats since the 1950s – newcomers may bring changes, but probably not dramatic ones. On the Agriculture Committee, Condit will be positioned well to serve the district's traditional constituency.

PERSONAL: elected 1989; born April 21, 1948 in Salina, Okla.; home, Ceres; education, A.A. Modesto College 1970, B.A. Stanislaus State College 1972; Baptist; wife Carolyn, two children.

CAREER: production worker, Riverbank Ammunition Depot, 1972-76; community relations, National Medical Enterprises, 1976-82; Ceres City Council, 1972-74, mayor 1974-76; Stanislaus County Board of Supervisors, 1976-82; Assembly 1982-89.

COMMITTEES: Agriculture.

OFFICES: Suite 1729 Longworth Building, Washington, D.C. 20515, (202) 225-6131.

415 West 18th St., Merced 95340, (209) 383-4455.

Suite B, 900 H St., Modesto 95354, (209) 527-1914.

DISTRICT REGISTRATION: 55% D, 36% R

1989 CAMPAIGN: Gary Condit - D   57% $417,000

Clare Berryhill - R   35% $207,000

RATINGS: None as of yet.

16th Congressional District
Leon Panetta (D)

This is one of the few districts in the California where there's been a noticeable shift to the left in the 1970s and '80s. The environmental fights, which always take on increased intensity in coastal areas, are in part responsible for the change as residents have become increasingly concerned about onshore land development and offshore oil drilling. The 16th District takes in some of the most scenic land on the

California Coast, including Big Sur and Monterey Bay. Preservation of those resources is not a partisan issue. Republican coast dwellers value their views and clean beaches as much as anyone else.

Another reason for the change is the growth of the University of California, Santa Cruz, at the extreme northern end of the district. The campus is a place where the 1960s were reborn and haven't left. The Santa Cruz City Council is every bit as revisionist as Berkeley's and Santa Cruz's sharp shift to the political port (it was once a Republican city) neutralizes GOP strongholds in Monterey, San Benito and San Luis Obispo counties which are also part of the district.

Leon Panetta

Rep. Leon Panetta is sometimes accused of not paying enough attention to politics in the sprawling district. But he hasn't needed to. His unpaid wife runs his district offices and is probably the more effective politician of the two. That's left the Republican-turned-Democrat free to concentrate on legislative duties and, in a relatively short time, he's become one of the most powerful Californians in Washington. In 1989, he took over chairmanship of the Budget Committee which makes him a major player in national fiscal policy. Budget is one of the committees whose members are limited to six years. That means President Bush will have to contend with Panetta all through his first term.

Colleagues claim no one in Congress has a better grasp of budget issues. Panetta is committed to dealing with deficits, even though some sacrosanct Democratic programs may have to be sacrificed to do it. If it's possible for Congress and the administration to forge new bipartisan reforms, Panetta undoubtedly will be the one who takes them there.

On the Agriculture Committee, Panetta has had to walk a fine line between the powerful growers in his district and the strident environmentalists. He's helped growers keep their cheap labor with amendments to immigration bills that preserved their guest-worker provisions. He also worked to expand childhood nutrition programs. That is an area in which Panetta has sincere conviction, but it also has the happy effect of increasing growers' markets. But he has been tough on controls of pesticides, as well. In the Reagan administration, he successfully thwarted an effort to preempt California's tougher pesticide laws.

PERSONAL: elected 1976; born June 28, 1938, in Monterey,Calif.; home, Carmel Valley; education, B.A. University of Santa Clara 1960, J.D. 1963; Roman Catholic; wife Sylvia, three children.

CAREER: U.S. Army 1963-65; aide to U.S. Sen. Thomas Kuchel, 1966-69; director U.S. Office of Civil Rights, 1969-70; executive assistant to mayor of New York, 1970-71; attorney 1971-76.

COMMITTEES: Agriculture; Budget; House Administration; Select Commit-

tee on Hunger.
OFFICES: Suite 339, Cannon Building, Washington, D.C. 20515, (202) 225-2861.
380 Alvarado St., Monterey 93940, (408) 649-3555.
701 Ocean Ave., Santa Cruz 95060, (408) 429-1976.
200 West Alisal, Salinas 93901, (408) 424-2229.
1160 Marsh St., San Luis Obispo 93401, (805) 541-0143.
DISTRICT REGISTRATION: 53% D, 35% R
1988 CAMPAIGN: Panetta - D   79% $252,336
Monteith - R   21% $ 69,563

RATINGS:	ADA	ACLU	ACU	AFL/CIO	CFA	LCV	NTU	USCC
	90%	82%	4%	75%	82%	88%	28%	33%

17th Congressional District

Charles "Chip" Pashayan Jr. (R)

What was supposed to have been a swing seat takes in a piece of Kern County north of Bakersfield plus Kings and Tulare counties and eastern Fresno County. The growers and small-town shop keepers of the 17th District had a tradition of electing Democrats, but that suddenly changed in 1978 when Charles "Chip" Pashayan, Jr., upset an incumbent. The Democrats made several runs at Pashayan, but he deftly beat them back and has been steadily climbing the rungs of the GOP's House leadership ladder. In 1988, he won a seat on the Rules Committee.

Pashayan's roots are in the district's powerful Armenian community. On the water subcommittee of Interior, he worked for the development projects that are so vital

Charles Pashayan Jr.

to San Joaquin Valley. He's also been a caustic critic of the United Farm Workers union which is headquartered in the southern end of the district. It's a posture that solidifies his support among most of the area's Republicans and a good number of Democrats as well. Tulare County Democrats seem to like to vote for GOP candidates.

Pashayan's successes on agricultural issues can be attributed in part to ex-Rep. Tony Coelho who shared Pashayan's farm-booster philosophy, if nothing else. With Coelho gone and the increasing clout of Rep. George Miller, D-Martinez, the battles won't be so easily won. Miller is an outspoken foe of water subsidies and Pashayan gave up his seat on Interior for the berth on Rules.

Pashayan went through a messy divorce in 1989 which included charges of wife-beating. Pashayan contested the allegations. So far, his ex-wife has shown no inclination to move back to the district, which is probably a relief to Pashayan. In any event, the divorce hasn't seemed to hurt him politically. During and since the divorce, Pashayan has spent much less time in the district. But that hasn't appeared to hurt him either. Redistricting in 1982 made the 17th solidly Republican as Democratic leaders shored up the districts of nearby Democrats.

PERSONAL: elected 1978; born March 27, 1941, in Fresno, Calif.; home, Fresno; education, B.A. Pomona College 1963, J.D. UC Hastings Law School, 1968, M.Litt. Oxford University 1977; Congregational; divorced.

CAREER: U.S. Army, 1968-70; practicing attorney, 1970-73 and 1975-78; attorney for U.S. Department of Health, Education and Welfare, 1973-75.

COMMITTEES: Rules; Standards of Official Conduct.

OFFICES: Suite 203 Cannon Building, Washington, D.C. 20515, (202) 225-3341.

1702 East Bullard, Fresno 93710, (209) 487-5500.

831 West Center St., Visalia 93291, (209) 627-2700.

804 North Irwin, Hanford 93230, (209) 582-2896.

201 High St., Delano 93215, (209) 725-7371.

DISTRICT REGISTRATION: 49% D, 42%R

1988 CAMPAIGN: Pashayan - R   72% $206,677

Lavery - D   29% $ 5,227

RATINGS:

ADA	ACLU	ACU	AFL/CIO	CFA	LCV	NTU	USCC
35%	48%	64%	34%	55%	19%	40%	57%

18th Congressional District

Richard H. Lehman (D)

The 18th District is another where the late Rep. Phil Burton outdid himself in gerrymandering its boundaries to create a Democratic district. The district corkscrews through blue-collar sections of Fresno and into Sanger where the current incumbent lives. It takes in all of Madera County, includes the sparsely populated counties of Mono, Tuolumne and Calveras, and then sneaks into the working-class neighborhoods of Stockton. A Democrat has to commit moral turpitude to lose here.

Richard H. Lehman

Rep. Richard Lehman is the lucky beneficiary of Burton's handiwork. Lehman – a one-time legislative aide who won a seat in the Assembly at age 28 – had backed the losing side in an Assembly leadership struggle and as a consolation prize, the 18th District was drawn to his specifications. In Congress, Lehman has become known as an environmentalist, especially when it comes to enhancing mountain wilderness areas. But, like other Central Valley Democrats, he also is an effective supporter of agribusiness interests.

For the working-class areas of his convoluted district, Lehman offers support for education, consumer protection and drug rehabilitation. That plays well in a district with one of the highest percentages of traditional family units in the state.

Lehman was just 34 when he entered Congress. If he chooses, he can look forward to a long career with ever-increasing responsibility in his party.

PERSONAL: elected 1982; born July 20, 1948, in Sanger, Calif.; home, Sanger; education, A.A. Fresno City College 1968, attended CSU Fresno, B.A. UC Santa Cruz 1971.

CAREER: California National Guard, 1970-76; legislative aide 1970-76; Assembly, 1976-82.

COMMITTEES: Banking, Finance and Urban Affairs; Interior and Insular Affairs.

OFFICES: Suite 1319, Longworth Building, Washington, D.C. 20515, (202) 225-4540.

Suite 210, 2115 Kern St., Fresno 93721, (209) 487-5760.

Suite 216, 401 North San Joaquin St., Stockton, (209) 946-6353.

48 West Yaney Ave., Sonora 95370, (209) 533-1426.

DISTRICT REGISTRATION: 60% D, 32% R

1988 CAMPAIGN: Lehman - D   70% $193,681

               Linn - R   30% $89,260

RATINGS:

ADA	ACLU	ACU	AFL/CIO	CFA	LCV	NTU	USCC
85%	74%	9%	93%	91%	75%	24%	25%

19th Congressional District

Robert J. Lagomarsino (R)

Rep. Robert Lagomarsino got the scare of his political life during his 1988 re-election bid. When the votes were counted, the veteran congressman won by slightly less than one percent out of 228,000 votes cast. It was the toughest race in his 30-year career as an elected official.

Lagomarsino and state Sen. Gary Hart, D-Santa Barbara, had spent more than $3 million, making it the most expensive congressional race in the nation. Hart says he's seriously thinking about a rematch in 1990 even though he'd have to give up his Senate seat to do it. Perhaps that will be enough to retire Lagomarsino, who would be 64, voluntarily; but the veteran congressman hadn't announced in late 1989 what he'd do.

It was a classic battle between a unreconstructed   **Robert Lagomarsino** liberal and a Reagan stalwart. Both agreed there should be no more offshore oil drilling off Santa Barbara County, but that's about all they had in common. The stand probably hurt Lagomarsino in the refinery town of Oxnard, which is in the Ventura County portion of the district. As a ranking Republican on the Foreign Affairs Committee, Lagomarsino also had been the administration's point man on Central American policy. It was bad enough that he'd been mauled by the liberals on the committee. Now, Hart was doing the same thing in his district. Fortunately for Lagomarsino, he's always been a fanatic about constituent service. That's probably what saved him.

Santa Barbara has long been considered one of the jewels of the coastal counties and an ideal retirement locale. Yet there are plenty of working folks, too, and a number of them lost their jobs when the Reagan administration mothballed much of Vandenburg Air Force Base. That portion of Ventura County, which is Lagomarsino's home base, still has major Navy installations. But its civilian employment is limited and most of the military personnel who bother to vote mail their absentee ballots elsewhere.

But if Lagomarsino decides on another term, he probably can count on fundraising support from Ron and Nancy Reagan. Their mountain-top ranch is in the district.

PERSONAL: elected 1974; born Sept. 4, 1926, in Ventura, Calif.; home, Ventura; education, B.A. University of Santa Barbara 1950, L.L.B. University of Santa Clara 1953; Roman Catholic; wife Norma Jean, three children.

CAREER: U.S. Navy, 1941-45; attorney, 1954-74; Ojai City Council, 1958, and mayor 1959-61; state Senate 1961-74.

COMMITTEES: Foreign Affairs; Interior and Insular Affairs.

OFFICES: Suite 2332 Rayburn Bldg., Washington, D.C. 20515, (202) 225-3601.

Suite 101 5740 Ralston St., Ventura 93003, (805) 642-2200.

El Paseo, Studio 21, 814 State St., Santa Barbara 93101, (805) 963-1708.

104-E East Boone St., Santa Maria 93454, (805) 922-2131.

DISTRICT REGISTRATION: 46% D, 41% R.

1988 CAMPAIGN: Lagomarsino - R   50% $1,470,674

                 Hart - D   49% $1,548,193

RATINGS:

ADA	ACLU	ACU	AFL/CIO	CFA	LCV	NTU	USCC
35%	30%	80%	13%	82%	38%	58%	93%

20th Congressional District

William M. Thomas (R)

If the late Rep. Phil Burton was the winning strategist in the redistricting battles of the 1980s, there had to be a loser. That was Rep. Bill Thomas, who spent a lot of time trying to salvage what he could for the Republican party. It wasn't possible to gerrymander Thomas out of his seat, but Burton did the next best thing; he gave him a seat that stretches from the Nevada border to the sea.

The 20th District includes remote Inyo County in the high desert, most of Kern County's farm and oil lands in the Central Valley, the desert region of Los Angeles County and the least populated areas of San Luis Obispo County. The far-flung constituency is separated by two major mountain ranges, and the highest (Mount Whitney) and lowest (Death Valley) points in the contiguous United States. It is an area served by little in the way of media. At least it's predominantly conservative and should provide Thomas with a safe seat as long as he wants it.

Bill Thomas

Thomas' home base is Bakersfield, the right-leaning farm and oil town at the heart of the district. To the east, more conservatives are clustered around the sprawling military bases in the Mojave Desert. To the south, the district dips into Palmdale and Lancaster, booming communities with socially conservative young families.

Thomas has become one of the Republican leaders in the House and is young enough expect more advancement. He is vice chairman of the National Republican Congressional Committee and he seems to know what buttons to push to get recalcitrant Republicans aboard administration bills. But there's a coolness with Rep. Jerry Lewis, the California delegation's most powerful member. A few years ago, Lewis beat Thomas in an election for the California seat on the Republican Committee on Committees. The committee dispenses assignments and the loss hurt Thomas' standing in the delegation.

Besides the party work, Thomas has been active on both the Budget and Agriculture committees. He's supported increasing the retirement age for Social Security benefits and was chief Republican sponsor of a bill to require uniform poll-closing hours across the nation so that early results from Eastern states don't influence the national outcome.

The former community college instructor has done a lot to try to bring young people into the party, using campaign funds to conduct talent searches for people to fill minor posts and holding weekend retreats for college students. He's also an inveterate tinkerer in both Kern County and the state party machinery, a fact that gave him unpleasant moments during and after the state GOP convention in February 1989. Some delegates showed up on the floor wearing anti-Thomas buttons. Thomas' behind-the-scenes power plays were denounced by some of his oldest allies: ex-Assemblyman Joe Shell of Bakersfield and state Senate Minority Leader Ken Maddy of Fresno.

In Kern County, there's a Thomas faction and then there's the rest of the GOP.

"The Thomas faction and its leader believe if you're not with us 1,000 percent, you're against us," said Assemblyman Phil Wyman, R-Tehachapi. "It's the kind of mentality you expect from a war lord." Maddy cautioned that Thomas needs to "slow down his activities and not get so wrapped up in the party fights." Thomas, however, contends that his opponents "don't want to broaden the base of the party. Those who are in a power base don't want it dissipated."

Despite that, Thomas can be expected to be in the thick of the next reapportionment battles whether his colleagues want him there or not.

PERSONAL: elected 1978; born Dec. 6, 1941, in Wallace, Idaho; home, Bakersfield, education, A.A. Santa Ana College 1959, B.A. San Francisco State University 1963, M.A. 1965; Baptist; wife Sharon, two children.

CAREER: instructor, Bakersfield Community College, 1965-74; California assemblyman, 1974-78.

COMMITTEES: House Administration; Ways and Means.

OFFICES: Suite 2402 Rayburn Building, Washington, D.C. 20515, (202) 225-2915.

Suite 220, 4100 Truxton Ave., Bakersfield 93309, (805) 327-3611.

Suite 115, 848 West Jackman, Lancaster, (805) 948-2634.

Suite 203, 1390 Price St., Pismo Beach 93449, (805) 773-2533.

DISTRICT REGISTRATION: 42% D, 48% R

1988 CAMPAIGN: Thomas - R   71% $329,354

Reid - D   27% $15,814

RATINGS:	ADA	ACLU	ACU	AFL/CIO	CFA	LCV	NTU	USCC
	25%	29%	78%	13%	45%	31%	60%	100%

21st Congressional District

Elton Gallegly (R)

Since the late 1960s, white families have been fleeing increasingly seedy sections of the San Fernando Valley.

New communities have sprouted up beyond the valley's west and northerly hills. Towns such as Simi Valley, which were barely more than crossroads 20 years ago, are now flourishing communities in the 21st district. The district still takes in some neighborhoods on the fringe of the valley, such as Northridge, Granada Hills, Chatsworth and Tujunga. But the bulk of its mostly white and upwardly mobile families live beyond the hills in Ventura County communities such as Thousand Oaks and Camarillo.

One of the newcomers to the Ventura part of the  **Elton Gallegly**

district in the '60s was an ambitious young man with a real estate license named Elton Gallegly. In time, the boom made him wealthy, he became mayor of Simi Valley and was elected to Congress.

Gallegly seems to fit the district well. He's a family man who's devoted to hard work and traditional values. And like many baby boomers, he's Republican but not doctrinaire.

In a short time, Gallegly has become identified with anti-drug legislation. He was elected to chair his freshman Republican caucus. In his second term, he won a seat on the coveted Foreign Affairs Committee. He appears to have a bright future in Congress if he chooses to stay there.

PERSONAL: elected 1986; born March 7, 1944, in Huntington Park, Calif.; home, Simi Valley; education, attended Los Angeles State College; Protestant; wife Janice, four children.

CAREER: real estate firm owner, 1968-86; Simi Valley City Council, 1979-80, Mayor 1980-86.

COMMITTEES: Foreign Affairs; Interior and Insular Affairs.

OFFICES: Suite 107, Cannon Building, Washington, D.C. 20515, (202) 225-5811.

Suite 110, 3901 Oakdale Ave., Chatsworth 91311, (818) 341-2121.

Suite 207, 200 North Westlake Blvd., Thousand Oaks 91362, (805) 496-4700.

REGISTRATION: 37% D, 53% R

1988 CAMPAIGN: Gallegly - R   69% $465,310
Stevens - D   29% $ 0

RATINGS:

ADA	ACLU	ACU	AFL/CIO	CFA	LCV	NTU	USCC
15%	9%	96%	13%	27%	31%	59%	100%

22nd Congressional District
Carlos Moorhead (R)

This solidly Republican district is skewered by the San Gabriel Mountains. South and within long reaches of the range are the more affluent suburbs of the Los Angeles smog belt: Glendale, Pasadena, San Marino, Temple, Sierra Madre, Arcadia, Monrovia, La Canada, La Crescenta and part of Burbank. Most of the residents tend to be white, older and well educated. Across the mountains are the newer and booming suburbs of Newhall and Saugus where younger families are found in townhouses that staircase up the hillsides.

The affable congressman from the area is Carlos Moorhead, the dean of the Republican delegation. Moorhead doesn't try to assert his leadership of the California Republicans very often, perhaps because he knows it would be a waste of time. GOP members have a history of independence and some seem to regard the solidly Republican Moorhead as not ideological enough to suit their tastes.

Moorhead busies himself with legislation in a variety of important areas – but none that attract much attention – such as patent and copyright law, energy conservation, natural gas deregulation and operations of the border patrol. Almost alone, he's battled with Pacific Northwest congressmen to give California a fair share of the federal low-cost power generated in that region.

He's the No. 2 minority member of the Judiciary Committee and is known for faithful constituent service. No doubt he'll retire from the seat one day. At this point, he seems unbeatable.

Carlos Moorhead

PERSONAL: elected 1972; born May 6, 1922, in Long Beach, Calif.; home, Glendale; education, B.A. UCLA 1943, J.D. USC 1949; Presbyterian; wife Valery, five children.

CAREER: U.S. Army, 1942-45 (retired Army Reserve lieutenant general); attorney, 1949-72; Assembly, 1967-72.

COMMITTEES: Energy and Commerce; Judiciary.

OFFICES: Suite 2346, Rayburn Building, Washington, D.C. 20515, (202) 225-4176.

420 North Brand Blvd., Glendale 91203, (818) 247-8445.

301 East Colorado Blvd., Pasadena 91101, (818) 792-6168.

DISTRICT REGISTRATION: 35% D, 55% R

1988 CAMPAIGN: Moorhead - R   70% $234,920

                 Simmons - D   26% $ 18,046

RATINGS:	ADA	ACLU	ACU	AFL/CIO	CFA	LCV	NTU	USCC
	10%	13%	96%	7%	27%	19%	61%	100%

23rd Congressional District

Anthony C. Beilenson (D)

From Beverly Hills to the shores of Malibu, the 23rd District takes in the area that many Americans imagine when "Los Angeles" is mentioned. But there also are the tidy apartments near Wilshire Boulevard, the gay enclave of West Los Angeles and the mansions of Pacific Palisades. Across the Santa Monica Mountains, the district takes in the comfortable suburbs of Van Nuys, Reseda, Canoga Park, Encino, Tarzana and Woodland Hills.

Although furs and Rolls Royces abound in the area, many of the residents are upper middle–class professionals. Most of the southern portions of the district are peopled by older, predominantly Jewish and liberal voters. Across the mountains, neighborhoods are more homogeneous but leaning toward conservative. Lower-income people are disappearing as their homes are snapped up by two-income couples with few, if any, children.

One might expect a glitzy liberal to represent this area in Congress. But Rep. Tony Beilenson is one of the more anonymous members of the delegation.

Beilenson typifies the Jewish professional of the district. He's a solid and conscientious performer whose skills as a legislator are widely respected in the House. He seems nearly devoid of partisanship, which sometimes annoys those who would like to see him use his seat on the Rules Committee to the greater advantage of Democrats. Those most annoyed with Beilenson are the

Anthony C. Beilenson

highly partisan members of the "west side" political organization headed by Congress members Howard Berman and Henry Waxman. Beilenson has steadfastly refused to kowtow to the group, despite their similar ideological positions, and once conducted a nasty squabble with Berman and Waxman over the changing of his district boundaries.

Beilenson is known for studying issues thoroughly and voting his conscience. He's an expert on the budget and was responsible for creating the Santa Monica Mountains National Recreation area. Credible Republicans have run against him in the district, but none have gotten very far.

PERSONAL: elected 1976; born Oct. 26, 1932, in New Rochelle, N.Y.; home, Los Angeles; education, A.B. Harvard University 1954, L.L.B. 1957; Jewish; wife Dolores, three children.

CAREER: attorney 1957-59; counsel to Assembly Committee on Finance and Insurance, 1960; counsel to California Compensation and Insurance Fund, 1961-62; Assembly, 1963-66; state Senate, 1966-77.

COMMITTEES: Budget; Rules; Select Committee on Intelligence.

OFFICES: Suite 1025, Longworth Building, Washington, D.C. 20515, (202) 225-5911.
Suite 14223, 11000 Wilshire Blvd., Los Angeles 90024, (213) 209-7801.
Suite 222, 18401 Burbank Blvd., Tarzana 91356, (818) 345-1560.

DISTRICT REGISTRATION: 57% D, 37% R

1988 CAMPAIGN: Beilenson - D   64% $140,486
Saloman - R   33% $100,956

RATINGS:	ADA	ACLU	ACU	AFL/CIO	CFA	LCV	NTU	USCC
	95%	96%	8%	75%	23%	94%	30%	50%

24th Congressional District

Henry A. Waxman (D)

The 24th District stretches from downtown Los Angeles to Beverly Hills, taking in all of Hollywood, Hancock Park and Los Feliz. Then it runs over the crest of the Santa Monica Mountains to include North Hollywood and Universal City.

Henry A. Waxman

Since World War II, the neighborhoods of this entertainment industry-connected area have been solidly Jewish and liberal. At the southern and seedier end of the district, an area where the Hollywood technicians and extras once lived, the residents are increasingly Hispanic and Korean. These minorities, however, tend to vote in small numbers. There are increasing number of gays, as well, who do vote.

Drawing on the extreme wealth of the district and one of the sharpest intellects in Congress, Rep. Henry Waxman has built one of the most important power bases in the Democratic Party. With ex-Assembly chum Howard Berman and to a lesser extent Mel Levine, both of whom followed Waxman to Congress, the most potent political machine in Southern California has been created.

The Berman-Waxman organization raises vast sums of money and conducts hardball campaigns, often with extensive use of direct mail. Most of the day-to-day operations are run by Berman's brother, Michael, and Carl D'Agostino, who own a campaign management firm known as "BAD Campaigns," but the congressmen are instrumental in recruiting promising candidates and seeing to it that their campaigns get infusions of money and workers. Their interests don't stop with the Congress. Their hands reach deeply into local and national politics as well. Gary Hart's presidential campaign was one of their causes until he crashed and burned.

Waxman, in the meantime, has bucked the House seniority system to grab key subcommittees where he advances his interests in health, clean air and geriatrics issues. Probably no Democrat has more influence on health issues. In the Reagan administration, he was the Democrats' first line of defense against weakening health and air programs. He's also a leader on abortion rights and funding for AIDS research. Waxman's seat is secure, a factor that allows him to carry one of the heaviest legislative loads in Congress. He's on the verge of being in the House's top leadership now. If the right openings occur, it shouldn't take much to propel him further.

PERSONAL: elected 1974; born Sept. 12, 1939, in Los Angeles; home, Los Angeles; education, B.A. UCLA 1961, J.D. 1964; Jewish; wife Janet, two children.

CAREER: attorney, 1965-68; Assembly, 1968-74.

COMMITTEES: Energy and Commerce; Government Operations; Select Committee on Aging.
OFFICES: Suite 2418, Rayburn Building, Washington, D.C. 20515, (202) 225-3976.
Suite 400, 8425 West Third St., Los Angeles 90048, (213) 651-1040.
DISTRICT REGISTRATION: 60% D, 28% R
1988 CAMPAIGN: Waxman - D   72% $191,334
            Cowles - R   24% $15,449

RATINGS:

ADA	ACLU	ACU	AFL/CIO	CFA	LCV	NTU	USCC
90%	100%	0%	88%	82%	88%	23%	21%

25th Congressional District

Edward R. Roybal (D)

As the sun sets over Santa Monica Bay, the skyscrapers of downtown Los Angeles cast long shadows over the city's Mexican-American barrio. Yet California's most heavily Hispanic district (57 percent), is anything but a slum. It's an area of nondescript apartment houses and stucco bungalows where the medium income is below the city's average. But it also is one where families flourish and the attitudes are optimistic. Most households have two working parents and extended families living under one roof are common. Lawns are neatly trimmed, vegetable gardens abound and people awake to the sound of crowing roosters.

The district takes in some tenement areas of downtown Los Angeles and then swings east and north to

Edward R. Roybal

Boyle Heights, East Los Angeles and Highland Park. A predominantly black portion of Pasadena also is included.

Rep. Edward Roybal, who's represented the area on the Los Angeles City Council and then in Congress since 1949, is so safe here that Republicans don't bother to oppose him. In 1978, the House reprimanded him for taking a $1,000 contribution from Korean businessman Tongsun Park and converting it to his own use. But that didn't seem to cost him anything at home. Constituents claimed he was a victim of discrimination.

Roybal has important seniority but has never been one of Congress' workhorses. But he's been a helpful vote for California on the Appropriations Committee and has shown that he can exert influence when an immigration issue is before the House. As chairman of the Select Committee on Aging, he's been active in shoring up Social Security. His daughter, Lucille Roybal-Allard, now represents part of the district in the state Assembly. She may try to succeed him when he decides to retire.

PERSONAL: elected 1962; born Feb. 10, 1916, in Albuquerque, N.M.; home, Los Angeles; education, attended UCLA, and Southwestern University; Roman Catholic; wife Lucille, three children.

CAREER: U.S. Army, 1944-45; program manager, Los Angeles County Tuberculosis and Health Association, 1945-49; Los Angeles City Council 1949-62.

COMMITTEES: Appropriations; chairman, Select Committee on Aging.

OFFICES: Suite 221, Rayburn Building, Washington, D.C. 20515, (202) 225-6235.

Suite 1706, 300 North Los Angeles St., Los Angeles 90012, (213) 894-4870.

DISTRICT REGISTRATION: 68% D, 21% R

1988 CAMPAIGN: Roybal - D   86% $67,957

No opponent

RATINGS:	ADA	ACLU	ACU	AFL/CIO	CFA	LCV	NTU	USCC
	95%	100%	0%	93%	91%	88%	14%	23%

26th Congressional District

Howard L. Berman (D)

From Rep. Howard Berman's home in Hollywood Hills, the Santa Monica Mountains tumble northward to the floor of the San Fernando Valley. Mansions have replaced the colorful shanties that once dominated the higher elevations. The middle-class homes on scraped-off slopes now sell for near-mansion prices. And even the bungalows in the heart of the valley are beyond the financial reach of the working-class people who are becoming fewer and fewer in the area. Many of them in Van Nuys and Panorama City are now being torn down to make way for the walled-in condo havens so popular with yuppies.

Howard L. Berman

Yet the area is still solidly Democratic with the help of carefully drawn boundaries that reach into Burbank. Jews are a potent political force in the district, but their numbers are declining. Hispanic neighborhoods straddle the Golden State Freeway. And there are black neighborhoods in Pacoima.

Berman shares the strongest political machine in Southern California with Reps. Henry Waxman and Mel Levine. Together, they have legendary fund-raising capability and substantial success at the ballot box. Berman is often the most politically assertive of the three, working hand in hand with two ace strategists and campaign managers, Berman's brother, Michael, and Carl D'Agostino. They're often accused of creating puppets and keeping them in power with contributions raised elsewhere. That's been said about Reps. Julian Dixon, Esteban Torres and Matthew Martinez. If that was the intent, it hasn't worked in the cases of Dixon and

Torres, who show substantial independence. Martinez, however, doesn't show much of anything.

Berman was a divisive force in the Assembly, fomenting a spiteful revolt against then-Speaker Leo McCarthy in 1980 that preoccupied the house for a year. If he'd been willing to wait two more years, McCarthy planned to leave the Assembly and Berman was his likely heir. But Berman had other plans. Willie Brown eventually emerged from the fray and won the speakership with Republican backing to begin his long reign. Brown then got rid of his potential rival by creating a new congressional district on the west side of Los Angeles.

Berman has been more of a team player in Congress. As an urban legislator, Berman has been well poised politically to be a stalwart defender of the United Farm Workers. He's been active on border and immigration issues, anti-apartheid legislation and other civil libertarian matters that play well in his district. On the Judiciary Committee, he also has been able to assist his show-business constituents with copyright and licensing protections.

PERSONAL: elected, 1982; born, April 15, 1941, in Los Angeles, Calif.; home, Los Angeles; education, B.A. UCLA 1962, L.L.B. 1965; Jewish; wife Janis, two children.

CAREER: attorney, 1966-72; Assembly 1973-82.

COMMITTEES: Budget, Foreign Affairs, Judiciary.

OFFICES: Suite 137, Cannon Building, Washington, D.C. 20515, (202) 225-4695.

Suite 506, 14600 Roscoe Blvd., Panorama City 91402, (818) 891-0543.

DISTRICT REGISTRATION: 57% D, 34% R

1988 CAMPAIGN: Berman - D   70% $409,233

               Broderson - R   30% $ 0

RATINGS:	ADA	ACLU	ACU	AFL/CIO	CFA	LCV	NTU	USCC
	95%	95%	4%	87%	100%	81%	22%	36%

27th Congressional District

Mel Levine (D)

In most parts of the country, the posh waterfront precincts of a major city would be solidly Republican. But this is Los Angeles and few things fit the norm. The 27th District starts at Pacific Palisades and takes in Santa Monica, Venice, Playa Del Rey, El Segundo, Torrance, Manhattan Beach, Hermosa Beach and Redondo Beach. It's an odd mixture of stately homes, counterculture habitats and refinery towns. In the liberal bastion of Santa Monica, the median home price hit $552,000 in 1989. Then the district reaches into solidly Democratic inland areas, some of which are black or Hispanic, including Inglewood, Lennox, and Lawndale.

Its perennially youthful congressman, Mel Levine, is one of the promising liberal

Democrats who was sorely disappointed when Sen. Alan Cranston announced he was going for a fourth term in 1986. Levine still hopes to go to the Senate one day – and would jump in 1992 if Cranston decides to retire – but in the interim, he labors to please a constituency so diverse that it includes leftover beatniks from the '50s, people who skateboard for a living by advertising bistros in Venice, refinery machinists, yacht salesmen, and financial and oil titans.

Levine got a scare in 1986 when former Los Angeles Ram Rob Scribner made a run at him. But he ended the race with a solid victory and went back to fighting against offshore oil development, for the interests of **Mel Levine** Israel and accountability in defense spending – issues that seem to please most of his constituents regardless of political philosophy. This is an area where even refinery workers belong to the Sierra Club. A Republican with celebrity status might give Levine another hard run, but Levine has done a lot to solidify his support since Scribner's attempt and would have a huge campaign war chest for the fight. He's a close ally of Reps. Howard Berman and Henry Waxman, but doesn't seem to be as driven to manipulate Los Angeles-area politicos as actively as his two mentors.

From his seat on the Interior Committee, Levine got Santa Monica Bay included in the National Estuaries Program. That was a vital step in the effort to clean up the severely polluted bay. He wrote the successful law that required former President Ronald Reagan to get congressional approval before sending troops to Central America.

PERSONAL: elected 1982; born, June 7, 1943, in Los Angeles, Calif.; home, Los Angeles; education, A.B. UC Berkeley, 1964, M.P.A. Princeton University 1966, J.D. Harvard University 1969; Jewish; wife Jan, three children.

CAREER: attorney, 1969-71 and 1973-77; legislative assistant to U.S. Sen. John Tunney, 1971-73; California assemblyman 1977-82.

COMMITTEES: Foreign Affairs; Interior and Insular Affairs; Select Committee on Narcotics Abuse and Control.

OFFICES: Suite 132, Cannon Building, Washington, D.C. 20515, (202) 225-6451.

Suite 447, 5250 Century Blvd., Los Angeles 90045, (213) 410-9415.

DISTRICT REGISTRATION: 73% D, 19% R

1988 CAMPAIGN: Levine - D   68% $398,597

              Galbraith - R   30% $ 15,239

RATINGS:

	ADA	ACLU	ACU	AFL/CIO	CFA	LCV	NTU	USCC
	95%	95%	4%	89%	91%	88%	21%	36%

28th Congressional District
Julian C. Dixon (D)

Democrats may control the House of Representatives, but not the Committee on Standards of Official Conduct, better known as the ethics committee. That is the fiefdom of Rep. Julian Dixon and Dixon is his own man.

Though a party loyalist on most issues, Dixon is aggressively non-partisan when it comes to issues of right and wrong. And that's true whether the subject of the investigation is someone as obscure as ex-Rep. Jim Weaver of Oregon (who speculated in commodities with campaign funds) or as powerful as Speaker Jim Wright of Texas (whose tangled financial deals eventually drove him from office and whose investigation gave Dixon his first taste of national notoriety). And no

Julian C. Dixon

sooner did the committee finish with the Wright investigation than it began its first investigation of a fellow California Democrat, Rep. Jim Bates, who was found guilty by the committee in October 1989 of sexually harassing staff members.

Congressmen called before Dixon's committee get a plodding but fair investigation. He showed the same temperament when chairing the Democratic convention's platform committee in 1984.

Dixon, who is black, also won't allow race to color his judgement. As a member of the District of Columbia Committee, he's demanded accountability by the city's black leadership. He's also showed no hesitation to brand Yassir Arafat a terrorist at a time when the Rev. Jesse Jackson was comparing the PLO's struggle to the battle for racial equity in this country.

In all things, Dixon is a conciliator and a fact-finder. Those are qualities he's used effectively to defuse antagonisms between Jewish and black communities in the Los Angeles area.

Dixon's district, the second most Democratic in the state, is the home of many of Los Angeles' middle- and upper-middle-class blacks. There are middle-class white and Hispanic portions, too. All seem to coexist in relative harmony. But street gang warfare in recent years has threatened the stability of the area. The 28th lies on the floor of the Los Angeles basin between downtown and the Los Angeles International Airport. The main communities are Inglewood, Culver City and Ladera Heights.

Dixon, a former state legislator, is allied with the Berman-Waxman organization in local politics and has been tabbed by the group to run for the Los Angeles County Board of Supervisors if and when the legendary south-central Los Angeles supervisor, Kenneth Hahn, retires.

PERSONAL: elected, 1978; born Aug. 8, 1934, in Washington, D.C.; home, Culver City; education, B.S. Los Angeles State College 1962, L.L.B. Southwestern University 1967; Episcopalian; wife Betty, one child.

CAREER: U.S. Army, 1957-60; Attorney, 1967-73; Assembly, 1972-78.

COMMITTEES: Appropriations; chairman, Standards of Official Conduct.

OFFICES: Suite 2400, Rayburn Building, Washington, D.C. 20515 - 202-225-7084.

Suite 208, 5100 West Goldleaf Circle, Los Angeles 90056 (213) 678-5424.

DISTRICT REGISTRATION: 73% D, 19% R

1988 CAMPAIGN: Dixon - D   76% $114,523

Adams - R   20% $ 0

RATINGS:

ADA	ACLU	ACU	AFL/CIO	CFA	LCV	NTU	USCC
85%	100%	0%	97%	55%	81%	20%	25%

29th Congressional District

Augustus Hawkins (D)

At the heart of California's most heavily Democratic district is Watts, scene of the infamous riots of the mid-1960s. Then, as now, the issues are poverty, crime, drugs, lack of communities facilities and substandard housing. But now there's a new element – street gangs. The area was mostly black when Watts was burning nearly a quarter century ago. Now, there are more Hispanics and the two cultures collide nightly in vicious gang warfare. The conflict is not all racial, however. It's often black against black or brown against brown in battles where crack cocaine figures prominently as the cause – or at least as a co-conspirator. The district also takes in working-class neighborhoods in Huntington Park, South Gate and Downey.

Augustus Hawkins

Since 1934, the man who has represented the area first in the Assembly and then in Congress has been Augustus Hawkins. Now in his 80s, Hawkins is the nation's senior black legislator and the oldest member of the California delegation. Some have called him the black Claude Pepper. Hawkins may not have Pepper's fire, but he has all his mental faculties and the willingness to work himself to exhaustion for programs that benefit underprivileged people.

Hawkins had to wait a long time for Carl Perkins to retire so that he could chair the Education and Labor Committee. Yet, as a committee member and as chairman since 1984, he's worked ceaselessly to boost the minimum wage, shore up Social Security, and expand job training, childhood nutrition and education programs. Most of the social legislation approved by Congress in the past quarter century has had elements added by Hawkins.

Ambitious politicians in the area – Assemblywoman Maxine Waters in particular – have been growing old waiting for Hawkins to retire. Hawkins seems ageless and shows no sign of stepping down.

PERSONAL: elected 1962; born Aug. 31, 1907, in Shreveport, La.; home, Los Angeles; A.B. UCLA, 1931; attended USC; United Methodist; wife Elsie.

CAREER: Realtor, 1931-35; Assembly, 1935-62.

COMMITTEES: chairman, Education and Labor; Joint Economic Committee.

OFFICES: Suite 2371, Rayburn Building, Washington, D.C. 20515, (202) 225-2201.

4509 South Broadway, Los Angeles 90037, (213) 233-0733.

2710 Zoe Ave., Huntington Park 90255, (213) 587-0421.

DISTRICT REGISTRATION: 73% D, 19% R

1988 CAMPAIGN: Hawkins - D   83% $65,833

                Franco - R   14% $ 4,629

RATINGS:	ADA	ACLU	ACU	AFL/CIO	CFA	LCV	NTU	USCC
	85%	100%	0%	96%	91%	75%	21%	15%

30th Congressional District
Matthew G. Martinez (D)

After the 1980 census, the late Rep. Phil Burton set out to draw two Hispanic districts in Los Angeles County. As a result, the 30th and 34th districts look like something left on the floor of a pretzel factory. At the 30th's southern tip are the factory and warehouse areas of Bell Gardens and Commerce. It twists through Monterey Park, Alhambra and San Gabriel, then zigzags northeasterly, taking in parts of El Monte, Baldwin Park and Azusa.

The district becomes more affluent the further north one travels. The neighborhoods are heavily Hispanic but there are growing numbers of Koreans, Chinese and other Asians who own many of the retail businesses along the crowded thoroughfares.

Matthew G. Martinez

On paper, the district should be fairly safe Democratic turf. But it hasn't turned out that way. Many of the upwardly mobile Hispanics and Asians appear to have left their Democratic roots in poorer neighborhoods. They're ticket-splitters and often favor candidates who promise less government intervention in their lives. And then there's their congressmen, Matthew Martinez, who seems to have trouble relating to the constituency. He's had a series of difficult primaries and runoffs. Even against an unknown in 1986, he carried only 63 percent of the vote.

Some claim Martinez is simply a creation of Rep. Howard Berman and never would have gained public office without the Berman-Waxman organization's cash and campaign moxie. Berman plucked Martinez from obscurity to run against an incumbent assemblyman, Jack Fenton, during a nasty Assembly leadership battle in 1980, then boosted him into Congress just two years later. Whatever his political origins, Martinez has been a less-than-impressive political figure. A California Magazine survey rated him the dimmest bulb in the delegation and one of the five worst representatives overall, someone who makes little impact even on his own district.

PERSONAL: elected 1982; born Feb. 14, 1929, in Walsenburg, Colo.; home, Monterey Park; education, attended Los Angeles Trade Technical School; Roman Catholic; divorced.

CAREER: U.S. Marine Corps, 1947-50; upholstery business, 1957-82; Monterey Park City Council, 1974-76; mayor, 1976-80; Assembly, 1980-82.

COMMITTEES: Education and Labor; Government Operations; Select Committee on Children, Youth and Families.

OFFICES: Suite 240, Cannon Building, Washington, D.C. 20515, (202) 225-3965.

Suite 201, 1712 West Beverly Blvd., Montebello 90640, (213) 722-7731.

DISTRICT REGISTRATION: 59% D, 31% R

1988 CAMPAIGN: Martinez - D   60% $460,622
                   Ramirez - R   36% $382,111

RATINGS:

ADA	ACLU	ACU	AFL/CIO	CFA	LCV	NTU	USCC
90%	83%	0%	99%	91%	56%	20%	23%

31st Congressional District
Mervyn M. Dymally (D)

The 31st District sprawls on both sides of the Harbor Freeway south of the Los Angeles city limits. It contains the gang-infested areas of Compton and Willowbrook, and the aging suburbs of Lynwood, Paramount and Bellflower plus a sizeable chunk of Gardena. About half of its people are black or Hispanic. There has been a noticeable influx of Asians in this decade. And there are still sizeable white neighborhoods in Bellflower and Gardena.

The district is solidly Democratic, so much so that Rep. Mervyn Dymally doesn't need to spend much time there. In fact, he doesn't spend much time in Congress either. Year after year, he's one of the best-traveled members of House, often mixing into Third World politics in places as far flung as Micronesia, Ivory Coast and his native Trinidad. Meanwhile, his legislative accomplishments are almost nil.

Often there's an odor to Dymally's activities. Dymally, however, usually contends that his critics are motivated by racism and greed. Suggestions that he was involved in corruption of the state's Medi-Cal system led to his defeat by Mike Curb after one term as lieutenant governor, but nothing was ever proven. He often accepts, some say solicits, free trips from special interests. One such trip in 1989 involved a visit to Uganda, where he tried to persuade the government to hire a friend and campaign contributor as an agent for U.S. aid sent to the country.

Dymally won the seat in 1980 in one of the most dramatic comebacks seen in California in recent years. He took almost half the vote in the primary despite the fact that two ex-congressmen were among his four opponents. He's won easily ever since and it seems nothing short of a conviction could boot him out.

Mervyn M. Dymally

PERSONAL: elected 1980; born May 12, 1926, in Cedros, Trinidad; home, Compton; education, B.A. California State College, Los Angeles, B.A. 1954, M.A. 1969, Ph.D. U.S. International University 1978; Episcopalian; wife Alice, two children.

CAREER: teacher, 1955-61; manager, California Disaster Office, 1961-62; Assembly, 1962-66; state Senate, 1966-75; lieutenant governor, 1975-79.

COMMITTEES: District of Columbia; Foreign Affairs; Post Office and Civil Service.

OFFICES: Suite 1717 Longworth Building, Washington, D.C. 20515, (202) 225-5425.

322 West Compton Blvd., Compton 90220, (213) 632-4318.

DISTRICT REGISTRATION: 72% D, 20% R

1988 CAMPAIGN: Dymally - D   72% $481,799

               May - R   26% $ 10,169

RATINGS:	ADA	ACLU	ACU	AFL/CIO	CFA	LCV	NTU	USCC
	90%	100%	0%	95%	100%	63%	21%	23%

32nd Congressional District

Glenn M. Anderson (D)

The 32nd District isn't shaped like anything tangible. It lurches from San Pedro through the Democratic areas of Long Beach and Lakewood and then reaches northward to clutch Hawaiian Gardens. The children of Yugoslav and Italian fishermen still inhabit the port areas. The Long Beach and Lakewood portions are a mixture of middle-class white and Hispanic neighborhoods. Hawaiian Gardens is also Hispanic, but Koreans may soon be dominant.

It's an ideal district for Glenn Anderson, whose long career in California politics dates back to 1940. As chairman of the Public Works and Transportation committee, he's had a dramatic impact on port and highway development in south Los Angeles. He's also been a good friend of water development interests and mass transit. But it's not all pork barrel. Anderson insists on seeing economic justifications for projects. Consumer protection is another of his interests. His amendments created a seat-belt law for children and forced states to raise their drinking age to 21 in order to be eligible for federal highway money.

Glenn Anderson

Anderson might have been governor had it not been for the Watts riots. Gov. Pat Brown was out of state and Anderson, then lieutenant governor, was blamed for being too slow to send in the National Guard. The next year, both Brown and Anderson were buried by the Ronald Reagan-Ed Reinecke landslide. Anderson went to Congress two years later. Although in his 70s, 12-hour days are still part of his routine, and would-be successors will have to bide their time.

PERSONAL: elected 1968; born Feb. 21, 1913, in Hawthorne, Calif.; home, San Pedro; education, B.A. UCLA 1936; Episcopalian; wife Lee, three children.

CAREER: mayor of Hawthorne, 1940-43; Assembly 1943 and 1945-51; U.S. Army, 1943-45; lieutenant governor, 1958-67.

COMMITTEES: Chairman, Public Works and Transportation.

OFFICES: Suite 2329, Rayburn Building, Washington, D.C. 20515, (202) 225-6676

300 Long Beach Blvd., Long Beach 90801, (213) 437-7665.

DISTRICT REGISTRATION: 56% D, 35% R

1988 CAMPAIGN: Anderson - D   67% $457,410

               Kahn - R   30% $ 20,608

RATINGS:	ADA	ACLU	ACU	AFL/CIO	CFA	LCV	NTU	USCC
	70%	55%	10%	83%	55%	63%	21%	0%

33rd Congressional District

David Dreier (R)

Although the lines have been redrawn many times, the 33rd District still contains large areas that Richard Nixon represented in Congress 40 years ago. It takes in Whittier, Nixon's home, then jumps the Puente Hills to include Covina, San Dimas, La Verne, Pomona and Glendora. Whittier is becoming more Hispanic, but no less conservative. The other suburbs are predominantly white, upper middle-class areas where life would be much more pleasing without the air pollution that piles up at the base of the San Gabriel Mountains.

Twenty-eight-year-old Rep. David Dreier went to Congress from this area not to make laws, but to undo them. He's a strident foe of government regulation in most of its forms. He's worked for a balanced budget, more federal lands and services in private hands, and deregulation of trucking, airlines, pipelines and banking.

Some of his senior Republicans colleagues on the Banking Committee find his ideological commitment tedious. But none can argue that he's anything but consistent. Dreier is more reminiscent of the Goldwater Republicans who demanded ideological litmus tests before full acceptance within party ranks. On that score, **David Dreier** he's in step with a large faction of his party in California. But his influence spans beyond there. He recruits GOP candidates for congressional races in Western states.

Dreier first beat a complacent incumbent Democrat. Then, in 1982, he beat Rep. Wayne Grisham when redistricting dumped them both in the new 33rd. He's had phenomenal success as a fund-raiser, but is little known outside his district. Within Republican circles, there's been some speculation that Drier could be appointed to the U.S. Senate if Pete Wilson is elected governor in 1990.

PERSONAL: elected 1980; born July 5, 1952, in Kansas City; home, La Verne; education, B.A. Claremont McKenna College 1975, M.A. 1976; Christian Scientist; unmarried.

CAREER: public relations, Claremont McKenna College, 1975-79; public relations, Industrial Hydrocarbons Corp., 1979-80.

COMMITTEES: Banking, Finance and Urban Affairs; Small Business.

OFFICES: Suite 441, Cannon Building, Washington, D.C. 20515, (202) 225-2305.

112 North Second Ave., Covina 91723, (818) 339-9078.

DISTRICT REGISTRATION: 42% D, 48% R

1988 CAMPAIGN: Dreier - R   69% $186,183

Gentry - D   26% $ 0

RATINGS:

ADA	ACLU	ACU	AFL/CIO	CFA	LCV	NTU	USCC
5%	0%	100%	1%	27%	44%	68%	92%

34th Congressional District

Esteban E. Torres (D)

This is another of the districts drawn by the late Rep. Phil Burton to insure Hispanic representation in Southern California. Slightly more than half of the residents have Hispanic surnames in an area that 30 years ago was made up almost exclusively of white suburbs. The district also has a higher concentration of families than any other in California.

The 34th District straddles the San Gabriel River southwest of Los Angeles. Pico Rivera, Baldwin Park, La Puente and the city of Industry lie in the northern section. To the south are South Whittier, Santa Fe Springs and Norwalk. Many of the residents work in aerospace, manufacturing, refinery and government jobs, and two-income families are common. A growing number of Asians are taking over the retail shops that clutter the main streets.

Esteban Torres

Most are traditionally Democratic, but conservative and committed to family values. The congressman, Esteban Torres, shares those family concerns and is strongly anti-abortion. But on most other matters, he's stridently liberal. His preoccupation with the welfare of Third World countries and encouraging large social programs from Washington doesn't play particularly well in this district. That helps explain why he's had well-financed challengers from time to time.

Torres helps compensate for his more-liberal-than-the-district views by campaigning almost non-stop from election to election. He's constantly in the district, attending community gatherings, visiting nursing homes and assisting Democratic hopefuls at other levels. One of his latest causes is the seriously polluted water table in the San Gabriel Valley. The issue has given him a lot of visibility, but meaningful cleanup is probably impossible even if billions were available to spend on the effort.

Torres' staff is considered one of the better in the delegation. And he also has another ace in hand, the fund-raising support of the Berman-Waxman machine. Like many of the residents, Torres got where he is by working hard and overcoming racial barriers. He went from assembly-line worker to union official, to poverty programs and then on to posts where he could promote his human concerns in President Jimmy Carter's administration. He remains committed to government as a force in improving social interaction in society. The district seems to be moving away from that orientation, but not quickly enough to threaten Torres' tenure.

PERSONAL: elected 1982; born Jan. 30, 1930, in Miami, Ariz.; home, La Puente; education, A.A. East Los Angeles Community College 1959, B.A. CSU Los Angeles 1963, graduate work at the University of Maryland and American University; no religious affiliation; wife Arcy, five children.

CAREER: U.S. Army, 1949-53; assembly-line worker, Chrysler Corp., 1953-63; United Auto Workers representative, 1963-68; director, East Los Angeles

Community Union, 1968-74; UAW representative, 1974-77; ambassador to UNESCO, 1977-79; special assistant to the U.S. President, 1979-81; president, International Enterprise and Development Corp, 1981-82.

COMMITTEES: Banking, Finance and Urban Affairs; Small Business.

OFFICES: Suite 1740, Longworth Building, Washington, D.C. 20515, (202) 225-5256.

Suite 101, 8819 Whittier Blvd., Pico Rivera 90660, (213) 695-0702.

DISTRICT REGISTRATION: 61% D, 30% R

1988 CAMPAIGN: Torres - D   63% $227,098

                 House - R   35% $149,886

RATINGS:	ADA	ACLU	ACU	AFL/CIO	CFA	LCV	NTU	USCC
	90%	87%	0%	98%	91%	75%	18%	23%

35th Congressional District

Jerry Lewis (R)

In an extremely short period of time by congressional standards, Rep. Jerry Lewis has risen to the most important leadership role among California's Republicans. As chairman of the House Republican Conference, Lewis is the third-ranking member of his party. He serves as a spokesman and strategist, and more often than not carries his party's position on the Appropriations Committee.

At one time, the ex-assemblyman flirted with statewide races. In 1989, he tried unsuccessfully to move up to minority whip in the House. He remains popular with his colleagues, however, and is still young enough to win a higher leadership post one day.

Jerry Lewis

Lewis is the ranking Republican on the Legislative Subcommittee of Appropriations chaired by fellow Californian Vic Fazio. They've become one of the best bipartisan teams in Congress by seeing to it that ideological concerns don't clutter their relationship. They know where they can agree and where they can't. No breath is wasted trying to score philosophical points. Soon after his election, Lewis established himself as an intellectual force in his party. His work was soon noticed on the Republican Research Committee, which turns out articulate reports on policy positions for the GOP. By 1985, he was its chairman. He's worked to reshape U.S. contributions to the International Monetary Fund and the World Bank so that there is more accountability in loans to Third World countries. And he played a role in stopping the Reagan administration from weakening the Clean Air Act, a law that is extremely important in smog-burdened portions of his district. In 1986, he chaired a GOP task force on drug legislation. One of his utterances at that time has come back to haunt him: "There's not any question," Lewis told Democrats, "that a couple of billion dollars is an awful lot more than we need to do an effective job."

Most of Lewis' constituents are packed into the southwest corner of his district around San Bernardino, Chino, Upland, Redlands and Loma Linda. From there, the district stretches across the Mojave Desert all the way to Needles on the Arizona line. Some of the desert areas, however, are growing very fast – particularly around Victorville. Retirees are a growing force in the 35th as are young families who've been forced eastward by housing prices in Los Angeles and Orange Counties. To the south, the district stretches into the resort area around Big Bear.

Lewis wins easily every two years.

PERSONAL: elected, 1978; born Oct. 21, 1934, in Seattle, Wash.; home, Redlands; education, B.A., UCLA 1956; Presbyterian; wife Arlene, seven children.

CAREER: insurance agent and manager, 1959-78; field representative to U.S. Rep. Jerry Pettis, 1968; San Bernardino School Board, 1965-68; Assembly, 1968-78.

COMMITTEES: Appropriations.

OFFICES: Suite 2312, Rayburn Building, Washington, D.C. 20515, (202) 225-5861.

Suite 104, 1826 Orange Tree Lane., Redlands 92373, (714) 862-6030.

DISTRICT REGISTRATION: 38% D, 52% R

1988 CAMPAIGN: Lewis - R   70% $337,814

                   Sweeney - D   28% $ 0

RATINGS:	ADA	ACLU	ACU	AFL/CIO	CFA	LCV	NTU	USCC
	5%	29%	90%	15%	30%	19%	45%	67%

36th Congressional District

George E. Brown Jr. (D)

Districts may change, but not Rep. George Brown. One of the House's oldest peaceniks, Brown continues to champion liberal causes despite dramatic gains in his district's Republican registration and nonstop efforts by GOP candidates to unseat him.

The cigar-chomping Brown comes from Quaker stock and is both a physicist and nuclear engineer. He was talking about global warming and the virtues of solar energy long before it was fashionable. In 1987, he quit the Intelligence Committee, saying he couldn't live with the committee's gag rules on topics that are general knowledge elsewhere.

Brown's long career in the House began in 1962. In

George E. Brown Jr.

1970, he nearly won the Democratic U.S. Senate primary and probably could have dumped GOP Sen. George Murphy. But that privilege went to neighboring House member John Tunney instead. Brown sat out for two years and was re-elected, but he returned to the House without those eight years of precious seniority.

He represents a district far different from the one that first sent him to Congress. It's been reshaped a half dozen times in an effort to stave off Republican encroachment. Monterey Park, where Brown was first elected to public office in 1954, is 20 miles from the district's nearest border. Today, Brown has the industrial sections of Colton, Rialto and Fontana, the city of Ontario, and Democratic areas of Riverside and San Bernardino.

Many of the people living in those smog-choked cities are there for lack of choices. They include many blue collar and older people who can't afford to move to more pleasant environs. In other areas where there were once fields and orange groves, stucco subdivisions are peopled with young families who tend to be economic conservatives. An increasing number of them are upwardly mobile Hispanics. Many of these newcomers hope to have enough equity in a few years to move elsewhere. Fortunately for Brown, many of the latter don't get around to voting because they'd be more likely to vote Republican if they did.

Republicans might have more success against Brown if they'd quit throwing candidates from the extreme right against him. Brown, however, is good on the stump, has an excellent staff and is a superb fund-raiser. Even with a more mainstream Republican opponent, those are hard pluses to overcome.

PERSONAL: elected in 1962 and served until 1971, re-elected in 1972; born March 6, 1920, in Holtville, Calif.; home, Riverside; education, B.A., UCLA 1946; United Methodist; wife Marta, four children.

CAREER: U.S. Army, 1942-45; Monterey Park City Council, 1954-58, mayor 1955-56; engineer and management consultant, city of Los Angeles, 1946-58; Assembly 1958-62.

COMMITTEES: Agriculture; Science, Space and Technology.

OFFICES: Suite 2188, Rayburn Building, Washington, D.C. 20515, (202) 225-6161.
657 La Cadena Dr., Colton 92324, (714) 825-2472.
Suite 116, 3600 Lime St., Riverside 92502, (714) 686-8863.
337 North Vineyard Ave., Ontario 91764, (714) 988-5105.

DISTRICT REGISTRATION: 53% D, 38% R

1988 CAMPAIGN: Brown - D   54% $532,897
                 Stark - R   43% $218,696

RATINGS:

ADA	ACLU	ACU	AFL/CIO	CFA	LCV	NTU	USCC
80%	100%	5%	90%	73%	75%	22%	25%

37th Congressional District

Alfred A. McCandless (R)

This fastest-growing district in California takes in all the Republican areas of Riverside County that Rep. George Brown didn't want. It stretches from the city of Riverside through Moreno Valley and Banning, and on to the lavish desert communities of Palm Springs and Palm Desert (President Dwight Eisenhower's winter golfing home). From there, it's on to Indio and the rich farmlands of the Coachella Valley, then across the scorching desert to Blythe.

The Palm Springs area is home to many movie stars and retired captains of industry, plus former President Jerry Ford and ex-Vice President Spiro Agnew. But there are many less-well-off retirees as well, living in condos and fading trailers. The service-sector is domi-

Alfred A. McCandless

nated by Hispanics, many of whom travel some distance to their low-paying jobs.

Their congressman is a desert native, Rep. Al McCandless, who was once a General Motors dealer in Indio. McCandless is one of the most conservative members of the delegation and is re-elected almost by acclamation.Outside the district, he's probably best known for the video privacy bill he authored after a keyhole reporter got hold of Judge Robert Bork's rental list during his unsuccessful Supreme Court confirmation bid. McCandless has shown interest in legislation benefiting handicapped people but devotes most of his time to mustering "no" votes against any bill with an appropriation attached.

PERSONAL: elected 1982; born July 23, 1927, in Brawley, Calif.; home, La Quinta; B.A., UCLA 1951; Protestant; wife Gail, five children.

CAREER: U.S. Marine Corps, 1945-46 and 1950-52; auto dealer, 1953-75; Riverside County Supervisor, 1970-82.

COMMITTEES: Banking, Finance and Urban Affairs; Government Operations.

OFFICES: Suite 435, Cannon Building, Washington, D.C. 20515, (202) 225-5330.

Suite 165, 6529 Riverside Ave., Riverside 92506, (714) 682-7127.

Suite A-7, 75-075 El Paseo, Palm Desert 92260, (619) 340-2900.

DISTRICT REGISTRATION: 43% D, 48% R

1988 CAMPAIGN: McCandless - R   64% $122,839

                 Pearson - D   33% $ 13,558

RATINGS:

ADA	ACLU	ACU	AFL/CIO	CFA	LCV	NTU	USCC
10%	10%	95%	2%	27%	19%	60%	92%

38th Congressional District

Robert K. Dornan (R)

In Orange County, it seems appropriate that a congressional district would have freeways for boundaries. The 38th is one of the most intensely congested areas of Southern California. Rush-hour gridlocks are routine and some residents support the idea of building toll roads that would separate the rich from the riffraff. The district begins at the Los Angeles County line and trends to the southeast between the Santa Ana and San Diego freeways. It ends at the Newport Freeway. The area, as the name suggests, was once covered with neatly spaced orange groves. After World War II, it became a lily-white, extremely conservative bedroom community.

Robert K. Dornan

The construction of Disneyland in the 1950s made Orange County a world destination, but few attitudes changed. In the 1950s and '60s, there were more John Birch Society memberships in Orange County than in all other California counties combined. The '70s saw an influx of Vietnamese, a few more Hispanics and the decline of some the neighborhoods, especially in the Garden Grove area. Today, there are more Vietnamese in the 38th than any other district in the nation.

The congressman who carries the torch for many of the lingering Bircher attitudes is Robert "B-1 Bob" Dornan, the flamboyant, sometimes profane former fighter pilot who never saw a defense appropriation he didn't like. Many people underestimate Dornan. A man who bases his campaigns on shrillness, hate and character assassination, they argue, can't go too far. Yet he shows remarkable staying power and fund-raising ability.

When Democrats couldn't defeat Dornan in his ocean-front Los Angeles County district, the late Phil Burton gerrymandered the district in 1982 (Rep. Mel Levine has it now) so that Dornan couldn't be re-elected. Undaunted, Dornan raised $1 million for an unsuccessful GOP Senate primary race against Pete Wilson instead. He then moved south to the 38th, took on five-term Democrat Jerry Patterson in 1984, and won. Gerrymandering had made the 38th a nominally Democratic district in 1982. But in 1984, it was the first congressional district in the nation where Vietnamese immigrants made an obvious difference. Dornan is their hero, the American who would restart the Vietnamese War if he could. In subsequent elections, even well-financed campaigns haven't been able to dislodge him.

Dornan introduces legislation, but little of it goes anywhere. Despite his identity with the long struggle to approve the B-1 bomber, others get most of the credit for getting it off the ground. Dornan is one of the most widely traveled members of Congress. Some of the junkets, to his credit, have helped close MIA and POW cases from the war years. He also brags that he's piloted every aircraft in the American defense arsenal plus some from Israel, England and France.

Wives of congressmen don't often make news outside their husband's districts, but Sallie Dornan became an exception in 1988 when she announced – wrongly – that her brother had AIDS. Dornan is fervently anti-gay, but he has shown compassion for AIDS victims and has voted for increased funding for medical research.Dornan helped influence national policy in 1985 by becoming the first die-hard conservative to endorse George Bush for the presidency. Up until then, many conservatives questioned whether Bush was "Republican enough." Dornan seconded Bush's nomination at the Republican National Convention, chaired Veterans for Bush and was co-chairman of Bush's California campaign. Many thought Dornan would get a prominent post in the administration. Democrats hoped so too, since such a loose cannon might damage Bush. It's also about the only hope they have of getting Dornan's seat back anytime soon. But as of this writing, the Bush administration hasn't called.

PERSONAL: elected 1976 and served until 1983, re-elected 1984; born April 3, 1933, in New York City; home, Garden Grove; education, attended Loyola University, Los Angeles; Roman Catholic; wife Sallie, five children.

CAREER: U.S. Air Force, 1953-58; broadcaster and TV talk-show host, 1965-73; president, American Space Frontier PAC, 1983-88.

COMMITTEES: Armed Services; Select Committee on Intelligence; Select Committee on Narcotics Abuse and Control.

OFFICES: Suite 301, Cannon Building, Washington, D.C. 20515, (202) 225-2965.

12387 Lewis St., Garden Grove 92640, (714) 971-9292.

DISTRICT REGISTRATION: 49% D, 42% R

1988 CAMPAIGN: Dornan - R   60% $1,755,892

                Yudelson - D   36% $186,892

RATINGS:	ADA	ACLU	ACU	AFL/CIO	CFA	LCV	NTU	USCC
	0%	5%	100%	8%	18%	13%	59%	91%

39th Congressional District

William E. Dannemeyer (R)

The safest Republican turf in California is unquestionably the 39th District, which takes in the center and eastern end of Orange County. This birthplace and launch pad for Richard Nixon is synonymous with conservative Republican values. Although Democrats have made some inroads locally, the 39th turns in the highest percentage of GOP votes in each statewide election. Many of those votes come from the district's major towns, Fullerton, Anaheim and Orange.

Despite the extreme partisanship that characterizes the 39th, the district has sent some excellent legislators to Washington. But William Dannemeyer, the current congressman, isn't one of them. Even many of Dannemeyer's fellow conservatives are embarrassed by his right-wing pronouncements that resemble those of extremist Lyndon LaRouche. That's one of the reasons Dannemeyer's been turned down in attempts to get better committee assignments.

There's no doubt that he gets popular support in the district for his stands against abortion and homosexuality, on prayer in the schools, and to allow parents to block teaching of evolution in classrooms. But his punitive AIDS measure on the statewide ballot in 1988 lost even in his own district.

William Dannemeyer

Dannemeyer says he's just trying to make the world safe from the AIDS scourge. Its victims release "spores" that spread the disease, he claims. To his credit, Dannemeyer has introduced some public health measures of value. But most of his AIDS rhetoric is intertwined with gay bashing, something he seems to relish. Dannemeyer loves to dwell on deviant sexual practices. At the GOP state convention in 1989, he introduced an anti-gay measure that described seamy sexual acts in detail. With Rep. Bob Dornan, he embarrassed the party leadership with unsuccessful resolutions to drive all gays out of the GOP. The setback, however, didn't quiet Dannemeyer. Bombastic accusations are his stock in trade.

Some Democrats recall that he was once one of theirs. Dannemeyer served two Assembly terms as a Democrat, but switched parties and lost a state Senate race. Later, he came back to the Assembly as a one-term Republican before going to Congress.

PERSONAL: elected 1978; born Sept. 22, 1929, in Los Angeles, Calif.; home, Fullerton; education, attended Santa Maria Junior College, 1946-47, B.A. Valparaiso University 1950, J.D. UC Hastings Law School 1952; Lutheran (Missouri Synod); wife Evelyn, three children.

CAREER: U.S. Army, 1953-54; attorney, 1954-55; deputy district attorney, 1955-57; assistant city attorney, Fullerton, 1959-62; Assembly 1963-66; municipal and superior court judge, 1966-76; Assembly 1976-77.

COMMITTEES: Energy and Commerce; Judiciary.

OFFICES: Suite 2351, Rayburn Building, Washington, D.C. 20515, (202) 225-4111.

Suite 100, 1235 North Harbor Blvd., Fullerton 92632, (714) 992-0141.

DISTRICT REGISTRATION: 33% D, 57% R

1988 CAMPAIGN: Dannemeyer - R   74% $250,737

                 Marquis - D   23% $2,893

RATINGS:	ADA	ACLU	ACU	AFL/CIO	CFA	LCV	NTU	USCC
	0%	9%	100%	5%	18%	6%	71%	92%

40th Congressional District

Christopher Cox (R)

Packed along the northern end of the Orange County coast is an almost unbroken line of artsy villages, walled housing tracts and shimmering, glass office buildings. Yachts and pleasure boats clog the shoreline for miles. As one moves south, development is less dense but equally presumptions. Inland a bit, are the Laguna Hills, where mountain lions still roam, and the vast holdings of the Irvine Company. From top to bottom, the district is wealthy Republican country and conservative as only Orange County can be. In the 1970s and '80s, the area has become almost a second downtown Los Angeles as companies have established regional offices and research parks amid acres of parking lots.

Christopher Cox

The district's well-traveled and lackluster congressman, Robert Badham, hung it up in 1988. The race to replace him was decided in the GOP primary (general elections are perfunctory exercises here) as 14 conservatives vied for attention and votes. The one who emerged by garnering 31 percent of the vote was one of the most interesting, attorney Chris Cox.

Cox, making his first try for public office, has a solid background. He was a Harvard lecturer with strong links to the corporate world, and he also had been a White House counsel. That impressed district residents, but probably not as much as personal campaign appearances on Cox's behalf by Oliver North, Robert Bork and Arthur Laffer.

The GOP delegation saw to it that Cox got good committee assignments. Now it will be interesting to see what he does with them.

PERSONAL: elected 1988; born Oct. 16, 1952, in St. Paul, Minn.; home, Newport; education, B.A. USC 1973; M.B.A., J.D. Harvard University 1977; Roman Catholic; unmarried.

CAREER: attorney, 1978-86; lecturer, Harvard Business School, 1982-83; White House counsel, 1986-88.

COMMITTEES: Government Operations; Public Works and Transportation.

OFFICES: Suite 510, Cannon Building, Washington, D.C. 20515, (202) 225-6511.

Suite 430, 4000 MacArthur Blvd., Newport Beach 92660, (714) 644-4040.

DISTRICT REGISTRATION: 30% D, 59% R

1988 CAMPAIGN: Cox - R   67% $1,110,126

               Lenney - D   30% $ 47,746

RATINGS: None as of this printing.

41st Congressional District

Bill Lowery (R)

Northern San Diego and its suburbs have tradition-
ally been a Republican stronghold. It's a favorite retire-
ment place for Navy people and boasts some of the
finest weather in the United States. In La Jolla, Pacific
Beach and Mission Bay, many of the lavish homes don't
have air conditioning because the nearby sea supplies
naturally cooled air. Democrats who work at the Scripps
Institute or in service-sector jobs usually can't afford to
live in the district. They commute from the smoggy
towns up the Mission Valley or from working-class
areas in central and south San Diego.

One might expect the district's congressman to be an
arch conservative. But Rep. Bill Lowery is a protege of   **Bill Lowery**
Sen. Pete Wilson and is a moderate in most things,
except defense matters. He's also one of the most conservation-oriented Republicans in the delegation – at least on district issues. That is appreciated in an area where
local environmental issues tend to be non-partisan. When it comes to national environmental issues, however, his votes are more traditionally Republican.

Lowery, like Wilson, is a strident opponent of offshore oil drilling. In 1989, he
was instrumental in negotiating not only a one-year extension of the offshore
drilling ban in California, but also for the first time got a delay on pre-lease activities
by oil companies. Lowery worries about endangered song birds and has worked to
resolve the problem of sewage coming across the border in the Tijuana River even
though the most fetid impact is not in his district. At the same time, he's in a position
to help take care of the Navy from his seat on the Military Construction Subcommittee of Appropriations.

There are some signs that Lowery may be growing restless in the House.
Whenever future San Diego mayoral candidates are discussed, he is usually high on
the list of possibilities. Lowery also been mentioned as a potential senatorial
successor to Wilson if he is elected governor in 1990.

PERSONAL: elected 1980; born May 2, 1947, in San Diego, Calif.; home, San
Diego; education, B.A. San Diego State University 1969; Roman Catholic; wife
Katie, three children.

CAREER: public relations 1973-77; San Diego City Council 1977-80, deputy
mayor 1979-80.

COMMITTEES: Appropriations.

OFFICES: Suite 438, Rayburn Building, Washington, D.C. 20515, (202) 225-
3201.

880 Front St., San Diego 92188, (619) 231-0957.
DISTRICT REGISTRATION: 38% D, 48% R
1988 CAMPAIGN: Lowery - R   66% $407,025
                   Kripke - D   31% $ 45,311
RATINGS: ADA   ACLU   ACU   AFL/CIO   CFA   LCV   NTU   USCC
             15%   23%   92%   8%   18%   19%   44%   100%

42nd Congressional District
Dana Rohrabacher (R)

One of the late Rep. Phil Burton's chief goals in redistricting Southern California was to provide a safe seat for Democratic Rep. Glenn Anderson in the 32nd District. As a result, the 42nd had to take in pockets of Republican communities that intrude on three sides of Anderson's stronghold. When Burton was through, the 42nd was unquestionably the screwiest-looking district in the state. The district has two blobs east and west of Los Angeles Harbor connected by a five-mile peninsula across the mouth the harbor. In some areas, that strip of land is only one-block wide.

To the west are the Palos Verdes communities and Torrance, with stately homes and business centers linked to Pacific Rim trade. On the east are Republican

Dana Rohrabacher

areas of Long Beach plus the affluent communities of Seal Beach and Huntington Beach. Politics here aren't as extreme as those of the large Orange County communities, but they remain solidly conservative.

Rep. Dan Lungren was safely spending his time here when Gov. George Deukmejian tapped him to become state treasurer in 1988. But the state Senate denied Lungren the seat, and he moved to Sacramento to begin preparations for a statewide race for attorney general in 1990. That left an opening and, as with most Republican seats, it was all over in the primary. Dana Rohrabacher, one-time editorial writer for the conservative Orange County Register and speech writer for former President Ronald Reagan, emerged from a down and dirty, eight-person race. Like Chris Cox to the south, Rohrabacher was helped by the appearance of Oliver North. There was enough bitterness in the race that Rohrabacher might face another primary challenge in 1990. If not, he's probably safely ensconced.

PERSONAL: elected 1988; born June 21, 1947, in Corona, Calif.; home, Lomita; B.A. CSU Long Beach 1969; M.A. USC 1971; Baptist; unmarried.
CAREER: journalist, 1970-80; speech writer for President Reagan, 1981-88.
COMMITTEES: District of Columbia; Science, Space and Technology.

OFFICES: Suite 1017 Longworth Building, Washington, D.C. 20515, (202) 225-2415.

Suite 306, 2733 Pacific Coast Highway, Torrance 90505 (213) 325-0668.

DISTRICT REGISTRATION: 36% D, 53% R

1988 CAMPAIGN: Rohrabacher - R   64% $494,487

                Kimbrough - D   33% $ 11,889

RATINGS: None as of this printing.

43rd Congressional District

Ronald C. Packard (R)

Ronald C. Packard

Northern San Diego County and a slice of southern Orange County make up the 43rd District. The huge Camp Pendleton Marine Corps Base sprawls though the center. To the north and south are the wealthy coastal towns of San Juan Capistrano, San Clemente, Oceanside and Carlsbad. Inland are pleasant retirements communities and some shabby trailer courts inhabited by G.I. families and civilian defense workers.

The climate is one of the most ideal in the United States. White, waspy retirees dominate most communities and crowd the golf courses. Spouses of Marines and a few Hispanics are available for the service-sector jobs. Politically, attitudes are in step with hard-core Orange County Republicans to the north. Yet San Clemente homeowners weren't so Republican that they welcomed having the Western White House in their midst during Richard Nixon's presidency. There were many complaints that property values were being hurt. Residents have high educational levels and intense interests in property and private enterprise. Most can afford insurance which liberates them from dependency on government health plans.

Their congressman, however, is anything but a right-wing ideologue. Rep. Ron Packard, a dentist, is a practical man with a commitment to assisting local government. He's taken on thorny problems such as Indian water rights and negotiated a settlement that pleased all sides. He's also made a mark in aircraft safety legislation.

At the time of his election, Packard was only the fourth person in American history to win a congressional seat in a write-in campaign. In the primary, with 18 contenders running for an open seat, he was second by 92 votes to a businessman named Johnny Crean. Crean spent $500,000 of his own money to convince voters that he was then-President Ronald Reagan's personal choice for the job. Reagan, however, had never heard of him. Packard triumphed in November. Since then he's had easy races.

PERSONAL: elected 1982; born Jan. 19, 1931, in Meridian, Idaho; home, Oceanside; education, attended Brigham Young University and Portland State University, D.M.D. University of Oregon 1957; Mormon; wife Jean, seven children.

CAREER: U.S. Navy 1957-59; dentist, 1957-82; trustee, Carlsbad Unified School District, 1962-74; Carlsbad City Council 1976-78, mayor 1978-82.

COMMITTEES: Public Works and Transportation; Science, Space and Technology.

OFFICES: Suite 316, Cannon Building, Washington, D.C. 20515, (202) 225-3906.

Suite 105, 2121 Palomar Airport Road, Carlsbad 92009, (619) 438-0443.

Suite 204, 629 Camino de los Mares, San Clemente 92672, (714) 496-2343.

DISTRICT REGISTRATION: 30% D, 56% R

1988 CAMPAIGN: Packard - R   72% $160,267

                 Greenebaum - D   26% $ 74,087

RATINGS:	ADA	ACLU	ACU	AFL/CIO	CFA	LCV	NTU	USCC
	5%	5%	100%	7%	18%	13%	57%	92%

44th Congressional District
Jim Bates (D)

Every sparkling city has its shabby underside. Most of San Diego's working-class white, black and Hispanic precincts have been packed into the 44th District to create a Democratic haven in the midst of one of the most Republican counties in the state. Chula Vista and National City make up the southern flank. From the downtown area, the district runs eastward through Lemon Grove and laps over into smoggy reaches of the Mission Valley. Most of the paychecks in this area come from blue-collar Navy jobs, small retail shops or the service sector. There's also a fair number of people on relief.

Jim Bates

Rep. Jim Bates has an easy time getting re-elected here, but his string may have run out. In October 1989, the House ethics committee concluded that Bates was guilty of sexually harassing two women staffers and approving improper campaign activity in his congressional office. Bates said he accepted the panel's judgment, but added, "I did not know what sexual harassment meant until this came up."

The charges surfaced in September 1988 when two former female aides said Bates had made sexually explicit comments to them and had touched them in ways they found offensive. That became the main issue in Bates' re-election campaign in

1988, but Bates spent a half million dollars and won anyway with 60 percent of the vote. It took until the following summer for the ethics committee to get around to the investigation.

Even before the charges became public, Bates was known for being abusive with his staff. His office has one of the highest turnover rates on the Hill. His temper has a low flash point and he had difficulty working with other congressmen. Among colleagues, Bates' voting record is so unpredictable that he's known as an unreliable ally in a legislative fight. Part of the problem seems to be Bate's propensity for telling people what they want to hear rather than what he will actually do. As a freshman, Bates so annoyed former Speaker Jim Wright over MX issues that he's had virtually no influence with the leadership. All that helped him make California Magazine's list as one of the five worst members of the delegation. Perhaps Wright's departure will be a plus for Bates. But his standing with the leadership really depends on the ethics committee conclusions. And with it going badly for Bates, he may draw both strong primary and general election opponents in 1990.

PERSONAL: elected 1982; born July 21, 1941, in Denver; home, San Diego; B.A. San Diego State University 1974; Congregationalist; wife Marilyn, one child.

CAREER: U.S. Marine Corps, 1959-63; Banker, 1963-68; Aerospace administrator, 1968-69; San Diego City Council, 1971-74; San Diego Board of Supervisors, 1975-82.

COMMITTEES: Energy and Commerce; Government Operations; House Administration.

OFFICES: Suite 224, Cannon Building, Washington, D.C. 20515, (202) 225-5452.

Suite 220, 3450 College Ave., San Diego 92115, (619) 287-8851.

Suite A, 430 David St., Chula Vista 92010, (619) 691-1166.

DISTRICT REGISTRATION: 55% D, 32% R

1988 CAMPAIGN: Bates - D   60% $480,679

                Butterfield - R   37% $218,388

RATINGS:

ADA	ACLU	ACU	AFL/CIO	CFA	LCV	NTU	USCC
95%	91%	8%	83%	82%	81%	49%	46%

45th Congressional District

Duncan Hunter (R)

The 45th District stretches across the bottom of California in an area that has seen momentous change in recent decades and is apt to see much more. At the coast, it begins in the old beach village of Coronado, runs south on the Silver Strand to Imperial Beach, and then swings east through middle-class and upper middle-class suburbs. Once clear of San Diego, the district takes in the rock piles of eastern San Diego County and all of Imperial County.

The San Diego portions are comfortably Republican. Imperial County is becoming solidly Hispanic, but the white grower class still controls the political scene. Immigration pressures, however, are eroding the white dominance everywhere but in the richest San Diego portions in the district. In the Imperial Valley, friction between growers and workers continues to mount. A wide range of border issues fester here: immigration, pollution, drug trafficking, and educational and social services for new arrivals.

It's going to be difficult for a mere mortal congressman to juggle the issues here in future years with the disparity between haves and have-nots, the racial conflicts and the inconsistent national policies on border

Duncan Hunter

issues. It would take a hawkish Republican who's a former poverty lawyer to satisfy the diverse elements. Rep. Duncan Hunter is exactly that. As an added bonus, he seems to limitless energy to pursue his goals.

Hunter was a combat officer in Vietnam, went to night law school, and began his practice in an old barber shop in San Diego's barrio. From that base, he went on to beat Democrat Lionel Van Deerlin, an 18-year veteran in Congress.

Hunter has annoyed some colleagues by stepping over them to get what he wants. But his talents also have been recognized by party leaders. He chairs the Republican Research Committee which is charged with developing GOP strategies for emerging issues. Among other things, Hunter is using the committee to focus on Hispanic recruitment for the party. He is also leading the charge to put the military into the forefront of drug interdiction efforts. California's GOP delegation hasn't many stars. But Hunter is definitely one with great promise.

PERSONAL: elected 1980; born May 31, 1948, in Riverside, Calif.; home, Coronado; B.S.L. Western State University 1976, J.D. 1976; Baptist; wife Lynne, two children.

CAREER: U.S. Army, 1969-71; attorney, 1976-80.

COMMITTEES: Armed Services; Select Committee on Hunger.

OFFICES: Suite 133, Cannon Building, Washington, D.C. 20515, (202) 225-5672.

366 South Pierce St., El Cajon 92020, (619) 579-3001.

Suite G, 1101 Airport Road, Imperial 92251, (619) 353-5420.

825 Imperial Beach Blvd., Imperial Beach 92032, (619) 423-3011.

DISTRICT REGISTRATION: 37% D, 49% R

1988 CAMPAIGN: Hunter - R   74% $489,395

              Lepiscopo - D   24% $ 8,136

RATINGS:	ADA	ACLU	ACU	AFL/CIO	CFA	LCV	NTU	USCC
	0%	0%	100%	21%	18%	13%	63%	77%

3

Governors command attention

To be governor of California in recent decades is to stand in the wings of the national political stage. Ronald Reagan proved most adept at moving into the spotlight, and George Deukmejian did his best to avoid it altogether. But the state's chief executive automatically commands attention, owing largely to the 47 electoral votes that make California enormously important in any presidential election.

Earl Warren, elected three times as governor, sought the Republican presidential nomination twice before going on to preside for 16 years as chief justice of the U.S. Supreme Court. Edmund G. "Jerry" Brown Jr. shone in a string of 1976 primaries as he made a characteristically tardy bid to seize the Democratic presidential nomination from Jimmy Carter, then tried to unseat Carter in 1980.

Brown's father, Edmund G. "Pat" Brown Sr., had been governor for two years when he first flirted with the possibility of a vice-presidential nomination. The former state attorney general, who defeated Republican William Knowland to win the governor's job in 1958, was eventually frustrated in his hopes for higher office. He turned his attention instead to the less glamorous business of building the staples of government known collectively as the "infrastructure." Three decades later, the elder Brown's accomplishments – a bond issue to increase water supplies to Southern California, more investment in the university system, faster freeway construction for a rapidly growing state – are remembered fondly by elected officials facing a new crush of growth.

Brown's terms as governor are also memorable for their contribution to capital punishment history in a state where voters have demanded that political leaders be willing to put violent criminals to death. An opponent of capital punishment who nevertheless believed it was his job as governor to carry out state law, Brown described the agony of his clemency decisions in death penalty cases in a book published in 1989. "It was an awesome, ultimate power over the lives of others that no person or government should have, or crave," he wrote. "Each decision took something out of me that nothing – not family or work or hope for the future – has ever been able to replace."

Brown, whose defeat of Republican gubernatorial candidate Richard Nixon in 1962 prompted the infamous "you won't have Nixon to kick around anymore" press conference, was looking forward in 1966 to running against a political neophyte named Ronald Reagan. But the mediagenic actor, railing against disorder on college campuses and appealing to an electorate unnerved by the Watts riots, denied Brown a chance to join Warren as a three-term governor. Reagan continued while governor to fine-tune the conservative message that would propel him to the presidency, but he was largely unsuccessful in matching his fiscal actions as governor with his anti-government rhetoric. The former Democrat, who bashed the bureaucracy and welfare state in his public appearances, signed what was then the largest tax increase in the state's history in order to shore up the sagging budget he inherited from Pat Brown.

Reagan was replaced by Jerry Brown, a self-proclaimed spokesman for a younger generation demanding change and imagination from its government. If Jerry Brown followed his father's footsteps to the governor's office, he seemed determined to carve out his own path once he got there. The father was a consummate political mingler; the son standoffish. Pat was a spender; Jerry a relative tightwad. Pat laid pavement; Jerry discouraged freeway construction in favor of car pooling and mass transit. Similarly, the younger Brown's contributions as governor were less concrete. More than anything else, his governorship is remembered for his personal idiosyncrasies: his refusal to live in the governor's mansion, the mattress on the floor of his austere apartment, his 1979 trip to Africa with singer Linda Ronstadt.

Brown used his appointment power to fill state jobs with a more diverse group of people, but some of those appointments became enormous liabilities with voters. Transportation Director Adriana Gianturco defended the much-hated "Diamond Lanes" imposed on drivers, who resented being forced to share rides. Supreme Court Chief Justice Rose Bird, ultimately ousted by voters in 1986, came to symbolize a criminal justice system seen as too sympathetic to the people it was supposed to punish. Deukmejian used both to score points in his gubernatorial campaigns.

Yet even Deukmejian, acknowledging that the state could not simply build its way out of its traffic congestion problem, would later emphasize car pooling as a necessary gridlock-reduction tool. Brown also takes credit for influencing his Republican successor on other fronts, including energy and technology. His emphasis on minority hiring, he says, helped push the Deukmejian administration in that direction.

California governors like to talk about the size of the state's economy, which would rank sixth or seventh worldwide if California were a separate nation. The governor's line-item veto gives California's chief executive more control over spending than the president has over the federal budget, a fact that Reagan often cited in seeking, but never getting, a line-item veto power as president. But in the last decade, the voters have decided to exercise their own muscle on the subject.

In 1978, anti-tax crusaders Howard Jarvis and Paul Gann tapped into an underlying anger about government spending with Proposition 13. Failure to display enough tax-cutting zeal that year cost several state legislators their seats and created a new corps of "Proposition 13 babies" in the state Legislature. It also marked the beginning of the end for Jerry Brown, who irreparably damaged his credibility by campaigning against the initiative, then embracing it with enthusiasm once it had passed. Brown was defeated by Republican Pete Wilson in his 1982 bid for the U.S. Senate and left the political scene for a six-year sabbatical.

Proposition 13 and its follow-up, a 1979 voter-imposed limit on government spending promoted by Gann, still shape California politics today, forcing any aspiring officeholder who wants to be taken seriously to tiptoe around the subject of taxes. But as spending limits are beginning to bind at state and local levels, pressure for more flexibility is growing. And as the political pendulum began to swing back toward the middle, Brown returned to campaign for and win the chairmanship of the state Democratic Party. "The time," he told party members, "is ripe for resurgence."

Whether the Democratic Party continues its decadelong, post-Proposition 13 fade or re-establishes itself in California is one of the unspoken themes of the 1990 campaign for governor, one that is intertwined with growing concern among Californians about a widely perceived deterioration in the quality of their lives.

Republicans – Deukmejian being the chief example – have prospered during the 1980s by aligning themselves with the Proposition 13-inspired mood of limited taxation and government spending; Democrats, who ordinarily favor a more activist government, were left befuddled by the onset of tax-cut fever. Some, like Brown, opportunistically embraced the trend, while others remained silent.

And beyond the governorship of the nation's largest state itself, the candidates are vying for that place on the national political stage. The next governor of California will automatically be catapulted into the ranks of potential presidents.

THE DUKE TAKES OVER

In 1982, California voters, fed up with Gov. Jerry Brown's slapdash style and nearly perpetual campaign for president, elected a governor who would give them some rest. They chose a chief executive who joked about his own lack of charisma, demonstrated little interest in higher office and didn't hobnob with rock stars.

Courken George Deukmejian Jr. preferred to stay at home with his pet beagles and play an occasional game of golf, at least in the early days of his governorship. His public passions, which were few, included a weakness for Jamoca almond fudge ice cream. People likened him to Ward Cleaver, and in his more casual moments, he did wear sweaters that would have looked right at home on the Beaver's dad.

Elected by the thinnest of margins over his Democratic opponent, Los Angeles

GUBERNATORIAL ELECTIONS 1902-1986

Year	Candidate	Votes	Percent
1902	George C. Pardee (R)	146,332	48.06%
	Franklin K. Lane (D)	143,783	47.22%
1906	James Gillett (R)	125,887	40.4%
	Theodore Bell (D)	117,645	37.7%
1910	Hiram Johnson (R)	177,191	45.9%
	Theodore Bell (D)	154,835	40.1%
1914	Hiram Johnson (Progressive)	460,495	49.7%
	John Fredericks (R)	271,990	29.3%
	J.B. Curtin (D)	116,121	12.5%
1918	William Stephens (R, Progressive, Prohibition)	387,547	56.3%
	Theodore Bell (Independent)	251,189	36.5%
1922	Friend Wm. Richardson (R)	576,445	59.7%
	Thomas Lee Woolwine (D)	347,530	36.0%
1926	C.C. Young (R)	814,815	71.2%
	Justus Wardell (D)	282,451	24.7%
1930	James Rolph Jr. (R)	999,393	72.1%
	Milton Young (D)	333,973	24.1%
1934	Frank Merriam (R)	1,130,620	48.9%
	Upton Sinclair (D)	879,537	37.7%
1938	Culbert Olson (D)	1,391,734	52.5%
	Frank Merriam (R)	1,171,019	44.2%
1942	Earl Warren (R)	1,275,287	57.0%
	Culbert Olson (D)	932,995	41.7%
1946	Earl Warren (R and D)	2,344,542	91.6%
	Henry Schmidt (Prohibition)	180,579	7.1%
1950	Earl Warren (R)	2,461,754	64.8%
	James Roosevelt (D)	1,333,856	35.2%
1954	Goodwin Knight (R)	2,290,519	56.8%
	Richard Graves (D)	1,739,368	43.2%
1958	Pat Brown (D)	3,140,076	59.8%
	William Knowland (R)	2,110,911	40.2%
1962	Pat Brown (D)	3,037,109	51.9%
	Richard Nixon (R)	2,740,351	46.8%
1966	Ronald Reagan (R)	3,742,913	56.6%
	Pat Brown (D)	2,749,174	41.6%
1970	Ronald Reagan (R)	3,439,664	52.8%
	Jesse Unruh (D)	2,938,607	45.1%
1974	Jerry Brown (D)	3,131,648	50.2%
	Houston Flournoy (R)	2,952,954	47.3%
1978	Jerry Brown (D)	3,878,812	56.0%
	Evelle Younger (R)	2,526,534	36.5%
1982	George Deukmejian (R)	3,881,014	49.3%
	Tom Bradley (D)	3,787,669	48.1%
1986	George Deukmejian (R)	4,506,601	60.54%
	Tom Bradley (D)	2,781,714	37.37%

Mayor Tom Bradley, Deuk-
mejian decided from the beginning to stick to the basics.
He said he was convinced voters wanted a competent manager, and he did little to deviate
from that mission. He did his
best to avoid any revenue-raising measures that might be
labeled tax increases, he built
prisons and he appointed
judges he said took a "com-
mon-sense" approach to fighting crime.

Deukmejian proposed to
his wife, the former Gloria
Saatjian, within a month of
their meeting at a wedding in
1956. But his methodical approach to the job of governor
suggested that his marriage
may have been his last impetu-
ous act. He kept strictly to his
official schedule, and he didn't
bombard Californians with too
many new ideas.

George Deukmejian

Unlike Brown, who seemed to have had his eye on the White House from the day
he first ran for the Los Angeles Community College board of trustees, Deukmejian
had to be coaxed into leaving his position as attorney general to seek higher office.
Those who did the coaxing were clearly disturbed at having the lieutenant governor
of the moment, ex-recording industry executive Mike Curb, as their candidate.

Always most motivated by crime and punishment issues, Deukmejian cited the
governor's power to appoint judges as a primary reason for his candidacy. His
interest in public safety, he said, sprang from his boyhood in the village of Menands,
a small community on the outskirts of Albany, N.Y. Born there on June 6, 1928, he
grew up taking rides in the motorcycle sidecars of the local police, whose
department was housed in the municipal building next door to Deukmejian's home.
"He was like a mascot, I think," his wife once said. "He seemed to gravitate toward
the building."

"Corky," as he was known in those days, also spent time at the local fire station.
He served as a volunteer firefighter before going off to attend St. John's University
School of Law in the big city of New York.

Named after his father, an immigrant rug merchant, Deukmejian also seemed to draw his law-and-order attitudes from his Armenian heritage. His father's sister died during the Armenian genocide in Turkey following World War I, and the slaughter was one speech topic that touched him to the point of tears.

"As Armenian-Americans, we know, perhaps better than most, that all the material comforts in the world are meaningless if the threat of violence and crime hangs over our heads," he said at a 1983 banquet hosted by the Armenian General Benevolent Union.

Deukmejian was not a politician from the outset. Following his law school graduation, he worked briefly for the state of New York in the department of audit and control, then completed a 16-month military tour of duty in Paris, where he helped to settle claims made by French nationals against the U.S. Army. Upon returning to the United States in 1955, he worked for the Texaco Co. in its land and lease department. He was appointed as a deputy county counsel for Los Angeles County. He set up his own law practice in Long Beach in 1958. Then began what will be, by the time his second term as governor ends in early 1991, a 28-year public service career.

A CAREER IN POLITICS

When Assemblyman Bill Grant, a Long Beach Republican, announced his retirement in 1962, Deukmejian won the open seat and served two terms in the lower house. He moved to the Senate in 1966, when a U.S. Supreme Court ruling created new seats in Los Angeles County. He went on to serve 12 years in the Senate, earning the post of Senate majority leader in 1970.

He first sought to become attorney general that year, but lost in the primary election. By 1978, as author of California's 1977 death penalty and "use a gun, go to prison" laws, Deukmejian had little trouble winning election as state attorney general.

The 1982 governor's race was a different story. Conventional wisdom and key political contributors had already picked Curb as the Republican front-runner when Deukmejian entered the race. His narrow victory in the primary was a setback for the Republican right-wing, which had labeled Deukmejian a "closet liberal." That victory was followed by an even narrower win against Bradley. In the closest race for California governor since 1902, he won by just 1.2 percent of the votes cast, actually losing to Bradley in votes cast on Election Day and winning on absentee votes cast before the election.

Four years later, Deukmejian trounced Bradley in a rematch, winning by more votes than any governor since Earl Warren locked up both the Republican and Democratic nominations before his re-election victory in 1946.

In the interim, he had bragged repeatedly that he had taken the state "from IOU to A-OK" by erasing a $1.5 billion budget deficit he inherited from Brown. He spent much of the campaign denouncing liberal members of a state Supreme Court that had overturned dozens of death penalty decisions. Voters responded by dumping three members of the court and electing Deukmejian to a second term.

In a state that serves as a breeding ground for national politicians, Deukmejian's success provided a source of constant speculation for the Capitol press corps.

Presidential and vice-presidential talk began; at one point during the 1988 presidential campaign he announced he was considering a favorite-son candidacy in a bid to capture the state's presidential delegates himself. He later discarded that idea, announcing instead that he was creating a political committee, Citizens for Common Sense, to gather grass-roots support for his policies and guide his political future.

Considered a top prospect for the vice presidency by many national pundits and political consultants, Deukmejian nevertheless insisted he would refuse an offer to join the ticket because he would not put his office in the hands of Democratic Lt. Gov. Leo McCarthy. "I am honored and very grateful for your consideration, but I must tell you that I cannot be considered for the office of vice president," Deukmejian wrote in a letter to George Bush. "As you know, if I were to assume the vice presidency, it would mean turning the entire executive branch of the nation's most populous state over to the Democratic Party."

In retrospect, his decision seemed to spring more from party loyalty than from lack of ambition. He later proposed that California's governor and lieutenant governor run as a team to prevent voters from splitting their tickets between the two offices, and said that he would have accepted an offer from Bush if McCarthy had not stood in the way.

Yet Deukmejian also seemed to lack the stamina and desire that drives other politicians who reach his level of prominence. With three children – Leslie, George and Andrea – he was a devoted family man. More comfortable with a nine-to-five lifestyle than a 24-hour campaign schedule, he once commented on the effort required to a reporter who asked whether he shared New York Gov. Mario Cuomo's interest in the presidency. "Cuomo seems to be able to get by on about four hours of sleep a night," Deukmejian said. "If he decides to do it, he'll have his hands full. It would be very difficult for me."

CHAMPION OF THE STATUS QUO

Critics often focused on his status-quo approach to the job. Even as he was touted as potential vice presidential material in 1988, Newsweek magazine suggested he might just be the dullest major politician in America. An editorial cartoonist portrayed him as "the official state slug," with slime dripping from his desk and chair.

Always popular in public opinion polls, Deukmejian saw his job rating with voters dip as he entered the "lame-duck" phase of his political career. Complaints that he was bland, boring and stubborn began to escalate into a more serious charge: that he lacked the vision or leadership qualities needed to move the state into the 21st century with its prosperity intact.

His response to critics took on an increasingly strident tone, reaching a crescendo in a dispute with the editorial board of the Los Angeles Times. Bristling at criticism of his state budget proposals, Deukmejian told the newspaper to "put up or shut up" in a letter to the editor. "California is not falling off a 'cliff' or sinking into an 'abyss' – to cite just two examples of the hyperventilated phrase-making that has become a staple of your 'Chicken Little'-style editorials," he wrote.

In January 1989, Deukmejian announced that he was ready to return to the private sector rather than seek a third term. Despite appeals from party leaders who wanted him to remain in office as California prepared for legislative and congressional reapportionment following the 1990 census, he rejected their worries that a strong GOP candidate could not be found to succeed him. He gave away a chunk of his political funds for Armenian earthquake relief and appeared ready to earn a larger paycheck in private life.

By the time Deukmejian announced that he was bowing out of the 1990 election, the two-term governor had already accomplished much of what he had set out to do.

He had said no to billions of dollars in state spending proposals, racking up one-year records for vetoing both bills and budget items.

He could point to a state unemployment rate half of that facing the state when he took office, thanks to job development he attributed to his no-new-taxes posture.

He had reconstructed the court with justices willing to impose a voter-approved death penalty, leaving the stage set for California's first execution since 1967. Before the end of 1989, half of California's judges were expected to be Deukmejian appointees, including five of the seven members of the state Supreme Court.

And he had pushed a massive construction program to more than double the number of state prison beds.

Yet California was beginning to want more in a governor than a warrior against taxes and crime.

POPULATION BOMB EXPLODES

Deukmejian was wearing out his welcome with business leaders, who liked lower tax bills as long the state provided the services they needed. At a time when businesses were increasingly finding they couldn't move their products and services freely on California's congested highways, the governor was opposing any hike in the state's road-building tax on gasoline.

In addition, a population explosion and the accompanying demand for increased state services were blowing the lid off a voter-imposed state spending cap that Deukmejian defended. In the fall of 1988, the voters ignored Deukmejian's opposition and approved two initiatives, one raising the cigarette tax to pay for health programs and another guaranteeing a specific proportion of the state's budget for schools.

All the while, Democrats complained that the state freeway system was a disgrace, prisons remained substantially overcrowded and the mental health system was in a state of collapse.

As his term drew to a close, Deukmejian was continuing to wrestle with the issues – road financing, state spending constraints and the need to provide services for an increasingly diverse population – that would determine his legacy in the job.

The Republican governor had begun with a bang in 1983, maneuvering his way out of a $1.5 billion budget deficit inherited from Jerry Brown's administration. Although the compromise he reached with legislative leaders that year relied on revenue-raising measures that touched nearly every Californian, including changes in motor vehicle license fees, few challenged his claim that he had led the state back from the brink of bankruptcy without a general tax increase.

A governor who tended conscientiously to fiscal matters, no matter how boring, was appealing to an electorate that had hoped for a steadier hand at the helm. And each July, Deukmejian would announce that he had signed a balanced budget requiring no tax increases and providing a "rainy day" emergency reserve that came to stand as a symbol of his fiscal restraint. "IOU to A-OK" became the rallying cry for his 1986 re-election.

But fallout from conformity with federal tax reform put the state on a financial roller coaster beginning in 1987. Discovering an unexpected tax windfall that year, Deukmejian overrode Democratic desires to spend the money on education and returned $1.1 billion to taxpayers, the first rebate of its kind in state history. His success was short-lived. The following spring saw a state budget deficit of at least $1 billion.

Deukmejian proposed a revenue-raising plan to cope with the unexpected shortfall, then abandoned it as key Republicans worried that it could undercut a "no new taxes" pledge by GOP presidential candidate George Bush. The governor denied any connection, declaring angrily that the press had misrepresented as tax increases his call for "temporary minimal adjustments" in the state tax code.

ISOLATION HAUNTS DEUKMEJIAN

The episode nevertheless was an example of the way in which Deukmejian and the Legislature worked together, or rather failed to work together. Democrats, gloating that Deukmejian had finally seen the error of his no-tax ways, preferred to delight in his discomfort rather than seize the opportunity to solve a problem.

But Deukmejian was also to blame. He had always kept members of the Legislature at arm's length, and this instance was no exception. He had developed the proposal unilaterally, and Republican leaders complained privately that they were informed, not consulted. To rank-and-file legislators, his suggestion came as a complete surprise.

The collapse of his plan, and the months of budget turmoil that followed, may have taught the governor a lesson. When another unexpected pot of money surfaced in 1989, he invited legislative leaders to negotiate how to divide it.

It wasn't the first time – or the last – that Deukmejian reversed himself.

In the 1986 campaign, Los Angeles Mayor Tom Bradley needled Deukmejian for lacking a passport. After his re-election, the governor devoted a large share of his second term to promoting trade, winging his way to such distant locales as Australia and the Philippines.

Deukmejian decided in 1986 to sign a measure divesting state holdings in companies with ties to South Africa, legislation he had opposed the year before.

Rather than raise the state's gas tax, Deukmejian shifted more responsibility for road-building to local government, signing a 1987 bill that gave counties the power to ask voters for sales tax increases to pay for transportation. But by 1989, with even Republicans who shared Deukmejian's determination to hold the line on state spending chafing at what they saw as a lack of gubernatorial activism, Deukmejian was campaigning for a measure to raise the state's gas tax and adjust the state's voter-imposed spending limit.

The gasoline tax/spending limit measure, hammered out with Democratic legislative leaders, was one of a series of agreements that Deukmejian reached with the Democrats in 1989 after announcing in January his plan to retire at the end of his second term. The announcement opened a window of opportunity for bilateral negotiations. The years of stalemate on major policy matters gave way to action on, among other things, solid waste management, compensation for injured workers and control of assault rifles. In a stark contrast with the arm's length relations of previous years, Deukmejian conducted a number of summit conferences with Republican and Democratic leaders.

STAGE SET FOR 1990 CAMPAIGN

With the "Iron Duke" image wearing thin, the 1990 race for governor promised in part to address fears that California was sinking into a state of mediocrity.

Under pressure from Proposition 73, through which voters imposed stricter fund-raising requirements for state campaigns, candidates for state constitutional offices were forced to declare their interest in a job before they could begin raising money. And U.S. Sen. Pete Wilson, a former Marine who had served as a state assemblyman and mayor of San Diego, emerged early as the handpicked candidate of state GOP leaders, including Deukmejian loyalists.

Fresh from an easy re-election win over Democratic Lt. Gov. Leo McCarthy in November, where he battled the one-term "jinx" that had plagued his recent predecessors in the seat, Wilson waited less than four months to announce he would run for governor. He began his campaign by calling for the increase in the state gas tax that Deukmejian had resisted.

Democrats were expecting a less tidy selection process, with two major candidates – state Attorney General John Van de Kamp and former San Francisco Mayor Dianne Feinstein – likely to face off in the primary.

Feinstein, who became San Francisco's political leader in 1978 following the assassination of former Mayor George Moscone, was elected to two full terms before stepping down early in 1988. More conservative than Van de Kamp on crime issues, she nevertheless was likely to fight an uphill battle to distance herself from San Francisco's liberal reputation.

Portraying herself as an outsider in the race for the nomination, Feinstein began by assailing the Democratic Party's "knee-jerk" liberalism and courting the conservative Democrats who had helped put Republicans Ronald Reagan and George Bush in the White House.

Van de Kamp, meanwhile, labored to shore up his law-and-order credentials and link himself with pro-choice forces in the abortion debate. In a tactic made more politically attractive by Proposition 73's restrictions on fund-raising for candidates, he proposed and began to raise money for his own statewide initiatives on ethics and the environment for the 1990 ballot.

Wilson appeared ready to ride the same anti-crime issues that had worked so well for Deukmejian in 1986. He lent his name to a victims' rights measure circulating for the 1990 ballot, and began early to remind people that Van de Kamp had once refused to prosecute Angelo Buono for multiple murders in the Los Angeles "Hillside Strangler" case.

While Deukmejian aides stressed that Wilson and the governor sang from the same political hymnal, Wilson appeared willing to highlight their differences. Seven years of Deukmejian's cautious leadership made Wilson sound daring when he talked about long-term planning for state building needs.

Although the governorship is California's biggest political prize, it's not the only one. Californians also elect, independently from the governor, lesser statewide officials who run separate state agencies and, as tradition dictates, plot campaigns to become governor. Most of the state's recent governors – Ronald Reagan is the only exception – occupied one of the lesser offices before taking the big step to the top.

PERSONAL: elected 1982; re-elected 1986; born June 6, 1928 in the village of Menands, New York; lives in Sacramento and Long Beach; graduate of Siena College in Loudonville, New York; St. John's University School of Law, J.D.; married to Gloria Deukmejian; three children: Leslie, George, Andrea.

CAREER: Texaco Co. land and lease department, 1955; deputy county counsel for Los Angeles County; private law practice, 1958-1962; Assembly 1962-1966; Senate 1967-1978; attorney general 1978.

OFFICES: Capitol (916) 445-2864; Los Angeles (213) 736-2373; Washington, D.C., 202-347-6894.

LEO McCARTHY HITS HIS LIMIT

Leo McCarthy, long considered a cut above most California politicians, found in 1988 that his squeaky-clean reputation and proven performance on a list of liberal issues were not enough to defeat incumbent Republican Sen. Pete Wilson in a lackluster Senate race. In early 1989, the two-term lieutenant governor, his senatorial campaign still in debt, announced he was not willing to step back onto a round-the-clock fund-raising treadmill in order to run for governor. Instead, to the disappointment of several younger Democrats who had been waiting for him to move up or out, McCarthy opted to run for re-election to the post that he has used to pursue such issues as environmental protection and nursing-home reform.

A workaholic and conscientious to a fault, McCarthy can also be sanctimonious and stubborn, qualities that rose to the surface during the prolonged strain of his Senate campaign. He had endured defeat before, however, most notably in an agonizing power struggle with then-Assemblyman Howard Berman that ended McCarthy's six years as Assembly speaker in 1980. The fight ultimately handed the speakership to fellow San Franciscan Willie Brown after McCarthy and Berman battled to a draw.

McCarthy went on to become lieutenant governor in 1982 and to win re-election in 1986, even when he was one of the few candidates willing to openly support state Supreme Court Chief Justice Rose Bird during her losing bid to retain her post. By then, however, he

Leo McCarthy

had changed his position on the death penalty – the issue that led to Bird's defeat – after years of opposition to capital punishment. Kidnapped as a college student by a man who had just murdered a police officer, McCarthy said his views on violent crime began to change years later when he met the officer's widow.

Born in New Zealand, McCarthy grew up in San Francisco as the son of a tavern owner and attended Catholic seminary as a teenager. He served on the San Francisco Board of Supervisors from 1963 to 1968. From there, he moved to the Assembly, where he soon earned a reputation as a family man who commuted home to San Francisco nearly every night rather than pursue Sacramento's political night life.

Although it appears he has now hit a dead end after three decades in California politics, McCarthy is refusing to return voluntarily to private life. He has not ruled out a future bid to become governor or another run for a Senate seat in 1992.

PERSONAL: elected 1982; re-elected 1986; born Aug. 15, 1930, in Auckland, New Zealand; lives in San Francisco; graduate of University of San Francisco, B.S.; and San Francisco Law School, J.D.; married to Jacqueline Burke; four children: Sharon, Conna, Adam and Niall.

CAREER: legislative aide to Sen. Eugene McAteer, 1959-1963; San Francisco Board of Supervisors, 1963-1968; Assembly 1969-1982; Assembly speaker 1974-1980.

OFFICES: Capitol (916) 445-8994; San Francisco (415) 557-2662; Los Angeles (213) 620-2560; San Diego (619) 238-3489.

JOHN VAN DE KAMP TRIES TO MOVE UP

John Van de Kamp, California's two-term attorney general, entered the 1990 governor's race in a peculiar political position. The state's top Democratic constitutional office holder had become a party heavyweight by winning a string of elections in a law enforcement career spanning nearly three decades. But he had not experienced a serious electoral challenge in years, undergoing little statewide scrutiny of his personality and his record. With the exception of an early loss to Barry Goldwater Jr. in a 1969 special congressional election, his most difficult race to date was a successful 1976 contest for Los Angeles County district attorney against Charles Manson's prosecutor, Vincent Bugliosi.

John Van de Kamp

The attorney general's office has long been a trampoline for those aspiring to be California governor. Earl Warren, Pat Brown and, most recently, George Deukmejian all bounced into the chief executive's chair by that route. For a man who is the state's "top cop," however, Van de Kamp's anti-crime credentials are not exactly his strong suit.

Unlike the majority of California voters, he personally opposes the death penalty, although he points with pride to his prosecutorial record in such cases. Yet that same record has posed problems for him. While serving as Los Angeles County district attorney in 1981, Van de Kamp had tried to dismiss murder charges against defendant Angelo Buono in the high-profile Hillside Strangler case, arguing instead that Buono be prosecuted for sex crimes. He was unsuccessful, and Buono ultimately was convicted on the more serious charges, pressed by then-Attorney General Deukmejian. Hoping to put that issue behind him, Van de Kamp admitted early in 1989 that he erred in his handling of that prosecution. He also took on a highly visible role in the effort to ban semiautomatic assault weapons, at one point waving an AK-47 rifle at legislators on the Assembly floor in a move that won him mention in national news magazines.

A quiet man, in keeping with California's current crop of "bland is beautiful" politicians, Van de Kamp owed much of his start in politics to a reputation as a capable lawyer and a name made a household word in Southern California by his uncles' bakery business. Born in Pasadena, Van de Kamp was appointed Los Angeles County district attorney in 1975, winning election in his own right in 1976 and again in 1980.

Since his 1982 election as attorney general, Van de Kamp has fashioned himself as a consumer advocate, taking on big business in a variety of antitrust cases. He has sided with trial lawyers against insurance companies on questions of liability and insurance reform, most recently fighting to defend Proposition 103, the initiative aimed at cutting Californians' insurance rates.

In his bid to strike early in the governor's race, Van de Kamp offended Democrats in the Legislature by vowing to clean up the special-interest "swamp" at the state Capitol. Although he promised to give all-but-certain GOP nominee Pete Wilson a run for his money, Van de Kamp left many party regulars lukewarm. Before taking on Wilson, he first had to earn what many believed to be his rightful claim to front-runner status in the Democratic primary by defeating former San Francisco Mayor Dianne Feinstein for the party's gubernatorial nomination.

PERSONAL: elected 1982; re-elected 1986; born Feb. 7, 1936 in Pasadena; lives in Pasadena; Dartmouth College, B.A.; Stanford University School of Law, J.D.; married to Andrea Van de Kamp; one child: Diana.

CAREER: assistant U.S. attorney 1960-66; U.S. attorney, Los Angeles 1966-67; deputy director and director, Executive Office for United States Attorneys 1967-69; special assistant, President's Commission on Campus Unrest 1970; Los Angeles federal public defender 1971-1975; Los Angeles County district attorney 1975-1982.

OFFICES: Sacramento (916) 445-9555; San Francisco (415) 557-2544; Los Angeles (213) 736-2304; San Diego (619) 237-7351.

GRAY DAVIS: AMBITION PERSONIFIED

As a California assemblyman, Gray Davis campaigned to find missing children and remove asbestos from school buildings. As state controller, he promotes the return of unclaimed property to Californians and lobbies against offshore oil drilling. But Davis is best known in California political circles for two prominent traits: his impressive fund-raising talents and his unbridled ambition to be governor someday.

Born Joseph Graham Davis Jr. in New York, Davis moved to California with his family at age 11. A graduate of Stanford University and Columbia University law school, he served two years in the U.S. Army in Vietnam.

In 1974, with a stint as finance director for Tom Bradley's successful mayoral race under his belt, the slim and soft-spoken Davis made his first run at statewide office. He filed for the Democratic nomination for state treasurer, then learned to his dismay that former Assembly Speaker Jesse Unruh had decided to enter the race. It was no contest. "I was the doormat Jess stepped on in his road back to political prominence," Davis later recalled.

Davis then went to work as the chief of staff for Jerry

Gray Davis

Brown, who became governor that year. Putting aside his own ambitions for the moment, he helped forge Brown's thrifty image and ran interference with the Legislature, surviving a continual power struggle among the young governor's top aides. By 1981, however, Davis was restless and ready to run for the state Assembly. Elected to the 43rd District representing west Los Angeles in 1982, he won reelection two years later.

Those years laid the groundwork for Davis' second statewide run. When veteran state Controller Kenneth Cory announced his retirement just days before the filing deadline in early 1986, Davis was already sitting on a $1 million campaign fund that enabled him to dash in and win the race. His 1985 effort to encourage companies to picture missing children on milk cartons, grocery bags and billboards had publicized his own name, too. The program featured prominently in his campaign ads.

Although controversial Supreme Court Chief Justice Rose Bird presided at his wedding in 1983, Davis sidestepped the issue in his race for controller, saying he did not want to prejudice cases involving the controller's office that someday could come before the state court. He emerged largely unscathed by the Bird-bashing and

Brown-battering leveled at Democratic candidates that year.
It remains to be seen whether Davis will prove equally adept at maneuvering into position to run for governor. Early polls showed him far behind other potential Democratic candidates for the 1990 contest, and the Capitol press corps was growing weary of his blatant appeals for media coverage. Davis spent much of 1989 biding his time, keeping abreast of court rulings affecting his ability to use his campaign cash and crusading to restore state family planning funds vetoed by Gov. Deukmejian. It's a safe bet, however, that he is not interested in serving indefinitely as the state's fiscal watchdog. He's indicated that he might step into the 1990 governor's race if Dianne Feinstein opts out.

PERSONAL: elected 1986; born December 26, 1942, in New York; lives in Los Angeles; Stanford University, B.A.; Columbia University Law School, J.D.; married to Sharon Ryer Davis; no children.
CAREER: chief of staff to Gov. Jerry Brown 1974-1981; Assembly 1983-1986.
OFFICES: Sacramento (916) 445-3028; Los Angeles (213) 852-5213.

BILL HONIG: THE EDUCATION WARRIOR
With reform as his battle cry, state schools chief Bill Honig marched into the 1980s waging political war on behalf of California schoolchildren. Crusading relentlessly for the new money and new attitudes that he said were needed to bring about wholesale changes in the state's classrooms, he spent much of the decade alternately feuding and making peace with Gov. George Deukmejian over spending for education.

Born Louis William Honig Jr. in San Francisco, he abandoned a career as a lawyer to become a teacher and was named to the state Board of Education by Gov. Jerry Brown in 1975. By 1982, he said he was angry enough about the lack of education leadership in California to challenge three-term incumbent Wilson Riles for state superintendent of public instruction. Upon his election, Honig plunged immediately into a massive legislative dispute over education reform, emerging with Deukmejian's commitment to a plan that provided hundreds of millions in extra dollars for schools. The landmark package also enacted a series of reforms: a longer school day and year, stricter school discipline, higher pay for entry-level teachers and more stringent high school curriculum requirements for English, social science, science and math.

But maintaining the progress proved difficult as enrollment grew and California experienced an influx of young immigrants requiring extra classroom attention. The demands coincided with new state spending constraints as California began to experience the effects of a budget-capping formula approved by voters in 1979. Honig again martialed his political forces to demand a "fair share" of the state budget for schools. He lost a major round with Deukmejian in 1987, when legislators decided to return a $1.1 billion surplus to taxpayers rather than find a way to divert the money to education. He returned in 1988 to win voter approval of

Proposition 98, a school-funding initiative that guarantees schools a portion of the state's general fund and the lion's share of any income that exceeds the spending limit.

Passage of the measure, however, immediately ignited a storm of counterlobbying from doctors, university officials, state employees and others, who said it paid for education at the expense of other vital state services. That set the stage for another initiative battle over state spending in 1990, one that could determine whether Honig succeeds in pressing the demands of the state's education community without isolating himself politically. He has endorsed the governor's transportation/ spending limit ballot measure while his major ally, the California Teachers Association, has refused to back it.

Bill Honig

Always seen by Deukmejian as a potent political threat, Honig has left open the possibility that he will someday mount his own campaign for the governor's seat. In 1988, after declining to state his party affiliation for six years, he rejoined the Democratic Party and was rumored to be in line for a federal post if the Democrats had won the White House. When the defeat of Democratic presidential candidate Michael Dukakis denied him that opportunity, most Capitol observers expected Honig to run for governor in 1990. But he bowed out of the 1990 race before it began, announcing that he would concentrate on winning a third term. Honig said he had an obligation to remain in the post and to continue to wage budgetary battles for schools following the passage of Proposition 98.

PERSONAL: elected 1982; re-elected 1986; born April 23, 1937, in San Francisco; lives in San Francisco; University of California, Berkeley, B.A., J.D.; San Francisco State University, M.Ed.; wife, Nancy Catlin Honig; four children: Michael, Carolyn, Steven and Jonathan.

CAREER: clerk for Chief Justice Matthew Tobriner 1963-1964; associate counsel in state Department of Finance 1964-1966; San Francisco corporate and individual lawyer beginning in 1967; elementary school teacher 1972-1976; superintendent of the Reed Union Elementary School District 1979-1982; state Board of Education 1975-1982.

OFFICES: Sacramento (916) 445-4688; San Francisco (415) 557-0193.

TOM HAYES: A NEWCOMER AND A NOVICE

Thomas Hayes

The August 1987 death of one of California's political giants, Treasurer Jesse Unruh, marked the beginning of a months-long political headache for Gov. Deukmejian. Given a rare opportunity to elevate a fellow Republican to a job that Unruh had transformed into one of the country's most powerful public-finance posts, Deukmejian turned first to Dan Lungren of Long Beach, a conservative congressman seen by Democrats as a formidable foe.

It was clear that Deukmejian hoped to groom Lungren, a longtime family friend, to replace him as governor someday, and the state Senate balked. Lungren was denied the job after the Senate rejected Lungren's appointment and the Supreme Court ruled that rejection by one house of the Legislature was sufficient to deny him confirmation.

State Auditor General Thomas Hayes was second choice and he was quick to admit it. "Boring is in these days, I guess, around the state Capitol," he said at his first press conference as a nominee. "I know that I was the second choice, but so was Avis. They tried harder, and so will I." An obscure state official with no political experience, Hayes had spent nearly 10 years auditing state agencies for the Legislature before Deukmejian nominated him for treasurer in September 1988.

Born in New York, Hayes moved to California with his Air Force father. Hayes is a Marine veteran who holds the Navy commendation medal for his service in Vietnam. He earned a master's degree in business from San Jose State University after leaving the military. He worked in the U.S. General Accounting Office before joining the California legislative analyst's office in 1977, then joined the auditor general's staff as assistant auditor general until 1979.

Hayes, who said he had never stated a party affiliation when registering to vote while auditor, re-registered as a Republican when he was nominated treasurer by the governor and began running for election to a full term soon after taking office. As a non-politician, he argued that voters would see him as the best qualified to manage California's investment portfolio and serve as chairman or member of more than 40 boards and commissions that oversee billions of dollars' worth of taxpayer financing. And Hayes did make some fundamental changes in the operations of the treasurer's office that seemingly reduced the overtly political processes Unruh had installed.

But even some Republicans questioned his ability to hold onto the post when Unruh's unfinished term expires in 1990. GOP dissatisfaction with Hayes, particularly among conservatives, was reflected immediately in a primary challenge by political consultant Angela "Bay" Buchanan, who served as U.S. Treasurer under former President Ronald Reagan. Also running is Democratic lawyer Kathleen Brown, sister of former Gov. Jerry Brown.

PERSONAL: appointed, took office January 1989; born Dec. 21, 1945, in Ossinging, New York; lives in Carmichael; bachelor's degree in management from San Jose State; San Jose State University, M.B.A.; wife, Mary Hayes; two children: Christy and Shannon.

CAREER: U.S. General Accounting Office 1972-1976; state assistant auditor general 1977-1979; state auditor general 1979-1988.

OFFICES: Sacramento (916) 445-5316; San Francisco (415) 557-1932; Los Angeles (213) 620-4467.

MARCH FONG EU STANDS PAT

March Fong Eu's own press releases bill her as the winningest woman in California politics, and it's difficult to dispute her claim. The first and only Asian-American to be elected to state constitutional office, Eu has served as California's chief elections officer since 1975. She was a four-term legislator when she won the secretary of state's post in 1974 and she was re-elected in 1978, 1982 and 1986.

Unlike former Gov. Jerry Brown, who served one term as secretary of state on his way to becoming the state's chief executive, Eu has failed to use the job as a launching pad for high office. Brown made the post a bully pulpit to push for political reform in the post-Watergate era. Eu largely sticks to more mundane tasks, including a thankless effort to boost voter registration and turnout in a state where campaigns dominated by money and media are driving voters away from the polls in droves. And she also has warned fellow Democrats that the party is in danger of slipping into minority status if they don't do a better job of registering members of the state's burgeoning Asian and Hispanic populations.

Eu tried to move up in 1987, when she declared herself a Democratic candidate for the U.S. Senate seat held by Republican Pete Wilson. But she demonstrated sketchy knowledge of federal issues in her early meetings with reporters and struggled in her efforts to get a fund-raising operation going.

Eu, who had been beaten by a robber in her Los Angeles area home one week after winning election to her fourth term, put her Senate campaign on hold to launch a signature drive for a proposed initiative she called Dimes Against Crimes. The crime initiative was one way to keep her name in the news, a technique she had used to great advantage as an assemblywoman campaigning to ban pay toilets in public buildings. But she

March Fong Eu

failed to raise enough money to qualify her initiative.

Ultimately, her biggest political liability proved to be her wealthy husband. Henry Eu, one of 13 sons of one of the wealthiest men in the Far East, refused to reveal details of his business interests, making it impossible for Eu to comply with the disclosure requirements of federal campaign law. She abandoned her Senate campaign in 1987 before it truly began, saying she was forced to choose between her candidacy and her marriage.

A third generation Californian of Chinese descent, Eu was born in Oakdale, Calif. The daughter of a laundry owner, she began her own professional career as a dental hygienist. Eu, who earned a doctor of education degree at Stanford University, moved in 1966 from a position on the Alameda County Board of Education to become the state's first Asian assemblywoman.

Eu has said she would like to be governor someday, but she plans to run for re-election in 1990. She wants to stay in the job to oversee the construction of a new state archives building, a project scheduled for completion in 1993.

If, and when, Eu gives up her position, one of the likely candidates to succeed her will be Matthew Fong, her son. But unlike his mother, Matthew is a Republican.

PERSONAL: elected 1974; re-elected 1978, 1982 and 1986; born March 29, 1922, in Oakdale, Calif.; lives in Los Angeles; University of California, Berkeley, B.S.; Mills College, M.Ed; Stanford University, Ed.D.; married to Henry Eu; two children: Matthew Fong Jr., Suyin Fong.

CAREER: Dental hygienist for Oakland public schools 1945-48; chairwoman, division of dental hygiene, University of California Medical Center in San Francisco 1948-51; supervisor of dental health education for Alameda County Board of Education 1956-66; Assembly 1967-74.

OFFICES: Sacramento (916) 445-6371; San Francisco (415) 557-8051; Los Angeles (213) 620-4382; San Diego (619) 237-6009.

SALARIES

Governor	$85,000
Lt. Governor	$72,500
Secretary of State	$72,500
Controller	$72,500
Treasurer	$72,500
Attorney General	$77,500
Supt. of Public Instruction	$72,500
Legislator*	$40,816
Chief Justice, Supreme Court	$115,013
Associate Justice	$109,677
Appellate Court (Four judges)	$107,963
Appellate Court (Other judges)	$102,823
Superior Court Judge	$89,851
Municipal Court Judge	$82,054
President, University of California	$165,000
President, state college or university	$83,200- $112,656
Chancellor, state universities	$128,532

* Legislators receive direct compensation totaling $63,392, including their per diem pay for attending legislative sessions (maximum $17,776) and their $4,800 car allowance. They also receive health, dental and vision benefits and a retirement plan valued at $2,741 annually (computed for a single legislator with no dependents).

4

The big bad bureaucracy

At 256,951 employees, the state bureaucracy that carries out the decrees of the governor and the Legislature still represents less than 1 percent of the state's population. There are, of course, another 250,000 county employees, hefty school district and special district payrolls and a substantial sprinkling of federal workers toiling at the countless chores that keep the state's people educated and healthy, its streets and work places safe and its commerce bustling. And behind all of them stands a virtual army of non-profit and profit-making entrepreneurs hired to undertake the state's pursuits – clinics, emergency rooms, hospitals, janitorial services, security specialists, mental health programs, drug treatment centers and a host of councils, commissions, think tanks and task forces.

Yet taken together, they hardly represent the threat to freedom or the drain on resources that some politicians like to portray them as being. Bureaucrats may be stolid, slow, constrained by red tape and devoted to the evenhanded distribution of blame for their failings, but their numbers are not overwhelming.

Nevertheless, the first task of any governor is to tame the previous administration's bureaucracy and put those countless workers to his or her own use. The Civil Service is designed to protect voters and taxpayers against political exploitation of the work force, but a carefully tailored system of Civil Service exemptions and gubernatorial appointments gives the chief executive the authority he needs to take the reins of government in hand. When Gov. George Deukmejian took office in 1983, for instance, he had approximately 550 exempt positions to fill in his executive offices and another 100 or so on state boards and commissions. In addition, he could look forward to reshaping the state's judiciary according to his conservative views as appointments became available – in all a significant pool of patronage that became his to dispense.

Deukmejian's key transition team consisted of Steve Merksamer, his chief of staff and executive secretary; Michael Franchetti, his nominee to be director of finance; and Kenneth Khachigian, a public affairs consultant with offices in San Clemente. Merksamer and Franchetti had worked for Deukmejian in the attorney general's office. Khachigian, who met Deukmejian at the 1968 Republican convention, had worked in the Nixon White House and helped write Nixon's memoirs.

Dr. Richard Gable, a political scientist at the University of California, Davis, analyzed the 144 appointments Deukmejian and this team made in the new governor's first 100 days in office. Typically, Gable concluded, the governor chose well-educated, white, male Republicans between 45 and 60 years of age. He filled 22 percent of his appointments with Democrats, keeping some from the Brown administration but shifting their responsibilities. Two appointees to the governor's own offices were black. Hispanics slightly outnumbered Asians. One woman was named to the Cabinet, six became gubernatorial secretaries or deputy secretaries and 12 helped fill the 69 sub-Cabinet positions that were available.

By the end of 1988, the State Personnel Board reported that the labor force overall either met or exceeded the 1980 parity standards for blacks, Asians, Filipinos, Pacific islanders, other minorities and females. Hispanics remained underrepresented in state government, as did American Indians and the disabled. Hispanics made up 13.8 percent of the state work force, compared to a 17.2 percent labor parity goal. Many of the minorities, moreover, had not achieved occupational parity. For example, the board said females continued to remain significantly underrepresented in all occupations except clerical work.

The State Work Force

Year	Governor	Employees	Employees per 1,000 population
1976-77	Brown	213,795	9.7
1977-78	Brown	221,251	9.9
1978-79	Brown	218,530	9.6
1979-80	Brown	220,193	9.5
1980-81	Brown	225,567	9.5
1981-82	Brown	228,813	9.4
1982-83	Transition	228,489	9.2
1983-84	Deukmejian	226,695	9.0
1984-85	Deukmejian	229,845	8.9
1985-86	Deukmejian	229,641	8.7
1986-87	Deukmejian	232,927	8.6
1987-88	Deukmejian	237,761	8.6
1988-89	Deukmejian	248,541	9.1 estimated
1989-90	Deukmejian	256,951	8.9 estimated

The disparity in female representation in the state work force was particularly evident in a 1989 study by the Senate Rules Committee that examined the prevalence of females on state and local boards and commissions. At the state level, women held only 27.6 percent of all board and commission appointments. In a sample of 18 counties, women held 34.3 percent of the positions, and in a sample of 24 cities, they held 35.5 percent. Women make up 51 percent of the state's population.

The actual size of the government's work force is measured in "personnel-years," which represent the number of full-time positions or their equivalent after deducting the salary savings that result when authorized jobs are left vacant. For example, a position that was filled only half of the year would represent a 0.5 personnel-year, while three half-time jobs that were filled would represent 1.5 personnel-years.

DUKE THE KNIFE WHITTLES AT BUREAUCRACY

When Deukmejian took office, the state work force stood at 228,489 personnel-years – a slight reduction from the year before. Although growth in the work force had been lagging behind the state's population growth for years – a product of the post-Proposition 13 budget crunch – and even behind the growth in state operational expenses, Deukmejian was determined to pare back the bureaucracy even more. His budget called for a reduction of 1,016 personnel-years, half a percent. He wanted to achieve the cut while increasing the state's prison and juvenile corrections work force by 1,078 personnel-years.

In the succeeding years, Deukmejian proposed cutback after cutback state personnel, all the while balancing the reductions with increases for the growing correctional system. As the state's population continued to balloon, the work force as measured as a ratio of employees per 1,000 residents declined. Most of the cuts came in the health and welfare programs, including the Employment Development Department. The towering Sacramento buildings that housed those programs became emptier and emptier as the state built more and more prisons to support the governor's crackdown on crime. Not until 1986-87 did the governor relent. He proposed a 3,253 personnel-year increase, including a 31 percent boost for prisons.

Critics would argue that the staff cutbacks represented reductions in service to the state's neediest people, the poor and unemployed. The administration insisted it was trimming fat, not muscle, and that services remained intact or even improved. Throughout, the legislative analyst's office repeatedly identified what amounted to a political numbers game the governor played with the staffing statistics. By introducing budgets with inflated midyear work force estimates, the analyst said, Deukmejian was able to give the appearance of paring back staff when, in fact, "the number of personnel-years proposed for the budget exceeded the number of actual personnel-years in the prior year." By 1987-88, Legislative Analyst Elizabeth Hill concluded, Deukmejian had, in effect, lost the war against his staff. His work force that year grew by more than 6,515 personnel-years. The staffing level the governor proposed for 1987-88 was the largest request in the state's history, Hill declared.

The days have long since passed when state employees depended upon the largess of the governor and the Legislature to increase their pay or improve their benefits. Under the Ralph C. Dills Act of 1977, the administration now negotiates memorandums of understanding on working conditions and wages with 20 recognized bargaining units, represented by 13 employee associations. The MOUs are legal contracts that may remain in force as long as three years.

California's bureaucracy includes everything from the Abrasive Blasting Advisory Committee to the Yuba Sutter Fair Board. There are commissions on the status

The Bargaining Agencies and Bargaining Units

Union	Employees	Percent in union
California State Employees Association (CSEA)		
Administrative, financial and staff services	25,056	43.9
Education and library	2,070	64.7
Office and allied	32,382	62.0
Engineering and scientific technician	2,592	58.9
Printing trades	770	78.4
Custodial and services	5,548	72.7
Registered nurse	2,278	67.4
Non-professional medical and		
social services support	1,789	60.1
Association of Trades and Maintenance (ATAM)		
(buildings, grounds, roads, equipment)	9,700	73.6
Association of California State Attorneys		
(attorneys and hearing officers)	1,913	58.2
California Association of Highway Patrolmen	4,7349	8.2
California Correctional Peace Officers Assn.	14,267	89.9
California Union of Safety Employees	5,063	74.1
California Department of Forestry Employees'		
Association (firefighters)	3,948	68.0
Professional Engineers in California Government	5,589	62.0
California Association of Professional Scientists	1,608	58.4
International Union of Operating Engineers		
(stationary engineers)	584	92.5
Union of American Physicians and Dentists	1,075	62.3
California Association of Psychiatric Technicians	7,594	48.0
American Federation of State, County and		
Municipal Employees	2,865	64.1

of women, government efficiency, water and heritage preservation, councils on the arts and job training and offices for small business, tourism and community relations. The most politically significant offices, however, fall under the nine umbrella agencies and departments whose leaders comprise the governor's Cabinet.

BUSINESS, TRANSPORTATION AND HOUSING AGENCY

This superagency oversees 14 departments dealing with housing, business and regulatory functions and transportation, including the California Highway Patrol, the state Department of Transportation (Caltrans), and the Department of Motor Vehicles.

Secretary John K. Geoghegan was appointed on Dec. 2, 1985. A former city manager of Union City, Geoghegan was executive secretary of the California Environmental Quality Study Council from 1970-72, executive secretary of the California Commission on Economic Development 1972-73, and then director of the state Department of Commerce under Gov. Ronald Reagan in 1973-75. From then until 1983 Geoghegan was vice president of the California Manufacturers Association, after which he worked for Shell Oil Co. until his appointment to the Cabinet. Salary: $96,517; Office: 1120 N St., Room 2101, Sacramento, 95814; (916) 445-1331; Employees: 37,000; '88-'89 budget: $5.4 billion.

John K. Geoghegan

Department of Alcoholic Beverage Control

Licenses and regulates the manufacture, sale, purchase, possession and transportation of alcoholic beverages within the state. Director: Jay R. Stroh; Salary: $90,526; Office: 1901 Broadway, Sacramento, 95818; (916) 445-6811; Employees: 421; '88-'89 budget: $21,970,000.

State Banking Department

Protects the public against financial loss from the failure of state-chartered banks and trust companies, including foreign banking corporations, money order or traveler's check issuers, and business and industrial development corporations. Superintendent: Howard Gould; Salary: $90,526; Office: 111 Pine St., Suite 1100, San Francisco, 94111-5613; (415) 557-3232; Employees: 192; '88-'89 budget: $12,282,000.

Department of Corporations

Regulates the sale of securities, licenses brokers and agents, and oversees franchises, various financial institutions and health plans. Also controls the solicitation, marketing and sale of securities, oversees companies that lend money or receive funds from the public, and deters unscrupulous or unfair promotional schemes. Commissioner: Christine Bender; Salary: $90,526; Office: 1107 Ninth

St., 8th Floor, Sacramento, 95814; (916) 324-9011; Employees: 356; '88-'89 budget: $22,271,000.

Department of Commerce

Primary department that promotes business development and job creation to improve the state's business climate. Director: Kenneth Gibson; Salary: $90,526; Office: 1121 L St., Suite 600, Sacramento, 95814; (916) 322-1394; Employees: 122; '88-'89 budget: $21,480,000.

Department of Housing and Community Development

Guides and supports public- and private-sector efforts to provide decent homes for every Californian, administers various low-income housing programs, directs grants or loans to local governments or non-profit housing agencies for low-income housing and administers standards for manufactured homes. Director: Julie Nauman; Salary: $90,526; Office: 1800 Third St., Suite 450, Sacramento, 95814; (916) 445-4775; Employees: 597; '88-'89 budget: $282,119,000.

Department of Insurance

Examines insurance companies to protect policy holders in the state and administers Proposition 103, the insurance reform initiative approved by the voters in November, 1988. Commissioner: Roxani Gillespie; Salary: $90,526; Office: 100 Van Ness Ave., 17th Floor, San Francisco, 94102; (415) 557-1126; Employees: 499; '88-'89 budget: $35,367,000.

Department of Real Estate

Guarantees that real estate agents and developers are competent and qualified, protects the public in offerings of subdivided property and investigates complaints. Commissioner: James Edmonds Jr.; Salary: $90,526;Office: 2201 Broadway, P.O. Box 187000, Sacramento, 95818; (916) 739-3600;Employees: 382; '88-'89 budget: $25,121,000.

Department of Savings and Loan

Protects the $96 billion in funds deposited in savings and share accounts held in state associations to assure that the saving and borrowing public is properly and legally served, supervising and regulating the industry to prevent conditions or practices that would threaten the safety or solvency of the institutions or be detrimental to the public. Commissioner: William Crawford; Salary: $90,526; Office: 600 S. Commonwealth Ave., Suite 1502, Los Angeles, 90005; (213) 736-2798. Employees: 140; '88-'89 budget: $9,488,000.

California Department of Transportation (Caltrans)

Builds, maintains and rehabilitates roads in accord with the five-year State Transportation Improvement Program, manages airport and heliport safety and access, helps small- and medium-sized communities obtain and maintain air service, regulates airport noise, helps local governments provide public transportation and analyzes transportation questions. Director: Robert Best; Salary: $90,526; Office: 1120 N St., Sacramento, 95814; (916) 445-4616; Employees: 17,081; '88-'89 budget: $3.3 billion.

California Highway Patrol (CHP)

Patrols state highways to ensure the safe, convenient and efficient transportation of people and goods, monitors school bus and farm labor transportation safety and oversees the transportation of hazardous wastes. Commissioner: M.J. Hannigan; Salary: $96,517; Office: 2555 First Ave., P.O. Box 942898, Sacramento, 94298-0001; (916) 445-7473; Employees: 8,592; '88-'89 budget: $542,669,000.

Department of Motor Vehicles

Registers vehicles and vessels, issues and regulates driver's licenses and oversees the manufacture, delivery and disposal of vehicles. Director: A.A. Pierce; Salary: $90,526; Office: 2415 First Ave., Sacramento, 95818; (916)732-0250; Employees: 7,984; '88-'89 budget $413,593,000

DEPARTMENT OF FOOD AND AGRICULTURE

This is one of three superdepartments whose directors (food, finance and industrial relations) are in the governor's Cabinet. This department is responsible for regulating – some would say protecting – California's food industry, governing everything from pesticide registration and enforcement to raw milk inspections. Other duties include weights and measures enforcement, assessment of environmental hazards for agricultural chemicals and other pollutants, protecting farm workers in their jobs, keeping foreign insects and weeds out of the state or eradicating them, maintaining plant inspection stations, meat and poultry inspection, predatory animal control, animal health programs and livestock drug controls, and agricultural marketing, statistical and laboratory services.

Director Henry Voss was appointed May 1, 1989, after an active chairmanship of the California Farm Bureau, a position he had held since 1982. A farmer's son, born in San Jose in 1932, Voss was forced by urbanization to move to Stanislaus County, where the Voss family currently owns 500 acres of peaches, prunes, walnuts and almonds near Ceres.

Voss is a recognized specialist in agricultural marketing and has led trade missions on behalf of California agriculture to Europe, Japan, Southeast Asia and Israel. In 1986, he was appointed by President Reagan to the National Commission on Agriculture and Rural Development, a blue ribbon panel set up to assess the 1985 farm bill. Upon Gov. Deukmejian's recommenda-

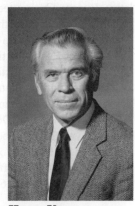

Henry Voss

tion, he was named by Senate Republican Leader Bob Dole to the Commission on Agricultural Workers, which will report to Congress on the Immigration Reform and Control Act of 1986. He is a member of Sunsweet Growers, Blue Diamond Almond Growers and Tri-Valley Growers, three of the state's leading agricultural cooperatives, and is a past president of the Apricot Producers of California and past chairman of the California Apricot Advisory Board. Salary: $96,517; Office: 1220

N St., Sacramento, 95814; (916) 445-7126; Employees: 1,998; '88-'89 budget: $187,454,000.

DEPARTMENT OF FINANCE

The Department of Finance serves as the governor's chief fiscal policy adviser, prepares the governor's January budget proposal and his annual May budget revision, reviews all departmental spending practices and proposals, administers the state budget after it has been adopted and signed, monitors all legislation that has fiscal implications for the state and recommends which bills and budget provisions should be adopted and which should be vetoed. The department also conducts research, produces revenue estimates, analyzes tax policy and tracks population changes.

The director, Jesse Huff, was officially appointed on Feb. 22, 1984, although he had been interim finance director since Jan. 4, the day after the Senate's stormy rejection of Deukmejian's first choice for the post, Michael Franchetti.

Huff was a legislative insider who had been a Republican employee in the Assembly and the Senate in various capacities since 1972, most notably as administrative assistant to Sen. Dennis Carpenter of Orange County and staff director of the Senate Minority Caucus. In 1978, he was liaison officer for the Joint Legislative Budget Committee, and in 1979, he became principal consultant to the Senate Minority Finance Committee. Deukmejian chose Huff in November 1982, to become Franchetti's chief deputy director and to help the transition from the outgoing Brown administration.

Jesse Huff

The Franchetti appointment ran into what proved to be politically fatal difficulties in the Senate over Franchetti's 1978 role, as a Justice Department official under then-Attorney General Deukmejian, in leaking a false rumor that then-Lt. Gov. Mervyn Dymally was about to be indicted. Dymally, Democrat, was never indicted and blamed the leak for costing him his re-election battle against Republican Mike Curb. Salary: $96,517; Office: State Capitol Room 1145, Sacramento, 95814; (916) 445-4141; Employees: 369; '88-'89 budget: $27,268,000.

DEPARTMENT OF INDUSTRIAL RELATIONS

The Department of Industrial Relations is responsible for enforcing California's occupational safety and health laws, administering the compulsory workers' compensation insurance law, adjudicating workers' compensation claims, negotiating in threatened strikes, enforcing laws and promulgating rules on wages, hours and conditions of employment, and analyzing and disseminating statistics on labor conditions.

The director, Ron Rinaldi, was appointed in February 1984, having served as interim director since the previous September. An Air Force veteran, he had joined the Department of Industrial Relations in 1967, during the administration of Gov. Ronald Reagan. In 1972, he served as secretary to Reagan's task force on workers compensation, and by 1973, he was deputy chief of the division of industrial safety. Before leaving office, Reagan appointed Rinaldi to serve as executive director of the newly created Cal-OSHA Standards Board. Gov. Deukmejian named Rinaldi chief deputy director of the department soon after taking office in 1983. Salary: $96,517; Office: 1121 L St., Suite 307, Sacramento 95814; (916) 324-4163; Employees: 2,215; '88-'89 budget: $157,106,000.

Ron Rinaldi

HEALTH AND WELFARE AGENCY

This superagency covering 11 major state departments administers the state's health, welfare, employment and rehabilitation programs serving the poor, the mentally ill, the developmentally disabled, the elderly, the unemployed and citizens with alcohol and drug addiction problems. The agency also administers Proposition 65, the Safe Drinking Water and Toxics Enforcement Act of 1986; is the state's lead agency in administering the Immigration Reform and Control Act of the same year; and manages the state's emergency medical services program. Five departments within the agency oversee long-term care services in residential and institutional settings for the aging, disabled, mentally ill and other needy citizens.

Secretary Clifford Allenby was appointed Dec. 31, 1986. He is a veteran of 26 years in state service and is perhaps the leading example of Gov. Deukmejian's turn toward government professionals, rather than party regulars, to manage some of the most complicated and controversial government agencies.

Allenby chaired a bipartisan task force on Medi-Cal reform in 1982 and became a deputy director of the Department of Finance in 1984, where he served as the administration's point man in budget negotiations with the Legislature. He has also served 17 years on the Elk Grove Unified School District Board of Trustees. In 1984, he was named the outstanding public administrator by the American Society of Public Administrators.

Clifford Allenby

Salary: $96,517; Office: 1600 N St. Room 450, Sacramento, 95814; (916) 445-1722; Employees: 39,634; '88-'89 budget: $25.2 billion (both state and federal funds).

Office of Statewide Health Planning and Development

Responsible for developing a statewide plan for health facilities, assuring that construction plans for health facilities conform to state building codes, maintaining a uniform system of accounting and disclosure for health facility costs and assuring that available federal and state assistance is provided to develop needed facilities. Director: Larry Meeks; Salary: $90,526; Office: 1600 Ninth St., Sacramento, 95814; (916) 322-5834; Employees: 305; '88-'89 budget: $28,289,000.

Department of Aging

State focal point for federal, state and local agencies that serve more than 4 million elderly Californians, working through 33 Area Agencies on Aging. The agencies manage programs that provide meals, social services and health insurance counseling and act as advocates for senior citizen issues. The department also manages the state's adult day health care centers, the Alzheimer's Day Care Resource Centers and the multipurpose senior services program, an experimental effort to keep the frail elderly from being unnecessarily admitted to skilled nursing homes or intermediate care facilities. The program expires June 30, 1990. Director: Alice Gonzales; Salary: $79,875; Office: 1600 K St., Sacramento, 95814; (916) 322-3887; Employees: 155; '88-'89 budget: $134,248,000.

Department of Alcohol and Drug Programs

Coordinates the planning and development of a statewide alcohol and drug abuse prevention, intervention, detoxification, recovery and treatment system, serving 300,000 Californians largely through programs operated by counties. The department is responsible for licensing the state's methadone treatment programs, multiple offender drinking driver programs and alcoholism recovery facilities. In addition, the department manages programs aimed at alcohol and drug abuse prevention, particularly among youth, women, the disabled, ethnic minorities and the elderly. The department expects to receive an increase of $22.5 million in the current fiscal year from the federal Alcohol, Drug Abuse and Mental Health Administration. Director: Chauncey Veatch III; Salary: $90,526; Office: 111 Capitol Mall, Sacramento, 95814; (916) 445-1940; Employees: 196; '88-'89 budget: $178,535,000.

Department of Health Services

Manages 11 health programs including the state's $6.8 billion Medi-Cal program (serving an average monthly caseload of 3.3 million people), the Office of AIDS and the controversial Family Planning program that Gov. Deukmejian seeks to eliminate. The department is in charge of preventive medical services, public water supplies, toxic substance control, environmental health, epidemiological studies, rural and community health, radiologic health, maternal and child health and the early detection of genetic disease and birth defects in newborns. The Food and Drug Program seeks to protect consumers from adulterated, misbranded or falsely advertised foods, drugs, medical devices, hazardous household products and cosmetics and to control botulism in canned products. A licensing office regulates care in some 6,000 public and private health facilities, clinics and agencies. Director:

Kenneth Kizer, MD, MPH; Salary: $90,526; Office: 744 P St., Sacramento, 95814; (916) 445-1248; Employees: 5,253; '88-'89 budget: $9.2 billion.

Department of Developmental Services

Coordinates services under the Lanterman Developmental Disabilities Services Act of 1977 for people with developmental disabilities, such as mental retardation, autism or cerebral palsy, to meet their needs at each stage of their lives through individual plans for each client's treatment within their home communities wherever possible. The department provides 24-hour care for more than 6,000 severely disabled clients through seven state developmental hospitals (Agnews, Camarillo, Fairview, Lanterman, Porterville, Sonoma and Stockton) and indirect care for 93,000 clients through a statewide network of 21 private, non-profit regional centers. Director: Gary Macomber; Salary: $90,526; Office: 1600 Ninth St., Sacramento, 95814; (916) 322-8154; Employees: 10,943; '88-'89 budget: $1.1 billion.

Department of Mental Health

Administers the Lanterman-Petris-Short Act, the Short-Doyle Act and other federal and state statutes that govern services to the mentally ill through county and community non-profit agencies and through the direct operation of the Atascadero, Metropolitan, Napa and Patton state hospitals and treatment programs for 600 clients at the Department of Developmental Services' Camarillo State Hospital. Services to the mentally ill include community education and consultation, crisis evaluation and emergency care, 24-hour acute care, 24-hour residential treatment, day-care treatment, outpatient care, case management and resocialization. The department also manages special programs for the homeless mentally ill, for mental illness associated with AIDS and other special categories. Acting director: Doug Arnold; Salary: $90,526; Office: 1600 Ninth St., Sacramento, 95814; (916) 323-8173; Employees: 7,641; '88-'89 budget: $1.2 billion.

Employment Development Department

Assists employers in finding workers and workers in finding jobs through a statewide data base, manages the unemployment insurance program, collects payroll taxes that support worker benefit programs, provides economic and labor market data and administers the Job Training Partnership Act. Under federal guidance, the department manages 130 field offices that provide job placement, employment counseling, vocational testing, workshops and referral services, targeted at groups such as veterans, older workers, disabled persons, youth, minorities, welfare families and migrant and seasonal farm workers. Director: Kaye Kiddoo; Salary: $90,526; Office: 800 Capitol Mall, Sacramento, 95814; (916) 445-8008; Employees: 9,985; '88-'89 budget: $4.5 billion.

Department of Rehabilitation

Helps rehabilitate and find employment for people with mental and physical handicaps. Director: P. Cecilio Fontanoza; Salary: $90,526; Office: 830 K Street Mall, Sacramento, 95814; (916) 445-8638; Employees: 1,863; '88-'89 budget: $246,762,000.

Department of Social Services

Administers the state's $7.7 billion welfare program for poor children, disabled and elderly residents; provides or manages social services, community care licensing and inspections, disability evaluations, refugee assistance and adoption services; manages the federal food stamp program; regulates group homes, nurseries, preschools, foster homes, halfway houses and day-care centers; administers programs designed to protect children, the disabled and the elderly from abuse or neglect, and manages the state's Greater Avenues for Independence workfare program. Director: Linda McMahon; Salary: $90,526; Office: 74 P St., Sacramento, 95814; (916) 445-2077; Employees: 3,566; '88-'89 budget: $9.3 billion.

YOUTH AND ADULT CORRECTIONAL AGENCY

This superagency oversees the Department of Corrections and the Youth Authority, which are charged with the responsibility for the control, care and treatment of convicted felons and civilly committed addicts, and the confinement and rehabilitation of juvenile delinquents. The agency has managed one of the most aggressive prison and prison camp construction programs in the nation during the Deukmejian years, adding more than 22,000 new prison beds to a system that had seen no new prisons in the previous 20 years. By June 1989, the state prison system was handling more than 79,000 inmates (average daily population), albeit in a system designed for 47,000. The agency also manages state parole programs and oversees the state Board of Corrections, the Youthful Offender Parole Board and the Board of Prison Terms. The agency considers itself the largest law enforcement organization in the United States.

Secretary Joe Sandoval was appointed on Oct. 12, 1988, having been Gov. Deukmejian's chief of the California State Police. Sandoval is a veteran of 26 years with the Los Angeles Police Department and was the first Hispanic officer to attend the FBI National Academy in Quantico, Va. He was the primary law enforcement officer at the University of Southern California athletes village for the 1984 Olympics. His last assignment in Los Angeles was commander of some 235 officers in the Hollenbeck area, a community of 300,000. He was a member of the Prison Industry Board from 1988 to 1989. Salary: $96,517; Office: 1100 11th St., Sacramento, 95814; (916) 323-6001; Employees: 35,000; '88-'89 budget: $2.5 billion.

Joe Sandoval

Department of Corrections

Manages 18 correctional facilities including eight reception centers that are expected to handle more than 82,000 inmates during the 1989-90 fiscal year. The department also manages parole programs, prison camps and a community correctional program designed to reintegrate released offenders to society. Director: E.

James Rowland; Salary: $90,526; Office: 630 K St., Sacramento, 95814; (916) 445-7682; Employees: 25,521; '88-'89 budget: $1.9 billion.

Youth Authority

Provides programs in institutions and the community to reduce delinquent behavior, help local agencies fight juvenile crime and encourage delinquency prevention programs. The department operates reception centers and clinics as well as 18 conservation camps and institutions for males and females throughout the state. Director: Clarence Terhune; Salary: $90,526; Office: 4241 Williamsbourgh Dr., Sacramento, 95823; (916) 427-6674; Employees: 4,962; '88-'89 budget: $365,317,000;

RESOURCES AGENCY

This superagency is responsible for departments and programs that manage the state's air, water and land resources and wildlife. The main departments are Water Resources, Forestry and Fire Protection, Parks and Recreation, Conservation, Fish and Game, Boating and Waterways, the Conservation Corps and the Energy Commission, Coastal Commission and State Lands Commission. The agency also oversees the Seismic Safety Commission, the Tahoe Regional Planning Agency, the Wildlife Conservation Board, the Santa Monica Mountains Conservancy, the state Coastal Conservancy, the San Francisco Bay Conservation and Development Commission, the Colorado River Board of California and the environmental license plate fund.

Director Gordon Van Vleck was appointed on Jan. 3, 1983. A graduate of Sacramento City College, Van Vleck is a third-generation cattleman and a business-man who is a past president of the National Cattlemen's Association and a former California Livestock Man of the Year. Van Vleck owns and operates the 3,000-acre Double V Bar Ranch near Plymouth in Amador County. He is a World War II veteran. Salary: $96,517; Office: 1416 Ninth St., Room 1311, Sacramento, 95814;(916) 445-3758; Employees: 13,364; '88-'89 budget: $ 1.4 billion.

Gordon Van Vleck

California Conservation Corps

A work force of some 2,000 young men and women who perform nearly 3 million hours of conservation work for the state of California each year, including flood patrol, fire restoration, tree planting, stream clearance, trail building, park maintenance, landscaping, home weatherization and wildlife habitat restoration. One of former Gov. Jerry Brown's more lasting creations, kept by the Deukmejian administration because of its popularity. Director: Robert Sheble Jr.; Salary: $79,875; Office: 1530 Capitol Ave., Sacramento, 95814; (916) 445-8183; Employees: 430; '88-'89 budget: $55,901,000.

Energy Resources Conservation and Development Commission

Responsible for maintaining a reliable supply of energy for the state's needs, siting new power facilities and encouraging energy conservation. Chairman: Charles Imbrecht; Salary: $86,533; Office: 1516 Ninth St., Sacramento, 95814; (916) 324-3000; Employees: 429; '88-'89 budget: $88,169,000.

Department of Conservation

Promotes the development and wise management of the state's land, energy, mineral and farmland resources, and disseminates information on geology, seismology, mineral, geothermal and petroleum resources, agricultural and open-space land, and container recycling and litter reduction. Director: Randall Ward; Salary: $79,875; Office: 1416 Ninth St., 13th Floor, Sacramento, 95814; (916) 322-7683; Employees: 492; '88-'89 budget: $144,482,000.

Department of Forestry and Fire Prevention

Provides fire protection and watershed management services for private and state-owned watershed lands. Responsibilities include fire prevention, controlling wildlife damage and improving the land and vegetative cover for economic and social benefits. Director: Richard Ernest; Salary: $90,526; Office: 1416 Ninth St., Sacramento, 95814; (916) 445-3976; Employees: 4,286; '88-'89 budget: $311,995,000.

Department of Fish and Game

Responsible for maintaining all species of wildlife, providing varied recreational use of wild species including hunting and fishing, providing for the scientific and educational use of wildlife and protecting the economic benefits of natural species, including commercial harvesting of wildlife resources. Director: Peter Bontadelli Jr.; Salary: $90,526; Office: 1416 Ninth St., 12th Floor, Sacramento, 95814; (916) 445-3531; Employees: 1,702; '88-'89 budget: $136,248,000.

Department of Boating and Waterways

Responsible for public boating facilities, water safety, water hyacinth control, beach erosion, small-craft harbor development (through loans and grants) and yacht and ship brokers licensing. Director: William Ivers; Salary: $73,221; Office: 1629 S St., Sacramento, 95814; (916) 445-2615; Employees: 58; '88-'89 budget: $40,307,000.

State Lands Commission

Administers state interest in more than 4 million acres of navigable waterways, swamp and overflow lands, vacant school sites and granted lands and tidelands within three miles of the mean high tide line. (One of few state agencies not controlled by the governor. State finance director Jesse Huff, Lt. Gov. Leo McCarthy and Controller Gray Davis comprise the commission and McCarthy and Davis, both Democrats, exert effective administrative authority.) Executive officer: Claire Dedrick; Salary: $77,299; Office: 1807 13th St., Sacramento, 95814; (916) 322-7777; Employees: 236; '88-'89 budget: $18,835,000.

California Coastal Commission

Charged with the state management of coastal resources, an area extending generally about 1,000 yards inland (but as much as five miles inland in some areas) and three miles seaward for the 1,100-mile length of the California coast, excluding San Francisco Bay. The commission was established in 1976 to succeed the California Coastal Zone Commission, a temporary agency created by the voters in 1972. The 15-member commission certifies local governments to manage the coastal zone in accordance with state-approved plans. Gov. Deukmejian attempted to abolish the agency in the early years of his administration and has since cut budgets sharply. Executive director: Peter Douglas; Salary: $71,644; Office: 631 Howard St., San Francisco, 94105; (415) 543-8555; Employees: 110; '88-'89 budget: $9,485,000.

Department of Parks and Recreation

Acquires, designs, develops, operates, maintains and protects the state park system, helps local park agencies through loans and grants, and interprets the natural, archaeological and historical resources of the state. State parks, recreation areas and historic monuments are designed to provide recreation, improve the environment and preserve the state's history and natural landscapes. The department is involved in underwater parks, a statewide trail network, state beaches and piers, coastal and Sierra redwood parks, an off-highway vehicle system and management of the Hearst San Simeon Castle and the Anza-Borrego Desert State Park. Director: Henry Agonia; Salary: $90,526; Office: 1416 Ninth St., Sacramento, 95814; (916) 445-6477; Employees: 2,876; '88-'89 budget: $221,426,000.

Department of Water Resources

Responsible for managing, developing and conserving the state's water, from flood control to drought responses and drinking water safety, under the provisions of the California Water Plan. The department operates Oroville Reservoir, the California Aqueduct and related facilities, and manages the key Delta water supply in conjunction with the U.S. Bureau of Reclamation. Director David Kennedy has undertaken a massive effort to resolve the state's long-standing water supply conflicts through private negotiation and has achieved some success. Salary: $90,526; Office: 1416 Ninth St., Sacramento, 85814; (916) 445-9248; Employees: 2,660; '88-'89 budget: $904,040.

SECRETARY OF ENVIRONMENTAL AFFAIRS

There is no environmental agency as such, the Legislature having rejected proposals to create one. The Cabinet-level secretary, who chairs the Air Resources Board, is responsible mainly for air pollution control efforts and acts as the administration's coordinator for offshore oil issues. The secretary advises the governor on appointments to the Air Resources Board, the Water Resources Control Board and the Waste Management Board and also oversees the Office of Offshore Development and the Hazardous Substance Cleanup Arbitration Panel.

Secretary Jananne Sharpless was appointed in August 1985. Sharpless began her state government career as an administrative assistant to the late Assemblyman John Veneman from 1967 to 1969, when she became a consultant on the Assembly

Agriculture Committee. From 1970 to 1973 she was a consultant to the Assembly Committee on Efficiency and Cost Control, after which she became a principal consultant with the Assembly Ways and Means Committee until she joined the Deukmejian administration in 1983. Prior to her appointment to the Cabinet, Sharpless served as chief deputy environmental secretary, primarily responsible for offshore oil leasing issues. Salary: $96,517; Office: 1102 Q St., P.O. Box 2815, Sacramento, 95812; (916) 322-4203.

Jananne Sharpless

Air Resources Board

Holds the primary responsibility for California air quality, including the establishment of clean air standards, research into air pollution, emissions enforcement and smog limitations on automobiles and industries. Chairwoman: Jananne Sharpless; Employees: 756; '88-'89 budget: $79,614,000.

State Water Resources Control Board

Manages state water rights and water quality control regulations, including timber and farm management practices, and oversees toxic site cleanups. The board has become a focal point of water supply and quality controversies. Chairman: W. Don Maughan; Salary: $86,533; Office: 901 P St., P.O. Box 100, Sacramento, 95801; Employees: 1,052; '88-'89 budget: $358,272,000.

California Waste Management Board

Responsible for establishing and maintaining a non-hazardous waste management program that protects the public health, reduces landfill disposal and enforces state waste disposal standards. Chairman: John Gallagher; Salary: $75,882; Office: 1020 Ninth St., Suite 300, Sacramento, 95814; (916) 322-3330; Employees: 86; '88-'89 budget: $5,612,000.

STATE AND CONSUMER SERVICES AGENCY

This superagency covers an array of departments and programs that include the departments of Consumer Affairs, Fair Employment and Housing, General Services and Veterans Affairs and the Fair Employment and Housing Commission, Building Standards Commission, State Personnel Board, State Fire Marshal, Franchise Tax Board, Museum of Science and Industry, the Public Employees Retirement System and the State Teachers Retirement System.

Secretary Shirley Chilton was appointed Jan. 3, 1983. She is a professor of managerial economics in the state university system, is a former vice president of the State Colleges and University Foundation and has an extensive background in business, including the distinction of becoming the first woman managing partner in the history of the New York Stock Exchange. She served as a consultant in economic development and enterprise zones for President Reagan, is a former League of Women Voters' "Woman of the Year" and a former Soroptimist "Citizen of the Year." Salary: $96,517; Office: 915 Capitol Mall, Suite 200, Sacramento, 95814; (916) 323-9493; Employees: 13,283; '88-'89 budget: $546,700,000.

Department of Consumer Affairs

Oversees the Bureau of Automotive Repair, the Contractors' State License Board and the Board of Medical Quality Assurance, the comparatively small Division of Consumer Services and 27 more small boards, bureaus and commissions that for the most part license and regulate "professional" services. They are the boards of Accountancy, Architectural Examiners, Barber Examiners, Behavioral Science Examiners, Cosmetology, Dental Examiners, Funeral Directors and Embalmers, Geologists and Geophysicists, Guide

Shirley Chilton

Dogs for the Blind, Landscape Architects, Examiners of Nursing Home Administrators, Optometry, Pharmacy, Polygraph Examiners, Professional Engineers, Registered Nursing, Certified Shorthand Reporters, Structural Pest Control, Examiners in Veterinary Medicine, Vocational Nurse and Psychiatric Technician Examiners and the Cemetery Board; the bureaus of Collection and Investigative Services, Electronic and Appliance Repair, Personnel Services and Home Furnishings; the Tax Preparers Program and the Athletic Commission. Director: Michael Kelley; Salary: $90,526; Office: 1020 N St., Sacramento, 95814; (916) 445-4465; Employees: 1,930; '88-'89 budget: $156,334,000.

Department of Fair Employment and Housing

Enforces the state civil rights laws that prohibit discrimination in employment, housing and public services and endeavors to eliminate discrimination based on race, religion, creed, national origin, sex, marital status, physical handicap, medical condition or age (over 40). Complaints are pursued before the Fair Employment and Housing Commission. Director: Talmadge Jones; Salary: $79,875; Office: 2016 T St., Suite 210, Sacramento, 95814; (916)739-4616; Employees: 236; '88-'89 budget: $13,187,000.

Office of the State Fire Marshal

Coordinates state fire services, adopts and enforces minimum statewide fire and panic safety regulations, controls hazardous materials and helps the film industry with special effects. State fire marshal: James McMullen; Salary: $79,875; Office: 7171 Bowling Drive, Suite 600, Sacramento, 95823; (916) 427-4161; Employees: 169; '88-'89 budget: $11,402,000.

Franchise Tax Board

Administers the personal income tax and the bank and corporation tax laws and the homeowners and renters assistance program, and performs field assessments and audits of campaign expenditure reports and lobbyist reports under the Political Reform Act of 1974. The members are state Controller Gray Davis; the chairman of the state Board of Equalization, Ernest Dronenburg Jr.; and state Director of

Finance Jesse Huff. Executive officer: Gerald Goldberg; Salary: $90,526; Office: 9645 Butterfield Way, Sacramento, 95827; (916) 369-4543; Employees: 3,850; '88-'89 budget: $184,534,000.

Department of General Services

Manages and maintains state property, allocates office space, monitors contracts, insurance and risks, administers the state school building law and helps small and minority businesses obtain state contracts. Also has jurisdiction over the state architect, the offices of Telecommunications, Local Assistance, Procurement, Energy Assessments and Buildings and Grounds, and the state police. Director: William Anthony; Salary: $90,526; Office: 915 Capitol Mall, Suite 590, Sacramento, 95814; (916) 445-5728; Employees: 4,329; '88-'89 budget: $522,226,000.

State Personnel Board

Manages the state civil service system including the Career Opportunities Development Program. Executive officer: Gloria Harmon; Salary: $79,246; Office: 801 Capitol Mall P.O. Box 944201, Sacramento, 94244-2010; (916) 322-2530; Employees: 297; '88-'89 budget: $16,572,000.

Public Employees' Retirement System

Administers pension, disability, health, Social Security and death benefits for more than 800,000 past and present public employees. Participants include state constitutional officers, legislators, judges, state employees and most volunteer fire fighters and school employees (except teachers) and others. Executive officer: Dale Hanson; Salary: $90,544; Office: 400 P St., P.O. Box 942701, Sacramento, 94229-2701; (916) 326-3829; Employees: 705; '88-'89 budget: $45,439,000.

State Teachers Retirement System

Administers the largest teacher retirement system in the United States with 325,445 members and 111,706 receiving benefits. Chief executive officer: James Mosman; Salary: $90,526; Office: 7667 Folsom Blvd., P.O. Box 15275-C, Sacramento, 95851-0275; Employees: 337; '88-'89 budget: $189,517,000.

Department of Veterans Affairs

Administers the Cal-Vet farm and home loan program, helps veterans obtain benefits and rights to which they are entitled, and supports the Veterans Home of California, a retirement home with complete nursing care and hospitalization. Director: Jesse Ugalde; Salary: $90,526; Office: 1227 O St., Sacramento, 94295; (916) 322-1796; Employees: 1,277; '88-'89 budget: $1.3 billion.

BOARD OF EQUALIZATION

The 1849 California Constitution advanced the notion that "taxation shall be equal and uniform throughout the state" and by 1879 the people made the Board of Equalization a constitutional agency to see to it. Today, the board boasts openly of its vast powers to affect "virtually every aspect of commerce and government in California," including the taxes paid by more than 900,000 businesses, 300 private utilities and some 4.5 million homeowners.

Operating in a quasi-judicial capacity, the board hears tax appeals and sets assessments on pipelines, flumes, canals, ditches, aqueducts, telephone lines and electrical systems – in a word, utilities. It acts in a quasi-legislative fashion to adopt rules, regulations and guidance for county tax assessors, and as an administrative body that adopts capitalization rates, classifies properties, sets the electrical energy surcharge rate and administers taxes on sales, fuel, alcoholic beverages, cigarettes, insurance, timber, hazardous waste, telephone services and city, county and transit district sales and uses. The board collects more than $16 billion each year in business tax revenues for the state and is the state's main revenue agency.

But does the board fairly administer these responsibilities? Or do politics and the influence of campaign donations seep into the board's decisions? Is the board a model agency for tax administration? Or is it an anachronism, outmoded, outdated and outpaced by the events it governs? As the board has assumed a more overtly political atmosphere in recent years, these and other questions are being raised.

The state Board of Equalization consists of state Controller Gray Davis and four members elected to four-year terms from districts so extensive that few of the electorate can be expected to know who his or her representative is. Some of the elected board members, however, are politically ambitious and consider their positions to be a rung toward higher office. Some have accepted political contributions from public utilities and other donors who later won favorable board consideration on tax appeals. And the board has seen a serious and often publicly acrimonious split, often pitting William Bennett, its senior member, against the other four. Bennett says the others are making tax decisions based on political considerations, often overruling staff recommendations.

The members and their districts are:

•William Bennett, representing the counties of Alameda, Alpine, Amador, Butte, Calaveras, Colusa, Contra Costa, Del Norte, El Dorado, Glenn, Humboldt, Lake, Lassen, Marin, Mendocino, Modoc, Napa, Nevada, Placer, Plumas, Sacramento, Santa Clara, Shasta, Sierra, Siskiyou, Solano, Sonoma, Sutter, Tehama, Trinity, Tuolumne, Yolo and Yuba. Office: 1020 N St., Sacramento, 95814; (916) 445-8081.

The outspoken Bennett began his fifth term on the board in January 1987. His government career began with 12 years of service as a deputy attorney general, followed by appointment in 1958 as chief counsel to the state Public Utilities Commission. He became a member of that commission in 1962. In World War II, he flew

William Bennett

15 missions over Europe. He has taught administrative and consumer law at Hastings College of Law, University of California, San Francisco.

Unlike his colleagues, Bennett accepts no campaign contributions and often is in the forefront of those who advocate reforming the board. "The practice of money and votes continues," he declared in a public letter in 1988. "And if indeed we continue to render tax decisions based upon purchased votes, then the agency properly should go into the pages of history."

•Conway Collis, whose district includes the counties of Fresno, Kings, Madera, Mariposa, Merced, Monterey, San Benito, San Francisco, San Joaquin, San Luis Obispo, San Mateo, Santa Barbara, Santa Cruz, Stanislaus, Tulare, Ventura and the northern and western portions of Los Angeles County. Office: 901 Wilshire Blvd., Santa Monica, 90401; (213) 451-5777.

After graduating from Stanford Law School, Collis served as counsel to the U.S. Senate Labor and Human Resources Committee and as a domestic policy adviser to Sen. Alan Cranston from 1974 to 1977, when he returned to California to direct Cranston's statewide field and finance operations. He was elected to the Board of Equalization in 1982 and re-elected in 1986.

Conway Collis

Although he voted to reduce the assessed valuations for utilities that had contributed heavily to his political war chest in 1988, Collis insists that he now refuses such contributions. Collis says he tries to act as an ombudsman for taxpayers, holding open office days to let taxpayers take their problems "to the top." In late 1989, Collis declared his intention to run for state insurance commissioner in 1990, touching off a scramble for his seat. Ex-Assemblyman Lou Papan and political reformer Brad Sherman were the first candidates out of the gate.

•Ernest Dronenburg Jr., the current board chairman and only Republican board member, whose district includes the counties of Imperial, Inyo, Kern, Mono, Orange, Riverside, San Bernardino and San Diego. Office: 110 W. C St., Suite 1709, San Diego, 92101; (619) 237-7844.

Dronenburg has degrees in finance and accounting and a business background. In 1978, he was the first Republican elected to the board in 24 years. Prior to his election, he was an auditor and field audit supervisor in the board's Business Taxes Department. He was the first board employee to join the board. Dronenburg defends the present board and the system it represents, arguing the citizens prefer elected rather than appointed tax officials.

Ernest Dronenburg Jr.

•Paul Carpenter, whose district includes the southern and central sections of Los Angeles County, including most of the city of Los Angeles and 74 other incorporated cities. Office: 4040 Paramount Blvd., Suite 103, Lakewood, 90712; (213) 429-5422.

Sen. Carpenter was elected to the Legislature from Orange County in 1972 and to the Board of Equalization in 1986. He holds a Ph.D. in experimental psychology from Florida State University. As an assemblyman and later as state senator, Carpenter was known as a player of political hardball who cultivated special-interest groups and ardently solicited their money for his campaign coffers.

Like Collis, Carpenter defends his vote in favor of lower assessments for public utilities that contribute to his campaigns on grounds that utility taxes actually come from the ratepayers and that the board's staff has a bias against taxpayers.

•Controller Gray Davis, member at large, declines to vote on tax matters relating to his campaign contributors. (Davis' biographical information appears in Chapter 3, pages 101-103.)

Paul Carpenter

BOARD OF EDUCATION

Establishes policy and adopts rules and regulations for the kindergarten through 12th grade where authorized by the Education Code. Major duties include selecting textbooks for grades kindergarten through eight, developing curriculum frameworks, approving district waivers from regulations and regulating the state testing program, teacher credentialing and school district reorganizations.

The 11 board members are Joseph Carrabino, Agnes Chan, Perry Dyke, Gloria Hom, Francis Lauffenberg, Maryela Martinez, Marion McDowell, Kenneth Peters, Jim Robinson, David Romero, Armen Sarafian. All are appointed by the governor. Office: 721 Capitol Mall, Room 532, Sacramento, 95814.

UC BOARD OF REGENTS

Governs the nine campuses of the University of California, five teaching hospitals and three major laboratories operated under contracts with the U.S. Department of Energy. The 18 appointed members serve 12-year terms since 1974, when terms were reduced from 16 years. The same amendment reduced the number of ex-officio members from eight to seven. During the transition, the board increased to 30 members but will decrease to 26 members by 1990. The long-term appointments as regents are considered to be among the most prestigious civic positions in California, much prized by the wealthy and politically well-connected. And because of their long terms, Regents often survive the terms of the governors who appointed them.

The regents (and end of their current terms) are Gov. George Deukmejian, president; Frank Clark Jr., chairman (2000); David Gardner, president of the university; Roy Brophy (1998); Assembly Speaker Willie Brown Jr.; Clair Burgener (2000); Yvonne Brathwaite Burke (1993); W. Glenn Campbell (1996); Tirso del Junco (1997); Jeremiah Hallisey (1993); Willis Harman (1990); state schools chief Bill Honig; Meredith Khachigian (1990); Leo Kolligian (1997); Vilma Martinez (1990); Lt. Gov. Leo McCarthy; Joseph Moore (1990); William French Smith (1998); Yori Wada (1992); Dean Watkins (1996); Harold Williams (1994); Jacques Yeager (1994); and student regent Guillermo Rodriguez (1990). Office of the secretary of the regents: 650 University Hall, Berkeley, 94720; (415) 642-0502.

TRUSTEES OF THE STATE UNIVERSITIES

Sets policy and governs collective bargaining; personnel matters, including the appointment of the system president and university chancellors; budget decisions and capital outlays. Members are appointed by the governor for eight-year terms. The trustees are Gov. George Deukmejian; Lt. Gov. Leo McCarthy; Assembly Speaker Willie Brown Jr.; state schools chief Bill Honig; Dr. Ann Reynolds, chancellor; Dr. Claudia Hampton (1994); Willie Stennis (1991); George Marcus (1989); Dixon Harwin (1990); Marianthi Lansdale (1991); Dean Lesher (1993); Theodore Bruinsma (1991); Dr. John Kashiwabara (1994); Thomas Bernard (1989); Roland Arnall (1990); Tom Stickel (1992); Martha Falgatter (1995); William Campbell (1995); Dr. Lyman Heine (1989); and John Sweeney (1989). Office: 400 Golden Shore, Long Beach, 90802; (213) 590-5506.

FAIR POLITICAL PRACTICES COMMISSION

Administers the voter-approved Political Reform Act of 1974 and the initiative reforms of Propositions 73 and 68 approved in 1988. The commission adopts regulations governing disclosure of conflicts of interest, campaign finances and lobbyist activities and is empowered to fine public officials and candidates. The commissioners are John Larsen, chairman; George Fenimore; Lim Lea; Michael Montgomery; and Stan Roden. Office: 428 J St., Suite 800, Sacramento, 95814; (916) 322-5660.

TRANSPORTATION COMMISSION

Administers state highway planning and construction and other state transportation programs, including mass transit and rail transportation services. Commission members are William T. Bagley, chairman; Joseph Duffel; Margie Handley; J. Thomas Hawthorne; Stanley Hulett; Assemblyman Richard Katz; Kenneth Kevorkian; William Leonard; Joseph Levy; Bruce Nestande; and Sen. Alan Robbins. Office: 1120 N St., Sacramento, 95814; (916) 445-1690.

5

Legislature–professional and paralyzed

Two facts crystallized the nature of the California Legislature of the late 1980s. First, it cost nearly twice as much on the average – $600,000 – to win a seat in the state Capitol as it did to win a seat in Congress. Second, legislators' resumes increasingly listed "professional legislative aide" as their previous occupation.

In short, those in the Legislature raised huge amounts of money to get there, and they were less willing to risk those sums on people who were not already "inside the building." First and foremost, the California Legislature became an institution of professionals looking out for professionals.

As individuals, California's legislators sometimes seemed an odd assortment. The voters sent to Sacramento drunkards and wheeler-dealers. They also sent a man who won a Bronze Star for heroism on the battlefields of Italy and a brave woman who, as a young congressional aide, barely survived her wounds from the Jonestown massacre in Guyana. There were the dedicated and the party animals, the ideological warriors and the pragmatists.

Among California's 120 lawmakers were two ex-cops, roughly 30 farmers, a doctor, a dentist, various small businessmen, a law professor, a handful of Vietnam veterans and a founder of the radical-but-defunct Students for a Democratic Society. Lawyers, who once comprised fully half of the Legislature, had steadily declined to less than one-third by the end of the 1980s. As the lawyers declined, ex-legislative aides rose – at least 33 incumbents were political aides at one time in their careers. Some seats were held by a third generation of aides, handed down from one legislative assistant to the next.

Legislators as a whole did not reflect the state at large. In 1989, there were 18 women lawmakers – just 15 percent of the Legislature in a state where more women than men voted in the 1988 election. Nine blacks held seats, matching their 7.5 percent share of the state population, but only seven lawmakers were Hispanic, or

131

6 percent of the membership, contrasting with 24.2 percent of the population. There were no Asian-American legislators, although Asian-Americans comprised more than 8 percent of the population.

The Democrats have held their majority grip on the Legislature throughout the decade, though they have slipped badly in the Assembly. By the end of 1989, the Assembly had 46 Democrats, 33 Republicans and one vacancy. The Senate had 24 Democrats, 14 Republicans, one independent and one vacancy.

Democrats sought at the opening of the decade to ensure their dominance with a gerrymandering of district boundaries during reapportionment. While some Democrats, especially legislative leaders, had such safe seats they barely noticed their election opponents, others were constantly campaigning because the Democrats had given themselves thin registration margins in many districts in order to stretch the number of seats they could hold. Conversely, many GOP members had such lopsided Republican districts that they could safely ignore their own re-election campaigns and devoted themselves to helping other Republicans get elected. In general, turnover was slow in the Legislature. The average length of a senator's tenure was 10 years, with Assembly members serving an average 7.5 years. As ex-staffers entered the Senate, most came from the Assembly. Moreover, they left through death as often as defeat. Since 1988, three have died in office while three lost re-election.

THE CONSTANT CAMPAIGN

Legislators of the '80s lived their life on a constant campaign much like their congressional counterparts in Washington. "It is the nearest thing to Congress outside Washington, D.C.," political scientist Alan Rosenthal of Rutgers University, a leading authority on state legislatures, once said. "California is way out there beyond where any other legislatures are in terms of political partisanship, full-time campaigning and the cost of campaigns. California is almost another nation."

When the Legislature was in session – generally eight to nine months of the year minus vacation recesses – lawmakers usually arrived Monday morning and were gone by mid-afternoon Thursday. By day, legislators juggled committee assignments, floor sessions and their own bills. By night, many made the fund-raiser circuit at downtown Sacramento watering holes frequented by lobbyists, staffers and other lawmakers. They spent their weekends toiling in their districts doing "constituent work," which was not very different from campaigning for office. Those from Southern California spent much of their life getting to and from airports.

While in Sacramento, a typical legislator would find issues flying in an endless succession. Even the best legislator could expect to have no more than a shallow understanding of most issues, and all had to rely on the Legislature's army of 2,400 staffers to point out the nuances. The details and compromises were often worked out by staffers and later blessed by the elected officials. Armed with a huge staff, legislators felt compelled to legislate on a wide variety of issues, creating a gridlock of bills.

In the professional Legislature of the 1980s, getting re-elected became all-important. Election methods became more sophisticated. Holding legislative leadership positions began to hinge not on parliamentary talents but on getting colleagues re-elected.

The Legislature had its own army of campaign managers, many of them parked on the state payroll between elections. Larry Sheingold, on the staff of Democratic Sen. Henry Mello, was loaned out to embattled Democrats and even worked on a Miami mayoral campaign. David Townsend, an ex-staffer to Sen. Robert Presley, opened his own political consultancy and managed Los Angeles Mayor Tom Bradley's losing bid for governor in 1986. And Richard P. "Richie" Ross, an ex-chief of staff and in-house elections guru for Assembly Speaker Willie Brown, D-San Francisco, went out on his own and elected a mayor of San Francisco, Art Agnos, and will manage John Van de Kamp's gubernatorial campaign in 1990.

RAISING THE MONEY

Getting the money to get elected – and stay there – became a predominant activity of the California Legislature in the 1980s. There was not a moment in the decade when a legislator was not under federal investigation for trading votes for campaign contributions. Two legislators were indicted in 1989 and a score more fell under a cloud of corruption investigations. The state's newspapers were replete with accounts of bills linked to campaign contributions.

In the first half of the decade, the Legislature endured a massive investigation into the passage of a bill that overturned local ordinances banning fireworks. The federal investigation into the activities of former fireworks mogul W. Patrick Moriarty yielded convictions of several Southern California officials, but only one legislator was dragged down – Democratic Assemblyman Bruce Young of Norwalk. His conviction was later overturned on appeal.

Legislators had no sooner caught their breath from the Moriarty affair when the FBI lifted the lid in August 1988 on an even bigger investigation, officially code-named Brispec for "Bribery Special Interest." Beginning in late 1985, undercover FBI agents posed as Southern businessmen in search of a bill to benefit their sham companies in return for campaign contributions. They spread more than $50,000 in contributions among Capitol figures.

The agents gathered enough evidence in their "sting" to obtain search warrants on the offices of Patrick Nolan, the Assembly's Republican leader at the time; his close associate, Assemblyman Frank Hill, R-Whittier; Assemblywoman Gwen Moore, D-Los Angeles; and Sen. Joseph Montoya, D-Whittier. By fall of 1989, Montoya was awaiting trial on a series of racketeering, bribery and money laundering charges. A cloud continued to hover above the others.

Not only had legislators become addicted to campaign contributions from those with business before them, they supplemented their personal incomes from such sources as well. The temptations were great, and only a handful of lawmakers declined to take outside income. Speaker Brown led the pack for years with gifts and honorariums from trade associations and others, pulling in $99,798 in 1988 alone. Nor were there any enforceable conflict-of-interest rules for legislators. The state Fair Political Practices Commission was prohibited by law from making legislators comply with the same rules that applied to local and regional officials.

In comparison with other high-achievers in society, legislators were not particularly well paid. Their 1988-89 salary was $40,816 a year in state salary and about $17,000 in living allowances, or $88 a day while the Legislature was in session. Many lawmakers earned lower salaries than their aides.

A consequence of the cozy relationships with those who provided outside income was that members of both parties introduced an avalanche of bills proposing tax breaks and other favors to narrow interests ranging from motorcycle dealers to fertilizer producers. At the same time, the Legislature witnessed an explosion of lobbying activity. A study by the Fair Political Practices Commission found that the cost of influencing lawmaking in 1988 was $82,896,801 – up by 29 percent from 1986, the last comparable end-of-session year. The money was spread among 293 lobbying firms, the top five netting $6.9 million that year. There were 374 clients – roughly half of them corporations – that spent at least $50,000 on lobbying during the year.

PARTISANSHIP TAKES OVER

In a sense, the Legislature is a young institution, transformed in 1966 when the voters approved Proposition 1-A, creating a full-time body. Whether they knew it or not, the voters had abandoned the idea of a "citizen legislator" whose primary career was something other than politics.

The move was the brainchild of then-Assembly Speaker Jesse Unruh, D-Los Angeles, who argued that going full time would give legislators the opportunity to master the complexities of a growing state and thus help break their dependence on lobbyists. By 1969, the California Legislature was rated the best in the nation by the Citizens' Conference on State Legislatures. Other states sought to emulate California. But by going full time, the Legislature became a career. It only awaited enough professional liberals and conservatives to create the conditions for paralysis.

The watershed year that ripened those conditions was 1978, the year of Howard Jarvis and Paul Gann's property tax initiative – Proposition 13. Middle-class voters, alarmed at rampant inflation, rebelled at the rising cost of their property tax bills (though many would become well-off by the inflated price of their homes). Proposition 13 capped property taxes and signaled an anti-government backlash that was to grip the 1980s.

Proposition 13 also brought to Sacramento a group of ideologically motivated conservatives who dubbed themselves "the Proposition 13 babies." They came equipped for warfare against the Democrats, who had held sway since the 1960s with few interruptions. The clubby atmosphere of old soon broke down, and both houses began churning with leadership intrigues. By 1980, Willie Brown had replaced Leo McCarthy as Assembly speaker and David Roberti replaced Jim Mills as Senate president pro tempore. Both rode to power on a wave of partisanship, although Browɴ actually needed Republican votes to gain the speakership.

THE STATE CAPITOL HOTHOUSE

Capitol life became a hothouse with its own hybrid flowers. "The Legislature is today in many ways a failed institution," said the gloomy Assembly Republican leader Ross Johnson in 1989. "The people who control the legislative process have become so wrapped up in the game – power for the sake of power – they've lost sight of the purpose the Legislature was created for: dealing with matters of public policy for the people of California."

One of the most well-known legislators of the decade reflected much of the institution's insularity: Assembly Speaker Willie Brown. His penchant for fast cars, expensive Italian clothes and beautiful women were legendary. He surpassed Jesse Unruh's seven-year record as speaker. The secret, Brown said, was in being "the member's speaker" – keeping everyone happy while sharing the credit for the policy agenda. Brown was more than a state Capitol player. He was one of the highest ranking black politicians in the country. His support was sought by national Democrats. He had prominence in 1988 as Jesse Jackson's campaign director. But Brown's reputation exceeded his power. Even the Rev. Jackson eventually learned that Willie Brown was one part reality, one part bluster and one part myth.

Brown's prominence was in part an unintended result of Republican election strategy. Year after year, Republicans mailed hit pieces featuring the black face of Willie Brown to voters in white suburbs. The hit pieces were often crude and sometimes crossed the line into racism. But the only tangible result was to implant in the public the perception that Brown was the strongman of the Legislature – a perception Brown basked in. Although Republicans made gradual gains in the Assembly, the election returns probably had less to do with Willie Brown than with local politics.

Brown's hubris nearly cost him the speakership to a cabal of upstart Democrats self-dubbed "The Gang of Five." He spent much of 1988 putting down the Democratic rebellion, and emerged a much weakened speaker. He also had to contend with increasingly vocal liberals in the Democratic caucus who dubbed themselves the "Grizzly Bears" (the nickname implied that they were an endangered species). Each faction had its hang-out. The speaker and other insiders preferred the swank Frank Fat's two blocks from the Capitol. The Gang of Five plotted nightly at Paragary's, a midtown California-cuisine restaurant. The proprietor, Randy Paragary, even put up a plaque marking the dubious Gang's spot in history.

In contrast to the flashy Brown, the most powerful of legislators was among the least known to the public – Senate President Pro Tem David Roberti. Through ruthlessness and smarts, Roberti, a Los Angeles Democrat, had held power in the Senate for as long as Brown in the Assembly. He had three challenges within his ranks during the decade and disposed of all swiftly. And, unlike Brown, Roberti used his position to consistently advance a liberal agenda. In 1989, Roberti won passage of a highly controversial bill restricting the sale of semiautomatic weapons, defeating the politically powerful National Rifle Association. Roberti also proved the sharpest thorn in Gov. George Deukmejian's side, blocking many of his political appointments and exacting a high price on numerous policy compromises.

Republican leaders also had their hands more than full during the decade, with the top posts changing regularly in both houses. In the Assembly, Bob Naylor was deposed in 1984 by Pat Nolan, who, faced with political and legal troubles, handed the job off to Ross Johnson in 1988. In the Senate, the Republicans shifted their posts back and forth between hard-line and pragmatic conservatives but were stymied badly in making headway toward becoming a majority.

Among the better known legislators, but certainly not the most influential, was Assemblyman Tom Hayden, one of the Grizzly Bears. The former student radical hung on to his Santa Monica seat through some close elections and pursued his causes inside the Legislature. But Hayden's biggest political influence was outside the Legislature promoting initiatives (like Proposition 65, the toxics measure) and using his statewide organization, Campaign California, in a number of local causes. The organization was instrumental in convincing Sacramento area voters in 1989 to close the troubled Rancho Seco nuclear power plant.

Other masters of the initiative process included Assembly Republican leader Ross Johnson of La Habra (Proposition 73 campaign finance limits) and Democratic Assemblyman Lloyd Connelly of Sacramento (Proposition 65 toxics). Their impact on the state was perhaps greater as initiative tacticians than as legislators.

ACHIEVEMENTS IN THE 1980s

The Legislature was not totally devoid of achievement in the 1980s. Since 1985, the Legislature has approved sweeping measures to reduce smog and garbage, passed a modest revision in workers disability compensation and took a step toward modernizing the state's transportation system by placing a measure on the June 1990 ballot to raise gasoline taxes. It passed a mandatory seat-belt law, lowered the blood-alcohol standard for drunken driving and summoned the political courage to approve restrictions on the sale of semiautomatic weapons. Legislators also garnered enough votes to require teenage girls to get parental consent before having an abortion and enacted the first far-reaching welfare reform since Ronald Reagan was governor, approving in 1985 a "workfare" plan called Greater Avenues for Independence, or GAIN. Finally, lawmakers and the governor stiffened numerous criminal laws and appropriated hundreds of millions of dollars throughout the decade for the most massive prison building program since the 19th century.

Such achievements, however, were usually under the threat of a more Draconian initiative from the outside. Indeed, a number of organizations found it easier – and cheaper than lobbying the Legislature – to draft their own law, gather enough signatures and take their measure directly to the voters.

Of the 5,000 or so bills that came before the Legislature in 1989 – and the 1,465 that were signed into law by Gov. Deukmejian that year – most dealt with mundane district issues or tinkered with business regulations. Indeed, the Legislature had become largely a regulatory body, spending considerable time refereeing "scope of practice" disputes between various medical professions (podiatrists and orthopedic surgeons waged one memorable battle over the right to perform surgery on the ankle) and dealing with licensure matters on trades ranging from building contractors to interior decorators.

Relations between the Legislature and the governor were stormy. The Legislature rejected Deukmejian's 1985 plan for re-organizing the state's toxic waste cleanup agencies, torpedoed numerous political appointments and exacted a high price for building a Los Angeles prison. But it wasn't just because Deukmejian was governor; the Legislature's relationship with Gov. Jerry Brown was difficult at best, another by-product of a Legislature with 120 professional politicians.

PARALYZED ON BASIC ISSUES

In the 1980s, the Legislature had been unable to find the solutions to basic issues, solutions that had somehow come more easily when it was a part-time institution. Some of the fault lay with the federal government, which under President Ronald Reagan had passed to the states increasing responsibilities without the money to pay for them. But even the traditional services California had prided itself on were caught up in the paralysis.

Legislators could not agree on how to modernize the state's water system or expand the universities. Although they patted themselves on the back for their transportation pact in 1989, their self-congratulations ignored the fact that they had only really agreed to let the voters decide on raising taxes. Efforts to reorganize the Los Angeles transit system foundered under its own weight. The state's school system gradually slipped from the top half to the bottom half in the nation. Passing a state budget each year became an act of supreme political will. The state was increasingly devoted to deficit spending in the form of floating interest-bearing bonds.

For legislative leaders, the growth of interest groups, and related power bases inside the Legislature, had made it far more difficult to cut deals and muscle legislation through. They had to work harder and harder to achieve less and less.

Legislative oversight of a vast state bureaucracy withered. Most oversight was done by budget subcommittees, and then only quickly while galloping through lengthy appropriation requests. Lawmakers complained that they got no credit for in-depth study of an agency. "If I am out inspecting Folsom Prison, I am missing committee votes," said one longtime Republican lawmaker. "A potential opponent will seize on that to show you are lazy."

The election of 1988 may well be remembered as the watershed year that set the stage for the 1990s. The voters rebelled against the campaign excesses of the 1980s by passing two restrictive initiatives on campaign finance – Propositions 68 and 73. The two were conflicting in their provisions, but not in their messages. The voters had had enough. The initiatives placed a cap on campaign donations and banned non-election-year fund raising. While the courts and the state FPPC spent much of 1989 interpreting the two initiatives, the Legislature reacted by passing its first far-reaching ethics reform package, restricting outside income, speaking fees and edging toward genuine conflict-of-interest rules.

The decade of the 1980s may be remembered as among the worst for the California Legislature; the decade of the 1990s could see its renewal.

BIOGRAPHICAL SKETCHES

The districts, political history and style for each legislator are sketched in the remainder of this chapter. After each sketch is biographical data, career information, committee assignments, ratings and key votes. Military service during a war is noted by listing the conflict served in (WWII, Korea and Vietnam) after the branch of service.

Ratings from a selection of nine lobbying organizations representing a wide spectrum of those active in Sacramento are also given. A score of 100 indicates the officeholder voted in agreement 100 percent of the time on the bills of interest to that organization. Lower scores indicate fewer votes in agreement. All of the ratings are for 1988, except those by the National Rife Association, which were from 1989, and the California Teachers Association, which were from 1987, the last year such ratings were available. Those who were newly elected in 1988 were only rated by the National Rifle Association.

The organizations are:

> **AFL**–The California American Federation of Labor-Congress of Industrial Organizations (AFL-CIO), the largest labor federation in the nation, based ratings for senators on 26 bills; for Assembly members on 30 bills. The issues included collective bargaining, workplace safety, job security protection and disability compensation.

> **PIRG**–California Public Interest Research Group, a nonprofit consumer and environmental organization founded in 1972, based its ratings of senators on 14 bills; Assembly members, 17 bills. Issues included limiting retail credit interest rate charges, clean air protections, preventing beer wholesaling monopolies and expanded child care.

> **CLCV**–The California League of Conservation Voters, an environmental-legal defense coalition of more than 100 groups, based ratings on 34 bills. Only legislators who voted on 60 percent of the bills rated by the organization received a score. Issues included hazardous waste reduction, wildlife protection,

restricting timber harvesting, acid rain studies and solid waste reduction.

NOW–California National Organization for Women Inc., a women's rights group, based its ratings for members of both houses on 11 bills. The issues included abortion funding, sex discrimination in private clubs, child and pregnancy care and pay equity.

CTA–The California Teachers Association, the largest labor union in the state, based its ratings on 19 bills from 1987 (no ratings were released in 1988). G is for good, scores between 80 and 100 (the organization added * for those with "exceptional service" or who carried its bills); S is for satisfactory, scores between 68 and 79; and U is for unsatisfactory, scores of 67 or less. Issues included cost-of-living raises for teachers, various adjustments to retirement programs, job protections in small school districts and class size reduction.

HAC–Health Access, a statewide coalition of nearly 100 health, medical, church, union, senior citizen and consumer advocate organizations, based ratings for senators on nine bills; for Assembly members, 22 bills. The organization favored bills providing universal access to prenatal care, long-term care for the elderly and comprehensive health insurance.

CofC–The California Chamber of Commerce, a statewide business group, based its ratings for members of both houses on votes on 25 bills. Bills included taxes, insurance liabilities, flood control, pesticide restrictions, child care tax credits and environmental restrictions.

CFB–The California Farm Bureau, an organization representing agriculture interests, based its ratings for senators on votes on seven bills; for Assembly members, nine bills. Issues included opposition to restricting pesticides, promoting marketing and adjustments to land-use regulation.

NRA–The National Rifle Association, based its ratings on its opposition to bills relating to firearms restrictions in 1989. In the Senate, the ratings were based on seven votes; in the Assembly, 10 votes. Issues included restricting the sale of semiautomatic weapons, increased penalties for concealed weapons, and extending the time lag for purchasing certain weapons.

KEY VOTES

A selection of 12 key votes are given for each legislator on a range of issues in the last five years. The bills and votes were selected by the editors and explanations for YES and NO are given below. If a legislator was not yet serving in the Legislature at the time of the vote, the bill has been deleted from their biographical data and is not shown. If the legislator was serving, but either abstained or missed the vote, their absence is noted with:—

The votes were compiled from the state Archive and Legitech, a computer retrieval service.

Divest S. Africa: AB 134 by Assemblywoman Maxine Waters, D-Los Angeles; signed by Deukmejian – The bill required the state to divest its investment portfolio from companies doing business in South Africa in protest of that country's policy of racial separation. The bill passed the Senate on Aug. 25, 1986, on a 27-11 vote and passed the Assembly on Aug. 27, 1986, on a 50-28 vote. YES favors divesting the state from companies doing business with South Africa; NO is against divestment.

Assault gun ban: SB 292 by Sen. David Roberti, D-Los Angeles, and AB 357 by Assemblyman Michael Roos, D-Los Angeles; signed by Deukmejian – Two bills to restrict the sales of semiautomatic military-style assault weapons worked their way through the Legislature in 1989. The bills were bitterly opposed by the National Rifle Association, and their passage marked a major setback to its fabled political power. The assault weapon restriction bills gained momentum after the massacre of children in a Stockton schoolyard by a crazed gunman wielding an AK-47. Since the bills were part of a package, the vote given here is a combination of the votes on both bills. The vote is shown if the member voted on at least one bill. Absences or abstentions are only noted if a member missed both votes. The Roberti bill passed the Assembly on April 17, 1989, by 41-34 and the Senate on May 4, 1989, by 29-8. The Roos bill passed the Assembly on May 18, 1989, by 41-35 and in the Senate on the same day by 27-11. YES favors restricting weapon sales; NO is against restricting weapon sales.

Clean Air Act: AB 2595 – Assemblyman Byron Sher, D-Palo Alto, signed by Deukmejian – The landmark bill expanded the powers of local air quality control districts and, for the first time, required a phased reduction of smog-causing emissions into the 21st century. Those in favor contended it marked a major step toward clean air; opponents argued that it allowed too much intervention in business and local government land-use planning. The bill passed the Senate on Aug. 29, 1988, by 25-4 and the Assembly on Aug. 31 by 47-27. YES is in favor of the bill and the new smog restrictions; NO is against the bill.

Lmt product tort: SB 241 – by Sen. William Lockyer, D-Hayward; signed by Deukmejian – The bill contained a series of procedural and substantive changes in the state's liability laws that were reached as part of a "peace accord" between doctors, lawyers and insurance companies during long negotiations that culminated in a meeting at Frank Fat's restaurant in the last week of the 1987 session. The final parts of the accord were written on a napkin. The bill was not seen by legislators until the final night of the year's session, and a number of lawmakers complained – to no avail – that they wanted more time to review it. The bill was seen as a test of Speaker Brown's ability to ramrod a bill and he succeeded. The bill passed in both houses on Sept. 11, 1987, approved by the Senate by 25-1 and the Assembly by 63-10. YES favors the bill and limiting liability laws; NO is against the bill.

Insurance reform: SB 103 by Sen. Alan Robbins, D-Van Nuys; killed in Assembly – The bill would have put into law the insurance reform provisions of Proposition 103's rate-rollbacks and other consumer-oriented insurance regulations. The bill was seen as a test of legislators' opinions on the consumer-oriented initiative. The bill passed the Senate on Feb. 9, 1989, by 27-9 and lost in the Assembly on April 6, 1989, by 49-22. The bill was granted reconsideration and voted on again on May 8, 1989, and again failed 49-21. The Assembly vote given here is for April 6. YES is for the bill and the insurance regulations; NO is against the bill.

Parent consent abortion: AB 2274 – by Assemblyman Robert Frazee, R-Carlsbad; signed by Deukmejian – Few issues have sparked more passion inside or outside the Legislature than abortion. The Legislature has routinely passed Medi-Cal abortion restrictions in the state budget, but those votes were essentially meaningless because the courts nullified the restrictions. Efforts to provide real restrictions on abortions had been bottled up in parliamentary maneuvers until the parental consent measure. The bill required that minor girls must have parental permission to get an abortion. However, the state has been under a court restraining order preventing enforcement of the law until the courts have ruled on its constitutionality. That order was upheld by the state Court of Appeal in October 1989. The bill passed the Assembly on June 25, 1987, by 46-28 and the Senate on Sept. 10, 1987, by 25-11. YES is in favor of requiring parental consent to get an abortion; NO is against such a restriction on abortions.

Cutting old trees (Assembly only): AB 390 by Assemblyman Byron Sher, D-Palo Alto; killed in Assembly – The bill called for a three-year moratorium on cutting old-growth timber on the state's North Coast, including redwoods and cedars. The measure was ambushed by the timber industry. The actual fight over the bill was played out with a set of "killer" amendments offered by Democratic Assemblyman Dan Hauser, who represents the North Coast and had received campaign contributions from the timber industry. The key amendment, requiring an appropriation for a University of California study on the old-growth timber, had the effect of converting the bill from a majority-vote measure into a bill requiring a two-thirds vote – a test it could never meet. The bill died in the Assembly a day after the amendments on a 42-27 vote, well short of the 54 votes needed for passage. The vote given here is on the amendment on June 29, 1989, that converted the bill. The amendment was adopted on a 40-29 vote. YES is for approval of the amendment, in effect voting to kill the bill and continue the cutting of old growth trees; NO is against the amendment and in favor of keeping the bill alive.

Ban insure donations (Senate only): SB 205 – by Sen. Gary K. Hart, D-Santa Barbara; killed in Senate – The bill would have banned candidates for state insurance commissioner from accepting campaign contributions from insurance companies. The bill was seen as a major test of the Senate's ability to clamp down on special interest money in campaigns. Opponents to the bill argued that a ban on insurance commissioner candidates could set a precedent for other offices – like their own. The bill needed a two-thirds majority (27 votes) to pass the Senate but it was defeated on a 15-19 vote on June 29, 1989. YES is in favor of banning insurance company contributions to candidates for insurance commissioner; NO is against the bill and for preserving the status quo.

End mob home rent cont: SB 1241 – Sen. William Leonard, R-Big Bear; signed by Deukmejian – Prohibits rent controls on new mobile home spaces that are offered for rent after January 1, 1990. Backers argued that local rent control ordinances had to be lifted to give incentives for building new mobile home parks. Organized mobile home organizations stayed neutral on the bill because it did not affect existing parks. The measure had no difficulty in the Senate, sailing through on a 37-0 vote on June 22, 1989. But liberal "Grizzly Bear" Assembly members opposed the bill, arguing that the bill penalized the elderly of the future. The Assembly on Sept. 1, 1989, passed the bill 41-24, with 14 members choosing not to vote. YES favors the repeal of rent control on new mobile home spaces; NO is for maintaining local rent control ordinances as they existed.

Child sick leave: AB 681 – by Assemblyman Terry Friedman, D-Los Angeles; vetoed by Deukmejian – The bill allowed employees to use the sick leave they were already entitled to for attending their sick children. Proponents said the bill recognized a modern economic fact of life – many families have two wage-earners. Without the bill, many employees would have to chose between their jobs and leaving their children unattended while ill. The bill was opposed by the California Manufacturers Association and the California Chamber of Commerce, which contended it, in effect, would have forced business to pay employees to care for their sick children. The bill passed the Assembly on June 26, 1989, by 43-29 and passed the Senate on Sept. 11, 1989, by 21-17. YES favored forcing business to allow sick leave to care for ill children; NO is against the bill.

Ban AIDS discrim: AB 65 – by Assemblyman John Vasconcellos, D-San Jose; vetoed by Deukmejian – The bill prohibited discrimination in employment against anyone stricken with acquired immune deficiency syndrome. Proponents argued that those with AIDS are sometimes fired from their jobs by fearful employers even though the disease is not easily transmitted. Opponents said the bill went too far in restricting businesses, like restaurants that have lost business when patrons found out a cook had AIDS. The bill passed the Assembly on June 29, 1989, by 46-32 and passed the Senate on Sept. 11, 1989, by 25-6 vote. YES favors banning discrimination against AIDS victims; NO is against the bill.

Expand death penalty: Efforts to expand the death penalty to include more "special circumstance" crimes have won majorities in both houses but have been thwarted from becoming law through parliamentary maneuvering. Thus, two bills are given reflecting death penalty votes, one for each house.

In the Senate: SB 1156 – by Sen. William Lockyer, D-Hayward; died in the Assembly – the Senate passed the bill by 26-5 on June 19, 1987, but it stalled in the Assembly Public Safety Committee and died without a vote. YES is in favor of expanding the death penalty to include new crimes; NO is against the bill and maintaining the current state of death penalty law.

In the Assembly: SB 44 – by Lockyer; died in the Senate – Because the Assembly Public Safety Committee would not let a death penalty bill leave its jurisdiction, a Senate bill awaiting a vote in the Assembly was amended on the floor to include expanding the death penalty so the bill could be sent to the Senate for a final vote. As amended, the bill passed the Assembly June 23, 1988, by 60-9 but died in the Senate without a vote. YES is in favor of expanding the death penalty to include new crimes; NO is against the bill and maintaining the current state of death penalty law.

Ban offshore oil: AB 284 – by Assemblyman Dan Hauser, D-Arcata; vetoed by Deukmejian – Required establishment of a "sanctuary" prohibiting offshore oil drilling within three miles of the Northern California coastline. Proponents argued that the northern coastline was too environmentally sensitive to risk disaster from offshore oil drilling. Opponents argued that California is not doing its share to provide the nation with oil and is too dependent on Alaskan crude for its own needs. The bill was largely symbolic, since it would not have affected oil leases within federal jurisdiction beyond the state's three-mile limit. The bill passed the Assembly on June 23, 1987, by 43-34 and passed the Senate on Aug. 12, 1988, by 28-6. YES is in favor of the bill and banning offshore drilling in state-controlled waters; NO is against the bill.

COMMON ABBREVIATIONS

CSU – California State University

D – Democratic party

inc. – incumbent (noted on incumbent candidates who lost)

J.D. – Juris doctor (the modern law degree designation is used)

L – Libertarian party

M.P.A. – Masters in Public Administration

P&F – Peace and Freedom party

R – Republican party

UC – University of California

USAF – U.S. Air Force

USC – University of Southern California

USMC – U.S. Marine Corps

WWII – World War II

SENATE
1st Senate District
John T. Doolittle (R)

This northernmost district loops from the Trinity Alps and Klamath Valley, across the top of the state – taking in snow-capped Mount Shasta – to the northeastern California border with Oregon and Nevada. It then moves south through the mountain counties of Lassen, Plumas, Sierra, Nevada, Placer and El Dorado along the northern reaches of the Sierra, including all of the Lake Tahoe basin. The district hooks eastward again, taking in the suburbs of Sacramento, Yuba City and Yolo County, including the university town of Davis. It is a sprawling district with widely divergent political and economic forces. And it has become one of the messiest election battlegrounds of the decade.

John T. Doolittle

The district's representative, John Doolittle, is the No. 2 Republican in the Senate. Handsome and energetic, Doolittle is easily the Senate's most rigidly ideological conservative. As GOP caucus chairman, Doolittle is responsible for getting his Republican colleagues re-elected. In that capacity, Doolittle presides over a tight-lipped and sometimes paranoid staff of ideological warriors directed by John Feliz, an ex-Los Angeles police detective. Doolittle and Feliz are both proteges of former Sen. Bill Richardson, for years the Senate's gun-toting conservative mastermind. Doolittle and Feliz are probably Richardson's most enduring legacies.

Doolittle was only 29 years old when he made his first try for public office in 1980. He was viewed as a sacrificial Republican lamb, running against Sacramento Democrat Al Rodda, the dean of the Senate. Doolittle won – hitting hard on crime issues in the Sacramento suburbs – and the Democratic dons of the Senate have never forgiven him for it. Two years later, the Democrats eliminated Doolittle's district during reapportionment. Doolittle was forced to run against Carmichael Assemblyman Leroy Greene in a new district that the Democrats had crafted specifically to favor a Democrat. Greene won. Doolittle still had two years left in his term, so for two years, he served without a district.

Democratic leaders, in drawing new districts for the region, had left longtime Republican Sen. Ray Johnson of Chico as the odd man out. In 1984, Doolittle challenged Johnson, and Republican leaders cast their lot with Doolittle. But Johnson, crying foul, bolted the party to run as an independent. Doolittle won, but not without some dirty tricks.

Doolittle and Feliz were eventually fined $3,000 by the state Fair Political Practices Commission for contributing $5,000 in campaign services to the Democratic candidate, Jack Hornsby, who had virtually no chance in the election, and in the hope of drawing off votes from Johnson, who had received some aid of his own from Democratic leaders.

Doolittle had another nasty race in 1988, pitted against Sutter County Sheriff Roy Whiteaker, who tried to capitalize on his fame-of-old from solving the Juan Corona murders. Doolittle again prevailed after mercilessly branding Whiteaker as soft on crime.

Doolittle is not particularly popular among his colleagues. He does not cavort at Frank Fat's or any of the other watering holes popular among legislators. He became caucus chairman in May 1987, not out of popularity but in the wake of the Republican's loss of a special election in Norwalk. In the leadership shake-up that followed, Doolittle got the second-ranking spot in a balancing act with moderate Ken Maddy of Fresno, the new GOP leader. Simply put, the Richardson wing in the Senate did not fully trust Maddy and put Doolittle in the job as insurance for conservative purity.

Since Richardson left the Senate, Doolittle has become the Republican that Democrats most love to despise – a role he no doubt relishes. Doolittle is considered a moral zealot on a number of issues: He is firmly against abortion and for the death penalty. His harangues against Rose Bird are legendary. He has carried legislation to ban the display of sexually explicit material at any business open to minors.

No issue, however, gets Doolittle more attention than AIDS. He has pushed legislation to require AIDS testing to get a marriage license, increasing prison time for those people who know they have AIDS and are convicted of committing sex crimes, and making it a felony for anyone to practice prostitution or donate blood with the knowledge they have the disease. Doolittle so far has been stymied by Democrats, many of whom dismiss him as a paranoid know-nothing. The label is unfair. Doolittle has made a studious effort to learn about the disease – more so than many of his detractors – but he approaches it, like so many other issues, with ideological blinders.

PERSONAL: elected 1980; born Oct. 30, 1950, in Glendale, Calif.; home, Citrus Heights; education, B.A. history UC Santa Cruz, J.D. McGeorge; wife, Julia Harlow; son, John Jr.; Mormon.

CAREER: lawyer; aide to Sen. H.L. Richardson; Senate Republican caucus chairman.

COMMITTEES: Business & Professions (vice chair); Agriculture & Water Resources; Insurance, Claims & Corporations; Judiciary. SELECT: Sierra/Cascade/Klamath Watersheds (chair); AIDS; Fairs & Rural Issues; Forest Resources; Mobile homes; Pacific Rim; Small Business Enterprises; Upper Sacramento Valley Economic, Resource & Rangeland Issues. JOINT: Fairs Allocation & Classification; Legislative Audit; Legislative Ethics; Revision of the Penal Code; Rules.

OFFICES: Capitol, (916) 445-5788; district, 720 Sunrise Blvd., 110-D, Roseville, 95661, (916) 969-8232/783-8232.

REGISTRATION: 46.3% D; 43.2% R

1988 CAMPAIGN: Doolittle – R   54%
                Whiteaker – D   46%

RATINGS:

AFL	PIRG	CLCV	NOW	CTA	HAC	CofC	CFB	NRA
18%	31%	44%	33%	U	78%	52%	71%	100%

KEY VOTES:

Divest S. Africa:	NO	Insurance reform:	NO	Child sick leave:	NO
Assault gun ban:	NO	Parent consent abortion:	YES	Ban AIDS discrim:	NO
Clean Air Act:	NO	Ban insure donations:	–	Extend death penalty:	–
Lmt product tort:	YES	End mob home rent cont:	YES	Ban offshore oil	–

2nd Senate District

Barry D. Keene (D)

The craggy north coast with its dwindling stands of old-growth forest remains out of the economic mainstream of the state. Illegal marijuana growing may well be its biggest cash crop. Quaint bed-and-breakfasts dot the Mendocino and Humboldt county coastlines. The district has a national park – Redwoods – though residents nearby have always resented it as a symbol of a lost timber industry. The new Pelican Bay state prison in Crescent City has brought a new economic base for some, but the unlikely spot for a prison is awkward for transporting prisoners and it has brought with it urban problems.

Barry D. Keene

A generation ago, California's scantly populated north coast voted Republican almost all the time, even though it had a majority of nominally Democratic voters. But its politics began to change in the late 1960s, when the decline of the timber industry was accompanied by an influx of counterculture refugees, dubbed "hippies." As the number of loggers has declined and the newcomers have become more numerous, the political pendulum has made a slow but steady swing to the left, with environmental and lifestyle issues becoming dominant in local politics. By the late 1980s, the region, stretching from the Oregon border nearly to San Francisco, was voting solidly Democratic from the top of the ticket to the bottom.

The harbinger of that change occurred in 1972, when a young Democratic attorney from Santa Rosa named Barry Keene defeated a young Republican attorney from Santa Rosa for a vacant state Assembly seat. Keene spent six years in the Assembly before moving into the region's state Senate district, which reaches nearly to Sacramento and includes fast-growing Solano County, as well as Del Norte, Humboldt, Mendocino and much of Sonoma counties.

Keene is one of the Capitol's most paradoxical figures. In his earlier days in the Legislature he was the archetypical young man on the make, climbing up the committee ladder and openly positioning himself to run for statewide office with high-profile moves, mostly in the medical field. An unabashed admirer of the Kennedys, Keene patterned himself – even his speaking style – on his idols.

But somewhere along the line after moving to the Senate, Keene lost his political zeal. The tall young man stooped and turned gray. He tried to persuade then-Gov. Jerry Brown to appoint him to the appellate court bench to no avail. In 1985, after helping Senate President Pro Tem David Roberti solidify his grip on the Senate's top political post, Keene moved into the No. 2 slot as majority floor leader.

Keene, the idealistic legislator, became Keene, the party appatratchik, hitting up lobbyists for campaign money and otherwise playing the inside game. And he also developed a reputation for personal erraticism, occasionally erupting into rages and firing his staff in wholesale lots. A magazine listed him as one of the worst bosses in California. Publicly, Keene displays a diffident, almost shy manner, but his psychological problems were indirectly confirmed when a newspaper revealed that he had been spending campaign funds on psychological counseling services.

Since turning his attention to party affairs, Keene has handled little major legislation and is content, apparently, to take care of local matters.

Republican strategists targeted Keene only once, in 1986, when the Republican leader of the time, James Nielsen, persuaded a personal friend, Solano County Supervisor Richard Brann, to take a run at Keene. Keene won handily and seems in little danger of losing his seat. The current registration margin of 56 percent to 32 percent makes the district Keene territory for the indefinite future.

PERSONAL: elected 1978; born July 30, 1938, in Camden City, N.J.; home, Benicia; education, B.A. prelaw and J.D. Stanford University; divorced; children, Susan, Mitchell, Joe, Tony, Patricia; Protestant.

CAREER: Sonoma County deputy district attorney 1967-1968; lawyer; businessman; school board member; Assembly 1972; Senate majority leader.

COMMITTEES: Budget & Fiscal Review; Business & Professions; Governmental Organization; Insurance, Claims & Corporations; Judiciary. SELECT: Forest Resources (chair); Calif. Wine Industry; Maritime Industry; Pacific Rim; Sierra/Cascade/Klamath Watersheds; JOINT: Fisheries & Aquaculture (chair); Legislative Retirement, Public Fund Investments.

OFFICES: Capitol, (916) 445-3375; district, 631 Tennessee St., Vallejo, 94590, (707) 648-4080; 317 3rd St., 6, Eureka, 95501, (707) 445-6508.

REGISTRATION: 56.4% D; 31.7% R

1986 CAMPAIGN: Keene - D   56%
Brann - R   41%
Elizondo - P&F   3%

RATINGS:	AFL	PIRG	CLCV	NOW	CTA	HAC	CofC	CFB	NRA
	90%	79%	95%	92%	G	78%	24%	42%	43%

KEY VOTES:

Divest S. Africa:	YES	Insurance reform:	YES	Child sick leave:	YES
Assault gun ban:	YES	Parent consent abortion:	NO	Ban AIDS discrim:	YES
Clean Air Act:	YES	Ban insure donations:	YES	Extend death penalty:	–
Lmt product tort:	YES	End mob home rent cont:	YES	Ban offshore oil:	YES

3rd Senate District

Milton Marks (D)

This district, which includes upscale, environmentally conscious Marin County and northern San Francisco, appears tailor-made for a Democrat – or a Milton Marks.

Marks has represented the area for 22 years, the first 19 as a moderate-to-liberal Republican. Throughout his legislative career, which began in the Assembly in 1958, Marks has been a maverick. He is a tireless campaigner who has built support through personal contact; he appears at everything from club lunches to bar mitzvahs in his district.

Marks took a brief respite from the Legislature in 1966, when Democratic Gov. Pat Brown appointed him to a San Francisco Municipal Court judgeship. But he

Milton Marks

returned to politics the following year, when California's new Republican governor, Ronald Reagan, supported Marks' successful effort to fill a vacant state Senate seat in a special election.

In the subsequent years, Marks steered an independent course in the Senate, often voting with Democrats on environmental, civil liberties and social issues, much to the consternation of his Republican colleagues. His credentials as a Republican got a brief boost in 1982, when, at the coaxing of the Reagan White House, he unsuccessfully challenged powerful Democratic Rep. Phil Burton, who died shortly after his re-election victory. Democrats, infuriated at Marks' challenge of Burton, challenged him in 1984, supporting Lia Belli, the wife of a prominent San Francisco attorney. But Marks easily won re-election.

Marks' big switch to the Democratic Party came in January 1986, when he cut a deal with Senate President Pro Tem David Roberti. In exchange for his change in affiliations, Marks, who had little clout inside the Republican caucus, immediately was made caucus chairman, the No. 3 position among Senate Democrats. Some Republicans said they weren't bothered by Marks' defection. "It's like losing a hemorrhoid," quipped ultraconservative Sen. H.L. Richardson, who once punched Marks when both were Republicans in the Senate. Yet Marks' defection was significant. It came at a time when Republicans were trying to make a move to take control of the Senate before reapportionment in 1991. Marks' defection made that possibility more remote.

Recent legislation by Marks reflects both his position as chairman of the Elections Committee and the concerns of his liberal district. He has carried bills to prohibit posting of guards at polling places – a direct response to a maneuver by Orange County Republicans in 1988 – and to purge voter rolls of non-voters in combination with programs aimed at increasing voter registration. He also has proposed making it a crime to raise veal calves in enclosures that do not meet minimum requirements and to give tax advantages to artists, a measure vetoed by Gov. Deukmejian.

Marks was one of the few state legislators to vote against a resolution urging that flag burning be made a crime.

PERSONAL: elected 1967 (special election); born July 22, 1920, in San Francisco; home, San Francisco; Army WWII (Philippines); education, B.A. Stanford University, J.D. San Francisco Law School; wife, Carolene Wachenheimer; children, Carol, Milton III and Edward David; Jewish.

CAREER: lawyer; Assembly 1958; municipal court judge (appointed in 1966 by Gov. Edmund G. Brown Sr.).

COMMITTEES: Elections (chair); Business & Professions; Housing & Urban Affairs; Judiciary; Natural Resources & Wildlife. SELECT: Maritime Industry (chair); AIDS; Calif. Wine Industry; Citizen Participation in Government; Pacific Rim; Small Business Enterprises. SPECIAL: UC Admissions. JOINT: Fisheries & Aquaculture; Legislative Budget; Refugee Resettlement, International Migration & Cooperative Development; State's Economy.

OFFICES: Capitol, (916) 445-1412; district, 350 McAllister St., 2045, San Francisco, 94102, (415) 557-1437; 30 N. San Pedro Road, 160, San Rafael, 94903, (415) 479-6612.

REGISTRATION: 58.6% D; 25.4% R

1988 CAMPAIGN: Marks – D 66%
Marshall – R 30%
Pickens – L 2%
Rodriguez – P&F 2%

RATINGS:

	AFL	PIRG	CLCV	NOW	CTA	HAC	CofC	CFB	NRA
	96%	93%	91%	84%	G	100%	20%	14%	0%

KEY VOTES:

Divest S. Africa:	YES	Insurance reform:	YES	Child sick leave:	YES
Assault gun ban:	YES	Parent consent abortion:	NO	Ban AIDS discrim:	YES
Clean Air Act:	YES	Ban insure donations:	YES	Extend death penalty:	NO
Lmt product tort:	YES	End mob home rent cont:	YES	Ban offshore oil:	YES

4th Senate District

James R. Nielsen (R)

Cutting across all or portions of eight north-central California counties, the 4th Senate District takes in Butte, Colusa, Glenn, Lake, Napa, Shasta, Tehama and Sonoma. The district includes the flatlands of the northern Central Valley and Redding, the largest city north of Sacramento. The district also includes spectacular river country, including the wild McCloud River, and a slowly dying timber industry.

Once it was considered a breach of protocol for one state senator to finance a campaign against another, regardless of party. But in the mid-1970s, conservative activist and fund-raiser Sen. H.L. Richardson shattered the tradition by financing a series of heavy-duty assaults on liberal Democratic senators. In three successive

James R. Nielsen

elections, three liberals fell, one of them being John Dunlap of Napa in 1978. Dunlap's successful challenger was Jim Nielsen, a young (then 34), little-known agricultural chemical salesman from Woodland.

A few years later, the Democrats ticketed Nielsen for oblivion by "folding up" his district during the reapportionment of legislative districts. But Nielsen adopted a clever counterstrategy, touring the neighboring district of Democrat Barry Keene and threatening to run against him. Keene, in turn, pressured Democratic leaders to draw a district for Nielsen. The resulting 4th District is a monster, certainly made to order for a Republican, with less than 50 percent Democratic registration, a strong conservative voting pattern and, for Nielsen, an agricultural flavor.

Nielsen won re-election in the new district in 1982, won again in 1986 and is preparing to seek a fourth term in 1990. In the meantime, however, he also won (thanks to Richardson's patronage) the Republican leader's position in the Senate, but lost it after suffering GOP losses at the polls. And he has undergone some odd personal changes as well.

The twice-divorced, thrice-married Nielsen dabbled in human potential development in his earlier years, but has since become a fundamentalist Christian. He created a stir in 1989 by declaring during a radio show that AIDS "may be God's way" of punishing "mankind (for) what kind of promiscuous society we've become." He reiterated that opinion later in a prepared statement, saying, "No one knows with certainty whether this is the case but I believe that God judges our lifestyles."

As a defrocked Republican leader and a conservative, Nielsen participates only occasionally in major legislative matters. He takes care of his district and the agricultural industry. In one celebrated case, Nielsen pressed the state to loosen regulation of a herbicide distributed by a chemical company that was still paying him a salary as a consultant.

Notoriety of a different sort came to Nielsen in 1986 as he was running for his third term. A newspaper revealed that Nielsen had paid nearly $75,000 to his second wife and a jointly owned consulting company out of his campaign funds without reporting his financial gain in state economic interest reports. The amount paid out of Nielsen's campaign fund, moreover, was almost exactly what he was paying his first wife in alimony and child support out of his own pocket. Nielsen had to do some fast explaining and amend his economic interest statements.

Some Democratic strategists believe that these and other incidents could make Nielsen vulnerable despite the Republican voting cast of the 4th District. Mike Thompson, an aide to Assemblywoman Jackie Speier, D-South San Francisco, will test the theory when he challenges Nielsen in 1990.

PERSONAL: elected 1978; born July 31, 1944, in Fresno, Calif.; home, Woodland; education, B.S. agricultural business CSU Fresno; wife, Marilyn; children, Prima and Brandi; Baptist.

CAREER: farmer; farm management consultant.

COMMITTEES: Insurance, Claims & Corporations; Agriculture & Water Resources; Appropriations; Natural Resources & Wildlife; Toxics & Public Safety Management. SELECT: Upper Sacramento Valley Economic, Resource & Rangeland Issues (chair); AIDS; Calif. Wine Industry; Pacific Rim; Planning for Calif. Growth; Sierra/Cascade/Klamath Watersheds; State Procurement & Expenditure Practices. SPECIAL: UC Admissions. JOINT: Fairs Allocation & Classification; Organized Crime & Gang Violence; Oversight on GAIN Implementation; Review of the Master Plan for Higher Education.

OFFICES: Capitol, (916) 445-3353; district, 1074 East Ave. Suite N, Chico, 95926, (916) 343-3546; 650 Imperial Way 103, Napa, 94559, (707) 253-7212; 50 Santa Rosa Ave., 305, Santa Rosa, 95404, (707) 523-1502; 2400 Washington Ave., 120, Redding, 96001, (916) 225-2201.

REGISTRATION: 49.% D; 40.4% R

1986 CAMPAIGN: Nielsen – R   64%

Cibula – D   36%

RATINGS:

AFL	PIRG	CLCV	NOW	CTA	HAC	CofC	CFB	NRA
32%	50%	68%	33%	U	79%	64%	100%	100%

KEY VOTES:

Divest S. Africa:	NO	Insurance reform:	YES	Child sick leave:	NO
Assault gun ban:	NO	Parent consent abortion:	YES	Ban AIDS discrim:	–
Clean Air Act:	NO	Ban insure donations:	–	Extend death penalty:	–
Lmt product tort:	YES	End mob home rent cont:	YES	Ban offshore oil:	YES

5th Senate District

John R. Garamendi (D)

This sprawling district covers all or part of eight counties, from the rural foothill counties of Alpine, Amador, Calaveras, Tuolumne and Mono to the city of Stockton and nearby Delta communities of San Joaquin County to part of Yolo County and an urbanized area of Sacramento County outside the Sacramento city limits. And this varied expanse is represented by one of the Capitol's most puzzling figures.

Perhaps the most Kennedyesque member of the Legislature, John Garamendi would appear to be the dream candidate: a handsome ex-college football star with degrees from Harvard and the University of California who served with his wife as a Peace Corps volunteer in Ethiopia; the son of Basque-Italian parents

John R. Garamendi

who carved out a rugged living on Nevada ranches and in the Sierra foothills; a bank officer; a land developer; and the devoted father of a handsome family.

Garamendi appeared destined for big things from the moment he won election to the Assembly in 1974. After only two years in the lower house, he moved up to the Senate, and four years later, in 1980, he became majority leader, the No. 2 spot in the Senate, in a leadership shake-up that made David Roberti president pro tem. But from that quick start, Garamendi's political career has become stuck, having fallen victim to, paradoxically, unctuous ambition and a stubborn unwillingness to play the political game by the rules.

Garamendi began to stumble in 1982, when he made a quixotic bid for the Democratic nomination for governor and got his ears boxed. He could have, and probably should have, run for a lesser statewide office but insisted on going for the top. He also passed up a chance to run for Congress.

Garamendi developed a reputation in the Senate for overweening ambition and was accused by Democratic colleagues of neglecting his duties as majority floor leader. Garamendi seemed unwilling to wheel and deal with the special interest sources of campaign money, one of the more unsavory aspects of life as a legislative leader. In 1985, he found himself replaced by Barry Keene. Garamendi made himself look foolish in the eyes of many observers when he tried to dump Roberti as pro tem and found himself standing alone. His run for state controller in 1986 was an equal failure.

Garamendi, a comparatively young man, still hankers after higher office, but given his recent record, his chances are not rated very highly. To succeed, Garamendi would have to place himself in the hands of professionals who could exploit his obvious attributes, but so far he has proved unwilling to do that. For the moment, he seems content to devote his time to his pet public policy issues, such as economic development and tax policy. Roberti has rehabilitated Garamendi a bit by giving him the chairmanship of the Revenue and Taxation Committee.

PERSONAL: elected 1976; born Jan. 24, 1945, in Camp Blanding, Fla.; Peace Corps; education, B.S. business UC Berkeley, M.B.A. Harvard University; wife, Patricia Wilkinson; children, Genet, John, Christina, Autumn, Merle and Ashley; Presbyterian.

CAREER: Banker and rancher; drafted by the Dallas Cowboys but did not play professionally; Assembly 1974.

COMMITTEES: Revenue & Taxation (chair); Bonded Indebtedness & Methods of Financing; Energy & Public Utilities; Governmental Organization; Natural Resources & Wildlife. SELECT: Fairs & Rural Issues; Forest Resources; Maritime Industry. JOINT: Science & Technology (chair); Arts; Quincentennial of the Voyages of Columbus; Oversight on GAIN Implementation.

OFFICES: Capitol, (916) 445-2407; district, 31 E. Channel St., 440, Stockton, 95202, (209) 948-7930.

REGISTRATION: 54.1% D; 36.6% R

1988 CAMPAIGN: Garamendi – D   69%

                    Lawrence – R   31%

RATINGS:	AFL	PIRG	CLCV	NOW	CTA	HAC	CofC	CFB	NRA
	79%	64%	–	92%	G	89%	24%	42%	14%

KEY VOTES:

Divest S. Africa: YES	Insurance reform:	YES	Child sick leave: YES
Assault gun ban: YES	Parent consent abortion:	–	Ban AIDS discrim: YES
Clean Air Act: –	Ban insure donations:	YES	Extend death penalty: YES
Lmt product tort:: YES	End mob home rent cont: YES	Ban offshore oil:	YES

6th Senate District

Leroy F. Greene (D)

The Capitol is not only where Leroy Greene spends most of his working hours, it is also in the middle of his senatorial district. The 6th District, which encompasses all of the city of Sacramento and most of the surrounding unincorporated area, was tailored to Greene's political specifications by Democratic leaders of the state Senate after the 1980 census.

In 1980, conservative Republican John Doolittle had stunned the Senate by upsetting one of its best-liked members, Democrat Al Rodda. What had been the Rodda district was reconfigured to lop off the most Republican-oriented suburbs and concentrate strength in Democratic-voting city precincts. And a clever change of district numbers forced Doolittle to stand for re-election in 1982, just two years into his four-year term.

Greene had spent 20 years in the Assembly representing a mid-Sacramento district, and with the change of boundaries, he was well-positioned to take on Doolittle in the newly created 6th District. Greene defeated Doolittle, but another change of district lines after the election created another new district in which Doolittle could run in 1984, and Doolittle remains in the Senate.

Greene, as the senator from Sacramento, represents one of the state's fastest-growing and fastest-changing metropolitan areas, one that is on the verge of assuming big-city status. Sacramento's traditional dependence on government payrolls is giving way to a surge in private industry, and with that change has come a decided shift to the right politically. The 6th District, however,  **Leroy F. Greene**
should remain solidly Democratic because most of the new industrial and commercial development is occurring in the suburbs outside the district.

As an assemblyman, Greene was an often acerbic, highly active legislator with a particular interest in education. A civil engineer who practiced in Sacramento for many years, the New Jersey-born Greene became chairman of the Assembly Education Committee and carried numerous bills to finance construction, reconstruction and operation of public schools.

Since moving to the Senate, however, Greene has moved into the background, no longer playing a leading role in shaping major legislation, seemingly content to support the Democratic Party line on issues and carry local-interest bills. He chairs the Senate Housing and Urban Affairs Committee, but it has not been a generator of major bills.

Greene survived a stiff challenge from Republican Sandra Smoley, a Sacramento County supervisor, in 1986, and there have been recurrent reports that he won't run for a third term in 1990, although he says he will.

PERSONAL: elected 1982; born Jan. 31, 1918, in Newark, N.J.; home, Sacramento; Army WWII; education, B.S. civil engineering Purdue University; wife, Denny Miller; daughter, Denny Lee Mazlak; no religious affiliation.

CAREER: civil engineer 1951-1978, owned firm; Assembly 1962; newspaper columnist; radio talk show host.

COMMITTEES: Housing & Urban Affairs (chair); Banking & Commerce; Business & Professions; Education; Energy & Public Utilities; Industrial Relations; Transportation. SELECT: Upper Sacramento Valley Economic, Resource & Rangeland Issues. JOINT: School Facilities (chair); Rules.

OFFICES: Capitol, (916) 445-7807; district, Box 254646, Carmichael, 95825, (916) 481-6540.

REGISTRATION: 56.5% D; 34.4% R

1986 CAMPAIGN: Greene – D   61%

Smoley – R   40%

RATINGS:	AFL	PIRG	CLCV	NOW	CTA	HAC	CofC	CFB	NRA
	87%	64%	95%	75%	G	100%	20%	42%	0%

KEY VOTES:

Divest S. Africa:	YES	Insurance reform:	YES	Child sick leave:	YES
Assault gun ban:	YES	Parent consent abortion:	NO	Ban AIDS discrim:	YES
Clean Air Act:	–	Ban insure donations:	NO	Extend death penalty:	YES
Lmt product tort:	YES	End mob home rent cont:	YES	Ban offshore oil:	YES

7th Senate District

Daniel E. Boatwright (D)

As the cities surrounding San Francisco Bay have exploded into the fourth-largest metropolitan area in the United States, that growth has oozed out "through the tunnel" in the Berkeley Hills into Contra Costa County. Where once a sleepy string of towns was connected by two lane roads, the Diablo Valley is now paved in concrete and glass towers. Walnut Creek even has a skyline.

In the 1930s, it was a long train ride to Oakland for basic services – like doctors – for the oil refinery workers in Avon, with not much in-between. Now the massive Bishop Ranch industrial park houses high-tech

Daniel E. Boatwright

industry and housing tracts cover the hillsides and valleys. The headquarters of Chevron are here, and its executives live nearby in places like the exclusive walled community of Blackhawk. And the region has a conservative bent more akin to Orange County than the rest of Northern California, reflected in the editorial pages of the newspapers belonging to aging right-wing publisher Dean Lesher.

Combative Democrat Dan Boatwright has been a central figure in Contra Costa politics for three decades. He has survived tough elections, a 1980s Internal Revenue Service investigation that sought $112,000 in back taxes for 1976, a 1984 civil trial in which he was charged and acquitted of taking money for official favors. Newspapers have written about the $10,000 Boatwright's law firm received from a client who also was seeking an $8.7 million tax break through a Boatwright bill. His girlfriend was a featured witness in his civil trial.

Along the way, Boatwright has been called the "Teflon senator" in honor of his ability to slough off negative media coverage without its damaging his political career – an ability much on display in 1988, when he easily turned back a

Democratic primary challenge from popular Contra Costa County Supervisor Sunne McPeak.

Boatwright certainly gives as good as he takes – and with an ego outstripping reality. In 1982, he had notions of running for lieutenant governor. He was muscled out of the way by Leo McCarthy. In 1986, he had notions of running for controller. Gray Davis muscled him out of the way.

In the hothouse of the state Capitol, Boatwright may be the Legislature's biggest bully. He and his assistant, Barry Brokaw, are known as two of the savviest operators "inside the building." When Boatwright was chairman of Appropriations, he arbitrarily killed without a hearing dozens of Assembly bills before his committee in a single day in 1986, setting off howls of protests from offended lawmakers. David Roberti stuck up for his demagogic chairman, but was repaid a year later when Boatwright tried to line up enough votes to depose Roberti as the leader of the Senate. Roberti swiftly sacked Boatwright as chairman of Appropriations, setting off a vintage Boatwright outburst:

"If he wants to sit up in his little ivory tower and be besieged every day for the rest of his term, he's come to the right guy," said Boatwright of Roberti. "I was a combat infantryman in Korea – had my ass shot off, and I know how to fight a war. If he wants war, he's got war ... I'll throw hand grenades, go get a big bazooka. I mean, I know how to fight a war."

However, no amount of public invective got Boatwright his job back (and he was not, by the way, wounded in Korea).

Roberti, who always eventually brings those he punishes back inside the tent, reached a detente with Boatwright in 1988. Roberti poured in hundreds-of-thousands of dollars, and drafted innumerable Senate staffers, to help Boatwright meet McPeak's challenge. Roberti bolstered Boatwright's status by giving him a new job, chairmanship of the newly created Bonded Indebtedness Committee. With Boatwright's sharp mind for all things financial, he has been in his element as the lawmaker principally responsible for ensuring that the legislative branch keeps tabs on the administration's efforts to expand the state's debt rather than raise taxes. And he has kept his mouth shut – at least for awhile.

PERSONAL: elected 1980; born, Jan. 29, 1930, in Harrison, Ark.; home, Concord; Army 1948-1952 Korea; education, B.A. political science and J.D. UC Berkeley; wife, Margaret Shedd; children, Daniel Jr., David and Donald; Protestant.

CAREER: lawyer; Contra Costa deputy district attorney 1960-1963; Concord City Council 1966-1972, mayor 1966-1968; Assembly 1972.

COMMITTEES: Bonded Indebtedness & Methods of Financing (chair); Appropriations; Banking & Commerce; Elections; Revenue & Taxation. SELECT: State Procurement & Expenditure Practices (chair); Tourism & Aviation. JOINT: Prison Construction & Operations.

OFFICES: Capitol, (916) 445-6083; district, 1035 Detroit Ave., 200, Concord, 94518, (415) 689-1973, 420 W. Third, Antioch, 94509, (415) 754-3011; 330 25th

St., 2, Richmond, 94804, (415) 236-3620; 2680 Bishop Drive, Suite 105, San Ramon, 94583, (415) 830-2871.

REGISTRATION: 53.3% D; 36.6% R

1988 CAMPAIGN: Boatwright – D   63%
Pollacek – R   37%

RATINGS:

AFL	PIRG	CLCV	NOW	CTA	HAC	CofC	CFB	NRA
83%	57%	94%	58%	S	89%	24%	57%	57%

KEY VOTES:

Divest S. Africa:	YES	Insurance reform:	YES	Child sick leave:	–
Assault gun ban:	YES	Parent consent abortion:	YES	Ban AIDS discrim:	YES
Clean Air Act:	YES	Ban insur donations:	YES	Extend death penalty:	YES
Lmt product tort:	–	End mob home rent cont:	YES	Ban offshore oil:	YES

8th Senate District

Quentin L. Kopp (independent)

Starting in San Francisco generally south of Market Street, this district takes in many of the city's older neighborhoods, the slums surrounding Hunter's Point, and stretches to the fog-shrouded suburb of Pacifica. Moving south down the peninsula, the district includes upscale Burlingame and Hillsborough, and the middle-class bedroom communities of South Francisco, Milbrae, Daly City and part of San Mateo.

Heavily Democratic, this district is as sure a bet for Democrats as there can be in politics, which is to say strange things can happen. The Assembly's "Lead-foot" Lou Papan (so named for his propensity for speeding tickets) thought he was such a shoe-in for winning the seat in 1986 that he had practically picked

Quentin L. Kopp

out his new office when longtime Sen. John Foran retired. But Papan, also sometimes called "The Enforcer," blew it. Republicans, mortified at the prospect of having the highly partisan Papan in the Senate, deserted their own candidate and threw their money behind San Francisco Supervisor Quentin Kopp, who entered the fray as an independent.

Kopp had run unsuccessfully for mayor in 1979 and had toyed with other political prospects over the years, becoming a fixture in San Francisco politics.

In the 1986 race, Papan mailed campaign pieces criticizing Kopp for appearing at a club that excludes Jews. But Papan did not count on one thing: Kopp is Jewish. The Bay Area Jewish community raised a howl, Papan apologized and lost the race.

Kopp has always been more interesting in San Francisco politics than in Sacramento. His scraps with Dianne Feinstein are legion. In fact, his scraps with nearly every San Francisco political figure from Willie Brown on down are legion. In March 1987, Kopp hinted around that he might (again) run for mayor with typical Kopp elocution: "Many people are importuning me to make the race." Instead, one of his aides managed the mayoral campaign of San Francisco Examiner columnist Warren Hinkel.

In the state Capitol, Kopp is viewed as a bit of drudge, nitpicking at bills and discovering parliamentary rules at inconvenient moments. With a voice like Walter Matthau's, his pompous allegiance to his alma mater, Dartmouth, leaves a number of his public university educated colleagues flat. Still, he has shown a shrewdness in his short tenure in Sacramento.

Although still registered as an independent, Kopp votes with the Democrats on leadership issues and a number of key budgetary matters. His sharpest move earned him a powerful post – and the wrath of the Deukmejian administration. A day before the 1988 confirmation vote on Dan Lungren as state treasurer, Kopp said he was behind the Deukmejian appointee all the way. On the day of the vote, Kopp switched, providing one of the last nails in Lungren's coffin and earning himself the gratitude of Senate President Pro Tem David Roberti. Democrat Wadie Deddeh, however, voted for Lungren and found himself stripped of the powerful chairmanship of the Transportation Committee. Kopp got Deddeh's job.

As a senator, Kopp has continually pushed for an early presidential primary date and been defeated at each outing. He also pushed a bill to ban transfers of campaign funds between candidates and limit donations. When that bill was defeated, Kopp joined forces with Republican Assemblyman Ross Johnson and Democratic Sen. Joe Montoya, and the three wrote the bill into Proposition 73. That initiative was approved by the voters in June 1988 and has provided no end of confusion in California's campaign laws.

PERSONAL: elected 1986; born Aug. 11, 1928, in Syracuse, N.Y.; home, San Francisco; USAF 1952-1954; education, B.A. government & business Dartmouth College; J.D. Harvard University; wife, Mara; children, Shepard, Bradley and Jennifer; Jewish.

CAREER: lawyer; San Francisco Board of Supervisors 1972-1986.

COMMITTEES: Transportation (chair); Housing & Urban Affairs; Local Government; Revenue & Taxation; Toxics & Public Safety Management. SELECT: AIDS; Planning for Calif. Growth; Small Business Enterprises; Upper Sacramento Valley Economic, Resource & Rangeland Issues.

OFFICES: Capitol, (916) 445-0503; district, 363 El Camino Real, 205, South San Francisco, 94080, (415) 952-5666.

REGISTRATION: 63.8% D; 22.2% R

1986 CAMPAIGN: Kopp – independent 47%
                        Papan – D   46%
                        Gray – R   8%

RATINGS: AFL PIRG CLCV NOW CTA HAC CofC CFB NRA
67% 93% 90% 75% S 89% 28% 42% 14%
KEY VOTES:

	Insurance reform:	YES	Child sick leave:	NO
Assault gun ban: YES	Parent consent abortion:	YES	Ban AIDS discrim:	YES
Clean Air Act: YES	Ban insure donations:	YES	Extend death penalty:	–
Lmt product tort: NO	End mob home rent cont: YES	Ban offshore oil:	YES

9th Senate District

Nicholas C. Petris (D)

Lining the middle section San Francisco Bay's eastern shoreline, the 9th Senate District takes in a polyglot
that includes the affluent, white Piedmont hills, the intensely poor black neighborhoods of Oakland and the
zany leftist environs of Berkeley and its University of
California campus. The district includes parts of
Alameda County, the one county where Tom Bradley
did well in his rematch with George Deukmejian in the
1986 race for governor. Stretching over the Berkeley
hills, the district includes the Contra Costa County
bedroom communities of Lafayette, Orinda and Moraga. The district is more than one-third black.

Democrat Nicholas Petris, one of the last unbending
liberals in the Capitol, is the only senator this district has

Nicholas C. Petris

known since the inception of the full-time Legislature in 1966. For years, the silver-
haired, courtly Petris has railed against growers for their treatment of farm workers;
pushed, without success, bills requiring warning signs in fields where pesticides
have been sprayed; and championed the rights of criminal defendants, mental
patients, the poor and the elderly. And he is a vocal champion of the state's
influential trial lawyers, standing against all efforts to tighten the state's "deep
pockets" tort liability laws, efforts he sees as victimizing consumers. Petris has one
characteristic rare in a Legislature of plodding speakers – Petris is eloquent.

The Deukmejian years have not been kind to Petris. It has been two decades since
Petris authored landmark legislation, like the Lanterman-Petris-Short Act that
brought major changes to the state's mental-health system, and the post-Proposition
13 world is not receptive to pleas to spend more on health care and education.

The cantankerous right-wing Republican Sen. Bill Richardson, now retired,
once claimed that Petris pulled the strings of Senate President Pro Tem David
Roberti. Although that's a vast overstatement, Petris' influence in keeping the
Senate Democrats left of center should not be underestimated. He still uses his
position on the Judiciary Committee as a bully pulpit and sits on the all-powerful
Rules Committee. Beyond policy matters, one of Petris' major interests is Greece.

He quotes from the Greek classics during his floor speeches and serves as the unofficial leader of the equally unofficial caucus of Greek-American legislators, often authoring resolutions that support that nation in its squabbles with Turkey.

PERSONAL: elected 1966; born Feb. 25, 1923, in Oakland, Calif.; home, Oakland; education, B.A. UC Berkeley, J.D. Stanford University; Army 1943-1946 WWII; wife, Anna S. Vlahos; no children; Greek Orthodox.

CAREER: lawyer, Assembly 1958.

COMMITTEES: Budget & Fiscal Review, and budget subcommittee 1 – education (chair); Housing & Urban Affairs; Industrial Relations; Judiciary; Revenue & Taxation; Rules. SELECT: Border Issues, Drug Trafficking and Contraband; Calif. Wine Industry; Substance Abuse. JOINT: Rules; Quincentennial of the Voyages of Columbus ; Legislative Budget; Review of the Master Plan for Higher Education.

OFFICES: Capitol, 445-6577; district, 1111 Jackson St. 7016, Oakland, 94607, (415) 464-1333.

REGISTRATION: 66.9% D; 21% R

1988 CAMPAIGN: Petris – D   75%

       Henson – R   21%

       Evans – P&F   4%

RATINGS:

AFL	PIRG	CLCV	NOW	CTA	HAC	CofC	CFB	NRA
94%	100%	100%	75%	G	78%	16%	14%	0%

KEY VOTES:

Divest S. Africa:	YES	Insurance reform:	YES	Child sick leave:	YES
Assault gun ban:	YES	Parent consent abortion:	NO	Ban AIDS discrim:	–
Clean Air Act:	YES	Ban insure donations:	NO	Extend death penalty:	NO
Lmt product tort:	–	End mob home rent cont:	YES	Ban offshore oil:	YES

10th Senate District

William Lockyer (D)

Taking in the San Francisco Bay's eastern shoreline south of Oakland, this Alameda County district includes the middle-class cities of San Leandro, Fremont and Hayward before extending over the hills to the Livermore Valley, with its housing tracts and nuclear weapons lab. Although it is a Democratic district, it has a conservative bent.

Democrat William Lockyer won the seat in 1982 after serving a decade in the Assembly. He had earlier worked as an aide to one of the Legislature's most powerful figures of the 1960s, Assemblyman Robert Crown.

Lockyer, as chairman of the Senate Judiciary Committee, has been a major force in the middle of the big issues of the last few sessions, including repeal of the business inventory tax, abortion, the death penalty and gun control.

Lockyer was among the clique of lawmakers and lobbyists who drafted a peace pact between major economic forces on a napkin at Frank Fat's restaurant two days before the end of the legislative session in September 1987 – a fabled meeting that culminated months of negotiations between doctors, lawyers and insurance companies over the state's liability laws. Lockyer got the related bill bearing his name through the Senate with little difficulty; Speaker Willie Brown ramrodded it through the Assembly over the strenuous objections of several liberal Democrats. Lockyer proudly displayed the napkin on the Senate floor.

In the spring of 1989, Lockyer presided over the heated hearings on Senate President Pro Tem David **William Lockyer** Roberti's bill to restrict semiautomatic assault weapons. Lockyer waffled for weeks, voted against the bill in committee, then voted for it in the Senate.

Lockyer can be charming, though sometimes ponderous, and his behavior is often erratic. His temper, when it flares, has gotten him in more trouble than most – and kept Bay Area headline writers employed. During a particularly tedious committee hearing in 1985, he cut short fellow Democratic Sen. Diane Watson of Los Angeles, leaving her sputtering, "Can I finish my thought?" Lockyer retorted, "Well, if you had a thought it would be great," and added that he was fed up with her "mindless blather." Lockyer later apologized, but Watson has barely spoken to him since. In June 1989, Lockyer barged into a private meeting between Roberti and a handful of other senators working out which big-ticket bills would move out of the Appropriations Committee. To their wonderment, Lockyer protested that he wanted a chance to make a pitch for his bills.

Lockyer once told the Oakland Tribune, "I would like people to know that I am a lovable eccentric and not a dysfunctional, strange one."

PERSONAL: elected 1982; born May 8, 1941, in Oakland, Calif.; home, Hayward; education, B.A. political science UC Berkeley, teaching credential CSU Hayward, J.D. McGeorge; divorced; daughter, Lisa; Episcopalian.

CAREER: teacher; school board member; legislative assistant to Assemblyman Bob Crown 1968-1973; Assembly 1973; passed bar examination 1988.

COMMITTEES: Judiciary (chair); Appropriations; Elections; Governmental Organization; Industrial Relations; Revenue & Taxation; Toxics & Public Safety Management. SELECT: Infant & Child Care & Development; Substance Abuse.

OFFICES: Capitol, (916) 445-6671; district, 22300 Foothill Blvd., 415, Hayward, 94541, (415) 582-8800; 4725 Thornton Ave., 104, Fremont, 94536, (415) 790-3605; 6140 Stoneridge Mall Road, 515, Pleasanton, 94566, (415) 847-6041.

REGISTRATION: 55.9% D; 32.1% R

1986 CAMPAIGN: Lockyer – D   71%
                Bergondy – R   29%

RATINGS:

AFL	PIRG	CLCV	NOW	CTA	HAC	CofC	CFB	NRA
94%	100%	100%	83%	G	89%	20%	42%	0%

KEY VOTES:

Divest S. Africa:	YES	Insurance reform:	YES
Assault gun ban:	YES	Parent consent abortion:	–
Clean Air Act:	YES	Ban insure donations:	NO
Lmt product tort:	YES	End mob home rent cont:	YES

Child sick leave:	YES
Ban AIDS discrim:	YES
Extend death penalty:	YES
Ban offshore oil:	YES

11th Senate District

Rebecca Q. Morgan (R)

Rebecca Q. Morgan

On its western shore, the 11th Senate District includes Half Moon Bay and then loops over the San Andreas fault to the bedroom communities of the San Francisco peninsula – San Mateo, Belmont, San Carlos, Redwood City, Woodside. Dropping into the San Francisco Bay's basin, the district includes California's fabled Silicon Valley, with its microchip industries, like Intel, that have grown up around Stanford University. Voters here are business oriented, but they lean to the left in their outlook and are decidedly environmentalist. The area has produced Republicans like maverick Pete McCloskey, moderate Ed Zschau and Shirley Temple Black.

The success of the Silicon Valley has come with a price. Once thought of as "clean industry," high-tech manufacturing has proved to be a big polluter. The valley holds a number of toxic waste sites on the federal Superfund cleanup list. Fairchild Camera, among the first discovered, used highly toxic solvents in its processing that leaked into the underground water supplies.

Republican Rebecca Morgan is very much a product of her district. Her husband, James, is a millionaire president of Applied Materials Inc., one of the Silicon Valley firms on the toxic cleanup list. The San Jose-based Silicon Valley Toxics Coalition once accused Morgan of having a conflict of interest by chairing an important toxics subcommittee in the Senate. Nonsense, she replied.

Morgan has steered an independent course, sometimes going against the Republican grain in the Senate by voting to uphold abortion rights and restrict semiautomatic assault weapons. Morgan made her own quiet protest against the U.S. Supreme Court's 1989 abortion rulings by removing from her office wall an autographed portrait of Associate Justice Anthony Kennedy.

She is generally popular among her colleagues, although she is not very good on her feet and is noted for missing some of the nuances. She has a reputation for vote switching during roll calls – not out of any scheming but because she did not understand the issue. And she is one of the biggest whiners in the Legislature, incessantly complaining that the press does not cover all of her important legislation.

Morgan has successfully focused on education issues. She won passage of a bill to tighten restrictions on "diploma mills" in 1989 and has pushed for a $207 million pilot project in the schools. Gov. Deukmejian signed into law her 1988 measure that appropriated $29.9 million in transit improvements statewide. With her moderate image, her access to business financing and her elegant demeanor, she may well have a statewide political future ahead of her.

PERSONAL: elected 1984; born Dec. 4, 1938, in Hanover, N.H.; home, Los Altos Hills; education, B.S. home economics Cornell University, M.A. in business administration Stanford University; husband, James C. Morgan; children, Jeff and Mary; Protestant.

CAREER: teacher; banker; school board member; Santa Clara County Board of Supervisors 1981-1984.

COMMITTEES: Education; Budget & Fiscal Review; Energy & Public Utilities; Revenue & Taxation; Transportation. SELECT: Infant & Child Care & Development (chair); Substance Abuse. SPECIAL: UC Admissions. JOINT: Review of the Master Plan for Higher Education; Science & Technology.

OFFICES: Capitol, (916) 445-6747; district, 830 Menlo Ave., 200, Menlo Park, 94025, (415) 321-1451.

REGISTRATION: 45.8% D; 41.2% R

1988 CAMPAIGN: Morgan – R   61%
Nolan – D   36%
Olson – L   3%

RATINGS:

AFL	PIRG	CLCV	NOW	CTA	HAC	CofC	CFB	NRA
40%	64%	75%	67%	G*	100%	40%	42%	43%

KEY VOTES:

Divest S. Africa:	NO	Insurance reform:	NO	Child sick leave:	YES
Assault gun ban:	YES	Parent consent abortion:	NO	Ban AIDS discrim:	YES
Clean Air Act:	YES	Ban insure donations:	NO	Extend death penalty:	YES
Lmt product tort:	–	End mob home rent cont:	–	Ban offshore oil:	YES

12th Senate District
Daniel A. McCorquodale (D)

This district – created by Democratic reapportionment craftsmen in 1982 to maximize the party's position – straddles two counties on either side of the Pacific Coast Range, one urban, the other rural.

To the east lies Stanislaus County, a mostly flat, agriculture-dominated region that includes the cities of Modesto, Turlock and Ceres. The area is increasingly

becoming urbanized, epitomizing the land-use balanc-
ing act between farmland and subdivisions facing much
of the rest of the San Joaquin Valley. To the west, in the
Santa Clara Valley, the district takes in the urbanized
Silicon Valley bedroom communities of Campbell,
Milpitas and the southern third of San Jose.

Representing both sides is Dan McCorquodale, a
large, shambling Democrat who lacks flash but is earning a reputation for class. The ex-Marine had an early
political career in the San Diego area, once serving as
the mayor of Chula Vista, but changed direction after
his first wife committed suicide, abandoning politics to
champion programs for the disabled.

Dan McCorquodale

McCorquodale returned to political life after relocat-
ing to the San Jose area and developed the technique, which he still practices, of
personally walking every precinct during every campaign. It's a good technique for
the naturally friendly McCorquodale.

On occasion, however, McCorquodale can get tough. He has ordered sergeants-
at-arms to remove outspoken witnesses from hearings. He has provided key votes
on bills that would help counties at the expense of cities. On occasion he has angered
environmentalists, though in 1988 they named him conservationist of the year. He
is generally more liberal than his district as a whole.

In 1982, McCorquodale narrowly defeated incumbent Republican Sen. Dan
O'Keefe. In 1986, Republicans tried bouncing back by waging a $1.3 million
campaign to defeat McCorquodale. But he worked hard and handily won a bruising
re-election battle over his GOP challenger, Santa Clara County Supervisor Tom
Legan. The victory was a bright spot for Senate President Pro Tem David Roberti,
who had lost a pair of Democratic races elsewhere. Shortly thereafter,
McCorquodale benefited from being on the winning side of an internal political
struggle and was named chairman of the Natural Resources and Wildlife Committee. He is expected to continue pushing environmental causes in the area of parks,
offshore oil drilling, timber harvesting, fisheries management and clean air.

PERSONAL: elected 1982; born Dec. 17, 1934, in Longville, La.; home, San
Jose; education, B.A. education San Diego State University; USMC 1953-1956;
wife, Jean; children, Daniel, Michael and Sharon; Protestant.

CAREER: special-education teacher; Chula Vista City Council and mayor;
Santa Clara County Board of Supervisors.

COMMITTEES: Natural Resources & Wildlife (chair); Transportation (vice
chair); Agriculture & Water Resources; Business & Professions; Health & Human
Services; Insurance, Claims & Corporations; Local Government; Public Employment and Retirement. SELECT: Citizen Participation in Government (chair);
Border Issues, Drug Trafficking & Contraband; Calif. Wine Industry; Forest

Resources; Maritime Industry; Mobile Homes; Small Business Enterprises. SPE-CIAL: Neighborhood Violence (chair). JOINT: Organized Crime & Gang Violence; Public Pension Fund Investments; State's Economy.

OFFICES: Capitol, (916) 445-3104; district, 4 N. 2nd St., 590, San Jose, 95113, (408) 277-1470; 1020 15th St, Suite B, Modesto, 95354, (209) 576-6231.

REGISTRATION: 52.7% D; 36.3% R

1986 CAMPAIGN: McCorquodale – D 56%
　　　　　　　　Legan – R 44%

RATINGS:	AFL	PIRG	CLCV	NOW	CTA	HAC	CofC	CFB	NRA
	97%	100%	95%	92%	G*	100%	20%	28%	43%

KEY VOTES:

Divest S. Africa:	YES	Insurance reform:	YES	Child sick leave:	YES
Assault gun ban:	YES	Parent consent abortion:	NO	Ban AIDS discrim:	YES
Clean Air Act:	YES	Ban insure donations:	NO	Extend death penalty:	YES
Lmt product tort:	YES	End mob home rent cont:	YES	Ban offshore oil:	YES

13th Senate District

Alfred E. Alquist (D)

Lying in the core of Santa Clara County, the 13th Senate District takes in the heart of San Jose and portions of Santa Clara, Sunnyvale and Mountain View. The area has mirrored the transformation and growth of California in the last 30 years. Where once there were orchards and canneries, now there are housing tracts, high-tech industries and traffic.

Democrat Alfred Alquist, the oldest member of the Legislature, has served long enough to roll with those changes. Elected to the part-time Assembly in 1962, Alquist was among the first class of "full-time" legislators elected to the Senate in 1966.

Alquist has had a generally successful career, though one with plenty of ups and downs. His landmark legis-

Alfred E. Alquist

lation has established earthquake construction standards for hospitals, and created the Seismic Safety Commission and the Energy Commission. Alquist has had his stamp on every major piece of earthquake preparedness legislation of the last three decades. He could take grim satisfaction in knowing that many of the laws he authored doubtlessly saved lives in the Oct. 17, 1989, Bay Area earthquake.

However, Alquist has become the Andrei Gromyko of the Legislature – he is iron-faced, publicly devoid of humor (although wryly funny in private), well past his prime, but still a force not to be crossed lightly.

At his peak, Alquist was chairman of the all-powerful Appropriations Committee. But in 1986, he agreed to relinquish his post to mollify critics of David Roberti within his own party. Roberti broke up his committee, splitting it in two. Alquist became chairman of a new Budget and Fiscal Review Committee, a panel chiefly responsible for the Senate version of the state budget each year. Alquist kept his imprint on the immensely complicated state spending plan, but he lost power over the daily workings of legislation, which go before the reduced Appropriations Committee, now chaired by Sen. Bob Presley. Each year Alquist and Assembly Ways and Means Chairman John Vasconcellos take turns chairing the budget conference committee, where the final legislative shape is given to the budget.

Alquist is known for a stormy temper, much in evidence in 1985, when he had a fabled shouting match with enfant terrible Assemblyman Steve Peace over an Alquist bill to establish a nuclear waste disposal compact with other states. Exactly what was said is still disputed; some witnesses (including Sen. Ken Maddy) claim Peace called Alquist a "senile old pedophile" while thrusting his right index finger toward him. Peace claims that he (only) called the elder senator a "pitiful little creature." Whomever was right was unimportant; an outraged Senate responded by killing all of Peace's remaining bills for the year.

Though Alquist has authored his share of major legislation, he has also had his share of petty, narrow-interest bills. In 1985, Alquist, an ex-railroad employee, won passage of a bill that would have required freight trains longer than 1,500 feet to have a caboose. Deukmejian vetoed it.

Alquist's wife, Mai, died in 1989. Ever outspoken, and a character in her own right in the halls of the Legislature, Mai Alquist had been her husband's political mentor and confidant for years. Without her, he may well choose to retire at the end of this term if not sooner.

PERSONAL: elected 1966; born Aug. 2, 1908, in Memphis, Tenn.; home, Santa Clara; education, attended Southwestern University; Army WWII; widower; son, Alan Russell; Protestant.

CAREER: railroad yardmaster; transportation supervisor; Assembly 1962.

COMMITTEES: Budget & Fiscal Review (chair); Constitutional Amendments (vice chair); Appropriations; Bonded Indebtedness & Methods of Financing; Governmental Organization. SELECT: Calif. Wine Industry (chair); Maritime Industry; Pacific Rim; Tourism & Aviation. SPECIAL: Neighborhood Violence; Solid & Hazardous Waste; JOINT: Fire, Police, Emergency & Disaster Services; Legislative Audit; Legislative Budget.

OFFICES: Capitol, (916) 445-9740; district, 100 Paseo de San Antonio, 209, San Jose, 95113, (408) 286-8318.

REGISTRATION: 54.5% D; 32.2% R

1988 CAMPAIGN: Alquist – D   65%

Bertolet – R   31%

Inks – L   4%

RATINGS:

AFL	PIRG	CLCV	NOW	CTA	HAC	CofC	CFB	NRA
88%	69%	95%	84%	G	89%	24%	42%	14%

KEY VOTES:

Divest S. Africa: YES	Insurance reform: YES	Child sick leave: YES
Assault gun ban: YES	Parent consent abortion: NO	Ban AIDS discrim: YES
Clean Air Act: YES	Ban insure donations: YES	Extend death penalty: NO
Lmt product tort: –	End mob home rent cont: YES	Ban offshore oil: –

14th Senate District

Kenneth L. Maddy (R)

Kenneth L. Maddy

This sprawling district takes in a big chunk of the farm-dominated San Joaquin Valley as well as some of the most scenic areas in the Sierra Nevada and Pacific Coast. From Yosemite on the east, to the Carmel Valley on the west and south to the northern tip of Santa Barbara County, the district includes all of four counties and parts of three others and was tailored to the man who has represented it for the past decade, Republican Ken Maddy. Republicans outnumber Democrats in three of those counties: Monterey, San Luis Obispo and Santa Barbara. But Democrats dominate in the remaining four counties: Madera, Mariposa, Merced and Fresno County, which includes the western part of the city of Fresno.

Clearly, Maddy has won successive elections by garnering support from many Democrats, which is not uncommon in the San Joaquin Valley. A political moderate who is popular with colleagues on both sides of the aisle, Maddy has parlayed his agricultural roots, concerns about health care and lifelong love for horses and horse racing into legislative successes.

Mixed in along the way, came tough campaigns and a couple of political and personal setbacks. In 1978, while still an assemblyman, he made a bid for governor with a campaign that got him nearly a half-million votes despite being an unknown entity from Fresno. And he made a couple of major political mistakes, like coming out against Proposition 13, which passed overwhelmingly, and admitting that he had twice smoked marijuana.

Having given up his Assembly seat to run for governor, Maddy was out of politics for a few months. But the resignation of Sen. George Zenovich quickly brought him back, and he won a hard-fought special election to fill the seat.

Handsome and articulate, Maddy saw his star rise quickly in the Senate, especially since his longtime pal, Bill Campbell, was the minority leader. Maddy became caucus chairman, the No. 2 party position, but he and Campbell lost a power struggle several years later to a conservative faction. In 1987, they returned in a countercoup, and Maddy became minority leader.

Maddy has been on everyone's list of rising Republican stars since his better-than-expected shot at the governorship in 1978. But while he has toyed privately and publicly with seeking statewide office again, he's never taken the plunge, except to apply for a gubernatorial appointment as state treasurer. He was under some pressure from supporters to run for governor in 1990 after George Deukmejian announced he would retire, but finally decided against a run and now seems content to end his active political career in the Senate. He has said publicly he intends to retire when he's 60 – or when there's a Maddy-supported highway bypass through Livingston, site of the only traffic light on Highway 99 in California and headquarters of the Foster Farms chicken empire Maddy now shares. Capitol insiders speculate that Maddy will seek another four-year term in 1990, then retire after it's completed.

Maddy's first marriage foundered after he won his Senate seat, and he later married the wealthy heiress to the Foster Farms chicken fortune, Norma Foster. That gave him the wherewithal to pursue his intense passion for thoroughbred horse racing. He also has emerged as a major player in the fashioning of horse racing legislation, including bills that have authorized off-track wagering in the state.

The Maddys also have become A-list socialites, not only in Sacramento and the San Joaquin Valley but in the playgrounds of the wealthy along Orange County's gold coast, where they maintain a weekend residence. And because of his good looks, money and political position, Maddy has become a star campaign fund-raiser in his own right for Republican candidates and causes.

PERSONAL: elected 1979 (special election); born May 22, 1934, in Santa Monica, Calif.; home, Fresno and ranch east of Modesto; USAF 1957-1960; education, B.S. agriculture CSU Fresno, J.D. UCLA; wife, Norma Foster; children, Deanna Hose, Don, Marilyn Geis, and stepchildren Jayne Waters, Ron Foster, Laurie Wesenberg, Suzi Sutherland, Janet Foster and Carrie Foster; Protestant.

CAREER: lawyer; horse breeder; Assembly 1970.

COMMITTEES: Health and Human Services (vice chair); Constitutional Amendments; Governmental Organization. SELECT: AIDS; Business Development; Calif. Wine Industry; Fairs & Rural Issues; Governmental Efficiency; Infant & Child Care & Development; Pacific Rim. JOINT: Revision of the Penal Code (chair); Legislative Audit; Arts; Quincentennial of the Voyages of Columbus; Refugee Resettlement, International Migration & Cooperative Development.

OFFICES: Capitol, (916) 445-9600; district, 3475 W. Shaw Ave., 105, Fresno, 93711, (209) 445-5567; 19901 W. First St., 2, Hilmar, 95324, (209) 667-3781; 895 Napa Ave., Suite A-6, Morro Bay, 93442, (805) 772-1287.

REGISTRATION: 50.6% D; 39.1% R

1986 CAMPAIGN: Maddy – R   69%

                LeSage – D   31%

RATINGS: AFL PIRG CLCV NOW CTA HAC CofC CFB NRA
44% 36% 67% 25% S 67% 44% 57% 71%
KEY VOTES:

Divest S. Africa: YES	Insurance reform:	NO	Child sick leave:	NO
Assault gun ban: NO	Parent consent abortion: YES	Ban AIDS discrim: –
Clean Air Act: –	Ban insure donations: NO	Extend death penalty: YES
Lmt product tort: YES	End mob home rent cont: YES	Ban offshore oil: –

15th Senate District
Rose Ann Vuich (D)

Agriculture is synonymous with this rural district in the southeastern corner of the San Joaquin Valley. The district encompasses all of Tulare County and the eastern part of Fresno County, including the eastern part of the city of Fresno.

Rose Ann Vuich

Without ever having set foot in the Capitol, Rose Ann Vuich in 1976 became the first woman elected to the state Senate. She had entered the race almost on a dare when the expected Democratic candidate backed out the day before the filing deadline. She upset the GOP nominee, longtime Assemblyman Ernest Mobley, by helping create the perception that he had done little to help Fresno get state money for a long-awaited crosstown freeway.

Vuich continues to practice the politics of local issues. The daughter of Yugoslav immigrants, she works her district religiously and capitalizes on strong ethnic and social ties throughout the region. Since arriving in Sacramento, she has easily won re-election, and in 1988 she ran unopposed. As she says at every district speech, the 15th District is Vuich country.

As the Senate's first woman member, Vuich handled her status with aplomb. She sought a woman's restroom for the Senate, and when a speaker would refer to the "gentlemen of the Senate," she'd ring a little bell. As the novelty of her situation faded (there are now four women senators) Vuich settled into her self-defined roles as advocate for the district, defender of agriculture and chairwoman of the Senate's banking committee.

Considered to be independent and strong-willed, Vuich has scratched out a reputation as a plain-speaking, tell-me-what-it-means legislator known to say, "All right, I won't vote" if pressed to take a position before all her questions have been answered.

She also once called herself "probably the best Democratic vote" Republicans have in the Senate. But that changed when her independence crossed paths with

Gov. Deukmejian. She refused to support two of the governor's bottom-line issues: a Los Angeles prison bill and his initial nominee for state treasurer, Dan Lungren. As a result, she earned a position on the governor's enemies list, and he has attacked her publicly, both in her home district and in the press.

With a campaign war chest approaching the half-million dollar level (a reserve she's built because she does not accept much money from state Democrats, nor dole out any among her colleagues), Vuich is a sure bet to win again in 1992, should she so choose to run. But her age and the recent health problems facing her brother, a lifelong roommate and de facto political consultant, may play more in her decision whether to run for a fifth term.

PERSONAL: elected 1976; born Jan. 27, 1927, in Cutler, Calif.; home, Dinuba; education, completed a business college accounting course; unmarried; Serbian Orthodox.

CAREER: owner of accounting firm.

COMMITTEES: Banking & Commerce (chair); Agriculture and Water Resources; Budget and Fiscal Review; budget subcommittee 2 — justice, corrections, resources & agriculture (chair); Transportation. SELECT: Fairs & Rural Issues (chair); Calif. Wine Industry; Pacific Rim. SPECIAL: Solid & Hazardous Waste (chair); JOINT: Rules (vice chair); Arts; Fairs Allocation & Classification.

OFFICES: Capitol, (916) 445-4641; district, 120 W. Tulare St., Dinuba, 93618, (209) 591-5005; 124 W. Shaw, Suite B, Fresno, 93704, (209) 445-5541.

REGISTRATION: 51.4% D; 39.1% R

1988 CAMPAIGN: Vuich – D   100%
no opponent

RATINGS:

AFL	PIRG	CLCV	NOW	CTA	HAC	CofC	CFB	NRA
65%	79%	81%	83%	G	89%	44%	85%	43%

KEY VOTES:

Divest S. Africa:	YES	Insurance reform:	YES	Child sick leave:	YES
Assault gun ban:	YES	Parent consent abortion:	YES	Ban AIDS discrim:	YES
Clean Air Act:	YES	Ban insure donations:	YES	Extend death penalty:	YES
Lmt product tort:	YES	End mob home rent cont:	YES	Ban offshore oil:	YES

16th Senate District

Donald A. Rogers (R)

With its population centered in Bakersfield, this expansive agricultural district is one of the nation's leading producers of food and oil. It covers Kings and Kern counties; the Mojave Valley and the high desert area of San Bernardino County, including much of Barstow; parts of Los Angeles County, including Lancaster, Palmdale and the eastern section of the Antelope Valley; and pieces of Pasadena (and its Rose Bowl) and Altadena.

After the 1980 census, the district was gerrymandered to take in more Democratic voters south of the Tehachapis near Pasadena as a desperate effort to save one of the last Democratic seats in a strongly conservative, increasingly Republican region.

The gerrymander worked for one election, saving veteran Democratic Sen. Walter Stiern's seat in 1982. But when Stiern retired four years later, Don Rogers, a former city councilman and four-term assemblyman from Bakersfield, won the seat.

It was one of the few victories in the GOP's long-range strategy to regain control of the Senate before the next round of reapportionment after the 1990 census. The victory helped shore up Rogers' credentials. In his two previous elections for the Assembly, he had come

Donald A. Rogers

within a sliver of losing to a Democrat. But voters, many of them conservative descendants of the Oklahoma migration, stuck with the Louisiana-born man who speaks with a twang and identifies with the oil industry through his career as a geologist.

The day Rogers arrived in Sacramento he introduced a bill to repeal the inheritance tax, which had forced some of his constituents to sell off their farmland. Frustrated when it got nowhere after 2 1/2 years, Rogers launched an initiative drive that placed the measure on the 1982 ballot. It passed with one of the largest majorities ever for an initiative.

Since then, Rogers has concentrated on bills dealing with agriculture, business and water. One recent measure called for shock absorber-type bases for certain buildings to help prevent damage in the event of earthquakes. Another measure allowed lower fat levels in eggnog, and was passed as an emergency measure so milk producers could capitalize on an upcoming holiday season. An ex-Marine, Rogers also pushed for special license plates for Pearl Harbor survivors and was a vocal opponent of a ban on semiautomatic assault weapons.

He didn't endear himself to his Democratic colleagues when he mailed a fund-raising appeal billing himself as the "commanding officer and founder of the Republican Air Force." The plea went on: "The RAF has remained high above the quagmire of Socialism and has effectively stayed the evils constantly trying to invade the California Legislature." It was a tongue-in-cheek allusion not only to Rogers' conservatism but his avocation of flying, one he shares with several other Republican legislators.

PERSONAL: elected 1986; born April 22, 1928, in Natchitoches, La.; home, Bakersfield; USMC 1946-1948; education, B.S. geology Louisiana State University; wife, Marilyn L. Miller; children, Mallorie, Grayson and Douglas; Mormon.

CAREER: oil geologist; owner of a geological consultant firm and partner in a petroleum firm; Bakersfield City Council 1973-1978; Assembly 1978.

COMMITTEES: Veterans' Affairs (vice chair); Agriculture & Water Resources; Bonded Indebtedness & Methods of Financing; Natural Resources & Wildlife; Public Employment & Retirement. SELECT: Fairs & Rural Issues.

OFFICES: Capitol, (916) 445-6637; district, 1326 H St., Bakersfield, 93301, (805) 395-2927.

REGISTRATION: 51.5% D; 39.4% R

1986 CAMPAIGN: Rogers – R   52%
　　　　　　　　　J. Young – D   48%

RATINGS:

AFL	PIRG	CLCV	NOW	CTA	HAC	CofC	CFB	NRA
10%	36%	39%	17%	U	67%	68%	71%	100%

KEY VOTES:

Divest S. Africa:	NO	Insurance reform:	NO	Child sick leave:	NO
Assault gun ban:	NO	Parent consent abortion:	YES	Ban AIDS discrim:	–
Clean Air Act:	NO	Ban insure donations:	NO	Extend death penalty:	YES
Lmt product tort:	YES	End mob home rent cont:	YES	Ban offshore oil:	NO

17th Senate District

Henry J. Mello (D)

This is one of the most diverse Senate districts in the state, not only geographically but politically and demographically. It contains some of the state's most beautiful beach communities – Carmel, Monterey, Pacific Grove and Santa Cruz – and some of the state's most productive farmland – Salinas, Watsonville and San Benito County.

The political spectrum ranges from the ultraliberal Santa Cruz to the conservative farm-area politics of Hollister. Its residents include the wealthy and movie stars – Clint Eastwood was briefly mayor of Carmel – as well as burgeoning Hispanic populations in cities like Salinas, Soledad and Watsonville.

Henry J. Mello

Henry Mello, a farmer and businessman, has attempted to walk a tightrope in response to his diverse constituency. He is a moderate and a bit of a nervous one at that. He has had a tendency on some controversial issues to try to give a little to each side. In 1989, for example, he voted in favor of a virtual ban of semiautomatic military-style assault weapons despite heavy pressure in his district from members of the National Rifle Association. Later in the year, when a key vote came up to require purchasers of rifles to wait 15 days between the time they buy rifles and the time they can be picked up, Mello, again under pressure from the NRA, called the waiting period "outrageous" and voted against it.

Mello's moderate course has made him, in effect, the swing vote on the five-person Senate Rules Committee, a powerful panel that decides to which committees legislation will be sent. The committee can also block confirmation of gubernatorial appointees. Mello generally sides with the two liberal Democrats on the committee, but on occasion has sided with the two Republicans.

One area of particular legislative interest for Mello has been senior citizens. He carried a bill to create the Senior Legislature, an annual gathering of senior citizen delegates from the throughout the state at which seniors set their legislative priorities. And Mello has frequently carried bills that the Senior Legislature has proposed, measures ranging from housing and day care to lunch programs and nursing homes.

Mello has, on occasion, generated controversy in his district by carrying bills to help local developers and other businesses in ways that some believe might have adverse environmental effects. And he has set himself up to charges that he is the Senate's big spender, having spent $618,022 in state funds in 1987 on his office and staff, more than any other member.

Under the auspices of being Democratic whip, Mello has built a political organization around staffer Larry Sheingold, who is lent out at election time to help embattled incumbents like Sens. Dan McCorquodale and Cecil Green. Sheingold, with his partner Rose King, have built a lucrative political consultancy on the side, and he was dispatched to San Diego to manage the special election of Lucy Killea for an open Senate seat in December 1989.

PERSONAL: elected 1980; born March 27, 1924, in Watsonville, Calif.; home, Watsonville; education, attended Hartnell Junior College; wife, Helen; children, John, Stephen, Michael and Timothy.

CAREER: farmer; Santa Cruz Board of Supervisors 1967-1974; Assembly 1976; Senate Democratic whip.

COMMITTEES: Rules; Agriculture & Water Resources; Banking & Commerce, Energy & Public Utilities; Health & Human Services; Natural Resources & Wildlife. SELECT: Calif. Wine Industry; Business Development; Citizen Participation in Government; Forest Resources; Mobile Homes. JOINT: Arts (chair); Quincentennial of the Voyages of Columbus (chair); Fairs Allocation & Classification; Fisheries & Aquaculture.

OFFICES: Capitol, (916) 445-5843; district, 1200 Aquajito Road, Monterey, 93940, (408) 373-0773; 701 Ocean St., 318A, Santa Cruz, 95060, (408) 425-0401; 240 Church St., 115, Salinas, 93901, (408) 757-4169; 92 Fifth St., Gilroy, 95020, (408) 848-1437.

REGISTRATION: 53.9% D; 33.6% R

1988 CAMPAIGN: Mello – D   71%

Damkar – R   29%

RATINGS:	AFL	PIRG	CLCV	NOW	CTA	HAC	CofC	CFB	NRA
	85%	71%	95%	75%	G	89%	24%	57%	71%

KEY VOTES:

Divest S. Africa:	YES	Insurance reform:	YES	Child sick leave:	YES
Assault gun ban:	YES	Parent consent abortion:	YES	Ban AIDS discrim:	YES
Clean Air Act:	–	Ban insure donations:	NO	Extend death penalty:	YES
Lmt product tort:	–	End mob home rent cont:	–	Ban offshore oil:	YES

18th Senate District

Gary K. Hart (D)

Running along a narrow corridor on the coast from Lompoc to Malibu, the 18th Senate District includes growth-controlled Santa Barbara, Oxnard, Ventura and the laid-back communities surrounding UC Santa Barbara. The district runs along the spine of the low but rugged Santa Ynez Mountains. The district has an environmentalist tilt but also is decidedly upscale and has a low Democratic voter registration, making it an increasingly volatile political battleground.

Gary K. Hart

Democrat Gary K. Hart – he has taken to using his middle initial to distinguish himself from that other Gary Hart – has managed to balance the sometimes conflicting political tendencies of his district. A former teacher, Hart is popular among growth controllers and environmentalists. He has ably chaired the Senate Education Committee and authored numerous dull-but-important education bills, including school bond acts in 1986 and 1988. While many child-care proposals died or were vetoed in 1988, Gov. Deukmejian signed a Hart bill offering state tax credits to employers who establish child-care programs for the use of their employees' children. Many employers are beginning to take advantage of the Hart bill.

Hart has also chaired the Senate Select Committee on AIDS, becoming the Legislature's chief expert on the disease since Art Agnos left the Assembly to become mayor of San Francisco. Hart authored legislation, vetoed by Deukmejian, that would have required AIDS education in the schools, as recommended by then-U.S. Surgeon General C. Everett Koop.

Hart is also a strong environmentalist, and has fought to close and cleanup the Casmalia Resources hazardous waste dump in his district, a site facing a $6 million fine from the U.S. Environmental Protection Agency. Hart's toxics legislation has gotten under the skin of the Deukmejian administration; for example, requiring the Department of Health Services to hold public hearings on the dumps like Casmalia.

When the political infighting gets rough, Hart often bows out–a trait that has contributed to his inability to move into a leadership role. In addition, Hart has become an in-house critic of the Legislature's institutional corruption of campaign contributions-for-bills, but he has avoided alienating his colleagues.

The tall and lanky Hart has grown decidedly bored with the Legislature. He ran for Congress in 1988 in one of the hardest fought congressional contests in the nation, falling less than 1 percentage point short of beating longtime Republican Rep. Robert Lagomarsino. Both national parties threw everything they could muster into the race. Ronald Reagan came down from his ranch in nearby Ed Davis' Senate district to stump for Lagomarsino. In the end, Lagomarsino won but was wounded, and Hart was encouraged to try again. Hart has given every indication that he will give up his state Senate seat in 1990 to run again for Lagomarsino's seat. And if he does, the 18th Senate District will be the site of a titanic partisan struggle because of its even-up political orientation.

PERSONAL: elected 1982; born Aug. 13, 1943, in San Diego, Calif.; home, Santa Barbara; education, B.A. history Stanford University., M.A. education Harvard University; wife, Cary Smith; children, Elissa, Katherine and Laura; Protestant.

CAREER: teacher; Assembly 1974.

COMMITTEES: Education (chair); Natural Resources & Wildlife (vice chair); Constitutional Amendments; Budget & Fiscal Review; Energy & Public Utilities; Transportation. SELECT: AIDS (chair); Border Issues, Drug Trafficking & Contraband; Children & Youth; Substance Abuse. JOINT: Review of the Master Plan for Higher Education (vice chair); Legislative Audit; School Facilities.

OFFICES: Capitol, (916) 445-5405; district, 1216 State St., 507, Santa Barbara, 93101, (805) 966-1766; 801 S. Victoria Ave., 301, Ventura, 93006, (805) 654-4648; 4881 Topanga Canyon Blvd., 202, Woodland Hills, 91364, (818) 716-2646.

REGISTRATION: 47.2% D; 40.4% R

1986 CAMPAIGN: Hart – D   65%
Holmdahl – R   33%
Wood – L   2%

RATINGS:

AFL	PIRG	CLCV	NOW	CTA	HAC	CofC	CFB	NRA
93%	93%	100%	75%	G	100%	20%	28%	0%

KEY VOTES:

Divest S. Africa:	YES	Insurance reform: YES	Child sick leave: YES
Assault gun ban:	YES	Parent consent abortion: NO	Ban AIDS discrim: YES
Clean Air Act:	YES	Ban insure donations: YES	Extend death penalty: –
Lmt product tort:	–	End mob home rent cont: YES	Ban offshore oil: YES

19th Senate District
Ed M. Davis (R)

The canyons and badlands of the northwestern San Fernando Valley hold amusement parks, old citrus groves and Highway 101. The 19th Senate District is made to order for Republicans, with new housing tracts and old money. Ronald

Reagan's ranch is in the district that stretches along the eastern rim of the Santa Ynez Mountains to include most of Santa Barbara and Ventura counties and the Los Angeles County communities of Newhall, Chatsworth and Granada Hills.

Representing the region is Ed Davis, a Republican who seems never to have hesitated to say exactly what he thinks and do exactly as he pleases. It is hard to imagine California politics without him.

As Los Angeles police chief, Davis wanted to hang hijackers at the airport, and he once wore a gag for the TV cameras when Mayor Tom Bradley tried to shut him up. His cops flushed out Patty Hearst's kidnappers by burning down their house.

Ed M. Davis

Liberals shuddered when Davis got elected to the state Senate after an earlier attempt for the U.S. Senate flopped. But in the state Senate, pipe-puffing Davis has followed a more diplomatic course, though he is just as independent. Davis incurred the wrath of conservatives by voting to protect homosexual rights, and he branded as "un-American" those who asked him to refuse support from homosexual groups.

Davis' continued aspirations for the U.S. Senate led to one of the most celebrated fiascoes in recent GOP history. In 1986, he was locked in a multicandidate race for the Republican U.S. Senate nomination. Cross-town rival Rep. Bobbi Fiedler allegedly offered to pay off his campaign debt if he would withdraw from the race. He considered it a bribe offer, and instead of taking the money he reported the incident to Los Angeles District Attorney Ira Reiner, who prosecuted Fiedler under an obscure state law. Davis and Fielder were irreparably damaged by the affair, and Ed Zschau won the nomination. Davis found himself booed at state party conventions and Fiedler beat the rap.

Although such Davisisms get the headlines, he follows a quieter course in the Senate. As a member of the Senate Judiciary Committee, Davis has steadily argued to do away with the state's determinant sentencing laws and return to the indeterminate sentencing procedures that he was familiar with as a police chief. Davis has begun to get a following on the issue. And although he voted against restricting the sale of semiautomatic weapons, Davis scolded lobbyists from the National Rifle Association for their unbending stubbornness on gun issues.

PERSONAL: elected 1980; born Nov. 15, 1916, in Los Angeles, Calif.; home, Santa Clarita; Navy 1942-1945 WWII; education, B.S. public administration USC; wife, Aileen "Bobbie" Trueblood; children, Chris, Michael, Mary Ellen; Episcopalian.

CAREER: chief Los Angeles Police Department; professor.

COMMITTEES: Judiciary (vice chair); Banking & Commerce; Budget & Fiscal Review; Education; Insurance, Claims & Corporations. SELECT: Border

Issues, Drug Trafficking & Contraband; Governmental Efficiency; Motion Picture, TV, Commercial & Recording Industries; Substance Abuse. SPECIAL: UC Admissions. JOINT: Quincentennial of the Voyages of Columbus; Fire, Police, Emergency & Disaster Services; Organized Crime & Gang Violence.

OFFICES: Capitol, (916) 445-8873; district, 11145 Tampa Ave., Suite 21B, Northridge, 91326, (818) 368-1171.

REGISTRATION: 37.2% D; 52.7% R

1988 CAMPAIGN: Davis – R   72%
Martin – D   25%
Starr – L   3%

RATINGS:

AFL	PIRG	CLCV	NOW	CTA	HAC	CofC	CFB	NRA
37%	64%	85%	50%	U	89%	48%	57%	57%

KEY VOTES:

Divest S. Africa:	NO	Insurance reform:	NO	Child sick leave:	NO
Assault gun ban:	NO	Parent consent abortion:	YES	Ban AIDS discrim:	YES
Clean Air Act:	–	Ban insure donations:	YES	Extend death penalty:	YES
Lmt product tort:	YES	End mob home rent cont:	YES	Ban offshore oil:	YES

20th Senate District

Alan E. Robbins (D)

The smog-shrouded eastern San Fernando Valley holds the middle-class bedroom communities of Van Nuys, Reseda, Panorama City, Mission Hills, Pacoima and other towns that blend one into the other. With pockets of Jewish, working-class and upscale voters, the valley votes generally Democratic with a conservative tinge.

When Democrat Alan Robbins first ran for the Senate as a 30-year-old upstart in a 1973 special election, he slung his coat over his shoulder, a la Bobby Kennedy, and heard hoots that he was nothing but a copycat phony who would never get anywhere. He won and has become a power-broker in the San Fernando Valley, and a very popular one at that.

Alan E. Robbins

Robbins has skated on the edge of political, personal and legal disaster more than once – and always come back from the brink. He stood trial in 1981 on charges that he engaged in sex with two 16-year-old girls, and was acquitted; the FBI tried to sting him in its "Brispec" undercover operation in 1988, and apparently failed; his former business associates have sued him, but settled out of court. Robbins provides no end of controversy, as when he has used his campaign fund to make loans to business associates. His activities keep Capitol reporters scurrying.

Robbins has turned out to be a political chameleon. He mirrors the political issue of the moment, be it opposition to busing for school integration, traffic jams or insurance rates. He is one of the shrewdest politicians ever to serve in the Legislature and a master at moving legislation, but he has become one of the most disliked and most distrusted lawmakers among his colleagues.

Robbins routinely carries one of the heaviest bill loads in the Legislature. By the end of the 1988 session, he had authored more than 120 bills, many enacted into law. He dives into such divergent subjects as animal rights, the death penalty, insurance, transportation and interstate banking.

No one is ever quite sure whose water he is carrying, as, for example, when he authored a banking bill to limit interstate banking to Western states – a bill rivaling one carried by Assemblyman Chuck Calderon to open up California banking to the rest of the country. At first it appeared Robbins was on the side of California bankers worried about Eastern encroachment. As it turned out, Robbins had moved against the California banks with legislation favoring savings and loans.

His role in banking legislation and other issues attracted the attention of the FBI, which subpoenaed legislative records on Robbins' banking bills. He was also among those the FBI tried to "sting" – apparently unsuccessfully – into asking for a bribe during its undercover investigation. Robbins eventually testified at the grand jury that indicted Sen. Joe Montoya.

Robbins is a master at amending bills during the final end-of-session rush each year, so cleaver that Sen. Bob Presley once stood up on the floor and asked his colleagues to keep a sharp eye out for Robbins' tricks. That distrust can have a detrimental effect on legislation; Robbins' efforts at reorganizing the Los Angeles transit district have fallen apart not just from cross-town conflicts (and greediness) but because many senators just do not trust Robbins to put together a fair bill.

In another instance of his wheeling and dealing, it was reported in 1985 that Robbins held investment in a Marina del Rey apartment complex at the same time he was involved in legislative efforts to ban rent control in that community.

As chairman of the Senate's insurance committee, Robbins has set himself up as the chief defender of Proposition 103's insurance regulation and rate rollbacks. He has not been known to miss an opportunity to bash state Insurance Commissioner Roxani Gillespie, but eschews ambitions of running for that office himself. Instead, Robbins is more interested in finding a cushy slot on the Board of Equalization, the Los Angeles County Board of Supervisors – or even as mayor of Los Angeles.

PERSONAL: elected 1973 (special election); born Feb. 5, 1943, in Philadelphia, Penn.; home, North Hollywood; education, B.A. political science and J.D. UCLA; divorced; children, Jacob and Leah; Jewish.

CAREER: lawyer.

COMMITTEES: Insurance, Claims & Corporations (chair); Banking & Commerce; Budget & Fiscal Review and budget subcommittee 4 – legislative, executive, business, transportation, housing & general government (chair); Transportation. SELECT: Governmental Efficiency (chair); Motion Picture, TV, Commercial & Recording Industries. JOINT: Courthouse Finance & Construction (chair).

OFFICES: Capitol, (916) 445-3121; district, 6150 Van Nuys Blvd., 400, Van Nuys, 91401, (818) 901-5555.

REGISTRATION: 56.7% D; 33.9% R

1986 CAMPAIGN: Robbins – D 65%

Davis – R 35%

RATINGS:

AFL	PIRG	CLCV	NOW	CTA	HAC	CofC	CFB	NRA
88%	50%	93%	58%	S	45%	20%	42% 1	00%

KEY VOTES:

Divest S. Africa:	YES	Insurance reform:	YES	Child sick leave:	YES
Assault gun ban:	NO	Parent consent abortion:	–	Ban AIDS discrim:	–
Clean Air Act:	YES	Ban insure donations:	YES	Extend death penalty:	YES
Lmt product tort:	–	End mob home rent cont:	YES	Ban offshore oil:	YES

21st Senate District

Newton R. Russell (R)

Democrats needn't apply in this Los Angeles County District that includes cities like Glendale, Lancaster, Palmdale, San Marino, Arcadia, Monrovia and part of Pasadena. The district's Republican registration stands at 55 percent, 20 points higher than that of Democrats.

Newton Russell has been in the Legislature for a quarter of a century, beginning his career in the Assembly in 1964 and moving to the Senate 10 years later. He is a hard-working, consummate conservative, rarely breaking from the Republican caucus line. In fact, it was something of a mild surprise when Russell reversed himself and supported a 1989 bill that would have heavily fined insurers who illegally canceled automobile policies following the passage of Proposition 103.

Newton R. Russell

In recent years, Russell has been most visible for his involvement in bills dealing with sex education at schools. In 1988, he successfully pushed a bill, signed into law by Gov. Deukmejian, that requires schools to encourage students to abstain from intercourse until they are ready for marriage and to teach honor and respect for monogamous heterosexual marriage. Russell said that measure was "not intended to preach morals. It is intended to give teens useful, factual tips." The following year, he introduced a bill that would require written consent of parent for children to receive sex education, and another to prohibit schools from providing any counseling to students other than career, academic or vocational without written consent of their parents.

Russell is also one of the Senate's resident parliamentarians, frequently rising to object to breaches of house rules. And those protests about parliamentary games led to a series of procedural reforms in the Senate, designed to prevent legislation from slipping into law without notice and full airing.

PERSONAL: elected 1974 (special election); born June 25, 1927, in Los Angeles, Calif.; home, Glendale; Navy WWII; education, B.S. business administration USC, attended UCLA and Georgetown University, no degree; wife, Diane Henderson; children, Stephen, Sharon Sclafani and Julia Gans; Protestant.

CAREER: insurance agent; Assembly 1964.

COMMITTEES: Banking & Commerce (vice chair); Energy & Public Utilities (vice chair); Local Government; Transportation. SELECT: Calif. Wine Industry; Children & Youth; Pacific Rim. JOINT: Rules; State's Economy.

OFFICES: Capitol, (916) 445-5976; district, 401 N. Brand Blvd., 424, Glendale, 91203-2364, (213) 247-7021.

REGISTRATION: 35.1% D; 55.6% R

1988 CAMPAIGN: Russell – R   68%
                   Gelber – D   28%
                   Scott – L   2%
                   Blumenthal – P&F 1%

RATINGS:

AFL	PIRG	CLCV	NOW	CTA	HAC	CofC	CFB	NRA
23%	43%	55%	42%	U	78%	72%	57%	71%

KEY VOTES:

Divest S. Africa:	NO	Insurance reform:	YES	Child sick leave:	NO
Assault gun ban:	NO	Parent consent abortion:	YES	Ban AIDS discrim:	NO
Clean Air Act:	–	Ban insure donations:	NO	Extend death penalty:	YES
Lmt product tort:	–	End mob home rent cont:	YES	Ban offshore oil:	NO

22nd Senate District

Herschel Rosenthal (D)

The heart of the liberal West Side of Los Angeles, the 22nd Senate District includes Santa Monica, West Los Angeles, Sherman Oaks, Pacific Palisades, Beverly Hills and the posh Brentwood and Bel Air neighborhoods.

Democrat Herschel Rosenthal is a product of the liberal political organization led by Reps. Henry Waxman and Howard Berman, and he is one of the most consistent liberals in the Legislature, although not nearly as articulate as Sen. Nicholas Petris. Rosenthal was among six senators who were overwhelmingly outvoted in July 1989 on a flag-burning resolution.

Rosenthal has made his legislative mark primarily in utilities law. He was the Senate Democrats' negotiator in breaking a tricky two-year stalemate over how to spend $154 million that California received from a national $2.1 billion judgment against several oil companies for overcharging during the 1974 oil crisis. The agreement reached in spring 1989 earmarked $60 million to start replacing about one-third of the state's unsafe school buses, and the rest was used to help poor people meet their utility bills and other energy and traffic projects.

Rosenthal is among the more traveled lawmakers, enjoying a steady stream of junkets courtesy of corporations, most of which have business pending before the public utilities committee he chairs. A few examples from 1987: Pacific Telesis paid $7,988 for Rosenthal's tour of London and Paris, including hotels, meals and theater tickets; Luz Engineering of Los Angeles (a major developer of solar energy projects in the California desert) paid $6,876 to send Rosenthal to Israel. In

Herschel Rosenthal

1988, he was the ninth highest recipient in the Senate of gifts and honorariums, pulling in a total of $16,351. Rosenthal's yearly financial disclosure statements are among the more entertaining for their restaurant and travel listings.

On the side, Rosenthal is a horse racing fanatic who owns all or pieces of several horses. This would also appear to have influenced his choice of attire. Rosenthal is one of the worst dressed members of the Senate. He often wears plaid jackets that look as if they were tailored from the blankets of his race horses.

Rosenthal lists himself among those Democrats who have been underwhelmed with his party's crop of candidates for governor. Rosenthal won notoriety in an otherwise boring summer of 1989 by trying to get actor James Garner to run for governor. Garner declined, reportedly telling Rosenthal it would mean giving up his $6 million a year income.

PERSONAL: elected 1982; born March 13, 1918, in St. Louis, Mo.; home, Los Angeles; Navy; education, attended UCLA; wife, Patricia Staman; children, Joel and Suzanne; Jewish.

CAREER: partner ADTYPE Service Co. Inc.; Assembly 1974.

COMMITTEES: Energy & Public Utilities (chair); Business & Professions; Elections; Governmental Organization; Health & Human Services; Industrial Relations; Toxics & Public Safety Management. SELECT: Motion Picture, TV, Commercial & Recording Industries (chair). JOINT: Quincentennial of the Voyages of Columbus; Oversight on GAIN Implementation.

OFFICES: Capitol, (916) 445-7928; district, 1950 Sawtelle Blvd., 210, Los Angeles, 90025, (213) 479-5588.

REGISTRATION: 58.9% D; 30.7% R

1986 CAMPAIGN: Rosenthal – D   68%

                                  Sias – R   29%

                                  Russell – L   2%

                                  Kirk – P&F   1%

RATINGS: AFL PIRG CLCV NOW CTA HAC CofC CFB NRA
96% 64% 100% 84% G 100% 16% 28% 14%

KEY VOTES:

Divest S. Africa: YES	Insurance reform: YES	Child sick leave:	YES
Assault gun ban: YES	Parent consent abortion: NO	Ban AIDS discrim:	YES
Clean Air Act: –	Ban insure donations: NO	Extend death penalty:	NO
Lmt product tort: YES	End mob home rent cont: YES	Ban offshore oil:	YES

23rd Senate District

David A. Roberti (D)

Turning 50 in the spring of 1989, David Roberti was at the pinnacle of his powers as the president pro tempore of the Senate, the top position in the Legislature's upper house. He could look back on his 23 years in the Legislature with the satisfaction of a successful politician who had steadily risen in strength and in stature – and grown ever more outwardly confident in his position. He had just beaten the much vaunted National Rifle Association by winning enactment of a law restricting the sale of semiautomatic military assault weapons. If he cared to, Roberti could look down the ornate Victorian hallway in the Capitol toward the chambers of Willie Brown and know that he had eclipsed the more flamboyant speaker of the Assembly,

David A. Roberti

who may be on the down slope of his career. And, in all likelihood, Roberti will be there greeting his third governor as leader of the Senate in 1991, his grip on the top post as firm as it has ever been.

Roberti, the son of Italian immigrants, has represented central Los Angeles in the Legislature since he was elected to the Assembly in 1966, then the youngest legislator at age 27. He moved up to the Senate in a July 1971 special election. Roberti's district looks like the Democratic coalition personified, taking in Jewish Beverly-Fairfax, gay-dominated West Hollywood, the older Catholic immigrant neighborhoods of the Wilshire District and Los Feliz (where Roberti lives) and some of the state's newest immigrants in Chinatown and Koreatown. No one has given Roberti re-election trouble, although feminist lawyer Gloria Allred once threatened to challenge him in his Democratic primary over his anti-abortion stance, a position that stems from his devout Catholicism. His tirades against Planned Parenthood are legendary.

Roberti and Brown were sworn-in as the leaders of their respective houses on the same December 1980 day, their coups triumphant. The forces that brought both to power were the same – the advent of the full-time Legislature in 1966 and the highly partisan atmosphere it engendered over the years. But their styles and personalities could not be more different.

Brown had noisily grabbed power by forming a coalition with Republicans (who thought he would be a weak speaker), while Roberti had quietly arranged the overthrow of President Pro Tem Jim Mills, who was planning to step aside anyway. Roberti had taken advantage of Senate Democratic fears that their leader was not partisan enough in the face of renewed Republican challenges.Democratic senators had been frightened by the election loss of Senate dean Al Rodda of Sacramento in a highly partisan, and decidedly ungentlemanly, contest with John Doolittle in 1980. While Mills, a Milquetoast Democrat, had entertained notions of handing off his mantle to the genteel Bob Presley, Senate liberals had other designs and elevated Roberti to pro tem on his promise to protect their seats in the upcoming reapportionment.

There would be no more Rodda incidents if Roberti could help it. Holding power in the Senate became dependent not on legislative prowess but on keeping incumbents re-elected, something he demonstrated in 1982, when he defended then-Sen. Alex Garcia, who was known mostly for his prolonged absences from the Capitol, against a Democratic primary challenge from then-Assemblyman Art Torres. Garcia lost anyway, but Roberti had demonstrated his fidelity to incumbents.

Although Roberti gained power on a partisan wave, he has proven a more complex politician. He enjoys cordial relations with many of his Republican colleagues. Some are even confidants, particularly Oceanside's Bill Craven, who sits with Roberti on the bipartisan Rules Committee that governs Senate operations.

In contrast to Brown's flashy clothes, fast cars and pretty women, Roberti is a pet-loving homebody who wears dark suits. His wife, June, is considered to be his closest political adviser. The San Francisco Chronicle once headlined a story about him, "The Unknown Man Running the Senate."

The frumpy, introverted Roberti has never been as prominent in politics outside the Capitol as Willie Brown. Although Brown has enjoyed a reputation as a fiery orator (won during his "Give me back my delegation" speech at the 1972 Democratic National Convention), Roberti has never been given full credit for his considerable oratorical skills. While the speaker has galavanted around the country and bragged he is the "Ayatollah of the Assembly," Roberti has steadily racked up a more solid legislative record. Roberti's bills have run the gamut from consumer protection, child welfare, hazardous waste, energy and crime. By throwing his full weight as leader of the Senate behind it, Roberti won passage in 1989 of a law restricting semiautomatic assault weapons and, later that year, convinced his nervous colleagues to embrace reforms of their ethical behavior in accepting outside income.

But while Roberti has shown tremendous skill in wielding and keeping power, he has exhibited twinges of jealousy toward the speaker. He tweaked Brown in a 1984 letter for mailing fund-raising appeals that referred to himself as "Speaker of the California Legislature."

"We don't have a unicameral legislature in California – yet," Roberti huffed. "If the vote were taken in the state Senate, you wouldn't have the votes to be elected Speaker of the Legislature. ... While I've heard you refer to yourself as the Legislature's Speaker, seeing it in writing was highly offensive to members of the Senate."

When George Deukmejian became governor he seems to have been sucked in by Willie Brown's reputation for legislative acumen and behaved as if the speaker was the source of all his troubles. As it turned out, Deukmejian's nemesis has been Roberti, even though the two served together in the Senate. Deukmejian got a quick education in revised Capitol politics when the Senate rejected his first nominee for state finance director, Michael Franchetti. Deukmejian's relationship with Roberti quickly soured, and in the years since, their relationship has resembled an elevator, constantly rising and falling.

Relations between Deukmejian and Roberti were never worse that when the Senate in 1988 dealt the death blow to Deukmejian's effort at naming his own successor. After the death of Democratic state Treasurer Jesse Unruh in 1987, Deukmejian named Dan Lungren, an obscure Republican congressman from his hometown of Long Beach, to fill the post. The plan was for Lungren to serve as treasurer for the remainder of Unruh's term, then run for governor or re-election as treasurer in 1990 or 1994, depending on Deukmejian's career plans. Brown and the Assembly went along, confirming Lungren. But Roberti called in every chit he had in defeating Lungren's confirmation in the Senate. An 11th-hour reversal by independent Sen. Quentin Kopp – and the administration's taking for granted Sen. Rose Ann Vuich – cost Lungren the confirmation.

Deukmejian displayed his ill humor thusly: "It is obvious that deals were made to ensure that Dan would be rejected in the Senate. It is also obvious that David Roberti is behaving more like a dictator than a statesman."

Deukmejian took the argument to the state Supreme Court, contending that Assembly confirmation was enough for Lungren to take office. However, the court – dominated by Deukmejian appointees – rejected the governor's arguments and upheld Lungren's rejection.

Roberti also exacted several pounds of flesh from Deukmejian's hide over building a prison in downtown Los Angeles. Initially, Roberti favored the administration plan to build a prison in an industrial section of downtown near the largely Hispanic neighborhoods of East Los Angeles. However, when residents raised objections with Sen. Art Torres, and he took their side, Roberti reversed position.

At first it appeared Roberti was protecting Torres' flank. But then it became apparent that the fight was something more, that it had become deeply personal for both Roberti and Deukmejian. The two hurled a stream of insults back and forth, each calling the other stubborn and dictatorial. Deukmejian called a special session in the fall of 1986 that proved fruitless. Roberti held the votes. Finally, with tempers calming after the November election, Roberti and Deukmejian reached a Rube Goldberg compromise with interlocking environmental impact reports that called for building a second Los Angeles prison in a Republican district somewhere in northern Los Angeles County.

The politics and heat of those battles masked something that cynics sometimes fail to see about David Roberti – he can be idealistic. In the Los Angeles prison affair, nearly everyone in both parties grew ever more impatient as the fight dragged into a special session in an election year. But Roberti held to a genuine belief that Deukmejian and the Department of Corrections were running roughshod over the residents of East Los Angeles. Roberti was willing to stake all on that proposition. The more Deukmejian appeared to be shoving a prison down the residents' throats, the more irate Roberti became. The prison battle became for Roberti a class struggle between country club Republicans and immigrant Democrats.

On another level, Roberti is the head of a huge organization that keeps the Senate lurching along. As pro tem, Roberti built a highly skilled staff, ruled initially with an iron-fist by Jerry Zanelli, who as executive officer of the Senate Rules Committee became a czar over the lives of lesser senators and staffers. However, Roberti has shed many of the people he brought with him. Roberti fell out with Zanelli, who became a lobbyist, and replaced him with Clifford Berg, a cool bureaucrat who has become the most powerful staffer in the Legislature, administering Roberti's huge staff, doling out office space and committee assignments to senators and overseeing Roberti's policy analysts. Berg is known as one of the Capitol's "Valley Boys" – a clique of staffers from the San Fernando Valley cutting across party lines (others include Republican Jerry Haleva and Democrat Barry Brokaw). Staffers working in the pro tem's office refer to their operation as "Roberti-land."

Roberti has faced three challenges to his leadership post, emerging from each struggle even stronger than before. Where Brown has sometimes dallied when challenged and then overreacted, Roberti has not hesitated. He has isolated his opponents quickly and ruthlessly cut them down. His first challenge came in 1983 from erstwhile ally Paul Carpenter of Norwalk. Three years later, John Garamendi took a run at Roberti, and found himself stripped of committee assignments within hours of approaching other senators about joining him in a coup. In 1987, conservative Democrats pressured Roberti on committee assignments – and Dan Boatwright took it as support for a coup. Boatwright, sputtering profanities in a hallway to reporters, found himself stripped of the plum chairmanship of Appropriations. But Roberti, not wanting to surround himself with malcontents, also brings the chastened rebels back into his fold after a measured time of exile. Carpenter, Garamendi and Boatwright were later given committee chairmanships.

Sometimes Roberti has had to scold his fussy Senate colleagues about compromise and pragmatism, as he did in the closing week of the 1989 session when a number of his colleagues balked at voting for a bill they had not seen.

"I wish the world were composed of 100 percent liberal Democrats," he said. "It would be great. I could solve all the problems my way without having to negotiate with Governor Deukmejian. My life would be perfect. But this is not the real world. ... But this terrible, terrible, state of California is just so complex everyone just doesn't seem to see it my way. And they expect me to go down to the governor and negotiate. I wish they didn't expect that. But they do."

Despite his lack of media appeal, Roberti has sometimes entertained ambitions of moving into statewide office. But it's more likely that he will continue as the Senate's top leader until well into the 1990s.

PERSONAL: elected 1971; born May 4, 1939, in Los Angeles, Calif.; home, Los Feliz neighborhood of Los Angeles; education, B.A. political science Loyola University, J.D. USC; wife, June Joyce; Catholic.

CAREER: lawyer; law clerk; deputy attorney general 1965-1966; Assembly 1966; Senate president pro tempore 1980.

COMMITTEES: ex officio member of all standing and joint committees; Rules (chair); Judiciary. SELECT: Small Business Enterprises (chair); AIDS; Infant & Child Care & Development; Motion Picture, TV, Commercial & Recording Industries; Tourism & Aviation. JOINT: Quincentennial of the Voyages of Columbus; Fire, Police, Emergency & Disaster Services; Refugee Resettlement, International Migration & Cooperative Development; Revision of the Penal Code; Rules.

OFFICES: Capitol, (916) 445-8390; district, 3800 Barham Blvd., 218, Hollywood, 90068, (213) 876-5200.

REGISTRATION: 59.3% D; 28.7% R

1988 CAMPAIGN: Roberti – D   68%
Larkin – R   26%
Nakano – P&F   3%
Foster – L   3%

RATINGS:

AFL	PIRG	CLCV	NOW	CTA	HAC	CofC	CFB	NRA
95%	86%	95%	83%	G*	100%	20%	42%	0%

KEY VOTES:

Divest S. Africa:	YES	Insurance reform:	YES	Child sick leave:	YES
Assault gun ban:	YES	Parent consent abortion:	YES	Ban AIDS discrim:	YES
Clean Air Act:	YES	Ban insure donations:	–	Extend death penalty:	YES
Lmt product tort:	YES	End mob home rent cont:	YES	Ban offshore oil:	YES

24th Senate District

Art Torres (D)

East Los Angeles is an area where one is just as likely to hear people speaking Spanish as English. Over 70 percent of the residents in cities like South Pasadena, Eagle Rock, Maywood, Commerce and Vernon are of Hispanic descent. This is also the Senate district with the lowest number of registered voters – further testament to its reputation as a haven for new immigrants, both legal and illegal.

In Art Torres, the residents of East Los Angeles have a bright, articulate and passionate representative. He is mediagenic, one of the best speakers in the Legislature, a devoted father and an affable-but-shrewd political operator. It is those qualities that for years have prompted political insiders to anoint Torres as the Hispanic with the best chance of being elected to statewide office. He himself has made it known that he someday wants to try to fulfill those predictions.

Art Torres

Yet Torres' political future has been clouded by recent personal problems, including estrangement from his wife and two arrests for drunken driving in Sacramento within 14 months. At the time of his first arrest in 1988, Torres was carrying a bill to take away the licenses of minors convicted of alcohol and drug related offenses.

Whether this Capitol enigma, in fact, has irreparably damaged his statewide chances remains to be seen. In a Ted Kennedy-like way, Torres is still courted by Democrats of national stature for support and endorsements. He has the ability to appeal to Hispanic voters and to mainstream Anglos.

Torres also remains one of the Senate's most active members. He has not only made his mark in the Legislature fighting for causes of importance to Hispanic voters, such as bilingual education and to block the siting of a prison in his district, but he has seized on statewide issues. He has pressed to crackdown on the disposal of toxic wastes, to improve child nutrition, to ban the importation of foreign produce tainted with pesticide residues, to raise the minimum wage and to set up a system to destroy vicious dogs and fine their owners.

He has also ventured into foreign affairs, including taking a trip to Hong Kong and Thailand to visit Amerasian refugees from Vietnam and to try to reunite them with American relatives.

Torres is a legislator who bears continued attention.

PERSONAL: elected 1982; born Sept. 24, 1946, in Los Angeles, Calif.; home, Los Angeles; education, B.A. government UC Santa Cruz, J.D. UC Davis, John F. Kennedy teaching fellow Harvard University; separated; children, Joaquin and Danielle.

CAREER: lawyer; Assembly 1974.

COMMITTEES: Toxics & Public Safety Management (chair); Appropriations; Education; Governmental Organization; Health & Human Services; Housing & Urban Affairs; Judiciary. SELECT: Tourism & Aviation (chair); AIDS; Business Development. SPECIAL: UC Admissions (chair); Neighborhood Violence. JOINT: Refugee Resettlement, International Migration & Cooperative Development (chair); Organized Crime & Gang violence; Review of the Master Plan for Higher Education; Science & Technology.

OFFICES: Capitol, (916) 445-3456; district, 107 S. Broadway, 2105, Los Angeles, 90012, (213) 620-2529.

REGISTRATION: 66.6% D; 22.7% R

1986 CAMPAIGN: Torres – D   72%
Prentiss – R   24%
Brown – L   4%

RATINGS:

AFL	PIRG	CLCV	NOW	CTA	HAC	CofC	CFB	NRA
97%	64%	100%	67%	G*	100%	20%	28%	0%

KEY VOTES:

Divest S. Africa: YES	Insurance reform: YES	Child sick leave: YES
Assault gun ban: YES	Parent consent abortion: YES	Ban AIDS discrim: YES
Clean Air Act: YES	Ban insure donations: YES	Extend death penalty: YES
Lmt product tort: YES	End mob home rent cont: YES	Ban offshore oil: YES

25th Senate District

William R. Leonard (R)

This district was carved out of cactus and rock by Democrats trying to gerrymander right-wing guru Bill Richardson into retirement. He did not see it that way and easily won the seat again in 1984 before deciding to retire on his own accord in 1988. The district takes in the upscale end of the eastern Los Angeles basin, including Redlands and Claremont, then bridges the rugged San Gabriel and San Bernardino mountains to span the Mojave Desert. Running north along the eastern edge of the Sierra, the district includes the remote towns of Bishop, Big Pine and other Owens Valley communities that depend on ranching, mining and tourism for their existence. The district is so immense that it abuts a district represented by a senator from Sacramento.

William R. Leonard

Richardson's successor is William Leonard, who is both smoother and more intellectual. But Leonard's conservatism is just as intense and rigid – with some surprises. The San Bernardino native son won the seat after serving 10 years in the Assembly. He had originally come to Sacramento as one of the "Proposition 13 babies," elected the same year as the property tax limitation initiative passed. His father, William Sr., has been a longtime figure in area politics and serves on the state Transportation Commission.

Leonard is unwavering in his opposition to gun control and is intensely anti-abortion. But he has for years introduced legislation to ban the internal combustion engine. While in the Assembly, he succeeded in winning Assembly approval in 1987 for a measure phasing in clean-burning methanol vehicles in the 1990s only to see the bill buried in the Senate by Democratic Sen. Ralph Dills of Gardena, chairman of the Governmental Organization Committee. Leonard has supported Democratic efforts to toughen smog laws, a subject of major concern to the eastern end of the Los Angeles basin he represents. In the Assembly, he was not afraid to buck his party leaders on that and other issues. Leonard has begun to assert himself in his first Senate term, authoring legislation that lowered the drunken driving blood alcohol level to 0.08 percent. He also authored a bill to end rent control laws on new mobile home spaces, a measure that asserts his laisser-faire conservatism.

PERSONAL: elected 1988; born Oct. 29, 1947, in San Bernardino, Calif.; home, Big Bear; education, B.A. history UC Irvine, graduate work CSU Sacramento; wife, Sherry Boldizsar; children, Michael, Tim and Jacob; Presbyterian.

CAREER: Real estate management; director San Bernardino Valley Municipal Water District 1974-1978; Assembly 1978.

COMMITTEES: Housing & Urban Affairs (vice chair); Budget & Fiscal Review; Natural Resources & Wildlife; Transportation; SELECT: Planning for Calif. Growth; State Procurement & Expenditure Practices.

OFFICES: CAPITOL (916) 445-3688; district, 400 N. Mountain View Ave. 19, Upland, 91786; (714) 946-4889.

REGISTRATION: 37.9% D; 51.8% R

1988 CAMPAIGN: Leonard – R   66%
                     Hester – D   34%

RATINGS: (except for NRA, ratings are for Leonard in the Assembly)

	AFL	PIRG	CLCV	NOW	CTA	HAC	CofC	CFB	NRA
	21%	26%	7%	17%	U	18%	96%	66%	100%

KEY VOTES: (includes votes by Leonard in the Assembly)

Divest S. Africa:	NO	Insurance reform:	NO	Child sick leave:	NO
Assault gun ban:	NO	Parent consent abortion:	YES	Ban AIDS discrim:	NO
Clean Air Act:	NO	Ban insure donations:	NO	Extend death penalty:	YES
Lmt product tort:	YES	End mob home rent cont:	YES	Ban offshore oil:	NO

26th Senate District

Joseph B. Montoya (D)

This eastern Los Angeles County district is mostly Hispanic, taking in Alhambra, San Gabriel, Monterey Park, Rosemead, Montebello, Pico Rivera, Irwindale and part of Whittier. The district also has a sizable and growing Asian population that could eventually produce an Asian-American legislator. The Southern California Edison mega-utility is headquartered in the district, as is a large gravel pit that the city of Irwindale wanted to convert into a football stadium for the Los Angeles Raiders. It is also the home of the Operating Industries Inc. dump, a mountain of Los Angeles' garbage sitting astride the Pomona freeway that is on the federal Superfund list as one of the most polluted corners of the United States.

Democrat Joseph Montoya has never had much difficulty winning in this Democratic district, perhaps giving him a fatal dose of hubris. Billing himself as a conservative Democrat, Montoya once led the charge on bills requiring parental consent for a minor to have an abortion. There was a time when Montoya talked of running for statewide office.

No more. Montoya was the first lawmaker charged in the federal undercover probe of Capitol corruption, named in a 12-count indictment with racketeering, extortion and money laundering. If convicted, Montoya faces a maximum sentence of 200 years in a federal prison and a $2.5 million fine. Two Assembly members, Charles Calderon and Sally Tanner, have indicated an interest in running for his seat should Montoya leave office.

Joseph Montoya

Montoya, chairman of the Senate's Business and Professions Committee, has been one of the sharpest Capitol operators of recent times. He came to the Legislature in 1972 as a modestly paid social worker. As a lawmaker, he has built an impressive real estate portfolio and shown a fondness for Cadillacs. Businesses big and small paraded before his committee looking for legal exemptions or trade monopolies. Federal prosecutors maintain Montoya and an aide, Amiel Jaramillo, used Montoya's position to extract cash from those with business before him. The indictment against Montoya is a breathtaking litany of Capitol horrors, accusing him of extorting payoffs from the National Football League Players Association, the Screen Actors Guild, actor Ed Asner, employment agency owners – and undercover FBI agents.

Nor is Montoya particularly liked by his colleagues, although they made a theatrical show of backslapping support in the Senate the day he was indicted. Most find him rough-hewn and crude. His quotes to reporters are often unprintable in family newspapers. He infuriated even allies while pushing his parental consent legislation with demagogic blasts at opponents.

Despite his seeming downfall, Montoya should not be taken lightly. He has had a major impact on California politics. He was one of three co-authors of Proposition 73, the campaign donation limit initiative approved by voters in June 1988. His co-authors, Republican Assemblyman Ross Johnson of La Habra and independent Sen. Quentin Kopp of San Francisco, seem to have had a convenient case of amnesia when it comes to Montoya.

PERSONAL: elected 1978; born April 30, 1939, in Rocky Ford, Colo.; home, Whittier; USAF; education, Mt. San Antonio Community College, B.A. UCLA; wife, Pilar Gonzalez; children, Cristina, Pilar, Joseph III and Marisa; Catholic.

CAREER: social services counselor; La Puente City Council, mayor 1968-1972; Assembly 1972.

COMMITTEES: Business & Professions (chair); Banking & Commerce; Energy & Public Utilities; Health & Human Services; Industrial Relations; Insurance, Claims & Corporations. SELECT: Pacific Rim (chair); Small Business Enterprises; Governmental Efficiency. JOINT: Legislative Budget; Review of the Master Plan for Higher Education; Rules.
OFFICES: CAPITOL (916) 445-3386; district, 11001 E. Valley Mall 3204, El Monte, 91731, (818) 575-6956.
REGISTRATION: 60.9% D; 29.3% R
1986 CAMPAIGN: Montoya – D   100%
                                                 no opponent

RATINGS:

AFL	PIRG	CLCV	NOW	CTA	HAC	CofC	CFB	NRA
84%	54%	–	17%	S	56%	16%	14%	29%

KEY VOTES:

Divest S. Africa:	YES	Insurance reform:	YES	Child sick leave:	YES
Assault gun ban:	YES	Parent consent abortion:	YES	Ban AIDS discrim:	–
Clean Air Act:	YES	Ban insure donations:	YES	Extend death penalty:	–
Lmt product tort:	YES	End mob home rent cont: YES	Ban offshore oil:	YES

27th Senate District

Bill Greene (D)

South-central Los Angeles is among the poorest and most crime-beleaguered areas of the state, and the 27th Senate District lies in its heart. Sandwiched between the Harbor and Long Beach freeways, the district includes South Gate, Compton, Huntington Park, Bell and Cudahy. More than half the residents are black; almost 40 percent are Hispanic. Gangs roam freely in this district; by midyear 1989, the area had the highest homicide rate in Los Angeles, with 177 killings out of the 395 committed in the entire city.

The district's troubles are mirrored in the man who represents it, Bill Greene.

Bill Greene

Democrat Greene, a bombastic senator with a gravely voice and short fuse, has one of the worst attendance records in the Legislature. In 1989, he missed more than 40 percent of his floor and committee votes, an average that only told part of the story. He has missed most of the key votes on major legislation in the last three years. Although he was around to vote for David Roberti's bill banning semiautomatic assault weapons, he missed the vote on Mike Roos' bill that was the second part of that legislative package.

In midsummer 1989, Greene finally admitted what Capitol insiders had long suspected – he was an alcoholic. Greene was arrested for drunken driving in Turlock, found urinating beside his car. He served two days in jail, then admitted himself into a 28-day treatment program, only to check out again after two days. Shortly before the Legislature resumed for its late summer session, Greene entered the Betty Ford Center in Palm Springs and disappeared for the remainder of the legislative year.

A former labor organizer, Greene has been chairman of the Industrial Relations Committee and a member of the powerful Governmental Organization Committee that oversees gambling and liquor legislation. However, Greene has been chiefly noted not for his legislation – which is negligible – but for his severe tongue-lashings directed at witnesses coming before his committees.

By being out of commission for much of 1989, he missed having any significant involvement in an issue – workers compensation reform – in which he had a long-standing interest. Greene lent his staff to Assemblyman Burt Margolin who engineered the pact signed by the governor. After he emerged from treatment, he said he was turning over a new leaf and would apply himself to legislation.

Greene has not always shown much regard for the niceties of campaign finance laws. He has never had to worry about re-election, racking up 87 percent of the vote in 1988. Instead, he has operated his campaign fund as a personal bank, paying himself $102,442 in the last decade with scant explanation on his disclosure forms for the payments. He has been fined twice by the state Fair Political Practices Commission for running afoul of campaign finance laws, the most serious offense in 1980 when Greene was fined $36,000 for using $5,208 in campaign funds to pay his personal income taxes. He paid the FPPC fine out of campaign funds.

PERSONAL: elected 1975 (special election); born Nov. 15, 1931, in Kansas City, Mo.; home, Los Angeles; USAF; education, attended Lincoln Junior College, Kansas City, University of Michigan; wife, Yvonne La Fargue; children, Alisa Rochelle and Jan Andrea.

CAREER: first black clerk of the Assembly; consultant to Speaker Jesse Unruh; legislative Assembly assistant to Lt. Gov. Mervyn M. Dymally; lobbyist for a labor union; Assembly 1967.

COMMITTEES: Industrial Relations (chair); Budget & Fiscal Review and budget subcommittee 3 – health, human services & labor (chair); Elections; Governmental Organization; Toxics & Public Safety Management. SELECT: Governmental Efficiency; State Procurement & Expenditure Practices. JOINT: Arts; Quincentennial of the Voyages of Columbus; Legislative Budget; Oversight on GAIN Implementation; Review of the Master Plan for Higher Education.

OFFICES: Capitol, (916) 445-2104; district, 9300 S. Broadway, Los Angeles, 90003, (213) 620-5600.

REGISTRATION: 84.5% D; 9% R

1988 CAMPAIGN: Bill Greene – D   87%
      Neely – R   10%
      Artz – P&F   3%

RATINGS:	AFL	PIRG	CLCV	NOW	CTA	HAC	CofC	CFB	NRA
	95%	54%	–	42%	G	56%	16%	28%	33%

KEY VOTES:

Divest S. Africa:	YES	Insurance reform:	YES	Child sick leave:	–
Assault gun ban:	YES	Parent consent abortion:	–	Ban AIDS discrim:	–
Clean Air Act:	–	Ban insure donations:	–	Extend death penalty:	–
Lmt product tort:	–	End mob home rent cont:	YES	Ban offshore oil:	–

28th Senate District

Diane E. Watson (D)

This southwest-central Los Angeles district is a
mixture of new-money harbor condos and old working-
class neighborhoods. Roughly half black, the district
includes Inglewood, Hawthorne, Lawndale, Venice,
Marina del Rey and Los Angeles International Airport.
Democrat Diane Watson has never had any trouble
getting re-elected here, although she once introduced a
bill to eject white Lawndale from her district.

Watson spent three short years on the Los Angeles
school board as one of its most vocal (and most televised) members in the 1970s during a period of high
racial tensions involving the district's forced busing
plan. She made quite a splash when she first came to
Sacramento in 1975; she was the first black woman
elected to the Senate, a club heretofore comprised primarily of old white men set in
their ways (symbolized by the high leather chairs in the back of their chambers). She
seemed to specialize in those years in crashing the party and opening the windows
– quite a shock for the old white men.

Diane E. Watson

However, Sacramento has gotten used to her. Most of the old boys have retired
or died, and many of the others are better at grandstanding than Watson. Though
she can still cause havoc (primarily for fellow Democrats with a pragmatic bent),
Watson doesn't generate much warmth from her colleagues and she has increasingly found herself isolated with few allies. Watson has crossed swords with her
colleagues on numerous issues ranging from welfare revision to setting ethical
standards – and lost. Her snits with Democratic Sen. Bill Lockyer are fabled, with
the two trading insults across the dais in the Judiciary Committee. She is also known
as one of the most difficult bosses in the Capitol, treating legislative staffers with
disdain.

Watson has, however, shown her loyalty to David Roberti during leadership tussles, and he has returned the loyalty.

As chairwoman of the Health and Human Services Committee, Watson's committee oversees the welfare system in the state, enabling her to position herself as one of the chief Deukmejian critics. In 1985, she filibustered a bipartisan legislative package for major welfare reforms (dubbed GAIN) that set up a "workfare" program for 190,000 recipients, most of them single mothers. Watson called it a "forced labor program," held a lengthy committee hearing in the waning hours of that year's session, but the bill passed over her objections.

She has for years bragged that she is the only Ph.D. in the Legislature. However, the circumstances of her advanced degree in education administration was called into question when the Sacramento district attorney's office investigated allegations in 1989 that she had used state staff and equipment to prepare her dissertation. District Attorney Steve White concluded that legislative record keeping was so shoddy that the allegations could not be proved or disproved and the matter was dropped.

Watson is among the most traveled legislators, taking numerous junkets worldwide from trade associations and others with business in the Legislature. She routinely uses her campaign fund for a wide range of expenses not traditionally associated with campaigning – like buying flowers. She voted against the 1989 ethics reform package that would tighten the rules for such spending, telling her colleagues that it "went too far."

PERSONAL: elected 1978; born Nov. 12, 1933, in Los Angeles, Calif.; home, Los Angeles; education, A.A. Los Angeles City College, B.A. education UCLA, master of science school psychology CSU Los Angeles, Ph.D. educational administration Claremont Graduate School; unmarried; Catholic.

CAREER: teacher; school administrator; textbook author; Los Angeles Unified School District board 1975-1978.

COMMITTEES: Health & Human Services (chair); Budget & Fiscal Review; Education; Judiciary; Public Employment & Retirement. SELECT: AIDS; Border Issues, Drug Trafficking & Contraband; Children & Youth; Citizen Participation in Government; Substance Abuse. SPECIAL: Neighborhood Violence; UC Admissions. JOINT: Oversight on GAIN Implementation (chair); Organized Crime & Gang Violence.

OFFICES: Capitol, (916) 445-5215; district, 4401 Crenshaw Blvd., 300, Los Angeles, 90043, (213) 295-6655.

REGISTRATION: 73.7% D; 18.1% R

1986 CAMPAIGN: Watson – D   72%
Vaquer – R   21%

RATINGS:	AFL	PIRG	CLCV	NOW	CTA	HAC	CofC	CFB	NRA
	95%	86%	100%	67%	G	89%	20%	14%	0%

KEY VOTES:

Divest S. Africa:	YES	Insurance reform:	YES	Child sick leave:	YES
Assault gun ban:	YES	Parent consent abortion:	NO	Ban AIDS discrim:	YES
Clean Air Act:	YES	Ban insure donations:	NO	Extend death penalty:	NO
Lmt product tort:	–	End mob home rent cont:	YES	Ban offshore oil:	YES

29th Senate District

Robert G. Beverly (R)

Hooking along the Los Angeles Harbor shoreline, on through the Palos Verdes Peninsula, the 29th Senate District takes in the beach towns of surfing safari yore, including El Segundo, Redondo Beach, Palos Verdes, San Pedro and parts of Long Beach.

In more recent years, however, property in the district has become too valuable for surfers' huts and the once-seedy beach towns are building glitzy hotels and shopping malls.

In the 1980s, developers sought to build a hotel in Manhattan Beach, sparking a local election, ending in a tie, asking residents if they wanted a hotel. The Legislature broke the tie with a bill in favor of the hotel. The district also has a base of high-tech industries, oil refineries, tourism and fishing.

Robert G. Beverly

Republican Bob Beverly, a former GOP leader in the Assembly, has never had much trouble holding this seat, though Republican Assemblyman Gerald Felando has long coveted it, leading to stormy relations between the two. That aside, Beverly is the insider's insider in the Capitol. He serves as one of two GOP representatives to the Senate Rules Committee; sits on the cushy Governmental Organization Committee, the overseer of liquor and gambling legislation; and is vice chairman of Appropriations. When legislators want a raise, they turn to Beverly to carry the potentially sticky bill, as he did in 1989 giving his colleagues a 5 percent raise.

Beverly is generally considered a moderate; he was a key swing vote for David Roberti's bill banning semiautomatic assault weapons. However, labeling Beverly does not do justice to his role he plays in the Senate. He shows himself motivated to a great extent not by ideology but by personal relationships.

Beverly may be a Republican, but he is certainly in the club that runs the Legislature. When Sen. Bill Lockyer crashed a meeting in David Roberti's office in the spring of 1989 to complain about secret budget deals, he found Beverly among those inside. When Assembly Speaker Willie Brown went to Lloyd's of London in 1986, among those he took with him was Beverly.

The jovial Beverly carries a lot of water for a lot of people. He authored the bill for Gov. Deukmejian that rebated $1.1 billion to taxpayers. A 1987 Beverly bill restored $86.6 million in aid to the state's urban school districts previously hatcheted by Deukmejian.

Other, lesser bills by Beverly are worthy of note. In the waning days of the 1989 session, he pushed a measure allowing members of the Signal Hill City Council to circumvent conflict-of-interest laws so they could vote on a proposed development that could boost their property values. He has pushed hard on a measure to exempt certain over-the-counter stock transactions from state regulation.

One of the most hotly contested measures behind the scenes was a Beverly bill to exempt employees of mortgage banking firms from having to hold a real estate license. And a Beverly bill signed by Deukmejian in 1986 allowed rental limousine firms to serve liquor without a license.

Beverly often presides over the Senate, his quick rulings and even temper at the rostrum are richly valued by Roberti and his colleagues.

PERSONAL: elected 1976; born July 1, 1925, in Belmont, Mass.; home, Manhattan Beach; USMC 1943-1946; education, attended UCLA 1946-1948, J.D. Loyola University; wife, Bettelu; children, Bill, Bob, Brian and Barbara; Protestant.

CAREER: city attorney; Manhattan Beach City Council, mayor 1958-1967; Assembly 1967.

COMMITTEES: Appropriations (vice chair); Rules; Banking & Commerce; Elections; Governmental Organization; Veteran's Affairs. SELECT: Business Development; Calif. Wine Industry; Forest Resources; Maritime Industry; Motion Picture, TV, Commercial & Recording Industries. SPECIAL: Solid & Hazardous Waste. JOINT: Quincentennial of the Voyages of Columbus; Fisheries & Aquaculture; Legislative Audit; Legislative Budget; Public Pension Fund Investments; Revision of the Penal Code; Rules.

OFFICES: Capitol, (916) 445-6447; district, 1611 S. Pacific Coast Highway 102, Redondo Beach, 90277, (213) 540-1611; 638 S. Beacon 508, San Pedro, 90731, (213) 548-0651.

REGISTRATION: 40.7% D; 48.2% R

1988 CAMPAIGN: Beverly – R   67%
Hachmeister– D 30%
Kelley – L   3%

RATINGS:

	AFL	PIRG	CLCV	NOW	CTA	HAC	CofC	CFB	NRA
	53%	71%	77%	67%	S	89%	60%	71%	43%

KEY VOTES:

Divest S. Africa:	NO	Insurance reform:	NO	Child sick leave:	NO
Assault gun ban:	YES	Parent consent abortion:	YES	Ban AIDS discrim:	YES
Clean Air Act:	YES	Ban insure donations:	NO	Extend death penalty:	YES
Lmt product tort:	YES	End mob home rent cont:	YES	Ban offshore oil:	YES

30th Senate District

Ralph C. Dills (D)

This Los Angeles County district is a blur of used car lots, tacky shopping centers and vast stretches of old and new working-class neighborhoods spanning Gardena, Compton, Lawndale, Lynwood, Harbor City and part of Long Beach. Stand-up comics joke about this part of the Los Angeles basin.

It is hard to think of the California Legislature without Gardena's longtime lawmaker, Ralph Dills, who arrived in the Assembly during the second term of Franklin D. Roosevelt and who once was known mostly as one-half of the Dills Brothers; his brother, Curly, was an Assembly member until his death.

Dills has had several careers, all of them lengthy. He was a saxophone player working jazz clubs in the 1930s,

Ralph C. Dills

then a teacher. An organizer in Democratic New Deal worker leagues, he won an Assembly seat in 1938. In his first 10 years in the Assembly, Dills authored the legislation creating California State University, Long Beach. He quit to accept a judicial appointment in 1949, then returned to Sacramento as a senator in 1967 in the first class of "full-time" legislators. As his campaign literature proclaims, "He's quite a guy!"

Dills became chairman of the powerful Governmental Organization Committee in 1970, a panel with an ironclad grip on liquor, horse racing, labor unions, oil leases and gambling legislation. Dills has long been known as the liquor industry's best friend in Sacramento. He has pushed legislation to give beer and wine distributors district monopolies – bills vetoed with a vengeance by Gov. Deukmejian as reeking with special-interest odor. He has also helped bury anti-smog bills, incurring the wrath of environmentalists, who are left wondering why the bills went to his committee in the first place.

As senior senator, Dills is entitled by protocol to preside over the floor sessions of the Senate, a largely ceremonial post but with power to gum up the works. His parliamentary calls and flowery mannerisms have irritated some of his younger colleagues, who have tried to get him to preside less often. Dills looks like a caricature of a politician – or used car salesman – from a bygone age, with blue-rinsed hair, outrageously colored polyester suits and unfashionably wide ties. He has responded by toning down his dress a little.

Dills does not visit his district as often as most of his colleagues visit theirs, preferring to make his home in the Sacramento suburbs. His voters do not seem to mind.

PERSONAL: elected 1966; born Feb. 10, 1910, Rosston, Tex.; home, Gardena;

education, graduate of Compton College and UCLA, M.A. from USC, J.D. Loyola University; wife, Elizabeth "Bette" Lee; three children, Leighton, Wendy and Gregory.

CAREER: saxophone player; teacher; lawyer; Assembly 1938-1949; municipal court judge 1952-1966.

COMMITTEES: Governmental Organization (chair); Appropriations; Bonded Indebtedness & Methods of Financing; Education; Veterans' Affairs. SELECT: Calif. Wine Industry; Governmental Efficiency; Mobile Homes. SPECIAL: Solid & Hazardous Waste; UC Admissions. JOINT: State's Economy (chair); Fairs Allocation & Classification; Organized Crime & Gang Violence; Refugee Resettlement, International Migration & Cooperative Development; Rules.

OFFICES: Capitol, (916) 445-5953; district, 16921 S. Western Ave., 201, Gardena, 90247, (213) 324-4969.

REGISTRATION: 67.5% D; 23.1 % R

1986 CAMPAIGN: Dills – D   72%
                 Gray – R   25%
                 Chauser – P&F   3%

RATINGS:

AFL	PIRG	CLCV	NOW	CTA	HAC	CofC	CFB	NRA
92%	71%	84%	92%	G*	100%	28%	57%	0%

KEY VOTES:

Divest S. Africa:	YES	Insurance reform:	YES	Child sick leave:	YES
Assault gun ban:	YES	Parent consent abortion:	NO	Ban AIDS discrim:	YES
Clean Air Act:	YES	Ban insure donations:	YES	Extend death penalty:	YES
Lmt product tort:	YES	End mob home rent cont:	YES	Ban offshore oil:	NO

31st Senate District
William P. Campbell (R)

Shaped something like a map of Vietnam, the 31st District bulges and stretches from Los Angeles County through Orange County, stopping just short of San Juan Capistrano. The district takes in La Habra, West Covina, part of Whittier, La Habra Heights, El Toro, Mission Viejo and Laguna Niguel. It was once the heart of orange grove country. Though there still are vegetable farms and groves tucked here and there, the district is now a vast stretch of housing tracts, high-tech industries and shopping centers.

Corpulent Republican William Campbell has had no trouble getting re-elected to this district. His engaging, sunny disposition makes him popular among his colleagues, and his joke-laced speeches put him in demand on the after-dinner circuit, helping to give him a sizable outside income.

Considered a moderate, Campbell was Senate Republican leader until a coup by hard-line Senate conservatives in 1983. He won the GOP nomination for controller in 1986, though that campaign went nowhere against Democrat Gray Davis. He is popular outside the Capitol as well – ex-Gov. Pat Brown's Institute for Public Affairs named him legislator of the year in 1989.

Campbell, however, is not all he seems. He is a skillful operator who has used his legislative talents to help some of the most notable special interests in Sacramento. He carried the bill on behalf of fireworks mogul W. Patrick Moriarty that would have overturned local ordinances banning fireworks. The measure was vetoed by Gov. Jerry Brown and was later the subject of a massive FBI investigation that resulted in the convictions of 10 people on an assortment of corruption charges at the local level, including Moriarty, who went

William P. Campbell

to jail for bribery and laundering campaign contributions (some convictions were overturned on appeal). Although never implicated in any criminal conduct, Campbell's name was indelibly cemented to the bill that was, on its face, a blatant example of the sort of special-interest "juice" bills that have become a hallmark of the California Legislature in the 1980s.

In the 1970s, Campbell was associated with Dr. Louis Cella, an Orange County businessman and political financier who also went to federal prison on tax fraud and embezzlement charges. During a two-year absence from the Legislature, Campbell was a lobbyist for Cella-owned hospitals and later received some of his campaign financing from Cella-connected sources.

Campbell has made his mark on California in other ways. He snuck an amendment into a $350 million trial court funding bill on the last night of the 1987 session on behalf of some of the most wealthy and exclusive cities in the state. The amendment forced counties to share revenues with cities that do not charge property taxes if the counties wanted a share of the court funds. Several counties chose not to take the state funds, defeating the purpose of the Deukmejian-sponsored court funding program.

Campbell at times has also worked against the Los Angeles delegation on transportation issues. On behalf of the trucking industry, Campbell in August 1989 pushed a bill to torpedo a proposal for a local law by Los Angeles Mayor Tom Bradley to limit truck traffic on Los Angeles city streets.

The Orange County Register, a diligent chronicler of Campbell's exploits, reported in the spring of 1989 that Campbell's office, through his top aide, Jerry Haleva, repeatedly pressured state officials to ease up on an asbestos removal company that was under official criticism for work on public buildings in California. The owner of the New Orleans firm, Gordon Goldman, and his company, Asbestos Environmental Controls, contributed $27,000 to Campbell's campaign funds.

Nor has the federal government ceased its interest in California's 1989 Legislator of the Year. The Register reported in July 1989 that the Small Business Administration wanted reimbursement for $49,300 it granted to Campbell for his annual "Conference on Women," contending he had misled it about fees for coordinating the event. Campbell's wife and a staff aide collected fat fees for organizing the affair.

In 1989, Campbell carried one of the legislative session's most controversial bills, which granted a $1.4 million tax break to wealthy East Bay developer Kenneth Behring, exempting from taxation rare autos that Behring had acquired and wants to donate to the University of California.

At one time Campbell was thought still to have statewide political ambitions, but in October 1989, less than a year after being re-elected, Campbell announced he will resign his Senate seat sometime in 1990 to become president of the California Manufacturers Association. Some thought it an appropriate end to his political career.

PERSONAL: elected 1976; born July 21, 1935, in Coraopolis, Penn.; home, Hacienda Heights; Army; education, attended Westminster College and Columbia University; wife, Margene Taylor; children, Stephanie, Michelle Smith and Kimberly Foster; Mormon.

CAREER: school administrator, Assembly 1966-1972; unsuccessful run for Los Angeles County Board of Supervisors; Assembly 1974.

COMMITTEES: Governmental Organization (vice chair); Industrial Relations (vice chair); Appropriations; Bonded Indebtedness & Methods of Financing; Health & Human Services. SELECT: Business Development (chair); Governmental Efficiency; Tourism & Aviation. JOINT: Fire, Police, Emergency & Disaster Services (chair); Legislative Budget (chair); State's Economy.

OFFICES: Capitol, (916) 445-2848; district, 1661 Hanover Road, 203, City of Industry, 91748, (818) 964-1443; 23161 Lake Center Drive, 205, El Toro, 92630, (714) 770-5533.

REGISTRATION: 35.7% D; 54.3% R

1988 CAMPAIGN: Campbell – R 69%
Graham – D 31%

RATINGS:

AFL	PIRG	CLCV	NOW	CTA	HAC	CofC	CFB	NRA
37%	46%	–	50%	S	78%	20%	42%	100%

KEY VOTES:

Divest S. Africa:	–	Insurance reform:	NO	Child sick leave:	NO
Assault gun ban:	NO	Parent consent abortion:	YES	Ban AIDS discrim:	–
Clean Air Act:	–	Ban insure donations:	NO	Extend death penalty:	YES
Lmt product tort:	–	End mob home rent cont:	YES	Ban offshore oil:	YES

32nd Senate District

Edward R. Royce (R)

Curving through Orange County like a horseshoe, the 32nd Senate District has traditionally voted Republican, but with a growing Asian and Hispanic population it could prove politically volatile in the future. The district takes in Westminster, Stanton, Fullerton and parts of Anaheim and Santa Ana and was supposed to be a "Hispanic seat," according to the Democratic drafters of a 1982 reapportionment plan. Instead, it went to an Anglo Republican, and a very conservative one at that.

Edward R. Royce

Winning his first elective office in 1982, Ed Royce is one of the quieter members of the Senate. He seldom speaks during Senate debates and generally seems to stay out of harm's way. He got the seat after he unexpectedly won a GOP primary in 1982.

A very serious conservative, Royce's favorite television show is William F. Buckley's Firing Line. His heroes are Adam Smith and Milton Friedman. Royce's legislative accomplishments include a 1987 bill sponsored by Mothers Against Drunk Driving requiring automatic revocation of a driver's license of anyone who refuses to take a roadside sobriety test. Other Royce bills have been aimed at protecting the privacy of crime victims

As chairman of the Senate Constitutional Amendments Committee, he has tried to leave his mark on ballot proposals, including one to alter the state's Gann spending limit. However, Royce chairs a committee in which he does not control a majority and has found himself out-voted 3-2 by the Democrats on major issues.

Royce has skirted the edges of a few low-grade controversies. Democrats accused him in the 1988 election of circumventing federal campaign laws to give $5,000 from his campaign fund to Republican Rep. Wally Herger of Yuba City. Herger gave the money back, and the Federal Elections Commission dropped the matter.

Royce also won passage of a bill requiring the Board of Medical Quality Assurance – the agency that licenses doctors – to review applications of University of Saigon Medical school graduates. The measure helped 33 influential Vietnamese doctors in his district, the center of the largest concentration of Southeast Asian refugees in the nation.

PERSONAL: elected 1982; born Oct. 12, 1951, in Los Angeles, Calif.; home, Anaheim; education, B.A. accounting and finance CSU Fullerton; wife, Marie Porter; no children; Catholic.

CAREER: corporate tax manager and controller.

COMMITTEES: Constitutional Amendments (chair); Public Employment &

Retirement; Business & Professions; Health & Human Services; Industrial Relations. SELECT: Border Issues; Drug Trafficking & Contraband; Governmental Efficiency; Substance Abuse. JOINT: Oversight on GAIN Implementation; State's Economy.

OFFICES: Capitol, (916) 445-5831; district, 305 N. Harbor Blvd., Suite C-1, Fullerton, 92632, (714) 871-0270.

REGISTRATION: 43% D; 47% R

1986 CAMPAIGN: Royce – R   66%
Hoffman – D   34%

RATINGS:

AFL	PIRG	CLCV	NOW	CTA	HAC	CofC	CFB	NRA
31%	62%	65%	25%	U	78%	56%	57%	100%

KEY VOTES:

Divest S. Africa:	NO	Insurance reform:	–	Child sick leave:	NO
Assault gun ban:	NO	Parent consent abortion:	YES	Ban AIDS discrim:	NO
Clean Air Act:	YES	Ban insure donations:	NO	Extend death penalty:	YES
Lmt product tort:	–	End mob home rent cont:	YES	Ban offshore oil:	YES

33rd Senate District

Cecil Green (D)

Straddling the border between Los Angeles and Orange counties, this district is decidedly industrial and working class. Homes are old but well-maintained. Their residents work at such places as Rockwell International and Powerine Oil Co., and they live in cities like Bellflower, Downey, Artesia, Norwalk and Buena Park.

The district is cross-hatched with five freeways and its population is about a quarter Hispanic. The voter registration has steadily slipped for the Democrats in the last decade, a circumstance that set the stage for a special election in 1987 that broke the records for legislative campaign spending and all bounds of reason.

The conditions for campaign insanity grew ripe in 1986, when Democrat Paul Carpenter – seeing his hold

Cecil Green

on the district slipping – abandoned the seat for a cushy postition on the state Board of Equalization. Looking at the registration figures, Republican strategists thought they had an excellent chance of winning in the subsequent special election. By the time the campaign was over, the two major parties had spent $3 million, mobilized hundreds of legislative employees going door-to-door, leased fleets of vans with car phones to ferry voters to the polls and purchased thousands of doughnuts to give voters as a reward for voting. In the aftermath, Republicans in the Senate laid the blame for the loss on their leaders, and unceremoniously dumped Sens. Jim Nielsen and John Seymour from their positions.

The winner was Democrat Cecil Green, ex-mayor and city councilman from Norwalk and the anointed candidate of Senate President Pro Tem David Roberti. Green heeded the advice of professional political mercenaries, while his Republican opponent, Assemblyman Wayne Grisham of Norwalk, did not. Grisham spent much of his campaign days on the golf course and could never adequately cope with charges that he had made sexual passes at a woman on his staff. Grisham so enraged his own supporters that his campaign manager, Dale Hardeman, opposed him in the Republican Assembly primary the next year. Grisham won his primary but went on to lose his Assembly seat in 1988.

As a senator, the affable Green has done little more than keep a seat warm for the Democrats. Soon after arriving in Sacramento, Green was quickly rewarded with the chairmanship of the dull-but-important committee that oversees the public employee retirement system and with seats on other choice committees, including Transportation.

So far, Green shows no signs of bucking his patron Roberti. When Green signaled he had an open mind on the nomination of Dan Lungren as state treasurer, he was quickly braced into line. In the meantime, voters in the 33rd District can look forward to more bloody battles between Sacramento political forces when Green's term comes up for re-election.

PERSONAL: elected 1987 (special election); born Sept. 24, 1924, in Riverside, Calif.; home, Norwalk ; Navy 1942-1952 WWII, Korea; education, attended CSU Long Beach; wife, Mary; child, Janyce; Lutheran.

CAREER: carpenter; contractor; commercial pilot; flight instructor; corporate manager; mayor; Norwalk City Council 1974-1987.

COMMITTEES: Public Employment & Retirement (chair); Agriculture & Water Resources; Education; Insurance, Claims & Corporations; Local Government; Transportation. SELECT: Substance Abuse. SPECIAL: Neighborhood Violence; UC Admissions. JOINT: Organized Crime & Gang Violence.

OFFICES: Capitol, (916) 445-5581; district, 12631 E. Imperial Highway, Building A 120, Santa Fe Springs, 90670, (213) 929-0016.

REGISTRATION: 52.1% D; 39.9% R

1988 CAMPAIGN: Green – D   51%
                  Knabe – R   49%

RATINGS:	AFL	PIRG	CLCV	NOW	CTA	HAC	CofC	CFB	NRA
	100%	71%	90%	75%	G	100%	20%	57%	71%

KEY VOTES:

	Insurance reform:	YES	Child sick leave:	YES
Assault gun ban: YES	Parent consent abortion:	YES	Ban AIDS discrim:	YES
Clean Air Act: YES	Ban insure donations:	NO	Extend death penalty:	YES
Lmt product tort: YES	End mob home rent cont: YES	Ban offshore oil	YES

34th Senate District

Ruben S. Ayala (D)

Tucked into the eastern end of the Los Angeles basin, this bow-tie-shaped district includes the bedroom communities of Pomona, the dairy farms and prisons of Chino and the boom towns of Fontana, Upland, Ontario and San Bernardino stretching along the I-10 corridor. Fontana, in particular, has undergone a remarkable turnabout in the last decade. Facing economic collapse when Kaiser Steel closed its World War II-vintage mill, the working-class, union town has come back from the dead with housing tracts and new businesses.

Democrat Ruben Ayala has held the seat without much trouble until recently. The overheated growth of western San Bernardino County has brought new resi-

Ruben S. Ayala

dents who don't know Ayala and who tend to vote Republican, and the core of his labor union supporters has faded as a local power. The western county just isn't the working class valley it once was. In 1990, Ayala faces a strong challenge from Republican Assemblyman Charles Bader of Pomona, who has been raising campaign money for more than a year before the election.

Ayala is an energetic legislator, jealously guarding the parochial interests of his district. He has kept a state building in San Bernardino by warding off the encroachments of Riverside's legislators to the south, and sought new escape-proofing measures for the cluster of prisons in Chino at the behest of middle-class homeowners terrified at the bloody massacre of a family in 1984 by an escapee. Ayala's choice committee assignments have given him a powerful weapon.

But ex-Marine Ayala's short temper and lack of patience are his worst enemies. As chairman of the Senate's principal committee on water issues, Ayala has labored for years to expand and modernize the state's water system with negligible success. To be sure, the task might defy even the most diplomatic and clever of lawmakers. But in the hands of the bullheaded Ayala, the effort in 1987-1988 took on the trappings of a personal war. Backed by Gov. Deukmejian, Ayala worked out a limited proposal to upgrade levees in the Sacramento River Delta, rehabilitation projects at the Salton Sea and elsewhere in the southern end of the water system. But the plan met unexpected opposition from the Northern California's Republican Sen. Jim Nielsen, and that was just too much for Ayala. Giving up in a burst of fury on the Senate floor, Ayala lashed out at all who had differences with him on the details. Ayala has no finesse.

PERSONAL: elected 1974 (special election); born March 6, 1922, in Chino, Calif.; home, Chino; education, attended junior college and UCLA Extension, graduated electronics school; USMC 1942-1946 WWII (South Pacific theater);

wife, Irene; children Bud, Maurice, Gary; Catholic.

CAREER: Insurance; Chino School Board 1955-1962; Chino City Council 1962-1964; Chino Mayor 1964-1965; San Bernardino County Board of Supervisors 1965-1973.

COMMITTEES: Agriculture & Water Resources (chair); Appropriations; Local Government; Revenue & Taxation; Veteran's Affairs. SELECT: Fairs & Rural Issues; Planning for Calif. Growth; Small Business Enterprises; State Procurement & Expenditure Practices; Upper Sacramento Valley Economic, Resource & Rangeland Issues. JOINT: Fairs Allocation & Classification; Legislative Audit; Organized Crime & Gang Violence; Rules.

OFFICES: Capitol, (916) 445-6868; district, 505 N. Arrowhead Ave., 100, San Bernardino, 92401, (714) 884-3165; 2545 S. Euclid Ave., Ontario, 91762, (714) 983-3566.

REGISTRATION: 50.9% D; 39.7% R

1986 CAMPAIGN: Ayala – D   66%

Turner – R   34%

RATINGS:

AFL	PIRG	CLCV	NOW	CTA	HAC	CofC	CFB	NRA
82%	57%	85%	50%	G	89%	44%	57%	0%

KEY VOTES:

Divest S. Africa:	YES	Insurance reform:	YES	Child sick leave:	NO
Assault gun ban:	YES	Parent consent abortion:	YES	Ban AIDS discrim:	NO
Clean Air Act:	YES	Ban insure donations:	YES	Extend death penalty:	YES
Lmt product tort:	YES	End mob home rent cont:	YES	Ban offshore oil:	NO

35th Senate District

John F. Seymour (R)

This district is part of the Republicans' magic kingdom of Orange County. It includes the communities of Tustin, Costa Mesa, Fountain Valley and parts of Santa Ana, Orange, Huntington Beach, Westminster, Irvine and Anaheim, the home of Disneyland.

John Seymour made his mark on local politics when, as mayor of Anaheim, he negotiated the Los Angeles Rams football team's move from the Los Angeles Coliseum to Anaheim stadium. And he pushed for local tax relief at the city level even before the passage of the tax-cutting Proposition 13 in 1978.

A successful Realtor, Seymour took his conservative, pro-business approach to Sacramento in 1982 when he won a special election to fill the district's

John F. Seymour

vacant Senate seat. And he quickly moved into the forefront of the Senate

Republican leadership, teaming with Sen. Jim Nielsen in 1983 to help topple Senate Republican leader William Campbell of Hacienda Heights and GOP Caucus Chairman Ken Maddy of Fresno.

Nielsen assumed Campbell's post as Republican leader, and Seymour moved into Maddy's No. 2 post. Together, they raised more money than any Senate GOP leadership team in history to be used toward their goal of making Republicans the majority party in the Senate before the 1991 redistricting. But the Nielsen-Seymour team was forced out after a 1987 election debacle in which their hand-picked candidate, then-Assemblyman Wayne Grisham, was ambushed by Democrat Cecil Green in an expensive special election that the Republicans were confident they would win.

Despite his drop from the leadership post, Seymour has remained one of the GOP's most visible Senate members. He has done this largely by carrying substantive bills and by gradually moving toward the center of the political spectrum.

When he was first elected, Seymour was predictably conservative – an outspoken opponent of abortion and rent control and a proponent of the death penalty – and he was not always willing to negotiate. But over time, Seymour has become more of a pragmatist, willing to not only listen and negotiate, but to join with Democrats in carrying legislation to benefit education, crack down on unsafe truckers and provide help to the homeless.

He has also proposed some innovative plans such as a measure to help parents provide for their children's education through tax-exempt savings accounts, an idea vetoed by Gov. Deukmejian, and has been a leader in getting legislation passed to increase penalties for drunken drivers.

Through his real estate connections, with whom he maintains close political and economic ties, Seymour is a formidable fund raiser. He was one of 50 Californians who contributed $100,000 to George Bush's 1988 presidential campaign.

Seymour will put his fund-raising abilities to a personal test in 1990, when he runs for the GOP nomination for lieutenant governor. And in 1989, the ambitious Seymour was already putting his ideological bent to a test. He announced in September that he had switched his position on the abortion issue. He said that while he was still personally opposed to abortion, he thought that the choice should be left to the woman. The switch angered conservatives, but it put him in the same camp as the likely Republican gubernatorial candidate, U.S. Sen. Pete Wilson.

PERSONAL: elected 1982 (special election); born Dec. 3, 1937, in Mount Lebanon, Penn.; home, Anaheim; USMC 1955-1959; education, B.A. finance UCLA; wife, Judy; children, John III, Jeffery, Lisa Houser, Sarena, Barrett, Shad; Protestant.

CAREER: owner real estate brokerage and management firm; Anaheim City Council and mayor.

COMMITTEES: Budget & Fiscal Review (vice chair); Education; Housing &

Urban Affairs; Revenue & Taxation; Transportation. SELECT: Substance Abuse (chair); AIDS; Children & Youth; Infant & Child Care & Development; Pacific Rim; Tourism & Aviation. SPECIAL: Neighborhood Violence. JOINT: Review of the Master Plan for Higher Education; School Facilities.

OFFICES: Capitol, (916) 445-4264; district, 2150 Towne Centre Place, 205, Anaheim, 92806, (714) 385-1700.

REGISTRATION: 33.1% D; 56.4% R

1988 CAMPAIGN: Seymour – R   74%
                Balmages – D   22%
                Quirk – P&F   3%

RATINGS:

AFL	PIRG	CLCV	NOW	CTA	HAC	CofC	CFB	NRA
35%	50%	69%	50%	S*	100%	72%	71%	71%

KEY VOTES:

Divest S. Africa:	YES	Insurance reform:	YES	Child sick leave:	NO
Assault gun ban:	YES	Parent consent abortion:	YES	Ban AIDS discrim:	YES
Clean Air Act:	YES	Ban insure donations:	–	Extend death penalty:	YES
Lmt product tort:	YES	End mob home rent cont:	YES	Ban offshore oil:	NO

36th Senate District

Robert B. Presley (D)

Riverside County's 36th Senate District stretches from the suburban environs of Riverside through the earth-toned stucco housing tracts of Moreno Valley, then to the San Jacinto Badlands, out through ritzy desert communities and pockets of rural poverty to the Colorado River in Blythe.

When Robert Presley won the seat in 1974 there were considerably fewer people living in that expanse of real estate. In the years since it has become the fastest-growing region of the state, and that creates no end of political problems for the Democratic incumbent. The newest residents, labeled disdainfully by those who have been there awhile as the Dreaded Orange County Influx, tend not to know their state legislators. And they are increasingly voting Republican.

Robert B. Presley

Presley has managed to win handily every four years through hard work and cleverness. A former Riverside County sheriff's deputy who rose through the ranks to become second in command, his law-and-order credentials are impeccable – and his exploits as a detective are still stuff of local lore. He won a Bronze Star in Italy in World War II for staying behind enemy lines with the wounded until an American counteroffensive came to the rescue.

As a senator, Presley is the area's preeminent politician – practically Riverside County's unofficial "mayor," resolving disputes between competing local power interests. He has cultivated the old power structure, personified by the "Monday Morning Group" of Riverside businessmen, and it has shown him unmatched loyalty.

Presley's soft Oklahoma drawl and folksy manners hide a stubborn streak and craftiness. Politically, Presley calls himself a conservative and hints periodically that he will become a Republican. In 1982, he ran a write-in campaign for the Republican nomination and won, thus enabling himself to run as the nominee of both major parties. He has carried major legislation for Republican Gov. Deukmejian on numerous occasions, including the enormously controversial construction of a Los Angeles prison, and has earned a reputation for taking on tough, no-win issues.

Nonetheless, Presley has cemented his relationship with Democratic President Pro Tem David Roberti, and reaped considerable benefits, not the least being the chairmanship of Appropriations, the Senate's most powerful committee next to Rules. As chairman he has won plaudits for fairness, but is not as fast with the gavel – or as ruthless – as his predecessor, Democratic Sen. Dan Boatwright of Concord.

Occasionally, Presley entertains thoughts of running for Congress if longtime Democratic Rep. George Brown ever retires. Meanwhile, white-haired Presley busies himself as one the hardest working and most successful legislators in Sacramento. His legislative achievements include authoring the state's vehicle smog-check program, reorganizing and strengthening the South Coast Air Quality Management District, bringing reason to chaotic child welfare laws and stiffening numerous criminal laws – not to mention building every new prison of the last decade.

PERSONAL: elected 1974; born Dec. 4, 1924, in Tahlequah, Okla.; home, Riverside; Army 1943-1946 WWII (Bronze Star, Italy); education, A.A. Riverside City College, FBI National Academy; wife, Ahni Ratliff; children, Marilyn, Donna and Robert; Baptist.

CAREER: Riverside County Sheriff's department 24 years, undersheriff (second ranking).

COMMITTEES: Appropriations (chair); Agriculture & Water Resources; Judiciary; Natural Resources & Wildlife. SELECT: Children & Youth (chair);Pacific Rim (vice chair); AIDS; Business Development; Fairs and Rural Issues; Infant & Child Care & Development; Mobile Homes; Planning for Calif. Growth. SPECIAL: Solid and Hazardous Waste. JOINT: Prison Construction and Operations (chair); Legislative Ethics (vice chair); Fire, Police, Emergency & Disaster Services; Legislative Audit; Revision of the Penal Code.

OFFICES: Capitol, (916) 445-9781; district, 3600 Lime Street, 111, Riverside, 92501 (714) 782-4111; 72-811 Highway 111 201, Palm Desert, 92260 (619) 340-4488.

REGISTRATION: 46.5% D; 44.5% R
1986 CAMPAIGN: Presley – D   61%
              Richardson – R 39%

RATINGS:

AFL	PIRG	CLCV	NOW	CTA	HAC	CofC	CFB	NRA
66%	86%	91%	67%	G	89%	40%	42%	57%

KEY VOTES:

Divest S. Africa: YES	Insurance reform: YES	Child sick leave: NO
Assault gun ban: YES	Parent consent abortion: YES	Ban AIDS discrim: YES
Clean Air Act: YES	Ban insure donations: YES	Extend death penalty: YES
Lmt product tort: YES	End mob home rent cont: YES	Ban offshore oil: YES

37th Senate District
Marian C. Bergeson (R)

This huge district, so large it is unwieldy, takes in a strip of upscale beach communities of Orange County – Newport Beach, Balboa Island, Laguna Beach to name a few – and then roughly one-third of Riverside County, including the burgeoning towns of Rancho California, Temecula and Hemet. To the south and east, the district includes most of North San Diego County, and all of fertile Imperial County. Its population is growing fast and the district, with an overwhelmingly Republican voter edge, will be carved up after the next census.

Marian C. Bergeson

Republican Marian Bergeson, a member of the Assembly for eight years, won the seat in 1984 after falling from favor among ideologically rigid Assembly Republican leaders. Bergeson has flourished in the Senate. She has shown an independent streak at times, and although conservative on issues like abortion, she has a practical bent.

However, Bergeson is another of those legislators who have grown weary of the Legislature. She made a major push to get Gov. George Deukmejian to appoint her state treasurer after Democrat Jesse Unruh died in 1987. He passed her over twice, along with several other Republican senators.

With her Orange County base, Bergeson has shown herself an able fund-raiser, and she is making a stab at running for lieutenant governor in 1990. The race for the GOP nomination has pitted her against another Orange County Republican senator, John Seymour of Anaheim, who has flip-flopped from anti-abortion to pro-choice. Bergeson remains anti-abortion, which should help her in the GOP primary but could cause her problems in the general election against Democrat Leo McCarthy. Polls show California voters overwhelmingly pro-choice.

The race in the early going seemed to be confined to the Orange County

Republican cocktail circuit, with neither candidate branching out from beyond the Santa Ana mountains. With no experience in a statewide race, Bergeson will need coaching. Although she is personally warm in one-on-one encounters, she has an awkward, wooden speaking style. She does look the part of a school board lady, which indeed is where she got her political start.

Some have said she is Democratic leader David Roberti's favorite Republican (though the distinction may be shared with Sen. Bill Craven). Indeed, she is the only Republican to chair a major committee in the Senate. As chairwoman of the Senate Local Government Committee, Bergeson presided over difficult hearings to reorganize the South Coast Air Quality Management District, and has attempted for years to streamline Caltrans' contracting policies for highway construction. She has also put herself in the middle of major school construction financing fights and has tried to deal with the thorny growth control issue. Possibly her most important assignment has been as the Senate Republicans' representative to the all-important yearly budget conference committee, putting the final touches on the state's spending plan. She is not as sharp as the Assembly Republican's representative – Bill Baker – but then, she could not possibly be as acid-tongued.

Bergeson has had a thankless time balancing the needs of her district. She tends to tilt toward Orange County – where her political roots and major contributors are – although the bulk of her district is in Riverside, San Diego and Imperial Counties. She has been caught more than once in the cross-fire of conflicting interests in her district. For example, in the fight over reorganizing the basin's smog district, she was drawn between Orange County and Riverside County – both wanting more representation on the district's board. She did her best to push for Orange County, but in the end acquiesced in letting smaller Riverside County have equal representation. At times, she shows scant knowledge of the communities in her district.

Some believe she was bamboozled a few years ago by a powerful irrigation district in Imperial County to sponsor legislation to help it drain more water from the Salton Sea. Only after angry residents of her district arranged a meeting with her did Bergeson modify her proposal; she seemed surprised at the residents' opposition. That may have been the best argument for breaking up this too-large district.

PERSONAL: elected 1984; born Aug. 31, 1925, in Salt Lake City, Utah; home, Newport Beach; education, B.A. elementary education Brigham Young University; graduate studies UCLA; husband, Garth Bergeson; children, Nancy, Garth Jr., Julie and James; Mormon.

CAREER: Newport Mesa school board 1965-1977; president of California School Boards Association; Assembly 1978.

COMMITTEES: Local Government, (chair); Bonded Indebtedness & Methods of Financing (vice chair); Agriculture & Water Resources; Appropriations; Transportation. SELECT: Planning for Calif. Growth (chair); Border Issues, Drug Trafficking & Contraband; Infant & Child Care.

OFFICES: Capitol, (916) 445-4961; district, 140 Newport Center Dr. 120,

Newport Beach, 92660, (714) 640-1137; 1101 Airport Road, Suite C, Imperial, 92251, (619) 353-8244.

REGISTRATION: 33.6% D; 56.2% R

1988 CAMPAIGN: Bergeson – R   71%

                     McCabe – D   27%

                     Sugars – L   2%

RATINGS:	AFL	PIRG	CLCV	NOW	CTA	HAC	CofC	CFB	NRA
	28%	71%	74%	58%	S	89%	44%	71%	43%

KEY VOTES:

Divest S. Africa:	NO	Insurance reform:	NO	Child sick leave:	NO
Assault gun ban:	YES	Parent consent abortion:	YES	Ban AIDS discrim:	–
Clean Air Act:	NO	Ban insure donations:	NO	Extend death penalty:	YES
Lmt product tort:	YES	End mob home rent cont:	YES	Ban offshore oil:	YES

38th Senate District

William A. Craven (R)

Sliced out of the upscale beach communities of North San Diego County, the safely Republican 38th District stretches along I-5 from the horse track of Del Mar to the Marine Corps base at Camp Pendleton. Much of San Diego County's growth over the last decade has been here. North County politics tends to focus on growth control. It is land of checker-board development, strawberry farms, real estate speculators and quick-buck artists. It is one of the most liveable corners of the state, where life is easy but homes are expensive.

William A. Craven

Republican Bill Craven has long been a figure in North County's civic and political life. An ex-Marine major, he epitomizes the Californians who have found their paradise in North County. Craven came from Philadelphia, settled in North County and served on the Oceanside Planning Commission – the town just to the south of Camp Pendleton. He won a seat on the county Board of Supervisors in 1970. Five years later, he was in the Assembly, and three years after that he was in the Senate.

Craven is often called David Roberti's favorite Republican. Democrat Roberti often looks to Craven for advice. The two have built a cordial, trusting friendship verging on a cross-party alliance. Craven is one of the barons of the five-member Rules Committee that runs the Senate. The chain-smoking Craven often presides over the committee in Roberti's absence. Craven has served as a bridge between the ideological poles of an increasingly fractured Senate. He is a club member who helps the house work. And the Republicans can't take Craven's vote for granted;

more than once Roberti has won a swing vote from Craven.

Craven's legislative accomplishments are solid though not flashy. After years of labor, he won approval of a state university expansion campus for his district that will be established in San Marcos. The administration building will be named after Craven. As chairman of the Select Committee on Mobile Homes, Craven is considered the Legislature's expert on mobile home legislation, an esoteric legal area of major interest to many of his older constituents.

PERSONAL: elected 1973, Assembly 1970; born June 30, 1921, in Philadelphia, Penn.; home, Oceanside; education, B.S. economics Villanova University; USMC 1942-1946, 1950-1953; wife, Mimi; children, William Jr., Patricia Worley and John; Catholic.

CAREER: leather business.

COMMITTEES: Rules; Elections; Agriculture & Water Resources; Business & Professions; Local Government. SELECT: Mobile Homes (chair); Business Development; Citizen Participation in Government; Maritime Industry; Neighborhood Violence; Substance Abuse. JOINT: Arts; Quincentennial of the Voyages of Columbus; Fire, Police, Emergency & Disaster Services; Legislative Ethics; Legislative Retirement (chair); Refugee Resettlement & International Migration; Rules.

OFFICES: Capitol, (916) 445-3731; district, 2121 Palomar Airport Road, 100, Carlsbad, 92008, (619) 438-3814.

REGISTRATION: 33.5% D; 52% R

1986 CAMPAIGN: Craven – R   85%

                       Mill – L   15%

RATINGS:	AFL	PIRG	CLCV	NOW	CTA	HAC	CofC	CFB	NRA
	49%	67%	82%	50%	G	67%	32%	28%	29%

KEY VOTES:

Divest S. Africa:	NO	Insurance reform:	–	Child sick leave:	NO
Assault gun ban:	YES	Parent consent abortion:	YES	Ban AIDS discrim:	YES
Clean Air Act:	YES	Ban insure donations:	NO	Extend death penalty:	–
Lmt product tort:	–	End mob home rent cont:	YES	Ban offshore oil:	–

39th Senate District

Vacant

Starting on Coronado Island, the 39th District hooks north across a narrow stretch of water to Point Loma. Then the district heads east by southeast, taking in the heart of San Diego's featureless Republican bedroom neighborhoods on the bluffs overlooking San Diego's sports stadium. Extending past San Diego State University and La Mesa, the district roughly follows Interstate 8 and the Mexican border into eastern San Diego County. It includes El Cajon, Santee, Lakeside and Alpine.

Republican Larry Stirling was elected to the Senate in 1988 after serving eight years in the Assembly, but to the total surprise of Capitol insiders, he quit after less than a year to take judgeship in the San Diego Municipal Court. Stirling's resignation could well cost the Republicans a seat in the Senate – and Republican leader Ken Maddy was said to be privately furious with Stirling for the move (Maddy was not even told about it in advance). Stirling's flight from Sacramento has set up a duel between Republican Assemblywoman Carol Bentley, who succeeded Stirling in the Assembly, and veteran Democratic Assemblywoman Lucy Killea, who hopes to overcome the Republican's registration edge with her firm pro-choice stance on abortion.

Larry Stirling

As Willie Brown's favorite Republican, Stirling chaired the Public Safety Committee – the only GOP Assembly member to chair a major committee for two sessions. However, Stirling was chairman in name only. He was consistently frustrated in his attempts to advance a stiff Republican criminal law agenda. The Democrats held the majority of votes on the committee and kept him at bay.

While in the Assembly as vice chairman of the Joint Committee on Prison Construction, Stirling's probing questioning was invaluable in correcting weaknesses in the state's massive prison building program – to the benefit of the taxpayers.

PERSONAL: resigned 1989, elected 1988; born Feb. 20, 1942, in Youngstown, Ohio; home, San Diego; Army 1965-1969 Vietnam; education, B.A. San Diego State University, J.D. Western State; divorced; children, Shenandoah and Benjamin; Presbyterian.

CAREER: lawyer; San Diego city administrative official; San Diego City Council 1977-1980; Assembly 1980.

REGISTRATION: 38.1% D; 49% R

1988 CAMPAIGN: Stirling – R   69%
Berkson – D   27%
Hall – L   4%

RATINGS: (except for NRA, ratings are for Stirling in the Assembly)

AFL	PIRG	CLCV	NOW	CTA	HAC	CofC	CFB	NRA
29%	42%	40%	50%	U	31%	72%	66%	100%

KEY VOTES: (includes Stirling votes in the Assembly)

Divest S. Africa: YES	Insurance reform: –	Child sick leave: NO
Assault gun ban: NO	Parent consent abortion: YES	Ban AIDS discrim: NO
Clean Air Act: NO	Ban insure donations: NO	Extend death penalty: YES
Lmt product tort: YES	End mob home rent cont: YES	Ban offshore oil: NO

40th Senate District

Wadie P. Deddeh (D)

The last decade has brought the transformation of downtown San Diego from fleabag sailor-bars to a glistening jewel of waterfront hotels and gleaming towers crowned by the unconventional Horton Plaza shopping center. The sailors and winos, however, are still around. Southward, arrayed along Interstate 5 are the South Bay communities of Chula Vista, National City, Imperial Beach, Bonita and San Ysidro (part of the city of San Diego).

Like downtown San Diego, much of the South Bay has also undergone monumental change in the last decade, but many pockets remain amazingly untouched. National City is still an expanse of shipyards and the "Mile of Cars." Chula Vista just to the south is

Wadie P. Deddeh

breaking out of its mold with ambitious plans for waterfront hotels and huge housing tracts. Imperial Beach is what California beach towns used to be – laid-back and a little bit seedy – but also going broke as a municipality. And all have one overriding common denominator – their proximity to Mexico, with a steady flood of illegal aliens, drugs and Tijuana's leaky sewage system polluting beaches and farms.

Democrat Wadie Deddeh has never been much of a force in either San Diego or state Capitol politics, although he has been working at it for three decades. He was elected to the Assembly in 1966, the year the Legislature went full-time. Deddeh won a seat in the Senate after the last reapportionment. He has carried legislation tinkering with transportation and tax laws, and tended to local bread-and-butter concerns like creating more judgeships. A native of Iraq, he spent much of the 1980s entreating President Ronald Reagan to appoint him ambassador to his native land – to no avail. Deddeh has been one of the Senate's biggest junketeers, accepting free trips to the Middle East, Europe and throughout the Pacific. He has shown minimal interest in Mexico and border issues, although he considers himself a foreign policy buff. He has left major border issues, like trade and pollution, to San Diego area Assembly colleagues Lucy Killea and Steve Peace.

Deddeh did not do well at his one chance to become a major force in the Senate. When longtime Transportation Committee Chairman John Foran decided to retire at the end of the 1986 term, Deddeh ascended to the chairmanship of the prestigious committee – one of supreme importance to his district with its creaky infrastructure. Less than two years later, Deddeh squandered his chairmanship by supporting Deukmejian's ill-fated nominee for state treasurer, Republican Dan Lungren. Senate President David Roberti sacked Deddeh as Transportation chairman and appointed in his place independent Sen. Quentin Kopp of San Francisco, who in the last hours before the Lungren vote switched from support to opposition. Roberti later resurrected Deddeh slightly by creating a new committee on veterans affairs for him to chair.

Deddeh recently underwent coronary bypass surgery. He may consider retirement at the end of his term in 1990.

PERSONAL: elected 1982; born Sept. 6, 1920, in Baghdad, Iraq; home, Chula Vista; education, B.A. English University of Baghdad 1946; M.A. education University of Detroit 1956; graduate work economics, government and political science San Diego State University; wife, Mary-Lynn Drake; son, Peter; Catholic.

CAREER: political science teacher, Southwestern Community College, Chula Vista; Assembly 1966.

COMMITTEES: Veterans' Affairs (chair); Appropriations; Banking & Commerce; Education; Health & Human Services; Insurance, Claims & Corporations. SELECT: Border Issues, Drug Trafficking & Contraband (chair); Pacific Rim; Planning for Calif. Growth; Substance Abuse. JOINT: Organized Crime & Gang Violence (chair); Legislative Retirement; Public Pension Fund Investments.

OFFICES: Capitol, (916) 445-6767; district, 430 Davidson St., Suite C, Chula Vista, 92010, (619) 427-7080.

REGISTRATION: 53.2% D; 34.2% R

1986 CAMPAIGN: Deddeh – D   69%
                   Hoover – R   29%
                   Beard – P&F   2%

RATINGS:

	AFL	PIRG	CLCV	NOW	CTA	HAC	CofC	CFB	NRA
	88%	93%	91%	67%	G	78%	20%	28%	86%

KEY VOTES:

Divest S. Africa:	YES	Insurance reform:	–	Child sick leave:	YES
Assault gun ban:	YES	Parent consent abortion: YES	Ban AIDS discrim:	YES
Clean Air Act:	YES	Ban insure donations:	–	Extend death penalty:	–
Lmt product tort:	YES	End mob home rent cont:	–	Ban offshore oil:	YES

ASSEMBLY
1st Assembly District

R. Stan Statham (R)

There's a little sign outside Assemblyman Stan Statham's Capitol office informing visitors that he represents "the 51st state."

That's not quite true, but the nine-county 1st Assembly District covers some 30,000 square miles of northeastern California, almost a fifth of the state and nearly as large as Maine.

As its size implies, the 1st District is mostly sparsely populated stretches of agricultural fields, rangeland, mountains and timber. There are few communities larger than small towns, the most prominent being Redding.

Although the district has a Democratic voter registration edge (48-41 percent), it, like the rest of the region, tends to vote Republican with monotonous regularity.

R. Stan Statham

Statham, who became known in the area by being a local television anchorman for a decade, won the seat in 1976 after Democratic Assemblywoman Pauline Davis retired. And he's won re-election easily ever since.

Despite his relative seniority among the fast-changing Republican membership of the Assembly, Statham has never achieved much power. That's because he comes from a rural backwater district and because his politics are decidedly more moderate than the prevailing right-wing slant in the GOP caucus.

Statham is part of a loose confederation of Republican rebel moderates known as the "Magnificent Seven" and has been mentioned as a candidate for GOP leader should the faction become more powerful.

Being a minority within a minority means that Statham isn't a player on major legislative matters. His wife, Lovie, however, has carved out a semi-career of her own as an organizer of political fund-raising events not only for Statham but other politicians.

Given the Republican bent to his district, Statham can probably remain in the seat for as long as he wants – which will be until a state Senate or congressional district becomes available.

PERSONAL: elected 1976; born April 7, 1939, in Chico, Calif.; home, Chico; Army 1956-1959; education, attended CSU Chico; wife, Lovie Plants; children, Devin and Jennifer; no religious affiliation.

CAREER: finance and banking; radio disc jockey; television anchor; news and public affairs director, KHSL-TV Chico, 1964-1975.

COMMITTEES: Finance & Insurance, Governmental Organization, Health, Judiciary. SELECT: Ethics.

OFFICES: Capitol, (916) 445-7266; district, 429 Red Cliff Drive, #200, Redding 96002, (916) 223-6300.

REGISTRATION: 48% D, 41.1% R

1988 CAMPAIGN: Statham – R   70%
               Caudle – D   30%

RATINGS: AFL   PIRG   CLCV   NOW   CTA   HAC   CofC   CFB   NRA
         28%   47%   31%   42%   S   36%   76%   77%   90%

KEY VOTES:

Divest S. Africa: NO	Insurance reform: NO	Child sick leave: –	
Assault gun ban: NO	Parent consent abortion: –	Ban AIDS discrim: YES	
Clean Air Act: NO	Cutting old trees: YES	Extend death penalty: YES	
Lmt product tort: YES	End mob home rent cont: YES	Ban'offshore oil: –	

2nd Assembly District

Daniel E. Hauser (D)

California's northwestern coast is so thinly populated that one state Assembly district stretches from the Oregon border 300 miles southward to within commuting distance of San Francisco. Once, the area voted Republican with some regularity, but as the traditional industries of lumber and fishing faded and as flower children of the 1960s moved in and established roots, the politics of the area began creeping leftward.

Democrats have replaced Republicans in all local legislative and congressional seats, including the 2nd Assembly District, which covers all or parts of Del Norte, Humboldt, Mendocino and Sonoma counties.

Barry Keene captured the seat for the Democrats in **Daniel E. Hauser** 1972 and he was followed four years later by Doug Bosco. Keene went to the state Senate and Bosco to Congress in 1982 and the third Democrat to win in the district was Dan Hauser, a one-time insurance adjuster and mayor of Arcata.

Hauser, in a victory for name-freakers everywhere, chairs the Assembly Housing Committee. But much of his time is occupied with avoiding being chewed up by the ceaseless environmental controversies that buffet his scenic and resource-rich district.

Environmentalists and logging and mining companies battle endlessly over regulations and laws. Hauser came into office as a Sierra Club candidate. He routinely offers bills and resolutions to ban offshore oil drilling. In more recent years, Hauser seems to have gravitated more toward the timber industry. Matters came to a head in 1989 when an environmental group-sponsored bill to put a three-year moratorium on logging old-growth forests came to the Assembly floor. Hauser offered industry-sponsored amendments that gutted the bill and were adopted after a sharp debate. The bill then died.

That and other instances have driven a wedge between Hauser and the increasingly militant environmentalists, but as the Democratic incumbent, he's unlikely to face a serious challenge from the left.

He has labored to produce a stream of dull-but-important housing bills. But beyond that, Hauser is considered to be a second-tier legislator who is unlikely to achieve major prominence.

PERSONAL: elected 1982; born June 18, 1942, in Riverside, Calif.; home, Arcata; education, B.A. American history Humboldt State University; wife, Donna Dumont; children, Dawn and Doug; Lutheran.

CAREER: insurance claims representative; Arcata City Council, 1974-1978, mayor, 1978-1982.

COMMITTEES: Housing & Community Development (chair); Agriculture; Local Government; Water, Parks & Wildlife. SELECT: California Wine Production & Economy. JOINT: Fisheries & Aquaculture (vice chair); Fairs Allocation & Classification; School Facilities.

OFFICES: Capitol, (916) 445-8360; district, 510 O St., Suite G, Eureka 95501, (707) 445-7014; 216 W. Perkins St., 107, Ukiah 95482, (707) 463-1508; 50 D St., 450, Santa Rosa 95404, (707) 576-2526.

REGISTRATION: 57.2% D, 31.1% R.

1988 CAMPAIGN: Hauser - D   75%
King - R   25%

RATINGS:

AFL	PIRG	CLCV	NOW	CTA	HAC	CofC	CFB	NRA
94%	84%	88%	92%	S	90%	32%	55%	40%

KEY VOTES:

Divest S. Africa:	YES	Insurance reform:	YES	Child sick leave:	YES
Assault gun ban:	NO	Parent consent abortion:	NO	Ban AIDS discrim:	YES
Clean Air Act:	YES	Cutting old trees:	YES	Extend death penalty:	YES
Lmt product tort:	YES	End mob home rent cont:	YES	Ban offshore oil:	YES

3rd Assembly District

Christopher R. Chandler (R)

Farms, mountains and wide open spaces are the main characteristics of this conservative, rural district that includes the Northern California counties of Colusa, Nevada, Sierra, Sutter and Yuba.

Chris Chandler, a Yuba City lawyer and real estate dealer, was handpicked by Assembly Republican conservatives to succeed Wally Herger, who was elected to Congress in 1986.

The substantial financial support given to Chandler by Assembly GOP leaders in the contested Republican primary that year temporarily angered party moderates who were supporting other hopefuls. But the schism was patched up and Chandler handily won a seat that Democrats had some fleeting hopes of capturing.

Chandler has been true to the conservative ideals his backers sought and has rarely strayed from the caucus line. He has concentrated primarily on carrying bills to benefit interests in his district. In 1988, for example, he

Chris Chandler

pushed a bill to suspend California water quality and toxics laws to allow rice farmers to use a specific chemical fungicide. He pushed a measure to prohibit the administration at California State University, Chico, from taking over student-run businesses. And he has adamantly opposed measures by San Joaquin Valley and Southern Californian legislators to increase water shipments from his district to theirs.

Chandler is among a group of a dozen legislators who were given "Free Speech" awards by Common Cause, a political watchdog organization, for refusing to take honorariums.

PERSONAL: elected 1986; born Jan. 20, 1951, in Marysville, Calif.; home, Yuba City; education, B.A. English UC Davis; J.D. McGeorge; wife, Cindy; children, Carolyn, Jessica and Emily; Episcopalian.

CAREER: lawyer.

COMMITTEES: Agriculture; Education; Governmental Efficiency & Consumer Protection. SELECT: State Public Procurement Practices. JOINT: Fairs Allocation & Classification, Review of the Master Plan for Higher Education.

OFFICES: Capitol, (916) 445-7298; district, 1227 Bridge St., Suite E, Yuba City 95991, (916) 673-2201.

REGISTRATION: 44.3% D, 44.5% R

1988 CAMPAIGN: Chandler - R   60%
Conklin - D   37%
Sweany - L   3%

RATINGS:	AFL	PIRG	CLCV	NOW	CTA	HAC	CofC	CFB	NRA
	10%	32%	7%	25%	U	31%	96%	77%	100%

KEY VOTES:

	Insurance reform:	NO	Child sick leave:	NO
Assault gun ban: NO	Parent consent abortion:	YES	Ban AIDS discrim:	NO
Clean Air Act: NO	Cutting old trees:	YES	Extend death penalty:	YES
Lmt product tort: YES	End mob home rent cont:	YES	Ban offshore oil:	NO

4th Assembly District

Thomas M. Hannigan (D)

More and more, this district is being transformed into a series of commuter cities for people who work in the San Francisco Bay Area. It contains all of Solano County, most of Vallejo and southern Yolo County, including the college town of Davis.

Tom Hannigan, a former U.S. Marine captain and Realtor, has developed a reputation as a thoughtful, honest and hard-working legislator since he was elected to the Assembly in 1978.

He began his political career in local government, serving as mayor of Fairfield and later as chairman of the Solano County Board of Supervisors. Accordingly, Hannigan has shown interest in trying to help solve local government funding problems. He was among the

Thomas M. Hannigan

early legislators who suggested that Proposition 13 and the state's spending limits needed some adjusting. He's proposed giving counties more money to encourage preservation of agricultural lands under the Williamson Act. He has also been acutely aware of his district's changing status, pushing to get rail service between Auburn and San Jose. And he pushed to help fund construction of the Vietnam Memorial in Capitol Park through a checkoff on the state income tax form.

For most of his Assembly career, Hannigan has been recognized as an expert in tax and financial matters, serving a stint as chairman of the Assembly Revenue and Taxation Committee through which all revenue-generating and tax break bills pass. In 1986, Hannigan set in motion a move to reform the state income tax.

The following year, however, Hannigan relinquished control over the committee when Assembly Speaker Willie Brown named him to replace embattled Mike Roos of Los Angeles as the Democrats' majority leader, one of the top leadership posts. At the time, Democrats were suffering from charges that they were putting politics over policy. Hannigan had a reputation for being more interested in issues than back-room maneuvering, public posturing and campaign strategy.

Since then, there has been some indication that part of Brown's naming of Hannigan to the post was aimed more at image polishing rather than substantive political reform. In fact, much of the overtly political work of raising money and getting candidates elected has simply been shifted away from the majority leader to Roos, who now serves as speaker pro tem, and Phillip Isenberg of Sacramento, who is assistant speaker pro tem.

Still, Hannigan's reputation generally has remained intact. His is one of the names consistently mentioned when speculation arises about a successor to Brown as Assembly speaker.

PERSONAL: elected 1978; born May 30, 1940, in Vallejo, Calif.; home, Suisun; USMC 1963-1966 Vietnam; education, B.S. business University of Santa Clara; wife, Jan Mape; children; Erin, Matthew and Bridget; Catholic.

CAREER: Fairfield City Council, 1970-1972; mayor, 1972-1974; Solano County Board of Supervisors, 1974-1978; owner and broker of Hannigan & O'Neill Realtors; Assembly majority floor leader.

COMMITTEES: Agriculture; Local Government; Public Employees, Retirement & Social Security; Transportation; Ways & Means. SPECIAL: Policy Research Management. JOINT: Rules.

OFFICES: Capitol, (916) 445-8368; district, 844 Union Ave., Suite A, Fairfield 94533, (707) 429-2383; 424 2nd St., Suite E, Davis 95616, (916) 753-0367.

REGISTRATION: 55.1% D, 32.1% R.

1988 CAMPAIGN: Hannigan - D   67%
                 Ford - R   33%

RATINGS:

AFL	PIRG	CLCV	NOW	CTA	HAC	CofC	CFB	NRA
95%	89%	100%	92%	S	90%	28%	44%	0%

KEY VOTES:

Divest S. Africa: YES	Insurance reform: YES	Child sick leave: YES
Assault gun ban: YES	Parent consent abortion: NO	Ban AIDS discrim: YES
Clean Air Act: YES	Cutting old trees: NO	Extend death penalty: YES
Lmt product tort: YES	End mob home rent cont: NO	Ban offshore oil: YES

5th Assembly District

Robert Timothy Leslie (R)

The evolutionary nature of politics in the Sacramento suburbs is crystallized in the 5th Assembly District.

Republican Jean Moorhead won the seat in 1978, but she later switched to the Democratic Party after a blowup with Republican leaders and in 1986 announced she would retire from the Legislature altogether.

The district had been altered in the post-1980 reapportionment to include more of fast-growing Placer County and although that shifted voting emphasis toward Republicans, Moorhead agreed to the change. The district now includes Sacramento County's northeastern suburbs, plus Roseville and Auburn.

Robert Timothy Leslie

Moorhead's decision to retire sparked a high-octane campaign by both parties to capture her seat because the district's registration, about

49 percent to 42 percent, made it potentially winnable by either party.

The Republicans went with Tim Leslie, a former lobbyist and legislative aide who had tried to unseat Moorhead in 1984 and lost by just 1,379 votes. Democratic leaders rebuffed a bid by Placer County Supervisor Terry Cook and anointed what they called "a macho man," Jack Dugan, a one-time New York policeman and retired Army colonel who had helped develop the California Conservation Corps.

But Dugan had an Achilles heel that didn't surface until a showdown debate between the two: he had never voted in a California election. Leslie blew out Dugan and easily won re-election in 1986.

Despite the theatrics of his campaign against Dugan, Leslie has been a low-voltage legislator, a backbencher who votes as GOP leaders decree, carries a few local interest bills and shows no signs of aspiring to greater things. He got a little notoriety by being on the Bay Bridge at 5:04 p.m. Oct. 17, 1989, during the earthquake. He told his tale to media and slipped back into obscurity.

PERSONAL: elected 1986; born Feb. 4, 1942, in Ashland, Ore.; home, Carmichael; education, B.S. political science CSU Long Beach; M.A. public administration USC; wife, Clydene; children, Debbie and Scott; Presbyterian.

CAREER: real estate; Assembly Ways & Means Committee consultant 1969-1971; lobbyist for County Supervisors' Association of California 1971-1980.

COMMITTEES: Human Services (vice chair); Judiciary; Education; Public Employees, Retirement & Social Security. SELECT: Youth & Drug Prevention. JOINT: Task Force on the Changing Family.

OFFICES: Capitol, (916) 445-4445; district, 1098 Melody Lane, 301, Roseville 95678-5133, (916) 969-3660.

REGISTRATION: 48.9% D, 41.7% R

1988 CAMPAIGN: Leslie - R   59%

            Byouk - D   41%

RATINGS:	AFL	PIRG	CLCV	NOW	CTA	HAC	CofC	CFB	NRA
	15%	37%	24%	42%	U	31%	88%	77%	90%

KEY VOTES:

	Insurance reform:	–	Child sick leave: NO
Assault gun ban: NO	Parent consent abortion: YES	Ban AIDS discrim: NO
Clean Air Act: NO	Cutting old trees: YES	Extend death penalty: YES
Lmt product tort: YES	End mob home rent cont: YES	Ban offshore oil: NO

6th Assembly District

Lloyd D. Connelly (D)

During the four terms Lloyd Connelly has represented this Sacramento area district, he has developed a reputation as one of the most earnest, honest and hardest-working legislators at the Capitol, and also one of the most controversial.

It is not uncommon to find the lawyer and former Sacramento city councilman at his office before dawn or after midnight. It also wouldn't be out of character to find him sleeping at a homeless shelter to take a first-hand look at the vexing social problem or running a marathon for relaxation.

Connelly has used his seemingly limitless energy on efforts to clean up the environment, improve public health and protect consumers. And he has been generally effective on behalf of those and other liberal causes.

Connelly has been able to shepherd through the Legislature a number of bills aimed at cutting down on the use of potentially harmful pesticides on produce or chemicals that may seep into groundwater supplies. He has fought to establish a tumor registry designed to warn public health officials of cancer clusters that might be

Lloyd D. Connelly

traced to environmental problems. He has pushed a bill aimed at reducing lead levels in paint that might poison children.

In 1989, he pushed for a bill to extend to rifle and shotguns the 15-day waiting period and background checks now required of handgun purchasers. But that bill was killed in the Senate under pressure from gun owner groups.

In addition to legislative accomplishments like those, Connelly has recently become a successful guru of statewide initiative drives, attempting to get voters to accept a broad liberal agenda that the Legislature has stalled.

In 1986, Connelly helped lead the charge for Proposition 65, a sweeping voter initiative to control toxic waste, which passed by a wide margin. In 1988, he successfully pushed Proposition 99, which raised the state's tobacco tax in an attempt to curb smoking and at the same time raise money for health programs.

And he is already talking about pushing initiatives in 1990 that would raise the alcohol tax and ban the use of suspected cancer-causing chemicals in food production.

Connelly's tendency to turn to initiatives has brought on criticism that he is impatient and that he gives up on the legislative process too soon. And his candid, independent and tenacious style has not endeared him to some of his colleagues.

Yet Connelly seems oblivious to most of the internal jockeying and posturing that goes on in the Legislature. In fact, sometimes Connelly seems oblivious to all that is happening around him – he is renowned for his absent-mindedness.

But when it comes to voting on bills, Connelly rarely lets a questionable one pass by. He carries around a list of such bills and others frequently ask to look at his "cheat sheets."

Connelly generally only gets token opposition from Republican candidates every two years. He seemingly has ambitions for higher office. He has been mentioned, for example, as a possible candidate for the newly elected position of insurance commissioner. And it's possible that due to population growth in the

Sacramento area, a state Senate or congressional district might be available in a few years.

PERSONAL: elected 1982; born Dec. 31, 1945, in Sacramento, Calif.; home, Sacramento; Army 1969-1970; education, A.A. American River College; B.A. government and speech CSU Sacramento; J.D. McGeorge; wife, the Rev. Jean Shaw; son, George; Catholic.

CAREER: lawyer; administrative assistant to Sacramento County Board of Supervisors 1971-1974; Sacramento City Council 1975-1982.

COMMITTEES: Aging & Long Term Care (chair); Environmental Safety & Toxic Materials; Judiciary; Natural Resources. SPECIAL: Medi-Cal Oversight. JOINT: Revision of the Penal Code (vice chair); Arts.

OFFICES: Capitol, (916) 445-2484; district, 2705 K St., 6, Sacramento 95816, (916) 443-1183.

REGISTRATION: 55.9% D, 34.9% R

1988 CAMPAIGN: Connelly – D   61%

                   Gates – R   39%

RATINGS:

AFL	PIRG	CLCV	NOW	CTA	HAC	CofC	CFB	NRA
96%	100%	100%	84%	S	95%	12%	33%	0%

KEY VOTES:

Divest S. Africa:	YES	Insurance reform:	YES	Child sick leave:	YES
Assault gun ban:	YES	Parent consent abortion:	NO	Ban AIDS discrim:	YES
Clean Air Act:	YES	Cutting old trees:	NO	Extend death penalty:	YES
Lmt product tort:	NO	End mob home rent cont:	NO	Ban offshore oil:	YES

7th Assembly District
Norman S. Waters (D)

After narrowly dodging a political bullet in the November 1988 election, incumbent Norman Waters has been walking a political tightrope in a growing, conservative district whose political landscape changes almost daily.

With a population that has jumped nearly 40 percent in five years and encompassing six Mother Lode counties and parts of two others, including the high-growth foothills east of Sacramento, this district's percentage of registered Republicans has steadily climbed upward—one of the predictable side effects of suburbanization.

With his district showing a comparatively slim 49.9 percent to 40.1 percent Democratic edge, Waters, a conservative Democrat given to abrupt remarks in public despite six terms in office, garnered only 50.41 percent of the vote against mortgage banker David Knowles. Out of 171,861 votes cast, Waters held off Knowles with a mere 1,403 votes. Coming to Waters' aid indirectly with money and manpower was Assembly Speaker Willie Brown, who, under attack at the time from a conservative band of Democrats, wanted to protect Waters – and Waters' vote.

An even closer race could occur in 1990 because Knowles in June of 1989 launched his 1990 campaign to oust Waters. Republicans smell blood, but may be running out of time. With a district that covers all of Alpine, Amador, Calaveras, El Dorado, Mono and Placer counties, plus parts of Sacramento and Tuolumne, legislative leaders expect Waters' district to be carved into at least two smaller ones when lawmakers tackle reapportionment in 1992.

A third-generation cattle rancher, Waters continues to proudly brandish a pro-agriculture, moderate-to-conservative legislative philosophy by promoting bills helping farming, senior citizens, law and order, and

Norman S. Waters

protection against child abuse. As chairman of the Assembly Agriculture Committee, he's well-positioned to protect his district's farmers and ranchers.

His liabilities, however, often stem from his style. Speaking off-the-cuff and on camera almost cost him the 1988 election, when he expressed frustration at the issues stressed by Knowles: "He talks about family values. He talks about praying and going to church and all this B.S."

Waters is a plodding legislator, often displaying that he knows next to nothing about his own legislation. During committee hearings on his bills, Waters stands by generally looking ignorant, letting the lobbyists present his bills and answer the questions. More than most, if he is without his crib-sheet on the Assembly floor, Waters cannot make a pitch for a bill.

PERSONAL: elected 1976; born July 1, 1925, in Plymouth, Calif.; home, Plymouth; Army Air Corps WWII; education, attended UC Davis Extension and Southwest Missouri State Teachers College, no degree; wife, Dona King; children, Mike, Fred, Bill, Tim and John; Protestant.

CAREER: Amador County Board of Supervisors 1970-1974; insurance agent; cattle rancher.

COMMITTEES: Agriculture (chair); Governmental Organization; Housing & Community Development; Water, Parks & Wildlife. SELECT: Child Abuse (chair); Calif. Wine Production & Economy. JOINT: Fairs Allocation & Classification.

OFFICES: Capitol, (916) 445-8343; district, 250 Main St., Placerville 95667, (916) 626-4954; 33 Broadway, Jackson 95642, (209) 223-3589; 48 W. Yaney St., Sonora 95370, (209) 532-0508; 14500 Musso Road, Auburn 95603, (916) 885-4384.

REGISTRATION: 49.9% D, 40.1% R

1988 CAMPAIGN: Waters – D   50%

Knowles – R   50%

RATINGS:	AFL	PIRG	CLCV	NOW	CTA	HAC	CofC	CFB	NRA
	71%	63%	67%	58%	S	85%	52%	99%	90%

KEY VOTES:

Divest S. Africa: YES	Insurance reform: YES	Child sick leave: YES
Assault gun ban: NO	Parent consent abortion: YES	Ban AIDS discrim: NO
Clean Air Act: NO	Cutting old trees: YES	Extend death penalty: YES
Lmt product tort: YES	End mob home rent cont: –	Ban offshore oil: NO

8th Assembly District

Beverly K. Hansen (R)

Beverly K. Hansen

The 8th Assembly District is the heart of the California wine region of Sonoma, Lake and Napa counties. It's scenic country, not only the center of the wine-making industry but a vacation destination of places like Lake Berryessa attracting a steadily increasing number of tourists whose presence, in turn, is sparking a nonstop debate over growth and development.

The district was represented for eight controversial years by the scion of a well-known wine-making family, Don Sebastiani. And when he stepped down in 1986 (after nearly losing his seat in 1984), a nasty fight erupted among Republicans over his successor.

The conservative Republican leaders in the state Assembly anointed 26-year-old goat rancher Martin McClure. But Bev Hansen, an aide to Republican state Sen. Jim Nielsen, wouldn't accept that decree.

Hansen whipped McClure and then triumphed over a Democratic candidate, Mary Jadiker, who had been tabbed by Democratic leaders to capture the Sebastiani seat after a strong showing two years earlier. Going into the last two weeks of the 1986 election, polls pegged Jadiker to win the seat. But a last minute blitz of mailers – and a series of neighborhood debates between the candidates where Hansen excelled – pulled her ahead.

With her double upset behind her, Hansen came to Sacramento with an independent mind-set that she's not relinquished. A moderate in a Republican caucus dominated by conservatives, Hansen has joined forces with other moderates in the so-called "Magnificent Seven" to steer their own course on such hot button issues as abortion.

As a Republican, a woman and a moderate, Hansen is still a triple minority. But she works the district hard and its voter registration is close enough that she can probably continue to win re-election, at least until reapportionment changes district lines.

PERSONAL: elected 1986; born, Aug. 18, 1944, in Oroville, Calif.; home, Santa Rosa; education, political science major UC Berkeley, no degree; divorced; children, Joe, Tim, Brett, Rick and Heather; Presbyterian.

CAREER: real estate; aide to Sen. Jim Nielsen 1981-1985.

COMMITTEES: Aging & Long-Term Care; Natural Resources; Public Employment, Retirement & Social Security; Transportation. SPECIAL: Policy Research Management. SELECT: Child Abuse; GAIN; Small Business.

OFFICES: Capitol, (916) 445-8102; district, 50 Santa Rosa Ave., 301, Santa Rosa 95404, (707) 546-4500; 1700 Second St., 380, Napa 94559, (707) 255-9084.

REGISTRATION: 52.6% D, 37.8% R

1988 CAMPAIGN: Hansen – R   64%
Ketron – D   33%
Marlow – (P&F)   4%

RATINGS:

	AFL	PIRG	CLCV	NOW	CTA	HAC	CofC	CFB	NRA
	26%	58%	60%	58%	U	63%	88%	66%	100%

KEY VOTES:

		Insurance reform:	YES	Child sick leave:	NO
Assault gun ban:	NO	Parent consent abortion:	YES	Ban AIDS discrim:	NO
Clean Air Act:	NO	Cutting old trees:	YES	Extend death penalty:	YES
Lmt product tort:	YES	End mob home rent cont:	YES	Ban offshore oil:	YES

9th Assembly District

William J. Filante (R)

Marin and southern Sonoma counties – the areas covered by this district – have a well-deserved reputation as the laid-back land of expensive homes, a beautiful coastline, white wine, rolling vineyards and hot tubs.

But the person these voters have chosen to represent them is anything but laid-back.

Dr. William Filante is the only physician in the state's Legislature and he still maintains a part-time ophthalmology practice.

What's more, Republican Filante represents a district that, judging from the numbers, should be in the hands of a Democrat. It is one of the few districts in the state where Democrats are gradually increasing in percentage of registrants, standing at 53.3 percent, compared with 33.8 percent who are Republicans.

William J. Filante

Those numbers make Filante a moderate out of political necessity.

He regularly breaks away from the conservative Assembly Republican caucus line on issues, most notably on the environment – a must in this scenic district – and those involving health. In 1989, he was one of two Assembly Republicans to buck the National Rifle Association and vote for the ban on semiautomatic military assault weapons.

Filante, as could be expected, is the Legislature's resident health expert and often is looked to by his colleagues to provide them with his best scientific view on bills.

He also is a fiscal conservative and regularly backs bills of interest to business.

Even though Filante's moderate views are closer to the Democrats' own than most Republicans', the Democrats regularly make runs at him because of the registration numbers.

Republicans, on the other hand, don't mind his occasional breaks with them. They only hope that Filante won't decide that practicing medicine full-time is more enjoyable than participating in politics.

PERSONAL: elected 1978; born Oct 22, 1929, in Brooklyn, N.Y.; home, Greenbrae; USAF flight surgeon 1955-1957; education, B.A. and M.D. University of Minnesota; internship Detroit Receiving Hospital; ophthalmology residency Los Angeles County General Hospital; wife, Margaret; children, Dave, Steve and Jan; Jewish.

CAREER: general practitioner; ophthalmologist; assistant clinical professor UC San Francisco; assistant chief, Department of Ophthalmology Mt. Zion Medical Center; instructor Pacific Medical Center, San Francisco; director Marin Municipal Water District; trustee Marin Community College District.

COMMITTEES: Rules (vice chair); Housing & Community Development; Health; Water, Parks & Wildlife. JOINT: Quincentennial of the Voyages of Columbus; Rules.

OFFICES: Capitol, (916) 445-7827; district, 30 North San Pedro Road, Suite 135, San Rafael 94903, (415) 479-4920; Post & English streets, Petaluma 94952, (707) 762-5706.

REGISTRATION: 52.6% D, 37.8% R

1988 CAMPAIGN: Filante – R   56%
Parnell – D   44%

RATINGS:

AFL	PIRG	CLCV	NOW	CTA	HAC	CofC	CFB	NRA
31%	68%	84%5	0%	U	63%	64%	33%	50%

KEY VOTES:

Divest S. Africa: YES	Insurance reform: YES	Child sick leave: –
Assault gun ban: YES	Parent consent abortion: YES	Ban AIDS discrim: YES
Clean Air Act: YES	Cutting old trees: NO	Extend death penalty: YES
Lmt product tort: YES	End mob home rent cont: YES	Ban offshore oil: YES

10th Assembly District

Phillip L. Isenberg (D)

This is a politically and geographically diverse district that stretches from downtown Sacramento to the Sacramento-San Joaquin Delta. It includes several small Sacramento County cities – Galt, Lodi and Elk Grove, which are rural in nature. It also includes farm areas of northern San Joaquin County and the Antioch area of Contra Costa County.

Democrat Phillip Isenberg, the former mayor of Sacramento, has represented the district since 1982 when he won the open seat by a landslide after the district was tailored to his needs by friendly Democrats. The boundary was altered slightly to include Isenberg's home, for instance, even though critics said it was an artificially crafted district.

Phillip L. Isenberg

He had his toughest re-election race in 1988 when his Republican opponent tried to paint him as soft on crime and as too close to liberal Assembly Speaker Willie Brown, who has served as something of a mentor to Isenberg. Still, Isenberg won by gaining 57 percent of the vote.

Isenberg remains a top lieutenant to Brown, who gave him his first job as a lawyer and for whom he once served as chief of staff to the Assembly Ways and Means Committee.

As assistant speaker pro tem, Isenberg is one of the Assembly Democrats' top political strategists and he plays a key role in trying to maintain the Democratic majority in the lower house. Some speculate he may be among those in line to succeed Brown. Others believe he will run for state Senate if and when Leroy Greene steps down. He has steadily moved up in the Democratic hierarchy, becoming chairman of the Judiciary Committee at the start of the 1988 session, a panel with responsibility over such hot-button issues as abortion and liability laws.

The owlish-looking Isenberg can be charming and witty or come off as arrogant and impatient. And while other politicians might prefer splashy headlines, Isenberg seems to relish the nuts and bolts of the government process. He is a political insider, knows parliamentary rules and is adept at quietly maneuvering behind the scenes.

While politics are clearly Isenberg's passion, he has made some significant policy contributions as well.

In 1989, he pushed through a new law to provide a state-subsidized health insurance program for Californians with pre-existing illnesses who would otherwise be uninsurable. He also played key roles in negotiating compromises on how to spend money from the state's newly increased tobacco tax and in the 50-year-old dispute over water diversions from eerily beautiful Mono Lake.

No other issue generates more passion in northern California than water and Isenberg has been right in the middle of the continuing war of words between the north and the central and southern parts of the state.

He has argued that less water from the north should go to San Joaquin Valley farms so that more would be available for fast-growing urban areas in Southern California. The position has shaken what has traditionally been a rock-solid alliance between southern and central California interests against the north.

PERSONAL: elected 1982; born Feb. 25, 1939, in Gary, Ind.; home, Sacramento; Army 1962-1968; B.A. social science CSU Sacramento; J.D. UC Berkeley; wife, Marilyn Araki.

CAREER: lawyer; Sacramento City Council 1971-1975, mayor 1975-1982; aide to Assemblyman Willie Brown 1967-1968; Ways & Means consultant 1971; assistant speaker pro tem.

COMMITTEES: Judiciary (chair); Elections, Reapportionment & Constitutional Amendments; Health; Revenue & Taxation; Water, Parks & Wildlife. SPECIAL: Medi-Cal Oversight. JOINT: Legislative Ethics; Refugee Resettlement, International Migration & Cooperative Development; Review of the Master Plan for Higher Education.

OFFICES: Capitol, (916) 445-1611; district, 1215 15th St., 102, Sacramento 95814, (916) 324-4676; 625 W. 4th St., 4, Antioch 94509, (415) 778-4510; 1200 W. Tokay, Room D, Lodi 95240, (209) 334-4945.

REGISTRATION: 56.3% D, 34.5% R

1988 CAMPAIGN: Isenberg – D   57%
Bowler – R   43%

RATINGS:

AFL	PIRG	CLCV	NOW	CTA	HAC	CofC	CFB	NRA
97%	89%	96%	92%	G	90%	16%	33%	0%

KEY VOTES:

Divest S. Africa: YES	Insurance reform:	YES	Child sick leave: YES
Assault gun ban: YES	Parent consent abortion:	NO	Ban AIDS discrim: YES
Clean Air Act: YES	Cutting old trees:	NO	Extend death penalty: YES
Lmt product tort: YES	End mob home rent cont:	NO	Ban offshore oil: YES

11th Assembly District

Robert J. Campbell (D)

Robert Campbell is one of the most consistently liberal members of the Assembly. And with the high percentage of blue collar workers and minority residents of a Bay Area district that stretches from Richmond to Pittsburg, he can afford to be.

Although Democratic registration in the district has gone down slightly, Democrats still outnumber registered Republicans by nearly 40 percentage points.

Campbell, a former insurance broker and Richmond city councilman, has only drawn token opposition, if any, since his election in 1980.
One of Campbell's key interests in the Assembly has been education funding. As chairman of the Assembly budget subcommittee that deals with education, he has significant influence on where education dollars will be spent. He has fought to restore funding cuts for community colleges and state universities as well as to limit tuition increases. His efforts have made him popular with the University of California Student Association who named him their Assembly "Legislator of the Year," in 1987.

Robert J. Campbell

Campbell's liberal leanings have also been evident on environmental legislation, civil liberties issues and measures to help minorities and recently arrived immigrants. He is one of a few legislators who have an announced policy of refusing to take fees for speaking. But Campbell has not been adept at playing the inside game; several legislators with less seniority have more clout. And he has developed a reputation for caving in to strong pressure from party leaders on special interest matters that other liberals resist.

PERSONAL: elected 1980; born Dec. 20, 1937, in Los Angeles, Calif.; home, Richmond; Army, National Guard Reserves 1961-1972; education, B.A. social science and history San Francisco State University, post-graduate studies UC Berkeley; wife, Diane Roark; children, Lisa and Kirk; Catholic.

CAREER: insurance broker; Richmond City Council 1975-1982.

COMMITTEES: Water, Parks & Wildlife; Ways & Means and subcommittee 2 – education (chair). SPECIAL: Policy Research Management (chair). JOINT: Quincentennial of the Voyages of Columbus; Legislative Budget; School Facilities.

OFFICES: Capitol, (916) 445-7890; district, 2901 MacDonald Ave., Richmond 94804, (415) 237-8171; 604 Ferry St., 220, Martinez 94553, (415) 372-7990; 2010 Railroad Ave., Pittsburg 94565, (415) 432-0147.

REGISTRATION: 63.9% D, 25% R

1988 CAMPAIGN: Campbell – D   73%
                Williams – R   27%

RATINGS:

AFL	PIRG	CLCV	NOW	CTA	HAC	CofC	CFB	NRA
98%	95%	96%	92%	G	95%	20%	44%	0%

KEY VOTES:

Divest S. Africa:	YES	Insurance reform:	YES	Child sick leave:	YES
Assault gun ban:	YES	Parent consent abortion:	NO	Ban AIDS discrim:	YES
Clean Air Act:	YES	Cutting old trees:	NO	Extend death penalty:	NO
Lmt product tort:	NO	End mob home rent cont:	NO	Ban offshore oil:	YES

12th Assembly District
Tom H. Bates (D)

If the incumbent had more pull, the 12th Assembly District probably would be more homogeneously constituted. But the district, which covers portions of Alameda and Contra Costa counties, seems to have been composed of the bits left over after Democratic leaders of the Assembly had drawn districts to the specifications of other members.

It includes the upscale portions of Oakland and some silk stocking suburbs in Contra Costa County, such as Pleasant Hill and Kensington, but the center of the district is Berkeley, home of the University of California and the spiritual center of all that is left-of-center in California politics.

Tom H. Bates

The bifurcated nature of the district is demonstrated in voter registration figures. Overall, it is safely Democratic with a 63 percent registration margin. But the Alameda County portions, including Berkeley, have a 4-1 ratio in favor of Democrats while the Contra Costa portions are about 3-2.

The man who has represented the 12th District since 1976 is Tom Bates and there's no question that the Alameda segment is his spiritual, as well as actual, home.

Bates is perhaps the Assembly's most consistently liberal member and his liberal credentials have been solidified by his recent marriage to Loni Hancock, the left-leaning mayor of Berkeley.

Although Bates ranks near the top in seniority in the Assembly, he has never wielded first-rank power, a reflection of his own rather quiet personality and the relative extremity of his politics.

Bates, an Alameda County supervisor for four years, has concentrated on liberal issues such as health care and only in recent years achieved a modicum of authority by becoming chairman of the Assembly Human Services Committee, which deals with welfare-related legislation.

He's a member of the "Grizzly Bears," an ad hoc coalition of liberals who congregate in the rear of the Democratic section of the house, and that has boosted his career of late because the group has, as a bloc, moved up in influence.

Bates been strongly identified with the University of California throughout his career. He not only represents the university's home campus in the Assembly, but was a member of Cal's 1959 Rose Bowl team. And as mayor of Berkeley, his wife often has found herself clashing with university officials over housing, parking and other jointly vexing issues.

The 12th District's strong Democratic bent means than Bates can continue in his seat through as many Big Games as he wants, and he'll most likely stick around until state Sen. Nicholas Petris retires, allowing Bates to move up to the Senate, or a congressional seat opens up.

PERSONAL: elected 1976; born Feb. 9, 1938, in San Diego, Calif.; home, Oakland; education, B.A. communications and public policy UC Berkeley; wife, Loni Hancock (mayor of Berkeley); children, Casey and Jon; no religious affiliation.

CAREER: real estate; Alameda County Board of Supervisors 1972-1976.

COMMITTEES: Human Services (chair) Governmental Organization; Revenue & Taxation; Natural Resources. SELECT: Child Care. JOINT; Oversight on GAIN Implementation.

OFFICES: Capitol, (916) 445-7554; district, 1414 Walnut St., Berkeley 94709; (415) 540-3176.

REGISTRATION: 63.3% D, 23.7% R

1988 CAMPAIGN: Bates – D   74%

                     Udinsky – R   24%

                     Phillips – P&F   2%

RATINGS:	AFL	PIRG	CLCV	NOW	CTA	HAC	CofC	CFB	NRA
	96%	100%	100%	84%	S	85%	16%	33%	0%

KEY VOTES:

Divest S. Africa:	YES	Insurance reform:	YES	Child sick leave:	YES
Assault gun ban:	YES	Parent consent abortion:	NO	Ban AIDS discrim:	YES
Clean Air Act:	YES	Cutting old trees:	NO	Extend death penalty:	NO
Lmt product tort:	NO	End mob home rent cont:	NO	Ban offshore oil:	YES

13th Assembly District
Elihu Harris (D)

The eastern shore of San Francisco Bay is a region of contrasts: of great wealth and great squalor, mind-bending scientific research and mind-destroying drug traffic, industry and social inertia.

Oakland, the Bay Area's second city, lies at the heart of the region, a black-governed city that contains all of its contrasts and contradictions. The highest death-toll in the Oct. 17, 1989 earthquake was here – the site of the now-infamous Nimitz freeway viaduct that collapsed, crushing motorists underneath it.

And the center of Oakland is also the center of the 13th Assembly District, which takes in nearby Alameda and Emeryville.

Its Democratic voter registration margin, approaching 75 percent, is the third highest in the Assembly, so what political squabbles exist are among Democrats. And there's a lot of squabbling.

The 13th District's seat has been occupied for the past decade-plus by Elihu Harris, an attorney who was only 31 when elected in 1978. Harris, a former legislative and congressional aide, has solidified his hold on the district, moved up the power ladder in the Assembly and now wants to move even further by becoming mayor of Oakland. Harris had been chairman of the Assembly Judiciary Committee, a taxing post, but gave up the chairmanship at the start of the 1988 session to devote more time to Oakland politics.

The current mayor, Lionel Wilson, hasn't decided whether he'll seek another term in 1990 but Harris is making all the moves to succeed him and might run even if Wilson takes another run himself.

To magnify his media visibility, Harris has made the financial plight of Oakland schools a personal crusade, incurring much anger among school district trustees.

PERSONAL: elected 1978; born Aug. 15, 1947, in **Elihu Harris**
Los Angeles, Calif.; home, Oakland; education, B.A. political science CSU Hayward; M.A. public administration UC Berkeley; J.D. UC Davis; wife, Kathy Neal; no children; United Methodist.

CAREER: lawyer; teacher; administrative assistant Assemblyman John J. Miller 1972-1974; staff assistant Rep. Yvonne Braithwaite Burke 1974-1975; executive director National Bar Association, 1975-1977.

COMMITTEES: Health; Judiciary; Transportation; Ways & Means. JOINT: Legislative Audit (chair); Refugee Resettlement, International Migration & Cooperative Development. SELECT: Ethics.

OFFICES: Capitol, (916) 445-7442; district, 1111 Jackson St., Room 5027, Oakland 94607, (415) 464-0339.

REGISTRATION: 73.3% D, 15.1% R

1988 CAMPAIGN: Harris – D 77%
Mangrum – R 20%
Dizon – P&F 3%

RATINGS:

AFL	PIRG	CLCV	NOW	CTA	HAC	CofC	CFB	NRA
94%	100%	100%	92%	S	90%	20%	33%	0%

KEY VOTES:

Divest S. Africa:	YES	Insurance reform:	YES	Child sick leave:	YES
Assault gun ban:	YES	Parent consent abortion:	NO	Ban AIDS discrim:	YES
Clean Air Act:	YES	Cutting old trees:	NO	Extend death penalty:	NO
Lmt product tort:	NO	End mob home rent cont:	–	Ban offshore oil:	YES

14th Assembly District

Johan M. Klehs (D)

Democrats don't worry much in this East Bay blue-collar district that includes the cities of San Leandro and Hayward, Castro Valley and part of Oakland.

Johan Klehs, a former aide to Sen. Bill Lockyer, has used his knowledge of how the legislative and political system work to his advantage. He has risen rather quickly to positions of political power, first as chairman of the Assembly Elections and Reapportionment Committee and now as chairman of the Assembly Revenue and Taxation Committee.

Johan M. Klehs

In heading the Assembly's tax committee, Klehs has broad influence on state tax issues and as such draws attention from large corporations seeking to influence tax matters as well as citizens who don't want to see their taxes raised.

Klehs is generally liberal in his political viewpoint, but at times can be unpredictable and abrupt. He is an archetypical political animal, the staffer who learned how to push buttons and then used that knowledge for his own benefit.

In recent years, he has proposed many high-profile tax-related bills on a variety of subjects.

He teamed with Controller Gray Davis to propose a constitutional amendment to give tax credits to individuals and corporations contributing toward research for an AIDS vaccine.

He joined Attorney General John Van de Kamp in proposing that corporate tax loopholes be closed to fund anti-drug programs.

He's also proposed letting first-time home buyers use Individual Retirement Accounts to purchase their homes without tax penalties and taking away tax-exempt status from social clubs that discriminate in their membership.

In 1989, Klehs carried one of 14 bills cracking down on semiautomatic assault rifles in the wake of the Stockton schoolyard massacre.

While Klehs isn't likely to get much of a challenge from Republicans, Hayward Mayor Alex Giuliani, a lifelong Democrat, has announced that he wants to challenge Klehs as an independent in 1990.

PERSONAL: elected 1982; born June 27, 1952, in Alameda, Calif.; home, Castro Valley; education, B.A. political science and M.A. public administration CSU Hayward, attended Harvard University John F. Kennedy School of Government; unmarried; Lutheran.

CAREER: Legislative assistant to Assemblyman Bill Lockyer 1973-1976; San Leandro City Council 1978-1982; account executive for a direct-mail advertising firm.

COMMITTEES: Revenue & Taxation (chair); Elections, Reapportionment & Constitutional Amendments; Governmental Organization; Health; Labor & Employment. SELECT: International Trade.

OFFICES: Capitol, 445-8160; district, 2450 Washington Ave., 270, San Leandro 94577, (415) 464-0847.

REGISTRATION: 64% D, 25.3% R
1988 CAMPAIGN: Klehs – D   73%
              Eaton – R   27%

RATINGS:	AFL	PIRG	CLCV	NOW	CTA	HAC	CofC	CFB	NRA
	98%	95%	96%	92%	S	90%	28%	33%	0%

KEY VOTES:

Divest S. Africa:	YES	Insurance reform:	YES	Child sick leave:	YES
Assault gun ban:	YES	Parent consent abortion:	NO	Ban AIDS discrim:	YES
Clean Air Act:	YES	Cutting old trees:	NO	Extend death penalty:	–
Lmt product tort:	YES	End mob home rent cont:	NO	Ban offshore oil:	YES

15th Assembly District

William P. Baker (R)

There aren't many Republican enclaves in the east San Francisco Bay area, but Democratic line-drawers made sure most of them were in the 15th Assembly District. It includes the Contra Costa County communities of Danville – William Baker's home – Walnut Creek, San Ramon, Orinda, Lafayette, Moraga and part of Concord as well as the Pleasanton area of Alameda County.

Baker fits this upscale, conservative district to a tee. A former budget analyst with the state Department of Finance, he has made tax and money matters his specialty. He is the Assembly Republicans' acknowledged fiscal expert and serves as the point man for them in virtually all major tax and budget negotiations.

William P. Baker

Along with his indisputable budget expertise, comes an acerbic wit. Baker is known to have angered more than a few of his colleagues after he's stared them down through his wire-rimmed glasses and dressed them down with sharp-tongued barbs. But Baker's sharp tongue can also be funny.

Baker came to Sacramento with a mission to cut spending and limit taxes. And while he has become more willing to negotiate over the budget with leaders of the Democratic-controlled Legislature, he has stuck close to his fiscal mission.

In 1989, for example, he carried a bill that would have required pharmaceutical companies to discount the prices they charge the state for drugs that are regularly prescribed to Medi-Cal patients. The measure was killed by high-powered lobbyists, but Baker saw it as a way to save the state millions.

Because of his GOP leadership position, he is often called upon by Deukmejian to carry bills for the administration. In 1989, he carried the governor's unsuccessful bill to let convicts in state prisons work for private employers.

PERSONAL: elected 1980; born June 14, 1940,in Oakland, Calif.; home, Danville; education, B.S. business and industrial management San Jose State University, graduate study international marketing research CSU Long Beach; Coast Guard Reserve (six months active duty); wife, Joanne Atack; children, Todd, Mary, Billy and Robby; Protestant.

CAREER: businessman; assistant to secretary of the Senate; budget analyst state Department of Finance.

COMMITTEES: Ways & Means (vice chairman); Elections, Reapportionment and Constitutional Amendments; Transportation. JOINT: Legislative Budget; Revision of the Penal Code.

OFFICES: Capitol, (916) 445-8528; district, 1801 N. Calif. Blvd., 103, Walnut Creek 94596, (415) 932-2537.

REGISTRATION: 36.8% D, 51.3% R

1988 CAMPAIGN: Baker – R   68%

                 Williams – D   32%

RATINGS:

AFL	PIRG	CLCV	NOW	CTA	HAC	CofC	CFB	NRA
10%	42%	15%	17%	U	18%	96%	55%	100%

KEY VOTES:

Divest S. Africa:	NO	Insurance reform:	–	Child sick leave:	NO
Assault gun ban:	NO	Parent consent abortion:	YES	Ban AIDS discrim:	NO
Clean Air Act:	NO	Cutting old trees:	YES	Extend death penalty:	YES
Lmt product tort:	YES	End mob home rent cont:	–	Ban offshore oil:	NO

16th Assembly District

John L. Burton (D)

San Francisco is such a polyglot that it cannot easily be divided into two social milieus. But in the grossest possible terms, the 16th Assembly District represents the wrong side of the tracks.

It's the easternmost portion of the peninsular city, encompassing the downtown business district, China-town, the waterfront (including Fisherman's Wharf), the seedy Tenderloin, the industrial area and the poor and mostly black Hunter's Point neighborhood.

Assembly Speaker Willie Brown's 17th District in-cludes the upscale and middle-class neighborhoods of western and northern San Francisco.

John L. Burton

Given the socioeconomic variety one can find within the 16th District, it's perhaps fitting that its representa-tive is the Capitol's only self-acknowledged ex-drug abuser, John Burton.

Burton, his late brother, Philip, Willie Brown and George Moscone, the mayor of San Francisco who was assassinated in 1978, were the founders of a political organization that has dominated San Francisco's major league politics for more than a generation.

The organization, which had declined in importance after the elder Burton's death in 1983, revived itself in 1987 to move then-Assemblyman Art Agnos into the mayor's office. That opened the door for John Burton, who had left Congress in 1982 as an admitted drug and alcohol abuser, to run for the Assembly again (he had served in the 1960s and 1970s before going to Congress).

The 1988 special election for Agnos' seat pitted Burton, who had undergone extensive and, he says, successful therapy for his substance abuse problems, against Roberta Achtenberg, an activist for lesbian and gay rights who was bidding to become the state's first openly homosexual legislator.

It was a sometimes bitter campaign but in the end, Burton's name and the organization's professional-class efforts won out and he returned to Sacramento.

Burton may have been the least fresh freshman ever to enter the Assembly, given his long political career and his close association with Speaker Brown.

Those attributes paid off with a series of important committee assignments, including chairmanship of the Public Safety Committee, which deals with always sensitive crime legislation.

Burton is, of course, a liberal and by nature an outspoken one, so he has evolved into one of the Legislature's most distinct characters, a man who prowls the chambers and the hearings rooms constantly, usually shunning a tie, making loud and sometimes rude commentaries on events as they unfold.

Burton's old-style liberalism is out of fashion, so his impact on the Assembly is more often theatrical than legislative. But he functions as a member of Brown's inner circle of close friends and advisers and the two represent a potent political force on behalf of San Francisco's parochial issues. And as Public Safety chairman, Burton gleefully kills Republicans' lock-'em-up anti-crime bills while crafting Democratic measures that give his party the edge on crime legislation.

The 16th District is lopsidedly Democratic and Burton can remain in the Assembly as long as he wants. That may not be long, especially if Brown steps down as speaker in the early 1990s.

PERSONAL: elected 1988 (special election); born Dec. 15, 1932, in Cincinnati, Ohio; home, San Francisco; Army 1954-1956; education, B.A. social science San Francisco State University, J.D. University of San Francisco Law School; divorced; children, Kimiko; no religious affiliation.

CAREER: lawyer; Assembly 1964-1974; U.S. House of Representatives 1974-1982.

COMMITTEES: Public Safety (chair); Aging & Long Term Care; Health; Water, Parks & Wildlife; Ways & Means. JOINT: Legislative Budget.

OFFICES: Capitol, (916) 445-8253; district, 350 McAllister St., 1064, San Francisco 94102, (415) 557-2253.

REGISTRATION: 69.5% D, 14.3% R

1988 CAMPAIGN:

Burton – D	78%
Mavrogeorge – R	15%
Meyer – L	3%
Ehman – P&F	5%

RATINGS:

AFL	PIRG	CLCV	NOW	CTA	HAC	CofC	CFB	NRA
96%	93%	100%	92%	NA	100%	12%	10%	0%

KEY VOTES:

Insurance reform: YES	Child sick leave: YES	Cutting old trees: NO
Assault gun ban: YES	End mob home rent cont: –	Ban AIDS discrim: YES

17th Assembly District
Willie L. Brown Jr. (D)

San Francisco's critics say the city has lost its economic and cultural vitality and become a sideshow for tourists. A similar criticism is often leveled at the man who has represented half of San Francisco in the Assembly for more than a quarter-century, Willie Brown.

However flashy he may be, Brown is not just another legislator. He has held center stage in the Capitol for most of that career and for nearly a decade has been the Assembly's speaker, having held the position longer than any other man.

Willie Brown is a star, and not just in San Francisco cafe society and the tight little world of Sacramento politics. He was the Rev. Jesse Jackson's national campaign chairman in 1988 and is one of the most influential black politicians in the country.

Willie L. Brown Jr.

Brown's 17th District is almost an afterthought in his political career. It's the more affluent western and northern sections of the city, but so overwhelmingly Democratic that Brown needn't spend more time on it than it takes to file his re-election papers every two years.

He was a man who seemed destined for big things from the moment he walked onto the Assembly floor as a freshman legislator, a flamboyant, left-leaning, angry-talking young street lawyer who had formed a homegrown political organization with like-minded liberals, the Burton brothers (Philip and John) and George Moscone, the son of a local fisherman.

Brown had an opinion on everything and would voice it to anyone who would listen. One of his first votes was against the re-election of the legendary speaker, Jesse Unruh, as speaker of the house.

But Unruh tolerated Brown, perhaps because both were raised dirt poor in Texas, both had emigrated to California after World War II to break out of their poverty and both had begun their political careers as left-wing rabble rousers.

"It's a good thing you aren't white," Unruh remarked to Brown one day after the latter had made an especially effective floor speech early in his career.

"Why's that?" Brown asked.

"Because if you were, you'd own the place," Unruh replied.

It turned out that Brown could own the place without being white.

Civil rights was the early focus of Brown's legislative career and no matter what the event, he was ready with a quote for the media.

When, for instance, black athletes Tommy Smith and John Carlos raised their hands in a "black power" salute at the 1968 Olympics, Brown said, "They will be known forever as two niggers who upset the Olympic Games. I'd rather have them known for that than as two niggers who won two medals."

Despite statements like that, Brown was developing a reputation among Capitol insiders for smart political work and in 1970, he took his first big step up the ladder when friend Bob Moretti became speaker and elevated Brown into the chairmanship of the powerful Ways and Means Committee.

Brown became a master of arcane matters of state finance, including the budget, and recruited a staff of young advisers who today form the nucleus of his Assembly senior staff.

California's political establishment was beginning to respect, if not like, the young politician and he expanded the consciousness of his presence nationwide in 1972 when, as the leader of the George McGovern faction from California, he arose at the Democratic National Convention during complex and bitter credentials fights.

"Give me back my delegation," Brown thundered on national television.

Moretti was planning to step down in 1974 to run for governor and he wanted to lateral the speakership to Brown. But Brown was to make the worst tactical error of his career in counting on the support of Hispanic and black members. Secretly, San Francisco's other assemblyman, Leo McCarthy, had courted the minority lawmakers, promising them committee chairmanships and other goodies. When the crunch came, they stood with McCarthy, who had snatched the speakership from under Brown's nose.

That was the beginning of an in-house exile for Brown, one that became even more intensive when he and some supporters plotted a coup against McCarthy that failed. At one point, Brown was given an office so small that he had to place his filing cabinets in the hallway outside.

The exile lasted for two years, during which, Brown said later, he underwent intense self-examination and concluded that he had been too arrogant in dealings with colleagues–like calling one member a "500-pound tub of Jello" in public.

McCarthy resurrected Brown's legislative career in 1976 by naming him chairman of the Revenue and Taxation Committee, a fairly substantial job, and that gesture paid off in 1979 when another bloc of Democratic Assembly members, led by Howard Berman of Los Angeles, tried to oust McCarthy from the speakership.

Brown declared loyalty to his old rival and maintained it during a year of often bitter infighting that culminated in the 1980 elections. Berman had seemingly won enough contested seats in 1980 to claim the speakership but the desperate McCarthyites cut a deal with Republicans to name Willie Brown as speaker.

The Republicans, who openly feared a Berman speakership, were promised some extra consideration by the new regime and although they later were to claim that Brown reneged, he always maintained that he stuck to the letter of the agreement.

Brown's speakership has been long and controversial. He has seen Democratic ranks whittled down due to Republican victories, but that may have resulted more from larger political trends over which he had no control. He has been accused of neglecting policy for politics, of shaking down special interests for millions of dollars in campaign funds, of presiding over a blatantly partisan reapportionment of legislative districts and of being too consumed with the inside game to deal with the fast-changing California society.

Brown does list making life easier for legislators as his chief accomplishment as speaker and there has been – at least until 1989 – a paucity of major legislative achievements. His legislative record is often compared, unfavorably, to that of Unruh, whose record for longevity he passed in the late 1980s. But Unruh also was speaker during simpler times, both politically and socially.

Brown has not remade the speakership, as Unruh did. Rather, he took the vast inherent powers of the office and shaped them into a personal tool. He is less innovator than implementer, something that extends to legislation as well. He says that he appoints competent people to staff and committee positions and gives them the tools to work.

Despite aging and mellowing, Brown has lost little of his controversiality among members of the larger public. But as speaker, he's answerable to only two constituencies: the voters of his San Francisco district and the 79 other members of his house. Brown could not be elected to statewide office, but he doesn't aspire to it.

Republicans use Brown as a tool to stir up their troops and raise money, portraying him as the political devil incarnate; but he says – with at least some validity – that it's thinly veiled racism. Likewise, he pins the racist label on critics, in and out of the media.

At least some of the controversiality that Brown wears like one of his $1,500 suits stems from his high-style personal life.

The Italian-cut suits, the low-slung sports cars and the flashy parties that he throws for personal and political reasons all contribute to the image, as do his liaisons with a string of attractive women (he's long separated from his wife, Blanche, a reclusive dance teacher).

But it's what Brown does to support that lifestyle that raises the most eyebrows.

He represents, as an attorney and quasi-lobbyist, a number of well-heeled corporate clients, most of them developers with business pending before local government officials in the Bay Area.

Occasionally, however, some of those clients also do business in Sacramento and Brown's actions have skirted the line of propriety. There have been published reports of Brown's pulling strings behind the scenes to the benefit of several of his corporate clients, but nothing concrete, or at least legally dangerous, has been proven.

Regardless of what he does in Sacramento, Brown's a power in and around San Francisco–and especially so since Art Agnos became mayor of the city with Brown's active assistance.

Former San Francisco Supervisor Terry Francois put it this way a few years ago, even before Agnos became mayor: "He engenders fear like you wouldn't believe. I have just become enthralled at the way he wields power. I don't know a politician in San Francisco that dares take him on. That includes the mayor, too."

The greatest threat to Brown's hold on the speakership came in 1987 when five Democratic members, all of whom had enjoyed close relations with the speaker, declared their independence.

The "Gang of Five," as the group was immediately dubbed, demanded procedural changes they said were reforms to lessen the power of the speaker. Before long they were actively demanding that Brown step down as speaker.

They could have formed a new majority with Republicans, but the GOP leader at the time, Pat Nolan, also had established a close relationship with Brown and protected the speaker's right flank. Brown stripped the five of their plum committee assignments in punishment and the war of nerves went on for a year. Eventually, the Republicans agreed to form a coalition with the Gang of Five, but the death of one Republican member prevented a new majority from forming and Brown bolstered his loyalists with enough victories at the polls in 1988 to eke out a paper-thin re-election as speaker.

As that threat faded, the question of how long Brown will remain as speaker becomes one of the most often asked in the Capitol.

There's no definite answer. Brown is secure again and says he wants to be speaker for the indefinite future. The betting in the Capitol is that he will remain at least through the post-1990 census reapportionment, to see how that process affects long-term Democratic strength.

Brown took a much more active role in shaping legislation in the 1989 session, personally authoring auto insurance and health care bills and engaging in summit meetings with Gov. Deukmejian on other issues. With the Gang of Five business behind him, Brown shows no signs of stepping down soon.

PERSONAL: elected 1964; born March 20, 1934, in Mineola, Tex.; home, San Francisco; National Guard Reserves 1955-1958; education, B.A. San Francisco State University, J.D. Hastings College of Law; wife, Blanche Vitero; children,

Susan, Robin and Michael; Methodist.

CAREER: lawyer, maintains a law practice while in office with large corporate clients including Southern Pacific Railroad; Speaker of the Assembly 1980 to present.

COMMITTEES: the Assembly speaker is a member of all committees.

OFFICES: Capitol, (916) 445-8077; district, 350 McAllister St., 5046, San Francisco 94102, (415) 557-0784; Southern California, 107 S. Broadway, 8009, Los Angeles 90012, (213) 620-4356.

REGISTRATION: 64.1% D, 19.4% R

1988 CAMPAIGN: Willie Brown – D 70%

Augustine – R 23%

Towers – P&F 5%

RATINGS:

AFL	PIRG	CLCV	NOW	CTA	HAC	CofC	CFB	NRA
93%	89%	92%	92%	G	90%	28%	33%	0%

KEY VOTES:

Divest S. Africa:	YES	Insurance reform:	YES	Child sick leave:	YES
Assault gun ban:	YES	Parent consent abortion:	NO	Ban AIDS discrim:	YES
Clean Air Act:	YES	Cutting old trees:	–	Extend death penalty:	NO
Lmt product tort:	YES	End mob home rent cont:	YES	Ban offshore oil:	YES

18th Assembly District

Delaine Eastin (D)

This is a district where Republicans think they have a chance to win. Although the numbers clearly favor Democrats – 54 to 32 percent – many of those Democrats are of the conservative brand, living in the cities of Fremont, Union City, Newark, Milpitas and parts of San Jose and Pleasanton.

But Delaine Eastin is considered a promising newcomer in Democratic politics and in her first re-election bid in 1988, she blew away her Republican opponent, gaining two-thirds of the votes cast.

Eastin is hard-working and ambitious. She is not as conservative as her predecessor, Democrat Alister McAlister, nor is she the liberal puppet of Assembly Speaker Willie Brown that GOP opponents have tried to portray her as being. Some have talked of Eastin as a future speaker.

Delaine Eastin

She is obviously aware of a need to walk a moderate line. In 1986, for example, she declined until late in the campaign to take a stand on whether she supported the retention of Chief Justice Rose Bird, a litmus test to many conservatives. She ultimately announced her opposition to Bird, causing the National Organization for

Women to drop its endorsement of her.

In the Legislature, Eastin has carried a solid list of bills including those aimed at helping consumers, such as pushing for a pilot project to see if it is feasible and economical to keep the Department of Motor Vehicles open on Saturdays to better serve drivers. She is a favorite of environmentalists for her pro-conservation positions and has become an advocate for senior citizens. She has also pushed hard for streamlining the San Francisco Bay Area's tangled web of transit districts.

Eastin's AB4 was part of the waste management package signed into law by Gov. Deukmejian in 1989, setting up market incentives for recycled products. A similar bill of hers was vetoed a year earlier but then embraced by Deukmejian.

PERSONAL: elected 1986; born Aug. 20, 1947, in San Diego, Calif.; home, Union City; education, B.A. political science UC Davis, M.A. political science UC Santa Barbara; husband, Jack Saunders; no children; non-denominational Christian.

CAREER: corporate planner; political science professor De Anza Community College; City Council Union City.

COMMITTEES: Governmental Efficiency & Consumer Protection (chair); Education; Environmental Safety & Toxic materials; Transportation. JOINT: Oversight on GAIN Implementation (chair); Quincentennial of the Voyages of Columbus.

OFFICES: Capitol, (916) 445-7874; district, 39245 Liberty St., Suite D-8, Fremont 94538, (415) 791-2151.

REGISTRATION: 54.1% D, 32.3% R

1988 CAMPAIGN: Eastin – D   67%

Curry – R   33%

RATINGS:

	AFL	PIRG	CLCV	NOW	CTA	HAC	CofC	CFB	NRA
	96%	89%	100%	92%	S	90%	24%	33%	0%

KEY VOTES:

		Insurance reform:	YES	Child sick leave:	YES
Assault gun ban:	YES	Parent consent abortion:	NO	Ban AIDS discrim:	YES
Clean Air Act:	YES	Cutting old trees:	NO	Extend death penalty:	YES
Lmt product tort:	YES	End mob home rent cont:	NO	Ban offshore oil:	YES

19th Assembly District

K. Jacqueline Speier

This safely Democratic district takes in the foggy, slightly funky, suburb of Pacifica and a southwestern corner of San Francisco, and moves down the peninsula to include Daly City, South San Francisco and Milbrae. Older housing tracts dot the hillsides while the flat areas are dominated by industry, Candlestick Park and the Cow Palace.

This district gave California one Louis J. Papan – aka "Leadfoot Lou," "the

Enforcer" and "Sweet Lou" – a man noted for his Rambo approach to politics. Papan had won the seat vacated by Leo Ryan, who went Congress and later lost his life at a South American airstrip when unhinged followers of the People's Temple gunned him and others down.

An ally of Willie Brown, Papan tried to move up to the state Senate in 1986 but his political career was cut short by Quentin Kopp. Papan left behind an open Assembly seat, one that Brown tried to fill with a hand-picked candidate in a Democratic primary, Mike Nevin. More than half of Nevin's $300,000 primary budget came from Brown or contributors associated with him, including other Democratic legislators.

K. Jacqueline Speier

However, neither Papan nor Brown calculated well in 1986. An underfinanced San Mateo County supervisor, Jackie Speier, won a close Democratic primary and then the general election.

Speier was an aide to Congressman Ryan on that ill-fated trip to Guyana in 1978. Shot five times at point blank, she lay wounded on an anthill for 22 hours until, near death, she was rescued by the U.S. Air Force and spent months in a hospital recovering. She is still partially paralyzed from her wounds.

After her 1986 election triumph, Speier's primary opponent wondered aloud whether she could function effectively in Sacramento. Perhaps she was brave, but bucking Willie Brown was not necessarily smart.

However, Speier has turned out to be among the savviest of the newest crop of legislators. She has eclipsed many others who have served longer, and she has won respect on both sides of aisle. Speier has two highly influential committee assignments – Ways and Means, and Assembly Rules. She is known as a sharp questioner of administration officials, and is a match for the acid tongue of Republican Bill Baker at Ways and Means.

Speier has pushed legislation on domestic violence, asbestos monitoring, requiring cholesterol labeling on food and other consumer protection measures. In her first term, perhaps a bit impetuously, she introduced a legislative ethics reforms bill. It went nowhere, but a number of her ideas were eventually incorporated into the leaderships' ethics package that moved in 1989.

Speier has voted with Brown in leadership tests, but she has shown an independent streak at times in her floor votes. She generally allies herself with the Assembly's "Grizzly Bear" liberals. If she stays in the Assembly, Speier has shown herself bright enough – and adept enough – to eventually move into a leadership position, possibly even becoming the Assembly's first woman speaker. However, many insiders have long suspected Speier has set her sights on moving into Leo Ryan's old congressional seat. Wherever she goes, her political future appears bright.

PERSONAL: elected 1986; born May 14, 1950, in San Francisco, Calif.; home, South San Francisco; education, B.A. political science UC Davis, J.D. Hastings College of Law; husband, Steve Sierra; son, Jackson Kent; Catholic.

CAREER: lawyer; San Mateo County Board of Supervisors 1981-1986; legal counsel to Rep. Leo J. Ryan 1969-1978.

COMMITTEES: Environmental Safety & Toxic Materials; Health; Judiciary; Rules; Ways & Means. SELECT: Assistance to Victims of Sexual Assault; Small Business (chair); Oil Spill Prevention & Response Preparedness. SPECIAL: Policy Research Management. JOINT: Rules.

OFFICES: Capitol, (916) 445-8020; district, 220 So. Spruce Ave., 101, South San Francisco 94080, (415) 871-4100.

REGISTRATION: 60.4% D, 25.5% R

1988 CAMPAIGN: Speier – D   77%
Silvestri – R   21%
Pepi – P&F   2%

RATINGS:

AFL	PIRG	CLCV	NOW	CTA	HAC	CofC	CFB	NRA
100%	95%	100%	92%	S	90%	24%	33%	0%

KEY VOTES:

	Insurance reform:	YES	Child sick leave:	–
Assault gun ban:	YES	Parent consent abortion: NO	Ban AIDS discrim:	YES
Clean Air Act:	YES	Cutting old trees: NO	Extend death penalty:	YES
Lmt product tort:	–	End mob home rent cont: NO	Ban offshore oil:	YES

20th Assembly District

Edward T. Lempert (D)

No Democrat had been elected to represent this San Mateo County district in 100 years until 1988 when young, idealistic Ted Lempert shocked first-term Republican Bill Duplissea. It was an upset of major proportions in a system which has been left with few political surprises because of redistricting.

Few Republicans or Democrats gave Lempert, an attorney who at 26 was already a longtime political activist, much of a chance to beat Duplissea. In fact, local Democrats casting about for a candidate asked his mother to run first, but she declined.

Lempert, a cheery, earnest, boyish sort, took his opportunity seriously. He pounded the sidewalks in hundreds of precincts in Burlingame, Hillsborough,

Edward T. Lempert

Foster City, Belmont, San Mateo, San Carlos and Half Moon Bay. He scored points questioning his opponent's ethical standards by concentrating on a bill Duplissea carried to benefit a local car dealer–a potent issue in the midst of a Capitol scandal over influence-peddling.

As part of his campaign, Lempert pledged to push for higher ethical standards in the Legislature and during his first term, he was true to his word. He introduced a package of eight bills that would have made major changes in the way the Legislature operates. Most of Lempert's bills stalled, but the Legislature ultimately passed a proposed constitutional amendment to set up a framework for ethical standards.

Lempert also pushed several other measures during his first term including ones that would allow prosecution for misleading advertising and would require video stores to maintain separate areas for adult films. He has already promised to help push a package of bills to set up an offshore oil spill prevention and cleanup plan for the state.

Lempert's major problem is re-election in a district that, because of registration, has a Republican voting tilt. But the San Francisco Peninsula's voters also have less partisan attachment than most and, as with Lempert's original victory, will vote for the individual, regardless of party.

PERSONAL: elected 1988; born June 14, 1961, in San Mateo, Calif.; home, San Mateo; education, B.A. public policy Princeton University; J.D. Stanford University; unmarried; Jewish.

CAREER: lawyer.

COMMITTEES: Economic Development & New Technologies; Education; Elections, Reapportionment & Constitutional Amendments; Transportation; Utilities & Commerce. SELECT: Ethics.

OFFICES: Capitol, (916) 445-8188; district, 1650 Borel Place, 229, San Mateo 94402, (415) 571-9521.

REGISTRATION: 45.2% D, 42.2% R

1988 CAMPAIGN: Lempert – D   52%

Duplissea (inc.)–R 44%

Genis – L   3%

RATINGS: NRA

0%

KEY VOTES:

Insurance reform: YES	Child sick leave: YES	Ban AIDS discrim: YES
Assault gun ban: YES	End mob home rent cont: –	Cutting old trees: NO

21st Assembly District

Byron Sher (D)

The silicon-chip empire of the Silicon Valley grew up around Stanford University. Thus it may be appropriate that a Stanford professor represents this generally upscale district that includes Mountain View, Palo Alto, East Palo Alto, and portions of Redwood City, Menlo Park and Sunnyvale.

Bearded Professor Byron Sher was mayor of Palo
Alto for two terms before he was elected to the Assembly in 1980. He has continued to teach law at Stanford
during the fall term, perhaps illustrating that the "full-
time" Legislature is not really full-time.

As chairman of the Assembly Natural Resources
Committee, Sher has emerged as one of the Legislature's chief environmentalists. He has pushed for adding rivers to the Scenic Rivers Act and he unsuccessfully tried to pass a three-year moratorium on lumbering old-growth stands along the North Coast. Sher's
major legislative accomplishment was in authoring the
state's landmark Clean Air Act that gave new powers
and responsibilities to local smog districts and requires

Byron Sher

localities to begin a phased reduction of smog emissions. He took a similar approach
in his 1989 legislation revamping the state's garbage management board, a law that
will lead to Californians sorting their trash for curbside recycling. The law, signed
by Deukmejian, requires localities to cut in half the trash sent to dumps by the year
2000.

On a local level, Sher has fought for years against Deukmejian's vetoes of bills
cleaning up leaking underground storage tanks, an issue of considerable concern to
the Silicon Valley with its high number of toxic waste sites.

Sher and his seatmate, Lloyd Connelly, collaborate in ferreting out special
interest bills and voting against them. The two are aligned with the Assembly's
"Grizzly Bears" faction of liberal Democrats who have tried to keep Speaker Willie
Brown on a leftward course.

Sher sparked the wrath of the speaker in 1987 when he spoke against a bill that
modified the state's liability laws, part of a peace accord worked out on a napkin at
Frank Fat's restaurant. When Sher asked for a Democratic caucus to discuss things,
Brown scowled "There will be no more caucuses tonight, Mr. Sher."

The speaker tried to move Sher to the chairmanship of the prestigious Judiciary
Committee at the start of the 1989 session, but Sher declined, preferring to stick with
Natural Resources and environmental issues.

PERSONAL: elected 1980; born Feb. 7, 1928, in St. Louis, Mo.; home, Palo
Alto; education, B.S. business administration Washington University, St. Louis;
J.D. Harvard University; wife, Linda; children, Adrienne, Benjamin and Katherine;
Jewish.

CAREER: law professor, Stanford University; Palo Alto City Council 1965-
1967 and 1973-1980; mayor, 1974-1975 and 1977-1978; commissioner of the San
Francisco Bay Conservation and Development Commission 1978-1980.

COMMITTEES: Natural Resources (chair); Environmental Safety & Toxic
Materials; Finance & Insurance; Governmental Efficiency & Consumer Protection.

California Political Almanac 249

JOINT: Arts; Prison Construction & Operations.

OFFICES: Capitol, (916) 445-7632; district, 785 Castro St., Suite C, Mountain View 94041, (415) 961-6031.

REGISTRATION: 53.6% D, 31.8% R

1988 CAMPAIGN: Sher – D   88%
                 Goodwyn – L   12%

RATINGS:

	AFL	PIRG	CLCV	NOW	CTA	HAC	CofC	CFB	NRA
	95%	89%	100%	17%	S	95%	24%	33%	0%

KEY VOTES:

Divest S. Africa:	YES	Insurance reform:	YES	Child sick leave:	YES
Assault gun ban:	YES	Parent consent abortion:	NO	Ban AIDS discrim:	YES
Clean Air Act:	YES	Cutting old trees:	NO	Extend death penalty:	–
Lmt product tort:	NO	End mob home rent cont:	NO	Ban offshore oil:	YES

22nd Assembly District

Charles W. Quackenbush (R)

Voter registration figures in this district make it a Republican stronghold. But residents of the affluent San Jose suburbs of Los Altos, Cupertino, Los Gatos, Campbell and Saratoga aren't hardcore conservatives yet can't quite be called moderates either. Enter Charles Quackenbush, a tall, youthful-looking ex-Army captain and high-tech entrepreneur who is conservative with a bit of an independent streak.

Quackenbush wasn't the first choice of the dominant hardcore conservative faction of the Assembly Republican caucus when he was elected to office in 1986, replacing Ernest Konnyu, who went on to a brief career in Congress. In fact, then-Assembly Republican leader Patrick Nolan pumped more than $164,000 into the

Charles Quackenbush

campaign of an Assembly staffer in an effort to defeat Quackenbush in the GOP primary.

But Quackenbush won the primary, bested Democrat Brent Ventura in the general election and now appears solidly entrenched in his seat, aligning himself with the more moderate faction of the Assembly Republican caucus.

During his first two terms in office, Quackenbush hasn't been in the forefront of many major legislative issues, save one. His was the key committee vote in support of a landmark Democrat-pushed bill to outlaw semiautomatic assault weapons in the state. Without his vote, the measure, which ultimately became law, could have died in committee.

In exchange for his vote, he got Democrats to outlaw weapons by specifically listing them rather than flatly banning all semiautomatic rifles. Quackenbush was also just one of two Assembly Republicans who supported the measure during the Assembly floor vote.

PERSONAL: elected 1986; born April 20, 1954, in Tacoma, Wash.; home, Cupertino; Army 1976-1981; education, B.A. American Studies, Notre Dame University; wife, Chris; children, Carrey and Charles; Catholic.

CAREER: owner of Q-Tech, an employment service for the electronics industry 1979-1989.

COMMITTEES: Governmental Organization; Health; Public Employees, Retirement & Social Security; Public Safety; Transportation.

OFFICES: Capitol, (916) 445-8305; district, 456 El Paseo de Saratoga, San Jose 95130, (408) 446-4114.

REGISTRATION: 40.7% D, 46.4% R

1988 CAMPAIGN: Quackenbush – R   63%
　　　　　　　　Yeamans – D　　37%

RATINGS:

AFL	PIRG	CLCV	NOW	CTA	HAC	CofC	CFB	NRA
14%	42%	35%	50%	U	50%	88%	66%	60%

KEY VOTES:

Insurance reform:	–	Child sick leave:	NO
Assault gun ban: YES	Parent consent abortion: YES	Ban AIDS discrim:	NO
Clean Air Act: NO	Cutting old trees: YES	Extend death penalty: YES
Lmt product tort: YES	End mob home rent cont: YES	Ban offshore oil: YES

23rd Assembly District

John Vasconcellos (D)

The city of Santa Clara and the Hispanic neighborhoods of East San Jose comprise the bulk of this South Bay Democratic stronghold that also includes Campbell and Alum Rock. Roughly one-third of the district is Latino.

For a quarter-century, this district in its various permutations has sent John Vasconcellos to the state Assembly. Only one other Assembly member has more seniority that Vasconcellos, Speaker Willie Brown. When Vasconcellos complained that the FBI had invaded "my house," he was not kidding; Vasconcellos has spent so much of his adult life in the Legislature that he is body and soul a part of it.

The transformations of John Vasconcellos practically mirror the social history of California since World War II. He began as an aide to Gov. Pat Brown and was eventually favored with an Assembly seat. He traded his dark suits and crew cuts for leather jackets and long hair in the '60s, storming the Capitol's halls with all the anger of the protest era. In the '70s and '80s, Vasconcellos became a convert to the inward-looking human awareness movement.

Some consider Vasconcellos a visionary, others consider him a flake. Whatever he is, Vasconcellos is nothing if not interesting. He was lampooned by the

Doonesbury comic strip for his legislation fathering the
state's self-esteem commission. He routinely talks not
in the language of politics, but in the lingo of encounter
groups. The San Jose Mercury News once dubbed him
"Mister Touchy Feely."

However, first and foremost, Vasconcellos is the
chairman of the vastly powerful Ways and Means
Committee, a committee that rules on the state budget
and all bills proposing to spend money. Although Vasconcellos embraces raising the self-esteem of citizens in
the abstract, his iron-fisted temperamental management
of his committee does not do much for the self-esteem
of many who come before it or the committee's staff.

John Vasconcellos

Vasconcellos is known for his severe tongue-lash-
ing and temper tantrums. He is one of the Capitol's most difficult bosses. He once
threatened to run a reporter over with his car. And during floor debates, Vasconcellos has been known to call those who disagree with him "stupid," which even by the
Assembly's low standards of decorum goes a little too far.

More energetic than Alfred Alquist in the Senate – his counterpart on the budget
– Vasconcellos every year wields enormous influence over the shape of the state's
spending plan, now topping $50 billion a year. Vasconcellos has stood firm on
maintaining health and welfare benefits, launching verbal bombs toward Gov.
Deukmejian each time the administration tries to tamper with them.

However, not all his fiscal ideas have been backed by his Democratic colleagues.
He was left out on a limb in 1987 when he proposed that the state should respond
to federal tax changes by raising income taxes and lowering sales taxes. The idea
made sense because sales taxes were no longer deductible while state income taxes
were. But the very idea of raising income taxes was totally taboo.

The speaker was said to have tried to ease Vasconcellos out of his Ways and
Means post at the start of the 1987 session in order to give the chairmanship to Mike
Roos. However, Vasconcellos would not go. Vasconcellos has been one of the
"Grizzly Bear" liberals who have been trying to keep the speaker true to his liberal
religion.

Vasconcellos is one the rare voices in Capitol life against the influence of special
interest money. He was one of the very few legislators – another was the Senate's
Bob Presley – who endorsed Proposition 68 in 1988 that would have set up public
financing for legislative campaigns, banned off-year fund raising and set donation
limits. The initiative was approved by voters but eclipsed by Proposition 73
donation limits because the latter measure got more votes. The conflict between the
two initiatives has landed in court, and at the end of 1989, was still unresolved.

With the Legislature's image increasingly tarnished because of federal investigations and less-than-flattering news coverage, the speaker turned to Vasconcellos

to chair a special committee on ethics. After months of labor, the committee produced a comprehensive package of institutional reforms. However, Senate President Pro Tem David Roberti upstaged the Assembly version with a proposal of his own and the speaker allowed it to pass. Vasconcellos was said to be privately furious with Brown for pulling the carpet out from under him.

Vasconcellos is popular on the lecture circuit. Unlike those of his colleagues who take "speaking fees" that are thinly veiled pay-offs, his speeches are legitimate. Vasconcellos has stumped nationwide for his self-esteem ideas, and they seem to be catching on in mainstream circles.He also teamed up with a cross-section of legislators to hold out on endorsing anyone for governor in 1990 until the candidates begin addressing issues near to his heart.

PERSONAL: elected 1966; born May 11, 1932, in San Jose, Calif.; home, San Jose; Army; education, B.A. and J.D. from University of Santa Clara; unmarried; no religious affiliation.

CAREER: lawyer; aide to Gov. Pat Brown.

COMMITTEES: Ways & Means (chair); Aging & Long-Term Care; Economic Development & New Technologies; Education. SELECT: Ethics (chair). JOINT: Review of the Master Plan for Higher Education (chair); Legislative Budget (vice chair); Legislative Audit.

OFFICES: Capitol, (916) 445-4253; district, 100 Paseo de San Antonio, 106, San Jose 95113, (408) 288-7515.

REGISTRATION: 59.5% D, 28.2% R

1988 CAMPAIGN: Vasconcellos – D   66%
Knapp – R   31%
Greene – L   4%

RATINGS:

AFL	PIRG	CLCV	NOW	CTA	HAC	CofC	CFB	NRA
91%	74%	100%	92%	G	81%	24%	33%	0%

KEY VOTES:

Divest S. Africa:	YES	Insurance reform:	YES	Child sick leave:	YES
Assault gun ban:	YES	Parent consent abortion:	–	Ban AIDS discrim:	YES
Clean Air Act:	YES	Cutting old trees:	–	Extend death penalty:	–
Lmt product tort:	–	End mob home rent cont:	–	Ban offshore oil:	YES

24th Assembly District

Dominic L. Cortese (D)

Dominic Cortese spent 12 years on the Santa Clara County Board of Supervisors before he was elected to the Assembly in 1980. It prepared him well for what has become his primary role in the lower house: an advocate for local government.

As chairman of the Assembly Committee on Local Government, Cortese has faced the challenge of attempting to figure out ways for local governments to operate in the wake of the property tax-cutting Proposition 13. One of his latest proposals was to permit – with voter approval – creation of county "service areas" that would allow assessments on residents for increased police protection. It was vetoed by Gov. Deukmejian.

Cortese, who comes from a third generation farming family from the San Jose area, is a political moderate who seems to fit his south San Jose district well. Nevertheless, Cortese faced a stiff challenge in 1988 from Republican Buck Norred who attempted to tie Cortese to liberal Assembly Speaker Willie Brown.

Dominic L. Cortese

One issue where Cortese has regularly broken with most Democrats is on abortion. A Catholic, he has consistently joined Republicans in voting in favor of limiting Medi-Cal funding of abortions for poor women. Cortese, on the other hand, tries to deflect criticism from pro-choice forces by saying that he believes in family planning, "the kind that doesn't encourage abortion."

While many of Cortese's measures deal with local government, he has carried a few others of note. At the behest of the wine industry, he proposed a modest increase in the state's liquor tax, an industry attempt to head off a possible initiative seeking a much larger hike. He also proposed to forbid telephone salespeople from calling people who put their names on a list declaring they don't wish to be bothered, a measure vetoed in 1989 by Deukmejian.

As an aside from the fun and games at the Capitol, Cortese has recently purchased an expansion team in the minor league Continental Basketball Association, the San Jose Jammers.

PERSONAL: elected 1980; born Sept. 27, 1932, in San Jose, Calif.; home, San Jose; Army 1954-1956; education, B.S. political science University of Santa Clara; wife, Suzanne; children, David, Rosanne, Mary, Thomas and James; Catholic.

CAREER: businessman and farmer, part-owner of Cortese Bros. grocery chain; Santa Clara County Board of Supervisors 1968-1980.

COMMITTEES: Local Government (chair); Agriculture; Governmental Organization; Health; Economic Development & New Technologies. SELECT: Child Abuse; Child Care; Calif. Wine Production & Economy (chair). JOINT: Quincentennial of the Voyages of Columbus; Legislative Audit; Organized Crime & Gang Violence; Refugee Resettlement, International Migration & Cooperative Development.

OFFICES: Capitol, (916) 445-8243; district, 100 Paseo de San Antonio Suite 300, San Jose 95113, (408) 269-6500.

REGISTRATION: 54% D, 34.3% R
1988 CAMPAIGN: Cortese – D   54%
                  Norred – R   46%

RATINGS:

AFL	PIRG	CLCV	NOW	CTA	HAC	CofC	CFB	NRA
94%	84%	96%	83%	S	90%	20%	44%	20%

KEY VOTES:

Divest S. Africa:	YES	Insurance reform:	YES	Child sick leave:	YES
Assault gun ban:	YES	Parent consent abortion:	YES	Ban AIDS discrim:	YES
Clean Air Act:	YES	Cutting old trees:	YES	Extend death penalty:	YES
Lmt product tort:	YES	End mob home rent cont:	–	Ban offshore oil:	YES

25th Assembly District

John Rusty Areias (D)

When framers of the post-1980 census reapportionment created the 25th Assembly District from bits and pieces of other districts, they dubbed it the "Steinbeck seat" because it encompassed the agricultural areas featured in John Steinbeck's novels.

The district straddles both sides of the coastal range, encompassing San Benito County, Gilroy and Morgan Hill in Santa Clara County, the growing Salinas area in Monterey County and western Merced County, including Los Banos.

Rusty Areias, a wealthy dairy farmer from Los Banos, fits the district well and never has been seriously challenged after winning his seat in 1982 although

John Rusty Areias

Areias' departure might leave it vulnerable to Republican penetration due to conservative voting patterns and relatively low Democratic registration.

Areias gained notoriety in 1988 as a member of the so-called "Gang of Five," a group of Democrats who challenged Assembly Speaker Willie Brown's authority despite having been favored by Brown with choice committee assignments. The challenge was turned back after months of bickering and Areias, who toyed briefly with running for the congressional seat vacated by Rep. Tony Coelho of Merced, is gradually returning to the fold as a player on the Democratic team.

Beyond balancing the sometimes diverse interests of his district, Areias has carved out a role for himself as an advocate of consumer interests, being one of the few legislators to oppose hikes in consumer loan rate ceilings. And with his personal wealth, good lucks, sharp suits and fast cars, he challenges Speaker Brown's position as the Legislature's party animal. Cosmopolitan magazine once named him as one of the nation's leading bachelors.

PERSONAL: elected 1982; born Sept. 12, 1949, in Los Banos, Calif.; home,

Los Banos; education, B.S. agriculture CSU Chico; unmarried; Catholic.

CAREER: managing partner family business, Areias Dairy Farms, Los Banos.

COMMITTEES: Aging & Long Term Care; Economic Development & New Technologies; Education; Governmental Efficiency & Consumer Protection.

OFFICES: Capitol, (916) 445-7380; district, 7415 Eigleberry, Suite B, Gilroy 95020 (408) 848-1461; 545 J St., Suite 14, Los Banos 93635 (209) 826-6100; 140 Central Ave., Salinas 93901, (408) 422-4344.

REGISTRATION: 53% D, 35.6% R

1988 CAMPAIGN: Areias – D   75%
Gilmore – R   23%
Hinkle – L   2%

RATINGS:

AFL	PIRG	CLCV	NOW	CTA	HAC	CofC	CFB	NRA
88%	74%	75%	75%	S	81%	36%	77%	10%

KEY VOTES:

Divest S. Africa:	YES	Insurance reform:	YES	Child sick leave:	YES
Assault gun ban:	YES	Parent consent abortion:	YES	Ban AIDS discrim:	YES
Clean Air Act:	–	Cutting old trees:	NO	Extend death penalty:	YES
Lmt product tort:	–	End mob home rent cont:	–	Ban offshore oil:	YES

26th Assembly District

Patrick W. Johnston (D)

This district takes in most of San Joaquin County, including Escalon, Linden, Manteca, Tracy, Ripon and Stockton, one of the most ethnically diverse and politically complex cities in California, and one that's in the middle of a growth boom born of the outward push of commuters from the Bay Area.

For years, Stockton's politics were tightly controlled by a tiny, semi-secretive oligarchy but in the mid-1970s, some newcomers challenged that control. A young rancher named John Garamendi won a local Assembly seat and quickly moved into the state Senate and he hired another young man, Patrick Johnston, as his aide.

Patrick W. Johnston

In 1980, Johnston, in an outgrowth of a power struggle then under way in the Assembly, challenged a Democratic incumbent assemblyman, Carmen Perino, in the primary. It was a nasty battle, reflecting not only the intensity of the Capitol squabble but the intensely personal nature of local politics as well. At one point, a Perino campaign aide was arrested in a murder-for-hire case.

Johnston defeated Perino but his struggle was just beginning. His tussle with Republican Adrian Fondse was one of the sleaziest in California history, complete with phony anti-Johnston mailings appealing to racial prejudices and other dirty tricks. The initial vote count showed Fondse to be the winner but a recount, certified by Johnston's fellow Democrats in the Assembly, unseated Fondse and declared Johnston the winner by 35 votes out of about 84,000 cast. None of his campaigns since have proved so rough, or so close, despite the Republicans bankrolling county Supervisor Doug Wilhoit's unsuccessful 1984 bid.

Johnston, a former journalist who once aspired to the priesthood, has achieved a reputation as a liberal reformer but has proven his adaptability while chairing the Finance and Insurance Committee, a major "juice committee" with jurisdiction over legislation affecting banks and insurance companies, whose members are showered with attention from industry lobbyists. Johnston has not been shy about accepting campaign contributions, trips and other goodies from special interests, but he also has won a reputation for even-handed operation of the committee that brings kudos from affected industries and consumerists alike.

Johnston found himself in the thick of battles over auto insurance and was a critic of both the industry and its self-appointed reformers, joining with consumer groups in pushing a no-fault system he said held out the best chance of keeping a lid on insurance rates. That effort failed.

As a liberal with a pragmatic bent, Johnston is considered to be one of the few Assembly members who could capture enough support to be elected speaker should Willie Brown step down or find himself forced out.

PERSONAL: elected 1980; born Sept. 3, 1946, in San Francisco, Calif.; home, Stockton; education, B.A. philosophy St. Patrick's College, Menlo Park; wife, Margaret Mary Johnston; children, Patrick and Christopher; Catholic.

CAREER: Reporter for a Catholic newspaper; probation officer, Calaveras County; chief of staff to Sen. John Garamendi 1975-1980.

COMMITTEES: Finance & Insurance (chair); Education; Governmental Efficiency & Consumer Protection; Judiciary. JOINT: Oversight on GAIN Implementation; State's Economy.

OFFICES: Capitol, (916) 445-7931; district, 31 E. Channel St., 306, Stockton 95202, (209) 948-7479.

REGISTRATION: 57.4% D, 34.7% R

1988 CAMPAIGN: Johnston – D 72%

Correll – R 28%

RATINGS:

AFL	PIRG	CLCV	NOW	CTA	HAC	CofC	CFB	NRA
87%	89%	89%	92%	G	90%	28%	33%	0%

KEY VOTES:

Divest S. Africa: YES	Insurance reform: YES	Child sick leave: YES
Assault gun ban: YES	Parent consent abortion: NO	Ban AIDS discrim: YES
Clean Air Act: YES	Cutting old trees: NO	Extend death penalty: –
Lmt product tort: YES	End mob home rent cont: YES	Ban offshore oil: YES

27th Assembly District

Vacant

This district, one of the fastest-growing in the San Joaquin Valley, is comprised of all of Stanislaus County and the Atwater-Snelling region of the northern tip of Merced County. The population center is Modesto, which in recent years has become a boom town for Bay Area commuters, with dozens of housing subdivisions sprouting in former fields.

Since the dawn of recorded time, at least a century, the area has been agricultural, but the influx of commuters is having an economic, as well as a political, impact. Shopping centers and other service industries are taking on added importance.

The conservative-Democrat tone of the 27th District is being altered in ways that are still not clear as the new residents sink roots. They may, or may not, shift the ideological tone of the district, but they move its orientation away from agriculture and toward more urban, or suburban, concerns.

Gary Condit danced to the district's conservative tune for years as he rose from Ceres councilman to mayor to county supervisor to assemblyman. A career politician with a largely one-note legislative platform, law and order, Condit benefitted from personal popularity and good luck. All of those qualities were on display in 1989 as Condit defeated Republican Clare Berryhill in the 15th Congressional District seat in a special election after the Democratic incumbent, Tony Coelho, resigned rather than face a prolonged investigation into his financial affairs.

Condit's congressional win touched off a new struggle for his Assembly seat and there was no shortage of candidates for the special election scheduled for late 1989. Among them were Republicans Carol Whiteside, mayor of Modesto; Turlock Mayor Brad Bates; Berryhill's campaign chairwoman Barbara Keating-Edh; Stanislaus County Supervisor Nick Blom; Modesto City Councilman Richard Lang; and former Air Force Maj. Chris Patterakis. Possible Democratic contenders were Condit's executive committee chairman, Tom Ciccarelli; Stanislaus County Supervisors Pat Paul and Sal Cannella; and Stanislaus County Democratic Central Committee chairman John Lazar.

REGISTRATION: 53% D, 37.8% R
SPECIAL ELECTION set for December 1989

28th Assembly District

Samuel S. Farr (D)

There are those who believe that the Central California coast is the most beautiful spot on earth. The political custodian of that stretch of California, and its many contradictory forces, is Sam Farr, whose 28th Assembly District runs from Santa Cruz to south of Monterey along the coast.

It's an area in which the forces favoring development and those favoring environmental preservation are locked in mortal combat, but Farr tries to sidestep as much of the controversy as possible, although he defines himself as an environmental protectionist.

The son of a state legislator and a one-time legislative staffer himself, Farr was a Monterey County supervisor before winning the Assembly seat in 1980.Given the high rate of turnover in the Assembly, that gives him a fairly high level of seniority, but he has seen the plums of power being passed into other hands.

To observers of the Assembly, Farr is known mostly as a talented amateur photographer who snaps pictures of his colleagues during floor sessions. He seems to lack the fire to engage in the sometimes brutal politics that lead to power. He chairs a minor committee dealing with technology.

Samuel S. Farr

Farr doesn't have any trouble getting re-elected in a district with an above-average Democratic voter registration and he'd been a leading candidate for the state Senate if Democrat Henry Mello decides to retire.

PERSONAL: elected 1980; born July 4, 1941, in San Francisco, Calif.; home, Carmel; Peace Corps; education, B.S. biology Willamette University, attended Monterey Institute of Foreign Studies and Santa Clara School of Law; wife, Sharon Baldwin; daughter, Jessica; Episcopalian.

CAREER: assistant administrative analyst for the Legislative Analysts' office 1969-1971; chief consultant to Assembly Constitutional Amendments Committee 1972-1975; Monterey County Board of Supervisors 1975-1980.

COMMITTEES: Economic Development & New Technologies (chair); Education; Natural Resources; Finance & Insurance; Governmental Efficiency & Consumer Protection. SELECT: Small Business. JOINT: Arts (vice chair); Quincentennial of the Voyages of Columbus; Fisheries & Aquaculture; Refugee Resettlement, International Migration & Cooperative Development; Review of the Master Plan for Higher Education.

OFFICES: Capitol, (916) 445-8496; district, 1200 Aguajito Road, Monterey 93940, (408) 646-1980; 701 Ocean St., 540A, Santa Cruz 95060.

REGISTRATION: 55.8% D, 31.3% R

1988 CAMPAIGN: Farr – D   71%

Skillicorn – R   29%

RATINGS:

AFL	PIRG	CLCV	NOW	CTA	HAC	CofC	CFB	NRA
93%	89%	92%	84%	G	95%	24%	44%	0%

KEY VOTES:

Divest S. Africa:	YES	Insurance reform:	YES	Child sick leave:	YES
Assault gun ban:	YES	Parent consent abortion:	NO	Ban AIDS discrim:	YES
Clean Air Act:	YES	Cutting old trees:	NO	Extend death penalty:	YES
Lmt product tort:	YES	End mob home rent cont:	–	Ban offshore oil:	YES

29th Assembly District

Carl Eric Seastrand (R)

This scenic Central California coastal district includes San Luis Obispo and parts of Monterey and Santa Barbara counties. It has farm-based communities like King City in the Salinas Valley and Santa Maria, and sleepy coastal towns like Pismo Beach and Morro Bay.

Eric Seastrand, a former stockbroker from Salinas, won the seat in 1982 after a series of unsuccessful runs for elective office. It's a seat that Seastrand could probably hold for as long as he wants. But since 1984, Seastrand has had a running battle with colon cancer.

At times, Seastrand has appeared gaunt and weak. Yet he continues to maintain a good Assembly attendance record, to deal with all with unfailing good humor and courtesy and to fly his plane home to Salinas most weekends.

Carl Eric Seastrand

Seastrand's illness seems to have tempered his staunchly conservative views. In 1989, he supported a Democratic bill to establish a program to provide insurance for people with serious illnesses who had been refused coverage by private companies, noting he would have been in trouble without insurance.

Two weeks after learning his cancer had reoccurred in 1987, he argued in favor of allowing the state to test experimental drugs on AIDS patients before federal approval was received. "When it is your life, you are going to use what is best for you even when all the doctors disagree," he said. Yet his pro-business bent shone through in 1989, when he argued against a bill to require employers to provide health insurance for workers, noting it would be too expensive.

Seastrand has been a staunch supporter of agriculture throughout his career. He also pushed a bill to make it easier to crackdown on distributors and producers of pornography.

PERSONAL: elected 1982; born Feb. 7, 1938, in Fresno, Calif.; home, Salinas; Army, USAF Reserve; education, B.S. political science San Jose State University; wife, Andrea; children, Kurt and Heidi; Presbyterian.

CAREER: stockbroker; Assembly Republican whip.

COMMITTEES: Agriculture; Finance & Insurance; Ways & Means.
SELECT: California.Wine Production & Economy; Child Abuse; Small Business.
JOINT: Fairs Allocation & Classification.

OFFICES: Capitol, (916) 445-7795; district, 523 Higuera St., San Luis Obispo 93401, (805) 549-3381.

REGISTRATION: 40.3% D, 47.4% R

1988 CAMPAIGN: Seastrand – R   67%
                  Bradford – D   33%

RATINGS:

AFL	PIRG	CLCV	NOW	CTA	HAC	CofC	CFB	NRA
10%	35%	12%	17%	U	31%	92%	66%	100%

KEY VOTES:

Divest S. Africa:	NO	Insurance reform:	NO	Child sick leave:	NO
Assault gun ban:	NO	Parent consent abortion:	YES	Ban AIDS discrim:	NO
Clean Air Act:	NO	Cutting old trees:	YES	Extend death penalty:	YES
Lmt product tort:	YES	End mob home rent cont:	YES	Ban offshore oil:	NO

30th Assembly District

James M. Costa (D)

The 30th Assembly District is mostly rural, but any resemblance to down-home, small family farming is purely coincidental. The game is agribusiness, agriculture on a large and scientific scale. The district covers all of Kings County, plus portions of Fresno, Madera and Merced counties, including Chowchilla, Madera, Mendota and part of the city of Fresno.

The district's growers supply foreign and domestic markets with commodities such as cotton, raisins, grapes, dairy products and beef cattle. Although agriculture is the economic backbone of the district, over half of its population resides in an urban setting, albeit one that still is closely tied to the agricultural industry.

James M. Costa

Once referred to as congressional timber, Jim Costa is a tenacious and skillful politician who works hard for his district but is also weighed down by political baggage that could limit his career.

With more than 10 years in the Assembly, Costa has become an ace legislative technician and one of Assembly Speaker Willie Brown's lieutenants. He began his career working for Rep. B.F. Sisk, then was an assistant to Rep. John Krebs and, finally, was administrative assistant to Assemblyman (now congressman) Richard Lehman before winning a seat in the Assembly. To the benefit of his farm district, Lehman watches over water-related matters as the chairman of the Assembly Water, Parks and Wildlife Committee.

On the upside of Costa's career, he's carried several big league bond issues, including one that would spend $1 billion on upgrading rail transportation if voters agree in 1990. On the downside, Costa has become one of the Capitol's big juice players, carrying legislation for special interest groups and accepting large amounts of campaign contributions, gifts and speaking fees. He pushed several anti-rent-control bills for landlords, which failed, as well as a measure for beer wholesalers that would have guaranteed them territorial monopolies, which eventually was vetoed by Gov. Deukmejian.

But it was Costa's arrest on the last night of the 1986 legislative session that brought him his greatest notoriety. Just weeks before he was to face voters for re-election, and while traveling in a state-leased car with a known prostitute at his side, Costa, who has never married, offered $50 to an undercover woman police officer to join them in a three-way sex act, Sacramento police said.

Nearly a week later, with his mother nearby, Costa admitted during a press conference in his home district that he made a mistake and committed an error in judgment. Later that month, he was fined $1 and given three years' probation. The episode would have likely spelled the end of a political career for anyone from a district with a different makeup of voters. But Republicans failed to capitalize on the mishap and Costa easily won re-election in the Democrat-dominated district.

Costa makes it clear he hopes to someday run for Congress, perhaps for any new congressional district that might be created in 1991.

PERSONAL: elected 1978; born April 13, 1952, in Fresno, Calif.; home, Fresno; education, B.S. political science CSU Fresno; unmarried; Catholic.

CAREER: aide to Rep. B.F. Sisk 1974-1975 and Rep. John Krebs 1975-1976; assistant to Assemblyman Richard Lehman 1976-1978.

COMMITTEES: Water, Parks and Wildlife (chair); Governmental Organization; Housing & Community Development; Transportation. JOINT: Fisheries and Aquaculture.

OFFICES: Capitol, (916) 445-7558; district, 1111 Fulton Mall, Room 914, Fresno 93721, (209) 264-3078; 512 N. Irwin, Suite A, Hanford 92320, (209) 582-2869.

REGISTRATION: 61.1% D, 30.7% R

1988 CAMPAIGN: Costa – D 72%

Hurt – R 28%

RATINGS:

AFL	PIRG	CLCV	NOW	CTA	HAC	CofC	CFB	NRA
78%	79%	89%	92%	S	85%	44%	66%	0%

KEY VOTES:

Divest S. Africa: YES	Insurance reform: YES	Child sick leave: YES
Assault gun ban: YES	Parent consent abortion: YES	Ban AIDS discrim: YES
Clean Air Act: YES	Cutting old trees: –	Extend death penalty: YES
Lmt product tort: YES	End mob home rent cont: YES	Ban offshore oil: NO

31st Assembly District

Bruce C. Bronzan (D)

This district centers on the heart of Fresno, the most strongly Democratic and liberal bastion, such as it is, in the San Joaquin Valley. It includes central Fresno County and most of the city of Fresno and surrounding cities of Clovis, Parlier,

Sanger, Reedley and Selma. Republicans maintain a strong presence and Bruce Bronzan, recovering from early stumbles, is careful not to offend his moderate-to-conservative, staunchly pro-agriculture constituency.

Articulate, friendly and energetic, sometimes to the point of being hyperactive, Bronzan is surrounded by loyal staff members and has quickly risen through the ranks of the Assembly. He has honed health-related issues into a specialty with the speed of an X-ray and, after Assemblyman Curtis R. Tucker of Los Angeles died, Bronzan was named in early 1989 by Assembly Speaker Willie Brown to replace Tucker as Health Committee chairman.

Bruce C. Bronzan

Bronzan, a loyal Brown lieutenant, has a strong liberal bent but has been the point person on conservative issues critical to his district. For instance, after the Alar food scare, and with threats of a statewide initiative banning many pesticides in the wings, Bronzan proposed a measure to expand food testing. Opponents in environmental groups described it as a shrewd maneuver designed to pre-empt their initiative drive. Bronzan also has carried numerous measures to revamp state health care systems, fix the workers compensation morass, cut exposure to cancer-causing asbestos, upgrade public safety, help AIDS victims, and improve the lot of the disabled and the mentally incompetent.

Politically, Bronzan weathered his most bruising campaign in 1988, when his Republican challenger, Doug Haaland, tried to keep Bronzan on the defensive by repeatedly focusing on Bronzan's open willingness to accept honorariums and gifts from many of the same special interest groups that have an interest in bills he carries, votes on or hears as chairman of the health committee. Bronzan defended his practices as essential to representing his constituency and to keep from going personally bankrupt. Bronzan was also criticized for his campaign and personal finances, including accepting $16,000 from a Sacramento lobbyist as part of a secured home loan. The state's Fair Political Practices Commission cleared Bronzan of any wrongdoing but the agency warned him it was not ruling out reconsidering similar cases in the future. Bronzan worked hard to offset the negatives and won re-election easily.

His articulation and drive–coupled with his ability to win in a district more conservative than he is–mark Bronzan as a Democratic comer who is likely to pop into a state Senate or congressional seat at the first opportunity and then explore statewide office.

PERSONAL: elected 1982; born Sept. 28, 1947, in Fresno, Calif.; home, Fresno; education, B.S. political science and teaching credential CSU Fresno; M.A. in urban studies Occidental College; wife, Linda Barnes; children, Chloe and Forest; Protestant.

CAREER: teacher; Fresno County Board of Supervisors 1975-1982; head of a drug and alcohol treatment program for Fresno Community Hospital.

COMMITTEES: Health (chair); Agriculture; Finance & Insurance; Human Services. SELECT: Calif. Wine Production & Economy. SPECIAL: Medi-Cal Oversight.

OFFICES: Capitol, (916) 445-8514; district, 2115 Kern 250, Fresno 93721, (209) 445-5532.

REGISTRATION: 58.1% D, 34.4% R

1988 CAMPAIGN: Bronzan – D   71%
                  Haaland – R   29%

RATINGS:	AFL	PIRG	CLCV	NOW	CTA	HAC	CofC	CFB	NRA
	90%	89%	92%	92%	S	85%	36%	77%	10%

KEY VOTES:

Divest S. Africa:	YES	Insurance reform:	YES	Child sick leave:	YES
Assault gun ban:	YES	Parent consent abortion:	–	Ban AIDS discrim:	YES
Clean Air Act:	YES	Cutting old trees:	NO	Extend death penalty:	YES
Lmt product tort:	YES	End mob home rent cont:	YES	Ban offshore oil:	YES

32nd Assembly District

William L. Jones (R)

Another agriculture-dominated district in the San Joaquin Valley, the 32nd Assembly District includes Mariposa County and the mountainous portions of Tulare, Fresno and Madera counties. It also has the cities of Dinuba, Porterville, Visalia and part of Clovis, plus the Kings and Sequoia Canyon National Parks. Business farming and ranching are key bywords here, and Republican Bill Jones, a businessman, row-crop farmer and cattle rancher, speaks the language.

Smart and articulate, Jones has carefully built a political career watching out for district interests such as agriculture, health, workers compensation, water, wine production, parks, education and local government. He was among those who helped work out the state's

William L. Jones

widely copied "workfare" program, where welfare recipients work to receive benefits. He has pushed measures to help reduce prison costs, increase highway funding for rural counties, keep rural hospitals open, recoup welfare overpayments and expand food inspections.

He has tangled with Democratic Assemblyman Byron Sher on water pollution issues, generally siding with the Deukmejian administration and farm interests that have sought a lenient approach to health standards for water. Sher, backing

California Political Almanac 264

environmentalists, reached an impasse with the administration in 1989 over progress – or the lack of it – in the state's program to adopt clean water standards, which resulted in the deletion of one-half of the budget from the Health Services budget for the water program. Sher and Jones eventually worked out an agreement to get the program going again.

As much as working the issues, Jones enjoys the politics. Part of a conservative-to-moderate faction of GOP Assembly members known as the "Magnificent Seven," Jones has openly challenged the Republican leadership for striking deals with Assembly Speaker Willie Brown, a San Francisco Democrat. For instance, the day after his re-election in 1988 to a fourth two-year term to the Assembly, he met with fellow party members in an effort to capture the title of minority leader. He lost to Ross Johnson of La Habra, but vowed to closely watch his performance.

In mid-1989, when Rep. Tony Coelho's 15th Congressional District seat became vacant, Jones briefly considered running for the seat. He legally could have run, although he did not live in the distirct. With Republican registration edging Democrats in his Assembly district, Jones can stay there as long as he wants. He enjoys being an assemblyman, aspires to higher, or at least more powerful, office and with his varied business and agriculture-related interests, he needn't worry about earning a living.

PERSONAL: elected 1982; born Dec. 20, 1949, in Coalinga, Calif.; home, Fresno; education, B.S. agribusiness CSU Fresno; wife, Maurine; children, Wendy and Andrea; Methodist.

CAREER: Chairman of the board of California Data Marketing, Inc., a computer service and direct mail firm; family partner in a 3,000-acre ranch and an investments firm.

COMMITTEES: Agriculture (vice chair); Environmental Safety & Toxic Materials; Economic Development & New Technologies; Ways & Means. SELECT: Calif. Wine Production & Economy; JOINT: Oversight on GAIN Implementation.

OFFICES: Capitol, (916) 445-2931; district, 1441 S. Mooney Blvd., Suite D, Visalia 93277, (209) 734-1182; 2497 W. Shaw, Suite 106, Fresno 93711, (209) 224-7833.

REGISTRATION: 44.2% D, 46.8% R

1988 CAMPAIGN: Jones – R   73%
Windham – D   28%

RATINGS:

AFL	PIRG	CLCV	NOW	CTA	HAC	CofC	CFB	NRA
15%	32%	32%	42%	U	31%	92%	88%	100%

KEY VOTES:

Divest S. Africa:	NO	Insurance reform:	NO	Child sick leave:	–
Assault gun ban:	NO	Parent consent abortion:	YES	Ban AIDS discrim:	NO
Clean Air Act:	YES	Cutting old trees:	YES	Extend death penalty:	–
Lmt product tort:	YES	End mob home rent cont:	YES	Ban offshore oil:	NO

33rd Assembly District
Trice J. Harvey (R)

This district covers the western portions of Tulare and Kern counties and the cities of Delano, Taft and parts of Bakersfield and Tulare. The chief industries are agriculture and oil and its politics are steadfastly conservative. Even Hispanic voters, who comprise 30 percent of the population, often vote Republican.

If state Republican leaders had had their way, Trice Harvey would not represent this rural-conservative district. And if Harvey had later had his way, a Democrat other than Willie Brown would be speaker of the Assembly.

Trice J. Harvey

In 1986, Harvey, then a Kern County supervisor, was the Republican candidate for the Assembly to replace Don Rogers, who had been elected to the Senate. Harvey had been endorsed by virtually all local GOP party leaders when then-Republican leader Pat Nolan abruptly turned against Harvey and backed his rival in the primary. Apparently Harvey's alliance with Bakersfield Congressman Bill Thomas, a bitter rival of Nolan in past Republican Party internal power struggles, prompted the turnabout.

Harvey beat Nolan's anointed candidate, Anna Allen, and went on to win the seat in a battle best-remembered for a controversial TV commercial. It depicted puppets representing Brown and the Democratic nominee, attorney Tom Fallgatter, in adjacent single beds. The "speaker" showered money on the candidate in what Harvey calls a "political purchase." Harvey's campaign also sent out phony letters of endorsement from President Reagan and campaign literature without identifying who paid for it, resulting in a $1,000 fine.

Two years later Harvey took revenge on Nolan during a boiling leadership struggle involving Speaker Brown and a group of dissident Democrats known as the "Gang of Five." Nolan had struck deals with Brown to keep him in office but Harvey didn't play along. He made motions to oust Brown and later to replace Brown with Democrat Charles Calderon. The resulting publicity played well in Harvey's district, where Brown is unpopular, but Brown stripped Harvey of his membership on the Assembly Agriculture Committee. Nevertheless, Harvey ended his freshman Assembly term with a flourish, and in the fall of 1988 he coasted easily to a second term.

Legislatively, having isolated himself from the Republican leadership, Harvey has concentrated on district issues such as oil and agriculture. He also has pushed efforts to limit importation of hazardous wastes into his district, a sensitive local issue. His bill to expand state efforts to learn the cause of high cancer rates among children in the city of McFarland was vetoed by Gov. Deukmejian, who said it duplicated existing efforts.

A native of Arkansas who still speaks with a southern twang, Harvey is also known for his role in helping write a happier ending to the "Onion Field" saga. Karl Hettinger was one of two Los Angeles officers kidnapped in 1963. His partner was killed by the kidnappers in an onion field outside of Bakersfield while Hettinger escaped, only to suffer years of emotional turmoil. Harvey befriended Hettinger, made him his aide for 10 years and persuaded Gov. Deukmejian to appoint Hettinger to complete the remaining 21 months of his term on the board of supervisors. Hettinger later won election on his own.

PERSONAL: elected 1986; born July 15, 1936, in Paragould, Ark.; home, Bakersfield; B.A. education CSU Fresno; wife, Jacqueline Stussy; children, Nick and Dinah Marquez; Morman.

CAREER: County health sanitarian; pharmaceutical salesman; school board member; Kern County Board of Supervisors 1976-1986.

COMMITTEES: Natural Resources; Aging & Long-Term Care; Labor & Employment.

OFFICES: Capitol, (916) 445-8498; district, 2222 E St., 3, Bakersfield 93301, (805) 324-3300; 115 South M St., Tulare 93274, (209) 686-2864.

REGISTRATION: 50.4% D, 41.4%

1988 CAMPAIGN: Harvey – R   67%
                  Powell – D   34%

RATINGS:

AFL	PIRG	CLCV	NOW	CTA	HAC	CofC	CFB	NRA
12%	42%	24%	25%	U	31%	92%	77%	90%

KEY VOTES:

	Insurance reform:	NO	Child sick leave:	NO
Assault gun ban:	NO	Parent consent abortion:	YES	Ban AIDS discrim:	NO
Clean Air Act:	YES	Cutting old trees:	YES	Extend death penalty:	YES
Lmt product tort:	YES	End mob home rent cont:	YES	Ban offshore oil:	NO

34th Assembly District
Phillip D. Wyman (R)

This district includes rugged Inyo County, the desert areas of eastern Kern County, the rapidly developing Antelope Valley of Los Angeles County and a portion of Bakersfield. It was already conservative when Phil Wyman, a rancher and attorney, was elected to the Assembly in 1978. And it's getting more conservative all the time.

The latest voter registration figures show that almost half of the voters are registered Republicans, a gain of nearly six percentage points in the past four years. Democrats, meanwhile, have dropped to 41 percent, a loss of six percentage points.

What that translates into is an extremely safe district for Wyman, a thin, chalky-

complected man who has been periodically chided by
some of his colleagues for his meek manner in the
Legislature where aggressive behavior is often valued.

Wyman briefly flirted with the idea of running for
state controller in 1986, but after five months abandoned his quixotic campaign and announced that he
would once again run for re-election. That abandoned
campaign, in turn, came five months after he indicated
he would run for the state Senate, another thought he
later reconsidered.

And while the two false starts hurt his credibility in
some GOP circles, it did nothing to hurt Wyman's
Assembly re-election bids. He continues to win by huge
margins; he gained 71 percent of the vote in 1988.

Phillip D. Wyman

As a legislator, Wyman is an orthodox conservative, rarely, if ever, breaking
from the party line. He has been most visible as an anti-abortion advocate, helping
to push through a law requiring minors to get parental consent before they can have
abortions. The law is being challenged in the courts.

Wyman is the Republican Willie Brown most loves to taunt. Once during a
committee hearing Wyman claimed the speaker's proposal to require vapor-recov-
ery systems on cars would cause them to "blow up like the Hindenburg." That
brought a pyrotechnic display from Brown, who told Wyman then and there he was
the Republican he would most like to get rid of and told him to report to his office
for a private chat.

PERSONAL: elected 1979 (special election); born Feb. 21, 1945, in Hollywood, Calif; home, Tehachapi; USAF 1969-1973; education, B.A. political science
UC Davis, graduate studies international law Ateneo de Manila University, Philippines, J.D. McGeorge; wife, Lynn Larson; children, Andrea Dee, Elizabeth Frances
and David Elliott; Protestant.

CAREER: lawyer; rancher.

COMMITTEES: Economic Development & New Technologies; Education;
Labor & Employment; Water, Parks & Wildlife. JOINT: State's Economy.

OFFICES: Capitol, (916) 445-3266; district, 5393 Truxtun Ave., Bakersfield
93309, (805) 395-2673; 556 W. Lancaster Blvd., 1, Lancaster 93534, (805) 945-
3544; 825 N. China Lake Blvd., Room B, Ridgecrest 93555, (619) 3750-5816.

REGISTRATION: 41% D, 49.5% R

1988 CAMPAIGN: Wyman – R   69%
Wilson – D   29%
Baucum – L   2%

RATINGS:	AFL	PIRG	CLCV	NOW	CTA	HAC	CofC	CFB	NRA
	12%	26%	8%	17%	U	22%	100%	66%	100%

KEY VOTES:

Divest S. Africa:	NO	Insurance reform:	NO	Child sick leave:	NO
Assault gun ban:	NO	Parent consent abortion:	YES	Ban AIDS discrim:	NO
Clean Air Act:	NO	Cutting old trees:	YES	Extend death penalty:	YES
Lmt product tort:	YES	End mob home rent cont:	YES	Ban offshore oil:	NO

35th Assembly District

Jack O'Connell (D)

Republicans think they might be able to win this district, which stretches from scenic Santa Barbara south to the farming community of Oxnard in Ventura County – but not until Jack O'Connell moves on.

O'Connell is a hard-working, quietly effective legislator who has built a following in his moderate, environmentally-conscious district through personal appearances and attention to local issues.

Republicans didn't even put up a candidate against him in 1988, although the district is only marginally Democratic. A few years earlier, GOP strategists thought they might be able to turn him out of office. Now, they're waiting for state Sen. Gary Hart, another popular Democrat from the area, to run for higher office so that O'Connell will run for his and open the seat.

Jack O'Connell

O'Connell, a longtime resident of the district, served as an aide to former state Sen. Omer Rains of Ventura. He, like Hart, is a former teacher.

Several of O'Connell's bills have been education and children-related. He pushed to extend program for gifted and developmentally disabled students at a time when they were threatened by partisan politics. He has sought increased penalties on drunken drivers who have children in their cars and for drug dealers who sell near schools. He also backed a measure to allow school districts to pass bond issues by a simple majority rather than two-thirds of the voters.

O'Connell drew the ire of gun enthusiasts in 1989 when he voted in favor of a bill to virtually ban semiautomatic assault weapons. An unsuccessful recall drive was started against him.

He also got involved in the controversial animal rights issue when he proposed making it a crime to use animals in certain laboratory tests.

O'Connell, showed an independent streak when he broke with the Democratic leadership in 1988 and voted in favor of confirming conservative former Rep. Dan Lungren of Long Beach as Gov. Deukmejian's nominee to replace the late Jesse Unruh as state treasurer.

PERSONAL: elected 1982; born Oct. 8, 1951, in Glen Cove, NY; home,

Carpinteria; education, B.A. history CSU Fullerton, teaching credential CSU Long Beach; wife, Doree Caputo; one daughter, Jennifer Lynn; Catholic.

CAREER: high school teacher; assistant speaker pro tem.

COMMITTEES: Education; Finance & Insurance; Rules; Ways & Means, and subcommittee 3 on resources, agriculture and the environment (chair). SELECT: Child Care. SPECIAL: Policy Research Management. JOINT: Rules; School Facilities.

OFFICES: Capitol, (916) 445-8292; district, Studio 127 El Paseo, Santa Barbara 93101, (805) 966-2296; 300 South C St., Oxnard 93030, (805) 487-9437.

REGISTRATION: 49.9% D, 37.1% R

1988 CAMPAIGN: O'Connell – D 93%

Bakhaus – L 7%

RATINGS:

AFL	PIRG	CLCV	NOW	CTA	HAC	CofC	CFB	NRA
97%	100%	88%	92%	G	90%	28%	55%	0%

KEY VOTES:

Divest S. Africa: YES	Insurance reform: YES	Child sick leave: YES
Assault gun ban: YES	Parent consent abortion: NO	Ban AIDS discrim: YES
Clean Air Act: YES	Cutting old trees: NO	Extend death penalty: YES
Lmt product tort: YES	End mob home rent cont: NO	Ban offshore oil: YES

36th Assembly District

Thomas M. McClintock (R)

Thomas McClintock

Not too many years ago, Ventura County was a quiet corner of California, a place of orange groves and oil wells separated from Los Angeles by a string of low mountains.

But freeways were punched through the mountains and Ventura County has, albeit with mixed feelings, become part of the Los Angeles-centered megalopolis. And as it has evolved from bucolic backwater to suburbia, Ventura County has moved rightward in its politics, becoming a dependable citadel of Republican voters.

Tom McClintock was eight years old when Willie Brown was first elected to the state Assembly in 1964. But McClintock, like Ventura County, grew up quickly and in 1982, at the relatively tender age of 26, he was elected to the Assembly from the 36th District.

McClintock, a one-time aide to Republican state Sen. Ed Davis, got started in politics young, claiming the chairmanship of the county GOP central committee at 22. He was the youngest legislator when elected and still comes across as boyish, although that doesn't hinder his self-proclaimed role as the Republicans' chief parliamentarian.

It's McClintock who arises on the Assembly floor to raise points of parliamentary order that often place him in open conflict with Speaker Brown. McClintock doesn't win many of those parliamentary squabbles since the majority Democrats retain the ultimate authority over conduct, but he keeps on raising his points.

The 36th District is so lopsidedly Republican that McClintock need not worry about re-election every two years, so he's free to concentrate on his parliamentary procedures and his interest in political history. And, scarcely into his 30s, he also can explore higher rungs on the political ladder. He came close to running for Congress in 1986 and is a likely candidate for a House seat after districts are reshuffled in the early 1990s, or perhaps for the state Senate.

PERSONAL: elected 1982; born July 10, 1956, in White Plains, N.Y.; home, Newbury Park; education, B.A. political science UCLA; wife, Lori; no children; Christian.

CAREER: administrative assistant to Sen. Ed Davis 1980-1982; minority whip.

COMMITTEES: Judiciary (vice chair); Governmental Efficiency & Consumer Protection; Public Safety. SPECIAL: Policy Research Management. JOINT: Review of the Master Plan for Higher Education.

OFFICES: Capitol, (916) 445-7402; district, 350 N. Lantana 222, Camarillo 93010, (805) 987-9797.

REGISTRATION: 37.5% D, 50.9% R

1988 CAMPAIGN: McClintock – R   70%
                   Webb – D   28%
                   Driscoll – L   3%

RATINGS:

	AFL	PIRG	CLCV	NOW	CTA	HAC	CofC	CFB	NRA
	11%	42%	15%	17%	U	22%	96%	44%	100%

KEY VOTES:

Divest S. Africa:	NO	Insurance reform:	NO	Child sick leave:	NO
Assault gun ban:	NO	Parent consent abortion:	YES	Ban AIDS discrim:	NO
Clean Air Act:	NO	Cutting old trees:	YES	Extend death penalty:	YES
Lmt product tort:	YES	End mob home rent cont:	YES	Ban offshore oil:	NO

37th Assembly District
Cathie M. Wright (R)

The Los Angeles suburbs continue to push out, filling geographic nooks with houses, shopping centers, schools and highways. Simi Valley, northwest of Los Angeles and straddling the Ventura County line, is one of those nooks, and it's also the center of the 37th Assembly District, which takes in portions of three counties.

Los Angeles suburbs tend to be Republican, and the 37th District is no exception with its 52 percent-plus GOP registration. That has made it easy for Republican Assemblywoman Cathie Wright to win re-election since first taking the seat in 1980.

As a double minority, a woman and a Republican, Wright hasn't played a big role in shaping legislation. But her extracurricular activities have made headlines at home and in Sacramento.

In 1989, there were a series of reports that Wright had interceded with state motor vehicle and judicial authorities to prevent her daughter, Victoria, from losing her driver's license for a series of traffic tickets.

Wright denied doing anything wrong but a report from the Ventura County district attorney's office concluded that she had tried to fix Victoria's tickets on several occasions and even solicited help from the Assembly's top Democrat, Speaker Willie Brown, in contacting judicial officials.

That incident led to another. Wright refused to go along with Republican efforts to deny Brown re-election as speaker in December, 1988, and for that, there were demands among Republicans that Wright be stripped of her seat on the Assembly Rules Committee. The GOP caucus voted to drop Wright from the committee but Brown, invoking another rule, protected her from being dumped.

Cathie M. Wright

Making the flap even more complicated has been a bitter feud between Wright and the Republican assemblywoman from the adjacent district, Marian LaFollette.

It's a feud that may be renewed when state Sen. Ed Davis retires because both women seem to have their eyes on his office.

PERSONAL: elected 1980; born May 18, 1929, in Old Forge, Penn.; home, Simi Valley; education, A.A. accounting Scranton Community College, Penn.; widow; daughter, Victoria; Catholic.

CAREER: insurance underwriter; school board; City Council and mayor Simi Valley 1978-1980.

COMMITTEES: Utilities & Commerce (vice chair); Environmental Safety & Toxic Materials; Finance & Insurance; Rules; Ways & Means. JOINT: Quincentennial of the Voyages of Columbus; Organized Crime & Gang Violence; Rules.

OFFICES: Capitol, (916) 445-7676; district, 250 E. Easy St., 7, Simi Valley 93065, (805) 522-2920.

REGISTRATION: 36.4% D, 52.7% R

1988 CAMPAIGN: Wright – R   73%

                    Marcus – D   25%

RATINGS:

AFL	PIRG	CLCV	NOW	CTA	HAC	CofC	CFB	NRA
14%	26%	15%	17%	U	22%	100%	55%	100%

KEY VOTES:

Divest S. Africa:	NO	Insurance reform:	NO	Child sick leave:	NO
Assault gun ban:	NO	Parent consent abortion:	YES	Ban AIDS discrim:	NO
Clean Air Act:	NO	Cutting old trees:	YES	Extend death penalty:	YES
Lmt product tort:	YES	End mob home rent cont:	YES	Ban offshore oil:	NO

38th Assembly District

Marian W. La Follette (R)

The further north and west one goes in the San Fernando Valley, the more Republican it becomes. The 38th Assembly District lies at the northwest extremity of the suburban valley, encompassing such communities as Woodland Hills, Northridge, Canoga Park and Calabasas. With its 49-42 percent registration edge in favor of Republicans, there's no question about the partisan identity of its member. Marian La Follette, who was active in local civic and GOP affairs before entering elective politics, won the seat in 1980 and has been re-elected easily ever since.

La Follette has rarely moved beyond lock-step attachment to the Republican Party line in the Assembly, nor has she advanced beyond backbencher status. Her

Marian La Follette

feud with the woman who represents the adjacent 37th District, however, has become one of the Capitol's longest-running melodramas.

La Follette and Republican Assemblywoman Cathie Wright are rivals in local GOP politics and both aspire to the state Senate seat now held by Republican Ed Davis when he retires. But La Follette is allied with Davis while Wright is connected to a rival faction.

PERSONAL: elected 1980; born Sept. 19, 1926, in Van Nuys, Calif.; home, Northridge; education, B.A. general education UC Berkeley; husband, John T. La Follette; children, Laurie, Curtis, Jackie and Philip; Protestant.

CAREER: teacher; businesswoman; Los Angeles Community College Board of Trustees 1969-1975.

COMMITTEES: Education; Human Services; Natural Resources; Water, Parks & Wildlife. JOINT: Arts; Revision of the Penal Code.

OFFICES: Capitol, (916) 445-8366; district, 11145 Tampa Ave., 17A, Northridge 91326, (8181) 368-3838.

REGISTRATION: 42% D, 48.9% R

1988 CAMPAIGN: La Follette – R   65%
                    Lit – D   36%

RATINGS:

AFL	PIRG	CLCV	NOW	CTA	HAC	CofC	CFB	NRA
16%	42%2	8%	50%	U	22%	92%	55%	71%

KEY VOTES:

Divest S. Africa: NO	Insurance reform: NO	Childsick leave: NO
Assault gun ban: –	Parent consent abortion: YES	Ban AIDS discrim: NO
Clean Air Act: NO	Cutting old trees: YES	Extend death penalty: YES
Lmt product tort: YES	End mob home rent cont: –	Ban offshore oil: NO

39th Assembly District

Richard D. Katz (D)

Republicans once thought they had a good chance of winning back this moderate San Fernando Valley district, which includes the largely Latino and black neighborhoods of Pacoima and San Fernando, working-class Sepulveda, rural Sylmar and upper-middle-class areas of Northridge. But Democrat Richard Katz has cruised to lopsided victories in his last two elections. Now, Katz, who once worried about just getting re-elected, is a key player in the Legislature and is thinking about running for statewide office.

Katz is, above all, a pragmatist. He is generally conservative on crime issues, a position in concert with his constituents and Californians as a whole. He tends to be moderate on fiscal issues, not adverse to spending

Richard D. Katz

money on government programs but not a classic tax-and-spend liberal. And he is generally liberal on social issues like abortion and the environmental.

That middle-of-the-road record has allowed him to brush away Republican attempts to exploit his position as one of liberal Assembly Speaker Willie Brown's top lieutenants, one of the GOP's favorite tactics in swing districts such as this.

Katz, in fact, has used his influence and skills to help elect more moderate Democrats. With his own re-election assured in 1988, Katz contributed staff and money to help Robert Epple defeat incumbent Republican Wayne Grisham in the 63rd District. He also helped prosecutor Christian Thierbach come within a whisker of defeating Republican Curt Pringle in a tight race in the 72nd District.

Aside from his role as political strategist, Katz, who was running a graphic arts and printing company when he was elected in 1980, also is a key player in the legislative arena. As chairman of the Assembly Transportation Committee, he has been a driving force behind the effort to put before voters in 1990 a measure to raise the gas tax to provide money for the state's highways and mass transit. A few years earlier, at the height of statewide concern about toxic pollutants, Katz pushed a tough new law regulating the way toxic waste can be stored and dumped.

He has also seized on issues with which the general public can relate, successfully sponsoring legislation to require gravel trucks to cover their loads with tarps to protect the windshields of cars traveling behind, raising the speed limit to 65 miles per hour on rural highways and making it easier for law enforcement officials to confiscate the assets of drug dealers.

Katz's critics contend that the measures are part of an agenda designed to give him exposure for a run at statewide office. Katz, meanwhile, makes no secret of his ambition to run for higher office. He announced in 1989 he would seek the

Democratic nomination for lieutenant governor in 1990, but then pulled out when Lt. Gov. Leo McCarthy said he would seek re-election. It won't be the last time he considers a statewide race.

PERSONAL: elected 1980; born Aug. 16, 1950, in Los Angeles, Calif.; home, Sylmar; education, B.A. political science San Diego State University; wife, Gini Barrett; no children; Jewish.
CAREER: graphic artist and printer.
COMMITTEES: Transportation (chair); Environmental Safety & Toxic Materials; Finance & Insurance; Water, Parks & Wildlife. SELECT: Small Business (chair); Ethics.
OFFICES: Capitol, (916) 445-1616; district 9140 Van Nuys Blvd., 109, Panorama City; 91402, (818) 894-3671.
REGISTRATION: 57.6% D, 34% R
1988 CAMPAIGN: Katz – D   73%
           Rendleman – R   25%
           Newton – L   3%

RATINGS:

AFL	PIRG	CLCV	NOW	CTA	HAC	CofC	CFB	NRA
85%	100%	100% 8	4%	S	90%	20%	33%	50%

KEY VOTES:

Divest S. Africa: YES	Insurance reform:	YES	Child sick leave: NO
Assault gun ban: YES	Parent consent abortion:	NO	Ban AIDS discrim: YES
Clean Air Act: YES	Cutting old trees:	NO	Extend death penalty: YES
Lmt product tort: YES	End mob home rent cont:	NO	Ban offshore oil: YES

40th Assembly District
Thomas J. Bane (D)

The more celebrated side of the Santa Monica Mountains is the southern slope, which includes the communities of Beverly Hills, Laurel Canyon, Coldwater Canyon and Hollywood. The northern side of the mountains is a relatively quiet collection of residential communities which flow into the San Fernando Valley: Studio City, Sherman Oaks, Encino and Van Nuys.

There are pockets of great wealth on the northern slope, but it lacks the show business glitter of the south side. Some stars, such as singer Michael Jackson, second-echelon performers and executives and professionals who spend their working hours over the hill make up much of the area's population. It's affluent, largely Jewish and Democratic in its voting patterns.

It's appropriate that the man who has represented the 40th District for many years, Tom Bane, fits all of those categories himself. Bane came into the Assembly in 1958, just as the legendary Jesse Unruh was transforming it into a powerful political instrument. As part of Unruh's closest circle of friends and advisers, Bane quickly became chairman of the Rules Committee, which handles Assembly

housekeeping functions and also directs the flow of
legislation. He quickly established himself as a hardball
player, using his power over office space, staff and other
prosaic matters to enforce discipline on Unruh's behalf.

Bane left the Assembly in 1964 to make an unsuccessful bid for Congress, then operated a savings and
loan business and 10 years later, returned to the Legislature from the 40th District. Almost immediately, he
found himself embroiled in a battle over the Assembly
speakership and, as part of the losing faction, spent the
rest of the 1970s in relative exile.

Another speakership battle broke out in 1980, this
one between then-Speaker Leo McCarthy and Howard
Berman, and once again Bane backed the loser, Ber-

Thomas J. Bane

man. But Willie Brown emerged from the confrontation as speaker and Bane's star
rose again. He resumed the chairmanship of the Rules Committee in 1986.

Bane is one of the Capitol's more controversial figures, not for what he says or
does publicly, which is little, but because of his high-handed, almost solitary
operation of the Rules Committee. Often, even other members of the committee are
kept in the dark about what Bane is doing in their name.

As Assembly Speaker Willie Brown once said of him: "Tom's theory is kind of
like mine. Someone may do something bad to you. The first time, it's an accident,
you have to figure. So the only way to avoid it again is to constantly be reminded
of it. Tom does that."

His "reminders" take the form of using the Rules Committee chairmanship to
reward loyalists and punish those who oppose him. As he does that, Bane continues
to function as the savings and loan industry's most loyal legislative ally, and the
industry has reciprocated by contributing lavishly to Bane's campaign treasury, one
that he rarely needs because of his safe district.

The most controversial aspects of Bane's legislative career have revolved about
his personal business affairs. In 1986, it was revealed that Bane had been promoting
a computer software package for Assembly offices that had been developed by a
firm jointly owned by his wife, Marlene.

No account of Bane's career is complete without mentioning Marlene, his one-
time campaign manager and legislative aide whom he married in 1981. Marlene
Bane has a small office near her husband's in the Capitol and has established a
lucrative political fund-raising business on the side, drawing hundreds of thousands
of dollars in fees from Speaker Brown and other politicians to tap into her extensive
network of would-be contributors.

She also suffers from lupus, a potentially fatal genetic disorder, and her husband
has carried a number of bills dealing with lupus research. But even that has been
controversial. Marlene Bane chairs a three-member state board that doles out grants

for lupus research and there have been published reports that scientists applying for the money also have been hit up for campaign contributions, some of which have been forthcoming, to Bane's and Brown's campaign treasuries.

The controversies show no signs of damaging Bane's standing in the 40th District, which continues to return him to Sacramento for term after term by overwhelming majorities. And he once told an interviewer: "The only time I'll retire is when they carry me out feet first."

PERSONAL: elected 1958, resigned 1964 to run for Congress, elected Assembly 1974; born Dec. 28, 1913, in Los Angeles, Calif.; home, Van Nuys; wife, Marlene; Jewish.

CAREER: president of board managing investment fund of Los Angeles City Employees Retirement System.

COMMITTEES: Rules (chair); Elections, Reapportionment & Constitutional Amendments; Finance & Insurance; Health & Community Development. SELECT: Genetic Diseases (chair). JOINT: Rules (chair); Fire, Police, Emergency & Disaster Services.

OFFICES: Capitol, (916) 445-3134; district, 5430 Van Nuys Blvd., 206, Van Nuys 91401, (818) 986-8090.

REGISTRATION: 55.2% D, 34.9% R

1988 CAMPAIGN: Bane – D 73%
Dahl – R 25%
Prah – L 2%

RATINGS:

AFL	PIRG	CLCV	NOW	CTA	HAC	CofC	CFB	NRA
87%	95%	87%	92%	S	90%	20%	33%	0%

KEY VOTES:

Divest S. Africa:	YES	Insurance reform:	YES	Child sick leave:	YES
Assault gun ban:	YES	Parent consent abortion:	–	Ban AIDS discrim:	YES
Clean Air Act:	YES	Cutting old trees:	YES	Extend death penalty:	YES
Lmt product tort:	YES	End mob home rent cont:	YES	Ban offshore oil:	YES

41st Assembly District

Patrick J. Nolan (R)

With a solid Republican majority, this district skirts the flatlands and canyons of the north-eastern Los Angeles basin, including La Canada, parts of Altadena, Glendale and Pasadena. The growth of the Los Angeles area has extended up into the San Gabriel Mountain canyons that periodically let loose torrential avalanches of rock and mud that wipe the homes away. The homes are re-built, are more expensive than ever and no one seems any wiser.

Republican Pat Nolan has never had any trouble in this district and has used it as his home base for trying to win a Republican majority in the Assembly and expand his own political horizons. Articulate and clever – but sometimes not as clever as he thinks – the former University of Southern California student politician and organizer for the staunchly conservative Young Americans for Freedom has shown himself a shrewd political strategist.

Nolan, one of a batch of Republicans elected to the Assembly in 1978, deposed Bob Naylor as Republican leader in 1984 and saw Republicans pick up three Assembly seats in 1986, despite his controversial penchant for attempting to override local party leaders and anoint GOP candidates from Sacramento. Nolan claimed full credit for the Republican victories in 1986, even though Democratic miscues were important factors, and predicted that the GOP was on its way toward capturing control of the lower house in time for the 1991 reapportionment.

Patrick J. Nolan

Nolan, one of the few Republican leaders who seems to genuinely enjoy politics, patterned his leadership after that of his Democratic counterpart, Speaker Willie Brown, raising vast campaign sums and choosing candidates. Even while bashing Brown as a campaign theme, Nolan reached an accommodation with the speaker that allowed him to pick the committee assignments for Republicans. Nolan insiders talked of his running for state attorney general in 1990.

Then Nolan ran into big troubles. His heavy-handed fund-raising came to the attention of the FBI, which was conducting an undercover investigation of Capitol influence-peddling, and his Capitol office was among those raided in August 1988. It seemed that Nolan had accepted $10,000 in campaign contributions from a sham undercover FBI company that was making the rounds in the Capitol looking for help on a bill. The FBI continued its investigation of Nolan, among others, through 1989.

Nolan's semi-secret, mutually supportive political understanding with Brown came to light when he refused to lend Republican support to efforts by a band of Democratic dissidents to dump the speaker – a position that engendered opposition within the GOP ranks. And when three Republican incumbents – Paul Zeltner, Bill Duplissea and Wayne Grisham – lost in 1988, Nolan saw the writing on the wall and resigned as Assembly Republican leader. He managed to hand-off the job to close associate Ross Johnson.

Both were embarrassed when one of their lieutenants, Assemblyman John Lewis, was indicted on forgery charges stemming from the distribution of letters of endorsement for Republican Assembly candidates carrying an unauthorized signature of then-President Ronald Reagan. There was testimony that both participated in the strategy sessions that led to issuance of the letters and one of the side effects of the affair was to poison relations between Nolan and the Reagan White House.

But Nolan did not slink very far into the background despite these setbacks. He has remained a key strategist for Assembly Republicans. A few short months after he quit as their leader, GOP Assembly members followed Nolan in holding up passage of the budget in 1989 while he fought to redefine the distribution of school money for gifted and disadvantaged programs to get more for the suburbs and less for the inner cities. Nolan made life miserable for non-Los Angeles Democrats by reading from computer lists showing how much money their districts stood to win if they followed his plan to spend less on Los Angeles and more on the rest of the state. In the end, Nolan won an agreement that left Los Angeles legislators fuming.

If Nolan can rid himself of the lingering federal investigation, he doubtless will renew his statewide political ambitions.

PERSONAL: elected 1978; born June 16, 1950, in Los Angeles, Calif.; home, Glendale; education, B.A. political science and J.D. USC; wife, Gail Zajc-MacKenzie; daughter, Courtney; Catholic.

CAREER: lawyer; reserve deputy sheriff, Los Angeles County.

COMMITTEES: Finance & Insurance; Rules; Utilities & Commerce; Ways & Means. SPECIAL: Policy Research Management. JOINT: Quincentennial of the Voyages of Columbus; Fire, Police, Emergency & Disaster Services.

OFFICES: Capitol, (916) 445-8364; district, 143 S. Glendale Ave., Suite 208, Glendale 91205, (818) 240-6330.

REGISTRATION: 40.8% D, 49.6% R

1988 CAMPAIGN: Nolan – R   58%

Vollbrecht – D   38%

Helms – L   2%

Kasimoff – P&F   1%

RATINGS:

AFL	PIRG	CLCV	NOW	CTA	HAC	CofC	CFB	NRA
10%	37%	11%	8%	U	22%	88%	77%	100%

KEY VOTES:

Divest S. Africa:	NO	Insurance reform:	NO	Child sick leave:	NO
Assault gun ban:	NO	Parent consent abortion:	YES	Ban AIDS discrim:	NO
Clean Air Act:	NO	Cutting old trees:	YES	Extend death penalty:	YES
Lmt product tort:	YES	End mob home rent cont:	YES	Ban offshore oil:	NO

42nd Assembly District

Richard L. Mountjoy (R)

The residential uplands of the San Gabriel Valley east of Los Angeles vote Republican and the 42nd Assembly District is the heart of the region.

Arcadia, Azusa, Glendora, Irwindale, Monrovia and San Marino are just a few of the dozen-plus communities contained within the district, which has a 51-40 percent Republican registration edge.

The 42nd District's man in the Assembly, Richard Mountjoy, fits his district perfectly: a middle-aged, white Republican businessman who joined the Legislature in 1978 as one of the self-proclaimed "Proposition 13 babies" and has lost none of his zeal for political infighting in the decade-plus since. He has become a point man for the Republicans in their ceaseless partisan wars with Democrats over legislative procedure, and he helped write a 1984 ballot measure aimed at curbing Speaker Willie Brown's powers. Given that preoccupation, Mountjoy participates only rarely in policy matters and devotes much of his time to plotting political strategy.

Mountjoy owns a construction company and was a city councilman and mayor of Monrovia before his election to the Legislature. Mountjoy usually flies his own plane between Southern California and Sacramento and survived one crash-landing at Sacramento's Executive Airport. He can keep on flying, and keep on

Richard L. Mountjoy

doing battle with the Democrats, for as long as he wishes, given the overwhelmingly pro-GOP tilt to his district.

PERSONAL: elected 1978; born Jan. 13, 1932, in Monrovia, Calif; home, Monrovia; Navy 1951-1955 Korea; wife, Earline; children, Michael, Dennis, Judy; Protestant.

CAREER: general contractor; commercial pilot; Monrovia City Council and mayor 1968-1976.

COMMITTEES: Elections, Reapportionment & Constitutional Amendments; Governmental Organization; Housing & Community Development; Rules. JOINT: Rules.

OFFICES: Capitol, (916) 445-7234; district, 208 N. First Ave., Arcadia 91006, (818) 446-3134.

REGISTRATION: 39.5% D, 50.9% R

1988 CAMPAIGN: Mountjoy – R   71%
                Boyle – D   29%

RATINGS:

AFL	PIRG	CLCV	NOW	CTA	HAC	CofC	CFB	NRA
8%	42%	15%	25%	U	18%	96%	44%	100%

KEY VOTES:

Divest S. Africa:	NO	Insurance reform:	–	Child sick leave:	NO
Assault gun ban:	NO	Parent consent abortion:	YES	Ban AIDS discrim:	NO
Clean Air Act:	NO	Cutting old trees:	YES	Extend death penalty:	YES
Lmt product tort:	YES	End mob home rent cont:	YES	Ban offshore oil:	NO

43rd Assembly District

Terry B. Friedman (D)

The heart of the liberal Democratic machine of Henry Waxman and Howard Berman, this district includes the upscale Jewish neighborhoods of West Los

Angeles, Brentwood, Westwood, and the student "ghetto" surrounding UCLA, and then extends eastward along Wilshire Boulevard to take in Beverly Hills.

The seat was held by Jerry Brown's ex-chief of staff, Gray Davis, who moved on to become state controller in 1986. Speaker Willie Brown tried to break the Berman-Waxman machine at its heart by backing his own candidate for the seat in 1986 in a Democratic primary. But it was not a good year for Brown, whose primary candidates did not do well.

The victor was Terry Friedman, a poverty housing lawyer who had long labored in the political trenches for Berman-Waxman. In 1972, Friedman was one of the principal organizers in West Los Angeles for George McGovern's presidential campaign.

Terry B. Friedman

After winning his primary, Friedman easily beat Republican businessman Marc Schuyler of Tarzana and has had no trouble keeping his seat.

As an Assembly member, Friedman has kept a close alliance with other Assembly "Grizzly Bear" liberals and is personally close to Burt Margolin. As a member of the Public Safety Committee, Friedman has stuck to a civil libertarian position and engendered criticism that he is too rigid a liberal.

Friedman has shown legislative ability, including winning passage of a bill to force employers to give sick time to employees to care for ailing family members. The bill was vetoed, but marked Friedman's emergence as a serious legislator.

PERSONAL: elected 1986; born Sept. 14, 1949, in Pasadena, Calif.; home, Los Angeles; education, B.A. American studies UCLA, J.D. UC Berkeley; wife, Elise Karl; no children; Jewish.

CAREER: staff lawyer Western Center on Law & Poverty 1976-1978; executive director Bet Tzedek Legal Services 1978-1986.

COMMITTEES: Education; Judiciary; Public Safety; Ways & Means and subcommittee 1 on health & welfare (chair).

OFFICES: Capitol, (916) 445-4956; district, 14144 Ventura Blvd., 100, Sherman Oaks 91423, (818) 501-8991.

REGISTRATION: 54.7% D, 35.2% R

1988 CAMPAIGN:

Friedman – D	62%	
Franklin – R	34%	
Leet – L	2%	
Hinds – P&F	2%	

RATINGS:

AFL	PIRG	CLCV	NOW	CTA	HAC	CofC	CFB	NRA
100%	100%	100%	92%	S	95%	12%	33%	0%

KEY VOTES:

		Insurance reform:	YES	Child sick leave:	YES
Assault gun ban:	YES	Parent consent abortion:	NO	Ban AIDS discrim:	YES
Clean Air Act:	YES	Cutting old trees:	NO	Extend death penalty:	NO
Lmt product tort:	NO	End mob home rent cont:	NO	Ban offshore oil:	YES

44th Assembly District
Thomas E. Hayden (D)

Thomas E. Hayden

This Los Angeles County coastal district includes comfortable Pacific Palisades, the beach houses and canyons of Malibu, portions of liberal West Los Angeles and the vaguely left-of-center environs of Santa Monica. The district should be safe for any Democrat, but the particular Democrat who occupies its seat happens to be one of the nation's most controversial figures, Tom Hayden.

Only two other words – Rose Bird – seem to evoke such strong loyalty or loathing in recent California political history.

To the public, Hayden is probably the best known member of the California Legislature, with the possible exception of Willie Brown. Hayden is the subject of scores of books, magazine and newspaper articles spanning three decades. He is certainly the only legislator whose life is charted by People magazine.

Hayden has a life that transcends the narrow world of the Legislature. Whatever he does in Sacramento is almost beside the point. As a founder of Students for a Democratic Society, and as one of the authors of the New Left's manifesto, The Port Huron Statement, Hayden's place in postwar American history is assured, for better or for worse. He was put on trial as one of the Chicago Eight, accused of fomenting the riot at the 1968 Democratic convention, and sentenced to five years in prison. Back then, Hayden was urged to go underground because friends feared he would be murdered in prison. Those were the days when Hayden vented speeches calling for "revolutionizing youth" through "a series of sharp and dangerous conflicts, life and death conflicts."

But Hayden drew back from the self-destructive revolutionary life. His Chicago conviction was overturned in 1972. His marriage to Jane Fonda won him star status and something the New Left had lacked: a sizable bank account.

With Fonda's money, Hayden rejoined the mainstream by running for the U.S. Senate in 1976 against Democratic incumbent John Tunney, who was perceived as being weak. Hayden lost and incurred the wrath of many Democratic leaders who accused him of weakening Tunney even further, leaving him vulnerable to Republican S.I. Hayakawa. In the wake of his Senate campaign, Hayden created the

Campaign for Economic Democracy (which, years later became Campaign California.) Hayden's groups have won success at the ballot box, most notably in helping to close Sacramento's troubled Rancho Seco nuclear power plant. The organization has pockets of strength in the Bay Area, Chico, Sacramento, and, of course, in Hayden's home base of Santa Monica. But his organizations also have suffered notable setbacks at the local level.

Hayden and Jerry Brown had a contentious relationship at first, but then reached a political deal: Hayden protected Brown's left flank and was given a series of high-profile appointments that, with Fonda's bankroll, carried him into an Assembly seat in 1982.

Hayden's fame and success came with a heavy price. There are those who will always consider him a traitor for having supported the Communist side during the Vietnam War and believe he should have been put on trial for treason.

Led by right-wing Orange County Assemblyman Gil Ferguson, Hayden's enemies tried unsuccessfully to have him ejected from the Assembly (many believed Ferguson's effort a cynical fund-raising ploy and, indeed, Republican Assembly campaign coffers have been enriched by the Hayden-haters). Some of Hayden's colleagues, particularly Ferguson, routinely refuse to vote for a Hayden bill regardless of its merits because his name is on it. And legislative life appears to have contributed to the breakup of his marriage with Fonda.

Why then does Hayden stay in the Assembly? The simple answer is that Hayden enjoys being a legislator. First and foremost, Hayden is a political junkie. He enjoys the rough and tumble. He has described it as being "an intellectual in action." And therein lies the hubris of Tom Hayden.

Hayden is the Legislature's loner. He counts only a handful of his colleagues as his friends, chief among them his seatmate, Tom Bates, who represents Berkeley. Hayden flies home to Santa Monica every night, the only legislator who makes a daily commute from Southern California.

While Hayden has made little dent on the Legislature, it can safely be said that the Legislature has made little dent on him. In his autobiography, "Reunion," he made little mention of the Legislature. His close friends remain outside the Capitol as do the central events of his life. Although Hayden at times seems bored in a sea of mediocrity, he remains one of the Legislature's most astute observers and original thinkers.

Hayden has mellowed with age. He occasionally votes with Republicans on crime issues and favors the death penalty (this coming from the ex-radical who once called for a "total attack on the courts"). As a legislator, Hayden has concentrated on the esoterica of toxic waste and higher education issues, particularly strengthening the state's community colleges. He has also concentrated on oversight of the University of California's Lawrence Livermore nuclear weapons lab, much to its discomfort.

Hayden was an indirect beneficiary of the 1987-1988 "Gang of Five" rebellion against Willie Brown. In sacking rebel Democrat Gary Condit as chairman of the

Governmental Organization Committee, the speaker had to reshuffle other chairmanships. To Hayden went the chairmanship of the Assembly Labor Committee, a post where he must deal with labor union honchos. Although Hayden has won plaudits as a competent committee chairman, the major labor issue of 1989 – workers compensation revision – was engineered by Assemblyman Burt Margolin.

Hayden may well run for statewide office again. He has toyed with running for insurance commissioner, but committed a major blunder during the Prop. 103 rate reform initiative campaign. Ralph Nader came to Hayden hat-in-hand looking for a contribution. Hayden refused, only to offer money later when the initiative looked like a sure bet. Nader was insulted. Consumer groups have come to regard Hayden as an opportunist – not the first time he has faced that epithet from critics on the left – and scowled at the idea of supporting Hayden for insurance commissioner.

But a more likely political move may be to Congress if, as seems likely, a Santa Monica-centered seat opens up in the 1990s.

PERSONAL: elected 1982; born Dec. 11, 1939 in Detroit, Mich.; home, Santa Monica; education, B.A. history University of Michigan; wife (estranged), Jane Fonda; children, Troy and step-daughter Vanessa; Catholic.

CAREER: founder Students for a Democratic Society; founder Campaign for Economic Democracy, Campaign California; author; teacher.

COMMITTEES: Labor & Employment (chair); Education; Environmental Safety & Toxic Materials; Revenue & Taxation. JOINT: Review of the Master Plan for Higher Education.

OFFICES: Capitol, (916) 445-1676; district, 227 Broadway 300, Santa Monica 90401, (213) 393-2717.

REGISTRATION: 60% D, 29.1% R

1988 CAMPAIGN: Hayden – D   61%
Stout – R   39%

RATINGS:

AFL	PIRG	CLCV	NOW	CTA	HAC	CofC	CFB	NRA
96%	89%	100%	84%	G	81%	12%	33%	0%

KEY VOTES:

Divest S. Africa:	YES	Insurance reform:	YES	Child sick leave:	YES
Assault gun ban:	YES	Parent consent abortion:	NO	Ban AIDS discrim:	YES
Clean Air Act:	YES	Cutting old trees:	NO	Extend death penalty:	–
Lmt product tort:	NO	End mob home rent cont:	NO	Ban offshore oil:	YES

45th Assembly District

Burt M. Margolin (D)

This heavily Jewish district extends along Sunset Boulevard to include Hollywood, North Hollywood, Fairfax (and CBS's Television City) and the posh homes of Laurel Canyon. It extends over the hills to include part of Burbank. Overwhelmingly Democratic, the district is a base for the Berman-Waxman liberal Democratic organization that dominates politics on the West Side; thus it's not surprising that one of its proteges has held this Assembly seat since 1982.

Democrat Burt Margolin has become a masterful legislative technician with a clear, liberal agenda. He had good training. Margolin was Congressman Henry Waxman's chief of staff in Washington and Congressman Howard Berman's legislative aide when he was an assemblyman in Sacramento. He is aligned with the "Grizzly Bear" bloc of liberals in the Assembly and is a dependable vote for environmental and consumer protection bills.

Burt M. Margolin

Margolin moved into his own in 1986 when he engineered the state's bottle-can deposit law. Coaxing reluctant environmentalists and industry lobbyists, Margolin fashioned a complicated compromise that set up the state's recycling container program – and allowed the battling interests to avoid thrashing it out with a costly ballot initiative.

In 1989, Margolin moved on to an even more arcane area of law – workers compensation. After marathon negotiations that stretched all summer long, Margolin was instrumental in working out a bill that increased benefits to injured workers and trimmed lawyer fees.

With a voice like Woody Allen, Margolin is invariably polite – and that may be the key to his success – that and his ability to master the nuances of complicated issues. He has ignored the barbs from every ideological quarter, whether it was Democrat Dick Floyd calling him an "aging hippie" for pushing the bottle deposit bill or Republican leader Ross Johnson blasting him as the great "impediment" to workers compensation revision. As it turned out, Margolin got his bill on each. And when a congressional seat on the west side opens up, it's fairly certain that Margolin will be there to claim it.

PERSONAL: elected 1982; born Sept. 28, 1950, in Chattanooga, Tenn.; home, Los Angeles; education, UCLA, no degree; wife, Laurie Post; son, Joshua David; Jewish.

CAREER: chief of staff to Rep. Henry A. Waxman 1975-1977 and 1980-1982; legislative consultant to Assemblyman Howard Berman 1978-1979.

COMMITTEES: Finance & Insurance; Health; Natural Resources. SELECT: Genetic Diseases. SPECIAL: Medi-Cal Oversight (chair).

OFFICES: Capitol, (916) 445-7440; district, 8425 W. 3rd, Suite 406, Los Angeles 90048, (213) 655-9750.

REGISTRATION: 59.5% D, 28.4% R

1988 CAMPAIGN: Margolin – D   69%
Frankel R   27%
Fausto – P&F   4%

RATINGS:	AFL	PIRG	CLCV	NOW	CTA	HAC	CofC	CFB	NRA
	98%	95%	100%	84%	S	95%	8%	33%	0%

KEY VOTES:

Divest S. Africa:	YES	Insurance reform:	YES	Child sick leave:	YES
Assault gun ban:	YES	Parent consent abortion:	NO	Ban AIDS discrim:	YES
Clean Air Act:	YES	Cutting old trees:	NO	Extend death penalty:	NO
Lmt product tort:	NO	End mob home rent cont:	NO	Ban offshore oil:	YES

46th Assembly District

Michael Y. Roos (D)

The locals call it "midtown," a compact swatch of Los Angeles west of downtown and east of the conspicuous consumption of Beverly Hills. It may be the most ethnically and culturally diverse portion of the planet's most heterogeneous city, a collection of Asian, Hispanic, Anglo, straight and gay neighborhoods whose residents range from the very wealthy to the very poor, plus the daytime, power tie-wearing occupants of Wilshire Boulevard skyscrapers.

One of the few unifying factors in midtown is that when it comes to politics, the overwhelming majority of its voters are Democrats and they vote consistently for the party's candidates, including their veteran state assemblyman, Michael Roos.

Michael Y. Roos

Actually, there aren't very many voters in Roos' 46th Assembly District. Its 72,000 registered voters are the second lowest total for any of the 80 Assembly districts, less than half the average Assembly district contains.

That makes it easy for Roos to get re-elected, even though he's been touched by scandal on more than one occasion.

Roos is the quintessential California professional politician who spent his early career as an aide to other politicians before moving into elective office himself in 1977 by winning the Assembly seat; a hothouse flower who was trained in and thrives in the political atmosphere of the Capitol but has few adult experiences outside the political arena.

The one-time Tulane University baseball player still retains a hint of his native Tennessee in his voice and is a highly visible and popular member of the Capitol's inner circle, presiding over most Assembly sessions as the speaker pro tem and serving as part of Speaker Willie Brown's leadership team.

His affability and boyish appearance notwithstanding, Roos is a consummate politician who once entertained hopes of becoming mayor of Los Angeles, before his public record was marred by scandal.

For four years, federal investigators delved into Roos' personal financial dealings with fireworks magnate W. Patrick Moriarty, including a questionable investment in a Moriarty condominium project at a time he was pushing a Moriarty fireworks regulation bill.

Moriarty was convicted of masterminding a broad scheme of political corruption, as was ex-Assemblyman Bruce Young. But in the end, Roos escaped prosecution, although his hopes of climbing further up the political ladder were dashed.

In the aftermath of the Moriarty affair, Roos attempted to resurrect his political career by attaching himself to several high-profile causes, most notably an effort to block the Raiders football team from leaving the Los Angeles Coliseum and sponsorship of a heavily publicized and ultimately successful measure to restrict sales of assault rifles.

But as those efforts were raising his positives, the FBI's sting investigation of Capitol corruption began producing indictments and Roos found his name once again making headlines as a subject of the new probe, this time for his handling of particular bills.

Although his hopes of becoming mayor or moving into some other powerful position may have faded, Roos probably can be re-elected in the 46th District as long as he wants. Some gay and Asian groups have promoted would-be successors in the past, especially in the wake of the Moriarty affair, but Roos has avoided all serious challenges.

PERSONAL: elected 1977 (special election); born Aug. 6, 1945, in Memphis, Tenn.; home, Los Angeles; education, B.A. political science Tulane University; M.P.A. USC; wife, Lorna; children, Shelby and Melissa; Catholic.

CAREER: chief deputy Los Angeles City Councilman Marvin Braude 1975-1977; executive director Coro Foundation 1972-1975; majority floor leader 1980-1986; speaker pro tempore.

COMMITTEES: Agriculture; Public Safety; Transportation; Ways & Means, and subcommittee 5 – public employees & bonded indebtedness (chair). SELECT: State Public Procurement Practices. SPECIAL: Policy Research Management. JOINT: Fire, Police, Emergency & Disaster Services (vice chair).

OFFICES: Capitol, (916) 445-7644; district, 625 S. New Hampshire Ave., 100, Los Angeles 90005, (213) 386-8042.

REGISTRATION: 60.1% D, 26.9% R

1988 CAMPAIGN: Roos – D 68%
Trias – R 26%
Lake – L 4%
Taves – P&F 2%

RATINGS:

AFL	PIRG	CLCV	NOW	CTA	HAC	CofC	CFB	NRA
90%	89%	92%	84%	G	95%	32%	33%	0%

KEY VOTES:

Divest S. Africa:	YES	Insurance reform:	YES	Child sick leave:	YES
Assault gun ban:	YES	Parent consent abortion:	NO	Ban AIDS discrim:	YES
Clean Air Act:	YES	Cutting old trees:	NO	Extend death penalty:	NO
Lmt product tort:	–	End mob home rent cont:	YES	Ban offshore oil:	YES

47th Assembly District

Teresa P. Hughes (D)

Roughly nine out of ten residents of this district, which includes central Los Angeles and the cities of Huntington Park, Bell and Cudahy, are either Latino or black. The percentage of registered Democrats is almost as high.

Teresa Hughes, a former social worker, teacher, school administrator and college professor, was first elected to represent the district in a special election in 1975. The seat is hers to keep for as long as she wants; Republicans generally don't even bother putting up anyone against her.

Hughes is most visible in the Legislature as chairwoman of the Assembly Education Committee, **Teresa P. Hughes** through which all legislation dealing with elementary, secondary and college education passes.

She has used her position to try to push for more school funding, affirmative action in state colleges, programs to reduce the drop-out rate and teen pregnancies among disadvantaged youths and to retain bilingual education and programs for gifted and developmentally disabled students.

Hughes, however, has not been as successful in the fractious Assembly as the Senate education leaders have in forging consensus on controversial issues and innovative programs.

In recent years, Hughes has also pushed several AIDS-related bills, including a 1987 measure signed into law that allows doctors to disclose AIDS test results to the spouses of people who have been tested. She has also backed legislation to require condom standards to make sure that the prophylactics block the AIDS virus.

PERSONAL: elected 1975 (special election); born Oct. 3, 1932, in New York City; home, Los Angeles; education, B.A. physiology and public health Hunter College; M.A. education administration New York University; Ph.D. in educational administration Claremont College; husband, Frank Staggers; children, Vincent and Deirdre; Catholic.

CAREER: teacher, school administrator; professor of education, CSU Los Angeles; aide to Sen. Mervyn Dymally 1973.

COMMITTEES: Education (chair); Housing & Community Development; Local Government; Public Employment, Retirement & Social Security. **JOINT:** Review of the Master Plan for Higher Education; State's Economy.

OFFICES: Capitol, (916) 445-7498; district, 3375 S. Hoover Ave., Suite F, Los Angeles 90007, (213) 747-7451.

REGISTRATION: 81.4% D, 11.2% R

1988 CAMPAIGN: Hughes – D   95%
                   Riley – R   5%

RATINGS:

AFL	PIRG	CLCV	NOW	CTA	HAC	CofC	CFB	NRA
95%	89%	92%	92%	G	90%	16%	33%	0%

KEY VOTES:

Divest S. Africa:	YES	Insurance reform:	YES	Child sick leave:	YES
Assault gun ban:	YES	Parent consent abortion:	NO	Ban AIDS discrim:	YES
Clean Air Act:	YES	Cutting old trees:	–	Extend death penalty:	YES
Lmt product tort:	–	End mob home rent cont:	YES	Ban offshore oil:	YES

48th Assembly District

Maxine Waters (D)

Republicans are an endangered species in the 48th Assembly District, which cuts across the heart of south-central Los Angeles, the city's black ghetto.

The 48th is California's most heavily Democratic district, with a whopping 84.2 percent registration, nines times the Republican proportion.

Maxine Waters, a bundle of angry energy who has represented the district since 1976, doesn't worry about re-election every two years. She spends her waking hours plotting strategy for her many causes in Sacramento, figuring out ways to confound her many enemies and waiting for the local congressman, octogenarian Gus Hawkins, to retire so that she can take her act to Washington.

Maxine Waters

It's quite an act. Around the Capitol, Waters is known as "Mama Doc" for her absolutist, take-no-prisoners approach to politics, one that's been her hallmark in a career in and around politics that has consumed most of her adult life.

Waters, a native of St. Louis, began that career as a Head Start teacher and civic organizer in Watts and then became an aide to Los Angeles City Councilman David Cunningham before winning her Assembly seat in 1976.

Her star rose rapidly after Willie Brown became speaker in 1980. She received several key committee appointments, especially those involving the state budget, and eventually became a member of the six-legislator committee that writes the final version of the budget. The appointments gave Waters the clout to wage war for "my constituency," as she calls it: the poor, the non-white and women.

It was in battling for expanded health care and other services to inner city neighborhoods that Waters' caustically combative nature became evident. She fought with everyone, but especially with Republicans and even more particularly with the Republicans who control the Los Angeles County Board of Supervisors over health and welfare spending in south-central Los Angeles.

Waters' most public fight, however, was for legislation, ultimately successful, to restrict state investments in firms that do business in South Africa. It was one of the rare issues on which Waters and Republican Gov. George Deukmejian agreed.

Along the way, Waters established herself as an important player in national politics, one of an inner circle of advisers to Jesse Jackson and his campaigns for the presidency in 1984 and 1988. She was instrumental in persuading Willie Brown to become Jackson's national campaign chairman in 1988.

But Waters' close ties to Brown backfired for both in 1986. At her behest, Brown anointed her son, Ed, as the Democratic candidate in another Assembly district in southern Los Angeles County, one not nearly as Democratic or as black as her own. Young Waters was defeated in a district that the Democrats should have won, and did win, two years later with another candidate.

Waters will remain a major player in Assembly politics as long as Willie Brown remains speaker or until Hawkins cedes his congressional seat. She also may run for the Los Angeles Board of Supervisors if Kenneth Hahn ever steps down. Should Brown leave the speakership, however, the long knives will come out.

PERSONAL: elected 1976; born Aug. 15, 1938, in St. Louis, Mo.; home, Los Angeles; education, B.A. sociology CSU Los Angeles; divorced; children, Karen Denise and Edward Keith.

CAREER: chief deputy to Los Angeles City Councilman David Cunningham 1973-76; partner in a public relations firm; founder, Black Women's Forum.

COMMITTEES: Elections, Reapportionment & Constitutional Amendments; Judiciary; Natural Resources; Ways & Means; (chair) Ways & Means subcommittee 4, state administration. SELECT: Assistance to Victims of Sexual Assault; State Public Procurement Practices. SPECIAL: Policy Research Management. JOINT: Public Pension Fund Investments (chair); Legislative Budget; Legislative Ethics; Organized Crime & Gang Violence.

OFFICES: Capitol, (916) 445-2363; district, 7900 S. Central Ave., Los Angeles 90001, (213) 582-7371.

REGISTRATION: 84.2% D, 9.6% R

1988 CAMPAIGN: Waters – D 100%
no opponent

RATINGS:	AFL	PIRG	CLCV	NOW	CTA	HAC	CofC	CFB	NRA
	95%	83%	96%	92%	G	85%	16%	33%	0%

KEY VOTES:

Divest S. Africa:	YES	Insurance reform:	YES	Child sick leave:	YES
Assault gun ban:	YES	Parent consent abortion:	NO	Ban AIDS discrim:	YES
Clean Air Act:	YES	Cutting old trees:	NO	Extend death penalty:	–
Lmt product tort:	NO	End mob home rent cont:	NO	Ban offshore oil:	–

49th Assembly District

Gwen A. Moore (D)

This Democratic stronghold is both a combination of working class and heavily black sections of Los Angeles and Culver City as well as fashionable oceanfront communities like Marina del Rey.

Gwen Moore, a former deputy probation officer and community college instructor, regularly receives more than two-thirds of the votes every two years when she seeks re-election.

Moore has been the Assembly's point person for several years on public utility and cable television issues as chairwoman of the Assembly Utilities and Commerce Committee. In that role, she has generally pushed utilities to justify proposed rate increases. And she successfully established a low-cost "lifeline" telephone rate for low-income people.

Gwen A. Moore

Moore, along with fellow Los Angeles Democrat Maxine Waters, was at the forefront of a movement to get the Legislature to prohibit investments of state pension funds in corporations doing business in South Africa. She's also pushed legislation on domestic violence and a bill that would require medium and large businesses to give unpaid leave to workers who want to care for sick children or parents.

Yet Moore's legislative accomplishments have been overshadowed recently by an ongoing political corruption probe at the Capitol by the U.S. Justice Department. She was the author of two bills that federal agents pushed through the Legislature that would have benefited two sham companies set up by the FBI to track influence peddling. Her office was one of a handful raided by the FBI. Moore has maintained she did nothing wrong and has not been charged with any wrongdoing.

With her connections to the Berman-Waxman political organization, Moore is being readied to run for Congress when the opportunity arises–perhaps when Rep. Julian Dixon seeks a seat on the Los Angeles County Board of Supervisors.

PERSONAL: elected 1978; born Oct. 28, 1940, in Detroit, Mich.; home, Los Angeles; education, B.A. sociology CSU Los Angeles, graduate study at USC, teaching credential UCLA; husband, Ron Dobson; child, Ronald Dobson; Protestant.

CAREER: probation officer; Los Angeles Community College trustee 1975-1978.

COMMITTEES: Utilities & Commerce (chair); Finance & Insurance; Governmental Efficiency & Consumer Protection; Health; Local Government. SELECT: State Public Procurement Practices.

OFFICES: Capitol, (916) 445-8800; district, 3683 Crenshaw Blvd., 5th Floor; Los Angeles 90016, (213) 292-0605.

REGISTRATION: 72.8% D, 18.4% R

1988 CAMPAIGN: Moore – D   77%
                   Givens – R   23%

RATINGS:

AFL	PIRG	CLCV	NOW	CTA	HAC	CofC	CFB	NRA
94%	89%	88%	92%	G	90%	24%	44%	0%

KEY VOTES:

Divest S. Africa: YES	Insurance reform: YES	Child sick leave: YES
Assault gun ban: YES	Parent consent abortion: NO	Ban AIDS discrim: YES
Clean Air Act: YES	Cutting old trees: –	Extend death penalty: YES
Lmt product tort: –	End mob home rent cont: YES	Ban offshore oil: YES

50th Assembly District

Curtis R. Tucker Jr. (D)

This district encompassing the El Segundo-Inglewood area of Los Angeles has a heavy minority population – about 55 percent black and 20 percent Latino. It is one of the hardcore Democratic districts in the state, with 77 percent of the voters registered as Democrats and only 16 percent as Republicans.

For 14 years, the district was represented by Curtis R. Tucker Sr., a former health department worker and Inglewood city councilman. He died in October 1988 of liver cancer, but it was too late to remove his name from the November ballot. Even in death, Tucker easily defeated his Republican opponent, gaining 72 percent of the vote.

Curtis R. Tucker Jr.

That set up a February 1989 special election, and Curtis R. Tucker Jr., a former Pacific Bell manager who was working as an aide to Assemblywoman Gwen Moore, emerged as the easy winner. With backing from Assembly Speaker Willie Brown and utilizing the name identification of his father, Tucker pulled away from a field of four, winning 71 percent of the vote.

Tucker has expressed interest in improving health care, the area in which his father specialized. A proponent of the death penalty, Tucker also listed cracking down on drugs and gang warfare as among his priorities. But it's too soon to tell whether he'll become a major player or remain on the back bench he now occupies.

PERSONAL: elected 1989 (special election); born April 6, 1954, in New Orleans, La.; home, Inglewood; education, B.A. history CSU Dominguez Hills; wife, Dianne; children, Christopher and Nicole; Catholic.

CAREER: consultant to Assemblyman Mike Roos 1983-1988; aide to Assemblywoman Gwen Moore 1988; manager Pacific Bell.

COMMITTEES: Aging & Long-Term Care; Human Services; Labor & Employment; Public Employees, Retirement & Social Security; Revenue and Taxation. SELECT: Assistance to Victims of Sexual Assault; Unlicensed Contractors. JOINT: Organized Crime & Gang Violence.

OFFICES: Capitol, (916) 445-7533; district, 1 Manchester Blvd., Box 6500, Inglewood 90306. (213) 412-6400.

REGISTRATION: 77.2% D, 15.7% R

1989 CAMPAIGN		
Tucker – D	71%
Davis – R	19%
Hill-Hale – D	7%
McGill – D	2%
Wright – D	1%

RATINGS: NRA
    0%

KEY VOTES:

Insurance reform: YES	Ban AIDS discrim: YES	Assault gun ban: YES
Child sick leave: YES	End mob home rent cont: YES	Cutting old trees: –

51st Assembly District

Gerald Felando (R)

In the Los Angeles area, the value of property is based largely on how close it is to the water – and thus how far upwind of the smog.

The people who live in the 51st Assembly District are, therefore, residing on some of the area's most valuable real estate, the stretch of coastal land south of Los Angeles International Airport and north of Long Beach.

Within the district are more than a dozen upscale communities – Rolling Hills, Rancho Palos Verdes, Manhattan Beach, Redondo Beach, etc. – and a couple of working class towns whose property values have been skyrocketing in recent years, Torrance and a part of San Pedro.

Gerald Felando

It's a solidly Republican district, with a 52 percent GOP registration, and the local political battles, therefore, pit Republican against Republican. A whale of a battle occurred in 1988, when the district's 10-year veteran, Gerald Felando, was challenged by Deane Dana Jr. His father, Los Angeles County Supervisor Deane Dana Sr., the local political powerhouse, poured tons of money into his son's campaign. Felando's rough-as-a-cob personality had opened the door for the challenge, but he survived and won re-election handily.

Felando is a dentist who grew up in San Pedro and maintains close ties to the commercial fishing industry, which has been one of his prime legislative interests.

Although one of the "Proposition 13 babies" elected in 1978, Felando is somewhat less conservative than many members of the group. In recent months, he's been undergoing chemotherapy for cancer.

PERSONAL: elected 1978; born Dec. 29, 1934, in San Pedro, Calif.; home, San Pedro; Coast Guard 1953-1957; education, D.D.S USC; wife, Joyce; children, Cynthia, Nicholas and Steven; Catholic.

CAREER: dentist.

COMMITTEES: Health; Ways & Means; Judiciary; Governmental Organization. JOINT: Fisheries & Aquaculture; Legislative Audit; Organized Crime & Gang Violence.

OFFICES: Capitol, (916) 445-7906; district, 3838 Carson St., 110, Torrance 90503, (213) 540-2123.

REGISTRATION: 36.8% D, 52% R

1988 CAMPAIGN: Felando – R   62%
                Wirth – D   35%
                Dobson – L   3%

RATINGS:

AFL	PIRG	CLCV	NOW	CTA	HAC	CofC	CFB	NRA
22%	54%	19%	25%	U	18%	80%	44%	100%

KEY VOTES:

Divest S. Africa: YES	Insurance reform: –	Child sick leave: NO
Assault gun ban: NO	Parent consent abortion: YES	Ban AIDS discrim: NO
Clean Air Act: NO	Cutting old trees: YES	Extend death penalty: YES
Lmt product tort: YES	End mob home rent cont: –	Ban offshore oil: NO

52nd Assembly District

Frank C. Hill (R)

Republican registration in this Los Angeles County district, which includes La Mirada, Walnut, La Habra Heights and portions of West Covina and Whittier, just keeps on growing. And a direct beneficiary of the GOP growth has been Frank Hill.

The 35-year-old Hill has been in the Legislature since he was 28. He has been in politics even longer, having served as the Whittier office manager for former U.S. Rep. Wayne Grisham and as an aide in Washington, D.C. to then-U.S. Sen. S.I. Hayakawa.

In Sacramento, Hill used his political skills to move quickly into a leadership position among Assembly Republicans, eventually serving as their liaison with Gov. Deukmejian.

An outspoken conservative, Hill gained some state-wide exposure as a leader in the successful initiative drive to declare English the state's official language in 1986. And while he supports more education funding in general, he also has become known for his opposition to mandatory bilingual education programs, arguing for giving local school districts control over making those decisions.

Hill is considered a strong voice for the liquor industry in the Capitol. In the closing days of the 1989 session, Hill made an impassioned floor speech against a fellow-Republican's bill lowering the blood-alcohol

Frank Hill

standard to .08 for drunken driving. The bill passed overwhelming and was signed by Gov. Deukmejian.

Hill indicated in the fall of 1989 that he will run for the state Senate seat being vacated by Republican Sen. Bill Campbell, who is leaving the Legislature to become president of the California Manufacturers Association. Hill got the immediate backing of Assembly Republican leader Ross Johnson, who also lives in the senate district and could have run for the seat.

However, Hill's bright political future has been clouded by an FBI probe of corruption at the state Capitol. Hill's office was one of the four searched in 1988 by agents as part of its undercover "sting" investigation into influence peddling in the state Capitol. He reportedly remains a focus of the probe. Despite the publicity–and virtually no campaigning in 1988 – he won re-election with 63 percent of the vote.

PERSONAL: elected 1982; born Feb. 19, 1954, in Whittier, Calif.; home, Whittier; education, A.A. political science Mt. San Antonio College in Walnut; B.A. political science UCLA; M.A. public administration Pepperdine University, Malibu; wife, Faye; children, Jenny and Greg; Episcopalian.

CAREER: Washington office manager U.S. Sen. S.I. Hayakawa 1976-1978; field director Rep. Wayne Grisham 1978-1982.

COMMITTEES: Ways & Means; Health; Governmental Organization; Utilities &Commerce. JOINT: Legislative Audit.

OFFICES: Capitol, (916) 445-7550; district, 15111 E. Whittier Blvd., Whittier 90603, (213) 945-7681.

REGISTRATION: 42.6% D, 47.8% R

1988 CAMPAIGN: Hill – R   63%
Perkins – D   37%

RATINGS:	AFL	PIRG	CLCV	NOW	CTA	HAC	CofC	CFB	NRA
	13%	39%	58%	42%	U	31%	80%	33%	100%

KEY VOTES:

Divest S. Africa:	–	Insurance reform:	NO	Child sick leave:	NO
Assault gun ban:	NO	Parent consent abortion:	YES	Ban AIDS discrim:	NO
Clean Air Act:	YES	Cutting old trees:	YES	Extend death penalty:	YES
Lmt product tort:	YES	End mob home rent cont:	–	Ban offshore oil:	NO

53rd Assembly District

Richard E. Floyd (D)

With a strong working-class bent, the district includes Gardena, Hawthorne and Carson with portions of the San Pedro area – though it never reaches the water. This Democratic district has grown increasingly conservative, and tempted the Republicans into trying to oust its incumbent, the bad-boy of the Assembly, Dick Floyd. The Republicans probably should have thought the better of it for all the trouble Floyd has caused them.

Richard E. Floyd

Floyd is one to never forget a grudge. In 1986, Republicans targeted him for defeat and mailed letters to voters in his district calling him a friend of drug dealers – which he most assuredly was not. The letters bore a forged signature from Ronald Reagan. Livid, Floyd demanded criminal prosecution – and he did not let up until state Attorney General John Van de Kamp won an indictment of Assemblyman John Lewis, the Republican's chief election strategist. Authorities say Lewis authorized the use of Reagan's name after the White House had balked at allowing it to be used.

Floyd is easily the loudest, most profane member of the Legislature – and proud of it. Not a last-night-of-the-session has gone by without Floyd bellowing a profanity directed at one of his Republican colleagues. During Gov. George Deukmejian's state of the state addresses, Floyd can usually be spotted tossing paper airplanes and making comments to anyone within earshot.

Among his more polite expressions has been to address Republican Pat Nolan as "the fat man" during floor debates. Those who complain that Floyd's chain smoking on the Assembly floor violates house rules, he dismisses as "whiners." And he once opposed the state's beverage-container deposit law as a tax, and called its author, fellow Democrat Burt Margolin, an "aging hippie." His microphone is often switched off – he is usually ruled out of order – but that has never been known to shut him up. He once threw coffee on reporters – and paid their dry cleaning bills. The coffee was actually directed at members of the Ways and Means Committee.

Floyd's histrionics aside, he can be a serious legislator. He was Sen. Ralph Dills' legislative assistant for years, and like his mentor, knows liquor and horse racing legislation inside and out. Floyd has been tight with labor unions as chairman of the Assembly's labor committee. In 1988, he was promoted to the chairmanship of the Assembly's governmental organization committee – the Assembly panel chiefly responsible for gambling and liquor legislation. He and Dills now hold full reign over what are politely called the "sin bills."

Floyd carried a full load of horse racing bills in 1989, including a measure to link the state Lottery with horse racing by having an Irish Sweepstakes-type lottery game tied to a race.

Whatever Dick Floyd's political future, it is bound to be entertaining.

PERSONAL: elected 1980; born Feb. 3, 1931, in Philadelphia, Penn.; home, Carson; Army 1948-1952 Korea; divorced; children, Lorene and Rikki; Protestant.

CAREER: Western regional sales manager for a tape manufacturer and propane equipment firm, 1957-1969; administrative assistant to Sen. Ralph C. Dills 1969-1980.

COMMITTEES: Governmental Organization (chair); Labor & Employment; Finance & Insurance; Human Services. JOINT: Fairs Allocation & Classification; Prison Construction & Operations.

OFFICES: Capitol, (916) 445-0965; district, 16921 S. Western Ave., 101, Gardena 90247, (213) 516-4037.

REGISTRATION: 60.2% D, 29.3% R

1988 CAMPAIGN: Floyd – D   59%
                  Bookhammer – R   41%

RATINGS:	AFL	PIRG	CLCV	NOW	CTA	HAC	CofC	CFB	NRA
	94%	84%	85%	67%	G	81%	20%	33%	90%

KEY VOTES:

Divest S. Africa: YES	Insurance reform:	YES	Child sick leave: YES
Assault gun ban: –	Parent consent abortion:	–	Ban AIDS discrim: YES
Clean Air Act: YES	Cutting old trees:	–	Extend death penalty: YES
Lmt product tort: YES	End mob home rent cont:	–	Ban offshore oil: YES

54th Assembly District

Willard H. Murray Jr. (D)

When Republican Paul Zeltner won this largely minority and blue-collar district in 1986 – thanks mostly to a tactical blunder by Assembly Speaker Willie Brown – Brown quickly proclaimed that Zeltner's days as a legislator were numbered.

Brown's prediction came true. Willard Murray, a former aide to Rep. Mervyn Dymally, edged the first-term lawmaker to reclaim a seat that had traditionally gone to Democrats.

It didn't take Murray long to get in the middle of controversy. Murray, whose southeast Los Angeles district includes cities plagued by Uzi-toting gangs, refused to support a measure that would restrict semiautomatic assault weapons. In so doing, he was sticking by the National Rifle Association, which had given him a key endorsement against ex-cop Zeltner, and going against the wishes of many in his district. Ironically, shortly after he was elected, Murray came under fire from the NRA for sending out an endorsement letter without their permission.

Murray was also the subject of controversy even before he was elected. During his campaign, he acknowledged that he had never graduated from UCLA despite campaign literature that said he had received a degree in mathematics.

Nevertheless, Murray squeaked by Zeltner in a district that includes his hometown of Paramount, Lakewood, Compton, Bellflower and a portion of Long Beach.

Williard H. Murry Jr.

Up until his election, Murray was best known for sending out slate-mailers to voters in the heavily black and Hispanic South-Central Los Angeles area.

In his first term, Murray has concentrated on anti-crime bills, introducing a measure that would increase penalties for possession of a machine gun. He has proposed improved services for veterans and a program to encourage college students to become teachers.

PERSONAL: elected 1988; born Jan. 1, 1931, in Los Angeles, Calif.; home, Paramount; USAF 1951-1954 Korea; education, attended CSU Los Angeles; wife, Barbara Farris; children, Kevin and Melinda Jane; Methodist.

CAREER: engineering; legislative consultant Rep. Mervyn Dymally; chief deputy Los Angeles City Councilman Robert Farrell; executive assistant Los Angeles Mayor Sam Yorty; senior consultant Assembly Democratic Caucus.

COMMITTEES: Education; Governmental Organization; Labor & Employment; Local Government; Utilities & Commerce.

OFFICES: Capitol, (916) 445-7486; district, 16444 Paramount Blvd., 100, Paramount 90723, (213) 516-4144.

REGISTRATION: 65.3% D, 27.3% R

1988 CAMPAIGN: Murray – D   52%
                              Zeltner (inc) – R   48%

RATINGS:
        NRA
        90%

KEY VOTES:

Insurance reform: YES	Child sick leave: YES	Cutting old trees: YES
Assault gun ban: NO	End mob home rent cont: NO	Ban AIDS discrim: YES

55th Assembly District

Richard G. Polanco (D)

When then-Assemblyman Richard Alatorre was named to preside over the reapportionment of legislative and congressional districts after the 1980 census, he didn't neglect his own. The 55th Assembly District is a compact, overwhelmingly Democratic and predominantly Hispanic portion of East Los Angeles.

Alatorre didn't remain in the 55th District seat very long. A federal lawsuit resulted in the redrawing of Los Angeles City Council districts, creating two Hispanic seats and he quickly claimed one of those in 1985. Alatorre has since become a City Council power and has been mentioned as a future candidate for mayor.

Richard G. Polanco

When Alatorre gave up his Assembly seat, a serious split developed among local Hispanic politicians over his successor, who was to be chosen by special election. Alatorre endorsed Richard Polanco, as did Assembly Speaker Willie Brown, and after a rough campaign and two elections Polanco emerged as the winner.

Polanco, a one-time aide to Alatorre and several other politicians, made a big mistake on his very first day in the Assembly. He was placed on the Public Safety Committee and voted for a bill to authorize a new state prison in East Los Angeles. There was, however, heavy opposition to the prison in the community and Polanco quickly reversed course and became a leading critic.

Polanco doesn't display the same gutty political instincts as Alatorre and has yet to climb out of backbencher status, although he tried to carve off a piece of the auto insurance controversy for himself by carrying some insurer-sponsored bills.

Given the nature of the district, Polanco probably can remain in the seat as long as he wants, awaiting an opportunity to move up to the Senate or Congress, or perhaps even the Los Angeles County Board of Supervisors if it, too, is reapportioned to create one or more Hispanic seats.

PERSONAL: elected 1986; born March 4, 1951 in Los Angeles, Calif.; home, Los Angeles; education, attended Universidad Nacional de Mexico and University of Redlands, A.A. East Los Angeles Community College; wife, Olivia; children, Richard Jr., Alejandro Gabriel and Liana Danielle; Methodist.

CAREER: special assistant Gov. Jerry Brown 1980-1982; chief of staff Assemblyman Richard Alatorre 1983-1985.

COMMITTEES: Health; Governmental Organization; Rules; Utilities & Commerce; Ways & Means. SELECT: State Public Procurement Practices (chair); Calif.-Mexico Affairs (chair). SPECIAL: Policy Research Management. JOINT: Rules.

OFFICES: Capitol, (916) 445-7587; district, 110 North Ave. 56, Los Angeles 90042, (213) 255-7111.
REGISTRATION: 66.4% D, 22.9% R
1988 CAMPAIGN: Polanco – D   75%
                   Alarcon – P&F   16%
                   Wilson – L   9%

RATINGS:

AFL	PIRG	CLCV	NOW	CTA	HAC	CofC	CFB	NRA
99%	89%	89%	84%	S	95%	24%	44%	10%

KEY VOTES:

Divest S. Africa: YES	Insurance reform: YES	Child sick leave: YES
Assault gun ban: YES	Parent consent abortion: NO	Ban AIDS discrim: YES
Clean Air Act: YES	Cutting old trees: YES	Extend death penalty: YES
Lmt product tort: NO	End mob home rent cont: YES	Ban offshore oil: YES

56th Assembly District

Lucille Roybal-Allard (D)

There are fewer than 60,000 registered voters – the lowest of any Assembly district – in this predominantly Latino district which includes part of east Los Angeles and the cities of Bell Gardens, Commerce, Maywood and Vernon. Moreover, only slightly more than half of that number voted in the 1988 elections.

And among those who voted, eight out of ten chose Democrat Lucille Roybal-Allard, a former United Way planner and daughter of a legendary figure in East Los Angeles politics, Rep. Edward Roybal.

Roybal-Allard came out of nowhere in 1987 to overwhelm a crowded field in a special election to fill the seat vacated by Gloria Molina, who was elected to the Los Angeles City Council. In fact, she had never run

Lucille Roybal-Allard

for political office before. But the family name proved unbeatable in a district that included areas that have been represented by her father for nearly four decades.

Roybal-Allard leaves little doubt that she's grooming herself to take over her father's congressional seat whenever he decides to retire. In the meantime, she is gradually and quietly learning the political ropes in the Assembly.

She has emerged as a liberal – often siding with an informal group of Democrats known as the Grizzly Bears, who share information on bills and ideas on how to vote on issues.

Roybal-Allard has spent a good chunk of her time working to protect her district. She has helped state Sen. Art Torres in the effort to keep the state from building a prison in her district. And she authored a bill to crack down on companies that constantly violate pollution laws, primarily because a company with a history of violations wants to build a hazardous waste incinerator in her district. That bill was vetoed by Gov. Deukmejian.

PERSONAL: elected 1987 (special election); born June 12, 1941, in Boyle Heights; home, Los Angeles; education, B.A. speech therapy; CSU Los Angeles; husband, Edward T. Allard III; children, Lisa Marie, Ricardo, Angela and Guy-Mark; Catholic.

CAREER: planning associate; past executive director National Association of Hispanic Certified Public Accountants; past assistant director of the Alcoholism Council of East Los Angeles.

COMMITTEES: Health; Transportation; Utilities & Commerce; Ways & Means. SELECT: Assistance to Victims of Sexual Assault (chair). JOINT: Organized Crime & Gang Violence; Refugee Resettlement, International Migration & Cooperative Development.

OFFICES: Capitol, (916) 445-1670; district, 5261 E. Beverly Blvd., Los Angeles 90022, (213) 721-5557.

REGISTRATION: 75% D; 15.1 R

1988 CAMPAIGN: Roybal-Allard – D 80%
Sheldon – R 14%
Munoz – P&F 7%

RATINGS:

	AFL	PIRG	CLCV	NOW	CTA	HAC	CofC	CFB	NRA
	100%	100%	100%	92%	S	95%	16%	33%	0%

KEY VOTES:

	Insurance reform:	YES	Child sick leave:	YES
Assault gun ban: YES	Parent consent abortion:	NO	Ban AIDS discrim:	YES
Clean Air Act: YES	Cutting old trees:	NO	Extend death penalty:	NO
Lmt product tort: –	End mob home rent cont:	NO	Ban offshore oil:	YES

57th Assembly District

Dave A. Elder (D)

The 57th Assembly District is an island of Democracy in a sea of Republicanism, created by Democratic leaders to include loyalist neighborhoods in the Long Beach-San Pedro area.

Dave Elder, a one-time budget analyst for the city of Long Beach and executive for the Port of Long Beach, won the district in 1978 and, with a 60 percent-plus Democratic registration, has had little trouble holding the seat since.

Elder is something of a loner in the clubby Capitol, specializing in arcane bills dealing with taxes, government finance and public employees' pensions. He chairs the Public Employees and Retirement Committee, which is perhaps the lowest-visibility committee in the house.

Periodically, Elder arises on the floor to raise some complicated question about a particularly complicated bill, but seems limited by his low-key personality to a subsidiary political role. If he has any hope of moving beyond the Assembly, it's probably to run for Glenn Anderson's congressional seat when the latter retires.

PERSONAL: elected 1978; born Feb. 10, 1942, in Los Angeles, Calif.; home, Long Beach; education, B.A. political science CSU Long Beach; wife, Linda Proaps; children, Jonathan and Nicholas; Catholic.

CAREER: budget analyst; general manager of the Port of Long Beach.

COMMITTEES: Public Employees, Retirement & Social Security (chair); Economic Development &

Dave A. Elder

New Technologies; Elections, Reapportionment & Constitutional Amendments; Revenue & Taxation. JOINT: State's Economy (vice chair); Organized Crime & Gang Violence. SELECT: Hazardous Materials, Pipeline, Chemical Plant & Refinery Safety (chair).

OFFICES: Capitol, (916) 445-7454; district, 245 W. Broadway, 300, Long Beach 90802, (213) 590-5009; 638 S. Beacon St., 307, San Pedro 90731, (213) 548-7991.

REGISTRATION: 60.9% D, 28.6% R

1988 CAMPAIGN:
Elder – D	69%	
Ball – R	27%	
Bellock – P&F	4%	

RATINGS:
AFL	PIRG	CLCV	NOW	CTA	HAC	CofC	CFB	NRA
89%	79%	83%	75%	G	95%	28%	33%	60%

KEY VOTES:

Divest S. Africa:	YES	Insurance reform:	YES	Child sick leave:	–
Assault gun ban:	NO	Parent consent abortion:	YES	Ban AIDS discrim:	YES
Clean Air Act:	YES	Cutting old trees:	YES	Extend death penalty:	YES
Lmt product tort:	YES	End mob home rent cont:	YES	Ban offshore oil:	YES

58th Assembly District

Dennis L. Brown (R)

Dennis Brown is a legislator who believes the less government, the better. He plays his belief to the hilt. He annually introduces fewer bills than any other lawmaker, rarely speaks in the Assembly and votes "no" with monotonous regularity. It must be a formula that voters like in his increasingly Republican Southern California shoreline district, which includes a part of Long Beach, Signal Hill and Orange County communities stretching from Huntington Beach to Seal Beach. Brown won re-election in 1988 with 62 percent of the vote.

Brown was a Republican Party activist and research director for a stock brokerage firm when he rode into the Legislature in 1978 as one of the self-proclaimed "Proposition 13 babies." On a rare occasion when he does take a bill, it often has something to do with taxes. He played a key role in the Legislature's 1987 effort to conform the state tax law to the federal one.

Brown is widely regarded as one of the most conservative members of the Legislature, consistently voting against social programs, environmental programs and regulation of business. It came as a mild shock, then, when Brown, in 1987, supported a bill that banned smoking on planes, buses and trains in California.

Dennis L. Brown

Brown's passion – and his role in Sacramento – is politics. He is a key strategist for Assembly Republicans. His involvement in campaigns in 1986 almost got him into trouble with the law, however. Brown was among four Assembly GOP leaders investigated for their roles in sending out mailings bearing the forged signature of President Reagan.

Brown, who is an ardent law-and-order proponent, declined to talk to investigators, citing his Fifth Amendment right against self-incrimination. Brown was never charged with a crime, but his name was mentioned several times in an attorney general's report of the investigation.

PERSONAL: elected 1978; born March 21, 1949, in Compton, Calif.; home, Long Beach; education, A.A. Cerritos College, B.S. finance and M.B.A. USC; unmarried; Protestant.

CAREER: stockbroker; part-time business instructor Pepperdine University.

COMMITTEES: Revenue & Taxation (vice chair); Finance & Insurance; Ways & Means.

OFFICES: Capitol, (916) 445-8492; district, 1945 Palo Verde Ave., 203, Long Beach 90815, (213) 493-5514 or (714) 895-3787.

REGISTRATION: 39.2% D, 50.2% R

1988 CAMPAIGN: Brown – R 62%
Kincaid – D 33%
Stier – L 2%
Green – P&F 2%

RATINGS:

AFL	PIRG	CLCV	NOW	CTA	HAC	CofC	CFB	NRA
5%	37%	4%	0%	U	18%	92%	77%	100%

KEY VOTES:

Divest S. Africa:	NO	Insurance reform:	–	Child sick leave:	NO
Assault gun ban:	NO	Parent consent abortion:	YES	Ban AIDS discrim:	NO
Clean Air Act:	NO	Cutting old trees:	NO	Extend death penalty:	YES
Lmt product tort:	YES	End mob home rent cont:	YES	Ban offshore oil:	NO

59th Assembly District

Charles M. Calderon (D)

This district has seen a huge influx of the state's newest immigrants – Asians. The district is largely Hispanic, including such areas as Pico Rivera. This is also a district that has two cities practically at war – Monterey Park and Montebello. The battlegrounds are many, but they include a huge dump that straddles the Pomona Freeway in Monterey Park. Montebello, downwind, wants it cleaned up.

Perhaps it was the better part of valor then that its Assembly member, Charles Calderon, moved from Monterey Park to the politically neutral end of his district in Whittier. His address change also helps Calderon position himself to run for the Senate seat held by Joseph Montoya, who has been indicted by a federal grand jury for bribery and racketeering.

Charles M. Calderon

Calderon, a balding ex-prosecutor, came to Sacramento, like many, naive in its ways. He fell in with a set of youngish Assembly members who hung out at Paragary's restaurant in Sacramento's mid-town. The group eventually plotted the overthrow of Speaker Willie Brown and became known as the "Gang of Five."

When the speaker started retaliating in 1987, Calderon tried to play politics on his terms – and failed. Calderon tried to defeat the speaker's handpicked candidate, Robert Epple, in a neighboring Democratic primary in 1988. Calderon got behind Pete Ohanesian, but Epple won.

Then at the start of the 1989 session, the rebels formed a brief alliance with Republican Assembly leader Ross Johnson that had Republicans voting for Calderon for speaker. The effort failed. Calderon is not speaker and the Gang of Five eventually reached a peace pact with Brown.

Calderon briefly broke with his Gang of Five pals during the 1989 session by supporting Assemblyman Byron Sher's bill for a three-year moratorium on old-growth timber harvesting. His old ally, Steve Peace, denounced Calderon's action as "the ultimate in hypocrisy."

Aside from his involvement in the endless petty intrigues of the Capitol, Calderon is generally a competent legislator. His chief legislative accomplishment was in shepherding interstate banking legislation through to the governor's signature – and dodging obstacles thrown in his way by Sen. Alan Robbins. Calderon's bill opened California to out-of-state banks over a phased-in period.

PERSONAL: elected 1982; born March 12, 1950, in Montebello, Calif.; home, Whittier; education, B.A. political science CSU Los Angeles, J.D. UC Davis; wife, Jeannine; children, Charles and Matthew James; unaffiliated Christian.

CAREER: lawyer; city attorney's prosecutor; school board member 1979-1982; legislative aide to Assembly members Richard Alatorre and Jack Fenton; special consultant to Secretary of State March Fong Eu.

COMMITTEES: Environmental Safety & Toxic Materials; Housing & Community Development; Natural Resources. JOINT: Revision of the Penal Code; Refugee Resettlement, International Migration & Cooperative Development.

OFFICES: Capitol, (916) 445-0854; district, 1712 W. Beverly Blvd., 202, Montebello 90640, (213) 721-2904.

REGISTRATION: 61.9% D, 28.3% R

1988 CAMPAIGN: Calderon – D   87%

                      Pencall – L   13%

RATINGS:

AFL	PIRG	CLCV	NOW	CTA	HAC	CofC	CFB	NRA
90%	58%	74%	84%	G	85%	32%	44%	10%

KEY VOTES:

Divest S. Africa:	YES	Insurance reform:	–	Child sick leave:	YES
Assault gun ban:	YES	Parent consent abortion:	YES	Ban AIDS discrim:	YES
Clean Air Act:	YES	Cutting old trees:	NO	Extend death penalty:	YES
Lmt product tort:	YES	End mob home rent cont:	YES	Ban offshore oil:	YES

60th Assembly District

Sally M. Tanner (D)

This heavily Democratic district in Los Angeles County is also heavily Latino – over 50 percent – and working class. It includes the cities of Baldwin Park, Bassett, El Monte, City of Industry, Valinda, La Puente, Rosemead and part of West Covina.

Democrat Sally Tanner, a former commercial artist and an administrative aide to an assemblyman and a congressman, is in her sixth two-year term, having succeeded now-state Sen. Joseph Montoya.

It is a district that Democratic Party officials say someday will likely be represented by a Hispanic, but for the time being, Tanner seems firmly entrenched, having defeated a Latino Republican challenger in 1988 by a 66 to 33 percent margin. One of 14 women in the

Sally M. Tanner

Assembly, Tanner is the chair of the Legislature's Women's Caucus.

Tanner has focused largely on environmental issues during her tenure. As chairwoman of the Assembly Committee on Environmental Safety and Toxic Materials, Tanner has made a major mark on toxic waste and air quality laws in the state. Respected by members of both parties, Tanner has authored many of the major toxic laws of the last decade and helped craft those carried by others. Tanner's interest is natural; her smoggy district suffers from very real pollution difficulties.

The underground water of the San Gabriel Valley is polluted from years of industrial abuses and there are several federal Superfund toxic sites in her district.

However, Tanner in 1985 was cheated out of what could have been her crowning legislative achievement by a fellow Democrat. After months of stormy negotiations with Deukmejian officials and nearly every industrial and environmental lobbyist in Sacramento, Tanner was on the verge of winning bipartisan passage for a total reorganization of the state's duplicative toxic cleanup agencies. But on the last night of that year's session, the Assembly's Rules Committee chairman, Louis Papan of Milbrae, held the bill hostage until Republicans would vote for an unrelated bill giving welfare cost of living increases to the elderly, blind and disabled. Despite Deukmejian's personal entreaties to Assembly Republicans, they would not budge and Tanner's bill died without a vote in a gridlock of stuck bills.

She is said to be eyeing the Senate seat held by Democrat Joseph Montoya, who is under federal indictment. Tanner will have to shoot it out with Assemblyman Charles Calderon if Montoya should leave.

PERSONAL: elected 1978; born Dec. 12, 1928, in East Chicago, Ind.; home, El Monte; education, attended Pasadena City College and the Art Center College of Design in Los Angeles, no degree; divorced; children, Timothy and Christopher; Catholic.

CAREER: newspaper graphic artist; department store advertising director; campaign manager and administrative aide Assemblyman Harvey Johnson 1964-1974 and Rep. George Danielson 1974-1977;

COMMITTEES: Environmental Safety & Toxic Materials (chair); Governmental Organization; Natural Resources; Labor & Employment.

OFFICES: CAPITOL (916) 445-7783; district, 11100 Valley Blvd., 106, El Monte 91731 (818) 442-9100.

REGISTRATION: 60.7% D, 30% R

1988 CAMPAIGN: Tanner – D   66%

Valasco – R   33%

Argall – L   1%

RATINGS:

	AFL	PIRG	CLCV	NOW	CTA	HAC	CofC	CFB	NRA
	95%	92%	–	42%	S	58%	4%	33%	0%

KEY VOTES:

Divest S. Africa: YES	Insurance reform: –	Child sick leave:	YES
Assault gun ban: YES	Parent consent abortion: YES	Ban AIDS discrim:	YES
Clean Air Act: –	Cutting old trees: –	Extend death penalty:	YES
Lmt product tort: YES	End mob home rent cont: NO	Ban offshore oil:	YES

61st Assembly District

Paul A. Woodruff (R)

This expansive San Bernardino County district includes the communities of upscale Redlands, the bedroom communities of Loma Linda and Yucaipa and the high desert towns of Barstow, Victorville, Needles and Crestline. Also included are the San Bernardino Mountain resorts of Big Bear and Crestline.

When longtime Assemblyman Bill Leonard decided to run for an open seat in the state Senate in 1988, he set off a free-for-all in the scramble to replace him. Seven Republicans announced their candidacies in a district where the Republican nominee was the all-but-certain winner.

In the end, the winner was Leonard's hand-picked successor, Paul Woodruff, who had worked for Leonard as an administrative assistant and campaign manager.

Woodruff, who still maintains a campaign consulting business, is a young, baby-faced legislator who

Paul A. Woodruff

spent his first term quietly sitting on the Republican back benches. Near the end of the 1989 legislative session, however, Woodruff was among those pushing for the inclusion of an open meeting requirement in the ethics reform package. He has generally followed the Assembly Republican pack in his voting record.

PERSONAL: elected 1988; born Feb. 13, 1960, in San Bernardino, Calif.; home, Yucaipa; education, B.A. political science CSU San Bernardino; unmarried; Protestant.

CAREER: aide Assemblyman William Leonard 1981-1988.

COMMITTEES: Education; Elections, Reapportionment & Constitutional Amendments; Revenue & Taxation.

OFFICES: Capitol, (916) 445-7552; district, 300 E. State St., 480, Redlands 92373, (714) 798-0337.

REGISTRATION: 39.2% D, 49.7% R

1988 CAMPAIGN: Woodruff – R   62%

Ford – D   35%

Harbour – L   3%

RATINGS: NRA
100%

KEY VOTES:

Insurance reform: NO	Child sick leave: NO	Assault gun ban: NO
Cutting old trees: YES	End mob home rent cont: YES	Ban AIDS discrim: NO

62nd Assembly District

William H. Lancaster (R)

The 62nd Assembly District covers a patch of middle-class suburbia east of Los Angeles, and the man who has represented the district for nearly two decades fits it perfectly. Bill Lancaster, the highest-seniority Republican in the Assembly, is the

Johnny Lunchbucket of legislators. He carries his quota of bills, diligently attends committee hearings and floor sessions and otherwise pays attention to his duty. He puts in his time, takes care of district concerns and is rewarded with easy-as-pie re-election every two years.

Lancaster is chairman of the Joint Legislative Ethics committee, a panel that seldom meets and is not to be confused with the Assembly Select Committee of Ethics that was chaired by Democrat John Vasconcellos and churned out a comprehensive ethics proposal in 1989. It remains to be seen if Lancaster and his largely defunct panel will be entrusted with enforcing the Legislature's new ethical standards.

William H. Lancaster

Lancaster was a Duarte city councilman and mayor, a field representative for the California Taxpayers Association and an aide to then-Rep. Charles Wiggins shortly before the latter won fame as one of the last defenders of Richard Nixon in the House Judiciary impeachment hearings in 1974. Lancaster left congressional employ after he was elected to the Assembly in 1972. He rarely engages in any of the partisan or factional infighting that marks the Assembly and seems content to punch the clock each morning and go home each night. He's likely to retain his seniority status for many years to come.

PERSONAL: elected 1972 (special election); born April 29, 1931, in Bakersfield, Calif.; home, Covina; wife, Treece Whitaker; children, Cort, Chris and Dianne; Protestant.

CAREER: City council, mayor of Duarte 1958-1965; aide to Rep. Charles Wiggins 1967-1972.

COMMITTEES: Finance & Insurance; Housing & Community Development; Local Government; Transportation. JOINT: Legislative Ethics (chair); Legislative Audit.

OFFICES: Capitol, (916) 445-9234; district, 145 Badillo St., Covina 91723, (818) 332-6271.

REGISTRATION: 40.8% D, 49.8% R

1988 CAMPAIGN: Lancaster – R   68%
Wendt – D   29%
Polson – L   4%

RATINGS:

AFL	PIRG	CLCV	NOW	CTA	HAC	CofC	CFB	NRA
17%	42%	29%	25%	U	31%	96%	66%	90%

KEY VOTES:

Divest S. Africa:	NO	Insurance reform:	NO	Child sick leave:	NO
Assault gun ban:	NO	Parent consent abortion:	YES	Ban AIDS discrim:	NO
Clean Air Act:	NO	Cutting old trees:	YES	Extend death penalty:	YES
Lmt product tort:	YES	End mob home rent cont:	YES	Ban offshore oil:	NO

63rd Assembly District

Robert D. Epple (D)

Reapportionment has eliminated all but a few truly competitive districts, where neither a Democrat nor a Republican has a clear advantage over the other. This is one of them, and in 1988, Democrat Robert Epple, a Norwalk attorney, was the surprise winner. He didn't win by much – 220 votes – but his defeat of incumbent Republican Wayne Grisham helped solidify the Democrats' majority in the Assembly.

Epple represents the kind of district that would appear strongly Democratic. It is comprised of the mainly blue-collar cities of Artesia, Cerritos, Downey, Hawaiian Gardens, Norwalk and part of Santa Fe Springs. But even Democrats here are conservative to moderate. Grisham, a former congressman, seized the

Robert D. Epple

seat in 1984 after Democrat Bruce Young, under investigation for his financial dealings with a campaign contributor, decided not to seek re-election.

Grisham, however, had proven to be a lackadaisical campaigner in a 1987 special election to fill a vacant Senate seat. And Assembly Speaker Willie Brown and other Democratic leaders smelled blood. They poured money and staff into the district and came out winners.

In his first term, Epple has gone to great lengths to walk the moderate line and to try not to give his opponents ammunition for charges that he is a Brown puppet. He bucked the Democratic leadership by voting against a highly publicized measure to restrict most military assault-type semiautomatic weapons, one of six Democrats to do so.

Among his bills, Epple carried a measure to increase the maximum home loans for Cal-Vet loans, a popular issue in his district.

PERSONAL: elected 1988; born Sept. 18, 1947, in Hollywood, Calif.; home, Norwalk; Army 1966-1970; education, Cerritos Community College and CSU Dominguez Hills, J.D. American College of Law; wife, Cheryl; Children, Nicole; Protestant.

CAREER: lawyer; tax consultant; Cerritos Community College board of trustees 1981-1988.

COMMITTEES: Finance & Insurance; Labor & Employment; Aging & Long-Term Care; Public Employees, Retirement and Social Security; Utilities & Commerce.

OFFICES: Capitol, (916) 445-6047; district, 13710 Studebaker Road, 202, Norwalk 90650, (213) 929-1796.

REGISTRATION: 56.5% D, 36% R

1988 CAMPAIGN: Epple – D   50%
                     Grisham (inc.) – R 50%
RATINGS: NRA
              30%
KEY VOTES:

Insurance reform: YES   Child sick leave: YES Ban AIDS discrim: YES
Assault gun ban: NO   End mob home rent cont: NO   Cutting old trees: –

64th Assembly District

J. Ross Johnson (R)

There's nothing mysterious about the 64th Assembly District. It's a hard-line conservative district in the heart of northern Orange County suburbia, covering such communities as Fullerton and Anaheim.

But Ross Johnson, the man who has represented the 64th District for the past decade-plus, is something of an enigma.

With a political intelligence that sometimes borders on brilliance, Johnson seems well-suited to his role as the Assembly's Republican leader. But lurking just beneath the surface of his public personality is an anger that bubbles up on occasion, rendering Johnson virtually incoherent with rage – a trait that leads some Democrats to bait him in public.

J. Ross Johnson

Johnson, an attorney who was active in local civic affairs prior to embarking on a political career, was part of the huge class of Republicans elected to the Assembly in 1978, a group that quickly dubbed itself the "Proposition 13 babies" and vowed to wage ideological war on liberals and Democrats.

The group asserted itself within months by lending support to a coup against the relatively moderate Republican leader of the time, Paul Priolo, that brought Carol Hallett into the leadership position.

Johnson helped Pat Nolan, the de facto leader of the Proposition 13 babies, engineer another coup on Hallett's successor, Robert Naylor, in 1984 and wound up as one of Nolan's top lieutenants. But in November, 1988, after Republicans lost several seats to the Democrats and Nolan had become entangled in an FBI investigation of Capitol corruption, he lateraled the leader's position to Johnson.

The switch from Nolan to Johnson – which staved off rumblings from moderates in the Republican caucus – had little to do with ideology. The new leader was every bit as conservative as the old leader. But it did make a difference in style.

Whereas Nolan was gregarious and loved the public stage, Johnson is a semi-introvert who, aides say, dislikes the limelight. And while Nolan had developed a mutually beneficial, cooperative relationship with Speaker Willie Brown – one that protected Brown from being dumped during a squabble with his own critics–Johnson has proclaimed a more adversarial attitude toward Brown. Nolan had refused to join a coalition with Democratic rebels to oust Brown; Brown had reciprocated by giving Nolan some powers over Republican committee appointments that shored up his own position.

When the Legislature reconvened in December, 1988, just a month after Johnson had assumed the leadership position, he publicly pledged support to one of the Democratic "Gang of Five" rebels as a replacement for Brown. But the speaker, having picked up three seats in the November elections, had enough votes to win a new term.

Johnson's partisan militancy quieted the critics within his own caucus, at least for the time being, although some of the old animosities arose again when–after vowing to keep out of local Republican politics, unlike Nolan–Johnson and other GOP leaders backed a primary candidate for a vacant Assembly seat in San Diego County in 1989. Another Republican, moderate Tricia Hunter, defeated the anointee in a battle marked by fierce debate over abortion and Johnson belatedly endorsed Hunter in the runoff.

While Nolan seemed to be consumed with politics as a game, Johnson displays a greater interest in political policy-making. He sat at the table as Gov. Deukmejian and legislative leaders hammered out a series of agreements on major policy issues in 1989 after years of unproductive wheel-spinning.

Personally, Johnson has devoted his energies to overhauls of the political system itself, although his precise motives for that interest, like so many aspects of Johnson's persona, have never been clear. He joined with two other legislators–a Democrat and an independent–to sponsor a campaign finance reform initiative (Proposition 73) in 1988 that imposes limits on contributions and transfers of funds. But some reformers saw the measure as a poison pill for a broader reform initiative (Proposition 68) on the same ballot. Since Proposition 73 received more votes, it superseded Proposition 68 in areas of conflict, such as its ban on public financing of campaigns. And its anti-transfer provisions seemed aimed at Speaker Brown's political powers.

Johnson is sponsoring another initiative for the 1990 ballot, this one a rewrite of a 1984 measure fronted by the late Paul Gann that would impose new rules on the Legislature's internal procedures and also require two-thirds votes on reapportionment plans. Democrats see the Johnson measure as a purely partisan hit.

Given the volatile history of internal Republican politics in the Assembly–four leadership changes in a decade–it's never certain that the current occupant of the position is safe. But for the moment, Johnson seems to be relatively secure and thus free to pursue his political causes, whatever they may be. A more precise calculation of his longevity must await the outcome of the 1990 elections.

PERSONAL: elected 1978; born Sept. 28, 1939, in Drake, N.D.; home, Brea; Navy 1965-67; education, B.A. history CSU Fullerton, J.D. Western State; wife,

Diane Morris; children, Susan and Molly; Protestant.

CAREER: iron worker; lawyer; legislative aide to Assemblyman Jerry Lewis, 1969-1973; Assembly Republican floor leader.

COMMITTEES: As Assembly Republican leader, Johnson does not serve on any committees.

OFFICES: Capitol, (916) 445-7448; district, 1501 N. Harbor Blvd., 201, Fullerton 92635, (714) 738-5853.

REGISTRATION: 35% D, 55.5% R

1988 CAMPAIGN: Johnson – R 72%

Heuer – D 28%

RATINGS:

AFL	PIRG	CLCV	NOW	CTA	HAC	CofC	CFB	NRA
13%	32%	10%	8%	U	18%	92%	55%	100%

KEY VOTES:

Divest S. Africa:	–	Insurance reform:	NO	Child sick leave:	NO
Assault gun ban:	NO	Parent consent abortion:	YES	Ban AIDS discrim:	NO
Clean Air Act:	NO	Cutting old trees:	YES	Extend death penalty:	YES
Lmt product tort:	YES	End mob home rent cont:	YES	Ban offshore oil:	NO

65th Assembly District

Charles W. Bader (R)

The west end of the San Bernardino Valley has experienced some of the most explosive growth of the last decade. Roughly following old Route 66, this district hardly resembles the ticky-tack conglomeration of towns of the '50s and '60s immortalized in the song of the same name. The district includes the old, upscale neighborhoods of Ontario and the new stucco housing tracts of Rancho Cucamonga, Montclair, Chino and Pomona. The district extends northward into the desert, including the small community of Adelanto that has been begging for years to get a state prison and thinking about legalized gambling, both without success.

Charles W. Bader

The district was once partisanly competitive. After the last reapportionment, however, it became safely Republican for Chuck Bader, an ex-condo manager who is a generally good-government conservative.

Bader in 1990 is attempting to take advantage of the tremendous middle-class growth in his area by challenging long-time Democratic Sen. Ruben Ayala for his seat. The two have spent much of 1989 raising money for what promises to be a costly and nasty race.

As a legislator, Bader has been critical, without sounding petty, of his own party leaders and aligned himself with the "Magnificent Seven" Republican rebels who sought to oust Pat Nolan as leader in 1986 and, once he was gone, became critics of Ross Johnson. That has not, however, kept Bader from supporting Nolan, for example, on such issues as redistributing school funds for 76 programs for the gifted and disadvantaged. And as a member of Ways and Means, Bader in May 1989 joined other Republicans and a handful of Democrats in voting for a capital gains tax cut that some critics contended was a $2 billion giveaway.

To challenge Ayala, Bader will have to give up his Assembly seat. He is attempting to hand it off to his chief aide, Jim Brulte, who should have no trouble winning the seat if he can get through a GOP primary.

PERSONAL: elected 1982; born March 19, 1940, in Los Angeles, Calif.; home, Pomona; Navy 1963-1966; education, B.S. business administration UCLA; wife, Rosanne; children, Ron and Steve; Lutheran.

CAREER: real estate management; Pomona City Council, mayor 1971-1981.

COMMITTEES: Education (vice chair); Environmental Safety & Toxic Materials; Finance & Insurance; Revenue & Taxation. SPECIAL: Policy Research Management. JOINT: Review of the Master Plan for Higher Education; School Facilities.

OFFICES: Capitol, (916) 445-8490; district, 203 West G St., Ontario 91762, (714) 983-6011.

REGISTRATION: 40.4% D, 50% R

1988 CAMPAIGN: Bader – R   67%
Chamberlain – D   31%
Gautreau – L   2%

RATINGS:

AFL	PIRG	CLCV	NOW	CTA	HAC	CofC	CFB	NRA
19%	42%	40%	42%	S	36%	92%	77%	100%

KEY VOTES:

Divest S. Africa:	NO	Insurance reform:	NO	Child sick leave:	NO
Assault gun ban:	NO	Parent consent abortion:	YES	Ban AIDS discrim:	NO
Clean Air Act:	YES	Cutting old trees:	YES	Extend death penalty:	–
Lmt product tort:	YES	End mob home rent cont:	YES	Ban offshore oil:	NO

66th Assembly District

Gerald R. Eaves (D)

Few districts in the state have undergone as much change in the last decade as the 66th Assembly District. Once solidly working class, the dusty neighborhoods of Fontana, Rialto, Colton and Ontario grew up around big factories, chief among them Kaiser Steel's huge plant in Fontana. The mill was put inland during World War II to escape shelling from Japanese submarines. After the war, the outlaw Hell's Angeles motorcycle gang began here. But in the 1970s the mill fell on hard times and closed. The future looked bleak. Housing prices remained stagnant.

In the 1980s, western San Bernardino County boomed precisely because those housing prices had stayed low. Big developers came in, built instant neighborhoods and new businesses grew around them.

And political loyalties just weren't what they used to be. When the state Fair Political Practices Commission found that Democrat Terry Goggin had committed a raft of financial indiscretions, he got dumped in a Democratic primary by Rialto Mayor Gerald Eaves, who went on to win the general election. Goggin had won the seat under similar circumstances, challenging a Democratic incumbent in the primary.

In Sacramento, the bearded Eaves has been chiefly noted for one thing — his membership in that rebel group known as "The Gang of Five." The five waged

Gerald R. Eaves

war for a year on Speaker Willie Brown for a variety of political and personal reasons. His fellow rebel, Steve Peace, has described Eaves as the most thoughtful among the bunch. Of the five, Eaves is certainly the quietest.

Eaves was the last of the five punished for his deeds by getting his committee assignments stripped, apparently because the speaker was trying to woo him away from the other four. But after that failed, Brown and his forces threw support behind a 1988 primary challenger, Joe Baca. Eaves won his primary, and re-election, and the Gang of Five made an uneasy peace with Brown in 1989.

PERSONAL: elected 1984; born May 17, 1939, in Miami, Ariz.; home, Rialto; education, San Bernardino Valley College and CSU San Bernardino, no degree; divorced; children, Cheryl, Michael and Laura; Protestant.

CAREER: Steel-mill laborer and manager; insurance agent; Rialto City Council and mayor 1977-84.

COMMITTEES: Governmental Organization; Transportation; Utilities & Commerce.

OFFICES: Capitol, (916) 445-4843; district, 224 N. Riverside Ave., A, Rialto 92376, (714) 820-1902.

REGISTRATION: 55.8% D, 35% R

1988 CAMPAIGN: Eaves – D   55%

Masters – R   41%

Snare – L   4%

RATINGS:

AFL	PIRG	CLCV	NOW	CTA	HAC	CofC	CFB	NRA
93%	63%	68%	92%	G	76%	40%	44%	40%

KEY VOTES:

Divest S. Africa:	YES	Insurance reform:	YES	Child sick leave:	--
Assault gun ban:	YES	Parent consent abortion:	YES	Ban AIDS discrim:	–
Clean Air Act:	–	Cutting old trees:	YES	Extend death penalty:	YES
Lmt product tort:	YES	End mob home rent cont:	NO	Ban offshore oil:	YES

67th Assembly District

John R. Lewis (R)

This major GOP stronghold includes Tustin, Orange, Yorba Linda, Villa Park and portions of Anaheim. The heart of Orange County, this is where Richard Nixon was born and the John Birch Society prospered. Since 1980, the district has been represented by John Lewis, whose roots in business have made him one of the most conservative members of the Legislature. He rarely rises to make a speech on the floor, instead making his statement by pushing his red button – for "no" – more often than most on bill after bill. He carries a relatively light bill load, not out of laziness but out of conviction that government should be minimal.

Although seldom heard from in public, Lewis is a major force in the Assembly Republican caucus, one of

John R. Lewis

the "cavemen" who have dominated the GOP caucus in the 1980s. For years Lewis has been the principal election strategist in the effort to wrest control of the Assembly away from the Democrats and is a much-in-demand designer of election tactics. Lewis has a dry wit and is sharply analytical about the Legislature–a detachment born, perhaps, of the fact that Lewis is one of the wealthiest members as the heir to a dog food fortune.

The 1986 effort was a watershed for the Assembly Republicans, the closest they have come to getting a majority by picking up several seats from the Democrats. But the effort cost Lewis dearly. In 1989, he was indicted by a Sacramento County grand jury and accused of forgery for sending out letters bearing the faked signature of President Ronald Reagan during the '86 campaign. Going to households in several hotly contested races, the letters accused Democratic incumbents of favoring drug dealers.

Lewis has pleaded innocent and contends that the indictment is political, arguing that state Attorney General John Van de Kamp ignored campaign dirty tricks committed by Democratic legislative candidates in seeking charges against him.

PERSONAL: elected 1980; born Nov. 2, 1954, in Los Angeles, Calif.; home, Orange; education, B.A. political science USC; wife, Suzanne Henry; no children; Protestant.

CAREER: aide to Assemblyman Dennis Brown; investment manager.

COMMITTEES: Finance & Insurance; Health. SELECT: Census.

OFFICES: Capitol, (916) 445-2778; district, 1940 N. Tustin 102, Orange 92665, (714) 998-0980.

REGISTRATION: 30.8% D, 59.3% R

1988 CAMPAIGN: Lewis – R   74%
                  Fink – D   26%

RATINGS:	AFL	PIRG	CLCV	NOW	CTA	HAC	CofC	CFB	NRA
	4%	21%	4%	0%	U	13%	84%	55%	100%

KEY VOTES:

Divest S. Africa:	NO	Insurance reform:	NO	Child sick leave:	NO
Assault gun ban:	NO	Parent consent abortion:	YES	Ban AIDS discrim:	NO
Clean Air Act:	NO	Cutting old trees:	YES	Extend death penalty:	YES
Lmt product tort:	YES	End mob home rent cont:	YES	Ban offshore oil:	NO

68th Assembly District

Steve W. Clute (D)

Winding like a desert serpent, the 68th District weaves and bobs through the Democratic neighborhoods of Riverside near the University of California campus and into Moreno Valley – an instant bedroom city created by developers stymied in their efforts to build in growth-controlled Riverside. The district weaves through the San Gorgonio Pass communities of Banning and Beaumont, then turns north through unpopulated Joshua Tree National Monument, avoiding the Republican territory of Palm Springs. Turning southward again, the district includes the rich farmlands of the Coachella Valley and stretches across the desert to the Colorado River in Blythe.

Steve W. Clute

The seat was vacated by the sharp-tongued and troubled Walter Ingalls in 1982 when he fell from favor by backing the wrong horse in the speakership wars of the early '80s. Steve Clute, an ex-Navy pilot, ex-airport manager – and total unknown with perfect teeth – got the nod from Speaker Willie Brown and won the seat. Clute was such an outsider that he walked precincts in the wrong district in his first campaign and was labeled – somewhat unfairly – as a carpetbagger. He did have some claim as a near-native; he was schooled in Pasadena and is a graduate of UC Riverside.

It is easy to mistake Clute's awshucks-flyboy-jock manner as that of a less-than-serious politician. He does at times appear out of place. But he is a tenacious, energetic campaigner, continually underestimated by his Republican foes, who every two years make him their No. 1 statewide target for defeat.

Clute is unfailing honest and remarkably thick-skinned. Generally, Clute sticks to himself when in Sacramento and boards in a small house with a Catholic priest. At home he is more at ease, working the district nearly every weekend in his state-leased four-wheel-drive truck with his brainy wife, Pam, a math instructor at UC Riverside.

California Political Almanac 316

Clute has preferred to stick to local issues like attempting to win a veteran's home in his district and plodding efforts at blocking plans for a tire burning incinerator just outside his district in Rialto. He has labored in the shadow of the more powerful and successful Democratic Sen. Robert Presley. Clute is often taken as a lightweight; one Democratic colleague once called him, behind his back, a "goofy galoot." Nor has he been accepted by Riverside's snooty old families and press. He has made some headway on both fronts but has a ways to go. And he did not help his cause any by skipping out on the last night of the session in 1989, leaving Family Planning $24 million in the lurch.

PERSONAL: elected 1982; born Dec. 8, 1948, in Chicago, Ill.; home, Riverside; Navy 1971-1977; education, B.S. social sciences UC Riverside, M.A. management Webster College, St. Louis; wife, Pamela Chaney; no children; Methodist.
CAREER: airport manager city of Rialto 1980-1982.
COMMITTEES: Ways & Means and subcommittee 6 on transportation (chair); Governmental Organization; Health; Transportation. SELECT: Youth & Drug Abuse Prevention (chair); Aviation; Small Business; Unlicensed Contractors. JOINT: Arts.
OFFICES: Capitol, (916) 445-5416; district, 3600 Lime St., 410, Riverside 92501, (714) 782-3222; 82-632 Highway 111, Indio 92201, (619) 347-0933.
REGISTRATION: 53.8% D, 37.9% R
1988 CAMPAIGN: Clute – D   55%
                  Carroll – R   45%

RATINGS:

AFL	PIRG	CLCV	NOW	CTA	HAC	CofC	CFB	NRA
84%	79%	85%	84%	G	81%	44%	66%	14%

KEY VOTES:

Divest S. Africa:	YES	Insurance reform:	YES	Child sick leave:	–
Assault gun ban:	YES	Parent consent abortion:	YES	Ban AIDS discrim:	NO
Clean Air Act:	YES	Cutting old trees:	NO	Extend death penalty:	–
Lmt product tort:	YES	End mob home rent cont:	NO	Ban offshore oil:	YES

69th Assembly District
Nolan Frizelle (R)

Bedrock conservative country is the best way to describe this Orange County district which includes Irvine, Fountain Valley and parts of Santa Ana, Costa Mesa and Huntington Beach.

Nolan Frizelle is every bit as conservative as his district. He is an optometrist by trade who has long been active in Republican politics and is the past state president of the California Republican Assembly.

Since his election in 1980, Frizelle has, for the most part, remained on the back benches in the Assembly, consistently voting the GOP caucus line. He is irascible, staunchly defends his point of view and is almost impossible to budge on an issue.

One local issue of statewide importance with which Frizelle is identified is toll roads. In an effort to alleviate Orange County's horrible traffic congestion, Frizelle for years proposed authorizing privately built toll roads. His early advocacy eventually led to the passage of bills authorizing toll roads operated by a joint-powers agency.

Another bill of note which carried Frizelle's name was a 1986 measure to give to legislators the same health benefits that state workers received. The provisions of the measure were actually amended into a bill introduced by Frizelle under an agreement between Democratic and Republican leaders.

Nolan Frizelle

PERSONAL: elected 1980; born Oct. 16, 1921, in Los Angeles, Calif.; home, Huntington Beach; USMC WWII; education, attended Stanford University, UC Berkeley, UCLA and USC of Optometry; wife, Ina; children, Roger, David, Diane, Robert, Sabina and Tim; Protestant.

CAREER: Optometrist.

COMMITTEES: Governmental Organization; Natural Resources; Utilities & Commerce. JOINT: State's Economy.

OFFICES: Capitol, (916) 445-8377; district, 17195 Newhope St., 201, Fountain Valley 92708, (714) 662-5503.

REGISTRATION: 32.2% D, 56.5% R

1988 CAMPAIGN: Frizzelle – R 70%
Fennell – D 30%

RATINGS:

AFL	PIRG	CLCV	NOW	CTA	HAC	CofC	CFB	NRA
11%	26%	11%	8%	U	18%	96%	66%	100%

KEY VOTES:

Divest S. Africa: NO	Insurance reform: NO	Child sick leave: –
Assault gun ban: NO	Parent consent abortion: YES	Ban AIDS discrim: NO
Clean Air Act: NO	Cutting old trees: YES	Extend death penalty: YES
Lmt product tort: YES	End mob home rent cont: YES	Ban offshore oil: NO

70th Assembly District

Gilbert W. Ferguson (R)

Imbedded on the tony beachfront of Orange County, this district includes Newport Beach, Balboa Island, Mission Viejo, Laguna Beach, San Clemente and San Juan Capistrano – towns that are the epitome of upscale California suburbanization. Condos, hotels and estates are jammed along the bluffs above the beach. The development here is one of the major reasons voters statewide approved the Coastal Protection Act in 1972, setting up the Coastal Commission and a system for statewide growth control along the shoreline.

Not surprisingly, this stronghold of BMWs and cellular phones has been the most Republican district in the state during the 1980s. However, it has pockets of Democratic voters, particularly in Laguna Beach which has a politically active gay community and turned out by the thousands when Michael Dukakis made a campaign stop in 1988.

The district is so safe for Republicans that there appears nothing that incumbent Gil Ferguson can do to get in trouble with voters back home. He can vote against the interests of Orange County on transportation issues. He can say outrageous things about every non-Anglo community in the state. He can pursue his conservative cause with a religious passion.

Gilbert W. Ferguson

Ferguson was elected to the Assembly in 1982 and became a core member of the conservative "cavemen" who made Pat Nolan the Republican Assembly leader.

Ferguson tends to shoot from the hip. For example, he railed against resolutions to make amends for interring Japanese-Americans in World War II. "The veterans of Pearl Harbor have read this, and they are outraged!" he said in August 1989, bringing Assemblyman Phil Isenberg to his feet, whose wife was among those interred in the war. "You should be ashamed!" huffed Isenberg.

Ferguson is best known for his effort to oust Tom Hayden from the Legislature. Ferguson has called Hayden a traitor for supporting the North Vietnamese during the war and refuses to vote for any bill with Hayden's name on it. Ferguson came close to winning enough votes to have Hayden bounced in 1986.

Until recently, Ferguson also ran a political action committee, Freepac, that doled out campaign money to Republicans.

Ferguson often reminds his audiences of his long military record. He fought in the bloody Tarawa and Saipan battles of World War II, the Inchon landing in Korea and he was on the first full-scale Marine assault in Vietnam in 1965. He has tried to act as a spokesman for veterans groups before the Legislature, although that is not universally welcome among Vietnam vets.

Aside from his pyrotechnics in the Assembly, Ferguson is a lackluster legislator, authoring little legislation of any note and showing scant interest in learning much about the bills before him in committees. He instead spins off elaborate theories about the forces of evil, which usually means Democrats and Communists. He insists that very-Republican U.S. Attorney David Levi was manipulated by Democrats into investigating the Republican honchos in the Assembly.

Ferguson had indicated an interest in running for statewide office but decided to run for the state Senate seat vacated by William Campbell. Ferguson will face Assemblyman Frank Hill, among others, in the GOP primary.

PERSONAL: elected 1984; born April 22, 1923, in St. Louis, Mo.; home, Balboa Island; education, attended USC, University of Maryland, B.A. Akron University; USMC 1942-1968 WWII, Korea and Vietnam; wife, Anita Wollert; children, Mark, Rhonda, Darrel and Jay; Protestant.

CAREER: career officer USMC; president of Corporate Communication, a Newport Beach advertising and public relations firm; corporate vice president of The Gilita Co., a housing development firm; newspaper publisher; columnist for Freedom Newspapers including the Orange County Register; artist.

COMMITTEES: Housing & Community Development (vice chair); Transportation; Local Government. JOINT: School Facilities.

OFFICES: Capitol, (916) 445-7222; district, 4667 MacArthur Blvd., 305, Newport Beach 92660, (714) 756-0665.

REGISTRATION: 27.3% D, 62% R

1988 CAMPAIGN: Ferguson – R   71%
                 Gallups – D   30%

RATINGS:

AFL	PIRG	CLCV	NOW	CTA	HAC	CofC	CFB	NRA
8%	39%	18%	42%	U	22%	92%	66%	100%

KEY VOTES:

Divest S. Africa:	NO	Insurance reform:	NO	Child sick leave:	NO
Assault gun ban:	NO	Parent consent abortion:	YES	Ban AIDS discrim:	NO
Clean Air Act:	NO	Cutting old trees:	YES	Extend death penalty:	YES
Lmt product tort:	YES	End mob home rent cont:	YES	Ban offshore oil:	NO

71st Assembly District

Doris J. Allen (R)

Democrats enjoyed a brief period of dominance in Orange County politics during the 1970s, but one-by-one, Democratic legislators fell to Republican challenges beginning in 1978.

The 71st Assembly District, in the central portion of the county, was one of the last Democratic bastions left, its seat held by Chester Wray. However, Wray was the subject of local derision, some of which made it into the newspapers, for his alleged lack of mental agility. And he fell in 1982 to Doris Allen, who had gained local prominence as a school district trustee and leader of an anti-busing campaign.

Allen, as a woman and a Republican, has not been part of the Assembly's ruling circles. In fact, she's

Doris J. Allen

feuded publicly with one of the more influential Republican leaders, Gerald Felando. The issue that divides Allen and Felando is the one that has become her legislative preoccupation: state regulation of fishing. She sees Felando, who represents San Pedro, as pushing the interests of commercial fishermen over those of sports fishermen.

Allen has found a forum to press her views on the issue by serving as the Republican vice chairman of the Assembly Water, Parks and Wildlife Committee.

PERSONAL: elected 1982; born May 26, 1936, in Kansas City, Mo.; home, Cypress; education, University of Wyoming, no degree, Golden West College, IBM School in Kansas City, Long Beach Community College and Hallmark Business School; divorced; children, Joni and Ron; Protestant.

CAREER: co-owner lighting business, Lampco.

COMMITTEES: Economic Development & New Technologies; Environmental Safety & Toxic Materials; Health; Labor & Employment. JOINT: Review of the Master Plan for Higher Education.

OFFICES: Capitol, (916) 445-6233; district, 5911 Cerritos Ave., Cypress 90630, (714) 821-1500.

REGISTRATION: 41.2% D, 49.5% R

1988 CAMPAIGN: Allen – R   70%

                   Brown – D   31%

RATINGS:

AFL	PIRG	CLCV	NOW	CTA	HAC	CofC	CFB	NRA
16%	44%	46%	50%	U	54%	92%	55%	100%

KEY VOTES:

Divest S. Africa:	NO	Insurance reform:	NO	Child sick leave:	NO
Assault gun ban:	NO	Parent consent abortion:	YES	Ban AIDS discrim:	NO
Clean Air Act:	YES	Cutting old trees:	YES	Extend death penalty:	YES
Lmt product tort:	YES	End mob home rent cont:	YES	Ban offshore oil:	NO

72nd Assembly District

Curtis L. Pringle (R)

The 72nd Assembly District is entirely in Orange County, the bastion of conservatism of California politics. Yet because of its working class and ethnic minority enclaves in cities such as Stanton, Westminster, Garden Grove, Santa Ana and Anaheim, this is one Orange County district where either a Democrat or a Republican has a chance to win.

For 12 years, the district–tailored by Democratic leaders to maximize their chances of holding it–was represented by Democrat Richard Robinson, who left office to seek a congressional seat in 1986, two years after he narrowly defeated retired naval officer and businessman Richard Longshore. Republican Longshore won the seat in 1986, but died in 1988.

Curtis L. Pringle

That set the scene for a furious partisan tug-of-war for the swing district between Democrat Christian F. Thierbach, a law-and-order prosecutor (employed by the Riverside County district attorney), and Republican Curt Pringle, a Garden Grove businessman. In the end, Pringle won by fewer than 800 votes out of more than 63,000 cast. But the victory was and continues to be mired in controversy. The Orange County Republican Central Committee hired uniformed guards to patrol polling places in heavily Hispanic precincts. Democrats charged that the guards were posted in an attempt to intimidate Hispanics. Democrats have asked that the courts overturn the election. The case is still pending.

Pringle continues in office and makes almost no impact on shaping issues in Sacramento, content to vote the party line.

PERSONAL: elected 1988; born June 27, 1959, in Emmetsburg, Iowa; home, Garden Grove; education, B.A. business administration and M.A. public policy CSU Long Beach; wife, Alexis Nease; son, Kyle; Methodist.

CAREER: member and chairman of Garden Grove Planning Commission 1986-1988; partner in Pringle's Draperies, a retail and wholesale manufacturing firm in Anaheim.

COMMITTEES: Revenue and Taxation; Local Government; Elections, Reapportionments & Constitutional Amendments.

OFFICES: Capitol, (916) 445-7333; district, 14550 Magnolia St., 201, Westminster 92683 (714) 895-4334.

REGISTRATION: 53.3% D, 38.1% R

1988 CAMPAIGN: Pringle – R   50%
                 Thierbach – D   50%

RATINGS: NRA
         100%

KEY VOTES:

Insurance reform: YES	Child sick leave:	NO Ban AIDS discrim:	NO
Assault gun ban: NO	End mob home rent cont:	– Cutting old trees:	YES

73rd Assembly District
David G. Kelley (R)

Falling within fast growing Riverside County, the oddly configured district includes Norco's horse ranch country on the county's west end and the affluent sections of Riverside and Corona. The district is sharply bisected by the Democratic 68th Assembly district, lopping off the bedroom community of Moreno Valley for neighboring Steve Clute. After circling to the south, the 73rd District picks up again in the farmland of San Jacinto and the mobile home parks of Hemet, stretching through the exclusive environs of Palm Springs and other decidedly Republican desert resorts.

Republican David Kelley has never had to work hard to stay elected to this district – and work hard, he doesn't. Kelley coasts through legislative life, heard

from occasionally with outbursts against farm worker
unions and the leaders of the Republican Assembly
caucus (whomever they may be at the time).

Kelley's intrigue against then-Republican leader Pat
Nolan got him temporarily stripped of his one important
assignment, a slot on the Assembly Agriculture Committee, where his bona fide expertise on farming and
water issues allow him to make a contribution. Kelley
later got the committee assignment back after he toned
down for awhile but recently he seems just as dead-set
against Republican leader Ross Johnson.

Kelley came to the Legislature relatively late in life.
He is a wealthy citrus farmer with acres of productive
trees in the Hemet-San Jacinto Valley. He was instru-
mental in helping George Deukmejian gain the trust of agricultural interests in the
1982 GOP gubernatorial primary, but Kelley got little in return.

David G. Kelley

Kelley makes occasional noises about running against Democratic Sen. Robert
Presley but has never risked trying. His ranch is actually in the senatorial district of
Republican Marian Bergeson, but Kelley is registered to vote at a mobile home he
owns in Presley's district. Kelley is an astute observer of the Legislature's ways and
foibles but has not, so far, converted that into much political success for himself.

PERSONAL: elected 1978; born Oct. 11, 1928, in Riverside, Calif.; home,
Hemet; education, B.S. agriculture, Calif. State Polytechnic University, Pomona;
USAF 1949-1953; wife, Brigitte; children, Sharon Marie, Bridget Ann, Margaret
Elizabeth, and Kenneth; Lutheran.

CAREER: citrus farmer

COMMITTEES: Agriculture; Environmental Safety & Toxic Materials;
Health; Water, Parks & Wildlife. JOINT: Fairs Allocation & Classification.

OFFICES: Capitol, (916) 445-7852; district, 6840 Indiana Ave., 150, Riverside
92506, (714) 369-6644; 777 E Tahquitz Way,200, Palm Springs 92262, (619) 323-
8301.

REGISTRATION: 40.6% D, 50.4% R

1988 CAMPAIGN: Kelley – R   67%

Parker – D   30%

Beers – L   3%

RATINGS: AFL   PIRG   CLCV   NOW   CTA   HAC   CofC   CFB   NRA
        15%   32%   11%   25%   U   22%   96%   88%   100%

KEY VOTES:

Divest S. Africa:	NO	Insurance reform:	NO	Child sick leave:	NO
Assault gun ban:	NO	Parent consent abortion:	YES	Ban AIDS discrim:	NO
Clean Air Act:	YES	Cutting old trees:	YES	Extend death penalty:	YES
Lmt product tort:	YES	End mob home rent cont:	YES	Ban offshore oil:	NO

74th Assembly District

Robert C. Frazee (R)

Expanding, upscale communities in southern Orange County and northern San Diego County like San Clemente, Camp Pendleton, Oceanside, Rancho Santa Fe and Carlsbad make up this district.

Robert Frazee is another conservative who mirrors his district. Frazee was president of a family-owned fresh-flower growing business when he was elected to the Assembly in 1978. Prior to that, he had been on the Carlsbad City Council for six years, including a stint as mayor. Quiet and courtly, Frazee is generally a pro-business, pro-development vote in the traditional Republican mold. But he has on a few occasions broken from some of his colleagues to try to find solutions for social problems in his district and others.

Robert C. Frazee

He has, for example, backed state funding for farm worker housing, in large part because he has been made aware of the problem in his hometown of Carlsbad, where farm workers are often found living in the brush beneath the plateaus where crops are grown. Frazee also has worked to try to rescue financially troubled trauma centers and emergency medical centers, problems that plague big cities.

The issue on which Frazee was most visible in recent years, however, was his 1987 bill that would require minors to get parental consent before getting abortions. That bill was signed into law but is still being challenged in court.

PERSONAL: elected 1978; born Sept. 1, 1928, in San Luis Rey, Calif.; home, Carlsbad; USMC 1950-1952; wife, Delores Hedrick; children, Susan Marie Kurner and Nancy Anne; Congregational.

CAREER: construction; horticulturist; Carlsbad City Council, mayor 1972-1978; chairman Assembly Republican caucus.

COMMITTEES: Local Government; Governmental Efficiency & Consumer Protection; Natural Resources; Water, Parks & Wildlife. SPECIAL: Policy Research Management. JOINT: Legislative Budget; Ethics Committee; Legislative Retirement; Public Pension Fund Investments; International Trade. SELECT: Unlicensed Contractors; Regional Government; Oil Spill Prevention & Response Preparedness; Calif. Wine Production & Economy.

OFFICES: Capitol, (916) 445-2390; district, 3088 Pio Pico Drive, 200, Carlsbad 92008, (619) 434-1749.

REGISTRATION: 31.2% D, 55.3% R

1988 CAMPAIGN: Frazee – R   69%
                       Melville – D   27%
                       Flanagan –L   4%

RATINGS: AFL   PIRG   CLCV   NOW   CTA   HAC   CofC   CFB   NRA
        18%   42%   22%   25%   U   54%   88%   77%   90%

KEY VOTES:

Divest S. Africa:	NO	Insurance reform:	NO	Child sick leave:	NO
Assault gun ban:	NO	Parent consent abortion:	YES	Ban AIDS discrim:	NO
Clean Air Act:	YES	Cutting old trees:	YES	Extend death penalty:	YES
Lmt product tort:	YES	End mob home rent cont:	YES	Ban offshore oil:	NO

75th Assembly District

Joyce F. "Sunny" Mojonnier (R)

The most exclusive – and Republican – sections of coastal San Diego County comprise this district, taking in the upscale neighborhoods of Coronado, La Jolla, Del Mar and its race track. The district extends eastward to take in the horse country of Poway and its instant housing tracts.

Sunny Mojonnier's last Democratic opponent spent less than $500 on his campaign, and barely noticing him, she breezed to an easy, third-term re-election. That does not mean, however, that all is well personally or politically for the outwardly cheery flower grower. Republican rivals are sharpening their knives for her in 1990, accusing her of rarely visiting her district.

Joyce F. Mojonnier

Personally, Mojonnier has undergone a messy divorce – her third – that has left her financially strapped. The San Diego Union and Los Angeles Times have published unflattering reports that Mojonnier has resorted to dipping into her campaign funds for personal expenses. She also used campaign funds in 1989 to send staffers to a fashion consultant.

Although Mojonnier's voting record on issues is impeccably conservative, she has ticked off the leaders of her party by failing to support them in the Assembly's petty world of leadership intrigue. At the start of the 1989 session, Mojonnier demonstrated her independence by voting not for Democrat Chuck Calderon for speaker, as she had been instructed by Republican leader Ross Johnson, but for Johnson himself – a kind of "in your face" gesture.

Mojonnier has many friends – and even admirers – in Sacramento. She is close to Speaker Brown, who has helped her with personal problems, and chummy with many of her colleagues. She won the undying gratitude – and a $10,000 "honorarium" – from the state's correctional officers for coming off her sick bed after a hysterectomy in 1987 to vote for building a Los Angeles prison.

PERSONAL: elected 1982; born Feb. 17, 1943, in Detroit, Mich.; divorced; children, Jenifer, Craig, Melissa and Marc; Jewish.

CAREER: flower growing and shipping firm; co-owner of travel agency.

COMMITTEES: Economic Development & New Technologies; Governmental Organization; Judiciary; Ways & Means. JOINT: Quincentennial of Voyages of Columbus (vice chair); Arts.

OFFICES: Capitol, (916) 445-2112; district, 3368 Governor Drive, Suite C, San Diego 92122, (619) 457-5775.

REGISTRATION: 33.5% D, 51.7% R

1988 CAMPAIGN: Mojonnier – R   65%
                      Christian – D   30%
                      Murphy – L   3%
                      Schoenberg – P&F 2%

RATINGS:

AFL	PIRG	CLCV	NOW	CTA	HAC	CofC	CFB	NRA
20%	53%	27%	50%	U	40%	88%	77%	100%

KEY VOTES:

Divest S. Africa:	NO	Insurance reform:	–
Assault gun ban:	NO	Parent consent abortion:	–
Clean Air Act:	NO	Cutting old trees:	YES
Lmt product tort:	YES	End mob home rent cont:	YES

Child sick leave:	NO
Ban AIDS discrim:	NO
Extend death penalty:	YES
Ban offshore oil:	–

76th Assembly District

Patricia Rae Hunter (R)

The district stretches from the plush suburbs northeast of San Diego, including Escondido, up the spine of "North County," with its avocado groves and housing tracts roughly following Interstate 15, and into the hot desert of Riverside County. It includes some of the state's fastest growing suburbs, desert retirement communities and small towns in the hills that seem a thousand miles removed from California's coast. The area is staunchly Republican, with a 54 percent to 33 percent registration advantage over Democrats.

Patricia Rae Hunter

It hardly seemed the place where a special election would attract national attention, but the primary and the run-off to fill the unexpired term of the late Bill Bradley did just that for one reason – they were among the first elections in America after the U.S. Supreme Court gave state's more power to restrict abortion. Forces on both sides of the issue poured money and people into the campaigns, and said a victory by their side would be a harbinger of things to come.

Republican Tricia Hunter, a Bonita nurse and former president of the state Board of Registered Nursing, narrowly survived the primary, then won the run-off, mostly on the strength of her pro-choice stand. She was the only pro-choice Republican in the field and got a big boost to her campaign from the California Abortion Rights

Action League, the National Organization for Women and the California Nurses Association.

Hunter's campaign made abortion one of the central issues of the election, drawing support not only from moderate Republicans but also from Democrats who understood that in their strongly Republican district Hunter was their best pro-choice vote. Hunter's Republican primary opponent, Poway business consultant Dick Lyles, was one of the staunchest opponents of abortion in the race. After Hunter beat him by barely 500 votes in the primary, Lyles mounted a strong write-in campaign with the help of the National Right to Life Committee. Still, Hunter won the run-off handily. The Democrats were never a factor.

Hunter, who spent much of her campaign insisting she has good Republican credentials, nonetheless is relatively moderate. She presented a problem for Assembly GOP Leader Ross Johnson, who promised to remain neutral, then ended up raising money for Lyles in the primary. Johnson, an opponent of abortion, mended a few fences by endorsing Hunter in the general election, but Hunter represents yet another caucus member who would be happy with someone else at the helm. In 1990, Johnson must decide whether to try to close the breach with Hunter or to support a primary opponent.

PERSONAL: Elected 1989 (special election); born June 15, 1952, in Appleton, Minn.; home, Bonita; education, B.S. nursing UC San Diego, M.A. nursing UCLA; husband, Clark Hunter; no children; Lutheran.

CAREER: surgical nurse; director surgical services Chula Vista Community Hospital; appointed by Deukmejian to state Board of Registered Nursing.

COMMITTEES: none assigned.

OFFICES: not opened.

REGISTRATION: 33% D, 54% R

1989 CAMPAIGN: Hunter – R   49%
                       Lyles – write-in   38%
                       Correia – D   13%
                       Boser – write-in   0.1%

RATINGS and **KEY VOTES:** newly elected.

77th Assembly District

Carol J. Bentley (R)

Expanding from the east-west artery of Interstate 8, this district includes the settled portions of eastern San Diego County, including El Cajon, La Mesa and portions of San Diego proper. The district is in the heart of San Diego's middle-class Republican communities and was represented for nearly a decade by Larry Stirling.

Stirling vacated the Assembly seat in 1988 and moved to the Senate upon the retirement of Sen. Jim Ellis. His successor, Carol Bentley, a personable – though unaccomplished – aide to Ellis, won a GOP primary against San Diego City

Councilwoman Gloria McColl. Bentley's election also signaled that the district's center of gravity had moved to El Cajon and the suburbs.

Thus was born from total obscurity a new San Diego area political figure who in less than a year stands to go even further. At the end of the 1989 session, Stirling quit the Senate to accept a judgeship in San Diego – and Republican leaders have quickly endorsed Bentley in a special election. However, Bentley's inexperience and relative obscurity could prove a problem even in a district where Republicans have a 10 point registration edge. The biggest anchor on her future could be her anti-abortion stance. A special election in nearby Escondido in August 1988 gave a victory to Tricia Hunter, a pro-choice Republican who was targeted for defeat by Sacramento GOP leaders. Other Republicans may emerge to challenge Bentley – and Democratic Assemblywoman Lucy Killea, who is pro-choice, is in the race for the Senate seat and taking heart in Escondido's election results.

Carol J. Bentley

PERSONAL: elected 1988; born Feb. 26, 1945, in Riverside, Calif.; home, El Cajon; education, B.S. business, San Diego State University; husband, David Bentley; no children; Presbyterian.

CAREER: administrative assistant to Sens. Jack Schrade and Jim Ellis 1980-1988; political campaign consultant.

COMMITTEES: Aging & Long Term Care; Governmental Efficiency & Consumer Protection; Public Safety.

OFFICES: Capitol, (916) 445-6161; district, 2755 Navajo Road, El Cajon 92020, (619) 464-7204.

REGISTRATION: 37.2% D, 50.2% R

1988 CAMPAIGN: Bentley – R   64%
Hornreich – D   32%
Deutsch – L   4%

RATINGS: NRA
90%

KEY VOTES:

Insurance reform: NO	Child sick leave: NO	Ban AIDS discrim: NO
Assault gun ban: NO	End mob home rent cont: YES	Cutting old trees: YES

78th Assembly District

Lucy L. Killea (D)

This San Diego district includes the older fashionable neighborhoods near the zoo and Balboa Park, including largely gay Hillcrest, and the stately Republican streets just to the east. The district extends eastward into the black sections of East

San Diego. The district is marginal for the Democrats and that has prompted a number of Republicans to try mounting a strong challenge against Democrat Lucy Killea.

What they have forgotten is that Killea is generally popular in her district and listens to good campaign advice. Killea, an ex-councilwoman with plenty of community contacts, has run several masterful campaigns, masterminded by Richie Ross and Craig Reynolds. In 1986 her television commercials may have been the best of the year, featuring her jogging on the beach to an upbeat jingle, "Running with Lucy Killea."

Killea's route to the Legislature is a bit unusual. Her **Lucy L. Killea** resume was already bulging before she got to Sacramento. Killea was an Army intelligence officer in World War II and was then detailed to the State Department as aide to Eleanor Roosevelt during the first general assembly of the United Nations. She went on to serve nine years in the CIA in the 1950s. Killea later lectured in history, and is a bona fide expert on Mexican border affairs, having served as executive director of Fronteras de las Californias before her election to the City Council in 1978.

While in the Assembly, Killea toyed with running for mayor after the demise of Roger Hedgecock in 1985, but she stepped back for another Democrat, the more charismatic Maureen O'Connor. In October 1989, Killea decided to run for a state Senate seat opened when Larry Stirling accepted a judgeship.

At first glance, it would appear Killea stands no chance – the Senate district has a 10 percent registration edge for Republicans. However, Killea is solidly pro-choice on abortion and her potential Republican rival, first-termer Carol Bentley, is anti-abortion. That could help Killea in a city that may be conservative on some issues but can be liberal on social issues.

As an Assembly member, Killea has focused primarily on her committee work devoted to the tedium of solid and hazardous waste issues, authoring numerous bills in that area, and was involved in the 1985 legislative effort that brought forth the state's "workfare" program. She has also concentrated on international trade incentives and Mexican border issues, both of major interest to the San Diego area. One of the most wooden speakers in the Legislature, she rarely speaks during floor debates.

Killea may well win a Senate seat. But it is seriously questionable whether the Democrats could keep her Assembly seat without her.

PERSONAL: elected 1982; born July 31, 1922, in San Antonio, Tex.; home, San Diego; Army 1943-1948 WWII; education, B.A. history Incarnate World College, Tex.; M.A. history University of San Diego; Ph.D. Latin American history UC San Diego; husband, John F. Killea; children, Paul and Jay; Catholic.

CAREER: State Department personal secretary and administrative assistant to Eleanor Roosevelt (delegate to United Nations 1946); Central Intelligence Agency 1948-1957; U.S. Information Agency 1957-1960; vice president Fronteras de las Californias; university lecturer; research and teaching assistant; San Diego City Council 1978-1982.

COMMITTEES: Economic Development & New Technologies; Rules; Transportation, Utilities & Commerce; Ways & Means. SELECT: Ethics; Waste Reduction, Use & Recycling (chair). JOINT: International Trade (chair); Quincentennial of the Voyages of Columbus; Organized Crime & Gang Violence; Oversight on GAIN Implementation; Rules.

OFFICES: Capitol, (916) 445-7210; district, 2550 Fifth Ave., 152, San Diego 92103-6619, (619) 232-2046.

REGISTRATION: 46% D, 41.1% R

1988 CAMPAIGN: Killea – D   60%

                   Wear – R   38%

                   McMillen – L   2%

RATINGS:

AFL	PIRG	CLCV	NOW	CTA	HAC	CofC	CFB	NRA
91%	89%	89%	92%	S	85%	20%	44%	30%

KEY VOTES:

Divest S. Africa:	YES	Insurance reform:	YES	Child sick leave:	YES
Assault gun ban:	YES	Parent consent abortion:	NO	Ban AIDS discrim:	YES
Clean Air Act:	YES	Cutting old trees:	NO	Extend death penalty:	YES
Lmt product tort:	YES	End mob home rent cont:	NO	Ban offshore oil:	YES

79th Assembly District

Peter R. Chacon (D)

The black and Latino neighborhoods of East San Diego comprise this safely Democratic district. Meandering along the dusty mesas, the district also includes Lemon Grove, Spring Valley and the airport. A tongue of the district extends down the middle of San Diego Bay to take in a small South bay neighborhood. While the rest of San Diego has grown and gotten richer, this area has only seen more crime and poverty.

Democrat Pete Chacon has served in the Assembly for two decades, having been plucked from the obscurity of a teaching career by Democratic leaders in need of a candidate. But he has never been much of a player either in Sacramento or San Diego. He has authored housing and bilingual education legislation, matters of large concern to his district.

Peter R. Chacon

Chacon was chairman of the Assembly's reapportionment committee, but lost the post during the last reapportionment. Once redistricting was finished, he got his chairmanship back – when it has mattered the least.

Inside the Capitol, Chacon is chiefly noted for keeping his family on the campaign payroll. He skated out from under an investigation by the state attorney general's office in 1989 for accepting a $7,500 honorarium from check cashing businesses, and then killing a bill that was odious to those businesses. While prosecutors said that the timing of the transaction was "suspicious," the investigation was dropped for lack of evidence.

In 1989, Chacon served as the Hispanic caucus chairman, but he showed ineptness when he went before the Fair Political Practices Commission seeking an exemption from Proposition 73 donation limits. It turned out he hadn't done his homework; he could have safely applied for a tax exempt status from Internal Revenue Service and saved everyone the trouble of untangling the campaign laws.

PERSONAL: elected 1970; born June 10, 1925, in Phoenix, Ariz.; home, San Diego; Army Air Corps 1943-1945 WWII; education, B.A. elementary education and M.A. school administration San Diego State University; wife, Jean Louise Picone; children, Chris, Paul, Ralph and Jeff; Catholic.

CAREER: school administrator.

COMMITTEES: Elections, Reapportionment & Constitutional Amendments (chair); Finance & Insurance; Governmental Efficiency & Consumer Protection; Housing & Community Development. JOINT: Quincentennial of the Voyages of Columbus; State's Economy.

OFFICES: Capitol, (916) 445-7610; district, 1129 G St., San Diego 92101, (619) 232-2405.

REGISTRATION: 58.3% D, 29.4% R

1988 CAMPAIGN: Chacon – D   65%
Gahn – R   27%
Shea – L   4%

RATINGS:

AFL	PIRG	CLCV	NOW	CTA	HAC	CofC	CFB	NRA
88%	79%	92%	75%	S	85%	32%	44%	0%

KEY VOTES:

Divest S. Africa:	YES	Insurance reform:	YES	Child sick leave:	YES
Assault gun ban:	YES	Parent consent abortion:	YES	Ban AIDS discrim:	YES
Clean Air Act:	YES	Cutting old trees:	YES	Extend death penalty:	YES
Lmt product tort:	YES	End mob home rent cont:	YES	Ban offshore oil:	NO

80th Assembly District

J. Stephen Peace (D)

This district begins along the shoreline of San Diego Bay, where the once sleepy bedroom communities of National City and Chula Vista have awakened in the 1980s. Chula Vista is building ritzy bayside hotels and home developers are paving the mesas above. The district extends eastward along the Mexican border to include all of Imperial County, a breadbasket farming region that is among the poorest in the state.

The problems of this district are those of Mexico, where the First and Third worlds crash headlong into each other. Illegal aliens and drugs are smuggled across the border at Otay Mesa and elsewhere. Sewage from Tijuana leaks across the border into San Diego and fouls the beaches and horse farms nearby. Eastward, the New River carries highly toxic industrial and agricultural poisons – like DDT – from Mexico into the Salton Sea in Imperial County.

J. Stephen Peace

The Democrat who has represented this district, Steve Peace, was once known for two things; he was the producer of "Attack of the Killer Tomatoes," a cult classic film, and he was Willie Brown's man to see in San Diego. If someone there wanted something from the speaker, they were advised to go see Peace. Socially chummy with the speaker, Peace was considered a genius at political strategy – and that may be why the speaker tolerated Peace so long. Many of Peace's colleagues could not stand him, considering him immature and obnoxious. His fabled fight with the Senate's Al Alquist (when witnesses heard Peace call Alquist a "senile old pedophile") earned him the undying hatred of the Senate but Brown protected him.

Then Peace and four of his colleagues turned on Brown, dubbing themselves the "Gang of Five" in 1987. They pulled parliamentary maneuvers for a year, tying the Assembly up in a world of petty intrigues. Peace again showed his strategic skill. For a year the five challenged Brown, eventually making peace in 1989.

As a legislator, Peace has paid attention to the border issues that so plague his district, working on getting a sewage treatment plant for the area. He has labored for years over a low-level nuclear waste compact with other states (which got him in trouble with Alquist) and has kept proposed nuclear waste dumps out of Democratic districts. And Peace still makes loud, ranting speeches on the floor on virtually any issue that strikes his fancy.

PERSONAL: elected 1982; born March 30, 1953, in San Diego, Calif.; home, Chula Vista; education, B.A. political science UC San Diego; wife, Cheryl; children, Chad, Bret and Clint; Methodist.

CAREER: partner Four Square Productions of National City, a film production firm; aide to Assemblyman Wadie Deddeh 1976-1980 and Assemblyman Larry Kapiloff 1980-1981.

COMMITTEES: Human Services; Revenue & Taxation; Water, Parks & Wildlife. SPECIAL: Policy Research Management. SELECT: Committee on Radioactive Waste Disposal & Fusion Technology.

OFFICES: Capitol, (916) 445-7556; district, 430 Davidson St., Suite B, Chula Vista 92010, (619) 426-1617; 1101 Airport Road B, Imperial 92251, (619) 352-3101.
REGISTRATION: 50.5% D, 37.1% R
1988 CAMPAIGN: Peace – D 59%
Baldwin – R 39%
Myrseth – L 2%

RATINGS:

AFL	PIRG	CLCV	NOW	CTA	HAC	CofC	CFB	NRA
79%	63%	67%	84%	S	72%	68%	88%	40%

KEY VOTES:

Divest S. Africa: YES	Insurance reform: YES	Child sick leave: YES
Assault gun ban: NO	Parent consent abortion: YES	Ban AIDS discrim: YES
Clean Air Act: –	Cutting old trees: YES	Extend death penalty: YES
Lmt product tort: YES	End mob home rent cont: NO	Ban offshore oil: YES

6

Lobbyists–a vital link in the process

When infamous lobbyist Artie Samish appeared on the cover of Collier's in 1949, posed with a ventriloquist's dummy on his knee, he etched an image into the political consciousness of California: lobbyists as puppeteers standing in the shadows pulling strings while legislators, the marionettes, danced vacuously on the public stage. Reality is much more complicated and far less sinister. Lobbyists are neither good nor evil. They have become, however, a linchpin in the legislative process.

Lobbyists are a critical link between lawmakers and the industries, professional associations, consumer advocates and other combatants in California politics. It is the lobbyists who carry the intricate information about the details of an industry or the desires of a professional group to the people who make the laws. The lion's share of the bills introduced in the Legislature are proposed and at least sketched out by lobbyists. They also help devise legislative strategies, manage bills, work with staff members, organize letter-writing campaigns, produce grass-roots pressure and, often, manage the media.

Legislative advocates, as they prefer to call themselves, are the experienced professionals in the multilayered, arcane world of California politics. They deal in a bewildering system that has more twists and turns and hidden hallways than the state Capitol. It is an environment in which the unguided can easily end up running a corridor that goes nowhere.

The lobbyists who are influential are successful for a host of reasons. Chief among them is the ability of their clients to make campaign contributions – or "participate in the political process," as it is euphemistically called in the lobbying trade. But that is only one tool, and few advocates remain effective for long using money alone. The vast majority of lobbyists also trade heavily on their knowledge

333

of the Legislature and the industries they represent, their political acumen, the grass-roots connections of their clients and, perhaps most important, their individual relationships with elected officials and staff.

LOBBYISTS GO BIG-TIME

One of most profound changes in the "third house," as the lobbying corps is known in Capitol jargon, is the shift to the full-service lobbying company. There are fewer and fewer one- or two-person operations that rely on their good will in the Capitol and their overall knowledge of the political system. Instead, as in Washington, D.C., a cadre of firms have sprouted with specialists, in-house attorneys, public relations experts – all of which look and run like law firms. In fact, to explain their role, lobbyists most often compare themselves with lawyers. They say they are advocates, plain and simple. They are hired to win today and again tomorrow and to protect their clients just as lawyers do whatever is necessary, and possible, to protect their clients. And California's massive growth has created even more demand for these advocates. As the booms continue in population, business and government, as society continues to increase in complexity, as every interest in the state becomes more and more interwoven with government, the demand for lobbyists increases.

In 1977, the secretary of state's office registered 538 lobbyists and 761 clients who hired lobbyists. In 1989, there were 826 lobbyists and 1,193 clients. Ironically, the passage of anti-government, anti-tax Proposition 13 in 1978 helped fuel that growth by centralizing financing of schools and local governments in Sacramento; interests with a stake in those finances, including local governments and schools themselves, muscled up by hiring more lobbyists in the capital.

The best measure of growth is the amount of money spent lobbying the Legislature. According to the Fair Political Practices Commission, $40 million was spent on lobbying during the 1975-76 session of the Legislature. In 1987, just the first half of the 1987-88 session, more than $75 million was spent by trade associations, corporations, utilities and others on lobbying. In 1988, $82.9 million was spent. The total for the 1987-88 legislative season was nearly 295 percent greater than 12 years before.

A GROWTH INDUSTRY

Lobbyists say privately that a major reason for the increased demand for their services is that everybody else is getting a lobbyist these days. Interests entering the legislative field feel like soldiers without rifles if they can not rely on the weapons of a good lobbyist.

But it is not just mutual armament in dealing with the Legislature that is sparking the explosion of lobbyists. Industries and interests are coming to realize that all levels of government, including state agencies and commissions, require expert representation. The state's gigantic bureaucracy can be even more unfathomable than the Legislature. A growing number of lobbyists are former state officials who have learned the pathways and players in key state agencies. And they are finding themselves in demand from a variety of interests with huge stakes in the decisions dealt out by the bureaucracy. For example, the state Department of Food and Agriculture and the state Department of Health Services have been playing key roles in defining and administering Proposition 65, the 1986 Safe Drinking Water Act. That law could have a multimillion-dollar impact on scores of businesses. As a result, chemical, pesticide, agricultural and other California companies with a stake have lobbyists working those agencies.

The labyrinthine legislative process and the ever-increasing demands on lawmakers' time and attention make it nearly impossible for someone outside of the inner political circles to have much of an impact on the workings of the Legislature. Given the lobbyists' essential role then, it would seem the door is open for them to play puppet masters in the way Artie Samish once did. But that is not the case. In fact, the same massive and complex system that makes lobbyists so vital prevents any one advocate or interest from asserting control. There are so many interests and there is so much pressure from every quarter, that it is virtually impossible for one lobbyist, or even a handful, to indiscriminately muscle bills through.

One reason for that is that it takes a monumental effort to push any measure burdened with controversy through the Capitol. The bill must survive at least two committees and a floor vote in each house, possibly a conference committee and other floor votes, then must win the governor's signature. Those are seven chances, at a minimum, to kill a bill. Passing it means winning at every step. Defeating it takes only one victory. And it is easy for many lobbyists, especially those representing single-issue interests, to confuse the issue or throw enough doubt into lawmakers' minds to get them to vote against a bill or at least to be absent so there are not enough votes to make it pass. For legislators, there is always less political damage in sticking with the status quo, whether by voting no or just by not voting. Lobbyists often simply encourage the old political ploy that many legislators use well – when in doubt, take a hike. In fact, much of what lobbyists do is defensive. They spend much more energy trying to kill bills that may hurt their clients than breaking new ground or pushing proposals.

ALL SHAPES, SIZES AND SKILLS

So with all those lobbyists wandering the Capitol representing all those interests, the teeming atmosphere of California politics looks at first glance as if it might fit the picture of the marketplace of ideas and interests envisioned by the framers of American democracy. But only at first glance. The Capitol is not a place where decision-makers blend those ideas and choose simply on merit. And if any one set of players is responsible for that, it would be lobbyists.

For one reason, lobbyists, like anyone else, come in a variety of levels of skill, influence and experience. The better ones often win regardless of the merits of their case, because victories in the Capitol are based on politics, not virtue. Each category of lobbyists brings its own weapons and weaknesses. Those categories include:

•Public interest lobbyists: Often called "white hat lobbyists," these are the people who work for consumer groups, good government organizations, environmentalists or any of those people who seem to represent the public at large. These lobbyists, for the most part, are the weakest in the Capitol. Their best weapon is public sentiment. Because of that, they are about the only lobbyists consistently willing to talk with reporters and to make their issues public. They often resort to calling press conferences to announce their positions or unhappiness, hoping it will generate enough of that public sentiment to influence the votes of legislators. But these lobbyists have little to offer lawmakers other than public approval. They usually have meager resources and no money. And, as often as not, they are fighting against powerful interests who have more lobbyists and more money. Unless the issue is something that will ignite the public – and there are few of those, since most Californians pay scant attention to the Legislature – these people spend much of their time working on damage control rather than outright victory.

•Organization lobbyists: These are the advocates who work for one specific organization, such as the California Association of Realtors or the Association of California Hospitals and Health Systems. Depending on the size of their organizations, these lobbyists can have tremendous resources, a large grass-roots network and fat campaign war chests to dole out. And depending on their causes, they too sometimes feel comfortable using the press and public sentiment to help push their issues. But organization lobbyists also have some disadvantages. Since their legislative goals have to be agreed upon by the association's directors and membership, they often have less flexibility to adjust in midstream. In addition, they spend a good deal of their efforts organizing their association, and trying to keep internal politics out of state politics.

•Contract lobbyists: These are the hired guns, the quintessence of what the public envisions as the lobbying corps. And for the major contract lobbyists and the powerful lobbying firms handling large client loads, that image generally fits. The most successful contract lobbyists are the very essence of political power. They are the ones who have been around the Capitol for years, who know the game from every angle and who have enough of a client list, campaign war chest, history in politics, stored up favors and political acumen to make lawmakers listen. But contract lobbyist come in many sizes and shapes. Some work for public-interest groups, which forces them to operate like those "white hat lobbyists." Others represent cities or semi-public entities and can distribute few campaign contributions. Still others work for smaller, less powerful companies or industries and have never gathered enough clout to make the Capitol's inner circles.

•Company lobbyists: Some of the larger companies that play in California politics have their own in-house lobbyists, who are often a cross between association and contract lobbyists. Company lobbyists are some of the real inside players in the Capitol, with the resources and money to be influential. And like many contract lobbyists – and legislators – they often are most comfortable functioning out of the glare of public scrutiny. Since they work for only one client, they generally have the flexibility to compromise and roll with the inevitable political punches. However, because they only represent one company, no matter how powerful, they usually need to work within coalitions or at least to try to eliminate opposition from companies within their industry. If they cannot, they can find themselves as one lone voice with little clout.

THE IMPORTANCE OF MONEY

For lobbyists, success goes to those who understand best the nature of influence. They understand timing, organization and the value of information. They have built relationships with legislators, consultants, even a key secretary or two. And, for the big-time lobbyists, they understand the connection between politics and money.

It is an absolute axiom of modern political life, especially in a state such as California, that a politician without money is not a politician for long. In these days of computer-aided, television-oriented, high-tech campaigns, no candidate without a healthy chunk of cash can hope to win. And if there is any group that is aware of this, it is the lobbyists. They have found themselves squarely in the middle of the campaign financing free-for-all.

Lobbyists have become the main conduits for contributions, as well as the pipeline to their clients for the requests for funds from politicians. But lobbyists are more the vehicle for those campaign contributions than the reason. Take lobbyists out of the picture and the interests that contribute and the legislators who raise money would still find ways to connect. In fact, many lobbyists portray themselves as victims of a system that requires nearly constant fund-raising. That view is in vivid contrast to the widely held image of lobbyists padding the halls of the Capitol hoping to corrupt legislators with the bundles of bills in their briefcases.

Victims or not, those with money still do win their share of Capitol battles. And the need for cash is a fact of life lobbyists frequently have to sell to their clients. Without money, the lobbyists lose access to legislators.

The actual impact of campaign contributions on the drafting of laws can be small since many other lobbyists and interests are also buying access. Generally, money plays the deciding role only in turf fights that do not affect a legislator's district or do not become an issue in the media, such as when two financial interests like banks and savings and loans battle over state regulations.

It is clear most lobbyists understand the impact of money: It is always easier to lobby for a client who has it. And the lobbyists with money almost never lose a key vote of great significance to their clients. Whether they are happy about it or not, lobbyists realize that if most other factors are equal, an interest with money will beat one without.

While the influence of money is not necessarily direct, it is thorough. For starters, the big-moneyed interests can afford to hire the best lobbyists, who in turn use that money to conduct public relations campaigns, to organize in the districts of legislators and to hire enough staff to make sure nothing is missed.

In addition, the skills of those top lobbyists often include the judicious deployment of the client's campaign contributions. Many lobbyists make sure a client's money goes to legislators in position to help that client, but they also funnel some of that money to the lawmakers who have been consistent friends. That in turn, adds clout to the lobbyist's own status independent of his or her clients.

When a lawmaker is approached by a top lobbyist such as Clayton Jackson, who counts insurance companies among his clients, that lawmaker is not simply thinking about the one employer whose cause Jackson may be advocating, but about Jackson's long list of clients, whose combined campaign contribution totals reached more than $2 million annually in recent years. Legislators have too little time to see all the people who want to argue their cases. And when push comes to shove and there are two lobbyists waiting in the office lobby, the one who will get in is always the one who has consistently contributed to campaigns.

ALL RELATIONSHIPS ARE PERSONAL

In fact, the investment of campaign money earns more than simple access because, as in any business, when two people have dealt with and grown to trust each other over the years, a relationship develops. This brings up another primary rule of California politics: Everything that happens in the Capitol comes down to basic human relationships, rather than institutional ones. Both lobbyists and legislators hold nothing more precious than their relationships with each other. If a lawmaker likes you and trusts you, he will listen to you. If a lobbyist thinks of you as a friend, he will make sure you receive useful information and equally useful campaign contributions.

In the storm that is Capitol politics, both legislators and lobbyists are grateful for any safe harbor they can find. For veteran lawmakers and influential lobbyists, those symbiotic harbors often grow into genuine friendships. And those friendships, creations of convenience though they may be, can have as much influence on California's laws as any other aspect of the state's politics.

The most marked advantage of a lobbyist's friendship with a legislator is that member's willingness to listen to a friend argue for or against a bill. That becomes even more significant during the end-of-session tempests, when hundreds of bills can be dispatched in a few hours. That is when bills are changing, members are under the gun and a lobbyist doesn't have time to document arguments about a set of amendments. Members are left with no choice but to ask the lobbyists if the changes are acceptable to his or her clients. If they trust each other, the lobbyist can look the legislator in the eye and tell him the truth – with neither feeling nervous.

A study done for former Assembly Speaker Jesse Unruh during the mid-1970s asked legislators what they thought was the most corrupting influence in politics. The answer that came back the most often was "friendship." One legislator said, "I never voted for a bad bill, but I voted for a lot of bad authors."

Former lawmakers are one rapidly growing class of lobbyists that begin with ready-made friendships in the Capitol. These people have worked together, seen each other almost every day, experienced the same pressures and developed the same interests. They have an emotional bond like university alumni. Approximately two-dozen former legislators lobby either full or part time. Others are not registered, either because they do not lobby enough to qualify as official lobbyists or because their contacts and connections are less direct.

The list of some of the more prominent or active among the former legislators includes former Sens. John Briggs, Clair Burgener, Dennis Carpenter, John Foran, Bob Wilson and George Zenovich; and former Assembly members Gordon Duffy, Jean Duffy, Joe Gonsalves, John Knox, Frank Murphy Jr., Robert Naylor, Paul Priolo and John P. Quimby. Even James Garibaldi, the dean of the lobbying corps who is known around the Capitol as "the Judge" for his years on the Superior Court bench, was an assemblyman in the mid-1930s.

In addition, former legislative or administration staff members turn their expertise and inside relationships into influential lobbying jobs, often focusing on the committees and subject areas in which they had been involved. There are dozens of lobbyists who were ex-legislative staff members, but the largest group is probably the legion of former aides to Assembly Speaker Willie Brown, which includes Kathleen Snodgrass, Jackson Gualco, John Mockler and Kent Stoddard.

Administration officials, of course, find themselves in great demand to lobby the agencies they once worked in. The ranks of administration-officials-turned-lobbyist include Michael Franchetti, Gov. Deukmejian's first finance director; David Swoap, once a health and welfare secretary; David Ackerman, a former deputy business, transportation and housing undersecretary; Rodney Blonien, an ex-corrections undersecretary; and former Deukmejian aide Timothy Flanigan. Former Deukmejian chief of staff Steven Merksamer must also be included in that list, although he is not a registered lobbyist. Merksamer's law/lobbying firm – Nielsen, Merksamer, Hodgson, Parrinello & Mueller – represents some of America's largest companies and is one of the most influential firms on the state scene.

There are also top lobbyists who were state officials in former administrations, including Richard B. Spohn, Gov. Edmund G. Brown Jr.'s director of the state Department of Consumer Affairs; and George Steffes, an aide to Gov. Ronald Reagan in the early 1970s.

A study in 1986 by political scientists Jerry Briscoe and Charles Bell, who were then at the University of the Pacific and the University of California, Davis, respectively, found 36 percent of the registered lobbyists had served in government. This steady stream from the Capitol to the third house periodically inspires "anti-revolving door" bills from lawmakers or outside groups such as Common Cause. Those proposals generally would prohibit state officials and lawmakers from lobbying their former houses or agencies for a year or two after leaving state service. But few of those bills have come close to passage and none has reached the governor's desk. In addition, both supporters and opponents of those proposals agree that it is not possible to legislate away the friendships that are an inherent part of the system.

The fact that former lawmakers and staffers are in demand as lobbyists underscores the changes in the third house in recent years. One of the biggest changes may be the nature of the relationships between lawmakers and lobbyists. Today, those relationships most often are based on shared interests and friendships. Sometimes families of lawmakers and lobbyists play together on weekends or holidays. That is a far cry from the days of shared duck hunting or drunken revelry in the 1930s, '40s and '50s, when Artie Samish said he supplied his legislative friends with "a baked potato, a girl or money."

While Samish, who was imprisoned for tax-evasion in 1956, was probably the most extreme case in California, many lobbyists used a few good meals or a round of drinks to create a bridge to lawmakers. With that bridge, they could then argue the merits of their cases. Those bridges were built on an old-fashioned, good-ol'-boy network. Some of the more well-known lobbyists ran up tabs of $1,500-a-month wining and dining legislators. And, not infrequently, lawmakers signed a lobbyist's name to a restaurant or bar tab even when the lobbyist was not there.

There also were regular, institutionalized social affairs paid for by a number of lobbyists and open to all lawmakers and many key members of the staff. The most spectacular of those was the "Moose Milk," a lavish lunch and open bar held Thursdays in the former El Mirador Hotel across from the Capitol. There also was the lunch at the Derby Club on Tuesdays and the "Clam and Corral" at the Senator Hotel on Wednesdays. The purpose was nothing more than good times, good will and, of course, access.

The era of good old boys has not entirely disappeared. That is apparent in the lack of women in the upper echelons of the lobbying corps. Although there are a number of women lobbyists who are influential and successful, most are connected with firms run by men, and virtually all of the top-earning lobbyists are men.

However, the backslapping days when legislators relied almost solely on lobbyists for everything from meals to information began to change in 1966, when Californians made their Legislature full time. That meant career politicians and full-time staff. No longer were lobbyists the only people who understood the state's industries and the fine points in the bills. Lawmakers and their larger staffs had more time and more information of their own.

And with the professionalization of the Legislature, lawmakers began to develop their own areas of expertise and fiefdoms to protect. Specialists, usually committee chairmen, emerged in banking, insurance, health and dozens of others fields. For lobbyists that had two implications.

THE OLD-BOY NETWORK BREAKS DOWN

First, that meant the lobbyists had to have better, more specific information. A simple, "trust me on this one," became less convincing. Lobbyist had to learn the fine points of the industries and clients they represented. And second, with power spread through the committee chairmen and their staffs, it became increasingly difficult for just a few lobbyists to handle most major legislation. So lobbyists, too, became specialists. Not only did they come to concentrate on specific subjects, but different lobbyists became valuable to clients because of their relationships with specific lawmakers. And many clients, especially larger companies or industries, hire two, three or even a half-dozen lobbyists to guard their interests. In those cases, one firm will act as the major lobbyist that tracks bills and plans the strategies, while the others are called upon to handle specific issues or committees or legislators.

The biggest step in the transformation of the lobbying corps from the days of camaraderie to a law-firm atmosphere was Proposition 9, the Political Reform Act passed in 1974. That initiative required detailed disclosure and limited the gifts and meals lobbyists could buy legislators to $10 a month. With that act, the Moose Milk and the free lunches and dinners disappeared, eventually to be replaced by an even more businesslike lobbying industry. In fact, that measure inspired a group of longtime lobbyists to form the Institute of Governmental Advocates, an association to lobby for lobbyists, which filed suit to set aside some of the more restrictive elements of the measure and succeeded.

With the increasing difficulty of establishing social relationships with lawmakers, the growing complexity of society and the heightened representation of interests in recent years, many people predict the slow extinction of the one-person lobbying operation. In its place has emerged the multiservice firm with a number of lobbyists, lawyers and public-relations specialists. Some small lobbying operations have merged together, others have joined with political consulting or public relations companies and still others have grown out of law firms. Whatever their origin, lobbying firms with big staffs, big client lists and big campaign war chests are coming to dominate the political landscape.

This has also changed the outside view of lobbyists. Potential clients are wooed not only by connections and understanding of the system, as in the old, one-person operations. Instead, the big firms advertise themselves as people with the wherewithal to handle every aspect of the legislative and political battle, be it pushing or killing legislation, fighting a legal challenge or filing an initiative. There has been a change in the relationship with lawmakers as well. Because lobbyists with large client lists have less time to deal with clients individually, they have less ability to impress upon their employers the reality of politics. Lobbyists often need to convince their clients to ask for tiny changes that take place over several sessions rather than to expect major revisions in the law. Without the ability to persuade their clients to go slow, lobbyists end up bringing more and more unfiltered demands to lawmakers, making it harder to reconcile requests from competing interests. The result: legislative stalemate, or lobbylock, as it is called in the Capitol.

The lobbyists

DONALD K. BROWN

If there is one person in Sacramento who epitomizes the public's age-old notion of a lobbyist, it is Donald "Big O" BrOwn. He is the quintessential "juice" – or money – player, an insider who uses power politics and who rarely lets legislators forget that standing behind him is a collection of clients that includes some of the biggest campaign contributors in the state.

BrOwn, who changed the legal spelling of his name to distinguish himself from another Donald Brown, is considered one of the most effective lobbyists in Sacramento. But unlike the other big juice players, Brown's clout is almost unconnected to technical expertise. Instead, it is based on his ability to direct, or withhold, huge amounts of campaign cash.

His client list, which has shrunk a bit in recent years, is still long and heavy with financial power. It includes the Summa Corp. and the empire of the late Howard Hughes, the Irvine Co., the California Manufacturers Association, the Pharmaceutical Manufacturers Association, the Southland Corp. and the state's mortgage brokers. Together, his clients give as much or more than the clients of any lobbyist in California. In 1988, BrOwn's firm, Advocation Inc., collected nearly $900,000 in lobbying fees, according to documents filed with the secretary of state.

Some lobbyists and staff members describe BrOwn as arrogant, others say he can be as personable as they come. All agree that his forte is politics, not policy. In fact, he makes it almost a point of pride that he stay in the background and out of the nitty-gritty.

Some lobbyists with whom he has worked say BrOwn leaves it to associates to do the lion's share of lobbying and bill-analysis, leaving him free to remind lawmakers of the ample campaign contributions of his clients. Staffers say they have been corralled by BrOwn, who told them little more than, "Go see so-and-so about his bill." The other lobbyists would handle the details. Brown just wanted them to know he thought the bill was important.

Yet for all the power politics, BrOwn does not appear the part. With his tweeds and soft shoes and thick mustache, he appears more a college professor than a hard-nosed lobbyist. And BrOwn is something of an enigma in Capitol politics because he so consistently stays out of the limelight. He tends to deal with legislative leaders. In fact there are a number of junior legislators who have never met him.

BrOwn also stays away from public appearances, rarely if ever testifying before committees and avoiding the press the way campers avoid poison oak. In fact, he even put a clause in one of his client contracts that prevented him from making press statements.

DENNIS CARPENTER

Dennis Carpenter in effect has never left the Legislature. Carpenter, a former FBI man, attorney, international cattle trader and Republican state senator from Orange County, has lost neither that air of belonging in the Capitol nor the connections to Orange County. But rather than representing the county's interests in debates on the floor, he works the hallways and offices for Orange County, one of his major clients.

The county and the Orange County Transportation Commission, however, are far from his only clients. In 1988, Carpenter's firm earned $1.2 million in lobbying fees, and much of that was before he picked up powerhouse clients RJR/Nabisco

Inc. and the Association of California Insurance Companies.

Carpenter's firm is one of the fastest growing lobbying operations in California, with five lobbyists, including his wife, Aleta, who was a school district lobbyist before the two married. When he took on the insurance industry as a client, not only did he get involved in one of the highest profile fights in the Capitol, the battle over auto insurance reform, but he also added another high profile lobbyist, Kathy Snodgrass. Snodgrass, a former staff member of Willie Brown's and still good friends with the Assembly speaker, has been doing a good chunk of the nuts-and-bolts lobbying for insurers for years.

But the firm has changed as it has grown. Carpenter recently separated from the man with whom he had set up his lobbying practice, former Democratic Sen. George Zenovich. The split was described an amicable, and Zenovich took a few clients, including Fresno County, to his own much lower key operation.

One of the major trends in California politics has been the increase in the number of former legislators who have joined the lobbying corps, and Carpenter is one of the most successful examples. He still has deep links inside the Capitol, and he has used those connections not only to influence legislation but to lure clients. Carpenter's success, however, is related to more than just his connections. Like many former lawmakers, he knows the system well, and he knows who else knows the system and what they can do for him.

He is a big, easy man who never seems pushed. His is the classic laid-back style, the kind where he stands with one shoe on the lower rail as he briefs someone on a bill. Not only does that make him easy to like, it makes him easy to underestimate as well. Carpenter's detractors say he does not work all that hard, doing just enough to get by and leaving many details to his associates. But even those detractors say he always seems to have time to chat in the friendly, old-boy style of a practiced politician.

JAMES GARIBALDI

James Garibaldi, known around Sacramento as "The Judge" and to intimates as "Gary," is the closest thing to royalty that exists in Capitol circles. He is treated with deference to his considerable influence; his age, 82; and, most important, his more than 40 years of lobbying.

Garibaldi is a throwback to the days when legislative business was done in richly panelled rooms on thickly padded leather couches. That, in fact, describes his office. He is a friendly, charming man who never seems out of sorts. Although slowed by age, Garbaldi continues to be one of the Capitol's most dignified figures.

And he still wields influence, although he has been cutting down his lobbying load in recent years. He does not make the walk across the street from his office to the Capitol as often as he used to, but when he does, it is to deal with legislative leaders. They usually listen.

Part of the reason he is still influential is that he knows the system and its nuances, and he is still a sharp man. His clients have been with him for years, and he knows the details of those industries as well as anyone in the Capitol. Plus, he is easy for legislators to deal with. He doesn't ask for much and he doesn't make threats. But his words carry the weight of his own legacy of influence.

Garibaldi is nothing if not adaptable, which goes without saying for a man who has survived as many years and changes in the system as he has. That adaptability shows in his lobbying strategy. Garibaldi once helped defeat a bill to legalize dog racing in California – an idea feared by his horse racing clients – by teaming with lobbyists who called it cruelty to animals. And he was instrumental in enacting a tax break for the horse racing industry at a time when the state government itself was feeling the financial pinch.

Garibaldi conducts himself with an air of authority. In the world of politics, that in itself lends him authority. A visit with Garibaldi takes on the feel of being granted an audience. New members are flattered to meet him, it almost confers a status on them. Plus, Garibaldi plays up the image of invincibility. His client list is still filled with blue-chip interests. It includes horse racing concerns, liquor dealers, the National Association of Securities Dealers, the California Association of Highway Patrolmen and the Leslie Salt Co. He is still among the top earning lobbyists, bringing in $570,000 in fees in 1988.

Garibaldi is a former assemblyman and Superior Court judge. He has literally grown up with some of his clients, for whom he has worked nearly all of his lobbying career. He was also instrumental in creating the Institute of Governmental Advocates, the lobbyists' lobbying organization.

JOE GONSALVES

Joe Gonsalves has been called by one legislator the sweetest man in the Capitol. Gonsalves, unassuming, soft-spoken, unerringly polite, is also one of the most consistently successful lobbyists, especially considering the issues he deals with .

Gonsalves, another former assemblyman, makes a specialty out of representing cities. His clients include nearly 20 municipalities, most of them smaller cities south and east of Los Angeles. And most are contract cities, which means they pay either private companies or other municipalities for many of their essential services. The problems of those cities often pose a dilemma for lawmakers because what one wants can be precisely what a neighboring community does not want. Legislators have to chose who to disappoint.

Gonsalves, more than any lobbyist in Sacramento, has been successful in pushing those interests. He does it with hard work, connections and by organizing local officials to lobby the Legislature and to bring pressure on lawmakers from back home. As one lobbyist said of Gonsalves, "If you're on the other side of his issue, you have serious problems."

Above all else, Gonsalves is persistent. He never lets legislators forget his issue. He covers all his bases with staff members. He dogs every bill from start to finish. But in that persistence, his approach is always gentlemanly and understated. He seems to fit into the process smoothly. Gonsalves wears neither the high-fashion nor expensive suits often worn by other lobbyists. Instead, his clothes, like his approach, are businesslike and straightforward.

Gonsalves worked alone for a number of years, but has been joined recently by his son, Anthony. Besides the cities, he also lobbies for several redevelopment agencies plus horse racing and dairy interests, a collection that earned him about $680,000 in 1988.

CLAYTON JACKSON

It is impossible to figure a formula for picking California's top lobbyist, but by any measure Clay Jackson has to be a contender. Never mind that his firm is consistently among the top earners, or that he is extremely influential, or that his clients give enormous amounts of campaign contributions. The man simply looks like a lobbyist.

He is a big 6-foot-6 and with his conservative gray suits and ever-present cigar, he is imposing, intimidating and impossible to ignore when standing in a back corner of a hearing room or in a Capitol corridor. And he wins.

As much as any lobbyist in Sacramento in recent years, Jackson has been involved in high-profile, high-stakes battles – most notably over insurance- and tort-reform legislation. As much as any one person in the Capitol, he is responsible for fending off repeated attacks on the state's insurance industry and was one of the driving forces behind the 1987 easing of liability laws that has come to be known as the Frank Fat's Napkin Deal because details were drafted on a restaurant napkin.

Besides the insurance industry – and Jackson has shifted clients there from California companies to the large, national insurance carriers after an internal blowup over strategy – he represents a number of power-hitting interests, including the Anheuser-Busch Cos., the California Hotel & Motel Association and state's independent thrift and loan companies. His clients paid his firm, Jackson/Barish and Associates more than $1.8 million in lobbying fees in 1988. That made him the top-earning lobbyist for the third straight year.

The financial clout of Jackson's clients is considerable. Some lobbyists say he would be far less effective without it. But many friends and foes say that is only a part of the reason for his success. Jackson may be as shrewd a political strategist as any working the halls of the Capitol. He knows the system. He knows the players. He is a master deal-maker. And he knows the minutest details of the industries he represents. One key to lobbying is knowing when little pieces of legislation might hurt or help a client, and there are times when Jackson sees those pieces as do few others.

It is hard to argue with someone who so thoroughly does his homework; it is even harder to argue when that person has both the physical and political stature of Jackson. Jackson's personal style – he can be charming and polite, or as tough as he needs to be – lends further impact to his arguments. When talking with legislators, Jackson's voice can convey both politeness and the firmness of a man who should not be trifled with. In a hearing room he often stands along a wall, making eye contact with members he is trying to influence, letting his presence alone remind lawmakers of his and his clients' interests.

In an arena where image often becomes reality, Jackson has done nothing to play down the reputation he has for being unbeatable.

JAY D. MICHAEL

Most lobbyists would trade an arm for the resources Jay D. Michael has to throw into political wars. Michael is the chief lobbyist for the California Medical Association, one of the most influential interests in the state, putting him on top of the pyramid of association lobbyists.

The CMA is one of the state's biggest givers to campaigns every year. With the proper handling, that alone would make the association influential. But the CMA is also well-organized, it has plenty of staff and it has influence with members in both parties because there are, after all, doctors in every legislator's district, and they are, for obvious reasons, influential civic leaders.

Yet even that impressive combination of money and organization does not make an interest powerful. The CMA has been a major force for years because Michael knows how to put those resources to work. A longtime lobbyist, Michael is an insider and a good strategist. His job is to protect the pocketbooks of doctors, and he has been extremely successful for a number of years.

Recently the CMA has been part of some unusual alliances that have resulted in high-profile, high-impact deals. Michael and the CMA were key players in the negotiations that brought about a major tort reform bill in 1987, a measure made famous by the drafting of some key points on a napkin at Frank Fat's restaurant a few blocks from the Capitol. Part of that bill extended protections for doctors against malpractice suits, protections that the CMA had first won in an earlier battle during the mid-1970s with the doctors' archenemies, the trial lawyers.

The CMA also was part of the coalition that pushed Proposition 99, the 1988 initiative that increased the cigarette tax by 25 cents a pack. One of the provisions of that initiative reimburses doctors for treating poor patients who have no way to pay their bills. Michael and the CMA later tried to barter CMA support for a ballot measure to increase the gas tax in exchange for even more of the Proposition 99 money, a campaign that failed but was noteworthy for an informal – and critics say infernal – alliance between the CMA and the tobacco industry.

Michael's access to political inner circles, where only the heavy-hitting lobbyists go, is a rarity for association lobbyists, who often must rely on their grass-roots organizing to wield influence. While Michael uses the CMA's grass roots well, his ability to use the system and the financial clout of doctors has put the CMA among the elite interests in the state.

Michael is an affable, approachable guy. His manner is understated and belies the influence he wields. And like so many of the top lobbyists, he would have opponents forget his connections and political acumen, which he mask with a friendly, hail-fellow well-met style.

RICHARD RATCLIFF

Richard Ratcliff has never really been among California's top-earning lobbyist, but he represents something that is fading from the scene, the one-person lobbying operation, especially one that is influential.

Ratcliff has been lobbying in Sacramento since long before the Legislature went full time. He has rarely had much campaign money with which to pry open doors, and he has rarely had a long client list to lend clout to his requests. But he has always been an insider respected for playing it straight. He is one of those rare lobbyists who is genuinely liked by almost every faction in the Capitol's wars. He has friends among old-boy staff members, legislative leaders and young reporters.

His appearance is almost always casual. Even on days when he must put on a tie under his tweed or corduroy coats in order to testify before a committee, he still is as likely as not to wear jeans and cowboy boots. And his beard, streaked with gray, makes him look even more like he belongs on a horse herding cattle rather than in the ornate halls of the Capitol trying to corral votes.

His client list is substantive, if not overwhelming – it earned him $198,000 in 1988 – and it includes chemical companies, du Pont and a coalition of international companies doing business in California. With those clients come complex issues, often involving tax law and international business. By necessity and inclination, Ratcliff deals much more with the intricacies of issues rather than politics. Although no lobbyist can be successful without understanding and using a good deal of politics, Ratcliff's best tools are his expertise and his ability to construct a compromise.

His approach is that of a man who is not certain he can answer a question. "Well, I'm not sure I'm the best guy for this," he might start, then launch into an explanation that covers excruciating details. His appearances before a committee are not statements that his clients oppose something – sometimes the only tack taken by some of the power-playing lobbyists. Instead, they are discourses about the issue, its background and complexities and, when his clients oppose a bill, a caution that lawmakers should move slowly.

Ratcliff also has long been a member of the inner circle of top lobbyists and is one of the leaders of the Institute of Governmental Advocates. He has spent a good deal of effort pushing a code of conduct for lobbyists that includes obligations to clients, legislators and the public and a caution against raiding other firms for clients – a practice that pits the big firms against the smaller operations, such as his.

GEORGE STEFFES

George Steffes is something of a bridge between the old and new styles of lobbying. The old way was dominated by personal connections and camaraderie; the new uses large firms and campaign money. Steffes is good at both.

A former aide to Gov. Ronald Reagan, Steffes goes back to the older days of lobbying, and he is one of those in the elite ranks who deal with legislative leaders and other elite lobbyists. That is evidenced by his leadership in the affairs of the

Institute of Governmental Advocates, and by his willingness to serve as a spokes-man for the lobbying industry.

He was one of the first major lobbyists to expand into a full-service firm, and he now runs one of the state's largest lobbying operations; it has six lobbyists and a large staff handling nearly 40 clients. Steffes is also an insider, with strong connections in the Capitol. He is considered a money player, well-versed in power politics. And like other top juice lobbyists, Steffes often gets other lobbyists to handle the day-to-day details while he works on strategy and politics, including the not inconsiderable job of recruiting and keeping clients.

But Steffes is also around the Capitol constantly, patiently waiting outside the Assembly and Senate rails to talk with legislators. He still uses as a lobbying tool his friendships with important lawmakers as well as a generally amicable approach.

While Steffes may not handle all the small details, he does his homework and he knows his issues. In playing the political game, he can be as hard-nosed as any lobbyist. In dealing with other lobbyists or staff members, he can be particularly demanding. And like many of the other lobbyists who succeed at playing hardball, Steffes gets away with it because of his clout, his understanding of politics and his powerful collection of clients.

He may have one of the broadest ranges of clients among all Sacramento lobbyists. Besides a number of horse racing interests, mining companies, hospital associations, foreign auto companies and insurers, Steffes' clients include Adolph Coors Co., American Express Co., Exxon Co. U.S.A., Hughes Aircraft Co. and Union Pacific Corp. That brought him slightly more than $1.3 million in fees in 1988.

The lobbying firms

A-K ASSOCIATES INC.

Once the perennially top-earning lobbying firm, A-K in recent years has scaled back its operation and undergone a rather substantial shake-up. At its peak, it had six California lobbyists, three more in Washington, D.C, and more than 40 clients. It still remains among California's elite operations – it earned about $550,000 in 1987 – but it is no longer head and shoulders above the pack.

In political circles, A-K is still regarded as a powerhouse, but is also noted for being involved in one of the bitterest rivalries over clients. The firm remains in the hands of its founders, S. Thomas Konovaloff and J. Michael Allen, but a brother of each of those men, Nicholai Konovaloff and Richard D. Allen, split from the firm, each to set up his own lobbying practice. When they tried to take some of the firms's business with them, the real lobbying began, the lobbying of clients. Nicholai Konovaloff landed a few big names, among them the R.J. Reynolds Tobacco Co., but A-K kept most of the heavy hitters, including the major tobacco interest, the industry-funded Tobacco Institute.

As an ironic result of this battle, A-K, possibly more than any other firm, became expert at wooing clients. Konovaloff and Allen went out and found businesses having governmental troubles and then convinced them that those problems could be solved by experienced lobbyists who knew the system and the players. Their success begat success. As they grew and offered more and more services, they built a reputation as big-time players, which became a self-fulfilling prophecy, as is so often the case in politics. Legislators, assuming A-K had substantial clout, gave the firm access and all due consideration, which gave it further clout. And clients, wanting the biggest of firms, signed up, making A-K the biggest of firms.

But A-K's stature also was earned through solid lobbying and consistent success. Both Konovaloff and Allen have good reputations as knowledgeable, hard-working lobbyists. They have built a number of close ties to key people in the Capitol, and they play the insiders game. They maintain those friendships, keep their issues out of the public spotlight, provide substantive information and whisper rather than shout their requests.

In addition, as one of the first full-service lobbying firms, A-K manages a client's interests from start to finish, whether the needs are legislative or legal. And their size gives them the ability to handle both large and small clients, as their eclectic client list shows. Besides the tobacco industry, they also work for surety companies, dental plans, Chrysler Corp. and a reclamation district, among others.

FRANCHETTI & SWOAP

It has never been a secret with whom Franchetti & Swoap have influence. George Deukmejian helped get this firm started in 1984, when the governor gave Michael Franchetti a strong endorsement during a fund-raiser, saying, "I always like to give a young lawyer a plug."

Franchetti was Deukmejian's first finance director, but amid partisan fighting over deep budget cuts, he was denied Senate confirmation and was forced to give up the post after a year. His partner, David Swoap, was Deukmejian's first health and welfare secretary. They represent two trends in the lobbying business – the increasing interest in lobbying administrative departments and agencies, and the growing number of former administration officials who have set up lobbying operations.

Of those former officials, Franchetti and Swoap have been the most successful. They focus much of their attention on their former colleagues in the governor's office, the Finance Department and the Health and Welfare Agency, but they continue to expand to lobby other agencies.

They handle some legislative lobbying chores, but they have few strong connections among lawmakers. Instead, they are often brought in as part of a team by other lobbyists who work the Legislature and need Franchetti and Swoap's influence on the administration. Franchetti and Swoap are used in those cases to work up administrative backing for or opposition to a bill, or they might be used after a bill has become law and is handed over to an agency for implementation.

But they are successful for more than just their connections. They often handle the technical aspects of issues rather than the political fights, making them function more like lawyers than lobbyists. So much of what happens in the agencies involves debates over seemingly small points of administering a law, but the cumulative impact of that kind of lobbying can be enormous.

The jump from administration to lobbying by a number of former Deukmejian officials in recent years has generated a number of anti-revolving door bills in the Legislature. Franchetti and Swoap, because of their success, were subject to a good deal of criticism. But none of the bills has passed, and Deukmejian has continued to defend them and other former top staff.

Their clients include a number of drug firms and hospitals, the California Chiropractic Association, Mobil Oil Corp. and PepsiCo Inc. In 1988, the firm brought in about $900,000 in lobbying fees.

HERON, BURCHETTE, RUCKERT & ROTHWELL

When Heron, Burchette, Ruckert & Rothwell set up shop in Sacramento in 1984, it signaled the day of the Washington, D.C., lobbying firms in California. As is the case in the nation's capitol, firms such as Heron not only trade on their expertise with issues, but on their range of services and their nationwide connections.

Heron is one the biggest and most successful of the Washington-based firms in California. Besides pounding the hallways of the Capitol, Heron manages trade associations, offers a phalanx of lawyers, handles public relations, organizes grass-roots campaigns and more. On top of that, the firm offers a full-service Washington operation to handle federal problems.

Like many of the larger firms that moved to Sacramento, Heron landed in a full sprint, picking up more clients and political clout immediately because it already had a substantial economic base and could hire respected solo lobbyists such as John Norwood and William Thomas. It now employs seven lobbyists and a huge staff.

Heron earned nearly $1.2 million in 1988 and has one of the longest client lists in Sacramento. It handles a range of agricultural interests – including those of rice, tomato, grape, almond and olive growers – plus truckers, pharmacists, insurance companies, insurance agents, energy companies and Best Western hotels. Heron's reputation in political circles is that of a solidly professional operation. Led by Norwood, none of the lobbyists particularly stands out, but the entire firm is well regarded and has substantial clout.

One of the reasons Heron has influence, with legislators and other lobbyists as well, is that Norwood and his staff have a reputation for working out compromises. That is different from the way some of the juice lobbyists work, and it makes everyone involved more comfortable. Opposing lobbyists come away with something and, more important, lawmakers don't have to disappoint anyone involved.

The problem with such large firms, some interests say, is that although Heron and some of the others have the resources to handles small clients as well as large, some smaller clients can feel they are unimportant or not getting the complete attention they would like.

NIELSEN, MERKSAMER, HODGSON, PARRINELLO & MUELLER

Most lobbying firms try to remain non-partisan, even if their major connections are with one party. That is hardly the case of Nielsen, Merksamer, Hodgson, Parrinello and Mueller. In fact, its rather substantial lobbying business grew out of its political activities.

Nielsen is more or less the official law firm of the California Republican Party, with people such as Steve Merksamer, Gov. Deukmejian's chief of staff during his first term; Bob Naylor, a former Assembly minority leader and state party chairman; Vigo "Chip" Nielsen, a longtime Republican activist; and Charles Bell, a counsel for the Republican Party. The firm handles every political chore, from raising money, to writing initiatives and ballot arguments, to handling election law.

Merksamer originally derived his stature from his connections to Deukmejian, but has gradually evolved as a top party figure in his own right. Merksamer and the firm have become one of the kingmakers of the Republican Party. They were one of the key groups that helped push Pete Wilson into the 1990 gubernatorial campaign.

The firm's style is that of some of the old-time Washington firms – full-service but everything revolves around politics. For example, it was heavily involved from the start in efforts to put the gas tax increase on the 1990 ballot.

But the corps of lobbyists, which includes Naylor, who is registered as a lobbyist, and Merksamer, who is not registered but acts as a high-level contact man to smooth out occasional problems, are also heavily involved in legislative battles. It was Merksamer and Naylor who were major organizers of the 1987 "Frank Fat's Napkin" tort-reform deal. They helped push almost every major economic power in the state – insurers, manufacturers, doctors, lawyers and more – into a multilevel compromise that also gave new protections to their clients, the tobacco industry.

Nielsen's lobbyists often trade on their connections to Deukmejian, and with their overall political clout and their influential clients, they have little trouble playing power politics in the Legislature.

Nielsen is the major California firm for the powerful tobacco lobby. It represents industry giants Philip Morris U.S.A. and R.J. Reynolds, plus the industry's public relations and political vehicle, the Tobacco Institute. Other powerful clients include the Irvine Co., the Southland Corp., General Mills, Summa Corp. and Waste Management Inc. That lineup in 1988 earned the firm more than $1 million in lobbying fees.

NOSSMAN, GUNTHER, KNOX & ELLIOT

One look at the list of clients would be enough to convince anyone that Nossman, Gunther, Knox & Elliot is a major player on the Sacramento scene. The firm has major insurance companies, some large municipal agencies, Avis Rent A Car, General Electric, Pearle Health Systems, the Recording Industry Association of America, lending institutions and some high-technology companies, among others.

All told, Nossman earned $1.3 million in 1988, and it has been one of the fastest growing lobbying firms in California, large or small. It is another of the full-service firms, with six lobbyists and everything from lawyers to public relations people to Washington connections.

Nossman uses its resources well. Its lobbyists are well-versed in the issues, and the firm can fight battles on every front. Nossman also uses the resources of its clients well, throwing their campaign contributions into the fray. Its lobbyists have been successful on a range of issues, and its reputation is that of the firm for clients who want to do whatever it takes to win.

Like many of the larger firms, Nossman is as good at recruiting and keeping clients as it is at fighting legislative battles. In a day when the big firms are gaining more and more of an advantage at persuading interests to use them, Nossman's John Knox, a former assemblyman, is regarded as one of the better people at winning over and satisfying clients, as well as one of the smartest politicians ever to serve in the Legislature.

But unlike some of the full-service firms, Nossman's lobbying efforts have become centered around one of its lobbyists, John Foran. A legislator for more than two decades, Foran was the former chairman of the Senate Transportation Committee and was regarded then as one of the more knowledgeable men in the state on transportation issues. He still has more connections in the Capitol than some current lawmakers.

Foran, who has dealt with a number of insurance and transportation issues for Nossman, goes far beyond that realm in his lobbying, however. As well as any legislator-turned-lobbyist, Foran made the switch from decision-maker to petitioner with ease. He was a well-liked legislator, an unassuming good-old boy and one of the insiders. As a lobbyist, he is still well liked.

His style is Mr. Nice Guy. Unlike some of the other top lobbyists, he seems never to be really pressuring anyone. And unlike a few of the top lobbyists who make a point of standing inside the rail that is outside the Assembly – a move that is partly an effort to send a message about their clout to lawmakers and other lobbyists – unassuming Foran, with as much clout as almost anyone, usually waits patiently outside the rail.

7

Press vs. politicians–never-ending war

An aide to Assembly Speaker Willie Brown once put out a 15-page guide with detailed advice for legislators on how to deal with the news media. On the cover of the guide was a cartoon with a farmer, sitting on a tractor, telling a reporter that the two of them are in the same business.

"We are?" the reporter asks.

"This here's a manure spreader," the farmer says.

That about sums up the relationship between most California politicians and the people who cover them for print and broadcast media around the state. Each group thinks that, as often as not, the other is spreading manure.

It has become a given in American politics in general that a certain tension and wariness is natural in the dealings between reporters and politicians. That is certainly the case in California. Gone are the days when the Capitol press corps and the state's political press were part of the inside establishment. Then, reporters and politicians ate and drank together, and neither group judged the other too harshly. All of that changed in the last 15 years. The creation of a full-time Legislature in the mid-1970s coincided with a generational change in the Capitol press corps and development of a more critical attitude in the wake of the Vietnam War and Watergate. Despite the occasionally chummy feelings between some reporters and politicians today, the press continues to move toward much harder reporting about campaign spending, conflicts of interest and ethical problems, not to mention giving thorough coverage to a continuing FBI investigation – an investigation that apparently began because prosecutors were reading about Capitol influence-peddling in newspapers.

A number of reasons account for the constant battles between reporters and politicians. For starters, politicians have an almost single-minded concern about their images, as might be expected of people whose careers depend upon public

353

approval. To project any image, they need the media. But often the publicity they get is not exactly what they want. For example, when politicians stage events hoping to score a few points with the public, political reporters, striving for the journalistic Grail of objectivity, feel compelled to throw in other views and counterarguments.

In the Capitol, many legislators have a list of complaints about the press. They say both privately and publicly that stories about recent FBI investigations, campaign contributions and political shenanigans stain the Legislature with a few broad strokes, obscuring the hard work and good intentions of many lawmakers. Reporters don't buy that argument. If anything, they feel their stories often make legislators look too statesmanlike. They say most stories deal with the substance and progress of bills and budgets, and that too few reports cover the wheeling and dealing that goes into most legislation, or the enormous influence that powerful interests exert in the Capitol.

INHERENT DIFFERENCES

But the differences between political reporters and the people they cover run much deeper than simply the nature of the stories. Politicians and news people generally have very different expectations.

In a sense, news people see it as their job to be the loyal opposition, always asking critical questions, always making elected representatives justify to voters why they should remain in office. When politicians try to tell only part of a story, news people feel it is their obligation to bring the other side to the public.

Such independence does not sit well with many career politicians, people who have spent much of their lives surrounded by partisan advocates. They do not easily accept the idea that reporters or editors can function without grinding personal or political axes. Instead, they assume, as they would of anyone who causes problems, that news people oppose them for ideological or overtly political reasons. In addition, legislators, administration officials and even the governor get angry when reporters do not show that most valued of political attributes – loyalty. Loyalty is everything to a politician. Reporters, instead, are loyal to their stories, not the people they write about. That leaves some politicians feeling betrayed when they joke with reporters, talk about movies or restaurants, their children's baby teeth, and then find a critical story the next day in the papers or on the news broadcast. Their frustration and enmity is made worse by their inability to get news people to negotiate or compromise. Everyone else in the system is willing to negotiate, except the media (although individual reporters may undertake negotiations with individual sources). Politicians know they need the press, but it is the one major piece of the political picture they cannot control.

Reporters, on the other hand, often feel they are being controlled too much. If a politician understands the news media's universally accepted rules of engagement – that every side gets to have a say, that the opinions of major figures such as the governor or the Assembly speaker usually are newsworthy, that reporters cannot simply say somebody is lying or distorting information, for example – they then can color the reporting of events. It is just such manipulation that has given rise to "spin doctors." While still less prevalent in Sacramento than in Washington D.C., political consultants and others, realizing reporters need quotes to flesh out a story and give each sides' arguments, have created a new art form of interpreting events – attempting to put "spin" on a story – to make their candidates look good.

BASHING THE PRESS

Efforts to control media coverage have heightened the tension in Sacramento in recent years as more and more politicians have taken to bashing the press as a means of discrediting stories. Former state Sen. Larry Stirling, now a San Diego Municipal Court judge, was one of the most consistent practitioners of this. Almost every story about ethical problems in the Legislature or the influence of campaign spending generated a response from Stirling, who would say that newspapers were either trying to boost circulation or crying wolf.

Gov. George Deukmejian has become especially adept at deflecting criticism by blaming the messenger. For instance, Deukmejian, who has made his fiscal frugality a cornerstone of his political image, ran into problems when a series of state fiscal agencies reported that the state had run a deficit for the 1987-88 fiscal year. Deukmejian, whose state Department of Finance predicted a year-end finish narrowly in the black, complained at length about the coverage of the story, and that complaint became part of the story. Deukmejian went so far as to don a symbolic black tie for a news conference in which he blasted the press for reporting what he called a debate between bookkeepers. Eventually, nearly everything written about the possible deficit contained Deukmejian's side, the agencies' side and Deukmejian's side again in the form of his complaint that there was no story to begin with.

It is hard to assess the impact that complaints such as Deukmejian's or Stirling's have on the public's perception of a story, but it is clear they have done little to cool the intense scrutiny of the Legislature and political campaigns that the media has undertaken in recent years.

A HARDER EDGE TO COVERAGE

While only the major papers, such as the Los Angeles Times, the Sacramento Bee and the San Jose Mercury, spend large chunks of news space and resources on long, investigative pieces on the Legislature and other Capitol stories, almost every one of the two dozen papers and news services that cover the Capitol regularly has added a harder edge to its coverage and focused more and more attention on ethics and political reform.

At the same time, many of the papers, including the Orange County Register, the Los Angeles Herald Examiner and the Los Angeles Daily News, are focusing their coverage on issues that affect their circulation areas and leaving broad, statewide topics to the wire services and other papers, such as the Times and the Bee, that offer their own wire services. In part, this emphasis on legislators and issues particular to a circulation area comes in response to newspaper marketing surveys that show readers are more concerned with local issues and events and have limited interest in state politics.

As newspapers have added more and more reporters in Sacramento, television news has moved away from Capitol coverage in any form. During the 1960s and 1970s, most large stations in San Francisco, Los Angeles and San Diego maintained bureaus in Sacramento, lured there by the glamour of Govs. Ronald Reagan and Jerry Brown and by the desire of many local stations to follow the networks' lead in covering hard news. The San Diego stations were the first to pull out, leaving a decade ago, and the last Los Angeles station left in 1983. KRON-TV in San Francisco, the last holdout, closed its Capitol bureau in 1988.

Television news has not entirely given up on California political coverage. Most major stations spend a good deal of resources covering statewide races and important ballot measures. But a recent University of Southern California study said stations outside Sacramento averaged barely one minute per news hour of coverage of the Legislature during a period of intense activity during the 1988 session.

Television is shying away from politics for a number of reasons, the most prevalent being economics. Television stations used to make money almost faster than they could count it, and the local news operations were their biggest earners. But now, television stations face increased competition on all fronts from cable networks, superstations and video recorders, as well as from talk and games shows on competing stations.

In response, station managers are listening more and more to their consultants, who produce survey after survey that say viewers are not particularly interested in politics. In addition, as smaller profits have lessened resources, expensive out-of-town bureaus have become expendable. Thus, with the exception of the major news stories such as the recent battle to restrict assault weapons, state politics are covered almost exclusively with short mentions of legislative action or a local visit by a politician.

NEW FORMS OF TV COVERAGE

There have been a few developments running counter to that trend. One has been the growth of Northern California News Satellite, which sells Capitol coverage regularly to about two dozen stations. However, much of that coverage is often used as brief stories rather than the more in-depth reports that bureaus might have supplied.

The other development is an increasing interest in creating some form of live coverage. One group of cable television operators and educators is pushing for a statewide system modeled after C-SPAN, which covers Congress. Key legislators, including Assembly Speaker Willie Brown and Senate President Pro Tem David Roberti, have held hearings on the idea.

The proposal for the C–SPAN-like system calls for creating The California Channel, which would sell to California cable systems gavel-to-gavel coverage of the Legislature, plus news conferences and programs with commentary and analysis of state politics. The promoters of the channel have asked the Legislature to install and run the equipment, allowing Capitol business to be televised to all Capitol offices. The California Channel then would patch into that feed, and send the coverage to cable networks. In addition, commercial stations would be able to use the broadcasts on their news shows. The consensus among those exploring the live coverage is that the impact on the Legislature would be about the same as C-SPAN's effect on Congress: Lawmakers would dress up, slim down and arrive on time, but soon they would forget about the cameras and go on with business as usual – possibly with a little less fooling around.

The interest on the part of legislators in televising their proceedings is another sign that California politicians are becoming more media savvy and are increasing their efforts to control the media coverage they receive. This is most visible in those campaigns where candidates and consultants have mastered the "bite of the day" technique of presenting splashy, often vague statements designed to boost their images rather than explain campaign issues. Campaign consultants also have become more adept at whispering in reporters' ears, attempting to plant story ideas that help them or hurt their opponents, or to put spin on everything involved in the campaigns, from polling to money-raising to issues.

At the same time, reporters are trying to do more than carry campaign statements to their readers and viewers. Most major papers are trying to examine candidates more carefully, over a longer period and on more issues than ever before. They are looking not only at voting records but consistency, ethics, financial holdings, spouses' activities and, occasionally, sexual behavior. As a result, there is an increased wariness developing. Where once reporters and candidates would relax after a campaign swing with dinner or drinks, both groups now keep their distance. And where once consultants would answer questions about their polling or money-raising honestly, now every utterance has the best face painted on it. So candidates are careful with what they say around reporters, and reporters believe only half of what they hear from candidates.

TELEVISION'S CRUCIAL ROLE

Media coverage is crucial to the success of political campaigns, especially statewide contests. There are thousands of miles to cover and dramatically varied constituencies to reach. In fact, just about the only effective way to reach the state's 13 million registered voters is through television. Candidates and initiative sponsors are eager to get on the local news, especially in Southern California, in order to reach potential voters, and local news stations are eager to cover big-name candidates and major ballot campaigns. Televisions news, despite all but abandoning the dull and gray day-to-day political coverage in the off season, is more interested in campaign coverage in California than ever before. Campaigns are exciting and colorful; they project what television covers well – movement, intensity and conflict.

Politicians and political consultants are thrilled by this turn. Local television news reaches many more people than newspaper stories, and because it is the magic of television, it has more impact. Plus, campaigns can occasionally get messages out without a balancing point of view by playing to TV's fascination with live technology. A live interview or live coverage of an event can give viewers a much less filtered theme or message than even a 15-second sound bite.

Outside of campaigns, consultants and politicians are working harder than ever to attract and control press coverage. While they want their names in the news, they ask a lot more from their publicity than just spelling the name correctly. Politicians and consultants are using more and more devices to gain favorable coverage.

Stunts – disguised as news conferences – are often used to call attention to issues. Recent examples include using an ambulance to deliver petitions to the Capitol from people supporting more money for emergency rooms, and lining up about 1,000 hospital administrators like a marching band spelling out H-E-L-P to ask for aid to hospital budgets. One of the more common moves is the press conference to announce the introduction of a bill, thus giving one or more legislators a chance to be identified with a newsworthy issue. Sometimes a serious effort to move the bill follows, but at times the bills are abandoned, having served their purpose. Another ploy is the ever-popular "spontaneous" statement during a legislative debate. As often as not, these are practiced beforehand and timed to fit a TV sound bite.

PROFESSIONAL MEDIA MANAGERS

The increased sophistication in the interplay with the media has moved politicians to seek professional help pursuing press coverage. Even legislators who are rarely quoted in their hometown newspapers are employing aides whose sole responsibility is to deal with the press or sometimes chase the press down in an effort to get the name of their boss in the paper. But on-staff press aides are only so effective. In greater and greater numbers, even unspectacular legislators who are not immediately running for higher office are hiring the services of a growing number of political public relations firms. Those firms also are being used by special interests pushing or resisting particular bills in the Capitol. In fact, it is not uncommon on almost any high-profile issue being fought out in the Capitol to have every side represented by PR people.

One big job for these firms is to put their clients, either politicians or special interests with a stake in legislation, in touch with the media. The major firms that engage in political PR around Sacramento – among them PBN Company; Stoorza, Ziegaus and Metzger; and Townsend and Company – all employ people who either were former members of the Capitol press corps or who dealt with the press at length in legislative offices. They know what reporters are interested in and how to get their client's views inserted into a story. And they realize that competition for reporters' time and interest is intense, so they can help their clients by making it easier and faster for reporters to get information or quotes.

Many PR people also try to call attention to their clients by putting them in touch with reporters through casual breakfasts or lunches or even backyard barbecues. No immediate news is expected from these events, but it makes those reporters and politicians feel more comfortable with each other and, as often as not, the politicians may find their names appearing in some stories a little more readily. In effect, this new breed of political PR consultant is a lobbyist of the media, working in conjunction with those who lobby the officeholders.

THE PRESS EXAMINES ITSELF

All the attention California's political press is attracting is beginning to be matched by the attention that the media is paying to itself. When a few legislators introduced bills to reduce press access to public records or to give public figures more power to sue for libel, a debate among the members of the Capitol press corps began over the role of journalists in fighting for access to information. Although none of those measures made it through the Legislature, that debate within the press is likely to continue between people who believe that reporters should actively lobby lawmakers to keep information public and those who argue that journalists have a responsibility to their readers and viewers and that by lobbying for anything, journalists compromise their objectivity.

This self-examination by the press has intensified since a Sacramento television reporter, who covered the Capitol and state government, was found in 1989 to have had a consulting contract with the California Highway Patrol for five years to teach them how to deal with the media. That reporter was removed from the Capitol beat by his station and reprimanded by the Capitol Correspondents Association, but Capitol reporters have continued to wrestle with the ethics of outside income – such as speeches to trade associations and free-lance writing for professional or industry publications – or possible conflicts of interest created by the jobs held by spouses.

Newspapers and News Services

ASSOCIATED PRESS

Sacramento bureau: 925 L St., Suite 320, Sacramento, 95814; (916) 448-9555.

Doug Willis, correspondent and political writer; John Howard, news editor; reporters: Rodney Angove, Steve Geissinger, Kathleen Grubb, Jennifer Kerr, Steve Lawrence; photographer Walter Zeboski.

The Associated Press is a news cooperative that has approximately 100 member newspapers and 400 broadcasters who receive AP reports in the state.

The Sacramento office is an all-purpose news bureau covering breaking stories from Fairfield east to the Nevada border and from Stockton north to the Oregon border. Roughly two-thirds of the bureau's time is spent reporting on California politics and state government.

Willis has been in AP's Sacramento bureau since 1969 and has directed the bureau since 1974. Howard came to the bureau as news editor in 1980 from AP's San Francisco office.

The AP staff is a veteran one: Angove, who joined AP in 1959, has spent 17 years in Sacramento; Geissinger moved to the bureau in 1984 from the Salinas Californian; Grubb joined AP in 1987 from the Vacaville Reporter; Kerr joined AP in 1973 and has been in Sacramento since 1978; Lawrence came to Sacramento in 1973 from AP's Los Angeles office; and Zeboski has been with AP since 1949, the last 23 years in Sacramento.

BAKERSFIELD CALIFORNIAN
Capitol bureau: 925 L St., Suite 1190, Sacramento, 95814; (916) 324-4585.
Michael Otten, bureau chief.
The bureau primarily covers news of interest to the Californian's Kern County circulation base.
Otten joined the paper in April 1989 after more than 30 years with the Sacramento Union, the last five of those years as Capitol bureau chief. Otten writes a political column for the Californian, and his column also appears in the Union.

CAPITOL NEWS SERVICE
1113 Capitol Ave., Sacramento, 95814; (916) 445-6336; Los Angeles office (213) 462-6371.
Fred Kline, editor; Thomas L. Nadeau, reporter.
A small, independent news service serving small dailies and weeklies. The news service was founded in 1939 and was taken over by Kline, a veteran newsman, in 1971.

CONTRA COSTA TIMES/LESHER NEWSPAPERS
Capitol bureau: 925 L St., Suite 348, Sacramento, 95814; (916) 441-2101.
Virgil Meibert, bureau chief.
The bureau covers local legislators, the effect of state government decisions on local communities and regional issues for six Lesher newspapers in the San Francisco Bay Area: the Contra Costa Times, Antioch Daily Ledger, Pittsburg Post-Dispatch, San Ramon Valley Times, Valley Times in Pleasanton and West County Times covering the Richmond-Pinole area.
Prior to becoming Lesher's Sacramento bureau chief in 1988, Meibert spent 24 years with the Oakland Tribune, the last 14 years as its Sacramento bureau chief.

COPLEY NEWS SERVICE
Capitol bureau: 925 L St., Suite 1190, Sacramento, 95814; (916) 445-2934.
Robert P. Studer, bureau chief; James P. Sweeney, political writer.
The bureau covers stories of particular interest to a group of Copley newspapers in the Los Angeles area – the Torrance Daily Breeze, the San Pedro News and the Santa Monica Evening Outlook. It occasionally helps two other Copley newspapers, the San Diego Union and the San Diego Tribune, which also have Sacramento bureaus. In addition, the bureau serves roughly 100 California clients, including daily and weekly newspapers and broadcasters who subscribe to the Copley News

Service.

Studer, who also writes analyses on statewide issues, has been with the Copley chain for more than 50 years and has been Sacramento bureau chief since 1974. Sweeney joined the bureau in 1985 from the Torrance Daily Breeze, where he had been an assistant city editor.

DAILY RECORDER

1115 H St., Sacramento, 95814; (916) 444-2355.

Patricia Rogero, reporter.

This Sacramento-based legal-profession newspaper is one of several owned by the Daily Journal Corp. of Los Angeles. It concentrates on news of interest to the legal community, lobbyists and Capitol staffers.

Rogero has been the Daily Recorder's Capitol correspondent since 1987 and was formerly the Los Angeles Daily Journal's Sacramento reporter.

GANNETT NEWS SERVICE

Capitol bureau: 925 L St., Suite 110, Sacramento, 95814; (916) 446-1036.

Rebecca LaVally, bureau manager; Jake Henshaw, reporter.

The bureau has two permanent writers and a rotating temporary reporter on loan from a Gannett newspaper. They cover stories of local and statewide interest to the chain's California newspapers: the Indio Daily News, Marin Independent Journal, the Palm Springs Desert Sun, the Salinas Californian, the San Bernardino Sun, the Stockton Record and the Visalia Times-Delta. The bureau also occasionally covers stories for the Reno Gazette Journal and USA Today.

LaVally had been in United Press International's Sacramento bureau for nearly 12 years – including the last four as bureau manager – when she joined GNS in 1989. She also writes a weekly political column for GNS. Henshaw came to Sacramento in 1987 from the GNS Washington bureau.

LONG BEACH PRESS-TELEGRAM

Capitol bureau: 925 L St., Suite 315, Sacramento, 95814; (916) 448-1893.

Lawrence L. Lynch, reporter.

This is one of two Knight-Ridder newspapers with bureaus in Sacramento, the other being the San Jose Mercury-News. The one-person bureau's main focus is stories of local interest to Long Beach readers, including coverage of local legislators and major statewide stories.

Lynch has been with the paper since 1970 in various positions, including political writer and editorial writer. He took over the Capitol bureau in 1989.

LOS ANGELES DAILY JOURNAL

Capitol bureau: 925 L St., Suite 325, Sacramento, 95814; (916) 445-8063.

Thomas L. Dresslar, bureau chief; Hallye Jordan, reporter.

The bureau covers news of interest to the legal community ranging from the death penalty to probate law. In addition to the Daily Journal, the bureau's work appears in the San Francisco Banner Journal and other Daily Journal Corp. publications.

Dresslar came to the bureau from the Daily Recorder in Sacramento in 1987. Jordan joined the bureau in 1987 from the Orange County Register.

LOS ANGELES DAILY NEWS

Capitol bureau: 925 L St., Suite 335, Sacramento, 95814; (916) 446-6723.

James W. Sweeney, bureau chief; Sandy Harrison, reporter.

The bureau's primary focus is on state government, political news of interest to its San Fernando Valley area readers and major statewide stories.

Sweeney transferred to Sacramento in 1988 from the Daily News city room, where he had covered local government and politics since 1984. Harrison joined the bureau in 1989 and had previously worked covering local government for the Daily News.

LOS ANGELES TIMES

Capitol bureau: 1125 L St., Suite 200, Sacramento, 95814; (916) 445-8860.

George Skelton, bureau chief; staff writers: Virginia Ellis, Ralph Frammolino (Orange and San Diego editions), Jerry Gillam, Mark Gladstone (Los Angeles County zone sections and San Fernando Valley edition), Carl Ingram, Paul Jacobs, Richard C. Paddock, Douglas Shuit, William Trombley, Daniel Weintraub.

Los Angeles office: John Balzar, (213) 237-4550, and Keith Love, (213) 237-7070, political writers.

The Los Angeles Times Sacramento bureau primarily takes a statewide approach to its coverage of Capitol issues. It does in-depth political analyses, personality profiles and investigative stories involving the state bureaucracy as well as daily coverage of the Legislature, the governor and other state agencies.

The Times also provides stories of local and regional interest to its primary audience of Los Angeles area readers. Two reporters within the bureau focus on news of local interest to Times editions in San Diego, Orange County, the San Fernando Valley and Los Angeles area zones.

Times stories also appear in newspapers that subscribe to the Times-Mirror wire service.

Skelton, a former Capitol correspondent for UPI who moved to the Times in 1974, is in his second tour of duty as the Times' Capitol bureau chief. He has also worked as a politics editor in Los Angeles and as White House correspondent for the Times.

The Times bureau includes Ellis, who came to Sacramento in 1988 from the Dallas Times Herald, where she was chief of its Capitol bureau in Austin; Frammolino, who moved to Sacramento in 1989 from the Times' San Diego edition; Gillam, the president of the Capitol Correspondents Association and a member of the bureau since 1961; Gladstone, who joined the bureau in 1984 and has been with the Times since 1981; Jacobs, who has been with the Times since 1978 and moved to Sacramento in 1983; Paddock, who has been with the Times since 1977 and in Sacramento since 1982; Ingram, a former UPI Capitol correspondent who joined the Times in December 1978; Shuit, who has been with the Times since 1967 and joined the bureau in 1980; Trombley, who has been with the Times since 1964 and who moved to Sacramento in 1989; and Weintraub, who moved to Sacramento in 1987 after four years in other Times assignments.

Balzar and Love are based in Los Angeles and cover statewide and national political stories. Balzar joined the Times in 1982 from the San Francisco Chronicle and had worked in the Capitol bureau before becoming a political writer in 1985. Love joined the Times in 1979 as an assistant metro editor from the New York Times and has been a political writer since 1983.

OAKLAND TRIBUNE

Capitol bureau: 925 L St., Suite 385, Sacramento, 95814; (916) 445-5424.
Kathy Zimmerman McKenna, bureau chief.
The bureau focuses on stories of interest to the East Bay and statewide stories.
Zimmerman McKenna transferred to Sacramento in 1988 from Oakland, where she had been covering City Hall for the Tribune.

ORANGE COUNTY REGISTER

Capitol bureau: 925 L St., Suite 305, Sacramento, 95814; (916) 445-9841.
Marc S. Lifsher and Chris Knap, correspondents.
Santa Ana office: Larry Peterson, political writer, (714) 953-2223.
The bureau's main mission is to cover political and government stories of statewide and local interest for the rapidly growing Orange County daily.
Lifsher joined the bureau in 1983 from the Dallas Times Herald. Knap came to the bureau in 1989 from the Register's city room, where he was the county government reporter. Peterson covers state and national politics from the main office.

RIVERSIDE PRESS-ENTERPRISE

Capitol bureau: 925 L St., Suite 325, Sacramento, 95814; (916) 445-9973.
Dan Smith, bureau chief.
Riverside: Joan Radovich, political writer, (714) 782-7567.
The bureau's main charge is to cover Riverside County legislators and issues of local interest as well as major breaking political and government stories.
Smith became the Press-Enterprise's Capitol correspondent in 1988. He has worked for the paper since 1984 and had previously covered local politics and government. Radovich, the paper's former City Hall reporter, became political writer in 1989.

SACRAMENTO BEE / McCLATCHY NEWSPAPERS

Capitol bureau: 925 L St., Suite 1404, Sacramento, 95814; (916) 321-1199.

William Endicott, bureau chief; Rick Rodriguez, deputy bureau chief; Dan Walters, political columnist; staff writers: Amy Chance, Thorne Gray, Stephen Green, Rick Kushman, Jon Matthews, James Richardson, Herbert A. Sample, Ray Sotero (Fresno Bee and Modesto Bee coverage).

McClatchy Newspapers: Martin Smith, political editor, P.O. Box 15779, Sacramento, 95852; (916) 321-1914.

Fresno Bee: Jim Boren, political writer, (209) 441-6307.

Modesto Bee: Kathie Smith, political writer, (209) 578-2348.

The Sacramento Bee's Capitol bureau primarily takes a statewide view in its coverage of issues and politics. It regularly offers political analyses, features and daily coverage of state government and political issues. In addition, bureau members work on in-depth special projects ranging from investigative reports on the Legislature to examination of emerging political trends. In election years, bureau reporters cover both statewide and national campaigns.

The impact of the Bee's political, legislative and state government coverage has increased in recent years with the growth of the McClatchy News Service. Fifty-two California newspapers subscribe to MNS, with many using stories covered by the Bee's Capitol bureau.

Bureau Chief Endicott took over The Bee's Capitol bureau in 1985, coming to the paper from the Los Angeles Times, where he had worked for 17 years in various positions, including San Francisco bureau chief, political writer and the last two years as the Times' Capitol bureau chief.

Rodriguez became deputy bureau chief in 1987 after a stint as an editorial writer. He came to the Sacramento Bee from the Fresno Bee as a Capitol bureau reporter in 1982.

Walters' column appears six days a week in The Bee and is distributed statewide by McClatchy News Service. He joined the paper as a political columnist in 1984 after 11 years with the Sacramento Union, the last nine in its Capitol bureau.

Martin Smith has been political editor of McClatchy Newspapers since 1977 and has been covering politics since 1965. He writes a political column three times a week that appears on The Bee's editorial pages and is distributed statewide by McClatchy News Service. He is a member of The Bee's editorial board.

The Bee's Capitol staff includes: Chance, who joined the paper in 1984 from the Fort Worth Star-Telegram to cover Sacramento City Hall and moved to the Capitol bureau in 1986; Gray, who moved to Sacramento from the Modesto Bee in 1983; Green, who moved to The Bee in 1978 from the Seattle Post-Intelligencer and to the Capitol bureau in 1985; Kushman, a former Sacramento Union reporter and television assignment editor who joined the bureau in 1987; Matthews, who joined the bureau in 1986 from the Anchorage Daily News; Richardson, who became the Riverside Press Enterprise's Capitol bureau chief in 1985 and moved to The Bee in

1988; Sample, a former Los Angeles Times reporter who joined the bureau in 1986; and Sotero, who moved to Sacramento in 1988 after five years with the Modesto Bee.

Boren and Kathie Smith cover local and statewide politics for their respective papers and assist in national coverage during presidential election years.

SACRAMENTO UNION
Capitol bureau: 925 L St., Suite 1190, Sacramento, 95814; (916) 440-0545.
Trinda Pasquet, reporter.

The main charge of this bureau is to cover news of local interest to Sacramento area readers. The Union generally relies on wire stories for its major breaking news.

Pasquet, the Union's former courthouse reporter, joined the bureau from the Union's city room in 1989.

SAN DIEGO TRIBUNE
Sacramento bureau: 925 L St., Suite 1190, Sacramento, 95814; (916) 445-6510.
Ron Roach, bureau chief.

The bureau's main mission is to cover news of interest to San Diego area readers and major statewide stories. Roach also occasionally writes commentaries and analyses. This is one of three Copley Newspapers bureaus in Sacramento.

He has been the Tribune's Capitol correspondent since 1978, coming to the newspaper after several years with the Associated Press, the last three as news editor of its Sacramento bureau.

SAN DIEGO UNION
Sacramento bureau: 925 L St., Suite 1190, Sacramento, 95814; (916) 445-9656.
Daniel C. Carson, bureau chief; Michael Smolens, staff writer.
San Diego office: Gerald Braun, John Marelius, reporters; (619) 299-3131.

This Copley newspaper's Sacramento bureau splits its time covering stories of local interest, including the San Diego area's 11-member legislative delegation, and statewide political and government stories. The two writers also regularly contribute to a political column and stories are distributed by the Copley News Service.

Carson has been with the Union since 1977 and in Sacramento since 1982, the last two years as bureau chief. Smolens, who formerly covered local government and political issues for the Union, joined the bureau in 1987.

Braun and Marelius cover statewide political issues and are based in the main office in San Diego.

SAN FRANCISCO CHRONICLE
Sacramento bureau: 925 L St., Suite 680, Sacramento, 95814; (916) 445-5658.
Rob Gunnison, Greg Lucas, staff writers; Vlae Kershner, economics editor.
San Francisco office: Jerry Roberts, political editor; Mark Z. Barabak, political writer, (415) 777-7123.

The Sacramento bureau's primary emphasis is on statewide government and political news. Chronicle Capitol bureau stories also move over the New York Times wire and are picked up by other subscribing California newspapers.

Gunnison moved to the Chronicle in 1985 from United Press International's Sacramento bureau, where he had worked for 11 years. Lucas joined the bureau in 1988 from the Los Angeles Daily Journal's Sacramento staff. Kershner, who joined the bureau in 1989, concentrates on economic and business issues in Sacramento.

Roberts, a longtime Chronicle staffer, has been the paper's political editor since 1987. He and Barabak, who joined the paper in 1984, do much of the local, state and national political reporting from the home office in San Francisco.

SAN FRANCISCO EXAMINER

Sacramento bureau: 925 L St., Suite 320A, Sacramento, 95814; (916) 445-4310. Steven A. Capps, bureau chief.

San Francisco office: John Jacobs, chief political writer, (415) 777-7868.

This Hearst paper's Sacramento bureau covers major statewide stories and stories of interest to San Francisco Bay Area readers.Capps joined the bureau in 1980 after spending three years with United Press International in San Francisco and Los Angeles.

Jacobs has been the paper's chief political writer since 1987. He joined the paper in 1978 from the Washington Post.

SAN JOSE MERCURY NEWS

Sacramento bureau: 925 L St., Suite 312, Sacramento, 95814; (916) 441-4601. Bert Robinson, Gary Webb, reporters.

San Jose office: Phil Trounstine, political editor, (408) 920-5657.

The Sacramento bureau relies on wire services to cover the bulk of daily Capitol stories and concentrates more on off-agenda and investigative stories of statewide and local interest. Stories also move over the Knight-Ridder wire and are picked up by other newspapers.

Robinson, who has been with the Mercury News since 1983, moved to the Sacramento bureau at the beginning of 1988. Webb came to Sacramento in 1989 from the Cleveland Plain Dealer, where he had been an investigative reporter in the statehouse bureau in Columbus.

Trounstine is responsible for national, statewide and local political coverage from the home office. He joined the paper in 1978 from the Indianapolis Star and has been political editor since 1986.

UNITED PRESS INTERNATIONAL

Sacramento bureau: 925 L St., Suite 1185, Sacramento, 95814; (916) 445-7755.

Chris Crystal, bureau manager; reporters: Robert Crabbe, Ken Hoover, Clark McKinley, Teresa Simons, Ted Appel.

UPI's Sacramento bureau is responsible for covering breaking news in the northeastern quadrant of California, although the bureau's emphasis is government news. It also offers political analyses and campaign coverage for its clients.

Chris Crystal took over as bureau manager in July 1989, moving from San Francisco. She has been with UPI for nine years and was a Washington correspondent from 1983 to 1987.

Staff writers include: Crabbe, who has been with UPI for 25 years, much of it in Asia, and in the bureau since 1980; Hoover, who joined the bureau in 1987 from the Los Angeles Daily News; McKinley, who has been with UPI for 16 years and in the Sacramento since 1978; Simons, who joined the bureau in 1988 from the News Pilot in San Pedro; and Appel, who transferred from UPI's Los Angeles bureau in 1989.

Magazines

CALIFORNIA JOURNAL

1714 Capitol Ave., Sacramento, 95814; (916) 444-2840.

Richard Zeiger, editor; A.G. Block, managing editor.

The California Journal, founded by a group of Capitol staffers as a non-profit institution, celebrated its 20th anniversary in 1989. The monthly magazine, which relies primarily on free-lance writers, takes an analytical view of California politics and government. It has a circulation of about 19,000. The California Journal also publishes various books about California government and politics. It became a for-profit organization in 1986 with Tom Hoeber, one of the founders, as publisher.

Zeiger took over as the magazine's editor in 1984. Prior to that, he had been with the Riverside Press-Enterprise for 16 years, the last seven as its Sacramento bureau chief. Block was a free-lance writer when he joined the magazine in 1983.

GOLDEN STATE REPORT

444 N. Third St., Suite 200, Sacramento, 95814; (916) 448-2653.

Ed Mendel, editor; Alice Nauman, managing editor.

This monthly magazine was started in 1985 to take an in-depth look at public policy issues, politics and personalities in state government. Its circulation is about 12,000 and the articles are primarily written by free-lancers.

Mendel became editor in January 1989 after 17 years with the Sacramento Union, the last eight in its Capitol bureau. Nauman has been the magazine's managing editor since its inception, a post she previously held with the California Journal.

Newsletters

CALIFORNIA EYE / THE POLITICAL ANIMAL

P.O. Box 3249, Torrance, 90510; (213) 515-1511.

Joe Scott, editor.

Scott publishes two biweekly political newsletters. The California Eye, begun in

1980, is aimed at analyzing and forecasting trends in state politics, while The Political Animal, started in 1973, takes a nationwide approach with some California news included. Scott also writes a twice-weekly column that appears in the Los Angeles Herald Examiner, the Sacramento Union and the San Diego Union.

CALIFORNIA POLITICAL WEEK

P.O. Box 1468, Beverly Hills, 90213; (213) 659-0205.

Dick Rosengarten, editor and publisher.

This newsletter takes a look at trends in politics and local government throughout the state. It was established in 1978.

Rosengarten is a former print and broadcast journalist who has also worked in public relations and as a campaign manager.

POLITICAL PULSE

926 J St., Room 1218, Sacramento, 95814; (916) 446-2048.

Bud Lembke, editor and publisher.

This newsletter, which looks at political news, trends and personalities, was started in 1985.

Lembke was a Los Angeles Times reporter for 21 years and a former press secretary to Senate President Pro Tem David Roberti. Subscribers receive 23 issues a year.

NEW WEST NOTES

P.O. Box 221364, Sacramento, 95822; (916) 395-0709.

Bill Bradley, editor and publisher.

Formerly called the Larkspur Report, this monthly newsletter aims to give a California perspective to political and economic affairs through Bradley's analysis.

Bradley was a senior consultant to former U.S. Sen. Gary Hart in his presidential bids. He also writes columns for Golden State Report, the Sacramento News and Review and California Business Magazine.

Radio

CALNET / AP RADIO

926 J St., Suite 1014, Sacramento, 95814; (916) 446-2234.

Steve Scott, correspondent.

Calnet produces a daily, half-hour program of news and commentary focusing on state government and political news. It is carried by public radio stations in 12 California markets.

Scott has covered the Capitol as a stringer for several radio stations since 1986.

He joined Calnet in 1988 and also strings for Associated Press radio.

KCBS-San Francisco

925 L St., Suite A, Sacramento, 95814; (916) 445-7372.

Jim Hamblin, correspondent.

Hamblin covers the Legislature and related government stories as well as other major breaking news for this San Francisco-based news radio station. Hamblin has covered state government and politics for 20 years and has been based in Sacramento since 1987.

KXPR/FM

3416 American River Drive, Suite B, Sacramento, 95864; (916) 485-5977.

Mike Montgomery, reporter.

This member station of the National Public Radio network is one of the few that regularly cover the state Capitol and government. Montgomery has been covering political and Capitol stories since December 1983.

Television

Los Angeles

KABC-TV

4151 Prospect Ave., Los Angeles, 90027; (213) 668-2880.

Mark Coogan, John North, correspondents. Bill Press, Bruce Herschensohn, political commentators.

Coogan and North are used as a team and are often sent together to cover major political events such as conventions or elections. Coogan, who started at KABC in 1976, spent 1979 and 1980 as the southern Africa bureau chief for ABC News, then came back to KABC as a political reporter in 1980. North, who started covering California politics in 1979 for KABC, also spent some time at the network until he came back to KABC in 1982.

The station also offers political commentary from Press, a liberal former aide to Gov. Jerry Brown who is considering running for insurance commissioner in 1990, and conservative Herschensohn, an unsuccessful candidate for the Republican nomination for U.S. Senate in 1986 who is contemplating another try in 1992.

KCBS-TV

6121 Sunset Blvd., Los Angeles, 90028; (213) 460-3553.

Ruth Ashton Taylor, political editor; Bill Stout, commentator; Harvey Levin, reporter.

Ashton Taylor, the political editor, began her television career in 1949 as a producer on Edward R. Murrow's original show. She moved from CBS to the network-owned station in 1966 in the capacity of political reporter.

Stout, whose commentary includes political issues, has been with KCBS for 24 years. He has been doing commentary since 1978. Levin, an attorney who covers some statewide political issues as well as the state's courts, came to KCBS from KNBC in 1988.

KNBC-TV

3000 West Alameda, Burbank, 91523; (818) 840-3425.

Linda Douglass, political editor.

This Los Angeles station covers national, statewide and local political stories. Douglass, the political editor, started at KNBC in 1985 after jumping across town from KCBS-TV, where she was a longtime political reporter.

Sacramento

KCRA-TV

3 Television Circle, Sacramento, 95814; (916) 444-7316.

Steve Swatt, Capitol correspondent.

Swatt has covered the Capitol, state government and politics full-time since 1979 for this NBC-affiliate. He also covers national politics during election years. Swatt has been with the station since 1969, joining it from United Press International's Los Angeles bureau. KCRA's Capitol reports are often picked up by other stations.

KOVR-TV

1216 Arden Way, Sacramento, 95815; (916) 927-3050.

John Iander, reporter.

This ABC-affiliate covers the Capitol as news stories occur. Iander has been covering politics since he came to the station in 1980, from the then-McClatchy Broadcasting Corp.

KTXL-TV

4655 Fruitridge Rd., Sacramento, 95820; (916) 454-4548.

Lonnie Wong, reporter.

Wong has been covering the Capitol and state government for radio and television since 1973. He has been with KTXL, an independent station that covers politics on a spot-news basis, since 1980.

KXTV

400 Broadway, Sacramento, 95818; (916) 321-3300.

Deborah Pacyna, Capitol correspondent.

Pacyna has covered state politics and government for this CBS-affiliate since 1984 and also covers national politics during election years. She came to the station from WPXI-TV in Pittsburgh, Pa.

NORTHERN CALIFORNIA NEWS SATELLITE
1121 L St., Suite 109, Sacramento, 95814; (916) 446-7890.
Steve Mallory, president.

NCNS is a video wire service that covers the Capitol, state government and other major breaking news for 15 subscribing television stations stretching from San Diego to Eureka to Medford, Ore. It offers voice overs, live interviews, election coverage as well as daily reports, all transmitted by satellite. In addition, its facilities are often used by out-of-town stations that travel to Sacramento to cover news.

NCNS made its first news transmission in July 1987 and has filled a void created by the closure of all out-of-town television news bureaus.

This is Mallory's second stint in Sacramento. He served as KNBC's Sacramento bureau chief for three years before moving to Beirut as an NBC correspondent in 1978. Subsequent assignments for NBC took him to London, Moscow and Tokyo before he returned to set up his company.

San Francisco

KGO-TV
900 Front St.; San Francisco, 94111; (415) 954-7777.
Jim Vargas, correspondent.

This ABC-affiliate formerly had a bureau in Sacramento but has been covering the Capitol and other statewide stories out of the main office.

Vargas covers state and local politics and government. He has been with the station since 1971 and formerly worked for KJEO-TV in Fresno.

KRON-TV
1001 Van Ness Ave.; San Francisco, 94109; (415) 441-4444
Rollin Post, political correspondent.

Post covers state and local politics and offers political analysis for this NBC-affiliate station. Post has been with the station since 1989 and has covered politics for San Francisco area stations since 1965. KRON had the distinction for several years of being the only out-of-Sacramento station to maintain a full-time Capitol bureau, but it closed its Sacramento operation in 1988.

8

California's movers and shakers

To the larger public, politics is an activity of politicians, the men and women who offer themselves for public office. But behind the candidates exists a complex network of professionals and amateurs who design, finance and manage the campaigns that voters see. These are the movers and shakers of politics, who have at least as much influence as the out-front candidates for office. Their motives range from ideological conviction to greed, and, if anything, their role is increasing as campaigns become more expensive and sophisticated.

California's power brokers are especially obscure because of the state's unique political system, features of which include weak party structures, non-partisan local governments and a multitude of locally based political organizations. Other major states such as Illinois and New York have more formalized political power structures. During Richard Daley's heyday as mayor of Chicago, for instance, no one doubted that he was the boss, not only in his city, but of the entire Illinois Democratic Party. Those who aspired to office, whether it was the clerkship of the smallest court or the president of the United States, had to clear through Daley or his minions.

Behind-the-scenes political power in California is wielded more indirectly. And in a state of media and money politics, rather than street-level organizations, those with access to money form the elite, a fact that becomes ever-more important as California's clout in national politics expands. The Los Angeles area has evolved into a source of national political money at least as important as the concrete canyons of New York and continues to gain strength as new campaign finance laws make direct contributions more difficult.

California has also developed a cadre of professional campaign organizers – "consultants," as they prefer to be called – who have pioneered in the sophisticated techniques of mass political communications: television, computer-directed mail and, most recent, prerecorded video tapes that combine the impact of television with the selectivity of mail.

THE HOLLYWOOD BRANCH

Every four years, a little ritual occurs. Those who aspire to the White House begin booking flights to Los Angeles International Airport, not to present themselves to voters, but to schmooz with a handful of men and women who reside within a few miles of one another on the West Side of Los Angeles. Most of those who make the pilgrimages to Los Angeles are Democrats because most of the West Side's political financiers are Democrats, connected to the huge, Los Angeles-based entertainment industry. But not a few of them are Republicans. Prior to the 1988 presidential primary season, Republican Bob Dole raised more money out of Hollywood than did Democrat Michael Dukakis.

Hollywood types tend to be passionate about their causes and free with their money, which is exactly what politicians want. It's been estimated that the Los Angeles region accounts for a fifth of all the money spent on presidential primaries.

"There's an increasingly mutual attraction between political people and entertainment people," Stanley Scheinbaum, an economist and political activist, has said. "The politicians like the glitz and the entertainment people like the power."

But Scheinbaum and others have qualms about the growing influence of entertainers – most of whom are naive – on politics through these in-and-out fundraising visits.

"I don't think it's healthy," he says. "Basically, a few rich people get that opportunity (to meet the politicians), and I don't think the influence of these kind of people should be any greater than of those folks in the ghettos and barrios."

Among the Democrats, two organized groups have emerged in recent years. One is the Hollywood Women's Political Committee, founded in 1984 by singer/actress Barbra Streisand. The committee specializes in the star-studded fund-raising extravaganza on behalf of liberal candidates and causes. Streisand, for instance, staged a big fund-raiser for California Sen. Alan Cranston at her Malibu ranch in 1986 and repackaged the entertainment as a television special, thus magnifying its financial impact. The second and newer organization is the Show Coalition, known as ShowCo, founded in 1988 by younger Hollywood figures, most of whom had been identified with Gary Hart's abortive presidential bid. ShowCo has not yet become a major fund-raising source but acts as an intermediary between politicians and entertainers, staging seminars and other non-financial events.

Sometimes the relationships between politicians and entertainers can backfire. State Assemblyman Tom Hayden, the former radical and estranged husband of actress Jane Fonda, took a group of "brat pack" actors to the 1988 Democratic convention in Atlanta for an immersion in politics. Among the young stars was Rob Lowe. Months later, it was revealed that Lowe had made explicit videotapes of sexual escapades with local girls during the convention.

Streisand and actor Robert Redford (who starred together in a semi-political movie "The Way We Were") are the prototypical Hollywood liberals, willing to devote time and money to their candidates and causes. While Streisand prefers to work directly for candidates, Redford takes a loftier, issue-oriented approach through a foundation that he has endowed. But they are not alone. Others who share their ideological commitment include Morgan Fairchild, who is especially close to Cranston; Sally Field; Cher; Gregory Peck; Ally Sheedy; Bette Midler; Goldie Hawn; Chevy Chase; and Bruce Willis.

Jerry Brown developed especially tight ties to the Hollywood Democrats during his eight years as governor and as a perennial candidate for president and U.S. senator. He was singer Linda Ronstadt's self-proclaimed "boyfriend" for a time, dated other Hollywood figures and made Lucy's El Adobe Cafe, a hangout for actors, his unofficial Los Angeles headquarters. Actors such as Warren Beatty, Jane Fonda and singers such as Ronstadt and Helen Reddy raised tons of money for Brown's non-stop campaigns, and director Francis Ford Coppola produced an ill-fated live television program in Wisconsin during Brown's second unsuccessful campaign for the presidency in 1980. Gary Hart was the Hollywood liberals' clear favorite for president in 1984 and again in 1988 until he was forced to withdraw. So far, none of the would-be presidents has won the heart of Hollywood Democrats for 1992, although several are trying hard.

Ronald Reagan personified the blurry line that separates politics and show business, and during his political career solidified the ties that bind many in Hollywood to the GOP. The most outwardly political of the Hollywood conservatives these days is Charlton Heston, who makes commercials for Republican candidates and has often been mentioned as a potential candidate himself, so often that he's developed a stock rejoinder: "I'd rather play a senator than be one." Heston's fellow Republican, Clint Eastwood, did pursue a brief political career as mayor of Carmel, but has since returned to his movie-making career full-time.

Comedian Bob Hope is a mainstay of Republican fund-raising events and, not surprisingly, most of the other Hollywood conservatives are of the older generation, such as Frank Sinatra, Fred MacMurray, James Stewart and Robert Young. But some newer and younger stars also side with the GOP, such as Sylvester Stallone, Tony Danza, Chuck Norris, Jaclyn Smith and strongman-turned-actor Arnold Schwarzenegger, who's married to Kennedy clanswoman Maria Shriver.

Hollywood politics, however, involves more than the men and women whose names are found on theater marquees and record labels. The business side of show business is also heavily involved in politics in terms of both personal conviction and financial betterment. The most prominent of the Hollywood tycoons who dabble in politics is Lew Wasserman, head of the huge MCA entertainment conglomerate, and he plays both sides of the partisan fence. Wasserman is a Democrat but had particularly close ties to Reagan from the latter's days as an MCA client and star of MCA-produced television programs. Republican Sen. Pete Wilson also has established a close relationship with Wasserman that forecloses aid to any would-be political rival. The entertainment industry, like any, has business in Washington and

Sacramento, mostly involving tax treatment on those incredibly complex movie and television deals. Wilson, for instance, endeared himself to the show biz moguls by protecting their interests during the writing of federal tax reform laws.

Movie mogul Jerry Weintraub is another Hollywood businessman who dabbles in politics. He served on Republican George Bush's finance team in 1988, although he's best known as a Democratic campaign contributor. And producer Norman Lear has made liberal causes his second career.

Much of the Hollywood hierarchy is Jewish and politicians who want its support must adhere to a strongly pro-Israeli line. That's why Jerry Brown, Alan Cranston, Pete Wilson, Ronald Reagan and any other California politician who aspires to the political big time in Washington can be counted in Israel's corner. In contrast, when Rep. Pete McCloskey ran for the Senate in 1982 as a critic of Israel, he bombed in Hollywood.

ELSEWHERE IN THE SOUTHLAND

Not everybody who writes a fat check to a politician in California is an entertainment industry figure. As a prosperous and fast-growing state, California has produced more than its share of wealthy people who give to candidates from both parties or – perhaps more important – can ask others to contribute as peers rather than political beggars.

Not surprisingly, Southern California aerospace executives tilt toward the Republicans with their promises of greater military spending. When, for instance, George Bush made a quick, money-raising trip to Southern California in 1988 while seeking the Republican presidential nomination, he stopped at the TRW aerospace plant in Redondo Beach, then headed for private fund-raising events at the Bel Air home of real estate tycoon Howard Ruby and the Rancho Mirage estate of publisher Walter Annenberg.

Donald Bren, head of the big Irvine Co. land development firm in Orange County, has emerged in recent years as a Republican financial power, joining such older kingmakers as auto dealer Holmes Tuttle, who was part of the group that persuaded Ronald Reagan to run for governor in 1966. (Most of those prominent early Reagan backers have since died.) Financier David Murdock is another Southern California business mogul with strong Republican connections, as is Lodwrick Cook, chairman of Atlantic Richfield Co. Philip Hawley, chairman of the Carter-Hawley-Hale department store chain, was once a major Republican player but with his company's shaky financial situation in recent years, his political star seems to have dimmed.

The Southern California business types who lean toward the Democratic side include Richard O'Neill, an heir to vast land holdings in Orange County who has been known to devote weekends to precinct-walking and once served as state Democratic chairman. Michael Milken, the junk bond whiz kid whose career crashed in scandal, was closely identified with several Democratic political figures, including Cranston and former Rep. Tony Coelho. Coelho, in fact, was forced to resign from Congress after revelations that he had acquired a bond through Milken under suspicious circumstances.

One of the towering figures of Southern California political financing defies easy categorization. Armand Hammer, oilman, philanthropist and private diplomat, has been an adviser to and fund-raiser for countless California politicians of both parties.

San Diego, which tries to isolate itself from Los Angeles, has developed its own infrastructure of political power brokers. Newspaper publisher Helen Copley is a powerhouse, as is Joan Kroc, who inherited the McDonald's hamburger empire and a baseball team from her late husband, Ray. Banker and deal-maker Richard Silberman was a big political player – even serving for a time in Jerry Brown's administration in Sacramento – and is married to a San Diego County supervisor, Susan Golding. But Silberman was indicted in 1989 on drug-money laundering charges.

Fast-food moguls represent a particular subspecies of political financiers in California. In addition to the Krocs, Silberman once headed the Jack-in-the-Box hamburger chain in partnership with Robert Peterson, whose wife, Maureen O'Connor, is the Democratic mayor of San Diego. And Carl's Jr. chain founder Carl Karcher is a patron of Republican and right-wing causes in Orange County.

Another subspecies is the political lawyer and the prime examples are to be found in the offices of a Los Angeles law firm headed by Charles Manatt, former Democratic national chairman, and ex-U.S. Sen. John Tunney. Mickey Kantor, one of Southern California's most effective political lawyers, is a member of the firm, and a former associate is John Emerson, who periodically takes time out from his practice to run campaigns, such as that of Gary Hart.

MOVERS AND SHAKERS OF THE NORTH

Northern California's power brokers tend to operate more quietly than their counterparts in Los Angeles and Hollywood. Among Republicans, no one is quieter or more influential than David Packard, a co-founder of the Hewlett-Packard computer firm and perhaps California's richest man, with a personal fortune exceeding $2 billion. Packard tends to support moderate to liberal Republicans; he was, for instance, instrumental in helping Tom Campbell unseat a conservative Republican incumbent, Rep. Ernest Konnyu, in 1988 in his home district on the San Francisco Peninsula.

Packard is the grand old man of Silicon Valley, the center of California's computer industry. As computer entrepreneurs have matured in business terms, they also have become civic and political leaders. One, Ed Zschau, won a seat in Congress and came within a few thousand votes of unseating Sen. Alan Cranston in 1986.

To date, the computer moguls have wielded influence mostly at the local level, helping San Jose and the rest of Silicon Valley develop an infrastructure to match their population and economic growth. But some, such as Packard, have moved beyond. His influence extends to the White House, and he has been a quiet prod to Gov. George Deukmejian on doing something about California's traffic problems.

Two other Northern California tycoons whose influence extends well beyond the state are the Bechtels, Stephen Sr. and Stephen Jr., who run San Francisco-based Bechtel Corp., a worldwide construction and engineering firm. At one time, it seemed as if half the Reagan administration in Washington consisted of ex-Bechtel executives, such as Secretary of Defense Caspar Weinberger and Secretary of State George Schultz.

Among Northern California Democratic financiers, none ranks higher than San Francisco real estate investor Walter Shorenstein. Shorenstein labors tirelessly on behalf of the party's coffers and is courted just as tirelessly by presidential hopefuls. In 1989, however, Shorenstein declared independence after ex-Gov. Jerry Brown became state party chairman. Shorenstein and Bruce Lee, a high-ranking United Auto Workers official, established a "soft-money" drive to aid Democratic presidential nominee Michael Dukakis in California in 1988 and decided to continue the separate organizational fund despite entreaties from Brown that they fold their operation into his party apparatus.

Another San Franciscan who has wielded a big stick in Democratic financial circles is attorney Duane Garrett, although his standing fell in 1988 after he attached himself to Bruce Babbitt's ill-fated voyage into presidential waters. And among San Francisco insiders, Henry Berman, a "consultant" to the Seagram's distilling family, carries much clout for his political fund-raising ability.

Shorenstein, Garrett and Berman are valued not so much for their personal wealth, which is fairly modest in the case of the latter two, but for their organizational ability. They can pull together a substantial amount of political money simply by making a few phone calls or placing their names on invitations.

Gordon Getty, who may be California's second-wealthiest man, is a different kind of political financier. Getty, a San Francisco resident, is an heir to the Getty oil fortune but devotes much of his time to private endeavors, especially composing classical music. Wife Ann Getty is a political junkie who lends her husband's name and her energies to political enterprises and was particularly active in ex-Gov. Brown's ceaseless campaigns.

The East Bay – Oakland, Alameda County and Contra Costa County – has developed its own coterie of political pooh-bahs. Jack Brooks, a part-owner of the Raiders football team, carries a lot of weight among Democrats, and developers Joe Callahan and Ken Hoffman play major roles at the local levels. Ken Behring, a developer and owner of the Seattle Seahawks football team, has also developed a reputation for political dealing at the local level with influence that stretches into the state Legislature.

Sacramento, another fast-growing area, has seen its developers become political heavyweights, and not just at the local level. The Northern California and Republican equivalent of the Manatt-Tunney law firm in Southern California also is to be found in Sacramento, this one headed by, among others, Steve Merksamer, a one-time top aide to Deukmejian. Merksamer and his colleagues at the firm represent top-drawer corporate clients in political affairs while Merksamer functions as a Republican insider and continues to informally advise Deukmejian.

Two of Sacramento's developers, Angelo Tsakopoulous and Phil Angelides, were big-money contributors and fund-raisers for fellow Greek-Americans Michael Dukakis and Art Agnos (mayor of San Francisco) in 1988, and Angelides, a former Capitol aide, has toyed with running for Congress himself. They exemplify another trend in political financing in California: the creation of groups that help people of similar ethnic backgrounds pursue their political careers. Frozen out of traditional sources of Republican campaign money, for instance, George Deukmejian tapped the state's large and wealthy Armenian-American community. Los Angeles lawyer Karl Samuelian organized the effort, and with Deukmejian's victory, he became a major power in Republican politics. Similar organization efforts have aided Asian politicians such as Los Angeles City Councilman Michael Woo and Sacramento Rep. Robert Matsui, while Los Angeles' large Jewish community has been a major source of campaign money for both parties, and not just for Jewish candidates.

Hispanics and blacks have yet to develop similarly powerful ethnic fund-raising networks, although black entertainers have helped such political figures as Los Angeles Mayor Tom Bradley. The most important black political financier in the state has been Sam Williams, a Los Angeles attorney who is close to Bradley.

DOWN ON THE FARM

In California's major agricultural valleys the financial and political powers are, not surprisingly, connected to agribusiness. The state's wealthiest agribusinessmen – and two of the most influential – are Modesto's Gallo wine-making brothers, Ernest and Julio. The secretive brothers have personal wealth estimated at nearly $1 billion and are powerful political figures in the Central Valley.

Further south, amid the cotton fields of the lower San Joaquin Valley, the powers are the Boswells and the Salyers, two agribusiness families whose holdings sweep across the now-dry expanse of Tulare Lake. The Boswells – the largest privately owned farming operation in the world with interests in other states and in Australia – and the Salyers play political hardball with campaign funds and high-priced lobbyists to protect their interests in Sacramento and Washington. And their major interests lie in protecting and enhancing the public water supplies vital to their farming operations.

Norma Foster Maddy has double-barreled political clout. She's not only the heiress to the Foster Farms chicken empire, but she's married to state Sen. Ken Maddy, the Republican leader of the Senate. And Maddy's partner in the horse racing business is John Harris, head of Harris Farms.

The wine-making families of the Napa and nearby valleys are major powers in local politics and the scion of one family, Don Sebastiani, briefly served in the state Legislature.

At last count, about 2 million California workers belonged to labor unions, a number that's holding steady even as labor's overall share of the expanding work force has slipped to under 20 percent. Despite that relative decline, California labor leaders remain powerful political figures, able to turn out bodies and distribute money at levels that are decisive in many political conflicts. A prime example occurred in 1987, when a big labor turnout helped Democrat Cecil Green capture a Los Angeles County state Senate seat that seemed destined to go Republican. Labor fired up its troops on an issue near to worker's hearts: Republican Deukmejian's unilateral closure of the state's occupational safety and health inspection agency. Later, labor obtained voter approval of a ballot measure reinstating the agency and won approval of a major increase in California's minimum wage. So while labor's ranks may have thinned, they still can be potent.

The leading labor figure in California is Jack Henning, an old-school orator and organizer who serves as secretary-treasurer of the California Labor Federation (the AFL-CIO umbrella organization) and is largely a one-man band. Henning walks the hallways of the Capitol personally to lobby legislation affecting labor's interests and battles privately and publicly with employers and politicians who don't follow his bidding. A major overhaul of the state's system of compensating injured workers in 1989 was Henning's major accomplishment of the decade and, some believe, the high note on which he will retire. But if Henning is ready to step down, labor doesn't have anyone immediately positioned to step into his shoes. Bill Robertson, the AFL-CIO's man in Los Angeles, is a secondary labor power, as is United Auto Workers official Bruce Lee.

Cesar Chavez was an enigmatic and influential figure of the 1970s as head of the farm workers' organization, but in more recent years, with a hostile Republican administration in Sacramento, his clout and that of the United Farm Workers Union have dropped like a stone.

Labor's major gains in recent years have been among public employees, and the leaders of their unions have seen their visibility and power increase, especially since they are free with campaign funds. Ed Foglia, who heads the California Teachers Association, is one of labor's new power figures. His stock rose when the CTA won voter approval in 1988 of a major overhaul of school financing. The large California State Employees Association is also a major source of campaign money, but it rotates its presidency often, which prevents any from becoming a figure of independent stature.

ORGANIZATIONS OF OTHER COLORS

The public employee unions exemplify another trend in California political financing: the increasing clout of large organizations with direct financial interests in political decision-making.

In the halls of government in Sacramento, big business doesn't loom very large. The groups that count – because they annually distribute hundreds of thousands of dollars to political campaigns – are the associations of professionals, such as the

California Trial Lawyers Association, the California Medical Association and the California Nurses Association. They approach fund-raising as a cost of doing business and operate their distribution operations in close consultation with their lobbyists, who daily walk the halls of the Capitol seeking to pass and kill legislation that impacts people they represent.

But that workaday attitude toward political financing also is accompanied by relative anonymity. The men and women who operate these and other associations aren't political kingmakers in the usual sense of the world, although they wield considerable political power. They are narrowly focused on their issues and disinterested in the larger political picture.

THE INITIATIVE ENTREPRENEURS

California's most powerful political agenda-setters these days are those who are most adept at writing, financing and organizing campaigns for the increasingly numerous ballot measures.

The prototypical initiative entrepreneurs were Howard Jarvis and Paul Gann, two old men (both have since died) who sponsored Proposition 13 in 1978. The financial and political impact of Proposition 13 made Jarvis and Gann, especially the former, into high-profile political figures and thus into political powerhouses in the media-heavy atmosphere of the 1980s. They were besieged with requests to lend their names to additional ballot measures and endorse candidates for office and engaged in both. Gann even became a candidate himself for the Senate in 1980, losing to incumbent Alan Cranston.

In the mid-1980s, a new crop of initiative designers arose, this time on the left side of the political ledger. To date, the most spectacularly successful has been Harvey Rosenfield, a young consumer advocate and Ralph Nader disciple who founded "Voter Revolt" and then put together a successful auto insurance reform initiative in 1988, winning in the face of a $60 million-plus opposition campaign financed by the insurance industry.

Rosenfield, whose penchant for publicity has been likened to that of Jarvis, immediately launched a second initiative campaign for the 1990 ballot, aimed at modifying Proposition 13 to remove its benefits from business property. And he, too, played political kingmaker by endorsing a candidate for the state insurance commissioner's position.

In Sacramento, meanwhile, an informal coalition of environmentalists is establishing its own ongoing initiative factory and already has several wins under its belt. Gerald Meral, the bearded, mild-mannered administrator of the Planning and Conservation League, operates as the consortium's coordinator, and he and his colleagues have devised a unique system of promoting their measures. Groups are invited to join the consortium and supply a quota of cash or signatures to entitle them to direct a share of the proceeds. The system was used on a park bond issue and a cigarette tax measure in 1988 and is being used for a big rail-bond issue and a liquor tax measure for 1990.

Assemblyman Lloyd Connelly, a liberal Democrat from Sacramento, has been closely allied with the Meral consortium and has become, in his self-effacing way, a powerful figure in setting the political agenda of the late 1980s. A much better known Democratic assemblyman, Tom Hayden, also is playing the initiative game. He was a force behind the anti-toxics initiative, Proposition 65, in 1986 and is pushing for the so-called "Big Green" environmental protection measure in 1990 that also has drawn the backing of Attorney General John Van de Kamp, the likely Democratic candidate for governor.

Republicans, too, are using the initiative as a tool of partisan and ideological warfare. Ross Johnson, the Assembly's Republican leader, has been especially active.. He co-sponsored a campaign finance reform measure, Proposition 73, that was approved by voters in 1988 and is backing one of the several reapportionment initiatives in 1990. But beyond Johnson, the right side of the initiative business is moribund after the deaths of Jarvis and Gann. Gann's daughter, Linda Gann-Stone, has taken over his "People's Advocate" organization, but she is little known and cannot automatically command the attention her father received. Jarvis' anti-tax movement has also fallen on slow times with his death, and the conservative forces await the rise of a new figure who can front initiatives. For the moment, even as the state edges rightward in its overall political orientation, the political left has captured the momentum in the use of initiatives to further its political agenda.

MERCENARIES OF THE POLITICAL WARS

Standing just behind the candidates and the front men for the initiative campaigns are legions of professionals to whom the explosion of political activity in California is a lucrative growth industry, so much so that pros who used to practice out of Washington and New York are shifting their operations to California. Professional signature-gathering firms, fund-raisers, media consultants, pollsters, campaign strategists, accountants and even attorneys who specialize in writing, attacking and defending ballot propositions have reaped tens of millions of dollars in the 1980s as the mercenaries of the initiative wars. The most obviously profitable of those campaigns was the $100 million battle over five insurance initiatives in 1988. One campaign consultant alone earned over $10 million in fees.

The consultants, however, aren't just paid soldiers in California's political wars. Whether they are helping candidates or fighting over ballot measures, they have also become major players in determining who runs or what proposal is put before voters. They, too, shape the political agenda. Some specialize in Democratic or liberal candidates and causes, while others exclusively work the Republican and conservative side. And a few plow the middle, working for whomever has the most money or the best chance of winning.

Although professional campaign strategists theoretically stand in the background while the candidate is out front, sometimes their importance is reversed. When Clint Reilly announced in 1989 that he was giving up his management of Dianne Feinstein's campaign for governor, it was a political event of the first magnitude since Reilly, a credentialed professional, had been one of the ex-San Francisco mayor's most valuable assets. Reilly's departure lowered Feinstein's political stock and forced her to engage in a damage-control operation.

Dozens of campaign management firms operate in California but only a relative handful command statewide attention. Reilly, who operates under the name of Clinton Reilly Campaigns, is based in San Francisco and specializes in Democrats such as Feinstein, but he earned his biggest fee, more than $10 million, as the major strategist for the insurance industry in the 1988 ballot battle. And he kept the money despite the industry's wipeout at the polls. Reilly managed Feinstein's mayoralty campaigns and has advised Bill Honig, who was elected as state superintendent of public instruction in 1982. Reilly also has done a number of local campaigns, including Gary Condit's 1989 victory in a special congressional election in the San Joaquin Valley. Abrasive and opinionated, Reilly is a controversial figure who feuded publicly for years with Assembly Speaker Willie Brown.

A rising star among the Democratic-oriented consultants is Richie Ross, who was Brown's chief political adviser until striking out on his own after Brown lost some Assembly races in 1986. Ross, headquartered in Sacramento, had two statewide victories in 1988: Proposition 98, a school financing measure, and Proposition 97, a labor-backed proposal to restore the state worker safety program canceled by Gov. Deukmejian. He also managed Art Agnos' come-from-behind campaign for mayor of San Francisco in 1987 and was tapped by Agnos to run the campaign for a new baseball stadium in 1989. Ross also is John Van de Kamp's gubernatorial campaign manager.

The most prominent Democratic campaign management firm in Southern California is BAD Campaigns, operated by Michael Berman, brother of Rep. Howard Berman, and Carl D'Agostino, a former aide to Ken Cory when Cory was state controller. BAD, based in Beverly Hills, specializes in candidates endorsed by the political organization headed by Reps. Howard Berman and Henry Waxman. The Berman-Waxman organization dominates politics on Los Angeles' West Side and dabbles in campaigns throughout Southern California. BAD also advised Gray Davis, the West Side Democrat elected as state controller in 1980.

Los Angeles-based Cerrell Associates functions mostly as a public relations company, but it also handles some Democratic campaigns. Firm owner Joe Cerrell has national influence in Democratic politics.

A newcomer to the upper ranks of Democratic consultants is Sacramento's Townsend & Co., owned by David Townsend. Townsend broke out of the local category in 1988, when his firm managed – unsuccessfully – the campaign against a statewide cigarette tax ballot measure. But Townsend is beefing up to go after other statewide candidates and issues.

Another striver is Glazer and Associates, based in North Hollywood. Owner Steven Glazer's bid for the big time, after working in subsidiary roles for a number of clients, will be Kathleen Brown's campaign for state treasurer in 1990. And in roughly the same category is Darry Sragow of Beverly Hills, who worked on Sen.

Alan Cranston's successful campaign in 1986 and Lt. Gov. Leo McCarthy's failed bid for the U.S. Senate in 1988 and now has stepped in to replace Reilly on the Feinstein effort in 1990. David Doak and Robert Shrum of Los Angeles are often called to advise Democratic campaigns on media strategy and theme-setting, leaving overall management to others.

REPUBLICAN RANKS SWELLING

There seem to be more professional Republican campaign management firms than Democratic ones, perhaps because the Republicans, as the minority party, lack the campaign-staff-in-place on the legislative payroll. While legislative staffers regularly take leaves from state service to go into the field to manage Democratic campaigns for the Legislature, Republicans usually call upon professionals.

For years, the GOP professional field was dominated by Stu Spencer and Bill Roberts. But with the latter's death and the former's semiretirement (he still is an on-call adviser), a new flock of GOP-oriented consultants has arisen. The hottest of them these days is Otto Bos, a former San Diego newspaper reporter who became then-Mayor Pete Wilson's press secretary and then segued into statewide politics when Wilson ran, successfully, for the U.S. Senate in 1982. Bos ran Wilson's second-term campaign in 1988 and now is in business for himself with Wilson, the Republican candidate for governor in 1990, as his chief client. Bos, George Gorton and Dick Dresner own a San Diego-based campaign consulting firm.

Until a few years ago, the splashiest Republican consulting firm was based in Sacramento and operated by two young former legislative staffers, Sal Russo and Doug Watts. They made a name for themselves as managers of Ken Maddy's spectacular, if failed, bid for the governorship in 1978, then hit the big time as operators of George Deukmejian's narrow victory for governor in 1982. They also managed the successful campaign against the Peripheral Canal in 1982 and even moved briefly into official positions in the new administration.

Russo and Watts added Ed Rollins, the former Reagan White House political director, to their firm and did much of the media work for Ronald Reagan's presidential re-election campaign in 1984. But after that spectacular rise, the firm fell on hard times and eventually broke up. Watts is now a New York-based political consultant while Russo has remained in Sacramento and has a new firm, Russo, Marsh and Associates. Before the breakup, Russo, Watts and Rollins crashed and burned on an unsuccessful 1986 campaign against a toxic waste initiative. More recently, Russo lost a special congressional election in the San Joaquin Valley to fill ex-Rep. Tony Coelho's seat. The word in political circles is that Russo and partner Tony Marsh need a winner bad.

Another GOP campaign consultant with a string of strikeouts is Los Angeles-based Ronald Smith, who specializes in moderate to liberal Republican candidates. Smith came close with then-Rep. Ed Zschau's campaign for the U.S. Senate in 1986 and has had to settle for wins at the local level, including Tom Campbell's congressional campaign in 1988 on the San Francisco Peninsula. Another consultant who concentrates on moderate GOP candidates is Joe Shumate of San Francisco. He's confined himself to local campaigns, and he scored a noteworthy win in 1988 when a pro-choice Republican, Tricia Hunter, won a hard-fought special election for the state Assembly in San Diego County.

The Dolphin Group of Los Angeles has tried to move into the big time, but so far has settled for pieces of larger campaigns and a few local efforts on its own. The firm is looking for a statewide ballot measure campaign in 1990.

Allan Hoffenblum of Los Angeles eschews statewide campaigns in favor of handling many Republican legislative and congressional candidates and has run up a high batting average. Gary Huckaby and Carlos Rodriguez, partners in a Sacramento firm, are trying to emulate Hoffenblum's approach with some success, as are Wayne Johnson and Ray McNally, who also operate their own firms in Sacramento.

Ken Khachigian was a speech writer for Reagan and Deukmejian and now hires out as a media and strategy specialist.

THE MIDDLE-OF-THE-ROADERS

While most California campaign consultants have partisan identification, some purposely avoid such labeling and concentrate, instead, on the increasingly lucrative ballot measure field. The granddaddy of these operations is Woodward & McDowell of Burlingame, known for its high-budget campaigns for and against major propositions for a generation. It was W&M, for instance, that persuaded Californians to adopt a state lottery in 1982, working with money from a major lottery supply firm.

But the campaign firm, operated by Richard Woodward and Jack McDowell, hit a wall in 1988. It lost a campaign to change the Gann spending limit in June and then had a mixed result on auto insurance initiatives in the fall. It successfully battled insurance industry-sponsored measures, but was unable to secure passage of its own insurance proposition, sponsored mostly by trial lawyers.

As the 1990 initiative battles shape up, W&M is still looking for a high-profile and well-heeled client. Sacramento's Townsend & Co. wants to break into the big-bucks initiative campaigns, but pulled out of an effort to persuade Californians to raise gasoline taxes, apparently fearful of adding a second loss to its embryonic record.

A winner in 1988 was Bill Zimmerman of Santa Monica and his partners, Jack Fiman and Daniel Dixon. Veterans of Gary Hart's 1984 presidential campaign and identified mostly with liberal or Democratic causes, the firm was instrumental in the success of Proposition 103, the one auto insurance measure to win, and is lining up similar work for 1990. Zimmerman and Co. clearly hope to cash in on the increasing willingness of liberals to use the initiative process, something they once shunned.

TESTING THE PUBLIC MOOD

The best known of California's public opinion pollsters is Mervin Field of San Francisco, whose California Poll has been a staple of newspapers and television broadcasts for decades. Field's California Poll has itself become a major factor in handicapping politicians by determining how much attention from the media and respect from potential contributors a candidate can command. But Field doesn't offer his services to individual politicians or campaigns.

When political strategists want to know what California voters are thinking to help tailor their campaigns, they must turn to the private political pollsters, some based in California and others based elsewhere but offering their services in the state. Like consultants, pollsters tend to be identified with one party or the other and some have long-standing relationships with consultants. Sacramento's Jim Moore, for instance, is known best for his efforts on behalf of candidates and causes managed by Richie Ross.

As with consultants, there seem to be more pollsters working the Republican side of the street than the Democratic. Besides Moore, the most heavily used Democratic-oriented polling firm is Fairbank, Bregman and Maullin of San Francisco. Partner Richard Maullin first achieved prominence as a strategist in the 1970s for Gov. Jerry Brown and served for years in Brown's administration before moving into private consulting. Among the firm's clients have been Sen. Alan Cranston and Los Angeles Mayor Tom Bradley.

There are three major Republican polling firms that handle all of the major GOP candidates. They are Arthur J. Finkelstein & Associates of Irvington, N.Y., whose California clients include state Sen. Ed Davis; Tarrance & Associates of Houston, who has handled polling for, among others, Gov. Deukmejian; and The Wirthlin Group of McLean, Va., a Republican White House favorite who has done work in California for Ed Zschau and former Lt. Gov. Mike Curb.

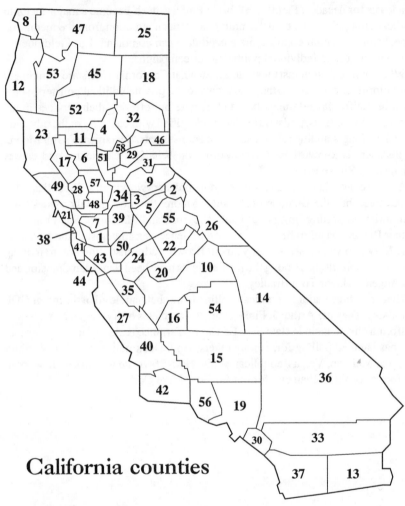

California counties

1. Alameda	16. Kings	31. Placer	
2. Alpine	17. Lake	32. Plumas	
3. Amador	18. Lassen	33. Riverside	46. Sierra
4. Butte	19. Los Angeles	34. Sacramento	47. Siskiyou
5. Calaveras	20. Madera	35. San Benito	48. Solano
6. Colusa	21. Marin	36. San Bernardino	49. Sonoma
7. Contra Costa	22. Mariposa	37. San Diego	50. Stanislaus
8. Del Norte	23. Mendocino	38. San Francisco	51. Sutter
9. El Dorado	24. Merced	39. San Joaquin	52. Tehama
10. Fresno	25. Modoc	40. San Luis Obispo	53. Trinity
11. Glenn	26. Mono	41. San Mateo	54. Tulare
12. Humboldt	27. Monterey	42. Santa Barbara	55. Tuolumne
13. Imperial	28. Napa	43. Santa Clara	56. Ventura
14. Inyo	29. Nevada	44. Santa Cruz	57. Yolo
15. Kern	30. Orange	45. Shasta	58. Yuba

9

County government–at the crossroads

Colonial Americans borrowed the concept of county government from Great Britain and as the United States expanded to 50 states, each of them, save one (Alaska) created its own set of counties.

Originally, a British county was, as the name implies, a territory administered by a count. Thus was born its dual nature, both a unit of local government and a subdivision of a larger central government.

It is that dual nature that lies at the heart of the crisis in county government in California, one so severe that some observers are saying counties should be abolished altogether.

That's not likely to occur, but as the 21st century draws near, California counties may undergo some fundamental changes to allow them to function in a world vastly different from the 19th century, post-gold rush California in which most were created.

There's nothing logical about the organization of California's 58 counties (including its one city-county combination, San Francisco).

More than half of the state's population is contained in seven counties of Southern California, for instance, while the remainder lives in 51 counties in the north. And they range in individual size from the more than eight million people of Los Angeles County to the 1,200 or so who call Alpine County home.

This reflects the fact that county boundaries were established according to 19th century economic and political conditions.

The relatively small, elongated counties of the old gold mining district along the Sierra foothills, for example, follow the dictum that no miner should be more than a day's horseback ride from a county seat so that he could file his mining claims. But in those days, Southern California was a largely unpopulated desert.

Originally, California had a few large counties. But as its population grew in the late 19th century, local boosterism and political tensions created the impetus for breaking up the big counties and creating many more smaller ones.

Mariposa County once contained most of Southern California, the lower San Joaquin Valley and the central coast. More than a dozen new counties were carved out of that vast territory as local ambitions flourished. One of them is the nation's largest county, San Bernardino.

San Francisco County once contained not only the city of San Francisco but what is now San Mateo County, to cite another example. San Mateo was created when the city and county governments were combined in San Francisco. A group of crooked politicians gave birth to the new county, via their friends in the Legislature, to continue to have a friendly milieu in which to practice their trade.

Cattle ranchers and farmers south of Los Angeles seceded to create Orange County, fearing domination by the municipal colossus then being formed.

The last of the breakaways occurred just after World War I, when Imperial County was carved out of the arid eastern reaches of San Diego County. Since then, the number has been fixed at 58, even though the state's population has increased many times over and its economy has undergone two or three evolutions.

And the irony of that is being driven home every day as local governments try to create new regional planning mechanisms to deal with such knotty issues as transportation and air pollution, issues that don't respect county boundaries. Local officials are, in effect, trying to recreate the large counties that were broken up in the 19th century.

The evolution of regional governments represents one possible direction for counties. As some see it, counties would cede their land-use planning and other large-scale functions to regional entities and evolve more and more into mere subagencies of the state.

From the earliest days of the state, counties conducted themselves along parallel lines with some inherent conflicts.

On one track, counties were purely units of local government, providing police, fire, transportation, judicial and other services to their residents, or at least to those not also residing in incorporated cities.

On the other, counties performed functions for the state, such as running welfare and health care systems for the poor.

Into the counties' treasuries came revenues from property taxes, sales taxes on transactions outside of cities, direct subventions from state and federal governments and other miscellaneous sources. In theory, the state was supposed to pay for most of what it required counties to do; in practice, the state aid never matched outgo and the difference came from local taxes, especially those on property.

The system worked, after a fashion, as long as there was elasticity in the local revenue base. County supervisors could adjust property tax rates to cover whatever was needed after the other revenues were tallied.

But it stopped working in the late 1970s, after California voters endorsed Proposition 13, the Jarvis-Gann property tax reduction initiative.

As state aid stagnated during the 1970s and property values soared, property tax bills skyrocketed. Angry homeowners trooped to the polls to vote for Proposition 13 in overwhelming numbers.

The effect of Proposition 13 on county governments was manyfold.

It was an immediate and massive loss of revenues amounting to billions of dollars each year. And that, in turn, resulted in a large infusion of state aid to cover some, but not all, of the gap.

As the state assumed a larger share of the counties' annual budgets, the focal point of policy-making shifted away from county boards of supervisors (five for each county except San Francisco) and to the Legislature in Sacramento.

But the new state aid never caught up with state-mandated levels of service, especially in the fast-growing health and welfare areas, despite state laws requiring such a match. Thus, county supervisors were compelled, especially in rural areas with stagnant economies, to shift more and more of their locally generated revenues to meet state mandates while purely local services declined.

The net result has been a more or less perpetual crisis in California counties that has been the topic of innumerable academic studies, seminars and journalistic examinations.

Politically, the crisis has manifested itself in a growing level of tension between the state and the counties. County supervisors are fond of denouncing state legislators and the governor for holding them in financial indenture, but some of them secretly enjoy having Sacramento as a convenient whipping boy. Proposition 13 and its aftermath have relieved them of the politically perilous annual chore of setting property tax rates. The measure essentially fixes tax rates.

At the same time, state legislators also enjoy having more direct power over counties through the budgetary process.

That's especially evident in the relationship between Sacramento and giant Los Angeles County.

The Los Angeles Board of Supervisors is controlled by three Republicans who keep a tight lid on health and welfare services to inner-city neighborhoods while playing to the demands for sheriff's patrols and other services from the suburbs.

Those policies put the supervisors at odds with the liberal Democrats who dominate the county's legislative delegation in Sacramento. They include Senate President Pro Tem David Roberti; Sen. Diane Watson, chairwoman of the Senate Health and Human Services Committee; and Assemblywoman Maxine Waters, a powerful member of the committee that writes the final version of the state budget each year.

The Democratic legislators use their power over county finances to pressure the Republican supervisors to do their bidding, sometimes successfully, other times not. The supervisors, in turn, call upon their fellow Republicans in the Legislature and the governor's office to protect their positions.

The Los Angeles supervisors have been called the "five little kings" for the vast power they wield, and they sit atop the supervisorial pecking order. State legislators and even congressmen would willingly give up their positions for a seat on the Los Angeles board.

To a lesser degree, supervisors in other densely populated, urbanized counties enjoy similarly elevated positions.

While they have been forced to relinquish much of their financial and budgetary authority to Sacramento, urban county supervisors still have vast powers over land use and other purely local matters.

That puts them squarely in the middle of California's expanding battle over growth, pitting environmentalists and their allies against land developers and associated business interests.

Traditionally, county supervisors have been politically conservative and pro-development, especially since their direct constituencies have been mostly in suburban or rural areas of the counties. A majority of current supervisors are Republicans.

And in counties such as Los Angeles, with its vast stretches of urbanized or suburbanized, but not unincorporated, territory, supervisors and pro-development forces have had a mutually beneficial relationship.

The supervisors approved the developers' projects almost without question and the developers reciprocated by pouring millions of dollars into the incumbents' political treasuries, thus rendering them nearly invulnerable to challenge at the polls.

But the rise of the anti- or slow-growth forces, even in traditionally Republican-voting areas such as Orange County, has scrambled the political picture. Few supervisors in fast-growing counties now portray themselves as advocates of growth, even though their voting records and lists of campaign contributors might say otherwise.

Los Angeles County Supervisor Mike Antonovich, who represents the fast-expanding northern section of the county, found himself facing a platoon of challengers in 1988, for example, and while Antonovich, long a friend of developers, survived a runoff, even he had to concede that the political chemistry has changed.

As California's population continues to expand by more than 5 million people a decade, the politics of growth will become even more dominant in counties feeling the impact.

Both large-scale land-use policies and individual projects will be subjected to more intense scrutiny and the old cozy relationship between supervisors and developers will be strained.

A growing sense that politically sensitive supervisors are incapable of dealing with big picture issues represents one threat to the continuation of county government along traditional lines.

The South Coast Air Quality District, which monitors air quality for most of Southern California, has been granted vast new powers by state legislation to deal with the region's worsening smog situation. And some of those new powers cut into the political turf traditionally occupied by counties and other local governments.

Some observers see in the district's new powers the beginnings of a true regional government that would make land use and other key decisions and leave counties, if they continue to exist, only with housekeeping matters.

And in some counties, that transition may already have occurred. San Diego County, for example, requires major development to occur only within a city, which negates much of the land-use power that has translated into political power in many counties. The city of San Diego has become, for all intents, the regional policy-making body for the county as a whole.

Another step along the path of county evolution may be replication of the San Francisco model, combining city and county governments into one unit.

A city-county consolidation failed at the polls in Sacramento County in the 1970s, but a new effort is being made because the rapid development of the county has resulted in overlapping and often competitive local governments.

Sacramento now has the state's largest proportion of urbanized unincorporated territory and its supervisors are concerned that much of the suburban sales tax base – an increasingly important source of revenue in the post-Proposition 13 world – might be siphoned off by the creation of new suburban cities.

The hunger for sales tax revenues to replace the lost property taxes has driven counties into bitter rivalries with one another and with city governments.

Local officials, offering above-the-table and hidden subsidies to developers, haggle with one another over the location of tax-generating shopping centers and "auto malls." There have even been accusations that slow-growth movements in one community are financed by boosters of another to capture revenue-producing development.

And to strengthen their competitive ability to lure development, some counties have moved into the "redevelopment" field formerly occupied by cities, using their powers to acquire land and borrow money cheaply as lures to investors.

The scramble for taxable development has become so intense that in many high-impact counties, land-use decisions are driven by that competition rather than by principles of good planning. And that has contributed to the demands for more comprehensive, regional approaches to major policy decisions.

While Los Angeles, Sacramento, San Diego and the other populous, urbanized counties try to deal with the effects of rapid and heavy growth, it's been a much different story among the state's more rural counties.

Some rural counties, especially those in the Sierra foothills, are experiencing booms of their own. They are close enough, in driving terms, to attract commuters and their weather is pleasant enough to attract pensioners. Indeed, retirement has become an industry unto itself in some foothill counties – and one that's likely to grow with the aging of the population.

But a broad swath of California, ranging from Del Norte, Siskiyou and Modoc counties on the state's far northern border to Imperial County in the extreme south, has missed out on the state's economic boom.

Their resource-based economies – timber, minerals, ranching and farming – have fallen on hard times. Their young fled to the booming metropolitan areas as local job opportunities disappeared, and their populations are stagnant in numbers and advancing in age. Tourism and recreation have eased the economic crisis in some areas, but those are even more seasonal and erratic than the traditional industries. They are too remote and their weather too severe to be attractive to retirees.

These rural counties have felt the post-Proposition 13 pinch the hardest since local wealth is largely property-based and local retail activity, which would generate sales tax revenues, is scant. Indeed, residents of rural counties often make special trips to urban areas, which have the shopping centers and chain stores that their hometowns lack.

And with chronically high unemployment (approaching 20 percent in some rural counties), the burdensome demands of health and welfare services are also persistently elevated.

Since Proposition 13 was passed more than a decade ago, the level of local services, such as sheriff's patrols and road maintenance, has declined markedly in rural areas because counties are required to meet the state "mandates" first before budgeting for the other programs.

That, in turn, has sparked a political backlash among rural residents who rate police protection and roads among their highest priorities. And rural supervisors have reacted by becoming increasingly militant on the closely related issues of revenues and state-mandated services.

Tehama County supervisors became celebrities – complete with national news magazine coverage – when they declared a revolt against state mandates. Neighboring Shasta County also received a flurry of publicity when it shut down its public libraries. And in Humboldt County, supervisors allowed paved roads to revert to gravel.

Officials in another rural county, Butte, filed suit against the state after gaining permission from county voters. They noted that state mandates rose from 45 percent to 65 percent of the county budget in the eight years that followed passage of Proposition 13.

The ballot measure that Butte County supervisors drafted and got passed by voters barred the county from spending any larger share of the county budget on welfare than it had spent in 1978-79, the first full year after Proposition 13's passage. Butte County took an even more drastic step in late 1989 by declaring itself ready to file bankruptcy. County supervisors said that projected income could not cover its obligations, even after eliminating virtually all optional services.

The state offered the county some relief by postponing payments for fire services that the state Department of Forestry provides to rural Butte County areas, but the crisis continued.

Although the Butte County law was probably invalid, it provided the legal framework for the county's suit, seeking validation of the measure and an order requiring the state to pay what county officials consider to be the state's fair share of welfare program costs. A local judge ruled for the county and the case went up on appeal.

It was one example of what came to be known as "Project Independence," a multipronged effort by counties to regain some of the financial flexibility lost with passage of Proposition 13 and its aftermath.

The counties wanted the state to pay for its mandates, as the law required, and/or provide more unrestricted revenues to counties.

Overall, county officials said, California counties went from having discretion over 30 percent of their annual budgets to just 5 percent in the decade that followed Proposition 13.

As a political and publicity tool, Project Independence – launched by the County Supervisors Association of California – had some results. In the late 1980s, as the state's own financial situation improved, it did start paying for more of its mandated services. And in 1988, Gov. George Deukmejian and the Legislature enacted a program to have the state assume virtually all costs of running the court system, thus removing it from county treasuries. But these steps merely relieved the immediate cash crunch in many counties, especially those in rural areas. And the militancy among supervisors for some permanent approach to their financial problems has continued to increase.

Specific proposals have ranged from abolishing counties altogether to obtaining a guaranteed form of revenue sharing through the sales tax. Some authorities believe that counties must create contractual, rather than dependent, relationships with the state to administer the big-ticket health and welfare programs. And there has been some discussion among supervisors of writing their own initiative to improve their political and financial standing and submitting it to voters.

Despite the militancy of county supervisors and despite the few relief programs enacted, the overall attitude toward county governments' plight among legislators and other state officials has been unsympathetic. The governor and the Legislature have continued to enact new mandates without payments to cover their costs and Deukmejian has told county officials publicly that they should use the court cost subvention funds to cover any unanticipated expenses for emergency health care and other expensive programs. There is, therefore, no immediate prospect that the counties' financial crisis will be resolved by the state.

A 1988 study by the University of California's Institute of Governmental Studies concluded that without radical surgery "future county government is likely to function as little more than an administrative arm of the state."

Alameda County

Area: 825.4 sq. mi.; Population (1988): 1,241,600; Voter registration (1989): D-63.3% R-24.5%; Unemployment (1989): 4.3%; County supervisors: Edward Campbell, Charles Santana, Don Perata, Mary King, Warren Widener; 1221 Oak St., Room 536, Oakland, 94612; (415) 272-6347.

Writer Gertrude Stein once said of Oakland, Alameda County's principal city, "There's no there there."

She didn't mean it that way, but the phrase has been interpreted ever since as meaning Oakland, and by extension the rest of Alameda County, lacked character.

Alameda County, situated on the eastern shore of the San Francisco Bay, has always existed in the cultural, political and economic shadow of San Francisco, despite all of the best efforts of the community boosters to establish a separate image.

And were it not in that shadow, Alameda County clearly would be one of California's most important areas. It contains as much social and economic diversity as can be found anywhere in the state – from the funky, 1960ish ambiance of Berkeley, home of the University of California's first and most important campus, to the wealth of Piedmont, the urban black social experiment of Oakland itself and the industrial communities of Fremont and San Leandro.

While Oakland struggles to shed itself of its crime-ridden image and claim a share of California's economic boom, the southern and eastern reaches of Alameda County are part of the California Sun Belt, with fast-growing suburban populations and the kind of economic development, strongly oriented to office operations, that is archetypical of the state in the 1980s.

Communities such as Livermore and Pleasanton are exploding with people and jobs and the Association of Bay Area Governments has projected that 70 percent of Alameda County's job growth between 1985 and 2005 will be in the southern and eastern parts of the county.

Alameda's diversity produces a certain level of political and social tension that is both geographic (Oakland and Berkeley vs. the suburbs) and socio-ethnic in character. And in that sense, the county is a microcosm of the state as a whole.

The suburbs are growing much faster than the older urban areas of the county and therefore are gaining political clout that may, in the long run, move the county's politics a bit to the right.

Alameda County, thanks to both Oakland and Berkeley, is as consistently left-of-center as nearby San Francisco, giving Democratic candidates for statewide office and president a substantial Bay Area base.

Democrats outnumber Republicans by a 2.5-1 ratio and the 64.7 percent vote that Alameda County voters gave to Michael Dukakis was second only to San Francisco's Democratic margin in 1988.

That Democratic tilt is reflected, too, in the county's all-Democratic legislative and congressional delegations and in the fact that within their own ranks, the Democratic legislators from the area are on the left side of the scale.

Assemblyman Tom Bates of Oakland is arguably the most liberal member of his house, as is, perhaps, Oakland Sen. Nicholas Petris. And Rep. Ron Dellums of Berkeley has a national reputation for tilting to the port – a fact that drives military advocates crazy since, by seniority, Dellums now wields a major influence over Pentagon spending.

The politics of Berkeley – known to its detractors as "Berserkeley" –are so far to the left that conventional liberals are, in relative terms, the local right-wing and the extreme left would embarrass the Kremlin. Berkeley established a national trend for left-of-center cities, most of them college towns, to involve themselves in issues of international politics and the global environmental. Gus Newport, the city of Berkeley's mayor for much of the 1980s, was a globe-trotting apostle for left-wing politics.

But while Berkeley's politics evolved out of the University of California and the "free speech," civil rights and anti-war protests of the 1960s, the politics of the campus itself are much more moderate these days. Student government, in fact, is dominated by the more conservative campus parties and the fraternity and sorority systems are stronger than ever, leading to some new twists on the traditional town vs. gown tensions.

University of California officials want to expand the campus and its supporting facilities, especially student housing, but city officials have resisted expansion. The standoff has meant an annual scramble for housing and one of the Bay Area's worst traffic problems. And UC officials have explored moving their statewide administrative offices out of Berkeley altogether. Alameda County's future, however, hinges more on economic trends than politics.

The Port of Oakland is a highly sophisticated doorway through which passes much of the commerce between California and the fast-growing economies of the Pacific Rim.

The rapidly expanding suburbs of the southern and eastern portions of the county include many high-tech plants, an extension of the nearby Silicon Valley. The Association of Bay Area Governments, the regional planning agency, projects a growth in total employment for Alameda County from just over a half-million jobs in 1980 to nearly 800,000 by 2005 – a growth that far outstrips population and thus makes Alameda County a destination for out-of-county commuters, many of them from the even newer suburbs in the San Joaquin Valley to the east.

Most of those new jobs, however, will be in trade and services and will be centered in the suburban portions of the county, rather than in the older communities, such as Oakland, along the bay. And that, in turn, means continued social problems for Oakland and environs.

Alpine County

Area: 726.6 sq. mi.; Population (1988): 1,210; Voter registration (1989): D-39.4% R-41.5%; Unemployment (1989): 2.7%; County supervisors: Donald Jardine, John Brissenden, Claudia Ann Wade, Eric Jung, John Bennett; P.O. Box 158, Markleeville, 96120; (916) 694-2281.

A brochure from Alpine County's Chamber of Commerce advises would-be visitors: "Get lost in Alpine County." It wouldn't be difficult to do.

This is California's smallest county in population, a tiny reminder of California's 19th century beginnings south of Lake Tahoe. And if anything, it's getting smaller. It lost 10 people between 1987 and 1988.

Not that local residents mind much. Most of them live in Alpine because they enjoy the solitude, which becomes even more intense when winter snows close all but a few roads.

Mining was the county's original reason for being, but ranching and later tourism – especially skiing during the winter – have become its economic mainstays.

Like the rest of the mountain regions of California, Alpine is politically conservative. But during the early 1970s, the tiny population base, however, sparked interest among homosexual activists, who proposed moving to Alpine en masse and establishing a friendly government. It never happened, but it kept the county stirred up for months.

Amador County

Area: 601.3 sq. mi.; Population (1988): 27,150; Voter registration (1989): D-51% R-40.6%; Unemployment (1989): 7.5%; County supervisors: Timothy Davenport, John Begovich, Edward Bamert, Steve Martin, Gale Cuneo; 108 Court St., Jackson, 95642; (209) 223-6470.

Like other counties in the "Mother Lode" east of Sacramento, Amador is experiencing the joys and pains of growth.

Its population, swollen by commuters and retirees, is among the state's fastest growing – nearly 11 percent just between 1987 and 1988.

The newcomers bring money into the county, and that economic base is augmented by the tens of thousands of tourists who flock to its consciously quaint old gold rush towns on weekends. The state, meanwhile, has built new prison facilities near Ione.

There is some social and political friction between the old-timers and the "flatlanders" who are becoming more numerous. The county was once conservatively Democratic in its political orientation but the influx of retirees and commuters seems to be moving it to the right – a fact most keenly felt by local Assemblyman Norm Waters, a conservative Democrat who came within a whisker of being defeated in 1988.

Butte County

Area: 1,664.8 sq. mi.; Population (1988): 172,600; Voter registration (1989): D-44.8% R-43.4%; Unemployment (1989): 9.3%; County supervisors: Haskel McInturf, Jane Dolan, Karen Vercruse, Edward McLaughlin, Leonard Fulton; 25 County Center Drive, Oroville, 95966; (916) 538-7224.

Butte County is the economic and political center of the vast area of California north and east of Sacramento. And as such, it reflects the ambivalence of the region, torn between a desire to participate in the economic boom that affects much of California and a fear that its quality of life would be adversely affected.

Bypassed by the construction of Interstate 5, the main north-south highway through California, Butte County has time to ponder its future. While its population has been growing, it has not yet experienced the double-digit growth that afflicts some of the rural counties that are more accessible.

The economic center of Butte County is not Oroville, its county seat, but Chico, home to the only branch of the state college system in the region and an attractive town of 35,000 with tree-lined streets and 19th century Victorian homes.

The presence of California State University, Chico, gives the community a lively political and cultural life. In the early 1980s, adherents of Tom Hayden's "economic democracy" movement seized control of the city government, only to be ousted a few years later by a right-wing reaction movement. Only Jane Dolan, Chico's liberal county supervisor, remains as a reminder of the left's brief hegemony.

The bulwarks of the local economy are the university, an agricultural industry dominated by orchard crops and tourism, much of it attracted by the state-owned Oroville Reservoir. But the university's Center for Economic Development and Planning is fostering an interest in wider economic development throughout the 12-county region centered in Butte.

The center sees the agricultural and other resource-based elements of the local economy continuing to lag and believes that the area, with its high quality of life and relatively low housing and other living costs, is primed for development.

Chico and the university notwithstanding, Butte County is a conservative area that votes Republican almost all the time. All local state and federal legislators are Republicans and George Bush easily bested Michael Dukakis in the 1988 presidential contest in the county. Within a few years, if current trends hold, Republican registered voters will outnumber Democrats.

That's the reverse of what was true only a generation ago, when all state and federal legislators from northeastern California were Democrats, albeit of a conservative bent. As such Democrats as Assemblywoman Pauline Davis and Congressman Harold "Bizz" Johnson left office, they were succeeded by Republicans. And in an interesting quirk, three of the six federal and state legislators from the area are Mormons, even though the LDS Church is not especially active in the area.

Calaveras County

Area: 1,036.4 sq. mi.; Population (1988): 30,300; Voter registration (1989): D-46.6% R-44.9%; Unemployment (1989): 11.1%; County supervisors: Michael Dell' Orto, Thomas Taylor, Robert Harris, Thomas Tyron, David Silveira; 891 Mountain Road, San Andreas, 95249; (209) 754-6370.

The most famous thing about Calaveras County is a fictional frog-jumping contest that became real. Writer Mark Twain described it in one of his whimsical tales about life in the gold rush era and the town of Angels Camp capitalizes on it by enacting a real version every spring.

The hordes of tourists that the frog-jumping contest attracts are a strong clue to the evolving nature of the local economy, which is moving away from mining and agriculture and toward tourism and retirees. Another sign is the precarious future of an asbestos mine, the nation's largest, which provides 5 percent of all of Calaveras County's jobs.

The county's population is growing faster than most of California, but not as fast as foothill counties closer to Sacramento.

But as it grows – mostly due to settlement of retired refugees from the state's urban centers – it also is continuing a slow shift to the right politically. Democrats are close, in fact, to becoming a minority.

Colusa County

Area: 1,155.8 sq. mi.; Population (1988): 14,950; Voter registration (1989): D-49.7% R-42.1%; Unemployment (1989): 16.7%; County supervisors: James Kalfsbeek, W.D. Mills, Kay Nordyke, William Waite, David Womble, 546 Jay St., Colusa, 95932; (916) 458-2101.

On any given day, a lot of people visit Colusa County. Few of them know it. Interstate 5, California's chief north-south highway, bisects the county an hour's drive north of Sacramento, but it bypasses the county seat, Colusa, and at 60 miles per hour, travelers can blink their way through Williams, which has fewer than 2,000 souls.

There are a few highway-related businesses in Williams, but the county's chief economic underpinning is agriculture. The Employment Development Department estimates farming provides nearly half of the county's direct employment. The chief crop is rice, which is subject both to the availability of water and the vagaries of international markets.

Colusa is too far from Sacramento or other major urban areas to experience suburbanization, and with its lack of recreational opportunities, it is not likely to become a haven for retirees. Thus, although its population is growing about as fast as California as a whole, Colusa's basic character is not destined for a big change soon.

Contra Costa County

Area: 797.9 sq. mi.; Population (1988): 753,500; Voter registration (1989): D-51.6% R-37.2%; Unemployment (1989): 4.2%; County supervisors: Tom Powers, Nancy Fahden, Robert Schroder, Sunne McPeak, Thomas Torlakson; 651 Pine St., 11th floor, Martinez, 94553; (415) 646-2371.

A generation ago, Contra Costa County was the quintessential Northern California bedroom suburb. The county's hills and valleys were a refuge for commuters who spent their working days in the employment centers of nearby Oakland and San Francisco – albeit those commuters affluent enough to afford the sophisticated country atmosphere of such communities as Walnut Creek, Moraga, Orinda and Lafayette.

But in more recent years, Contra Costa itself has seen an explosion of employment as huge complexes of offices, such as San Ramon's Bishop Ranch, have been developed. The county, or at least those portions along Interstate 680, became a destination for commuters who had moved even further east, into the San Joaquin Valley, in search of affordable housing.

Between 1985 and 1990, Contra Costa County's employment is expected to increase by some 21 percent. The explosion of development along I-680 has coined a new phrase, "Contra Costapolis," and also sparked a no-growth backlash among county residents fed up with hours-long traffic jams. Increasingly, local politics of the 1980s became defined by that single issue, and politicians caught on the wrong side – i.e. too cozy with developers – felt the lash of resentment.

The issue came to a head in 1985, when anti-growth candidates won a series of local elections and slow-growth ballot measures were adopted.

In many ways, the county is a microcosm of California. Along the outer reaches of San Francisco Bay, communities such as Martinez, Pittsburg and Antioch exist as blue-collar bastions, filled with oil refineries and other industrial facilities, although they, too, are experiencing suburban housing development. And Richmond, located on San Francisco Bay itself, has a large and Democratic-voting black population.

The county's voter registration matches almost exactly that of the state, but Michael Dukakis scored one of his rare victories in the county, thanks to a major turnout effort in blue-collar and black precincts.

The major political battle in the county in 1988, however, wasn't the presidential contest but a bitterly fought Democratic primary that pitted the county's controversial state senator, Daniel Boatwright, against county Supervisor Sunne McPeak, an ambitious political climber. Boatwright won, but only after spending heavily.

Contra Costa's dominating political figure is not a politician, but Dean Lesher, the outspoken octogenarian who publishes the Contra Costa Times newspaper. Lesher battles ceaselessly against anti-growthers and for the establishment of a state college campus in the county, known locally as "Dean Lesher U."

Del Norte County

Area: 1,003 sq. mi.; Population (1988): 19,750; Voter registration (1989): D-49.5% R-34.5%; Unemployment (1989): 14.5%; County supervisors: Helga Burns, Ray Thompson, E. Joyce Crockett, Glenn Smedley, Mark Mellett; 450 H St., Crescent City, 95531; (707) 464-7204.

Del Norte County is about as far north as one can get and still be in California. For generations, the twin underpinnings of the local economy were cutting trees and catching fish. Both industries fell on hard times during the 1970s and 1980s, and local boosters pushed hard to add a third element: keeping bad guys locked up. That dream was realized when the state began construction began on Pelican Bay State Prison.

Del Norte began experiencing a rare surge in commercial investment as the prison took shape near the Oregon border north of Crescent City and the $30 million annual payroll moved toward reality. Suddenly, one of the state's most chronically depressed areas was beginning the look like one of its more prosperous.

The new state prison was a political plum secured by the county's state senator, Barry Keene, the Senate's Democratic floor leader. Keene is one of several Democrats who have been winning regularly along the state's north coast, one of the few California regions to move to the left in its political orientation in recent years.

El Dorado County

Area: 1,804.8 sq. mi.; Population (1988): 116,700; Voter registration (1989): D-44.9% R-44.4%; Unemployment (1989): 5%; County supervisors: Robert Dorr, Patrica Lowe, James Sweeney, Eugene Chappie, John Cefalu; 330 Fair Lane, Placerville, 95667; (916) 626-2464.

The names of the county and its county seat, Placerville, reveal their origins as one of the centers of the 19th century gold rush. In the late 20th century, El Dorado County is at the center of another land rush.

Retirees and commuters alike are packing into El Dorado County, seeking cleaner air, friendlier social climates and more reasonable living costs. But their sheer numbers threaten to destroy those very qualities. As one recent arrival put it in a newspaper interview: "Everywhere I look I'm threatened."

Between 1980 and 1988, the county's population surged by 36 percent as developers converted pastures into "ranchettes." Population growth is highest in the communities, such as Cameron Park and El Dorado Hills, closest to Sacramento, and water shortages have become common.

Despite the growth, or perhaps because of it, El Dorado is turning to the right politically. Democrats barely outnumbered Republicans in 1988 and are destined to become the county's minority soon.

Fresno County

Area: 5,998.3 sq. mi.; Population (1988): 606,000; Voter registration (1989): D-55.8% R-36.7%; Unemployment (1989): 11.7%; County supervisors: Deran Koligan, Sharon Levy, Doug Vagim, A. Vernon Conrad, Judy Andreen; 2281 Tulare St., Room 300, Fresno, 93721; (209) 488-3531.

Fresno County is the middle of California – geographically, culturally and politically. Its major city, Fresno, is big enough – over 300,000 – to have some metropolitan advantages, and some urban ills. But it remains, at heart, an overgrown farm town that is largely ignored by the state's opinion-molders in San Diego, Los Angeles, Sacramento and San Francisco. The ambivalence of its image was captured perfectly by a satirical television movie, "Fresno."

It was in Fresno County that the term "agribusiness" was coined, and large-scale, scientific agriculture remains the heart of both its economy and its cultural being. Crops as varied as cotton and grapes abound in the fertile flatlands of Fresno, the nation's most productive agricultural county.

But as the unofficial capital of the San Joaquin Valley, Fresno has also developed an infrastructure of educational, medical and governmental facilities to serve a broader region. And its location, equidistant between Los Angeles and San Francisco, and its relatively low labor and land costs have sparked a flurry of non-agricultural industrial development.

More than a third of Fresno County's population is Hispanic, but, as in other areas of the state, Hispanics have not yet developed into a substantial political force. Economic and political power remains in the hands of Anglos.

Fresno County and the remainder of the San Joaquin Valley mirror larger political trends in the state: nominally Democratic but tending toward the conservative and willing, often eager, to elect Republicans.

That puts the valley into the swing position when it comes to close statewide races and explains why candidates for governor, senator and president spend disproportionately large amounts of scarce campaign time in and around Fresno's isolated media market. It was on one such swing through the valley that Michael Dukakis chose to declare his born-again liberalism, an odd locale given the slightly right-of-center tilt to the local electorate and perhaps symbolic of his botched campaign effort in the state.

Centrism is the dominant political credo of Fresno and environs. Right-wing Republicans and left-wing Democrats can't get elected to anything. Local government is the spawning ground for most legislators and congressmen, who tend toward the pragmatic.

Chief among them, and typical of the breed, is state Sen. Ken Maddy, the Senate's Republican leader and a one-time gubernatorial possibility who is married to the heiress of the Foster Farms chicken empire–the perfect combination of politics and agribusiness.

Glenn County

Area: 1,319 sq. mi.; Population (1988): 23,200; Voter registration (1989): D-46.7% R-43.5%; Unemployment (1989): 13.3%; County supervisors: Joanne Overton, George Edwards, Dick Mudd, Daniel Cooper, Jim Mann; P.O. Box 391, Willows, 95988; (916) 934-3834.

The 19th century courthouse in Willows is a symbol for all of Glenn County: quiet, bound to tradition, slow to change.

The bisection of the county, and Willows, by Interstate 5, the state's main north-south freeway, has had only a superficial impact on either. There are a few highway-related businesses, but otherwise the city and the county remain what they've been for generations, an agricultural area whose economy is tied to the value of farm products. Farming and government account for half of Glenn County's employment.

Jim Mann, a dairy farmer turned county supervisor, is trying to change that. Mann works for a regional economic development center in nearby Chico and is trying to offset chronically high unemployment by promoting the area as a site for light industry, stressing the comparatively low cost of living and the good transportation access. But so far, such development efforts are just in the speculative stage. Like the rest of the region, Glenn County is politically conservative and votes Republican most of the time.

Humboldt County

Area: 3,599.5 sq. mi.; Population (1988): 114,900; Voter registration (1989): D-58.6% R-31.3%; Unemployment (1989): 9.5%; County supervisors: Stan Dixon, Harry Pritchard, Wesley Chesbro, Bonnie Neely, Anna Sparks; 825 Fifth St., Eureka, 95501; (707) 445-7509.

Eureka (population 25,000) is the political, economic and cultural center of California's remote, beautiful north coast, an area in transition. The region was settled by loggers, who felled giant redwoods and cut them into timbers to shore up gold mines in the mid-19th century. Cutting and processing timber and catching and processing fish were Humboldt County's economic mainstays for generations, even after a substantial, if seasonal, tourist industry developed after World War II.

Both of those resource-based industries have fallen on hard times in more recent years, however, and many of the area's young men and women moved away to seek employment. As they left, they were replaced by urban refugees, universally dubbed "hippies," and the economic and political transformation of the area began.

Marijuana became a substantial, if illegal, cash crop, environmentalism, once a dirty word, became a powerful movement and the politics of the area, once conservative, began moving leftward with liberal Democrats replacing Republicans in legislative seats.

Imperial County

Area: 4,597.4 sq. mi.; Population (1988): 111,100; Voter registration (1989): D-54.8% R-34.3%; Unemployment (1989): 18.3%;County supervisors: Luis Legaspi, Bill Cole, James Bucher, Abe Seabolt, Jeanne Vogel; 940 W. Main St., El Centro, 92243; (619) 339-4220.

If it weren't for the fact that farmers can often grow three crops a year, it's doubtful whether anyone would live in the Imperial Valley.

Much of the valley, which occupies California's southeastern corner, lies below sea level and is covered with sand. Summer temperatures can reach 120-plus degrees in the shade, if one can find shade in the almost treeless landscape.

Imperial was the last California county to be created, carved off San Diego County just after World War I. There's a lively commerce in both goods and human bodies over the Mexican border south of El Centro, and Imperial County has California's highest concentration of Hispanic residents, nearly 56 percent in the 1980 census. That demographic fact is accompanied by an economic one; Imperial has the state's highest unemployment rate and is chronically near the top in terms of poverty.

Local boosters hope that a fledgling winter vacation industry – a kind of poor man's Palm Springs – will brighten the local economy.

Inyo County

Area: 10,097.9 sq. mi.; Population (1988): 18,100; Voter registration (1989): D-41% R-49.1%; Unemployment (1989): 5.1%; County supervisors: H.B. Irwin, Robert Campbell, Lawrence Calkins, Keith Bright, Paul Payne; P.O. Drawer N, Independence, 93526; (619) 878-2411.

There's only one word to describe Inyo County: empty.

That's only in terms of people, however, because Inyo, wedged onto the eastern slope of the Sierra, next to Nevada, contains some of the state's most spectacular, if starkest, natural scenery.

Inyo is California's second largest county in size, but the federal government owns more than 85 percent of its land. Extraction of minerals from Inyo's arid mountains, ranching and tourism are the county's chief economic activities, and hating Los Angeles – which locked up the area's water supplies in back-room maneuvers a half-century ago and which supplies hordes of summer and weekend visitors – seems to be the chief local pastime. Mining has been on the wane in recent years and local leaders have been looking for something – perhaps a state prison – to replace the lost employment.

Politically, Inyo's few voters lean to the right and give Republican candidates big majorities.

Kern County

Area: 8,170.3 sq. mi.; Population (1988): 511,400; Voter registration (1989): D-47.9% R-43.4%; Unemployment (1989): 11.5%; County supervisors: Roy Asburn, Ben Austin, Pauline Larwood, Karl Hettinger, Mary Shell; 1415 Truxton Ave., Bakersfield, 93301; (800) 322-0722.

If California is, as many believe, a microcosm of the United States, Kern County is its Oklahoma. There are oil wells, farms and country music recording studios. And many of the county's inhabitants trace their ancestry to the waves of migrants from Oklahoma, Texas and Arkansas before, during and after World War II.

When the oil and farming industries are down, Kern County is down. When they are up, the county rolls in money. There have been efforts to diversify the county's economy, taking advantage of its location 100 miles north of the Los Angeles megalopolis. And they have been partially successful. But for the foreseeable future, farming and oil will be the area's economic mainstays.

True to its cultural roots, Kern County is very conservative politically. It elects Republicans to its legislative and congressional seats and gives GOP candidates at the top of the ticket big margins. As elsewhere, the county's large Hispanic minority is politically impotent.

Kings County

Area: 1,435.6 sq. mi.; Population (1988): 92,000; Voter registration (1989): D-54.5% R-36.1%; Unemployment (1989): 12.7%; County supervisors: Les Brown, Joe Hammond Jr., Dom Faruzzi, Nick Kinney, Abel Meirelles; Government Center, Hanford, 93230; (209) 582-3211.

Kings County, sliced from a corner of neighboring Tulare County in the late 19th century, has achieved a remarkable economic diversification to accompany its large-scale agricultural base.

Starting in the early 1960s, the county developed such non-agricultural projects as a tire factory, a U.S. Navy base (Lemoore Naval Air Station) and a carpet mill. In more recent years, the state has built two large prisons in the small farming towns of Avenal and Corcoran.

The county seat, Hanford, has even developed a mild tourism industry centered on its town square, with its old-fashioned ice cream parlor and 19th century buildings redeveloped into shops. A small Chinatown includes one of the state's finest gourmet restaurants.

That non-farm development has given it a more stable economy than many other San Joaquin Valley counties and also fueled a relatively high rate of population growth.

Politically, Kings mirrors the valley: conservative-voting on most issues, but willing to elect Democrats who don't tilt too far to the left.

Lake County

Area: 1,326.5 sq. mi.; Population (1988): 51,400; Voter registration (1989): D-54.8% R-36%; Unemployment (1989): 12.3%; County supervisors: Voris Brumfield, Gary Lambert, Walter Wilcox, Karan Mackey, L.D. Franklin; 255 N. Forbes St., Lakeport, 95453; (707) 263-2367.

Lake County's name says it all. The county's major scenic and economic asset is Clear Lake, California's largest natural body of fresh water. Dotted along the lake are dozens of small communities that subsist on summer tourism, fishermen and the retirees.

There are so many retirees settling in Lake County, a three-hour drive from San Francisco, that the median age of residents is about 15 years higher than the state median. There are some other elements to the county's economy, such as ranching and geothermal power development, but retirees' pension checks are becoming steadily more important.

The Clear Lake Basin is a favorite hunting ground for archaeologists, incidentally, because of its centuries of human habitation. One stone tool fragment from the area has been dated at 10,000 years old.

Lake's retirees tend to be of the working class variety, so the local politics remain pro-Democratic. Michael Dukakis even won there in 1988.

Lassen County

Area: 4,690.3 sq. mi.; Population (1988): 26,450; Voter registration (1989): D-51% R-37%; Unemployment (1989) 11.9%; County supervisors: Hughes deMartimprey, James Chapman, John Gaither, Gary Lemke, Helen Williams; 707 Nevada St., Susanville, 96130; (916) 257-8311.

The biggest employer in Lassen County is the California Department of Corrections. Except for the prison at Susanville, Lassen, in California's northeastern corner, is mostly timber and ranching country, with an overlay of summer tourism. It shares Lassen National Volcanic Park with three other counties, but the volcano that gave the county its name, Mt. Lassen, is actually in Shasta County.

Many – perhaps most – of Lassen's residents are happy the county has missed out on the industrialization and population growth afflicting much of California. Indeed, when the state proposed to expand its prison and add another 200 jobs, it was opposed by local residents, who would prefer to leave things as they are: quiet and peaceful.

Lassen's population is growing slowly and many of the newcomers are retired refugees from urban centers, trading in the equity on their homes for the quietude of the country.

Politically, the county emulates the rest of northeastern California: conservative, with a don't-tread-on-me attitude toward government and taxes.

Los Angeles County

Area: 4,079.3 sq. mi.; Population (1988): 8,604,300; Voter registration (1989): D-55.4% R-35%; Unemployment (1989): 4.2%; County supervisors: Peter Schabarum, Kenneth Hahn, Ed Edelman, Deane Dana, Michael Antonovich; 500 W. Temple St., Los Angeles, 90012; (213) 974-1411.

Los Angeles County is the 800-pound gorilla of California and its politics, containing more than 30 percent of the state's population and wielding cultural, economic and political influence that is global in scope.

It is the new American melting pot, the destination for immigrants from dozens, perhaps hundreds, of other societies around the globe, and the newcomers, in turn, are changing the face of Los Angeles.

Los Angeles, both the city and the county, has huge enclaves of Hispanics, Koreans, blacks, Armenians, Chinese and other ethnic groups, and each plays its own role in shaping the unique society that evolved from a dusty outpost of the Spanish colonial empire.

Newcomers and old-timers alike participate in an economy that is marked mostly by its diversity, ranging from heavy manufacturing to burgeoning trade with the Pacific Rim, high-tech assembly lines, entertainment and sweatshop garment factories in downtown tenements.

Other communities may throb, but the city of Los Angeles and the dozens of other cities and towns that comprise Los Angeles County hum with the 24-hour-a-day freeway traffic that is its most notable physical feature.

What would be rush-hour level traffic anywhere else can be found in Los Angeles at any hour and during the morning and late afternoon commute periods, millions of Angelenos find themselves in slowly oozing streams of vehicles, most of them holding no more than one person.

That vehicular preoccupation has given Los Angeles one of the nation's worst smog problems and given rise to new mechanisms to deal with it, including the establishment of a regional body with vast new powers to control the way people live, work and transport themselves.

But any solution to the smog problem, if there is one, is decades away, and in the meantime, the freeways become more crowded and slower moving.

It's a problem that's worsened by the inexorable shift of population out of the center city and into the suburbs on the edge of the San Fernando Valley and in the Mojave Desert. Commuters seeking affordable homes pay the price in terms of ever-longer periods spent in their cars going to and from their jobs, even though there's a slow spread of employment into the suburbs as well.

The influx of immigrants, most of them from Asia or Latin America, and the continuing white flight to the suburbs, added more than 1.1 million to Los Angeles County's population between 1980 and 1988. That growth is more than twice as much as any other county, although in percentage terms it's a bit under the statewide population expansion for the same period.

The slower-than-average population growth, coupled with the tendency of Hispanic and Asian immigrants not to vote, means that Los Angeles County is losing a bit of its overall political clout vis-a-vis the rest of California.

The county, too, tends to divide rather evenly in a political sense. It's a bit more Democratic in registration than the state as a whole, but many of its Democrats tend to vote Republican at the top of the ticket, which means that neither party can emerge from the county with a commanding majority on Election Day. The strongly pro-Republican tilt in the remainder of Southern California more than offsets the slight Democratic edge in Los Angeles and gives the region an overall and very dependable GOP flavor in races for senator, governor and president.

Within Los Angeles County itself, politics tend to run to extremes. The state's most conservative and most liberal officeholders can be found in its legislative and congressional delegations.

The central and western portions of the county – downtown Los Angeles, heavily black south-central Los Angeles, heavily Hispanic East Los Angeles and the wealthy Beverly Hills, Santa Monica and Westwood areas on the West Side – are strongly Democratic. State Senate President Pro Tem David Roberti, the house's top Democratic leader; ex-radical Tom Hayden, now a state assemblyman; and Reps. Howard Berman and Henry Waxman, who head a powerful political organization, are among the powerful Democrats from the west side.

But Long Beach – Gov. George Deukmejian's home town – and the Anglo suburbs on the fringes of the county vote Republican, while the San Fernando Valley is a toss-up, Democratic in the south part, Republican in the north.

A third of the county's population is Hispanic and at least 10 percent is Asian, but neither of these fast-growing ethnic groups has become politically influential. So far, politics in the county is an Anglo and black business, as reflected in the ethnic identity of all but a few officeholders.

The county Board of Supervisors, for instance, is composed of five Anglo men despite the fact that Anglos are less than half of the county's population. These five positions are among the most powerful political offices in the nation, which is why their holders are called "the five little kings" by political insiders. The supervisors have huge personal staffs and without an elected head of county government, wield vast power over land use, transportation, health care and other matters.

The county's split political personality is revealed in the makeup of the board, three Republicans and two Democrats.

The Democrats once controlled the board, but former Gov. Jerry Brown indirectly handed control to the Republicans by naming a liberal black woman, ex-Rep. Yvonne Brathwaite Burke, to a coastal district vacancy in the late 1970s. She lost in the next election to a Republican, Deane Dana, and the GOP has been in control ever since. The other Republicans are Mike Antonovich and Pete Schabarum, who represent suburban districts, while the two Democrats are Ed Edelman, who represents the largely Jewish west side, and Kenneth Hahn, a legendary political figure who has represented overwhelmingly black south-central Los Angeles for decades and continues to function despite debilitating health problems. Hahn ran again and won in 1988 in the face of public calls from black leaders to step aside. They feared that if Hahn died in office, Republican Deukmejian would name his successor and enhance GOP control of the board.

The GOP majority is a source of huge frustration to local Democrats, who have attempted to regain control to no avail during a series of elections in the 1980s. The split has resulted, however, in pitched battles between the supervisors and Los Angeles Democrats in the Legislature, who control county purse strings.

It's unlikely that the GOP dominance will be upset at the polls anytime soon, despite some anti-growth backlash in the fast-growing suburbs. But it could be challenged in the courts, oddly enough, via a lawsuit by the Republican-controlled U.S. Department of Justice.

The department has filed suit alleging that the county supervisorial districts illegally exclude Hispanics from representation and is demanding that the lines be redrawn and/or the board be expanded to accommodate the large Hispanic population. The suit is being taken seriously since a similar suit forced the Los Angeles City Council to redraw its lines and create two Hispanic seats. A redrawing of the district lines or an expansion of the board would likely end the decadelong GOP control of the board, while also breaking its unspoken but strong racial barrier.

Among county government insiders, it's considered most likely that the board would be expanded to seven members so that the incumbents' seats could be protected. One new district, it's believed, would be created in the Hispanic central and eastern portions of Los Angeles, while another new one would be centered in the southern San Fernando Valley.

Speculation about who would occupy the two new seats is rampant in Los Angles political circles. Two Hispanic City Council members, Richard Alatorre and Gloria Molina, are strong possibilities for the east Los Angeles seat. They are rivals rather than allies in city politics. At one time, the betting would have favored state Sen. Art Torres, but his two drunken driving arrests have depressed a once-soaring political career. The only certainty, really, is that the Hispanic seat would be taken by a Democrat.

That would make the San Fernando Valley seat the hinge point for partisan control of the board and there's no shortage of potential candidates among local state legislators, city council members and civic leaders. Chief among them is Democratic state Sen. Alan Robbins, a controversial figure for two decades. Robbins, who once aspired to become mayor of Los Angeles, led anti-busing campaigns in the 1970s and became embroiled in a sensational trial on charges of having sex with a teenage girl in his Capitol office (he was acquitted). In more recent years, he has seized upon transportation-related issues, such as traffic congestion and auto insurance, as vehicles for publicity.

Madera County

Area: 2,147.1 sq. mi.; Population (1988): 82,500; Voter registration (1989): D-53.4% R-38.6%; Unemployment (1989): 12.7%; County supervisors: Rick Jensen, Alfred Ginsburg, Gail McIntyre, Jess Lopez, Harry Baker Jr.; 209 W. Yosemite Ave., Madera, 93637; (209) 675-7700.

Madera County is farm country, and far enough removed from the state's urban centers to avoid, at least for the time being, the dubious benefits of suburbanization. Its population is growing, up more than 30 percent between 1980 and 1988, and much of the growth is in foothill areas popular with retirees.

A portion of Yosemite National Park lies in Madera County, and it as well as other recreational sites, such as Millerton and Bass lakes, bring a steady stream of tourists through the county.

The city of Madera and surrounding communities are undergoing a modest amount of industrialization, spillover from the Fresno area to the south, but agriculture – especially grapes and dairy products – remains the economic linchpin, accounting for a third of employment.

Despite the seemingly strong Democratic registration edge typical of San Joaquin Valley counties, Madera votes conservatively, and its growing Hispanic population – nearing a third – remains largely powerless.

Marin County

Area: 588 sq. mi.; Population (1988): 229,900; Voter registration (1989): D-52.2% R-34.2%; Unemployment (1989): 2.8%; County supervisors: Bob Roumiguiere, Harold Brown, Albert Aramburu, Gary Giacomini, Robert Stockwell; Civic Center, Room 315, San Rafael, 94903; (415) 499-7331.

They make jokes about Marin County. They write books about Marin County. They even make movies about Marin County. It's that kind of place. The northern anchor of the Golden Gate Bridge, Marin County is a spot of unparalleled natural beauty, of woods and mountains and spectacular seashore.

Those seeking peace or alternative lifestyles gravitated to the county and gave it a particular ambiance unlike any other community in the state, a heady combination of bohemianism, money and libertine social attitudes, overlaid with an almost religious sense of environmental protection and social exclusivity.

It may say it all to note that one Marin County supermarket offers more than a dozen brands of ice cream, venison from New Zealand and chemical-free beef from Colorado, so certified by the store's own chemical testing machine.

As the San Francisco Bay suburbs boomed in the early 1970s, Marin County made a conscious choice to hold the line on population growth, long before such movements became popular elsewhere.

Marin residents succeeded. Between 1980 and 1988, for example, its population grew only 3.3 percent, a sixth of the statewide rate. But the success of the growth-control movement had side effects that most Marinites preferred to ignore: an incredible escalation of housing costs that drove out the non-affluent (its median income is over 50 percent higher than neighboring Sonoma County) and increasing traffic problems resulting from commuters' being forced northward toward Sonoma. Marin, like other close-in suburbs, has also seen a sharp increase in employment development, which brings commuters into the county and makes traffic even worse.

But Marin, despite those obvious impacts, remains dedicated to keeping its population low and its natural attributes relatively unaffected by the human maelstrom swirling around it – an island of beatitude and affluence. One coastal community even refuses to have signs directing traffic to itself, so intense is the desire for isolation.

A major showdown on the growth issue occurred in 1989, when voters decided the fate of a large residential and office development on the site of the former Hamilton AFB. Despite the shortage and high cost of housing and support from such prominent Democrats as Lt. Gov. Leo McCarthy, the project was rejected.

Politically, Marin was once steadfastly Republican but has been edging leftward as environmentalism has become a more potent political force. The only Republican officeholders who survive are those who embrace the cause.

Mariposa County

Area: 1,460.5 sq. mi.; Population (1988): 14,500; Voter registration (1989): D-45.5% R-42%; Unemployment (1989): 8.1%; County supervisors: Arthur Baggett, Sally Punte, Eric Erickson, George Radanovich, Gertrude Taber; P.O. Box 784, Mariposa, 95338: (209) 966-3222.

Once, in the mid-19th century, Mariposa County covered a huge swath of California, including most of the San Joaquin Valley and Southern California. But year after year, the county's boundaries were whittled down to form new counties, 11 in all. What's left are 1,460.5 square miles of scenic beauty that include the most famous and most visited portions of Yosemite National Park.

Each year, hundreds of thousands of visitors are exposed to Mariposa County's rolling foothills, quaint gold rush era towns and craggy mountains. And each year, a few more decide to stay, which is why the county's population grew by more than 30 percent between 1980 and 1988.

The county's population has nearly tripled since 1960, with many of the newcomers being retirees, who bring with them conservative political attitudes that are turning the county into a Republican bastion.

The state projects that Mariposa's population will continue to grow rapidly, reaching 20,000 by the turn of the century as the demand for recreational opportunities continues to expand.

Mendocino County

Area: 3,510.7 sq. mi.; Population (1988): 76,100; Voter registration (1989): D-54.6% R-31.9%; Unemployment (1989): 10.9%; County supervisors: Marilyn Butcher, Nelson Redding, Lis Henry, John Cimolino, Norman DeVall; Courthouse, Room 113, Ukiah, 95482; (707) 463-4221.

Mendocino County, like the remainder of Northern California's rugged and scenic coast, was once timber country. And felling and processing the trees of the densely forested areas of the county remains an important economic element. But in the last generation, the county has undergone a socioeconomic and political evolution.

A wave of urban emigres hit the county in the 1960s and 1970s and created a new economy rooted in tourism, crafts and, although illegal, the cultivation of high-quality marijuana.

The extremely quaint little coastal towns such as Elk and Mendocino acquired rafts of bed-and-breakfast inns and trendy restaurants to serve weekenders from the Bay Area. And in the late 1980s, the southernmost parts of the county started experiencing suburbanization as Bay Area commuters pressed ever-outward, searching for affordable housing.

Politically, the socioeconomic change has tended to move Mendocino County leftward, with liberal Democrats replacing conservative Democrats in elected offices.

Merced County

Area: 2007.7 sq. mi.; Population (1988): 171,200; Voter registration (1989): D-57.3% R-33.3%; Unemployment (1989): 13.4%; County supervisors: Wyatt Davenport, Ann Klinger, Michael Bogna, Dean Peterson, Anthony Whitehurst; 2222 M St., Merced, 95340; (209) 385-7366.

Merced County advertises itself as the gateway to Yosemite National Park, but its future appears to be tied less to the mountainous eastern end of the county than to the western portions, which are on the verge of suburban explosion.

The mind may boggle at the prospect, but Los Banos, a quiet and somewhat isolated farm town on the west side of the San Joaquin Valley, is laying plans to become part of the San Francisco Bay megalopolis as rising housing costs drive commuters ever-further from the central cities. In this case, the upgrading of Highway 152 to a full freeway will allow commuters to drive from Los Banos into the southern portions of the Santa Clara Valley south of San Jose.

Even without such suburbanization, Merced County's population has been growing 50 percent faster than the state as a whole, up more than 27 percent between 1980 and 1988. And its politics, which had been conservative Democrat, seem to be edging rightward with the growth.

Modoc County

Area: 4,340.4 sq. mi.; Population (1988): 9,200; Voter registration (1989): D-46.9% R-43.3%; Unemployment (1989): 10.7%; County supervisors: John Schreiber, Melvin Anderson, Don Polson, Mick Jones, John Coulson; P.O. Box 131, Alturas, 96101; (916) 233-3939.

A form letter that Modoc County employment officials send to would-be job seekers says it all. The weather can be extreme, the economy is seasonal and "Modoc County (has) virtually no growth," the letter bluntly informs those who think that the isolated, rugged and beautiful county would be an earthly paradise.

The few thousand souls who live in Modoc County, located in California's upper right-hand corner, like it just fine the way it is, although there are laments that a lack of job opportunities drives the young into the booming cities hundreds of miles to the south.

Timber and cattle ranching are the mainstays of the local economy, although government – local, state and federal – is the largest employer. Increasingly, summer homes are being built by urbanites seeking isolation. There are so many summer residents, in fact, that something of a political schism has developed between them and the year-round residents. Apart from that, the politics are solidly conservative.

Mono County

Area: 3,103 sq. mi.; Population (1988): 9,500; Voter registration (1989): D-36.4% R-45.3%; Unemployment (1989): 3.2%; County supervisors: Robert Stanford, Dan Paranick, Don Rake, William Reid, Andrea Lawrence; P.O. Box 715, Bridgeport, 93517; (619) 932-7911.

The dominant feature of Mono County – and the focal point of its politics – is Mono Lake, with its other-worldly geologic features.

The lake, which has shrunken markedly in the last half-century, is a constant reminder that the county's fate is largely in the hands of Los Angeles.

Los Angeles, through a series of subterfuges, gained control over water supplies on the eastern slope of the Sierra and pipes much of that water southward to slake its thirst. Local residents are caught in the political and legal battle over whether the diversions should continue uninterrupted or whether more water should be allowed to flow into Mono Lake and thus save the scenic and ecological wonder from further shrinkage.

Mono Lake is another symbol, that of the tourism industry that has gradually replaced ranching and mining as the chief source of local employment. The Mammoth Lakes area has become an important skiing area, contributing to that economic evolution.

Monterey County

Area: 3,324.1 sq. mi.; Population (1988): 348,100; Voter registration (1989): D-50.1% R-36.8%; Unemployment (1989): 11.7%; County supervisors: Marc Del Piero, Barbara Shipnuck, Dusan Petrovic, Sam Karas, Karin Strasser Kauffman; P.O. Box 1728, Salinas, 92902; (408) 424-8611.

Even in a state that's blessed with great natural beauty, Monterey County is something special. Its attractions are so abundant – a combination of rugged coastline, quaint towns and nearly perfect weather – that they have become the focal point of Monterey County politics.

Bluntly put, those who have already captured a piece of Monterey for themselves are increasingly active in protecting it against incursions from outsiders.

Almost any development project, from a hotel to a highway, is certain to spark controversy, and politics in Monterey, Carmel and other Monterey Peninsula communities are driven by that reality.

The mayorship of Monterey and the balance of power on the City Council shifted out of the hands of pro-development forces in the early 1980s after Monterey underwent a surge of hotel construction, including erection of a downtown hotel dubbed "Sheraton General" for its hospital-like appearance.

At the same time, however, the peninsula's economy is almost entirely driven by the tourist industry. The result is non-stop political churning over the future of the area, a two-hour drive from San Francisco. The battle of Monterey achieved national publicity when actor Clint Eastwood ran for and won the mayorship of Carmel on a pro-development platform.

Outside of the Peninsula, most of Monterey County is agricultural. Although Monterey and Salinas, the two major cities, are only a few miles apart, economically and socially they are two different worlds.

Salinas and other inland communities are driven by the prices of the vegetables they produce in such abundance, but they are also beginning to feel the impact of creeping suburbanization, of spillover commuter development from the San Jose area to the north.

The politics of Salinas and environs are being altered by suburban incursion and by the slowly emerging strength of Hispanics, who represent a large minority population. Hispanics, who are more than a third of the population of many communities, have been politically powerless, but key court decisions have opened avenues of political activity at the local level, especially in Salinas, which shifted to a district form of city voting after a court decision directly affecting nearby Watsonville.

The economic and social contrasts found within the county are mirrored in its politics – liberal-environmentalist along the coast and more conservative inland. Overall voting patterns are similar to those of the state as a whole, but will change in response to both suburban development and Hispanic political activity.

Napa County

Area: 796.9 sq. mi.; Population (1988): 106,300; Voter registration (1989): D-51.2% R-39.1%; Unemployment (1989): 4.6%; County supervisors: Robert White, Fred Negri, Mel Varrelman, Paul Battisti, John Mikolajcik; 1195 Third St., Napa, 94559; (707) 253-4386

Once upon a time – and not too many years ago – the Napa Valley was a little-known, if attractive corner of California.

No more. As wine-drinking evolved into a secular religion among baby boomers in the 1970s and 1980s, the Napa Valley became their mecca. Napa County's once quiet agricultural valley, an hour's drive from San Francisco, evolved with astonishing speed into a tourist draw. New wineries popped up like mushrooms and the valley acquired a full quota of inns, hotels, restaurants and other tourist-oriented facilities.

In the early 1980s, there was a backlash among residents fed up with weekend traffic jams. While new development controls, rising home prices and a lack of local jobs has kept population growth scant, the battles over tourist-oriented development remain intense, most recent being a squabble over a proposal to run a "wine train" through the valley.

Politically, Napa has been a bastion of conservatism, but the growth control battles seem to be pushing it a bit to the left.

Nevada County

Area: 992.2 sq. mi.; Population (1988): 77,200; Voter registration (1989): D-40.8% R-47.2%; Unemployment (1989): 6.6%; County supervisors: Todd Juvinall, James Callaghan, Jim Weir, Bill Schultz, G.B. Tucker; 950 Maidu Ave., Nevada City, 95959; (916) 265-1480.

Nevada County is archetypical of the fast-growing Sierra foothill region of California. Between 1980 and 1988, it recorded a whopping 49.5 percent population growth, the second-fastest rate of any county in the state, as increasing numbers of retirees, commuters to the booming Sacramento area and urban escapees settled into the area.

The county has developed a home-grown electronics industry and an underground marijuana-growing economy. The Nevada City-Grass Valley area has developed into a regional commercial and cultural center, and there is a thriving arts community in North San Juan. The combination of scenic beauty and mild climate continues to draw both visitors and those looking for new roots. And the major question facing the county is whether to impose some stricter curbs on development.

Nevada County, like other foothill communities, has been moving to the right politically. Republicans outnumber Democrats, reflecting the leave-me-alone philosophy that dominates the region.

Orange County

Area: 785.1 sq. mi.; Population (1988): 2,261,100; Voter registration (1989): D-34.7% R-55.2%; Unemployment (1989): 2.9%; County supervisors: Roger Stanton, Harriett Wieder, Gaddi Vasquez, Don Roth, Thomas Riley; 10 Civic Center, Santa Ana, 92701; (714) 834-3100.

No corner of California more typifies the state's postwar development than Orange County, a patch of coastline and rolling hills immediately south of Los Angeles. Prior to World War II, Orange County was cattle ranges (controlled mostly by big Spanish land-grant ranchers such as the Irvines and the O'Neills), vegetable fields and citrus orchards. After World War II, and especially after 1955, the county exploded with suburban development. It achieved national, and even international, notoriety as the home of Disneyland, the planet's first theme amusement park, and as a hotbed of right-wing politics.

As the British Broadcasting Corp. said in a 1976 documentary on Orange County: "This is the culmination of the American dream." That dream was a home in the suburbs, two cars and a ski boat in the garage and a barbecue in the back yard. And Orange County reproduced it hundreds of thousands of times in the space of a single generation.

Anaheim was a city of 35,000 when Walt Disney opened his amusement park in 1955, and over the next 30 years its population increased ninefold, matching what was happening in Orange County as a whole.

Orange County became the state's second-most populous county, but it continued to exist in the shadow of the much-larger Los Angeles to the north. Even its professional sports teams, the Los Angeles Rams football team and the California Angels baseball team, don't take their names from the county. And Orange County is the largest urban area in the country not to have its own network television service.

If, however, Orange County had become California's quintessential bedroom community in the 1950s and 1960s, the 1970s began to produce a change. Population growth slowed as new suburbs began to develop to the east in Riverside County. In addition, the county became a center for the development of California's post-industrial economy, one rooted in trade, services and high-tech fabrication.

Although no one city dominates Orange County, Irvine and nearby Costa Mesa are its center. The region's dazzling new performing arts center is in Costa Mesa, and the county's airport, named for the late actor and county resident John Wayne, lies just outside the city. Together with the development of the University of California's Irvine campus and the community of Irvine, the two cities have created a cultural locus that had been lacking during the county's go-go phase of rapid growth. This area, sprawled on either side of Interstate 405, contains dozens of high-rise office buildings, hotels, cultural facilities and restaurants. Only downtown Los Angeles rivals the area's concentration of office space. UC Irvine has become a center for biotechnological research and development and the county has more than

700 high-tech companies.

The development of the Irvine-centered commercial and cultural complex has also signaled a shift of emphasis from the older cities of Santa Ana and Anaheim in the north to the central and southern parts of the county. The older communities, meanwhile, found themselves with large and growing Hispanic and Southeast Asian communities, neither of which has become politically active or powerful.

As Orange County developed into an employment center, the commute patterns also changed, and that change produced traffic congestion that is the overriding local preoccupation. Layered over the local traffic was a new influx of tens of thousands of cars from suburbs in Riverside and elsewhere – suburbs created in response to the skyrocketing home prices in Orange itself. Traffic, in turn, has fueled a local anti-growth movement that has drawn support from both conservatives and liberals, but failed to pass a no-growth ballot measure in 1988.

As home prices went up, population growth slowed. Between 1980 and 1988, the county gained only 300,000 residents, a growth of 17 percent, which was lower than the state as a whole. In the mid-1980s, San Diego supplanted Orange as the state's second-most populous county.

Orange County's politics have always been conservative, even though Democrats achieved a very short-lived plurality of voter registration in the mid-1970s. If anything, the Republican grip on the county has solidified in more recent years, and the GOP now has a quarter-million voter advantage. That makes a big Republican turnout in Orange critical to statewide GOP candidates.

One by one, the Democratic state legislators and congressmen who had won office in the 1970s bit the dust in the 1980s, and the county now has all-Republican delegations in both Sacramento and Washington, a fact that hurts the county's bread-and-butter goals in the Democratic-controlled Legislature and Congress.

And the Republicans who hold office in the county tend to be of the flamboyantly right-wing category, such as Reps. Robert "B-1 Bob" Dornan and William Dannemeyer, who has become a leading anti-homosexual rights crusader in Washington, and Assemblyman Gil Ferguson, a former Marine officer whose major cause has been to oust ex-radical Tom Hayden from the Legislature.

The odd quality of local politics was illustrated by an incident in 1988. Local Republican officials hired armed guards to stand outside polling places in a severely contested state Assembly election. The guards carried signs warning that illegal aliens and non-citizens could not vote.

Democrats claimed that the action discouraged Hispanics from voting while Republicans said they were guarding against a feared invasion of illegal voters. It resulted in a lawsuit seeking to set aside the election of Republican Curt Pringle.

The county may, however, be on the verge of producing some statewide political figures. Two Orange County state senators, John Seymour and Marian Bergeson, are poised to run for lieutenant governor in 1990, and Supervisor Gaddi Vasquez is being groomed by GOP leaders to become a major Hispanic political figure.

Placer County

Area:1,506.5 sq. mi.; Population (1988): 156,400; Voter registration (1989): D-46.4% R-43.9%; Unemployment (1989): 5.1%; County supervisors: Robert Mahan, Alex Ferreira, George Beland, Susan Hogg, Mike Fluty; 175 Fulweiler Ave., Auburn, 95603; (916) 823-4641.

Fast-growing Placer County represents three distinct pieces of the varied California landscape.

The western portion of Placer County, centered in and around Roseville, has evolved in recent years into a high-growth residential and industrial suburb of Sacramento County with an expanding offshoot of the Silicon Valley computer complex. The middle part of the county, centered in Auburn, the quaint, gold rush-era county seat, is foothills and it, too, is growing rapidly with commuters, retirees and urban expatriates. And the eastern part of the county is high-mountain country, including the northern shore of Lake Tahoe, which is also feeling development pressure.

The common denominator – and a major reason for the county's growth – is Interstate 80, the major east-west highway that connects San Francisco and Sacramento with the rest of the continent.

The county's population has grown by a third in the 1980s, and it will continue to expand at that rapid clip – an expansion that has the effect of moving the area's politics rightward, toward the Republican Party.

Plumas County

Area: 2,618.4 sq. mi.; Population (1988): 20,000; Voter registration (1989): D-50.8% R-38.1%; Unemployment (1989): 17.6%; County supervisors: Jim Smith, John Schramel, Donald Woodhall, Joyce Scroggs, Bill Coates; P.O. Box 207, Quincy, 95971; (916) 283-0280.

The folks who live in Plumas County often feel more affinity, both culturally and economically, with Nevada than with expansive, fast-changing California. Indeed, Reno, 80 miles to the southeast, is the nearest big town, and much of the county's economic activity crosses the state border. Seventy percent of the county's land is owned by the federal government, mostly by the Forest Service, and the troubled lumber industry is the mainstay of the local economy, supplemented by tourism. It shares with other rural counties a chronically high unemployment rate. Plumas' population is growing, albeit slower than the state as a whole, as retirees and others seeking relief from the pressures of urban life find refuge in the area's heavily forested lands.

Overall, the county's politics are predictably conservative, although there has been a years-long battle for control of the Board of Supervisors that has included charges of election-rigging.

Riverside County

Area: 7,243 sq. mi.; Population (1988): 977,400; Voter registration (1989): D-45% R-46.1%; Unemployment (1989): 6.3%; County supervisors: Walt Abraham, Melba Dunlap, Kay Ceniceros, Patricia Larson, A. Norton Younglove; 4080 Lemon St., Riverside, 92501; (714) 787-2010.

Riverside County is Southern California's new boom area. It and neighboring San Bernardino County are gaining population at a breakneck rate reminiscent of what occurred in the San Fernando Valley and Orange County in the two decades that followed World War II. And the cause of that growth is the same: young families searching for affordable suburban homes.

While median home prices soared to the quarter-million-dollar mark in Los Angeles and Orange counties, developers subdivided large tracts of arid Riverside County and sold houses for less than half that amount. The desire for the most archetypically Californian value, a single-family home in the suburbs, was so strong that newly minted Riverside residents were willing to put up with commute times as long as two hours each way to the job centers closer to the coast, although late in the 1980s there were signs of job development to match the soaring population growth.

Riverside County, which began the decade with 663,199 in population, experienced a nearly 50 percent gain in the first eight years of the decade, making it – by far – the fastest growing large county in the state. The impacts of that growth have been many, ranging from suddenly crowded freeways to a worsening of the county's chronic smog problems.

Untold acres of orange groves – which had been the county's chief economic support until the real estate boom hit – were uprooted to make room for the new subdivisions and that, in turn, sparked an anti-growth backlash in the mid-1980s.

Growth issues remain the county's major political preoccupation but the suburban-style expansion is having an ideological impact on Riverside similar to what occurred in Orange County after World War II – a move to the right. Not too many years ago, Riverside was solidly Democratic, but in 1988 Republicans pulled ahead in registration and the remaining Democratic officeholders, especially Assemblyman Steve Clute, faced perilous times.

Riverside County's shift to the right is exacerbated by the presence of Palm Springs, an affluent retirement community that is a bastion of Republican votes. Given its high rates of population growth, Riverside is likely to benefit from post-1990 census reapportionment, and that will mean more opportunities for Republicans.

As long as Southern California's population continues to expand at a high rate, demographers expect that the net impact will be felt most keenly in inland areas such as Riverside, and the big question is whether it will be just a bedroom community or develop its own economic and employment base to match.

Sacramento County

Area: 1,015.3 sq. mi.; Population (1988): 975,300; Voter registration (1989): D-55.1% R-35.6%; Unemployment (1989): 5.1%; County supervisors: Grantland Johnson, Illa Collin, Sandra Smoley, Jim Streng, Toby Johnson; 700 H St., Suite 2450, Sacramento, 95814; (916) 440-5451.

There is no area of California that has been more affected by the growth and social change of the 1980s than Sacramento County. For decades, the Sacramento area slept while other urban areas boomed. It was known as a terminally dull government community, filled with civil servants who labored not only for the state government agencies but for dozens of federal offices as well.

At one point, more than 40 percent of the Sacramento County's work force collected public paychecks, and the metropolitan area, which included most of the county as well as chunks of neighboring counties, seemed to be nothing but a collection of endless suburban tracts, interspersed with shopping centers, including the first one ever built in California, shortly after World War II.

In the late 1970s, however, the Sacramento region began to awake from its long slumber. Soaring housing costs and traffic congestion in the Bay Area began pushing development outward, and Sacramento, with its low housing costs and relatively easy lifestyle, became an attractive destination for employers who were relocating. Government continued to be the economic backbone of the area, but the hottest growth was in the private sector. Public employment eventually declined to less than a third of the total payroll.

Downtown Sacramento began sprouting high-rises, some of them tall enough to qualify as skyscrapers; fields were converted into post-industrial and high-tech job centers; and dozens of subdivisions sprang forth. By 1989, Sacramento had been featured on the cover of a national newsmagazine touting it as one of the country's best places in which to live, and it had become the fastest growing region in the state. Professional sports and growing cultural amenities attested to Sacramento's being poised on the brink of becoming a major metropolitan area, on a par with such second-tier cities as Denver, Kansas City and Atlanta.

But there are downside impacts to the heady growth that Sacramento is experiencing, such as increased traffic congestion and worsening air quality. And the area is beset by perhaps the worst mish-mash of governmental authority in the state. The city of Sacramento is only a fifth of the metropolitan area, and the county has the highest proportion of unincorporated, urbanized area of any in the state.

One attempt at city-county consolidation failed in the mid-1970s and another, born of growth and the crazy-quilt system of local government, is being formulated. If it's successful, Sacramento would become the state's third-largest city, behind Los Angeles and San Diego, and half-again as large as San Francisco.

The non-expansion of the area during periods of high growth elsewhere in the state and the evolution of dozens of special districts to provide urban services is a amento County's past leadership vacuum.

Because the area has been a governmental center, it has not developed the private sector, corporate leadership that is vital to developing the social, political and cultural structures of a fully integrated community. In more recent years, some of the land developers who have profited from Sacramento's growth have stepped into that role, but it's not yet fully formed.

Traditionally, with its high number of government employees, Sacramento County has been dependably Democratic in its voting patterns. But with suburbanization and private-sector job development, that, too, has been changing.

Democrats still dominate in the city, but the fast-growing suburbs have developed more conservative voting habits that often translate into Republican wins.

The shift of local voting patterns was signaled in 1978, when Republican Jean Moorhead captured a suburban state Assembly seat. Moorhead later became a Democrat, but she gave up her seat. It's now held by a very conservative Republican, Tim Leslie. The trend continued in 1980, when another very conservative Republican, John Doolittle, ambushed a Democratic state senator, Al Rodda, who seemed impregnable. Doolittle appealed to suburbanites on the crime issue.

The Republicans have held their gains and may have additional opportunities after reapportionment becuase of high population growth in the suburbs. GOP candidates at the top of the ticket, meanwhile, have been doing well in the former Democratic stronghold.

San Benito County

Area: 1,397.1 sq. mi.; Population (1988): 34,500; Voter registration (1989): D-51% R-38.2%; Unemployment (1989): 16.6%; County supervisors: Richard Scagliotti, Ruth Kesler, Rita Bowling, Curtis Graves, Mike Graves; 440 Fifth St., Hollister, 95023 ;(408) 637-4641.

San Benito County lies in a little recess of public consciousness, overshadowed by its larger and/or more glamorous neighbors, Santa Clara and Monterey counties. But that may be changing.

As the extended Bay Area continues to march southward, San Benito County seems to be poised for growth. In a small way, it's already happening. Between 1980 and 1988, the county experienced a 38 percent population spurt, twice the statewide average, and as Highway 152, the major east-west route through the county, evolves into full freeway status, even more commuter-oriented development appears certain.

The question is whether this growth will overwhelm the slow-paced, rural lifestyle that has been San Benito's hallmark. Another question is whether the county's very large Hispanic population – San Juan Bautista is the headquarters of El Teatro Campesino, the farm worker's theater – will assume political power in keeping with its numbers or continue to play a secondary role.

San Bernardino County

Area: 20,164 sq. mi.; Population (1988): 1,284,900; Voter registration (1989): D-43.6% R-46.4%; Unemployment (1989): 5%; County supervisors: Marsha Turoci, Jon Mikels, Barbara Crum Riordan, Larry Walker, Robert Hammock; 385 N. Arrowhead Ave., San Bernardino, 92415; (714) 387-4811.

San Bernardino County – or San Berdoo, as it's almost universally called – is huge. It's the largest county in the United States, and its 20,000-plus square miles constitute more than an eighth of California. But most of those square miles are unpopulated stretches of desert, and more than three-fourths of them are owned by the federal government.

Politically, culturally and economically, most of what counts in San Bernardino lies in the western portion nearest to Los Angeles, and that's a sore point with residents of the other parts of the county. There was an effort in 1988, ultimately rejected by voters, to divide San Bernardino County and create a new county, called Mojave, in the desert regions.

The western slab of San Berdoo is, in conjunction with neighboring Riverside County, what boosters call the "Inland Empire," and that once-fanciful name is taking on new weight with the region's monumental boom in both population and economic and political importance.

Commuters in search of affordable housing are converting the once-grimy industrial towns of western San Bernardino County, such as Rialto and Fontana, into bedroom communities. The county's population expanded by 43.6 percent between 1980 and 1988 as hundreds of subdivisions took root and began peddling their pieces of suburban paradise.

Along with the growth has come environmental impact – smog is persistently heavy – and social dislocation. There is some job development, especially around Ontario International Airport, but the job-people mix is a continuing headache for local leaders.

The heavy industry that had been San Bernardino's economic underpinning, typified by the now-cold steel works at Fontana, is giving way to shopping centers, freight handling and other post-industrial economic activities. Dairy farmers around Chino, who used to supply much of the Los Angeles area's milk, are finding that their odoriferous activities are not compatible with the dreams of the new suburbanites.

Politically, San Berdoo has historically been blue-collar Democrat, tending to vote conservatively and Republican at the top of the ticket and Democratic for local and state offices. But with suburbanization has come partisan change, and in 1988, Democrats dropped below Republicans in registration. Local Democratic office-holders, therefore, are feeling the pinch, and Republicans look at San Bernardino County, both because of its growth and its changing vote patterns, as a source of future victories.

San Diego County

Area: 4,280.6 sq. mi.; Population (1988): 2,370,100; Voter registration (1989): D-39.7% R-46.8%; Unemployment (1989): 3.8%; County supervisors: Brian Bilbray, George Bailey, Susan Golding, Leon Williams, John MacDonald; 1600 Pacific Highway, San Diego, 92101; (619) 531-5198.

San Diego is the California of popular legend, of sunny days, sparkling beaches, red-tiled roofs and palm trees. And a lot of folks want a piece of that legend, which makes San Diego County a very popular destination for retirees and other seekers of the good life, so popular that it has become the second-most populous county in the state.

But the startling growth that San Diego has achieved over the past generation, more than doubling in population since 1960, also raises the question: If everyone wants the San Diego lifestyle, won't that destroy its attractive qualities? The answer, to many San Diegans, is yes. And that's why growth and its control have become the overriding political issues of the county. San Diego, in brief, is trying to achieve the fine balance between prosperity and quality of life and – as almost everyone will volunteer – avoid becoming another Los Angeles.

The fear of becoming Los Angeles is just one of the ways San Diego, despite its size and boosterism, exists in the shadow of the colossus to the north. Politicians refer to San Diego as the "cul-de-sac" in which political ambitions become lost, although since the city of San Diego's 1970s mayor, Pete Wilson, became a U.S. senator and a leading candidate for governor, some of that assessment has faded.

For most of the 20th century, San Diego has been known mostly as a Navy town and as a center for aircraft production. But beginning in the mid-1960s, San Diego County began experiencing economic diversification and strong population growth, driven by both domestic migration and international immigration, much of it across the nearby U.S.-Mexican border.

The fastest-growing segment of the county now is the north, which has become a center for retirees drawn by the pleasant weather. The San Diego Association of Governments has estimated that between 1980 and 2000 central San Diego County will grow by only 12 percent but outlying suburbs will expand by 100 percent or more.

In a state of diverse geography, incidentally, San Diego can boast of having the most variation within one county. Within the space of a few miles, one can experience ocean beaches, rolling hills, snowy mountains and sandy desert. That diversity is unto itself an attraction because it caters to so many personal tastes.

The strong anti-growth sentiment within the city of San Diego is encouraging development in the suburbs, especially those along the county's northern edge, although the anti-growth backlash has spread into some of those communities as long-settled residents resist the tides of newcomers.

Two recent events crystallized San Diego's uncertainty about its future and its collective fear about becoming another Los Angeles. Voters rejected a couple of growth restriction ballot measures in 1988, but when San Diego Gas and Electric Co. proposed to merge with Los Angeles-based Southern California Edison, there was a fierce backlash among local residents and politicians of both parties.

Politically, San Diego has always been something of a paradox. A tolerant attitude toward lifestyles and a strong blue-collar manufacturing base have not prevented San Diego from being largely Republican territory. But at the same time, local Republican leaders have tended to be from the centrist, moderate wing of the party, rather than from the right wing, as are many of the GOP leaders in Orange County, to the north. In addition, a core of Democratic activists keeps the party fairly well represented in legislative and congressional seats.

A conflict between centrist and conservative Republicans erupted in northern San Diego County in August 1989 after Assemblyman Bill Bradley died of cancer. The special election to fill Bradley's seat was called just after the Supreme Court reopened the abortion issue, and it quickly became nexus of the battle between two Republicans in the mostly Republican district. When the dust had settled, a pro-choice Republican nurse, Tricia Hunter, had bested an anti-abortion conservative endorsed by many Republican leaders in the Assembly. It was a symbolic setback for conservatives and a renewal of the moderate bent in local GOP politics.

The archetypical San Diego politician is Pete Wilson, a one-time Republican state legislator who later became mayor and then catapulted into the political big leagues by defeating Jerry Brown to win a U.S. Senate seat in 1982. Wilson won re-election in 1988 and now is running for governor. Wilson became an ardent advocate of "managed growth" during his term as mayor and has angered right-wingers with his liberal policies on such lifestyle issues as abortion and environmental protection.

San Diego politicians, regardless of party, tend to sail the same centrist course, conservative enough but not too conservative. But the ambitions of others to follow in Wilson's footsteps have been thwarted by the odd penchant for scandal that dogs local politics, personified by the conviction of Wilson's successor, Roger Hedgecock, on corruption charges.

Because San Diego County is growing so much faster than the state as a whole, it will continue to become more important in relative terms. By 2010, nearly 1 in 10 Californians will also be a San Diegan.

And because it's continuing to edge toward the Republicans politically (Democrats are the minority party and shrinking in relative terms), San Diego will become more important to the GOP in statewide contests. A low turnout in San Diego in 1986, for example, spelled defeat for then-Rep. Ed Zschau's very tight race against Democratic U.S. Sen. Alan Cranston.

One might argue, in fact, that just as Pete Wilson accurately reflects not only San Diego's politics but those of the state as a whole, the county has become the bellwether for California.

San Joaquin County

Area: 1,436.2 sq. mi.; Population (1988): 456,600; Voter registration (1989): D-54.8% R-37.4%; Unemployment (1989): 10.9%; County supervisors: William Sousa, Douglass Wilhoit, Ed Simas, George Barber, Evelyn Costa; 222 E. Weber St., Stockton, 95202; (209) 944-3113.

It wasn't too many years ago that San Joaquin County was farm country, part of California's vast Central Valley. But the crop being grown in many fields these days is housing for San Francisco Bay Area refugees.

San Joaquin County's population is up more than 30 percent just since 1980, and it's a change most noticeable in the once-sleepy farm town in the county's southern and western corners, such as Tracy and Manteca.

The change is less dramatic in San Joaquin County's principal city, Stockton, but it is slowly making the transition from agricultural center, with a veneer of non-farm industry, into a regional retail and service hub that includes two colleges, most notably the University of the Pacific.

San Joaquin voters mirror those in the Central Valley in registering Democrat but often voting conservatively. Stockton, however, with its ethnic diversity and industrial base, is a dependable Democratic area.

San Luis Obispo County

Area: 3,326.2 sq. mi.; Population (1988): 207,300; Voter registration (1988): D-40.9% R-46.7%; Unemployment (1989): 4%; County supervisors: Harry Ovitt, William Coy, Evelyn Delany, James Johnson, David Blakely; County Government Center, San Luis Obispo, 93408; (805) 549-5450.

Midway between San Francisco and Los Angeles, blessed with a scenic blend of coastline and mountains and boasting near-perfect weather, San Luis Obispo, both city and county, represents a version of California heaven that an increasing number of Californians want, judging from the county's soaring population, up more than a third since 1980.

It's not difficult to understand the attraction for those who, seeking respite from the pressures of urban life, cash in their inflated home equities and head either north or south along Highway 101. But the influx of newcomers is putting pressure on local housing costs and threatening, at least in the minds of many, to damage the very qualities that make "SLO-town," as local college students call it, so pleasant.

For the moment, San Luis Obispo County seems to be weathering the assault, mostly because it has a well-balanced economy rooted in agriculture, tourism and the civil service payrolls of a state college, a maximum security prison and a state hospital.

Politically, despite the presence of the college and so many public employees, San Luis Obispo is Republican and unlikely to change.

San Mateo County

Area: 530.8 sq. mi.; Population (1988): 628,500; Voter registration (1989): D-52.6% R-34.4%; Unemployment (1989): 2.7%; County supervisors: Mary Griffin, Tom Huening, Anna Eshoo, Tom Nolan, William Schumacher; 401 Marshall St., Redwood City, 94063; (415) 363-4000.

San Mateo County, a swath of the San Francisco Peninsula directly south of San Francisco itself, isn't very large in terms of area, but contained within its boundaries are vast social and economic extremes. Portions of the hilly county, communities such as Hillsborough and Atherton, are about as wealthy as California gets. Average incomes in those communities of gently winding, tree-shaded streets and stately homes approach $100,000 a year; these are the residences of choice for high-powered business executives and professionals, many of whom have their offices in San Francisco. Northern San Mateo County, the area nearest to San Francisco and containing San Francisco International Airport, is blue collar and middle class, with incomes a third of those found in the wealthier areas. And at the southern edge of the county there's East Palo Alto, a mostly black community struggling to survive, with incomes a fourth of those in the affluent communities.

San Mateo is experiencing a pattern that's become typical of California's closer-in suburban areas: relatively scant population growth coupled with soaring home prices and expansive employment. Between 1980 and 1988, the county's population grew by only 7 percent. In effect, San Mateo and other accessible suburbs are becoming employment centers unto themselves and thus evolving more into a receiver of commuters rather than suppliers, a situation that makes for changed and confused traffic patterns.

It's a pattern that's very visible in Marin and Contra Costa counties in Northern California and Orange County in Southern California. And as with these other areas, the employment growth is found mostly in white-collar and service categories.

The Association of Bay Area Governments estimates that between 1985 and 2005, San Mateo will add more than 90,000 new jobs, with finance, insurance and real estate accounting for much of the total. The new office complexes along the Bayshore Freeway attest to that trend. An entirely new subcenter is developing in Foster City, created 30 years ago by filling in a portion of San Francisco Bay.

San Mateo has the political diversity to reflect its socioeconomic variety. The blue-collar and less-affluent areas are rock-solid Democratic, while the affluent middle of the county tends to be Republican, albeit of the moderate, pro-environment, libertarian lifestyle variety personified by ex-Rep. Pete McCloskey, the area's best known political figure. That tradition was reinforced in 1988, when an iconoclastically conservative Republican congressman, Ernie Konnyu, was defeated after serving a single term by moderate Tom Campbell in the GOP primary. Campbell, who was endorsed by most local GOP leaders, went on to win the seat once held by McCloskey.

Santa Barbara County

Area: 2,744.7 sq. mi.; Population (1988): 343,100; Voter registration (1989): D-43.5% R-43.5%; Unemployment (1989): 4.6%; County supervisors: Gloria Ochoa, Tom Rogers, William Wallace, DeWayne Holmdahl, Toru Miyoshi; 105 E. Acapamu St., Santa Barbara, 93101; (805) 681-4200.

Santa Barbarans live, or think they live, with a perpetually hungry animal. The animal is Los Angeles, the pulsating powerhouse to the south. Santa Barbarans fear that it threatens to engulf their pleasant lifestyle and convert their area into just another suburb. Thus, "quality of life," however defined, is the dominant political and social issue of the area. To some, it means a never-ending anger at the presence of oil-drilling platforms off the Santa Barbara coast, with the latent danger of another serious oil spill. That's why "GOO," standing for "Get Oil Out," adorns the bumpers of many local cars. And to others, it means resisting proposals to develop new hotels along the Santa Barbara waterfront, or additional subdivisions of homes.

Santa Barbara County is growing, albeit somewhat slower than the state as a whole. But overall, local activists have managed to block most major development and to retain Santa Barbara's easy-going lifestyle. The price for that is a soaring local real estate market that precludes all but the affluent, thus creating a somewhat elitist social atmosphere that's reinforced by the trendy, expensive shops one finds in Santa Barbara's attractive downtown business district.

Outside of the city, the Santa Barbara lifestyle is self-consciously rural. Ex-President Ronald Reagan's ranch typifies life in Santa Barbara's horse country, and there are several small communities that serve these affluent rustics. There's a military presence on the northern edge of the county, near Santa Maria, in the form of the Vandenberg Air Force Base space center, from which many satellite-carrying rockets are launched.

Politically, Santa Barbara County has the unique distinction of having on paper a tie between Democrats and Republicans. At last count, in 1989, each party claimed 43.5 percent of the registered voters, with Republicans actually outnumbering Democrats by 66 souls. That tie translates into something of a split political personality. Santa Barbara tends to vote Republican at the top of the ticket and the local congressman, Robert Lagomarsino, is a Republican. But both state legislators from the area are liberal Democrats who have withstood Republican challenges. They have survived by campaigning hard and by stressing the local lifestyle and environmental protection issues that are dominant. But one, state Sen. Gary Hart, failed in 1988 in a bid to knock off Lagomarsino.

Hart, a popular local figure, must now decide whether to give up his Senate seat in 1990 to run against Lagomarsino again, or wait until 1992, when reapportionment will have changed district boundaries. If Hart does make another run for Congress, the battle over his Senate seat–now with less than 50 percent Democratic registration–will be a barnburner.

Santa Clara County

Area: 1,315.9 sq. mi.; Population (1988): 1,430,400; Voter registration (1989): D-50.5% R-36.5%; Unemployment (1989): 3.8%; County supervisors: Susanne Wilson, Zoe Lofgren, Ron Gonzales, Rod Diridon, Dianne McKenna; 70 W. Hedding St., 10th floor, San Jose, 95110; (408) 299-2323.

Santa Clara County is the engine that drives the economy of the San Francisco Bay Area, and the fuel for the engine is the computer industry. Between 1980 and 1985, nearly half of all the new jobs in the nine-county region were created in Santa Clara County, and most of those had something to do with "Silicon Valley," which is less a geographic term than a generic description for the interrelated, computer-oriented, high-tech industries found in Santa Clara County and immediate environs.

The Association of Bay Area Governments estimates that between 1985 and 2005, Santa Clara will add nearly 400,000 new jobs, more than half of them in manufacturing and wholesale trade. And while the high-tech companies of Silicon Valley have experienced their peaks and valleys, the tendency over the long term has been upward. The 1989 unemployment rate of 3.8 percent was well under the statewide average and one of the lowest found in any California county.

But economic success has had its price, or prices. They have included high levels of toxic contamination from chemicals used in the high-tech plants, incoherently sprawling suburbs, sky-high home prices ($250,000 is about the median) and legendary traffic jams.

While the county has continued to gain population, high home prices and traffic have removed some of the bloom from the rose in recent years. Through the first eight years of the decade, Santa Clara's population grew about half as fast as the state as a whole. That fact, coupled with continued high rates of job growth, means that Santa Clara has evolved into a commuter destination. Each morning, hundreds of thousands of high-tech industry workers and other commuters snake their way into the central portion of the county.

Santa Clara County's highway system was not designed to handle both local traffic and the daily influx of commuters and the result has been some of the state's worst traffic jams.

The saving grace is that Santa Clara's business and political leadership recognized relatively early that it was developing a king-size traffic headache and moved decisively to deal with it. Santa Clara, the fourth most populous county in the state, was the first county (in 1985) to enact a local sales tax override to finance transportation improvements, a step that other congested areas have since adopted. It was approved by voters because local industry put its financial muscle behind it.

New highway projects and a light-rail system centered in the county's largest city, San Jose, are among the fruits of the years-long transportation program. Transportation and other infrastructure improvements are made easier because Santa Clara virtually controls the state budget process. A San Jose senator, Alfred

Alquist, chairs the Senate's budget committee while the Assembly's is chaired by San Jose Assemblyman John Vasconcellos.

Despite the county's effort, however, the mismatch of job development and population will continue to cause strains. As ABAG said in a 1985 report, "Because of the health of the economy of Santa Clara is of importance to the region's economy, short and long-term solutions to Santa Clara's infrastructure and housing problems are essential."

The sales tax override campaign also marked another evolution for the county: the maturation of the high-tech industry and its executives into a civic force. Some – David Packard most prominently – have become compelling political and civic figures, and the industry is providing the financial and political muscle for the redevelopment of downtown San Jose.

San Jose, which recently surpassed San Francisco to become the state's third-largest city and is more than half non-Anglo, is the county's political, economic and population center and is seeing a dramatic downtown renaissance. But there are other communities of importance.

Palo Alto, on the county's northern edge, is famous as the home of Stanford University. Indeed, it was the presence of Stanford that gave rise to the high-tech industry in the first place. Palo Alto, with its university atmosphere, tree-shaded streets and old houses, is also a magnet for high-income suburbanites, and in recent years, the city has experienced a phenomenon better known in Beverly Hills: developers' acquisition of small- to medium-sized homes, which are then enlarged or replaced by larger houses for sale to well-heeled executives and professionals. It's a trend that many in Palo Alto fear will destroy the quiet, faintly academic tone of their community.

South of San Jose, along Highway 101, the one-time farm towns of Morgan Hill and Gilroy (the latter bills itself as the garlic capital of the world) are experiencing major population expansions as fields and orchards are bulldozed for new housing subdivisions and industrial parks.

With its population and economic clout, Santa Clara County has become an area of great political importance. Generally, it has been faithfully Democratic in its voting patterns, a reflection of its working-class history. But as home prices soar and affluence raises its ugly head, Santa Clara's politics seem to be edging right toward the center.

Ed Zschau, a Silicon Valley executive-turned-Republican-congressman, came within a whisker of unseating Democratic U.S. Sen. Alan Cranston in 1986, and he says he'll try again in 1992. Rod Diridon, a county supervisor, has displayed ambitions to move up the ladder. And San Jose's young, energetic mayor, Tom McEnery, is on everyone's list of potential future governors. The distinguishing quality of all of these politicians is their moderation, neither too liberal nor too conservative. And that pretty well describes the prevailing political climate in the county as a whole.

Santa Cruz County

Area: 439.6 sq. mi.; Population (1988): 226,400; Voter registration (1989): D-58.5% R-29.4%; Unemployment (1989): 9.1%; County supervisors: Janet Beautz, Robley Levy, Gary Patton, Sherry Mehl, Fred Keeley; 701 Ocean St., Santa Cruz, 95060; (408) 425-2201.

Three decades ago, Santa Cruz was a fading seaside resort looking for a new identity. It found one, but it's not to everyone's liking.

For decades, Santa Cruz had been a working-class resort area. But with that role fading, local boosters sought an economic replacement and settled on attracting a University of California campus. The effort succeeded, but the campus' unconventional and unstructured design (it opened in 1965), the advent of the hippie era and Santa Cruz County's scenic beauty all combined to transform the area within a few years.

What had been a quiet, conservative, seaside community became the capital of bohemian California. The county's politics turned sharply to the left and became hostile to new development – especially so after Santa Cruz began attracting commuters from the nearby Silicon Valley.

And for the foreseeable future, the wars over development will continue to dominate local politics.

Shasta County

Area: 3,850.2 sq. mi.; Population (1988): 139,600; Voter registration (1989): D-47.1% R-43%; Unemployment (1989): 11.4%; County supervisors: John Reit, Bob Bosworth, Frances Lynn Sullivan, Molly Wilson, Pete Peters; 1500 Court St., Room 207, Redding, 96001; (916) 225-5556.

A seminal event in the history of Shasta County was the completion of Shasta Dam nearly a half-century ago. Lake Shasta became the center of a vast recreational empire. A generation later, the completion of Interstate 5 – providing direct and convenient highway access from the rest of California – was an event of equal importance.

While the major employers in Shasta and its major city, Redding, continue to be resource-oriented manufacturing, principally lumber and mineral products, the area's climate (hot summers, mild winters) and recreational opportunities are drawing urban "equity refugees," the empty-nesters and retirees seeking less hectic lifestyles. As a result, Shasta County's population has been expanding faster than average, although official unemployment remains relatively high. Local boosters hope to put Shasta on the map in a big way by attracting one of the three new University of California campuses now in the planning stages.

Politically, Shasta is conservative and becoming more so, voting Republican consistently.

Sierra County

Area: 958.6 sq. mi.; Population (1988): 3,600; Voter registration (1989): D-49.3% R-37.1%; Unemployment (1989): 18.3%; County supervisors: Donald McIntosh, Nevada Lewis, Jerry McCaffrey, Donald Bowling, S. Craig McHenry; P.O. Drawer D, Downieville, 95936; (916) 289-3295.

Sierra County may be the second least populous California County. And its unemployment rate of 18.3 percent may be tied for first place in that dubious category. But local politics don't hinge on such mundane matters as economic growth and population change. Few though they may be, Sierra County's residents fight old-fashioned political turf battles that would seemingly be more appropriate in Chicago or Boston.

The division is mostly geographic, the eastern side of the county against the western. And Sierrans fight over such things as whether the county seat should remain in Downieville, in the west, or be moved to Loyalton, in the east. At one point, a male county supervisor was sued for sexual discrimination by a female supervisor. All of this makes the twice-monthly board meetings the best show in the county.

When not fighting with each other, Sierrans usually vote conservatively, although there's a vociferous liberal, environmental contingent.

Siskiyou County

Area: 6,318.3 sq. mi.; Population (1988): 43,300; Voter registration (1988): D-51.6% R-37.2%; Unemployment (1989): 14.6%; County supervisors: Norma Lee Frey, Ivan Young, Roger Zwanziger, Patti Jackson, George Thackeray; P.O. Box 338, Yreka, 96097; (916) 842-8081.

A half-century ago, there was a semi-serious political drive mounted in the northernmost California counties and the southernmost Oregon counties to break away and create a new state, called "Jefferson." Residents of the area felt that they were being dominated and ignored by the urban population centers. Secessionist fever cooled, but there remains a residual feeling – one very evident in scenic and sparsely populated Siskiyou County – of colonial status.

The fate of Siskiyou's timber industry, which accounts for at least one of every 10 jobs, is keyed, for instance, to battles over preservation or use of federally owned timber in the county. And there's an equally emotional battle over proposals for a major ski resort on Mount Shasta, the dormant volcano that is Siskiyou's most dominant landmark.

Those battles aside, Siskiyou County has an interesting socioeconomic phenomenon: a substantial black population that grew out of workers imported from the South by lumber mills. In 1986, Charles Byrd became California's only elected black sheriff.

Solano County

Area: 872.2 sq. mi.; Population (1988): 313,100; Voter registration (1989): D-54.7% R-32.8%; Unemployment (1989): 5.9%; County supervisors: Osby Davis, Lee Simmons, Sam Caddle, Don Pippo, Jan Stewart; 580 W. Texas St., Fairfield, 94533; (707) 429-6218.

Solano County used to be a predictable part of California. Vallejo was an industrial city, the site of a major Navy shipyard and other water-oriented industries. Fairfield was the county seat but otherwise a farm town on the edge of the Central Valley. Benicia was a sleepy little bit of history, the site of a former military arsenal and, briefly, a 19th century California capital. And Vacaville was another farm town that also had a state prison.

All of that used to be true. But the relentless expansion of people and jobs out of urban centers has transformed Solano County in ways that no one could have imagined just a few years ago.

Vallejo has become a tourist center with the re-location of Marine World Africa USA on a former golf course. Industry – most prominently a big Anheuser-Busch brewery – has come to Fairfield. And throughout Solano County, the sounds of hammers and saws at work have become part of the background noise as field after field has been transformed into new subdivisions, shopping centers and other physical evidence of rapid population growth. Solano County's population shot up by a third between 1980 and 1988, and there's no indication that it will slow down.

Solano County, in effect, is being squeezed from two directions. While the western portion of the county is transformed into a suburb of the Bay Area, the eastern portion, including the once-sleepy farm town of Dixon, falls within the orbit of fast-growing Sacramento. The county's location midway between the two major Northern California urban complexes also makes it attractive to industrial developers. The Association of Bay Area Governments, a regional planning agency, predicts that Solano will add 58,000 jobs and about 150,000 residents between 1985 and 2005.

The growth is most evident along Interstate 80, the freeway that connects Sacramento and the Bay Area, and especially along the intersections of I-80 with Interstate 680 near Fairfield and Interstate 505 near Vallejo.

Away from the freeways, the county's ambiance remains largely rural – and local residents want to keep it that way.

Not unexpectedly, the county is experiencing growing pains: traffic jams, overburdened water and sewage treatment facilities, etc. And the growth also has fueled a growing backlash among local residents worried that their bucolic lifestyles will be inundated by the rising flood of newcomers.

Traditionally, Solano County has been considered Democratic territory – especially blue-collar Vallejo. But with suburbanization has come a noticeable shift to the right politically, with Republicans looking to the county as a site of future gains.

Sonoma County

Area: 1,597.6 sq. mi.; Population (1988): 365,800; Voter registration (1989): D-55.4% R-33.9%; Unemployment (1989): 5%; County supervisors: Janet Nicholas, James Haberson, Tim Smith, Nick Esposti, Ernest Carpenter; 575 Administration Drive, Santa Rosa, 95403; (707) 527-2241.

In 1986, the Sonoma County Planning Department told county supervisors that the county's population was growing so fast that it had already reached the point that had been predicted for the turn of the century. And there's no end in sight.

As Marin County virtually shut down development in the 1970s, pressure shifted directly to the north, rapidly converting the one-time "Chicken Capital of the World," Petaluma, and Santa Rosa, the county seat, into suburban enclaves. And the transformation has continued as Santa Rosa develops a significant employment base of its own and becomes a destination point for commuters from housing developments even further up Highway 101, the main north-south artery, which often resembles an elongated parking lot.

The Association of Bay Area Governments notes that Sonoma County's population tripled between 1950 and 1980, with half of that growth coming in the last decade. It's expected to increase by another 44 percent between 1985 and 2005.

Jobs are growing more slowly, so Sonoma is expected to continue in its role as a bedroom community, at least until after the turn of the century. But the very qualities that have made Sonoma County so attractive – the rural lifestyle and stunning natural beauty – may be threatened by the sheer immensity of the growth. And that makes growth and related issues the driving force in local politics. A recent poll of residents listed traffic as the most important issue, followed by education and development.

An anti-growth backlash has arisen, with environmentalists and chicken farmers forming unusual political alliances to stave off the rapid conversion of agriculture land into subdivisions and shopping centers. Petaluma was the site of an early development battle when local officials, desperately trying to stave off suburbanization of agricultural community in the 1970s, passed a law limiting housing development to 500 units a year. The ensuing lawsuit reached the U.S. Supreme Court, which ruled in Petaluma's favor and thus validated local growth-control laws.

Politically, Sonoma County has a split personality. The western portion, home to a large gay community and environmental activism, is Democratic and liberal, while the rapidly suburbanizing eastern portion is conservative and Republican.

Sensibly, politicians have divided the county more or less along north-south Highway 101 while drawing congressional and legislative districts. Sen. James Nielsen and Assemblywoman Bev Hansen, both Republicans, represent the wine country in the eastern portion of the county, while Sen. Barry Keene and Assemblyman Dan Hauser, both Democrats, have the west.

Stanislaus County

Area: 1,521.2 sq. mi.; Population (1988): 340,200; Voter registration (1989): D-53.3% R-37.8%; Unemployment (1989): 12.9%; County supervisors: Pat Paul, Rolland Starn, Nick Blom, Raymond Clark Simon, Sal Cannella; 1100 H St., Modesto, 95354; (209) 525-6414.

Nowhere in California is the socioeconomic phenomenon of suburbanization more starkly evident than in Stanislaus County.

For decades, this San Joaquin Valley county was purely agricultural, home of some of the nation's best-known products, such as Gallo wine and Foster Farms chicken. But its location in proximity to the San Francisco Bay Area and, more important, to the freeways leading to the Bay Area ordained that it would explode with houses and shopping centers as population expanded and young commuters searched for affordable homes. Stanislaus' population swelled by nearly 28 percent between 1980 and 1988.

As the socioeconomic character of the area changes, so do its politics, away from agriculture and toward issues more identified with suburban life, some of which conflict with farming. Stanislaus and its major city, Modesto, are engaged in a great internal debate over their future – one characterized by a Modesto Bee series as "Growth–Pain and Progress."

Sutter County

Area: 607 sq. mi.; Population (1988): 61,700; Voter registration (1989): D-41.4% R-50.5%; Unemployment (1989): 16.3%; County supervisors: Larry Montna, Joseph Benatar, Tom Pfeffer, Ron Southard, Barbara LeVake; 463 Second St., Yuba City, 95991; (916) 741-7106.

Yuba City and its sister city just across the river, Marysville, found themselves in the spotlight of national publicity in 1986 when Rand McNally listed the area as the worst place to live in the United States. The ranking was based on statistics, and the area was dragged down by its high unemployment rate, among other factors. High unemployment is a sticky problem in agricultural Sutter County, but the county may be on the verge of an economic boom.

Highway 99, which links Yuba City-Marysville with Sacramento, 40 miles away, will be a four-lane freeway within a few years, and there are indications that the population boom in the Sacramento area will soon create intensive suburbanization of Sutter – especially the southern reaches of the county, which are within a few miles of downtown Sacramento. A recent county-commissioned study makes that prediction and developers are quietly acquiring tracts of farmland in anticipation.

Politically, Sutter County is very conservative, with a Republican registration majority, and is likely to remain so.

Tehama County

Area: 2,976 sq. mi.; Population (1988): 46,700; Voter registration (1989): D-49.6% R-38.5%; Unemployment (1989): 11.2%; County supervisors: Vance Wood, Phil Gunsauls, Floyd Hicks, Bill Flournoy, Burton Bundy; P.O. Box 250, Red Bluff, 96080; (916) 527-4655.

A 1988 article in California magazine described them as "The Revolutionary Junta of Tehama County." Time magazine told the same story, albeit more briefly, in an article entitled "Going Broke in California."

Tehama County supervisors put themselves in the spotlight when they threatened to shut down county government completely because Proposition 13 and a stingy state government had left them without enough money to take care of all their legal responsibilities.

Beyond that spurt of publicity, Tehama County scarcely registers in the consciousness of most Californians. Its chief city, Red Bluff, sometimes makes the weather charts as the hottest place in the state, but that's about it.

Tehama County subsists on agriculture – cattle ranching mostly – and timber production, but much of the potential commercial activity is siphoned away by the relatively larger and more vigorous communities of Redding and Chico. That leaves the county with relatively low sales tax revenues, which exacerbates the financing problem.

Trinity County

Area: 4,844.9 sq. mi.; Population (1988): 14,000; Voter registration (1989): D-48.3% R-37.1%; Unemployment (1989): 18.1%; County supervisors: Stan Plowman, Dee Potter, Arnold Whitridge, Howard Myrick, Patricia Mortensen; P.O. Drawer 1258, Weaverville, 96093; (916) 623-1217.

Nothing is more pervasive in Trinity County than a sense of disconnection to the 20th century.

Weaverville, the county seat and only semi-major city, still contains 19th century storefronts built during the gold rush era. And much of the county's scant population is scattered in homesteads and tiny crossroads communities.

Most of Trinity County's residents are happy in their isolation. They cut timber, raise cattle, pan for gold and grow marijuana to support themselves and wish the rest of the world would leave them alone.

As legend has it, Weaverville was the inspiration for the fictional kingdom of Shangri-la, and there is something mystical about the Trinity Alps, the magnificent and sometimes impenetrable range of mountains occupying much of the county. It's unlikely Trinity will share in any of the socioeconomic changes sweeping the state. It's a lengthy and difficult drive from any population center and offers scant appeal to developers.

Tulare County

Area: 4,844.9 sq. mi.; Population (1988): 297,500; Voter registration (1989): D-49.4% R-41.2%; Unemployment (1989): 11.2%; County supervisors: Clyde Gould, John Conway, Delores Mangine, LeRoy Swiney, Gary Reed; 2800 W. Burrel, Visalia, 93291; (209) 733-6271.

Superficially, Tulare County looks like any other San Joaquin Valley farm county and its principal city, Visalia, just like any other farm town. But in this case, appearances are deceiving.

Tulare County and Visalia have striven for economic diversification with uncommon vigor, and it's paid off with the establishment of dozens of industrial facilities.

Tulare County's central location and its nearby recreational opportunities in the Sierra aid the economic development effort. So has an almost entrepreneurial approach to government by Visalia. Despite the obvious fruits of development, unemployment runs at twice the state average, a reflection of the seasonal nature of agriculture, which remains the top industry.

Tulare's next big development effort will be directed at securing one of the proposed new University of California campuses.

Politically, Tulare is medium-conservative, voting for Democrats only when they avoid the liberal label.

Tuolumne County

Area: 2,292.7 sq. mi.; Population (1988): 46,300; Voter registration (1989): D-51% R-39.3%; Unemployment (1989): 9.9%; County supervisors: Larry Rotelli, Greg Hurt, Nell Farr, Norman Tergeson, Charles Walter; 2 S. Green St., Sonora, 95370; (209) 533-5521.

Tuolumne County came into being in the California gold rush and 130 years later finds itself in the midst of a new one. A huge new gold mine, working the spoils of generations of mining operations in the area, opened in 1986 and gave the county a much-needed steady payroll.

But in overall economic terms, gold mining is less important than the development of Tuolumne's scenic wonders. Its population is growing fast – more than 36 percent between 1980 and 1988 – and, like other foothill counties, most of that growth is composed of retirees and other urban escapees. Drawn by the county's mild climate, slow-paced lifestyle and recreational opportunities, the newcomers are fueling the economy with their pensions and the investment of equity from the sale of homes in urban areas. Thus construction of homes and other facilities and the provision of retail services have become industries unto themselves.

Politically, Tuolumne is conservative and, if anything, likely to become more so as its population grows.

Ventura County

Area: 1,863.6 sq. mi.; Population (1988): 646,700; Voter registration (1989): D-41% R-47.5%; Unemployment (1989): 4.9%; County supervisors: Susan Lacey, Madge Schaefer, Maggie Erickson, James Dougherty, John Flynn; 800 S. Victoria Ave., Ventura, 93009; (805) 654-2929.

Not too many years ago, one could have accurately described Ventura County as rural. Its dominant industries were citrus fruit and other forms of agriculture and oil. The pace of life was slow. Los Angeles was an hour's drive away.

But within an astonishingly brief period, Ventura County has become a suburban offshoot of the ever-expanding Southern California megalopolis.

As freeway routes were punched through the coastal hills from the San Fernando Valley and into the cities of Oxnard, Santa Paula and Ventura, developers began acquiring large tracts of agricultural land and converting them into housing subdivisions, shopping centers, office complexes and industrial parks.

One area of the Ventura County has been dubbed "Gallium Gulch," a takeoff on Silicon Valley, because it has become a center for development of gallium arsenide into a commercial product. The new technology has drawn some of the largest names in American industry.

Meanwhile, as the farm economy continues to stumble along, farmers are encouraged to sell off their lands to developers, and the socioeconomic conversion of the county becomes more intense with each passing year.

In more recent times, Ventura County has begun to exploit its coastal resources as well, seeking some of the recreational and vacation activity that the rest of Southern California has long enjoyed. The city of Ventura, long accustomed to having tourists pass through en route to Santa Barbara to the north, is now developing marinas, hotels and other facilities to capture their dollars. It is also – a la Santa Barbara – beginning to emphasize its historic roots as a mission town (the official name of the city is San Buenaventura, after the local mission).

As Ventura County continues to evolve economically, it is changing socially. The agricultural and blue-collar workers who once found the county an affordable place in which to live now find home prices soaring. And the county is experiencing other growing pains as well, including heavy traffic on Highway 101, the major route connecting it with Los Angeles, and on other highways.

The socioeconomic change is especially evident in Oxnard, a one-time farm town that had a very large Hispanic population. Its proximity to the ocean and freeways connecting to the San Fernando Valley and Los Angeles are converting Oxnard into a bedroom town at an astonishing rate.

And as Ventura County suburbanizes and grows, its politics are becoming more conservative. It has a Republican voter majority, and Democratic candidates are finding that an ever-steeper hill to climb.

Yolo County

Area: 1,034 sq. mi.; Population (1988): 135,000; Voter registration (1989): D-55.5% R-32.3%; Unemployment (1989): 8%; County supervisors: Clark Cameron, Helen Thomson, George DeMars, Betsy Marchard, Cowles Mast; 625 Court St., Woodland, 95695; (916) 666-8195.

It's rare to find the kind of closely spaced socioeconomic and political diversity that one encounters in Yolo County, just west of Sacramento.

Woodland, the county seat, is a farm town on the verge of becoming a suburb of Sacramento. West Sacramento is, as the name implies, already a suburb, but it is constantly fighting the image of being a low-income, quasi-slum, quasi-red light district.

West Sacramento has recently incorporated and is counting on a huge, upscale marina-commercial-residential project along the Sacramento River to upgrade its image.

Davis – or the People's Republic of Davis, as its detractors call it – is the quintessential university town, with a high degree of political activism that extends down to the street-light level. Mostly, it's trying to resist developer pressure to become still another Sacramento bedroom town, and mostly failing.

This socioeconomic mix also gives Yolo extremely diverse politics that range from Davis' liberalism to Woodland's conservatism.

Yuba County

Area: 639.1 sq. mi.; Population (1988): 56,800; Voter registration (1989): D-48.3% R-39.7%; Unemployment (1989): 13.3%; County supervisors: George Deveraux, Thomas Belza, Bill Harper, Michelle Mathews, J.E. McGill; 215 Fifth St., Marysville, 95901; (916) 741-6461.

Yuba County is next door to Sutter County. The county seats, Marysville and Yuba City, respectively, are just one river apart. But because of their geographic configuration, the two counties seem destined to develop along different lines.

Much of Sutter lies next to Sacramento County and is therefore likely to become suburban in nature. But most of Yuba County lies well to the north of Sacramento County and is likely to remain rural for the foreseeable future.

Marysville itself may be destined for semi-suburban status as the highways connecting it and Yuba City to Sacramento and the burgeoning high-tech industrial areas in nearby Placer County are upgraded to freeway status.

In addition, the area can count on a steady payroll from Beale Air Force Base, which not only escaped the recent round of base closures but will be enhanced by shifts of units from other bases.

Yuba County, with a less than 50 percent Democratic registration, votes conservatively and Republican most of the time.

10

Cities–business as usual

The evolution of local governments in California during the 19th and early 20th century bequeathed cities with the leftovers of power. But what seemed to be a deliberate weakening of municipal power became, in the post-Proposition 13 political environment, a blessing.

California cities have not only survived while other local governments, most notably school districts and counties, have struggled, but they are prospering. Cities are free of the big-ticket health, welfare and educational responsibilities, have major sources of revenue that are independent of the severely limited property tax and have evolved into semientrepreneurial agencies with wide powers to acquire and develop land in an economic atmosphere that favors expansion.

The resurgence of city governments has not only affected existing ones, but has sparked the creation of several dozen new ones. Since Proposition 13 was enacted in 1978, incorporations have been occurring at twice the rate as that of the same period preceding its passage.

Since 19th century California was not only rural in character but dominated by farmers, miners and others with a rural outlook, cities were almost an afterthought. The most important unit of local government to those early Californians was the county, and county governments acquired the responsibilities for health care, welfare and other social programs that in other states are often the province of municipalities. Education, which is also a municipal responsibility in some states, was placed under the direction of independent school districts. And other local services, such as fire protection and parks, were often provided by units of local government called special districts. In addition, cities, like other units of local government, became non-partisan.

While cities, including some large ones, did evolve in this atmosphere, much of

California's population still lives in unincorporated territory – an odd fact for the nation's most urbanized state. A million residents of Los Angeles County live outside city boundaries, and in a number of rural counties, city-dwellers are a minority. That's true even of Sacramento County, whose total population is about a million. One county, Alpine, has no incorporated cities, not even its county seat. The other extreme is San Francisco, which has California's only combined city-county government and thus no unincorporated territory.

California's decades-old taxation system retarded both the development of new cities (incorporation) and the expansion of existing ones (annexation). Property owners were required to pay property taxes to their county governments and separate taxes to city governments, even though some of the services were duplicated. As a result, efforts to expand municipal government often ran into opposition from homeowners unwilling to pay higher taxes.

There was stubborn opposition to annexation or incorporation, too, from the special districts that had mushroomed in the postwar era to provide services to unincorporated areas of the state. These districts provided parks and recreation services, fire protection, water and sewer services and other specialized services, each controlled by its own elected trustees, each having its own administrative structure and each levying its own taxes. Special district officials saw city expansions as threats to their existence and often used their political clout to block them. An arcane government agency called the Local Agency Formation Commission in each county is the referee for such turf battles. LAFCOs are composed of city, county and special district officials themselves and are the forges in which local governments are formed, shrunken and expanded.

In 1978, the cities' tax disadvantage vanished with the passage of Proposition 13, which placed an overall cap on property taxes and thus removed the penalty for the creation of new cities. The new political atmosphere coincided with a big growth spurt in California's population, one felt most keenly in the suburbs.

The growth, the removal of the property tax penalty and a rising desire of suburbanites to shape their communities through local land-use decisions sparked a renaissance in city governments. More than 30 new cities have been formed since Proposition 13 passed, most of them in the suburbs and some of them boasting substantial populations.

Archetypical is Moreno Valley, which sprawls along the freeway connecting Riverside and Palm Springs. In 1980, it was just a collection of widely dispersed homes in the desert. But the outward movement of young families looking for affordable homes and Moreno Valley's freeway-close location created a boom as dozens of subdividers built tracts of new homes. By the time Moreno Valley became a city in 1984, it already had about 100,000 residents.

Karen Hall, an analyst of local government change in Sacramento, puts it this way: "A lot of communities feel that boards of supervisors aren't listening to their desires and taking their interests to heart, especially in planning and land-use issues.

They're tired of being a forgotten stepchild."

A major spur to the creation of new cities is another quirk of California tax law: The local portion of sales taxes is returned to the local government in which the sale occurred. If the sale occurs in unincorporated territory, the tax goes into county coffers, but if it occurs in a city, the municipal government benefits. The reduction in property tax revenues because of Proposition 13 has made the local sales tax an increasingly important source of funds, and today the boundaries of would-be cities are drawn specifically to include shopping centers, auto dealerships and other high-volume retail areas.

For that same reason, many cities have concentrated on encouraging land uses with high potential for generating tax revenues, often using their "redevelopment" powers to acquire and repackage land for private developers. Annexations of unincorporated territory have in many cases hinged on such development or redevelopment deals, deals so common that redevelopment has lost its veneer of removing blight and has, instead, become almost entirely a tool of economic development. One city even declared a golf course blighted so that redevelopment funds could be used to develop a tourist attraction.

County officials, who once encouraged the formation of new cities as a way of relieving themselves of expenses for law enforcement, fire protection and other services, have become hostile to incorporations and annexations in many areas because of the revenue crunch.

The relationships between cities and counties varies widely. Some counties – Santa Clara for example – insist that new urbanized development occur within city boundaries, while others have bitterly resisted such municipal expansion. And in some counties, city and county officials have negotiated elaborate revenue-sharing agreements to avoid direct conflict.

"It's not clear what happens if cities and counties can't agree on a division of tax revenues," says Paul Valle-Riestra, a staff attorney for the League of California Cities. "The law doesn't provide any black and white resolution of how property taxes should be shared or whether there is authority for cities and counties to share other sorts of revenues, such as sales tax."

In the absence of any law forbidding such agreements, they are being negotiated in some counties while relationships remain hostile in others.

A major battleground is Sacramento County, which has California's highest proportion of unincorporated urbanized territory.

As Sacramento County's population grew after World War II, largely because of expansion of state and federal government employment, the city of Sacramento's municipal leadership resisted expansion of city boundaries. Thus, most of the county's growth occurred in hundreds of square miles of unincorporated suburbs north and east of the city. By the thousands, homes, shopping centers and office complexes were developed along suburban corridors. By the 1970s, the city was hemmed in. It could expand into vacant land north and south, but the Sacramento River on the west and the unincorporated suburbs on the northeast and east were barriers to growth.

A proposal to merge city and county government into a metropolitan government failed in the mid-1970s, in part because of the pre-Proposition 13 tax situation. By the 1980s, several of the unincorporated suburban communities were actively pursuing creation of city governments, which waved a red flag in front of county supervisors. Fearing the loss of sales tax revenue, the county officials stalled incorporation—most notably in Citrus Heights—while frantically pursuing a revised city-county merger, which is still pending.

But control of taxes is not the only factor in the creation of new cities. Growth has produced an anti-growth backlash in many communities, and this has spurred creation of city governments to make land-use decisions.

One new city, West Hollywood, was founded in 1984 through the efforts of gay activists seeking a haven for their lifestyle and the enactment of a rent control law. Residents of the waterside Marina del Rey area of Los Angeles County, who are overwhelmingly renters, sought incorporation for the same reason, but landlords and their allies retaliated with a unique state law that, in effect, prevents creation of a city of Marina del Rey. The mostly black San Mateo County community of East Palo Alto was formed in 1983, and it has struggled financially.

Three unincorporated Yolo County communities just across the Sacramento River from Sacramento were merged into West Sacramento in 1987. The acquisition of a privately owned water system to improve water quality was a major factor in West Sacramento's incorporation, but once formed, the city gave full vent to its newly acquired redevelopment powers to cash in on the Sacramento area's population and economic boom.

With county boundaries unchanged since 1919 and school district lines rarely changing, cities are California's most rapidly evolving form of local government. And big city mayorships have become tickets into the political big time, something that wasn't true until just recently.

Pete Wilson converted his successful reign as mayor of San Diego into a seat in the U.S. Senate and a candidacy for the governorship in 1990. The Democratic candidate for governor in 1982 and 1986 was Los Angeles' longtime mayor, Tom Bradley. John Seymour's major accomplishment as mayor of Anaheim was to lure the Rams professional football team to the city's sports stadium, and he parlayed that into a state Senate seat. He's now running for lieutenant governor. Dianne Feinstein, the mayor of San Francisco for a decade, came within a whisker of becoming the Democratic candidate for vice president in 1984, the year the party convention was held in her city. And as ex-mayor, she's running for governor in 1990.

A number of other small-town mayors have moved into state legislative and congressional seats.

Los Angeles

Population (1989): 3,400,500; Voter registration (1989): D-61.8% R-28.6%; Mayor: Thomas Bradley; City Council: Zev Yaroslavsky, Joel Wachs, Joy Picus, John Ferraro, Michael Woo, Ruth Galanter, Ernani Bernardi, Robert Farrell, Gilber Lindsay, Dave Cunningham, Marvin Braude, Richard Alatorre, Gloria Molina, Joan Milke-Flores; 200 N. Spring St., Los Angeles, 90012; (213) 485-2121; Incorporated: 1850.

"Los Angeles" is a term with many meanings. It's a generic term for dozens of Southern California communities in several counties. It's a county. It's a state of mind. And it's the city of Los Angeles, by far the largest city in California, the second largest in the nation and, in cultural and economic terms, one of the most powerful influences in the history of mankind.

The city's boundaries follow no logical pattern. They encompass the concrete towers of a downtown business district still trying to find its identity, vast suburban tracts of the San Fernando Valley and canyons populated mostly by coyotes and jack rabbits. Other cities and unincorporated portions of Los Angeles County abut the city's boundaries. Even within the city there are identifiable communities, virtually cities unto themselves, such as Hollywood, as well as separate incorporated cities such as San Fernando. And although Los Angeles is separated from the Pacific Ocean by other cities, it has established a narrow corridor linking it to the city-operated port.

In the beginning, it was just a loose collection of ranchos and missions, one of the most remote outposts of the Spanish empire. And well into the 20th century, it was a slow-moving, sprawling assemblage of bungalows and low-rise commercial buildings, lacking any distinguishing feature, a town that could have been any Midwestern farm city.

But the onset of World War II propelled Los Angeles, with the rest of California, into the industrial age. As factories, warehouses, docks and other facilities were rapidly built to serve the war, Los Angeles began to wake up. Its population doubled and redoubled as hundreds of thousands of war workers poured into the city.

The naturally arid region had assured itself of a dependable water supply, thanks to some clandestine and not altogether savory dealings by local landowners, and the San Fernando Valley and other one-time ranch lands were rapidly converted into housing tracts.

Los Angeles' boom continued unabated after the war. Factories that had turned out bombers began making airliners. The automobile, a necessity in such a low-density city, sparked the development of the freeway, a new form of highway that was disconnected from stop signs and traffic lights. The state's first freeway, connecting downtown Los Angeles with Pasadena, the traditional home of mon-eyed families, is still carrying cars.

With so many new people coming into town, with so much money to be made and with so little sense of civic identity, Los Angeles was ripe for corruption. Three decades after the fact, the movie "Chinatown" accurately captured the ambiance of Los Angeles in the 1940s. The police were corrupt. The city officials were corrupt. The newspapers were corrupt. Everybody was corrupt. Los Angeles was a civic joke, its downtown area a seedy slum, its once-extensive trolley system ripped out by money-grubbing bus companies, its development governed by which subdivider was most willing to grease the right palms.

Slowly, Los Angeles developed a sense of civic pride that extended beyond the latest land deal. Slowly, the city's notoriously corrupt Police Department was cleaned up by William Parker, a reformist police chief. The Los Angeles Times, once considered to be the nation's worst large newspaper, came under the control of Otis Chandler, a member of the family that had owned it for generations, and the new publisher cleaned house, turning the Times into a major institution that aspires to national prominence. Los Angeles developed a cultural infrastructure to match its fast-growing population: art museums, a symphony, charities and other amenities to help the nouveau riche – including those from the movie industry – acquire a veneer of social respectability.

But as the city's upper crust began developing a social sense, the city itself was undergoing vast social change. What had once been a purely white-bread city evolved, slowly at first and then with breakneck speed, into the new American melting pot. Economic and political refugees poured into Los Angeles from every corner of the globe – a phenomenon aided in no small measure by the Los Angeles-based movie and television industry, which had made the cityscape familiar to worldwide audiences.

A substantial black community that had been established during and after World War II, drawn from the South by industrial job opportunities, was augmented by Hispanics, Asians, Israelis, Arabs, Armenians and countless immigrants from dozens of other ethnic groups and nationalities. Soon, the newcomers established new ethnic enclaves or expanded those already in place. South-central Los Angeles is mostly black. East Los Angeles is mostly Hispanic. On the edge of downtown Los Angeles are long-established pockets of Chinese- and Japanese-Americans. Just west of downtown is Koreatown, a more recent phenomenon. And further west, one finds predominantly Jewish neighborhoods.

As the immigrants moved in and multiplied, the Anglos moved out to the suburbs, some of which – such as the San Fernando Valley – are within the city limits. The late 1980s found Los Angeles to be one of the nation's most ethnically diverse cities, with Anglos in the minority. More than a third of the city's population is Hispanic and blacks and Asians account for another 25-plus percent.

For decades, Los Angeles' politics, like the city itself, was a whites-only business. Mayors – honest or crooked – were all men who professed a conservative ideology, and none showed more than token ability to project an image outside the city itself. The City Council was also dominated by white men.

Racial relations were, like much of the Los Angeles lifestyle, conducted at long distance. If anything, the 1965 riots in the overwhelmingly black Watts section of Los Angeles widened the gulf between Anglos and non-Anglos. It was a more violent replay of the "Zoot suit riots," which had pitted Hispanics against white servicemen during World War II.

All of that seemingly changed in 1973, when Tom Bradley, a black ex-athlete and former Los Angeles policeman, won the mayorship. Bradley projected hope to minorities and pro-development moderation to the white business and political establishment. And he has survived, winning re-election four times, by continuing to walk that tightrope.

Bradley's chief mayoral accomplishment – one made in close collaboration with the business community – has been the revitalization of the city's downtown core. Oil companies, banks and other major corporations dumped money into the Bunker Hill project to give the downtown core a skyline, even though the lower reaches of the area remain somewhat seedy.

Beyond that, Bradley has delivered city government that is reasonably efficient, reasonably honest and reasonably inclusive, especially when compared to those of the nation's other big cities.

Bradley, an intensely proud and private man, thought that his record of moderation and progress warranted a broader stage, and he ran for governor in 1982 as Jerry Brown stepped down to seek a U.S. Senate seat. The Democratic Party thought it had a winner in Bradley, especially following the nomination of George Deukmejian, the lackluster attorney general, after a bitterly contested Republican primary.

The public opinion polls confirmed that Bradley was the favorite. Even surveys of voters leaving polling places on Election Day had Bradley the winner. But when all of the votes had been counted – including several hundred thousand absentee ballots that the Republicans had semisecretly encouraged – Deukmejian had eked out a paper-thin victory, sending Bradley back to Los Angeles.

Bradley's gubernatorial ambitions had been hurt by the state's changing political climate and by the presence on the ballot of a very controversial gun control measure, which brought out a heavy turnout of conservatives. And there also were assertions that racism played a role in the outcome.

Three years later, Bradley faced a tough re-election campaign himself but won and, driven more by pride than realism, ran for governor again in 1986. This time, Deukmejian's victory was a landslide.

In 1989, Bradley ran for his fifth term as mayor amid widespread speculation that his career was on the wane. A young city councilman, Zev Yaroslavsky, was running all-out. He had the backing of the powerful political organization headed by U.S. Reps. Howard Berman and Henry Waxman, which dominates politics on Los Angeles' affluent west side, an area long a source of Bradley support. Yaroslavsky also exploited a newly minted aversion among west-siders and San

Fernando Valley residents to development.

The Berman-Waxman organization is the single most powerful political force in Los Angeles, with influence that reaches to Sacramento and Washington. It even has its own professional campaign arm headed by Berman's younger brother, Michael, and his partner, Carl D'Agostino. (The firm is known as "BAD Campaigns.") The organization taps into the wealthy west side professional and entertainment industry community for money, and it backs candidates for local and state offices. It was instrumental in Gary Hart's 1984 presidential primary victory in California. Berman-Waxman is neo-liberal, pro-environment and very strongly supportive of Israel in foreign policy matters. Its support of Yaroslavsky over Bradley was the local version of the black-Jewish split that has become a national phenomenon.

But a funny thing happened to Yaroslavsky on his way to the mayor's mansion. A memorandum written by Michael Berman and D'Agostino, and leaked to local media, questioned Bradley's intelligence and urged Yaroslavsky to be more aggressive in his attacks on the mayor. "The reason why BAD thinks you can beat Bradley is you've got 50 IQ points on him (and that's no compliment). But your IQ advantage is of no electoral use if you don't use it," the memo said.

Yaroslavsky tried in vain to distance himself from the damaging memo and his advisers, but in the end, he opted out of the mayoral race, leaving Bradley with no impediments to winning a fifth term. Or so it seemed. A few months later, Yaroslavsky was probably kicking himself for not taking the plunge. Bradley was forced into a runoff with an obscure black city councilman named Nate Holden, and he won with only a few votes to spare.

The turnaround in the mayor's fortunes stemmed from a series of newspaper revelations about his personal finances, especially consulting fees he had accepted from two banks that were given deposits from city funds. The scandal continued to blossom even after Bradley was re-elected, and by late 1989, Bradley faced the possibility of prosecution for failing to disclose his financial dealings with the banks. The Justice Department, meanwhile, was examining Bradley's financial connections with junk bond king Michael Milken.

Bradley moved a step back from the political abyss when City Attorney James Hahn – son of legendary county Supervisor Kenneth Hahn and a rising political star himself – concluded in August 1989 that Bradley should be fined for improper reporting of his personal finances but should not be prosecuted.

While Hahn's conclusion protected Bradley from immediate prosecution, the Justice Department investigation was continuing and Bradley's overall reputation was severly damaged.

It is a crippled Bradley, therefore, who pursues his fifth term in the mayor's office. But perhaps it's a metaphor for the city he governs. Los Angeles seems to be a city under siege, moving ever closer to the apocalyptic city portrayed in the science fiction movie "Blade Runner" and ever further from the sun-drenched oasis of popular legend.

Ethnic diversity has produced social friction, including more than 400 gang-related murders a year. Drug abuse is rampant in lower-income neighborhoods and upper-income mansions. Smog is worsening, traffic congestion grows exponentially and polls indicate that most Los Angelos think their quality of life has deteriorated. One survey found half of those polled had considered moving out of the city.

Los Angeles is a city that still works; a huge reservoir of civic energy is evident in such enterprises as the 1984 Olympics. But it's also a laboratory in which the ability of people holding widely different social and cultural values to tolerate each other is being tested. The city's politics are beginning to reflect its social friction.

Under pressure from the U.S. Department of Justice, the city redrew the boundaries of its 15 City Council districts to create two seats for Hispanics. But those seats, now occupied by ex-state legislators Richard Alatorre and Gloria Molina, represent only a fraction of the latent Hispanic political power in the city. With more than a third of Los Angeles' population, Hispanics could claim at least five of the 15 City Council seats. Blacks, with a third of the Hispanic population, have three seats as well as the mayorship. There is one Asian city councilman, also of recent vintage, Michael Woo. The reason for this is that blacks vote at least in proportion to their numbers while both Hispanics and Asians have been virtually invisible politically. Even the two Hispanic council members find themselves on opposite sides of the political fence, Alatorre being allied with Bradley and Molina with the Berman-Waxman organization and other liberal forces.

Development is emerging as the city's overriding political issue, one that reached the ballot directly in 1989 in the form of a measure dealing with plans for oil development on city-owned coastal land. The plans were promoted by Occidental Petroleum and its longtime chairman, Armand Hammer, a close Bradley political ally.

Environmental protection has become a popular cause on the west side, albeit one that in the minds of many non-Anglos is tinged with racial exclusivity. Bradley has been pro-development in league with business and labor groups, but anti-development forces have been gaining strength on the City Council. Pat Russell, a Bradley ally who served as City Council president, was defeated in her coastal district on the development issue just before Bradley himself faced re-election, a portent of the issue's potency.

The battle over development has become, in effect, a battle over the quality of Los Angeles life, and anti-development fervor stems from concern over crowding and pollution – and, perhaps, unspoken worries about social change.

Whatever happens to Bradley in the current scandals, it's likely he is Los Angeles' last black mayor as well as its first. Political power in Los Angeles in the 1990s and beyond will depend on how well organized the burgeoning Hispanic and Asian populations become, and how militant the anti-development, quality-of-life movement becomes.

San Diego

Population (1989): 1,086,600; Voter registration (1989): D-44.2% R-42.5%; Mayor: Maureen O'Connor; City Council: Ron Roberts, H. Wes Pratt, Abbe Wolfsheimer, Gloria McColl, Bruce Henderson, Ed Struiksma, Judy McCarty, Bob Filner; 202 C St., San Diego, 92101; (619) 236-5555; Incorporated: 1850.

Despite the boastful local motto, "America's Finest City," San Diego always seems a bit defensive about itself. Mostly, it tries to convince the world – and perhaps itself – that it's not just another suburban satellite orbiting around Los Angeles, the colossus to the north, but a first-rank American city in its own right.

The truth probably lies somewhere in between. Blessed with near-perfect weather and a world-class natural setting, San Diego is an impressive metropolis. But despite all, it exists, and probably always will exist, in the shadow of Los Angeles, especially in the minds of those outside the state.

The relationship between California's two largest cities is more psychological than actual. There is enough distance and open ground between them to avoid any physical contact. San Diegans like to say that Camp Pendleton, the giant Marine Corps training base midway between the two cities, is their last line of defense.

San Diego isn't a suburb. It was an important corner of California, the site of very early Spanish missionary settlements, when Los Angeles was still a collection of mud huts. It was an important seaport in the 1830s, recorded faithfully in Richard Henry Dana's "Two Years Before the Mast." Rather, San Diego is what Los Angeles used to be before smog and congestion began their erosive effects, and San Diegans fear more than anything that they will be sucked into the same spiral. To some extent, it's already occurred. San Diego's air quality and traffic congestion have grown steadily worse, and its leaky sewage system brings no end of embarrassments when it spills onto beaches.

Thus, any – even the most infinitesimal – evidence of creeping Los Angelesization brings forth armies of San Diegans ready to do battle. Local jingoists worked themselves into a lather, for instance, when San Diego Gas and Electric Co. proposed to merge with Los Angeles-based Southern California Edison. What should have been a simple utility transaction (does electric current have a municipal identity?) became a secular crusade.

San Diego has a tense relationship to the south with another municipal neighbor larger than itself – Tijuana, with more than 1.5 million people, most of them poor. The contrast between Tijuana and San Diego could not be more striking; it is where the Third World bumps into the First World. And like matter meeting anti-matter, the collision is often explosive. Drugs and illegal aliens steadily flow across the border into San Diego.

A routine sight every evening are the campfires of Mexican nationals lining up along the border to dash into San Diego after dark. Mexican and American police have exchanged gunfire along the border, mistaking each other for bandits. And among the worst environmental problems facing San Diego is that the city is downhill from Tijuana, which discharges its sewage into a river flowing into the United States. Tijuana's sewage regularly pollutes San Diego beaches. San Diego is a city, more than any other in the state, that requires a foreign policy.

When it's not being paranoid about Los Angeles and Tijuana, and is considered on its own merits, San Diego offers a lesson in government that works better than most in California. San Diego is one of the most livable – and laid-back – cities in the country. Shopping malls have replaced town halls as the center of community life. San Diego's beach culture is fabled; the yearly "Over the Line Tournament" has elevated a local softball-style beach game into an international phenomenon. Tans are competitive, surfers still say "dude" and wear shorts to high school. Even the cops sometimes wear shorts on patrol.

Faced with incredible development pressure in the 1970s and 1980s, San Diego city officials, working closely with a tightly knit power structure, adopted what they called "managed growth." The city expanded its boundaries to take in previously unincorporated and undeveloped land and minimized the disjointed sprawl that has afflicted other fast-growing communities such as Los Angeles, San Jose and Sacramento. The city limits stretch some 50 miles north from the Mexican border. While independent suburbs exist, they are not the tail that wags the municipal dog. City government has become, in effect, the regional policy-making body.

Having controlled its frontiers, San Diego retained and even enhanced its downtown core, converting an old red-light district into a pleasing collection of shops, and took advantage of its harbor setting. Towering hotels now line the waterfront, and the innovative Horton Plaza multistory shopping center is successfully drawing suburbanites back into the inner city.

The traditional mainstay of the San Diego economy has been national defense. In the 19th century, the Navy seized the most attractive and usable bits of land on the fine natural harbor and later an aircraft industry developed to serve military needs. The needs of the city, however, sometimes conflicted with the needs of the Navy. It took years to win approval of a bridge across the bay linking San Diego to Coronado. The Navy vetoed the bridge, arguing that an enemy could demolish it and bottle up the fleet.

The military community, which includes countless retirees, remains strong. But in more recent years, San Diego has developed a non-military industrial and research base, much of it high-tech in nature, and has become a world-recognized center for health research and treatment. Conventions and tourism have evolved into a major source of jobs and tax revenues for the city, one it is attempting to enhance through hotel development and a big new convention center. The single most powerful force for development is the Port Commission, which has used revenues from the airport and other facilities to bankroll the downtown projects. Its members are appointed by the city councils surrounding the bay, with three of the seven commissioners appointed by San Diego.

San Diego developed its centrist approach to growth matters under the mayorship of Pete Wilson, a moderate Republican who yearned for higher office. Wilson ran unsuccessfully for governor in 1978 and was on the verge of trying again in 1982 when he was persuaded by Republican Party leaders to segue into a bid for the U.S. Senate against then-Gov. Jerry Brown. Wilson bested Brown after a hard-fought campaign in which Brown's negatives assumed more importance than Wilson's positives. He easily won re-election in 1988, defeating Democratic Lt. Gov. Leo McCarthy. Within a few weeks after that victory, he responded to another call by the GOP hierarchy: run for governor in 1990 to give the party its best shot of retaining the governorship after the retirement of George Deukmejian. Wilson complied and heads into 1990 with the Republican nomination sewed up and as the front-runner against the Democratic hopefuls.

Wilson's two U.S. Senate victories, coupled with his front-running candidacy for governor in 1990, have obliterated the "San Diego cul-de-sac" syndrome – the widespread belief that San Diego politicians could never break into the big time because Los Angeles and its politicians dominate media attention.

Wilson was successful as mayor because he positioned himself between pro- and anti-growth factions and acted as a project-by-project mediator. His successor, Roger Hedgecock, an ex-county supervisor, seemed cut from the same cloth and also seemed headed for an equally rapid ride on the political elevator. An articulate moderate Republican – he was once the head of the local Sierra Club chapter – Hedgecock won a hard-fought special election in 1983, his principal opponent Democrat Maureen O'Connor. In his first months as mayor, Hedgecock rang up an impressive tally of accomplishments, including allocation of funds to expand the city's pioneering trolley system and voter approval of the downtown convention center. Hedgecock, as expected, ran for a full term on his own in 1984 and, as one local politician said, "It was looking more like a coronation than an election."

But as Hedgecock headed into a runoff election with Dick Carlson, a local businessman and former television newscaster, some dark clouds began forming. He became entangled in one of the financial scandals that periodically sweeps through San Diego's financial community. This one revolved around financier J. David Dominelli. Dominelli's brokerage firm collapsed in 1984 – it turned out to be nothing more than a Ponzi scheme that bilked hundreds of investors out of millions of dollars. And it soon became evident that several hundred thousand dollars of Dominelli's ill-gotten money had found their way into Hedgecock's 1983 mayoral campaign. Hedgecock never reported the secret donations, circumventing San Diego's $250 per contributor campaign donation limits. Dominelli's girlfriend, Nancy Hoover, helped Hedgecock turn his shabby house into a mansion with home remodeling funds that were never reported on Hedgecock's state-required personal financial disclosure forms.

The steady stream of revelations touched off a series of official and journalistic investigations. Although under indictment by the time of the voting, he won re-election. Hedgecock stood trial on 12 counts of perjury and one of conspiracy, dealing with allegations that he funneled money illegally into his 1983 campaign. In the end, Hedgecock stood convicted and was stripped of his mayorship. His nemesis, Maureen O'Connor, a former council member and port commissioner, emerged from self-imposed oblivion and won election to succeed the man who had broken the law to beat her in 1983.

O'Connor also seems destined for bigger things. Her victory marked a shift of city hall control from Republican to Democrat, albeit of the same centrist mold, and also from a man to a woman. Her mayorship, in fact, has become the centerpiece of a quiet revolution in San Diego: the advent of women into powerful positions within San Diego's economic and political structure.

While O'Connor runs city hall, Helen Copley runs the influential local newspapers, the Union and the Tribune, and Joan Kroc oversees the McDonald's hamburger empire and the Padres baseball team. Susan Golding (whose husband, politico-financier Richard Silberman, is at the center of still another scandal) sits on the county Board of Supervisors and a number of other political and economic power positions are held by women.

O'Connor's political origins, however, are not so much with a political party, as with the glitzy glamour set of San Diego. She is independently wealthy. Her ailing husband, Robert Peterson, founded the Jack in the Box fast food chain. O'Connor is also a friend of Ted Kennedy, and parties with his crowd occasionally.

O'Connor, like Hedgecock and Wilson, rode into office as an advocate of environmental protection, a cause that has become more intense as the development pressure has increased. Several growth control measures have reached the ballot. One, in 1985, was approved; another, in 1988, was defeated. Concern over growth and its effects remains, however, the most potent local issue.

While O'Connor would appear to be well-positioned to move into statewide office, a la Wilson, she suffers from some political liabilities, including a wooden public style. She's more effective working behind the scenes, where mediagenic qualities are less important. O'Connor has seemed strained at times to find a common touch. She is known as aloof and moody. As mayor, she once posed as a bag woman and lived on the street for a night – and reaped plenty of media attention.

Unlike other major cities, San Diego's politics are almost entirely the province of middle- and upper-middle-class whites. There are substantial black and Hispanic populations, but proportionately they remain small minorities, which is a bit surprising, given San Diego's location next door to Mexico. Blacks and Hispanics are regularly elected to the City Council and Board of Supervisors, but remain far from the inner circles of power. Democratic Assemblyman Pete Chacon has served in the Legislature since the 1960s, but despite his longevity, he is anything but a major player in San Diego or Sacramento.

Each year hundreds of thousands of Mexican immigrants, documented and undocumented, pass through San Diego, but few remain. Most head northward, toward Los Angeles and its insatiable appetite for cheap labor, or into the fields of the agricultural valleys. The higher concentrations of Hispanics, moreover, tend to be found not in San Diego itself but in smaller suburban communities.

While San Diego County as a whole (now the state's second most populous) is a Republican stronghold and growing more so with each passing election, the city's politics are more varied. Democratic officeholders such as O'Connor tend to be centrist-liberals while Republicans tend to be centrist-conservatives. But voters venture out further in both directions along the political scale. The more liberal elements coalesce around the environmental protection and anti-growth issues, while the city's big military contingent, both active and retired, is a bastion of political conservatism.

Outside of Wilson, San Diego's best-known Republican politician has been Larry Stirling, a city councilman, state assemblyman and state senator until his resignation in late 1989 to take an appointment to the Municipal Court bench. The city's three congressmen, Democrat Jim Bates and Republicans Duncan Hunter and Bill Lowrey, tend to be fairly anonymous, as are most California congressmen. They tend to constituent matters and take care of the Navy's needs.

Democratic Assemblywoman Lucy Killea is local environmentalism's chief emissary to Sacramento. Democratic Assemblyman Steve Peace, who represents southern portions of the city, is an erratic schemer best known for his membership in the "Gang of Five" that attempted to topple Willie Brown from the Assembly speakership in 1988. Democratic Sen. Wadie Deddeh, representing the downtown and the South Bay, is largely a big disappointment, squandering his chairmanship of the vital Senate Transportation Committee to vote for Gov. Deukmejian's ill-fated nominee for state treasurer, Dan Lungren.

Growth and its effects will continue to be San Diego's overarching political issue for the foreseeable future, although there's a strong undercurrent of concern about crime. San Diego's proximity to the border has made it a haven for smugglers and turned the city into the Miami of the West. San Diego is considered the nation's capital for methamphetamine, a drug many experts predict will overtake cocaine as the country's narcotics nightmare; there were more garage labs turning out "crank" than in any other city in the country. In the mid-'80s, San Diego endured an excruciating series of murders of its police officers and became the most dangerous city in America for police officers based on the ratio of officers-to-population.

The location of a new airport is another pressing issue. The current airport, named after aviation hero Charles Lindbergh, is a model of convenience, once the traveler is on the ground, because it's just blocks from the center of the city. But airliners dodge tall buildings to land and noise restricts its hours of operation.

San Diego is expanding the airport's terminal facilities while seeking a new site. The most logical would be atop Mira Mesa north of downtown, but the Navy operates a major fighter pilot training facility on the site and shows no interest in giving it up. Another perennial site is Otay Mesa near the Mexican border.

San Jose

*Population (1989): 738,400; Voter registration (1989): D-53.8% R-33.8%;
Mayor: Tom McEnery; City Council: Lu Ryden, Judy Stabile, Susan Hammer,
Shirley Lewis, Blanca Alvarado, Nancy Ianni, Iola Williams, Patricia Sausedo,
James Beall Jr., Joe Head; 1st and Mission Sts., San Jose, 95110; (408) 277-4000;
Incorporated: 1850.*

A startling number of Californians have found the way to San Jose, so many that
the one-time suburb of San Francisco has surpassed its much better known neighbor
to become the state's third largest city.

But while the numbers (700,000-plus) are bigger than Boston, Denver, Atlanta
and Seattle, San Jose is still struggling to find its civic identity. In cultural, economic
and other terms, it still lags behind San Francisco, producing something of a
collective inferiority complex that local leaders are trying to overcome with one of
the state's most ambitious redevelopment programs.

San Jose's high-octane expansion was fueled by the dramatic growth of the high-
tech industry in the Santa Clara Valley, the one-time agricultural region that became
"Silicon Valley" within the last generation. The presence of Stanford University in
nearby Palo Alto brought together a collection of invention-minded engineers, and
they literally created the computer industry in garages and small shops. The industry
erupted in the 1970s and 1980s and created tens of thousands of new jobs. And with
that industrial revolution came a megaton explosion of population growth, most of
it in the form of domestic and foreign immigrants. San Jose, California's oldest city
(1777) and one-time state capital, was nothing more than a sleepy little farm town
before being blasted out of its somnambulism.

Throughout the state, and indeed throughout the nation, San Jose is held up as an
example of how not to deal with growth. Homes, shopping centers and business
complexes sprang up everywhere, with no thought given to transportation or other
infrastructure services. Local officials were seemingly powerless, or unwilling, to
say no to the developers or compel them to submit to some larger vision of civic
development. San Jose and other Santa Clara County cities competed, rather than
cooperated, and developers played political leaders off each other.

The results, at least in hindsight, were logical. Downtown San Jose acquired the
look of a bombed-out city as department stores abandoned downtown locations and
shopping centers blossomed amid the new residential tracts. "Do you know the way
to San Jose?" became a joke as well as the title of a popular tune. Traffic became
a nightmare as commuters tried to move in all directions at the same time on a road
system designed during Santa Clara Valley's agricultural days. And, eventually,
home prices soared to stratospheric heights as demand outstripped supply. It was,
on a smaller scale, not unlike what happened to Los Angeles in the immediate
postwar era.

San Jose continued to grow, in part because the city was annexing large blocs of vacant land on its southern border in anticipation of development. But it was becoming something of a joke. A writer for Sunset magazine – published just a few miles away in Menlo Park – referred to it as "the classic mid-20th century nowheresville."

A decade ago, San Jose grew tired of being the butt of the joke, of constantly having to defend itself. San Jose's civic leaders, many of them newly minted high-tech millionaires, decided to create for themselves a real city. The transformation of attitude was signaled by the 1982 election of Tom McEnery as mayor.

McEnery passes for aristocracy in a city where ancient history is defined as the precomputer age. He's a third-generation resident whose family has long been identified with downtown property interests and has also been prominent in local – and sometimes state and national – Democratic politics.

In 1976, when McEnery was still in his 30s, he took up a quasi-political career with an appointment to the city Planning Commission. He was named to the City Council two years later. The advent of district City Council elections in 1980 saw him emerge as the city's top vote-getter, and in 1982, he was elected mayor, succeeding Janet Gray Hayes.

During the Hayes regime, San Jose had become known as the favorite city of Gov. Jerry Brown, a graduate of nearby Santa Clara University Law School. Santa Clara faculty members trooped to Sacramento to take jobs in the Brown administration, and Brown showered attention on San Jose and its woman mayor, a strong Brown supporter.

The city's political clout in Sacramento was advanced even further, meanwhile, by a quirk of political fate. Two San Jose legislators, Assemblyman John Vasconcellos and Sen. Alfred Alquist, became chairmen of the Legislature's two most powerful committees, Assembly Ways and Means and Senate Finance, respectively. The two panels control all major legislation as well as the state budget. As a result, Sacramento has lavished money on San Jose – money for a new state office building (named for Alquist) and money for an innovative light-rail system, for example.

But despite these advances, downtown San Jose was still a municipal nightmare when McEnery was elected mayor on a promise to provide strong-minded leadership where none existed. Nor was he shy about enunciating San Jose's problems and how they developed.

"They weren't making the decisions in smoke-filled rooms at City Hall," he told one interviewer. "They were making them in smoke-filled private offices. Developers were allowed to reach out and gobble up square miles, which stretched the city's services to the limit."

Using the office as a bully pulpit, McEnery began preaching urban renewal. As he put it in a 1987 speech: "We have the opportunity to guide our cities to the future – not the state, not the federal government. We have the responsibility for resuscitating the life and heart of our cities, the downtown. For cities are living things. They can thrive and they can die. Some are growing up while others are growing old. They can be nurtured or nullified by those in city government and the community. In the history of our cities we find how our lives change."

Brashly outspoken, the young mayor also tried to instill some civic pride in San Jose by bashing San Francisco. He routinely refers to San Francisco, 50 miles to the north, as a dying city, and he has had the audacity to attempt to lure the Giants baseball team away from the metropolis that calls itself "The City." The mutual disdain that one finds between San Jose and San Francisco is as intense as any municipal rivalry in the state, although McEnery and San Francisco Mayor Art Agnos did bury the hatchet long enough to undertake a joint trade mission to Asia.

But McEnery has been more than words. During his mayorship, which will end in 1990 under the city's two-term limit, San Jose has completed the first phase of the trolley system; begun a huge downtown redevelopment project that includes a convention center, a Fairmont hotel and a high-tech museum; undertaken improvements to the airport with the aim of luring more international flights from San Francisco; and begun planning for a major sports complex. A big corporate center is planned south of the downtown area, the arts and the theater are beginning to draw attention from high-tech high rollers and many high-rise office buildings are under construction or on the drawing boards.

A strong indication of San Jose's new can-do attitude was the 1984 voter approval of a countywide sales tax override to help finance construction not only of the trolley system but of badly needed freeway and street improvements. San Jose – its relationship with Jerry Brown notwithstanding – was hit hard by the Brown administration's cutback on highway construction because it occurred just at the peak of the city's expansion. As the logjam over highways continued into the 1980s, civic and business leaders agreed to go it on their own. They got legislative permission to seek the sales tax boost, and business groups put up the money for a clever campaign – keyed to rush-hour radio ads – to persuade voters to approve it. In the years since, other counties have emulated Santa Clara's example.

San Jose is by no means complete. The downtown area is still low-voltage by the standards of other similarly sized cities, lacking major shopping facilities and other attractive amenities. And San Jose is still trying to cope with a cultural revolution created by the influx of thousands of Hispanic and Southeast Asian immigrants. It's still doubtful whether it will ever remove itself from the shadow of San Francisco. But compared to what was happening a decade ago, San Jose has undergone a remarkable transformation.

McEnery, as one might expect of someone so assertive, has engendered his share of criticism. Critics have said that his preoccupation with recreating downtown is a moral, if not legal, conflict of interest because of his family's extensive property holdings in the area, and he has been accused of neglecting the needs of the poor and non-Anglo populations in his quest for high-profile civic identity.

McEnery answers all of the critics and continues to promote his redevelopment program with an intensity that naturally raises speculation about his political future. In a state known for its bland officeholders, McEnery stands out with such take-charge statements as:

"Anyone who has served as the mayor of a major city has been in the crucible of fire. Mayors operate on the front line. They can't pass the buck. If anything goes wrong in this 161-square-mile city, I'm expected to fix it. If you promise the voters that you are going to cut down trees, you'd better have somebody out the next morning with axes."

Not surprisingly, McEnery is a maverick even within the Democratic Party. He chides party leaders for being too lockstep liberal and too unwilling to deal with issues pragmatically. In a sense, McEnery is a classic neo-liberal, or "Atari Democrat," as some call them: tough on law-and-order, liberal on lifestyle, skeptical of government. And there are those who think his next stop should be the governor's office in Sacramento. But McEnery professes disdain for climbing up the political ladder, saying he is content to live in San Jose after his stint in City Hall is finished and perhaps teach about politics and government at the college level.

"I want to be remembered as a mayor who cared about what he was doing for San Jose and had no other agenda than to make this city considerably better off than he found it," McEnery told an interviewer. "This is too fantastic a place to live, with too many opportunities, to run off and enter a New Hampshire primary or run for governor. And I don't see thousands of people writing and begging me to run for governor."

One reason for that lack of fan mail is that San Jose exists in a media shadow. No matter how accomplished its politicians, they struggle to achieve notoriety outside the city – a problem that plagued those of another California city, San Diego, for decades. One person who has achieved such notoriety is Assemblyman Vasconcellos, who has a statewide and even national following for his commitment to the "human potential" movement, especially to programs that enhance self-esteem as an antidote to crime, drug abuse and other social ills. Some of that attention – such as weeks of devotion in the "Doonesbury" comic strip – is derisive, but it has made Vasconcellos the best known local political figure outside of the area.

McEnery, Vasconcellos and virtually all other local officeholders are Democrats, and San Jose is a stronghold of party strength in an era when the Democrats' hold on voters is slipping statewide. But, like McEnery, most are not liberals of the traditional variety. There is a centrism in local politics that extends to Republicans as well. Occasionally, the suburbs elect Republicans to the Legislature or Congress, but they must adhere to a moderate philosophy or find themselves turned out in subsequent elections.

Given their population growth, Santa Clara County and San Jose itself are likely to pick up more clout when legislative and congressional district boundaries are redrawn after the 1990 census. More legislative and congressional representation is likely and a shuffle of local seats is looming.

San Francisco

Population (1989): 731,700; Voter registration (1989): D-65.4% R-18.3%; Mayor: Art Agnos; City Board of Supervisors: Wendy Nelder, Tom Hsieh, Terence Hallinan, Nancy Walker, Harry Britt, Angela Alioto, Doris Ward, Willie Kennedy, Bill Maher, Jim Gonzalez, Richard Hongisto; 400 Van Ness Ave., San Francisco, 94102; (415) 554-5184; Incorporated: 1850.

San Franciscans, a notably self-possessed clan, scarcely acknowledged the 1989 event that was front-page news elsewhere. The state Department of Finance, in its periodic updating of population data, calculated that San Jose, 50 miles to the south, had outstripped San Francisco to become the state's third most populous city behind Los Angeles and San Diego.

So what, San Franciscans shrugged. They had the cable cars, the tall buildings, the banks, the bay, the opera, the Giants, the 49ers and the tourist business. San Jose just had the people and, they seemed to say, not very interesting people at that.

Smugness aside, San Francisco is a city in transition and not all of the trends are positive. It has lost its maritime trade to more modern ports, such as Oakland, just across the bay. Its industrial base, including the famous fishing industry, has shrunken. It has lost its position as the West's financial capital to much-hated Los Angeles. It is continuing to lose white-collar office jobs to suburban centers such as those in Contra Costa and San Mateo counties. It is losing middle-class whites to the suburbs and gentrification has driven many blacks out of the city as well.

But San Francisco has retained its allure for tourists and conventioneers and has become, in effect, the capital of Asian California. The gay rights movement is just the latest manifestation of San Francisco's well-known tolerance for unconventional lifestyles, a colorful tradition rooted in the city's founding as a port of entry for gold rush fortune seekers and continued through decades of boom and bust, crooked mayors, earthquakes and fires.

The danger represented by the combination of those trends is that San Francisco will become a caricature of itself, a place where only the wealthy and the poor live, a city dependent on the fickle and seasonal tourist trade.

San Francisco is California's most intensely political city, one whose politics resemble those of New York or Chicago more than Los Angeles or San Diego. Every San Franciscan, or so it seems, belongs to some political pressure group. They range from lifestyle- and ethnic-oriented groups to neighborhood associations, and they exist to oppose – strenuously – anything they envision as representing a threat to their particular value systems. Republicans are an endangered species in a city that a couple of generations ago was a GOP stronghold, so most of the political plotting pits Democrat against Democrat on issues that are unique to San Francisco.

Political generalizations are dangerous amid such diversity, but there is a broad issue that explains much of the city's recent political history: development. Although San Francisco's population is stagnant, or even declining a bit, and much of its employment base has fled for more hospitable climes, there is a continuing pressure to develop hotels and other tourist-related facilities and retail facilities. San Francisco's business community bases its hopes for prosperity on the city's continued attractiveness to out-of-towners, either shoppers from the suburbs or out-of-area tourists and conventioneers. But development, in the minds of many, threatens the "real San Francisco," however that may be defined in the minds of anti-growth activists. Hence the years-long struggle.

The politics of the city swerve back and forth as first one group and then the other achieves dominance. That's why San Francisco has freeways that stop in mid-air, disgorging their automotive streams onto city streets at the most inopportune places, and why every proposal for change faces an immediate and adverse reaction.

The pro-development mayorship of Joseph Alioto was followed by the liberal reign of George Moscone. But his tenure was cut short by an assassin's bullet, bringing another pro-development mayor, Dianne Feinstein, into office. When Feinstein's second full term, the maximum allowed by law, ended in 1987, the great debate over San Francisco became more intense.

John Molinari, a one-time Republican allied with the business community, was pitted against Art Agnos, a former social worker who had been one of the city's two state Assembly members (the other is Willie Brown, a legendary politician and speaker of the Assembly since 1980). Molinari was the candidate of the status quo while Agnos attempted – with great success – to galvanize groups united by their distaste for business as usual: gays, environmental activists, ethnic minorities, etc.

Agnos, a first-generation Greek-American, came to San Francisco from Massachusetts as a social worker and wound up as an aide to Leo McCarthy. McCarthy is one of San Francisco's longest-lasting political figures, serving as a city supervisor, a state assemblyman (he was Brown's predecessor as speaker) and, since 1983, as California's lieutenant governor.

Agnos was McCarthy's chief of staff in Sacramento, then acquired his own Assembly seat in 1976 and moved out of McCarthy's shadow when the latter became lieutenant governor. Agnos achieved a reputation in Sacramento as a hard-nosed, but pragmatic technician. His biggest accomplishment was putting together a bipartisan coalition, including Republican Gov. Deukmejian, to enact a "workfare" program for welfare recipients. His biggest setback was Deukmejian's veto of his legislation to bar discrimination against homosexuals in employment.

Along the way, Agnos obtained substantial personal wealth, thanks to dealings with Angelo Tsakopoulos, a Sacramento land developer who, Agnos said, had promised to make him rich and thus free to practice politics without worrying about his family's financial position. Those connections would later haunt Agnos when he was fined for failing to fully reveal his financial dealings with Tsakopoulos.

Agnos' battle with Molinari, a conventional Italian-American politician and perennial mayoral hopeful, was, in effect, an attempt to reactivate a liberal organization that had dominated San Francisco's politics for a generation until fate dealt it a double blow, the deaths of two of its leaders.

The Burton brothers, Phillip and John, Willie Brown and George Moscone had created the organization in the halcyon days of the 1960s. Both Burtons went to Congress after serving in the Assembly, Brown climbed up the ladder in the Assembly and Moscone became a state senator and later mayor.

Phil Burton became a dominating presence in Congress and nearly became speaker before dying in 1982. Brother John struggled in the shadow of his older brother, developed a serious drug abuse problem and left Congress after Phillip died. In 1988, he won a special election to return to the Assembly.

Moscone's 1975 mayoral campaign represented the Brown-Burton-Moscone organization's crowning achievement in city politics. Power had been wrested from the old-line establishment, and gays, ethnic minorities and other "outs" became the "ins." But his assassination (along with that of gay rights leader Harvey Milk) by a political rival, Dan White, in 1978 reversed that flow of power as Feinstein succeeded Moscone and then won two terms on her own.

Agnos and his campaign manager, Richie Ross, a longtime aide to Speaker Brown, devised a novel campaign that stressed neighborhood organization. A centerpiece of the campaign was a widely distributed paperback book that laid out an ambitious agenda of social and political change. As San Francisco Examiner columnist Bill Mandel wrote, "The choice between Molinari and Agnos is a choice between the potential for too little and the potential for too much, between no ideas and almost too many new ideas." San Francisco voters opted for the uncertainty of an Agnos mayorship over Molinari's predictability.

Agnos' first year was dominated by a whopping budget deficit left behind by Feinstein. His second year was overshadowed by a police brutality scandal; by a threat from Bob Lurie, the owner of the Giants baseball team, to leave the city if a new stadium wasn't built to replace windy Candlestick Park; by the specter of thousands of homeless men and women camped in front of city hall; and by a killer earthquake.

In tone, his reign has been left-of-center, as exemplified by an Agnos-sponsored law giving spousal benefits to the long-term partners of homosexual city employees. One local newspaper columnist routinely refers to him as "Red Art."

But experience has also smoothed off some of Agnos' rougher corners. No longer does he go out of his way to antagonize business leaders. He dons a tuxedo to hobnob with the rich and powerful at civic events, and – most tellingly – he has alienated some of the most left-wing political elements among his supporters.

The trend is evident in his handling of the Giants crisis. The earlier Agnos might have told Lurie to take his Giants to San Jose; the newer model promised to come up with a satisfactory stadium. Ultimately, Agnos proposed a downtown stadium and placed the proposal on the ballot as an indirect referendum on his mayorship.

The longer-term questions about San Francisco and its politics center on its diversity. It is the nation's most ethnically diverse city, and the most noticeable element of that diversity are the Asians, who have broken out of Chinatown and Japantown and, with expanding economic power, become important factors in virtually every neighborhood in the city. So far, that personal and economic clout has not manifested itself in political terms. Only one of San Francisco's city supervisors is Asian, and Asians have very low rates of voting participation.

Blacks, once an important social and political element, are declining in number, unable to keep up with soaring housing costs, but they continue to enjoy political power disproportionate to their number. Hispanics from a dozen nations are a major population subgroup, but, as in other California cities, have not yet become a decisive political bloc. One city supervisor is Hispanic.

Beyond ethnicity, the population breaks down into countless ideological and lifestyle groups, the most visible and powerful of which is the gay community. There's even a residue of conservatism to be found in middle-class neighborhoods and personified by state Sen. Quentin Kopp, a Democrat-turned-independent.

The old power structure seems to be breaking down, but none is arising to replace it. Rather, dozens of interest groups battle constantly among themselves for power and influence at City Hall. Any high-profile issue – the new Giants stadium, for example – brings forth legions of activists. Agnos is trying (with a fair degree of success) to maintain a governing coalition. But it's a constant struggle in which any wrong move brings out the long knives among political rivals and media critics. For the moment, the old Brown-Burton-organization seems to be dominant, even though two of its principals are gone.

John Burton captured Agnos' old Assembly seat, defeating a gay candidate, and the organization provided the push for political activist Nancy Pelosi's ascendency into Congress, replacing Sala Burton. (Phillip Burton's widow succeeded him in office and then died herself in 1987). Brown remains speaker of the Assembly despite several serious challenges.

But in San Francisco's fast-changing political climate, nothing lasts forever. Gays are demanding more political power to accompany their rising economic clout, and the city is likely to produce the state's first avowedly gay state legislator. Asians are the city's latent political powerhouse, but, at least to date, lack a charismatic leader.

The city, meanwhile, continues to become less like a mini-New York, dominated by banks and big business, and to resemble more a collection of identifiable communities with employment concentrated in smaller businesses. A 1988 study by Bank of America – whose institutional decline parallels that of the city – concluded that San Francisco's future depends on the expansion of small business, and it's in the neighborhood-based businesses that much of the city's economic vitality and political activism is found. Gays have been especially successful in translating neighborhood businesses into economic and political clout. Asians seem to be following that model as well, but blacks and Hispanics have not moved into the entrepreneurial channels.

Long Beach

Population (1989): 419,800; Voter registration (1989): D-51.4% R-38.3%;
Mayor: Ernie Kell; City Council: Wallace Edgarton, Dr. Thomas Clark, Jan Hall,
Ray Grabinski, Warren Harwood, Clarence Smith, Jeffrey Kellogg, Evan Braude;
333 W. Ocean Blvd, Long Beach, 90802; (213) 590-6555; Incorporated: 1897.

Long Beach is the Rodney Dangerfield of California cities. It doesn't get much respect.

While the numbers – 400,000-plus population, fifth largest in the state – say big city, the image is that of a conservative, business-dominated, boring and tightly white town; "Iowa by the sea" as some wags have put it.

Some of that image is rooted in reality. And if anything, it was exacerbated in early 1989, when Long Beach achieved a rare bit of national notoriety. A black police officer from nearby Hawthorne, who has made a personal crusade of police brutality toward minorities, drove along Long Beach streets in civilian clothes while a clandestine NBC-TV film crew tracked him. The policeman, Don Jackson, was stopped by two Long Beach policemen and their brutal treatment of him, including shoving his head through a plate glass window, was captured on videotape. It was broadcast repeatedly and Long Beach received a civic black eye.

But times in Long Beach may be changing. The city, which has always existed in the shadow of Los Angeles, is showing signs of economic revival and civic renewal. The Jackson incident forced Long Beach to take a look at itself. Among other things, it resulted in the creation of a police review board to oversee law enforcement actions in a city that blacks and other minorities say has been openly hostile.

In the meantime, its location near the Pacific Ocean, which means clean air to smog-conscious Southern Californians, and its modern port facilities are creating a development boom. And it hasn't hurt Long Beach to be California Gov. George Deukmejian's hometown. The blandly conservative Deukmejian may be a living metaphor for the city, but his occupancy of the governor's office has meant some patronage, such as the appointment of local residents to state boards and commissions, securing some political convention business and seeing the construction of a big state office building.

The convention center is booked months in advance, new hotels are popping up everywhere and the Port of Long Beach has launched a development project that will double its capacity in 20 years to take advantage of the burgeoning trans-Pacific shipping trade – a trend that also has spurred new corporate interest in moving to the city.

Long Beach, whose municipal coffers benefit from having oil wells on city-owned tidelands, is finally seeing some return from its once-scorned purchase of the Queen Mary luxury liner. The floating hotel and tourist attraction is complimented by a museum housing Howard Hughes' huge flying boat, the "Spruce Goose."

The Queen Mary was acquired when Long Beach was mired in a years-long economic slump, its downtown area a shabby slum, its retail trade sucked dry by suburban shopping centers. Today, job expansion and Long Beach's seaside location have led, not unexpectedly, to gentrification. Developers are buying up homes in older neighborhoods, razing them and erecting high-density condo and apartment buildings. That has meant instant riches for some low-income Long Beach residents who had purchased their homes decades earlier, but it's also created something of a political backlash with the creation of a homegrown slow-growth movement.

The controversy came to a head during the 1988 election to choose a new mayor, Long Beach's first to be chosen by citywide ballot. Pro-development businessman Ernie Kell won the mayorship but was very nearly forced into a runoff by his opponents, Councilwoman Jan Hall and slow-growth advocate Luanne Pryor. Kell's close call has resulted in a more moderate approach to growth at City Hall with a new general plan that down-zones property that had been earmarked for high-impact development.

While Kell is the mayor, much of the day-to-day responsibility for running the city lies with James Hankla, a former Los Angeles County administrator who takes an entrepreneurial approach to the city. Hankla is considered to be a strong city executive.

Long Beach has always been a city noted for its tightly knit power structure, whose members are mostly white businessmen. For decades, the major political and civic force was the local newspaper, the Long Beach Press-Telegram, and its owners, members of the Ridder family. Some outside accounts depicted the Ridders as baronets who decided everything of importance and passed down their decisions to city officials for implementation.

The definitive account of the Ridder family's influence in Long Beach was published in the rival Los Angeles Times, whose controlling family, the Chandlers, also exerts heavy political influence in Los Angeles. That fact led some to wonder whether the piece on the Ridders reflected journalistic interest or the fact that the Times has an extremely low level of circulation penetration in Los Angeles County's second largest city.

Whether these accounts were correct or overblown, there's no doubt that the Press-Telegram and the Ridders were powerful entities. But in more recent years, that, too, has changed. The Ridder newspapers in Long Beach and San Jose have become part of a larger chain, now known as Knight-Ridder. The Press-Telegram remains a strong local influence, but its executives don't exert the behind-the-scenes influence they once did. With the emergence of neighborhood-based anti-development groups, more activism by minorities and other trends, Long Beach seems to be opening up.

It's still conservative, a Democratic voter registration edge notwithstanding. But it's not quite as rigid as its reputation would indicate.

Oakland

Population (1989): 356,300; Voter registration (1989): D-76.3% R-12.8%; Mayor: Lionel Wilson; City Council: Marge Haskell, Mary Moore, Aleta Cannon, Richard Spees, Wilson Riles Jr., Carter Gilmore, Leo Bazile, Frank Ogawa; 1 City Hall Plaza, Oakland, 94612; (415) 444-2489; Incorporated: 1852.

When it was revealed in mid-1989 that Oakland's school system was on the verge of bankruptcy and was beset by corruption, favoritism and plain thievery, it wasn't very surprising. Oakland is Wednesday's child in California's family of cities–full of woe.

Every time Oakland seems ready to surmount its crushing social and economic problems, some new and debilitating crisis emerges to tarnish the city's image. Oakland's baseball team, the A's, rises during the 1980s as a powerhouse, and the city mounts an effort to re-acquire the Raiders professional football team that had made the city famous. But gang crime and drug abuse soar to all-time levels. The city undertakes an ambitious downtown redevelopment scheme, but a sparkling new hotel suffers from low patronage, and the city must undertake a financial rescue. New buildings go up, then an earthquake kills dozens.

And so it has gone in Oakland, at least two steps back for every three forward, struggling to maintain a separate identity while existing so close to San Francisco, struggling to overcome an image of crime and violence, struggling to recreate a new employment base while white-collar jobs leapfrog over the city from San Francisco to the suburbs.

Oakland's moderate black mayor, Lionel Wilson, ponders his city's plight with characteristic equanimity. "It's no worse off than most cities," he tells an interviewer, "and better off than some."

But in 1989, Oaklanders were matching the A's home run output in homicides and seemed destined to break the record of 146 set in 1987. And Oakland acquired a new nickname, "Cokeland," for the rampant drug trade that was highlighted when the funeral of a prominent pusher became the media event of the year.

It wasn't too long ago that Oakland was considered by San Franciscans and others to be a dull outpost of conservatism, personified by the Oakland Tribune and its owners, the Knowland family. But white flight to the suburbs and a growth in the black population, including refugees from the soaring housing prices in San Francisco, created the circumstances for an assumption of political – and sometimes economic – power by blacks. By the 1960s, the city had become a center of black power militancy, the headquarters of the Black Panther Party.

Wilson, a former judge, emerged from the social maelstrom in 1976 to become mayor, a black man who was militant enough to draw support from the Black Panthers but moderate enough to placate the white business establishment. Then-Gov. Jerry Brown singled out Oakland for special attention from Sacramento and with the downtown redevelopment program, it seemed as if Oakland would pull out of its socioeconomic hole. But as the 1980s have worn on, many of Oakland's problems – especially crime and drugs – have worsened. And the politics of the city have become fragmented.

Wilson, now well into his 70s, clings to power. Critics call him "The King," and his five allies on the City Council – a bare majority – have been dubbed "The Clones." Three other council members, nicknamed "The Gang of Three" or "The Three Stooges" by Wilson's camp, routinely oppose the mayor. The three opponents are an odd trio: Wilson Riles Jr., a left-of-center political consultant and son of the former state superintendent of schools; Mary Moore, a liberal activist; and Richard Spees, a Republican and retired Kaiser Industries executive.

The 1990 election for mayor is shaping up as a political showdown. Wilson has not yet said whether he will seek a fourth term. One of his City Council allies, Leo Bazile, has already declared he will run if Wilson doesn't. Bazile and Riles have been especially bitter enemies, clashing constantly during council meetings. And state Assemblyman Elihu Harris has already declared he will run, regardless of what Wilson does.

Harris has seized upon the most recent of Oakland's crises, the near-bankruptcy of the school system, as his vehicle for media attention. The schools are governed by a separately elected board whose politics, if anything, are more convoluted than those of the City Council. The Oakland Tribune, California's only major black-owned newspaper, has reported that a controlling clique known as "The Family" fostered a climate of corruption and favoritism in the school district. Several investigations are under way into embezzlement allegations and other instances that amount to a systematic looting of the school system – to the ultimate detriment of its mostly black and mostly poor students.

Oakland's community college district has already undergone the indignity of having the state step in to run its operations while providing bailout funds, and the K-12 school system seems headed down the same path.

The expose of the Oakland school district's political and financial problems marked a coming of age for The Tribune.

The Knowland family had blundered by refusing to move aggressively into the suburbs of the East Bay and they were forced to sell as the newspaper lost circulation and advertising revenues. The Gannett chain wound up with The Tribune when it acquired another chain and sold The Tribune, in turn, to Robert Maynard, a former Washington Post journalist, on extremely favorable terms. The newspaper continues to struggle financially, but under Maynard is becoming a force in the community.

There are signs of hope for Oakland. After years of intensive recruitment, the city has finally interested a couple of major employers – including the federal government – and retailers in locating in the downtown area. And the city symphony, once bankrupt, has been reborn.

But Oakland remains a troubled corner of California.

Sacramento

Population (1989): 339,900; Voter registration (1989): D-64.3% R-27.1%; Mayor: Anne Rudin; City Council: David Shore, Joseph Serna Jr., Douglas Pope, Lyla Ferris, Thomas Chinn, Kim Mueller, Lynn Robie, Terry Kastanis; 915 I St., Sacramento, 95814; (916)449-5011; Incorporated: 1850.

Sacramento, a municipal Rip Van Winkle, had a long nap. California's capital city is now awakening and may be on the verge of recapturing the major-city status it enjoyed in the mid-19th century.

Sacramento was the western terminus of the emigrant trail after the city's founding by pioneer John Sutter, and it was the headquarters for the California gold rush. It was also the western terminal for the short-lived Pony Express before four Sacramento merchants, known as the "Big 4," became the impetus behind the transcontinental railroad. But after occupying that central place in the history of California and of the West, Sacramento found itself bypassed by the rise of other Western cities, and it settled into decades of relative obscurity before bursting out in the 1970s as an alternative to the congestion and high costs experienced in those other cities. Low housing prices, a stable labor force, moderate weather and cheap land attracted employers and Sacramento's population explosion began.

Physically, the change in Sacramento in the past decade has been startling. The oldest part of the city, adjacent to the Sacramento River, has been transformed into a living historic park. The downtown area is sprouting high-rise office buildings and hotels, each taller and more striking than the last, fed by a new light-rail system connecting the central core with the suburbs. Downtown development is so intense that the city is drawing international investment interest.

Sacramento has acquired a professional basketball team and is bidding for football and baseball teams. And the economy of the city and the surrounding metropolitan area has been shifting away from its traditional dependence on government payrolls as private developers, drawn by the region's low land and housing costs, have invested hundreds of millions of dollars.

The overall impact has been to make Sacramento one of the fastest growing metropolitan areas in the nation, and, according to major publications, one of the most desirable in which to live. There are problems, such as burgeoning traffic congestion, deteriorating air quality and crowded schools and parks. But their resolution may be dependent on first untangling the state's most convoluted system of local governance.

The city itself, at just over 300,000, contains scarcely a fifth of the metropolitan area's population because earlier city leaders resisted annexation. Sacramento is surrounded by more than a dozen unincorporated communities served by myriad special districts. These overlapping units of local government rarely work in concert and often work in competition with one another. Creating some form of broader metropolitan government is high on the list of Sacramento's priorities if it is to cope successfully with the effects of rapid growth. One city-county merger was rejected by voters in the mid-1970s and another is being put together. If it succeeds, Sacramento would be the state's third largest city, with a population approaching 1 million.

Lacking control over the larger metropolitan area, the city government itself is curiously, almost quaintly, old-fashioned. City Council members are part-timers, and the mayor is scarcely more than a figurehead. Real power lies in the office of an appointed city manager.

City politics are both amateurish and professional, the former because of the structure of the city government and the latter because so many local political figures are moonlighting from their professional jobs in the Capitol and state government. One of the city's state assemblymen, Phil Isenberg, personifies the genre. He was a state legislative staffer, then went into law practice and city politics, rising to the mayor's office before running for the state Legislature. He and other local officeholders are Democrats because the city – in contrast to the suburbs – is solidly Democratic territory.

The current mayor, Anne Rudin, is a former nurse and political activist who relishes her amateur status. She came within a whisker of losing the mayorship, however, after opposing the rezoning of property north of the city for development that included a sports arena and a new basketball team.

The most politically savvy of the City Council members – and, some believe, the real political power in the city – is Joseph Serna, a former Capitol staffer who now teaches politics at California State University, Sacramento.

Because it has been a government town for so long, Sacramento has lacked the civic power structure that defines so many major cities. The biggest employer in town is the state, and its chief executive, the governor, is only a transient resident.

But with the advent of private development in the last decade, that's beginning to change a bit. Land developers such as Phil Angelides, Angelo Tsakopoulos, Richard Benvenuti and Gregg Lukenbill are exerting civic influence, for good or ill. There's an opera company, a ballet, a symphony, several noteworthy museums and a very active theater community. Sacramento, in brief, is beginning to acquire the cultural amenities that distinguish what local boosters say Sacramento could become, a world-class city.

Unlike San Jose, another rising California city, Sacramento has been established long enough and is far enough removed from San Francisco to have its own civic identity. But Sacramento, like San Jose, has until recent years existed in San Francisco's cultural shadow. Sacramentans have defended their city by describing it as being "so close" to either San Francisco or Lake Tahoe.

All of that seems to be changing. Sacramento, with its historic sites, has even developed tourist and convention trades of its own. And its size is attracting the kind of retail trade that goes with big-city status. In that sense, it's already surpassed San Jose, whose downtown area is just beginning to shake off the effects of decay.

Fresno

*Population (1989): 317,800; Voter registration (1989): D-58.2% R-34.4%;
Mayor: Karen Humphrey; City Council: Les Kimber, Tom Bohigian, Rod Anafo-
rian, Craig Scharton, Tom MacMichael, Chris Petersen; 2326 Fresno St., Fresno,
93721; (209) 488-1563; Incorporated: 1885.*

There's a certain similarity to San Joaquin Valley cities. Typically, they were
founded as rail centers to serve the surrounding farming areas. As a result, they are
bifurcated by railroad tracks and Highway 99, which later paralleled the tracks.
Newer development tends to be on the northern edge of town (because, researchers
have concluded, during the days before indoor plumbing the wealthier residents
tended to move upwind, setting development patterns that have lasted for more than
a century) and heavy equipment dealers are the most prominent citizens.

Fresno fits most of those specifications and, to the casual observer, just seems to
be a larger specimen. Certainly the satirical television series "Fresno" did nothing
to dissuade non-Fresnans that the city is just an overgrown farm town. But there's
more to Fresno than that. Its reputation for conservative politics notwithstanding,
city residents actually vote Democratic and liberal. George McGovern, Walter
Mondale and Michael Dukakis all won in Fresno. But they lost badly in the more
rural portions of Fresno County, so the overall county voting patterns tend to be
conservative and even a bit Republican. Fresno's new mayor, ex-television newscaster Karen Humphrey, exemplifies the more liberal trend in city politics.

The city is growing – northward, of course; but it is nearing its physical limit, the
San Joaquin River, which is also the county line. Humphrey has adopted a go-slow
approach to growth, resisting expansion pressures fueled by the city's relatively low
housing prices and labor costs. But the City Council remains pro-development.

Fresno and other communities in the Central Valley are finding themselves
attractive to non-farm industries that are being forced out of major metropolitan
areas by housing costs, transportation snarls and environmental restrictions.

Fresno's downtown area has, on a smaller scale, all of the problems that any city
has these days: crime, drugs, traffic congestion and a decline in retail business in the
face of competition from suburban shopping centers. It's also got a problem that
most cities don't face: severe water contamination. Chemicals from surrounding
farms have been seeping into the city's wells, forcing a number to be shut off.

Fresno, like most of the San Joaquin Valley, is a city of strong ethnic divisions.
Hispanics comprise at least a quarter of the city's population, but with their low
voting rates they remain largely powerless. There also is a substantial black
population. And Fresno is the unofficial capital of Armenian America, the result of
immigration patterns in the early 20th century. Armenian-Americans are prominent
in local grape and fruit growing operations, and they hold two City Council seats,
one seat on the county Board of Supervisors and one in the House of Representatives.

Anaheim and Santa Ana

Anaheim – Population (1989): 244,300; Voter registration (1989): D-38.5% R-51.7%; Mayor: Fred Hunter; City Council: Miriam Kaywood, William Ehrle, Irv Pickler, Tom Daly; 200 S. Anaheim Blvd., Anaheim, 92805; (714) 999-5166; Incorporated: 1876.

Santa Ana – Population (1989): 237,300; Voter registration (1989): D-49.5% R-41.2%; Mayor: Dan Young; City Council: John Acosta, Patricia McGuigan, Daniel Griest, Miguel Pulido, Rick Norton; 22 Civic Center Plaza, Santa Ana, 92701; (714) 647-5400; Incorporated: 1886.

In Orange County, it's sometimes difficult to know where one city ends and another begins. To the outsider, they run together, an endless collection of freeways, housing tracts, commercial strips and almost non-existent downtown areas. But to the more discerning eye, there are differences, such as those that exist between Orange County's two largest cities, Anaheim and Santa Ana.

Although both have existed for more than a century, they were scarcely more than farm villages until well after World War II. Anaheim had scarcely 35,000 residents when Disneyland was built in in the mid-1950s. Santa Ana, a few miles down the road, existed mainly as a sleepy county seat. The big population and development boom hit both in the 1960s, and today the population of each approaches a quarter-million.

Anaheim, with Disneyland at its center, acquired a countless number of satellite facilities: motels, fast-food stands, a convention center and, most prominently, Anaheim Stadium, home of the baseball California Angels and the football Rams. And as Orange County grew, so did Santa Ana's government complex.

The cities developed different sociopolitical atmospheres. Anaheim is conservative, with a solid Republican voting majority, and white. It divides geographically, between the flatlands in the older part of the city and the newer developments in the hills to the east. For decades, Anaheim was unabashedly pro-growth, but developers' interest in buying and clearing older single-family homes to make way for high-density developments sparked a reactive neighborhood preservation movement. Attorney Fred Hunter seized upon that sentiment to win the mayorship in 1988, promising a more even-handed approach to development. Santa Ana is one of the county's few pockets of Democratic voting and has large Hispanic and Asian populations, which have become politically and economically potent.

There's more than a little rivalry between Orange County's two major cities. Both are planning 20,000-seat indoor sports arenas in hopes of attracting professional basketball and/or hockey, and there's a race to see which project will rise first.

Although both continue to grow in population, the longer-term prospect is for slowing growth as residential development shifts to lower-cost areas. But both cities remain hot areas for economic development, both tourist-related facilities and offices. The one-time suburbs are becoming commuter destinations themselves.

Appendix A

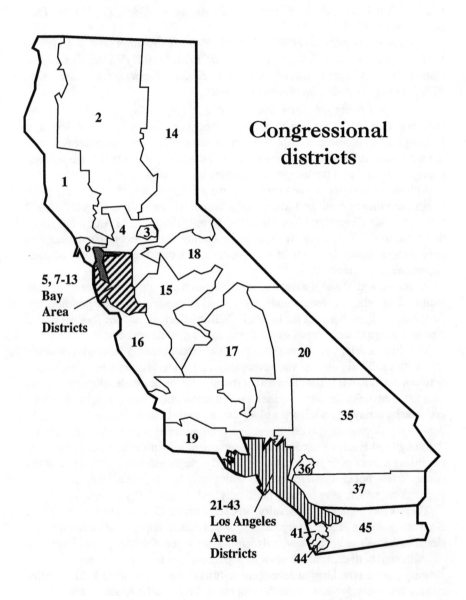

Congressional
districts

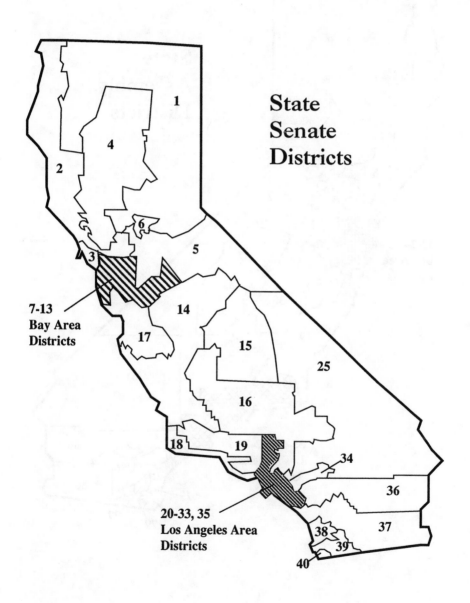

State
Senate
Districts

7-13
Bay Area
Districts

20-33, 35
Los Angeles Area
Districts

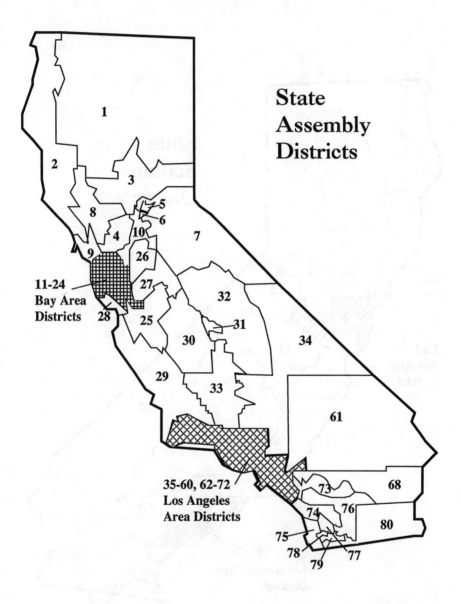

State
Assembly
Districts

11-24
Bay Area
Districts

35-60, 62-72
Los Angeles
Area Districts

Index

C

CofC, see Chamber of Commerce
Cole, Bill 403
Collin, Illa 419
Collis, Conway 128
Colusa County 398
Commerce, Dept. of 114
Common Cause 219, 339
Condit, Gary 49, 257, 283, 382,
"Conference on Women" 200
Congressional Districts: 1st 33; 2nd 34;
  3rd 35; 4th 36; 5th 38; 6th 39; 7th 40; 8th
  41; 9th 43; 10th 44; 11th 45; 12th 46;
  13th 47; 14th 48; 15th 49; 16th 50; 17th
  52; 18th 53; 19th 54; 20th 55; 21st 57;
  22nd 58; 23rd 59; 24th 61; 25th 62; 26th
  63; 27th 64; 28th 66; 29th 67; 30th 68;
  31st 69; 32nd 70; 33rd 71; 34th 72; 35th
  74; 36th 75; 37th 77; 38th 78; 39th 79;
  40th 81; 41st 82; 42nd 83; 43rd 84; 44th
  85; 45th 86
Connelly, Lloyd D. 136, 222-224, 248,
  381
Conrad, A. Vernon 401
Conservation, Dept. of 122
consolidation of city/county 391, 441
Consumer Affairs, Dept. of 125
Consumer Federation of America 23
Contra Costa County 399
Contra Costa Times/Lesher Newspapers
  360
Conway, John 435
Coogan, Mark 369
Cook, Lodwrick 375
Cook, Terry 222
Cooper, Daniel 402
Copley News Service 360
Copley, Helen 376, 450
Coppola, Francis Ford 374
Corporations, Dept. of 113
Corrections, Board of 120
Corrections, Dept. of 185, 120
Cortese, Dominic L. 252-254
Cory, Kenneth 102, 382
Costa, Evelyn 424
Costa, James M. 260-261
Coulson, John 412

County Supervisors Association of
  California 393
Cox, Christopher 81
Coy, William 424
Crabbe, Robert 366
Cranston, Alan 21,24-28, 30, 46, 65, 373,
  375, 376, 382, 385, 423, 428
Cranston, Kim 26
Craven, William A. 183, 211-212
Crawford, William 114
Crean, Johnny 84
Crockett, E. Joyce 400
Crown, Robert 160
Crystal, Chris 366
CTA, see California Teachers Association
Cuneo, Gale 396
Cunningham, David 288, 440
Curb, Mike 14, 70, 92, 93, 116, 385
Cutting old trees - key votes 141

D

D'Agostino, Carl 61, 63, 382
Daily Recorder 361
Daly, Tom 467
Dana, Deane Sr 293,406-407
Dana, Deane Jr 293
Dannemeyer, William E. 19, 79-80, 416,
Danza, Tony 374
Davenport, Timothy 396
Davenport, Wyatt 411
Davis, Ed 175-177, 269, 271, 272, 385
Davis, Joseph Graham "Gray" 101-103,
  122, 125, 129, 156, 199, 235, 280, 382
Davis, Osby 431
Davis, Pauline 216, 397
Parks & Recreation, Dept. of 123
deadwood on voter rolls 9
death penalty, expand - key votes 142
Deddeh, Wadie P. 214-215, 451
del Junco, Tirso 129
Del Norte County 400
Del Piero, Mike 413
Delany, Evelyn 424
Dell'Orto, Michael 398
Dellums, Ron 19, 41-42, 395

Almanac 476

DeMars, George 437
deMartimprey, Hughes 405
Deukmejian, Courken George Jr. 6, 11,17,
26, 29, 88, 89, 90-98, 105, 109-111, 117,
129, 130, 136, 137, 140, 141, 142, 149,
166, 170, 184, 194, 196, 197, 199, 203,
204, 208, 209, 236, 242, 244, 248, 251,
253, 261, 266, 289, 294, 300, 322, 349,
355, 378, 379, 383, 385, 393, 444, 457,
460
DeVall, Norman 411
Developmental Services, Dept. of 119
Deveraux, George 437
Dills, Curly 197
Dills, Ralph C. 189, 197, 295; Ralph C.
Dills Act of 1977 112
Diridon, Rod 427, 428
Dixon, Daniel 384
Dixon, Julian C. 63, 66, 290
Dixon, Stan 402
Doak, David 383
Dolan, Jane 397
Dole, Bob 373
Dolphin Group 384
Dominelli, J. David 449
Doolittle, John T. 144-146, 153-154, 183,
420
Dornan 19, 20, 78, 80, 416
Dorr, Robert 400
Dougherty, James 436
Douglas, Helen 3
Douglas, Melvyn 3
Douglas, Peter 123
Douglass, Linda 370
Dreier, David 71
Dresner, Dick 383
Dresslar, Thomas L. 361
Drexel Burnham Lambert 26
Dronenburg, Ernest Jr 125, 128
Duffel, Joseph 130
Duffy, Gordon 339
Duffy, Jean 339, also Moorehead
Dugan, Jack 222
Dukakis, Michael 373, 378, 394, 399, 466
Dunlap, John 150
Dunlap, Melba 418

Duplissea, Bill 246, 277
duPont 347
Dyke, Perry 129
Dymally, Mervyn M. 69, 116, 287, 296

E

Eastin, Delaine 243-244
Eastwood, Clint 374
Eaves, Gerald, R. 312-313
Edelman, Ed 406, 407
Edgarton, Wallace 460
Edmonds, James Jr. 114
Education, State Board of 129
Edwards, Don 19 44
Edwards, George 402
Ehrle, William 467
Eisenhower, Dwight 4
El Dorado County 400
Elder, Dave E. 300-301
Ellis, Virgina 362
Emerson, John 376
Employment Development Department
119
Endicott, William 364
Energy Resources Conservation &
Develop. Comm. 122
Engle, Clair 5, 6, 295
Epple, Robert D. 273, 303, 308-309,
Equalization, Board of 126-129
Erickson, Eric 410
Erickson, Maggie 436
Ernest, Richard 122
Eshoo, Anna 425
Esposti, Nick 432
ethics 194, 245, 251; see also "Brispec";
Moriarty, W. Patrick
Eu, March Fong 10, 106-108

F

Exxon Co. U.S.A. 348
Fahden, Nancy 399
Fair Employment & Housing, Dept. of 125
Fair Political Practices Commission 33,
130, 134, 138, 144, 192, 262,330,334

Hart, Gary K. 54, 142, 174-175, 268, 376, 426
Harvey, Trice J. 265-266
Harwin, Dixon 130
Harwood, Warren 460
Haskell, Marge 462
Hauser, Daniel E. 141, 143, 217-218, 432
Hawkins, Augustus 67
Hawley, Philip 375
Hawn, Goldie 374
Hawthorne, J. Thomas 130
Hayakawa, S.I. 29, 30, 281, 293
Hayden, Thomas E. 136, 281-283, 318, 373, 381, 397, 407, 416
Hayes, Janet Gray 453
Hayes, Thomas 105-106
Head, Joe 452
Health Access 139
Health Planning & Development, office of statewide 118
Health & Welfare Agency 117-120
Hedgecock, Roger 449
Heine, Dr. Lyman 130
Henderson, Bruce 447
Henning, Jack 379
Henry, Lis 411
Henshaw, Jake 361
Herger, Wally 34, 201, 218
Heron, Burchette, Ruckert & Rothwell 350
Herschensohn, Bruce 369
Heston, Charlton 374
Hettinger, Karl 404
Hewlett-Packard 376
Hicks, Floyd 434
Hill, Elizabeth 111
Hill, Frank C. 133, 293-295
Hinkel, Warren 157
Hoffenblum, Allan 384
Hoffman, Ken 377
Hogg, Susan 417
Holden, Nate 445
Holifield, Chet 19
Hollywood 373-375
Hollywood Women's Political Committee 373
Holmdahl, DeWayne 426

Hom, Gloria 129
Hongisto, Richard 456
Honig, Louis William "Bill" Jr 103-105, 130, 382
Hoover, Ken 366
Hoover, Nancy 449
Hope, Bob 374
Hornsby, Jack 145
Housing & Community Development, Dept. of 114
Howard, John 359
Hsieh, Tom 456
Huckaby, Gary 384
Huening, Tom 425
Huff, Jesse 116, 122, 126
Hughes Aircraft Co. 348
Hughes, Howard 342
Hughes, Teresa P. 287-288
Hulett, Stanley 130
Hull, Tupper 362
Humboldt County 392, 402
Humphrey, Karen 466
Hunter, Duncan 86, 451
Hunter, Fred 467
Hunter, Patricia Rae 325-326
Hunter, Tricia 310, 384, 423
Hurt, Greg 435

I

Iander, John 370
Ianni, Nancy 452
Imbrecht, Charles 122
Immigration Reform and Control Act 117
Imperial County 388, 403
incorporation of cities 438-441
Indio Daily News 361
Industrial Relations, Dept. of 116-117
Ingalls, Walter 315
Ingram, Carl 362
Initiatives 16
Institute for Public Affairs 199
Institute of Governmental Advocates 341, 344, 347, 348
Institute of Governmental Studies, University of California 393

Insurance, Dept. of 114
Insurance reform – key votes 143; see also
  Proposition 103
insurance donations, ban – key votes 142
Inyo County 403
Irvine Co. 342, 351, 375
Irwin, H.B. 403
Isenberg, Phillip L. 220, 229-230, 465,
Ivers, William 122

J

Jackson, Clayton 338, 345-346
Jackson, Don 460
Jackson, Patti 430
Jackson, the Rev. Jesse 66, 135, 289
Jacobs, John 366
Jacobs, Paul 362
Jadiker, Mary 226
Jaramillo, Amiel 190
Jardine, Donald 396
Jarvis, Howard 8
Jarvis-Gann 16, 90, 380, 381
"Jefferson" 430
Jensen, Rick 409
Johnson, Grantland 419
Johnson, Harold "Bizz" 397
Johnson, Hiram 3, 17, 24
Johnson, J. Ross 135, 136, 158, 190, 264,
  277, 284, 303, 309-311, 312, 322, 324,
  326, 381
Johnson, James 424
Johnson, Ray 144
Johnson, Toby 419
Johnson, Wayne 384
Johnston, Patrick W. 255-256
Jones, Mick 412
Jones, Talmadge 125
Jones, William L. 263-264
Jordan, Hallye 361
Jung, Eric 396
Juvinall, Todd 414

K

KABC-TV LA 369

Kalfsbeek, James 398
Kantor, Mickey 376
Karas, Sam 413
Karcher, Karl 376
Kashiwabara, Dr. John 130
Kastanis, Terry 464
Katz, Richard 130
Katz, Richard D. 273-274
Kauffman, Karin Strasser 413
Kaywood, Miriam 467
KCBS-SF 369
KCBS-TV LA 369
KCRA-TV Sac 370
Keating, Charles H. Jr 26
Keating-Edh, Barbara 257
Keeley, Fred 429
Keene, Barry D. 146-148, 150, 152, 217,
  400, 432
Kell, Ernie 460, 461
Kelley, David G. 321-322
Kelley, Michael 125
Kellogg, Jeffrey 460
Kennedy, David 123
Kennedy, Ted 450
Kennedy, Willie 456
Kern County 404
Kerr, Jennifer 359
Kershner, Vlae 365
Kesler, Ruth 420
Kevorkian, Kenneth 130
Key votes, Assembly 140-143
KGO-TV SF 371
Khachigian, Kenneth 110, 384
Khachigian, Meredith 130
Kiddoo, Kaye 119
Killea, Lucy L. 173, 213, 214, 327-328,
  451
Kimber, Les 466
King, Mary 394
King, Rose 173
Kings County 404
Kinney, Nick 404
Kizer, Kenneth MD 119
Klehs, Johan M. 234-235
Kline, Fred 360
Klinger, Ann 411

S

Torres, Esteban 63, 72-73
tort, limit product – key votes 140-141, see
  also Frank Fat's Napkin Deal
Townsend & Co. 358, 382, 384
Townsend, David 133, 382
toxic waste initiative, see Proposition 65
Transportation Commission 130
Transportation, Dept. of, see Caltrans
Trinity County 434
Trombley, William 362
Trounstine, Phil 366
Tsakopoulous, Angelo 378, 457, 465
Tucker, Curtis R. Jr 291-292
Tucker, Curtis R. Sr 262, 291
Tucker, G.B. 414
Tulare County 435
Tunney, John 6, 29, 76, 281, 376
Tuolumne County 435
Turoci, Marsha 421
Tuttle, Holmes 375
Tyron, Thomas 398

U

Ugalde, Jesse 126
Union Pacific Corp. 348
United Auto Workers 377,379
United Farm Workers union 52, 64, 379
United Press International 366-367
University of California, Board of Regents
  129-130
Unruh, Jesse 4-6, 15, 102, 105, 134, 239,
  241, 274, 338,
USA Today 361

V

Vagim, Doug 401
Valle-Riestra, Paul 440
"Valley Boys" 185
Valley Times 360
Van de Kamp, John 14, 16, 97,98, 100-
  101, 133, 235, 295, 381
Van Vleck, Gordon 121
Vargas, Jim 371
Varrelman, Mel 414

Vasconcellos, John 142, 166, 250-252,
  453, 455
Vasquez, Gaddi 416, 415
Veatch, Chauncey III 118
Ventura County 435
Ventura, Brent 249
Vercruse, Karen 397
Veterans Affairs, Dept. of 126
Visalia Times-Delta 361
Vogel, Jeanne 403
Voss, Henry 115
voter registration 9-12
"Voter Revolt" 380
Vuich, Rose Ann 169-170, 184

W

Wachs, Joel 440
Wada, Yori 130
Wade, Claudia Ann 396
Waite, William 398
Walker, Larry 421
Walker, Nancy 456
Wallace, William 426
Walter, Charles 435
Walters, Dan 364
Ward, Doris 456
Ward, Randall 122
Warren, Earl 3, 5, 88
Wasserman, Lew 31, 374
Waste Management Inc. 351
Water Resources, Dept. of 123
Waters, Ed 289
Waters, Maxine 68, 140, 288-290, 389,
Norm Waters, Norman S. 224-226, 396
Watkins, Dean 130
Watson, Diane 161, 193, 389
Watts, Doug 383
Waxman, Henry A. 61
Webb, Gary 366
Weintraub, Daniel 362
Weintraub, Jerry 375
Weir, Jim 414
West County Times 360
White, Dan 458
White, Robert 414

XYZ

This book was written and output entirely on The Sacramento Bee's typographic equipment. The writers initially wrote their copy on Coyote terminals on a SII computer system. The copy was then transferred electronically to a Macintosh IIx with a Radius double screen, using Smartcom software for the translation. The copy was edited in Microsoft Word 4.0, and page layout was done with Aldus Pagemaker 3.01 software, using Adobe Systems Inc. type fonts Caslon 3 and Times for headlines and text, respectively. Maps were drawn in MacDrawII using information provided by state agencies. The pages were output through a Linotronic VT-600W Postscript printer.

California Political Almanac staff

Amy Chance joined The Sacramento Bee in 1984 as a city government reporter and moved to the newspaper's Capitol bureau two years later. Formerly a reporter for the Fort Worth Star-Telegram, Chance now covers California's governor and other state politicians. A graduate of San Diego State University, she began her career as an intern at the Los Angeles Times.

Thorne Gray joined The Sacramento Bee's Capitol bureau in 1983 after 17 years with The Modesto Bee, where he covered government, environment, water and energy issues. He is a graduate of Cornell University and holds a master's degree in journalism from Northwestern University. At the Capitol bureau, he has covered health issues and the state budget.

Stephen Green has worked for The Sacramento Bee since 1978 as both a writer and editor. Since 1985, he's covered state government and politics from the Capitol bureau. Previously, he worked for the Portland (Ore.) Journal, the Seattle Post-Intelligencer, the Associated Press in Philadelphia and the National Observer in Washington, D.C. The Spokane native holds bachelor's and master's degrees in journalism from the University of Oregon.

John L. Hughes worked for three years as The Sacramento Bee's Capitol bureau news editor before taking his current job as the editor of the paper's letters section. He has held a number of editing positions at The Bee, including work at the 1984 Democratic National Convention in San Francisco, since joining the paper in 1980.

Rick Kushman joined The Sacramento Bee's Capitol bureau in 1987. He has worked as assignment editor at KXTV-TV, the CBS affiliate in Sacramento, as the city hall reporter for the Sacramento Union and at the San Luis Obispo Telegram-Tribune. He holds a bachelor's degree from the University of California, Davis, and a master's degree from Stanford University.

James Richardson, a native Californian, is a graduate of UCLA. He has been covering the state Capitol since 1985, first as a correspondent for the Riverside Press-Enterprise and then with The Sacramento Bee. He was previously a local political reporter with The San Diego Union. Richardson has been active with Investigative Reporters and Editors Inc.

Lori Korleski Richardson has been The Sacramento Bee's home and garden section editor since 1987. Prior to joining the paper, the University of Houston graduate worked as an assistant news editor at The Orange County Register. She has also worked at the Dallas Times Herald, St. Petersburg (Fla.) Times and The Beaumont (Texas) Enterprise.

Rick Rodriguez became deputy Capitol bureau chief of The Sacramento Bee in 1987 after a stint as an editorial writer for The Bee. He joined the Capitol bureau as a reporter in late 1982 from The Fresno Bee and began his career at his hometown paper, the Salinas Californian. A graduate of Stanford University, Rodriguez has also studied in Guadalajara, Mexico.

Ray Sotero has been in The Sacramento Bee's Capitol bureau since 1988 and covers the San Joaquin Valley for the Fresno and Modesto Bees. A 1979 graduate of the University of Nevada, Reno, Sotero has worked for The Modesto Bee, the (Boise) Idaho Statesman and at the Reno Gazette-Journal as an intern. He was reared in San Fernando.

Dan Walters has been a journalist for 30 years, half of which have been spent covering the Capitol, first for the Sacramento Union and since 1984 for The Sacramento Bee. He writes the only daily newspaper column about California politics, which appears in some 45 papers, and is the author of *The New California: Facing the 21st Century*.